Sophocles' Oedipus

A NEW VERSION BY FRANK McGUINNESS

Sophocles (496–406 BC) is believed to have written well over one hundred plays, of which only seven survive: *Women of Trachis*, *Ajax*, *Antigone*, *Oedipus the King*, *Electra*, *Philoctetes* and *Oedipus at Colonus*.

Frank McGuinness was born in Buncrana, Co. Donegal, and now lives in Dublin and lectures in English at University College Dublin. His plays include: *The Factory Girls* (Abbey Theatre, Dublin, 1982), *Baglady* (Abbey, 1985), *Observe the Sons of Ulster Marching Towards the Somme* (Abbey, 1985; Hampstead Theatre, London, 1986), *Innocence* (Gate Theatre, Dublin, 1986), *Carthaginians* (Abbey, 1988; Hampstead, 1989), *Mary and Lizzie* (RSC, 1989), *The Bread Man* (Gate, 1991), *Someone Who'll Watch Over Me* (Hampstead, West End and Broadway, 1992), *The Bird Sanctuary* (Abbey, 1994), *Mutabilitie* (NT, 1997), *Dolly West's Kitchen* (Abbey, 1999; Old Vic, 2000), *Gates of Gold* (Gate, 2002), *Speaking Like Magpies* (Swan, Stratford, 2005) and *There Came a Gypsy Riding* (Almeida, London, 2007). His widely performed versions include Ibsen's *Rosmersholm* (1987), *Peer Gynt* (1988), Chekhov's *Three Sisters* (1990), Lorca's *Yerma* (1987), Brecht's *The Threepenny Opera* (1991), *Hedda Gabler* (1994), *Uncle Vanya* (1995), *A Doll's House* (1997), *The Caucasian Chalk Circle* (1997), Sophocles' *Electra* (1998), Ostrovsky's *The Storm* (1998), Strindberg's *Miss Julie* (2000), Euripides' *Hecuba* (2004), Racine's *Phaedra* (2006) and Ibsen's *The Lady from the Sea* (2008).

D1353534

SOPHOCLES

Oedipus

a new version by
Frank McGuinness

from a literal translation by
Ciaran McGrogarty

faber and faber

First published in 2008
by Faber and Faber Limited
Bloomsbury House
74-77 Great Russell Street, London, WC1B 3DA

Typeset by Country Setting, Kingsdown, Kent CT14 8ES
Printed and bound by CPI Group (UK) Ltd, Croydon, CR0 4YY

A CIP record for this book
is available from the British Library

ISBN 978–0–571–24223–8

2 4 6 8 10 9 7 5 3

For Maria and John

Oedipus, in this version by Frank McGuinness, was first performed in the Olivier auditorium of the National Theatre, London, on 8 October 2008. The cast was as follows:

Oedipus Ralph Fiennes
A Priest David Burke
Creon Jasper Britton
Teiresias Alan Howard
Jocasta Clare Higgins
Stranger from Corinth Malcolm Storry
Shepherd Alfred Burke
Messenger Gwilym Lee
Chorus Patrick Brennan, Edward Clayton, Sam Cox,
    Russell Dixon, Darren Fox, Richard Freeman,
    Seymour Matthews, Neil McCaul, Paul McCleary,
    Stanley Page, Steven Page, Christopher Saul,
    David Shaw-Parker, Robert Willox

Director Jonathan Kent
Designer Paul Brown
Lighting Designer Neil Austin
Music Jonathan Dove
Movement Director Denni Sayers
Sound Designer Paul Groothuis

Characters

Oedipus

Priest

Chorus

Creon

Teiresias

Jocasta

Stranger from Corinth

Shepherd

Messenger

Children of Oedipus

OEDIPUS

Thebes.

Oedipus

    My people, my friends, you come before me – why?
    You are begging, you are praying – why?
    The city, why is it sore with weeping?
    Why is this whole city suffering?
    I want no messenger to stand here and tell me –
    I have come here myself, Oedipus.
    You all know who it is I am.
    Old man, I turn to you – speak out.
    I want to give you all the help I can.
    My heart's sore, for you are a black pity.

Priest

    Oedipus, you rule my land.
    Young and old, we gather before you.
    Boys without beards are here, and men like myself –
    I'm a priest of Zeus, pelted with age.
    We crowd the temples, the market place,
    The shrines – the entire city.
    We are like a sea that sweeps all before it.
    Our corn turns into cruel weeds.
    Meat turns to manure in our mouths.
    Women give birth to buckets of blood.
    God is on fire – his fever is plague.
    That is all he heaps on our heads.
    The city of Thebes is thronged with ghosts.
    Hell drinks a toast to our drought.
    We know you are not a god –
    Not one here burdens you with that,

But we salute you, best of men
In our eyes and the eyes of the gods.
You put a stop to the Sphinx –
She sings no more for her human supper.
We were freed from her worship.
You alone pitted yourself against her –
We did not need raise a finger.
Yourself and some god saved the day.
Now, Oedipus, great, good Oedipus,
We beg you, help us, hear us –
You must know some secret –
Some divine who can help us –
Some oracle to tell us what to do.
You've proved yourself man for this job.
Oedipus, you've saved us once before.
We salute you again as our saviour.
You tamed the birds of good omen.
They talked to you, took food from your hand.
Do the same now – save us.
Let us live on and walk this earth.
Would you rule a wrecked kingdom?
Bare, barren, is that your city's curse?

Oedipus

I know you suffer – you suffer very much.
Each and all of you, I know what you want.
I tell you this – what you suffer,
I suffer with you – I suffer more.
You feel your own pain, great pain,
But mine is your own, my own, my city's.
No, I have not been asleep, not dreaming –
I have wept my wet eyes dry.
I have walked every street wide –
I could find only one cure.
Creon, my brother, my wife's brother,
I have sent him straight to Delphi.

Let him learn what the gods want –
What have I to do? What have I to say?
How can I save Thebes, my home?
He's taking longer than I would like.
He should be home soon from his journey.
When he comes back, I'll do what needs doing –
I'd be the sorry man should I not –

Priest

You've chosen your time – Creon's coming.

Oedipus

Apollo, listen to me – bring us luck, Lord.

Creon enters.

You have the look of a man with good news.

Creon

The news is good – things might be rough,
If you face them down, you'll do all right.
Behave yourself well, and all's for the best.

Oedipus

What was the word of the god?

Creon

Should I speak to you alone?
Do you wish all to hear?

Oedipus

Tell all assembled –
I suffer more for them than for myself.

Creon

The god spoke and I listened:
There is poison in this land –
We feed on it, so we fester.
Apollo demands we drain it out.

Oedipus

    How do we purge ourself –
    What causes this catastrophe?

Creon

    Blood will have blood –
    Blood will drench this city –
    We must drive this man out.

Oedipus

    Which man – who does the god expose?

Creon

    Before your time we had a leader –
    Laius, he ruled this land well, my king.

Oedipus

    I've heard of him, but never set eyes on him.

Creon

    He was killed –
    Apollo demands we punish his killers.

Oedipus

    That crime was committed years ago –
    What traces of it survive?
    Those who did it, where on earth can they hide?

Creon

    In this very city, Apollo insists –
    That's where he escaped,
    The man we seek, and we allow him.

Oedipus

    Where was he murdered, Laius?
    The house – the fields – another country?

Creon

    On the way to Delphi –
    To consult the oracle.
    He left the palace and never returned.

Oedipus

No one went with him?
Was there no witness?

Creon

All dead – apart from one.
He ran away, terrified –
Certain of one thing only.

Oedipus

Which is what?
It may seem like nothing –
Who knows where it will lead?

Creon

He said robbers chanced on them –
It was a gang gutted him.

Oedipus

What possessed them to do it?
Laius was your king – a great crime –
What stopped you searching –?

Creon

The Sphinx – her song –
Her riddle ringing in our ears –
Devouring all and sundry.
Forget the mystery of his murder.
We had more pressing problems.

Oedipus

Apollo was right – you are right –
The dead man deserves justice.
I will be your ally.
I am on this country's side.
I am on God's side.
I must tackle this.
The fierce hand that held him down,
It might do the same to me.

I help myself in harming him.
People of Thebes, I will do what's to be done.
We either stand with God or sink.

Priest

Hear the wisdom of this great man.
We came looking for what he's promised.
May Apollo save us,
May he stop the plague.

The Chorus enters.

Chorus

My back's bent with woes.
Our people are all sick.
There is no reason –
There is no remedy
We can think of to save us.
The good earth turns evil.
Our women cry bearing children,
For none survive, none are saved.
All beat their bloodied wings west
To the god of death,
Faster than fire burning all before it.

In the city all things pass.
Youngsters lie unlamented,
Plague does not pity them,
It feasts on their faces.
Young wives, their grey mothers,
Root themselves at the altars
Raising plaintive voices,
Repeating the one wail –

Golden daughter of Zeus,
Show us succour –
Look on us with love.

Sweet voice of Zeus,
Heal me, hear me –
I am raw red,
My heart is fire.
Sweet voice of Zeus,
Hear me, heal me.

Apollo, save us.
Shining fire of Artemis,
Lighten this darkness –
Come to our aid.
Shield us from the sword
Of a godless god –
The plague without pity.
Apollo, save us –
Come to our aid.

Oedipus
This shall be dealt with, rest assured.
This unfortunate story, sad deed –
Though it happened before I came here,
I still have to confront it,
My duty as a citizen of our Thebes.
That is why I proclaim this warning –
If any of you know how this man,
This Laius, met his mysterious end –
I order you tell me all that you know.
If you're afraid you have hidden
Or held back relevant information,
Be assured of my leniency.
If a foreigner did this foul deed –
If the killer is not our kindred –
Speak out, speak up – you'll not suffer.
I'll pay out a handsome price.
If a friend did it and you're frightened,
You want to keep this quiet,
Well, that – concern – will cost you dear.

I speak as leader of this land.
Remember, I rule the roost here.
No one is to serve this soiled man,
No one is to speak to him,
No one is to partner him in prayer
Nor give him as much as a sip of water.
Haul him out of your house.
He is the poison – he is the plague.
The god Apollo has stated this clearly.
That's why I am his right-hand man,
A mate to the god and the godforsaken corpse.
Whoever did this – be it one or many –
I hope he may hear what I ask for.
May misery always attend him
As his eternal damned destiny.
If this filth warms himself at my fire
And I welcome him, I call upon myself
The curse I hurl upon his head.
Laius was noble – this man was your king.
You must find out how he died.
You can't leave this for others to clear up –
That would be a dark, dirty trick.
I now have the power he possessed.
I own the bed and the bride he bedded.
By that man she was barren
But I will fight to the death for him
As if he were my flesh, he were my blood.
I will not stop until I still the hand
That stained this illustrious honour.
I pray to the gods they grant no favour
To any who'd abuse this solemn vow –
May his killers know neither harvest nor home,
May hatred waste their women and children.
The rest of Thebes approves my reasons.
They are just, and the gods join with me.

Chorus

You put me under oath, lord –
I answer you.
I cannot name his killer.
Apollo asks the question –
He must answer it.

Oedipus

And he will answer it.
But no man can make a god obey –
They do as they desire.

Chorus

May I suggest a second way?

Oedipus

A third, if it pleases you –
Tell me –

Chorus

Ask Teiresias –
Ask the blind priest.
He sees like Apollo.
Ask – learn from him, lord.

Oedipus

I've sent for him – twice.
Creon bid me do it.
No sign of him.
Why is it taking so long –?

Chorus

There are other rumours.
Travellers set on him – Laius –
They killed him on the road –

Oedipus

I've listened to that one –
No one's seen any who saw it.

Chorus

With your curse ringing in his ear,
If he's clever he'll clear out of Thebes.

Oedipus

Words won't frighten whoever did this.

Chorus

This is the man who'll catch him.
Let them lead in the prophet of the gods.
He is the loneliest of men,
For he can speak only the absolute truth.

A Boy leads in Teiresias.

Oedipus

Teiresias, keeper of all secrets,
That which we do, that which we dream,
Your blind eyes can see the plague,
And you alone can save us.
Apollo has sent us his oracle –
Find the killers of Laius, kill them,
Or send them fleeing from this city –
That way only can Thebes be cleansed.
You have seen visions in a bird's voice,
Traced your prophecies in a thousand sighs,
Do not spare us your sacred wisdom.
Save yourself, save your home, save me.
Cure us all from the curse of the dead man.
You know –

Teiresias

There is no point in knowing what to do
When all that will happen is beyond help.

Oedipus

Why has your heart lost hope –?

Teiresias

    Let me go home – you'll face your fate easier.
    And I'll face mine, if you trust me.

Oedipus

    I find you no friend to this city.
    You do not care for its codes of honour,
    Keeping us in the dark –

Teiresias

    You are speaking out of order.
    So – I will be silent –
    I do not wish to suffer as you will.

Oedipus

    In God's name, don't turn your back on us.
    We'll throw ourselves to our knees before you,
    Begging –

Teiresias

    You understand nothing – all of you.
    But I will shut my sorrows away.
    To speak of them is to speak of yours.

Oedipus

    Do I hear what you are saying?
    You know something but tell nothing,
    So you intend to do the dirty –
    Aid and abet the state's destruction?

Teiresias

    I spare myself and I spare yourself.
    You keep on questioning – please quit.
    You'll learn nothing out of me.

Oedipus

    You beggar belief – are you saying
    We would as soon get blood from a stone
    Than your hard heart should soften and speak?

Teiresias

You blame my hard heart – look long at your own.
What hides in there?
See that before censuring me.

Oedipus

Who wouldn't harden, hearing your words?
They dishonour the whole city.

Teiresias

What will out will out –
I cannot bury it in clay.

Oedipus

All the more reason to tell me –

Teiresias

I've said my say – no more.
Raise your voice, roar –

Oedipus

I intend to – I'll spare no one.
I'll tell you what I make of it all –
You were part and parcel of this plague –
You didn't dirty your hands – no –
But you were in on the act –
You were the brains behind the plot –
If those dead eyes watching me could see,
I swear you'd have done the deed alone.

Teiresias

Is that so? Stand by your statement.
Never speak another syllable to me.
Never speak to these people.
There is a stench of something festering,
And its source is yourself.

Oedipus

You start this story –
You say it to my face –

Tell me this, pray –
How will you get away with it?

Teiresias
I will walk away.
Truth can't be chained.

Oedipus
What gives you this power?
Your gift of prophecy –

Teiresias
No, you give it.
You forced me to speak.
I did not want to.

Oedipus
Speak what? Speak again –
Enlighten me more.

Teiresias
Did it not dawn on you earlier?
Are you tempting me to talk?

Oedipus
Speak up – speak out –
I do not know what –

Teiresias
The man who was murdered, you murdered him.
You are who you are seeking to find.

Oedipus
Say that again.
Say it – and laugh.
I'll leave that laugh – blind man –
On the other side of your face.

Teiresias
Will I say more?
Will I make you more angry?

Oedipus

Speak till the skies fall.
It will all be said in vain.

Teiresias

You live in sin and do not know it.
You do not see the filth you are in.

Oedipus

Will you continue in this slander?
Are you revelling in it?

Teiresias

The truth is to be told.

Oedipus

It will be, but not by you.
Your eyes are blind,
Your ears are blind,
Your mind is blind.

Teiresias

I shed a tear for you taunting me.
Soon the world will be tormenting you.

Oedipus

You've lived too long in the night.
I see the sun – so do all here.
You can never, ever harm me.

Teiresias

Your fate is not in my power.
You won't fall through me.
Apollo's seen to that.
He's taking special care of you.
You are in his hands.

Oedipus

Whose plan is this?
Yours or Creon's?

Teiresias

    Creon cannot harm you.
    You and you alone do that.

Oedipus

    Jealousy is a strange thing –
    I did not ask for power –
    The city placed it in my hands –
    Wealth, the kingship –
    A skill to rival all other skills,
    To be the best of men.
    And I trusted Creon,
    My friend from the start –
    He plans to be rid of me –
    Plots with this prophet,
    This crafty chancer,
    Blind when he so chooses,
    Sharp when it's his interest.
    That he makes out clearly.
    So you claim a curious gift,
    You can read the future.
    Where is your second sight?
    Thebes was once tormented –
    By the Sphinx – that dirty dog.
    Where were you then?
    Did you save the city?
    A torrent of men tried.
    No luck – until this lad,
    This ignorant Oedipus –
    He put a stop to her.
    No help from birds screeching –
    I received no omens from the gods.
    I solved the riddle –
    Using my five wits I did.
    That's the man you take on,
    The man you'd kick out –

In cahoots with Creon.
The two of you will regret this,
Attempting to take the throne.
If you were not skin and ancient bone,
You would feel the force of my fist.

Chorus
The two of you speak in anger.
There is no need for this.
We should study the oracle.

Teiresias
Yes, you are king –
But I have right of reply.
I am not your servant,
I am Apollo's.
You mock my being blind –
There is sight in your eyes,
Yet you do not see your danger.
You do not see where you live,
Nor with whom you live.
Do you not know whose you are?
You have spat on your kith and kin
In this life and next.
Your father and your mother –
They both curse you –
They will drive you from this land,
A man in terror.
You will see only darkness.
No home will harbour you.
The mountain will echo your moan.
Look at your happy marriage,
Slap yourself on the back,
A reward for your goodness?
It will drench you in sin –
Drown you in sin after sin –

You are your own children.
Face up to that fate.
Slap Creon down into the dirt,
Shut my filthy mouth –
You are still mortal,
And you are marked –
You will be removed.

Oedipus

Do I have to listen to this man?
Go and die.
Do it quickly.
Get away from this house –

Teiresias

I came only because you called me.

Oedipus

Was I to know you would speak such scandal?
A long time before I send again –

Teiresias

You think me a fool –
But your parents thought me wise –

Oedipus

Which parents?
Stay.
Who were my parents?

Teiresias

This day you'll see your real self,
And it will destroy you.

Oedipus

All you speak in are riddles –

Teiresias

Aren't you the best man to solve them?

Oedipus

You mock what is meat and drink to me.
It made my name –

Teiresias

And it will take it from you.

Oedipus

If that saves the city, that is fine –

Teiresias

I will go now – lead me, child.

Oedipus

Lead him out, yes.
You are in my way here.
Out of sight you are out of mind.
You'll anger me no more.

Teiresias

I've said what I've come here to say.
I look you straight in the face.
I don't fear you – you can't harm me.
But I do say this to you, though –
A long time you've searched high and low,
Looking loudly for the killer of Laius.
That man is here in this city.
He claims to be from another country.
But he is native – born in Thebes.
That all-seeing, superlative man,
He will be blinded and will be beggared,
Tripping his way to a strange land,
Pointing to earth with a long stick.
To his children he is father and brother,
To his mother he is husband and son.
The father he killed, he's filthied his bed.
Go inside and ponder on these things.
If I'm a liar, laugh at my prophecies.

Oedipus and Teiresias leave in separate directions.

Chorus

Whose hands are soiled with this blood?
Who does the oracle accuse?
Time for him to flee like the wind,
For Apollo follows with fire and lightning –
That man at the mercy of merciless fate.

Divine judgement decrees no refuge,
No peace, no home for the guilty soul.
He wanders through cave, rock and wild wood
Like an animal crazed in crazy flight,
For the sentence of death Apollo has sworn
Will haunt him the days of his dying life.

I hear Teiresias – his wisdom disturbs me.
Where will I turn today – tomorrow?
I do not believe him – cannot deny him –
Is hope abandoning this great city?
Why should he insult our mighty king?

Zeus and Apollo know all's to be known.
The prophet's a smarter man than myself,
But I'll hold my tongue till proof's on the table.
Oedipus had brains to beat the Sphinx hollow.
He saved Thebes, and for that I stand by him.
I will not convict him in thought or deed.

Creon enters.

Creon

Oedipus the King condemns me –
An innocent, I stand accused.
His words tear my heart.
Does he think I would do –
Does he think I would say –
Anything to make him suffer?
To harm him and his own?

I'd sooner take my life.
It is no small matter
To be charged in this manner –
A threat to my state,
A threat to my friends,
The worst crime that can be levelled –

Chorus

He was speaking in anger.
Reason did not enter –

Creon

Teiresias was lying,
Lying at my prompting –
That's what he clearly said.

Chorus

He did imply –

Creon

He condemned me.

Chorus

Don't ask me to confirm –
Leave that to those who rule –
Ask him himself –
He comes from the house.

Oedipus

Do you dare show your face?
Do you dare stand here?
You did kill that man –
You, who'd steal my kingdom.
In the name of the gods,
Tell me this –
Do you think I'm a fool?
That I'm a coward?
What put you up to it?
Did you think this could be hidden?

I'd be in blissful ignorance –
I'd forgive and forget, perhaps?
You'd seize power, would you –
Without men, without money?
To take the throne you need both.

Creon
Are you listening to yourself?
If not, listen to me.
I will stand up for myself –
Judge me then –

Oedipus
Do not try to dazzle me with words.
You are too clever for me,
But you are my enemy –

Creon
I will have my say –
I will speak in my defence –

Oedipus
Do not dare claim you're innocent –

Creon
You are arguing without reason.
Is that right?
I accuse you –

Oedipus
No, I accuse you.
Killing a kinsman –
Getting away with it –
That is –

Creon
Not right – I agree –
How have I offended in this way?
What pain have I inflicted?
Tell me.

Oedipus

You persuaded me – did you not –
I must send for that prophet?

Creon

You must, yes – I still maintain –

Oedipus

How long since Laius –?

Creon

Since Laius did what?

Oedipus

Was taken from this world –
Taken by violent hands?

Creon

It was not today or yesterday.

Oedipus

Was that prophet – that Teiresias –
Was he then in the practice –

Creon

He was wise – he was revered –

Oedipus

Did he make mention of my name then?

Creon

Never – not while I was near him.

Oedipus

And you combed the earth for the killer?

Creon

We had to search hard – no clue was left.

Oedipus

Why did this revered man –
This wise man, Teiresias –
Why was he silent in his wisdom?

Creon
    I don't know.
    When I don't know things,
    I keep my mouth closed.

Oedipus
    But you'll speak if you wish me well.
    You'll say –

Creon
    What? Let me know –
    I'll deny you nothing.

Oedipus
    If that man and you were not working as one,
    He would never speak of my killing Laius.

Creon
    You know best if he says that.
    You've questioned me –
    May I question you now?

Oedipus
    Ask – I am innocent of murder.

Creon
    My sister, are you married to her?

Oedipus
    The world and his wife know I am.

Creon
    You and she – you rule this country equally?

Oedipus
    She has everything she wants from me.

Creon
    And am I not an equal to you both?

Oedipus

You are indeed –
That makes you more disloyal –

Creon

Not if you would use your head – think.
First things first –
I like to lie in peace at night,
I do not quake in my bed.
I have no desire – no design – to be king.
I have ample power – I am content,
The mark of a sensible man.
My life lacks one thing – that is fear.
I do not now – I never will want it.
I have command, I have influence,
But not the cares of state – sweet deprivation.
I know the ways of pleasure – they please me.
To me all bow and scrape, they bend the knee,
For I have your ear – they need to be nice to me.
Why throw that aside for the sake of your crown?
No sane man courts such stupidity.
I have no time nor truck with treachery –
I would hang terrorists from the trees.
Do you want proof? Go straight to Delphi.
Ask the oracle – did I speak as I found?
If I have plotted with the priest,
String me up without judge or jury.
Don't confuse good men for bad or bad for good –
Don't damn with the dimmest evidence.
Losing a friend is like losing one's life –
You'll learn that in time – let time pass its sentence,
It reveals all, the just and unjust man.

Chorus

He's spoken well – spoken carefully,
Not rash – nor rushed his words like guilty men.

Oedipus

The thief thinks fast to rob you blind.
The honest man thinks faster.
That's what I must do –
If I stall, he succeeds.

Creon

What do you want to do then?
Throw me out of the land?

Oedipus

That is too good for you.
I want you to die.
Make an example of your envy.

Creon

Nothing I say will shift you from this?

Oedipus

Nothing.

Creon

You don't see what is in front of you –
You're not thinking –

Oedipus

I'm thinking most of my own interest –

Creon

You should be thinking as much of mine –

Oedipus

You are foul as filth –

Creon

And if you are wrong entirely –

Oedipus

I must still rule –

Creon

Not if you rule badly –

Oedipus

Thebes, my love – my city, Thebes –

Creon

It is also mine –
Not yours alone.

Chorus

My lords, quiet – quiet.
Jocasta comes from the palace.
You must settle this with her help.

Jocasta enters.

Jocasta

Why do you indulge in this inane quarrel,
Raising your voices to the roof of Heaven?
Grown men calling each other childish names,
Are you not numb with shame, stirring this up?
This land labours under poisonous plague.
Let this be, or love will soon turn to hate.

Creon

You are the same blood as myself –
Your husband claims an inhuman right.
He gives me one of two cruel choices –
Exile, or instant death.

Oedipus

He has committed crimes against us, wife.
He is wicked – beware of his witchcraft.

Creon

All you accuse me of –
May I die – may I be damned –
If there's a word of truth –
One – in your countless charges –
I swear to the gods –

Jocasta

Oedipus, believe this –
Hear his oath –
Respect his sacred vow –
Listen to him – to me –
Good people, beg him –

Chorus

My lord, we do beg you –
Do right, listen –

Oedipus

What do you want me to do for you?

Chorus

This is an innocent man –
He has never choked on lies –
Respect his oath.

Oedipus

Do you know what you ask?

Chorus

I do know.

Oedipus

Spell out what you mean.

Chorus

You are accusing a friend –
Be sure of what you're saying.
That's what we're asking.

Oedipus

Then you wish to destroy me –
That or I depart from this land.

Chorus

I swear by the sun –
The supreme being –

May I be damned in Hell,
Friendless, godless
If that is what I think.
My soul is worn to shreds.
The country wastes away –
Will you add to our woes,
Imagining evil?

Oedipus

Then let him go – let me die,
Exiled, disgraced, dishonoured.

Oedipus turns to the Chorus.

I give you my heart.

Oedipus turns to Creon.

I give him my hatred.

Creon

A fierce forgiveness.
I taste your bitter word,
And leave you to yourself.
Endure that as you're best able.

Oedipus

Get out of my sight.

Creon

I'll do so.
You don't see who stands before you,
But they know who I am.

Creon exits.

Jocasta

What has happened?

Chorus

Stories were flying –
Suspicions aroused –

One word borrowed another –
Bother stirred.

Jocasta
On both sides?

Chorus
Yes.

Jocasta
And what ensued?

Chorus
Enough was said.
More than enough.
Leave well enough alone.
The land's on its knees.

Oedipus turns to the Chorus.

Oedipus
You've brought this about –
Your benign advice.
You softened my heart –
My head would not have stopped me –

Chorus
My lord, I will insist
Till I'm blue in the face,
If I don't stand by you,
Call me mad, without wit,
A meandering fool.
You have steered my country,
My loved, loved country
Through a sea of troubles.
Be our good captain again.

Jocasta
Tell me as well –
Why are you so angry?
Answer me, my lord.

Oedipus

I love you more than any other,
So I will tell you straight.
The cause is Creon.
He plots against me.

Jocasta

Explain the quarrel to me.

Oedipus

He says I stand here –
The killer of Laius.

Jocasta

He alone accuses you?
Do others dare say the same?

Oedipus

His own breath smells sweet.
Others do his dirty work.
A wicked, preaching prophet,
That's who delivers the verdict –

Jocasta

Cast aside that panic.
Listen and learn from me.
No man has second sight –
No such thing as prophecy.
I can quickly prove that.
An oracle came to Laius once.
I don't say from Apollo.
No, from his followers.
They say he would die –
Laius himself would die –
At the hands of his own child.
But we know the real story –
Laius was killed by robbers –
Foreigners – where three roads meet.

Our child, when three days old,
No more, no less –
Laius pierced his feet together.
Threw him into another's hands.
Let the baby die abandoned,
Alone on a bare mountain.
So Apollo did not succeed –
The child did not kill his father.
Laius did not die as he most feared,
At the hands of his son.
That's what the prophets warned –
That's what they decreed.
Pay no heed to such hoaxes.
When a god wants something to happen,
He has no need of dark doings.
It will all come into light.

Oedipus
My hair stands on end –
My soul shivers –
Hearing you speak, lady.

Jocasta
What threatens you like this?

Oedipus
Did I just not hear you say –
Laius died where three roads meet?

Jocasta
That is certain.

Oedipus
Where, precisely, did it come to pass?

Jocasta
A place called Phocis – the road branches there.
It leads to the same spot –
From Daulis, into Delphi –

Oedipus
When, precisely, did it come to pass?

Jocasta
Shortly before you came to the city
And took power –

Oedipus
Zeus, what have you decided to do to me?

Jocasta
Oedipus, why does this put the fear of God in you?

Oedipus
Not yet – not yet –
Laius, what kind of man was he?
First flush of youth,
Weighed with age –
What was he like?

Jocasta
A fine looking man – sturdy –
His hair sprinkled with white –
His shape – much like your own –

Oedipus
What have I done – what crime?
I didn't know –
I did not know –
I have put myself under curse –
Curse after curse –

Jocasta
I am frightened looking at you, my lord.
What is it you are saying?

Oedipus
So, he may have seen it all – the prophet.
And I am in blind panic.

But you can make it all clear –
Say one thing more –

Jocasta
Ask, I'll answer, no matter what –
I'm afraid –

Oedipus
Did he travel alone?
Did he travel with men –
Armed men – like a ring around him –
Did he have many –

Jocasta
Five altogether.
A servant as well.
Laius was in a chariot – alone –

Oedipus
Clear as daylight, God help me.
Lady, who spoke these words to you?

Jocasta
A servant – he came home –
The only one who survived.

Oedipus
Where is he now?

Jocasta
He came back – he begged me –
He touched my hand gently –
He asked to be sent to the fields
To shepherd the flocks of sheep –
As far as he could be from the city.
I sent him – he was a worthy slave –
He'd deserved better thanks than this.

Oedipus
Could he come back quickly to us?

Jocasta
   It is possible – why order that?

Oedipus
   I have loosened my tongue and should not have –
   That is why I want to see him.

Jocasta
   He will come then.
   My lord, what do you dread?
   Don't you think me fit to hear it?

Oedipus
   My father was Polybus, from Corinth.
   My mother's name Merope, a Dorian.
   I was the man to beat in that city.
   Then something happened, something strange –
   It shocked me more than it should have.
   The wine was flowing once – nine sheets to the wind,
   One fool berated me – I was a bastard –
   Worse, I was neither parent's son.
   I did take that hard, but I kept my head.
   Next day I questioned my father, my mother.
   They were incensed at that ignorant lout
   And would placate me with their displeasure,
   But it did not stop my fear, my foreboding.
   It was like something growing inside me.
   I said nothing to my mother, my father.
   In secret I went myself off to Delphi.
   Apollo listened, he gave me his answer –
   I should fill with shame standing there.
   He set it all out – the terror – the sorrow –
   I must grow afraid of the word mother –
   I would breed beasts with my – with my mother –
   A tribe too terrible to show their face.
   I would kill the father who'd fathered me.
   I heard these tidings, I fled from Corinth –

Keep it far from me as stars in the sky.
I went where I'd never see that happen –
Murder my father, mate with my mother.
I came to where you say that man was slain.
Jocasta, I will tell you the whole truth.
I was walking near where three roads meet.
I came across a man in a chariot and his servant.
The two tried to send me spinning –
The old man hell bent to force me from the road.
I raised my fist – lashed out at the driver –
The old man watched – waited for me to pass –
He took his horses' whip – he sliced my head –
I paid him back in kind – paid him double –
This was the hand that dealt the heavy blow.
He no longer rode in his chariot.
I killed him stone dead – I killed them all.
If this stranger and Laius were one and the same,
Where is there a man more miserable –
A man the gods hate more – than this wretch?
He'll be hurled from any decent house –
Friend, stranger, turn their backs – he is bad luck.
I am the one cursed this curse on myself.
These are the lethal hands that took his life.
And I defile the bed of this dead soul.
Am I an evil man – filthy and foul?
I must flee from Thebes – flee from the city.
Great gods in Heaven, don't let me see the day –
If this happens, let me hide from men's eyes
Rather than be stained with the sin of all sins.

Chorus
My lord, you fill us with fear.
Wait and find out who was there.
Have hope –

Oedipus
One hope, one only – wait for the shepherd.

Jocasta
When he appears, what will you ask?

Oedipus
If your stories agree, I am innocent.

Jocasta
What did I say hit you hardest?

Oedipus
You said robbers killed the king –
Not one man, but many robbers.
If he confirms that, I'm clear.
One man is not a multitude.
If he pins blame on one person,
Let blood pour on my head alone.

Jocasta
The world knows what happened – he can't deny it.
The whole city heard it – not just my ears.
If he should change his tune, what matter?
He still cannot prove what was prophesied –
A child of mine would murder his father.
No chance of that – the poor creature perished.
That's how much heed I pay to veiled visions –
Do they tell us if we're coming or going?

Oedipus
Wisely spoken – still, send for the shepherd.
This business has begun – finish it.

Jocasta and Oedipus exit.

Chorus
I put my faith in fate,
Holy in word and deed.
Believe in divine laws,
Born in high Heaven.
That's where I find my god –
Eternal, endless God.

God that does not forget,
God that does not grow old.

I fear the man that's proud,
Proud as the full belly.
Fear the tyrant's claw,
Clutching at high Heaven.
Beware the grip of God,
Masterful, mighty God,
God that does not relent,
God that defeats the proud.

I see men on the make,
Scorning law and justice,
Blaspheme in blessed shrines,
Cursing high Heaven.
They tempt the wrath of God,
Avenging ruthless God,
God that does not forgive,
God that can dance on death.

I put my fate in fire,
Blazing on Mount Olympus.
I hear Apollo speak
From the earth's deep bowels.
That's why I serve the gods,
Eternal, endless Zeus.
God that does not forget,
God that does not grow old –
But if his sacred truth
Lied in the ears of Laius,
There is no oracle,
And the gods themselves die.

Jocasta enters.

Jocasta
Oedipus is in agony –
Everything is an ill omen,

He sees strange things in all he hears,
No peace from the past nor in the present.
All he wants are warning voices.
I can give him no consolation,
So I stand in supplication to you,
Apollo, most adored divinity,
We see our ship's captain cowering in fear –
Scupper this terror, shelter us from harm.

A Stranger from Corinth enters.

Stranger
Where is the house of Oedipus, strangers?
Tell me if you know where he himself is.

Chorus
This is his palace – he is inside –
Stranger, this lady is mother to his children.

Stranger
I wish her and hers prosperity –
A happy marriage for all eternity.

Jocasta
I return the soft greeting, stranger.
You are welcome for your fine words.
Tell me why you're here – what do you wish?

Stranger
Good fortune on your house and husband, lady.

Jocasta
Where do you come from?

Stranger
Corinth, and I'm here with news to warm your heart.
How could it not, though it cause pain as well –

Jocasta
What is it – why should we laugh and cry?

Stranger
Corinth wants to crown Oedipus its king –

Jocasta
The old man Polybus gives up power?

Stranger
He is in the grip of his cold grave.

Jocasta
Are you saying Polybus is dead?

Stranger
May God strike me down if I lie.

Jocasta
Go give this great news to Oedipus.
What do you make of this marvel?
Now, is there a shred of truth in oracles?
Oedipus long fled far from that city,
Fearing he would take his own father's life –
Now the man dies at the hands of fate.

Oedipus enters.

Oedipus
My noble wife, why have you sent for me?

Jocasta
Listen to this man – learn the lovely truth –
This is all the gods boil down to – baseless –

Oedipus
Who is this fellow – what has he to say?

Jocasta
He comes from Corinth.
He brings word.
Polybus no longer exists.
Your father is dead.

Oedipus

Stranger, what are you saying?
Tell me your message.

Stranger

He is dead and gone –
Done and dusted –
I'll repeat it –

Oedipus

How did he die –
Disease – in a dispute –?

Stranger

He went gently –
Old bones break easy.

Oedipus

An illness took the poor man?
That's how he passed –?

Stranger

Not one but a long litany, over time.

Oedipus

Douse the flames at Delphi –
Strangle the screeching birds –
So I would kill my father?
He is buried beneath the ground.
I did not lift a finger.
My sword is still sheathed.
Did he desire to see his son?
That is how he perished –
That way I willed his death?
You sweep all before you, Polybus –
To hell with prophecies.
They are worth nothing now.

Jocasta
Long ago, did I not foresee this?

Oedipus
I still feared –

Jocasta
These things no longer trouble your heart –

Oedipus
I must not still look at my mother's bed –

Jocasta
What has a man to fear,
When luck is on his side?
Nothing is ordained,
No rhyme nor reason.
Our life is all random –
Lead it as you're able.
Forget this foolish stuff,
Marry your mother?
Many a man's mad dream.
Be free of a child's fancy.
That's the way to thrive –
Take life easy.

Oedipus
I would give the ear to your easy words
If the woman who bore me was not alive.
She is, and I shrink back, though you spoke well.

Jocasta
See the light shine from your father's grave –

Oedipus
I see it clearly –
But I fear my mother –
Alive –

Stranger

Who is this woman you fear?

Oedipus

Merope – she lived with Polybus –

Stranger

Why does that woman worry you?

Oedipus

A terrible oracle sent from the gods –

Stranger

What did it say – are we allowed to know?

Oedipus

Apollo decreed I'd lie with my mother,
And spill my father's blood with my own hands.
I have since kept safe distance from Corinth,
Yet longed to look into my parents' eyes.

Stranger

Fear of this kept you away from there?

Oedipus

I had no wish to murder my father.

Stranger

My lord, why don't I free you from this fear?
I come with good news, but can add better.

Oedipus

You would then be very warmly thanked.

Stranger

This was my real reason for arriving –
I wanted to get my foot in first –
Before you came back to Corinth –

Oedipus

I will never, ever go near my parents' city –

Stranger

You really don't know what you're doing, child.

Oedipus

Doing what? Tell me, in the name of the gods –

Stranger

You avoid going home because –

Oedipus

I am petrified of Apollo –
He will put me to the test –

Stranger

Your parents may pollute you –

Oedipus

That chills me to the bone –

Stranger

You don't know you've nothing to fear there –

Oedipus

How not if they were my parents?

Stranger

You have no connection to Polybus.

Oedipus

My father –

Stranger

Is no more to you than I am.
Him and myself, equals.

Oedipus

How – you are nothing to me.

Stranger

Neither is the man you call father.

Oedipus

Why did he call me his son?

Stranger

I gave you to him as my gift.

Oedipus

Yet he loved me –
But I was another man's –

Stranger

He had no children before you appeared –
He needed no persuading –

Oedipus

You gave me to him.
Did you buy me –
Stumble on me –?

Stranger

Cithaeron – in the glens –
The mountains of Cithaeron –
That's where I found you.

Oedipus

What brought you to Cithaeron?

Stranger

I was in charge of the flocks.

Oedipus

You worked as a shepherd –

Stranger

I was your saviour, son, that day.

Oedipus

When you took me in your arms –
Was I in any pain at all?

Stranger

You were – your feet should bear witness –

Oedipus

You bring up an old injury – why?

Stranger
Because your feet were pierced together –
I freed you –

The Stranger points to Oedipus' feet.

It's how you got your name, Oedipus –

Oedipus
'Lame child' – who first called me that –
Wrapped in swaddling clothes –
Who first called me that?
Father or Mother?
Speak –

Stranger
I don't know.
Ask the man gave you to me.

Oedipus
Another handed me to you?
You didn't come on me yourself?

Stranger
Another shepherd –

Oedipus
Who was he? Describe him.

Stranger
From the house of Laius.

Oedipus
Who ruled this land long ago?

Stranger
His herdsman, yes.

Oedipus
Is this man alive?
Might I see him?

Stranger

The people here would know that best.

Oedipus

Does one of you know this shepherd?
Have you seen him here or in the fields?
Answer – it's time to reveal these things.

Chorus

I think it's the man you sent for –
Jocasta would be best to tell you.

Oedipus

Lady, the man we've ordered to come –
Is this the fellow he speaks about?

Jocasta

Why concern yourself with all of this?
Pay no heed – forget what's said.
Idle chatter – words in the wind.

Oedipus

I cannot do that.
I want to know the secret of my birth.
I do not know who I am.
That lies buried –

Jocasta

Leave it there.
Don't search further.
Value your life.
I ask in the name of the gods.
My heart is sore enough.

Oedipus

Be brave.
I may be base-born.
A child of a slave –
Slave after slave –
You are still of sovereign blood –

Jocasta

For that reason, obey me.
I beg you –
Don't do this.

Oedipus

I will not obey –
I will see what I am.

Jocasta

I think only of you –
I act only for the best.

Oedipus

And your best is not my best.

Jocasta

May you never know who you are.

Oedipus

Someone fetch me the man I wait for.
This woman, let her leave us to find out.
Let her sweat in the lap of luxury.

Jocasta

You are lost – lost.
I'll say nothing again.

Jocasta exits.

Oedipus

Let whatever happens happen.
I wish to know what I am,
Though I be the lowest of the low.
Perhaps my lady's too delicate
To stomach my rough station.
I call myself a lucky child,
A man marked by good fortune –
Fortune's minded me like a mother,
Sharing gifts small and big.

49

When that is what I'm cut from,
How could I conceal my ancestry?

Chorus

Come the next moon
I will sing out,
Not of Olympus
But great Cithaeron.
I praise Cithaeron,
Exalt Cithaeron –
Nurse and mother
To my sweet master.
You saved Oedipus
To please Apollo.

O great god Pan,
To you I sing –
Did you give birth to
Divine Cithaeron?
I praise Cithaeron,
Exalt Cithaeron –
Bacchus is drunk
In your high mountains.
Did he create you
To rear and ravish?

The Shepherd is seen entering.

Oedipus

Is this the man we have been waiting for?
He seems to be exactly the right age.
My friends, you have the advantage of me –
You have set eyes on this shepherd before.

Chorus

I recognise him straight away –
A mere shepherd, but Laius trusted him.

Oedipus
Stranger from Corinth, is this the man?

Stranger
Who you are looking at, yes.

Oedipus
Old man, answer as best as you can –
Were you once in the service of Laius?

Shepherd
I was not bought as a slave –
I was raised in this house.

Oedipus
What was your work?

Shepherd
Minded sheep most of my life.

Oedipus
Where were you a shepherd?

Shepherd
Cithaeron, sometimes.
Other places as well.

Oedipus
You know this man?
You met him there?

Shepherd
My memory is not the best.

Stranger
That is no wonder, master.
I can help him remember.
He knows too well what I know.
The mountains of Cithaeron –
We herded our sheep together,

Six months at a time,
Spring, into autumn.
Come winter, we bade farewell.
My flock to my own fold,
His to the barns of Laius.
Is that what happened or not?

Shepherd
A long time ago, but that's true.

Stranger
Do you remember giving me a child?
I might rear him as my own? Speak up –

Shepherd
Why? What makes you ask –?

Stranger
This man – he was an infant then?

Shepherd
Are you hell bent on harming us?
Will you not hold your tongue?

Oedipus
Don't scold him, old man.
It's you needs the reprimand.

Shepherd
Best of masters, what have I said wrong?

Oedipus
Not telling about the boy this man asks –

Shepherd
He knows nothing – a waste of bloody breath –

Oedipus
Your lack of manners will leave you weeping.

Shepherd
What do you want to know?

Oedipus
The child he mentions –
Did you hand it over?

Shepherd
I did, and wish I had died that day.

Oedipus
You'll get that wish, if you don't tell the truth.

Shepherd
Worse will happen if I do speak.

Oedipus
This man insists on taking his time –

Shepherd
I said what I've said before –
I gave it to him.

Oedipus
From where did you receive the child?
Your own house, or another?

Shepherd
No – not my own – another's.

Oedipus
From one of these men assembled?
From what family –?

Shepherd
Master, question me no further.

Oedipus
If I have to ask these things again,
I will kill you myself.

Shepherd
The household of Laius.

Oedipus

A slave's child, was it?
Or a blood relation?

Shepherd

That is what scares me most.
What I have to say –

Oedipus

What I have to hear.
And I must listen carefully.

Shepherd

They said it was his child – Laius.
Your lady inside – ask her.
She is best fit to answer.

Oedipus

Did she give you the child?

Shepherd

Yes.

Oedipus

To do what?

Shepherd

Kill it.

Oedipus

That she, the bitch, gave birth to?

Shepherd

She was afraid of awful omens.

Oedipus

Which were?

Shepherd

Story was he'd slaughter his parents.

Oedipus
Why give it then to this man?

Shepherd
I pitied the baby, master.
I thought he'd carry it far away –
Back to where he belonged.
He'd save him from a savage fate.
But if you're who he says you are,
You know all I cannot speak of.

Oedipus
All has now come out very clear.
Light, I look on you for the last time.
I am cursed to the backbone.
I lay with a woman I should not –
I struck down an old man I should not –
I am damned – all has come out clear.

Oedipus exits.

Chorus
I can hear sore weeping,
Sound of the human soul,
Starting when we first breathe,
Lasting till blood colds.
Oedipus, I sorrow,
For happiness is gone –
Pity the poor hero,
Unrivalled, unenvied.
I can hear sore weeping.

His were golden arrows
Whose path Zeus controlled.
He heard the Sphinx singing,
Solved that strange beast's riddle.
Its answer is, myself –
Then Thebes fell at his feet.

Honour was his house guest,
Fortune his best of friends.
His were golden arrows.

All is crazed and chaos,
Where once there was just calm.
All harmony is now
The hoarsest raven's caw.
Your crying eyes are red,
You stained the marriage bed –
Unspeakable to say –
The child knifes the father.
Why did earth not swallow
This sacrilegious crime?
All is crazed and chaos.

Time takes no prisoners.
It spares no man nor beast.
United, unholy,
Husband and wife have sinned.
Begetter, begotten,
You are both in one man.
I loved you more than life –
You lulled me to my death.
Child of Laius, I curse you.
I close my eyes to you.
Time takes no prisoners.

A Messenger comes from the house.

Messenger
I speak to you old men of Thebes,
What deeds will you hear –
What deeds will you see?
They will break your hearts,
If you love the house of Thebes.
The rivers of earth

Cannot wash these walls clean.
They hide so much horror
Brought down upon our heads –
Sorrows stripped stark naked,
Accusing us of sin.

Chorus
We are weeping for what we know –
What more can you add to that?

Messenger
The queen is dead –
Jocasta dead.

Chorus
Why did this happen?
How did this happen?

Messenger
By her own hand.
You have been spared the sight of the worst.
I saw it all – that woman in wretched pain.
She ran through the palace – a thing possessed.
She saw the marriage bed – her hands clawed her hair –
She smashed the door shut, she called out to Laius,
As if his ghost could gather her in his arms.
She remembered giving birth to their boy –
The son who slayed his father – who slayed herself
Taking her in marriage, her children's father,
Her child her husband – I saw her tears trip her.
I heard the queen's voice rip Heaven asunder.
How did she take her own life? I do not know –
Oedipus was shouting – he burst into the room –
Screaming we should not see this woman's end.
But we looked on him in his blind panic –
A mad, cornered bull, demanding his own sword.
He asked where was his wife who was not his wife.

He was her child, her own flesh and her blood.
Their blood and their flesh passed through their
  children.
In his madness no man dared go near him,
As if some power was present inside him –
A terrible spirit, leading him, shrieking.
His fists beat at the double doors, breaking the bolts.
They fell apart, we can see straight into the hall –
See a woman hanging, the rope still swinging.
When he found her, a mighty roar flew from him.
He loosened the knot, he laid her on the ground.
And what he did next – I still dread to see it.
There were pinned on her clothes brooches cut from
  gold –
The woman had dressed herself in her finery –
He raised and rammed them into his eyeballs.
These were his words – here's what he shouted,
He would no more see the suffering he'd caused.
His eyes now would be at home in the darkness.
They would not know those he still wished to know.
He repeated this curse over and over –
His hands all the while destroying his eyes.
At each blow their blood bathed his cheeks red,
Not in drops but a dark downpour of rain.
This burden is shared by the two suffering –
Man and wife who've brought this horror on their
  heads.
Well may we yearn for the joys of yesteryear –
Aye, they were days when the world was a pleasure.
Now there's lamentation, ruin, shame and evil.
Men, name your poison – we'll drain it to the dregs.

Chorus
  The poor man in pain – can comfort be offered?

Messenger
  He cries out –

Open the gates –
Show all of Thebes –
He is his father's killer –
He is his mother's –
The word is too soiled –
I cannot stain your ears.
He wants to be banished.
He'll wait no longer.
Curse upon curse
He hammers upon himself.
The man is blind –
He needs someone to lead him.
This sickness devours him.
You'll see that yourself.
The gates open.
Prepare for a sight
A stone would pity.

Oedipus enters, blind.

Chorus

I bear witness to the end of the world.
What madness – what god descended on you?
Whose hand hurled you into this black pit?
Poor man, I cannot – I cannot look at you.
I have so much to ask and to learn from you,
But you send a shiver through my soul.

Oedipus

I walk in a cloud of darkness.
An evil wind blows through it.
But it will last for ever –
No change to night or day.
My heart is torn in torment,
Pierced by swords of sorrow.
The memory of what I was –
The memory of what I did –

They sting through to my bones.
Where do my two feet tread?
Where does my voice carry?

Chorus

A place like jet and ebony –
Too terrible to say.
Your grief is great.
Your heart has twice broken.

Oedipus

Friend, you've proved you're loyal.
You still care for the blind fellow.
Though I can't see, I know it's you –

Chorus

You have done a hideous thing, man.
Why stab the light from your eyes?
Which of the gods forced you?

Oedipus

Apollo, friends – it was Apollo.
He delights – he dances to see me suffer.
This hand alone stole my sight from me.
When nothing is there, why need I see?

Chorus

I can give you no answer.

Oedipus

All that was sweet is spilt and gone.
Lead me out of this place quietly.
A man most hateful to the gods,
A ball to kick beneath their feet,
Without bearings, in all directions –

Chorus

Fate has raised its fist and felled you in one blow.
Would I had never so much as known you.

I cannot give you comfort nor counsel.
Better to die than to live and be blind.

Oedipus
I refuse your counsel and your comfort.
I did what I did for the best – don't preach.
My father and mother wait for me in Hades.
Hanging is too good for their hideous son.
How can I see them and not bleed tears?
I thought the gods shone from my children's eyes.
They were born for me to look at – no more.
Most noble, most notorious in all Thebes,
I turn my back on its towers and temples.
I hear its gods scorn me, their statues speak –
You have revolted the whole race of Laius.
Would I be able to look straight in the eye –
How can I face people, filth that I am?
Let me mutilate this body of mine.
Slice off my ear to suit my blind eyes.
Hide me away and let me hear nothing –
It is sweet to turn myself into deaf stone.
Why did you save me, mountains of Cithaeron?
Take me, kill me, on the spot I was found.
I was the ancient house of Corinth –
Polybus, my father, a beautiful man –
I boasted his blood bred my strong features.
What was festering beneath that fine mask?
I am the stem, the root of all evil.
I call to mind where I murdered my father –
The hidden glen, woodlands, the three roads meeting,
Drenched with his blood drunk from my bare hands.
Do you remember the deeds I have done?
What did I do next, coming to this city?
Who did I marry? Let me remember.
Did I have children – where did they come from?
The same seed and womb that gave birth to me?

What are the words to answer my questions?
Husband and wife are mother and son,
Brother is father to kith and kindred –
Human beings turned to inhuman beasts.
No worse, there is none than what I have done.
In the name of the gods, get me from this city.
Kill me – drown me – never more set eyes on me.
Feel free to touch me – I will not taint you –
I am the sole carrier of my crimes.
They will not infect you – fear not – obey –

Chorus

Ask Creon to do what you demand.
He is now guardian in place of you.

Creon enters.

Oedipus

What can I say to this man?
What right have I to a hearing?
Night and day I have wronged him.

Creon

Oedipus, I have not come here to blame,
Nor will I throw insults back at your face.
You have lost all time for human law –
Have respect for the loving light of the sun,
The father that feeds and sustains us all.
Do not stand exposed in your grief and guilt.
The earth and the sacred skies reject you.
Get him inside the house as soon as we can.
Those he belongs to alone should see this.
That is what pity and kinship demand.

Oedipus

Against all hope, you come to see me,
A good man giving a hand to a bad one –
In the name of the gods, obey me in one thing.
I speak for your benefit, and not mine.

Creon

What is it you beg of me?

Oedipus

Drive me from this land –
Where no mortal man comes near.

Creon

Know that is what I would intend –
First I must find out what God wants.

Oedipus

Did the oracle not make that obvious?
I killed my father – the sinner must die.

Creon

That seems the case, but I'll see where we stand –
Better be certain what needs to be done.

Oedipus

You will speak up for this poor man here?

Creon

You'll surely believe in the god now.

Oedipus

I demand one thing only from you.
I beg you, bury that woman in the house.
Show due ceremony – she is of your blood.
Banish me to wild mountains, my Cithaeron,
Where my benign parents buried me alive,
That way we might not destroy each other.
I now can fear neither plague nor sickness.
Soft-hearted Death has something else in store.
Ah, misfortune – let me meet it head on.
Don't worry about my sons for my sake.
They are men, they will manage whatever.
As for my girls, are they not a pity?
We sat each night sharing food at meal time.

They'd have given me the bite from their mouth.
Care for them – care for them – let me touch them.
If I could just put my hands upon them,
It would be as it was when I could see.

The Children of Oedipus enter.

Sobbing – do I hear my small ones sobbing?
Can Creon pity and bring me my youngsters?
Am I thinking – am I saying right?

Creon
Right.
They console you now, as always.

Oedipus
God guide you for that – guide you gentler than I was.
Children, where are you? Come here to my hands.
They are your brother's that butchered my eyes.
Eyes once shone brightly, as did your father
Who made you his own where he first was made.
I weep for you, not able to see you.
I can taste the bitter rest of your days,
Abused and abandoned, sentenced to life.
What company will show you kindness?
You'll come home crying, hungry, from the feasts.
You'll want to dream of your wedding day.
No one will take you – who would risk ruin?
What man would court that cruel connection?
Your dowry is death – father killed father
And made the beast with his own mother.
These are the taunts to be thrown against you.
Who will marry you? No one, my daughters –
Beautiful, barren – white-skinned, grown wrinkled.
You are their father and mother now, Creon.
The two who reared them are dead in the grave.
I've left them with no home, no husband.
Save them from the sins I have committed.

64

Good man, grant me this – let me touch your hand.
Children, I would have given you much advice
Had you been grown into big girls and boys –
Now all I ask is that you pray for me.
Lead a good life, better than your father's.

Creon
Enough crying – enough – the house, come in.

Oedipus
I'll do as I'm told –
Even if I don't want to.

Creon
Time cures all things.

Oedipus
You know what I require –

Creon
You tell me – I'll listen.

Oedipus
See you send me far from this land.

Creon
You want what only the gods give.

Oedipus
But I am the man the gods despise most.

Creon
Well then, you'll soon get what you want.

Oedipus
Would you say so?

Creon
I do not say what I do not mean.

Oedipus
Lead me away from here now.

Creon

Let go of your children.

Oedipus

Don't take them away from me.

Creon

Don't try to rule the roost – that's over.
You had your day – it's turned into night.

Oedipus, Creon, the Children and Servants exit.

Chorus

Look on Oedipus, lament him.
Remember and respect his deeds.
With envy we once eyed that man,
Now lost in a storm of sorrow.
The grave is waiting for us all.
Our comfort lies in the cold clay.
Turn to dust, and be contented.

Le coeur a ses raisons
Que la raison ne connait
   point.

                    Pascal

THE MODERN LIBRARY
OF THE WORLD'S BEST BOOKS

PENSÉES

THE PROVINCIAL
LETTERS

PENSÉES

THE
PROVINCIAL
LETTERS

by

BLAISE PASCAL

THE
MODERN LIBRARY
NEW YORK

Pensées translated by W. F. Trotter

The Provincial Letters translated by Thomas M'Crie

Random House IS THE PUBLISHER OF

THE MODERN LIBRARY

BENNETT A. CERF · DONALD S. KLOPFER · ROBERT K. HAAS

Manufactured in the United States of America

Printed by Parkway Printing Company   Paper by Richard Bauer & Co.

Bound by H. Wolff

CONTENTS

THE PROVINCIAL LETTERS

INTRODUCTION

No two writers could be more antagonistic in thought and spirit than Voltaire and Pascal. Yet the heretical Voltaire was extravagant in his praise of the writings of the moderate and pious Pascal, saying: *"The Provincial Letters* were models of eloquence and pleasantry. The best comedies of Molière have not more wit in them than the first letters; Bossuet has nothing more sublime than the last ones. . . . The first work of genius that appeared in prose was *The Provincial Letters*. Examples of every species of eloquence may there be found. There is not a single word in it which, after one hundred years, has undergone the change to which all living languages are liable. We may identify this work with the era when our language became fixed."

A century intervened between the writing of Pascal's two major works and Voltaire's judgment of their literary worth. In that time the violence attending the publication of *The Provincial Letters* was forgotten, and there remained only the clarity of Pascal's thought, the persuasiveness of his ideas and the magnificence of their expression in literary form.

Two hundred years later still, in our own time, the circumstances of embittered dissension under which Pascal wrote are entirely eclipsed by the ever-increasing appeal of his style, the ingenuity of his reasoning, his delicate wit and irony and, above all, the flawless discernment of his prose, which has been a model for writers of nearly every nationality and every century since the seventeenth.

The brief thirty-nine years of Pascal's life were a consecration to his intellectual passion for truth, as it found expression in his scientific contributions, to his search in the realm of the spirit for a moral and religious explanation of human existence and to his career as a writer whose clarity and eloquence are unique in literature.

In 1626, three years after his birth on June 19, 1623, at Clermont in Auvergne, Blaise Pascal's mother died. He was left with his older sister, Gilberte, and his younger sister, Jacqueline, in the care of his father. Stephen Pascal undertook the education of his three children. His instruction in literature and science was as enthusiastic as it was severe. Occasionally the father took his son to meetings of the Academy of Science, where soon the youth's curiosity was aroused.

At the age of eleven, Blaise Pascal wrote a treatise on the cessation of sounds in vibrating bodies when touched. The father was impressed. Always the pedagogue, he feared a too rapid development in his son and deliberately interrupted his study of geometry, of which the youthful Blaise was becoming more and more enamored, in order to give him a more general conception of the principles of scientific inquiry. Nonetheless, the child mathematician, secretly and without aid, mastered the Euclidian elements. Before he was sixteen years old he wrote a paper on Conic Sections which not only won the respect of the mathematicians of Paris, but even brought applause from the father, who forthwith rescinded his edict against the study of geometry.

What has become known as Pascal's "first conversion" occurred as a consequence of an accident to his father. Stephen Pascal had the misfortune to break his hip and he was treated by physicians who were devoted to the Jansenist cause. They succeeded not only in curing their patient, but also in winning the son to their doctrines.

It was at this time that Blaise Pascal set himself the task of constructing a machine for arithmetical calculations. He was then an adult of nineteen. After devising and discarding more than fifty models, he perfected one contrivance which, for its time, was something of an international marvel. From his labors with the intractable machine, Pascal turned his mind to the consideration of problems of atmospheric pressure which had puzzled scientists from Galileo to Torricelli. Pascal set himself the task of observing columns of mercury at different elevations. With the aid of M. Perier, who had married his sister Gilberte, the experiments were carried out with a precision and with results that were to astound the scientific world. Pascal had established the simple fact that changes in altitude and weather, affecting a column of mercury in a glass tube, could be accurately recorded. The world owes the barometer to his painstaking investigations.

Following his experiments in atmospheric pressures, Pascal devoted himself to a consideration of the general laws of the equilibrium of fluids and laid down the principles upon which the hydrostatic press is based, as well as the foundations for the modern science of pneumatics. The law of pressure, known as Pascal's Law, establishes that pressure applied to a confined fluid at any point is transmitted through the fluid in all directions undiminished.

From his studies in air and fluid phenomena, Pascal returned to his first love—mathematics—and wrote several notable treatises which raised him, even before he was twenty-seven, to a secure place among the world's foremost mathematicians. During this period he evolved his ingenious research on the Arithmetical Triangle and proceeded to create the structure for his historic studies in the doctrine of probabilities.

It should be borne in mind that this concentrated application in mathematics and the physical sciences was carried on while Pascal was afflicted with almost continuous illness. At eighteen his constitution was so seriously undermined that he, in his own words, "never lived a day without pain." When he was twenty-four he was stricken with a paralytic stroke which deprived him of the use of his limbs for months.

During this period of his illness, and while he pursued his manifold scientific activities, Pascal lived with his father and sister Jacqueline. Under their care and influence, his thoughts turned more and more to the study of Christian doctrine and the practice of its faith. In these he found solace immediately after the death of his father in 1651. The passing of Stephen Pascal and a long-felt vocation for the Church led Jacqueline to renounce the world by entering the convent at Port-Royal.

Alone in Paris, worldly interests claimed much of Pascal's time for two years, but again he found himself absorbed in his scientific studies. In 1654, he narrowly escaped death when his carriage was stopped at the brink of the Seine at the moment two of the horses harnessed to it had fallen into the river. Nervously shocked by the incident, Pascal decided to follow Jacqueline's example and all but embraced the monastic life. A mystical experience soon afterward so profoundly affected him that it became his "second conversion," compelling him to abandon his pursuit of science until just before his death. He became more and more attracted to the group which identified itself with the Abbey of Port-Royal des Champs, near Versailles.

At this moment in its history the Catholic Church was involved in a doctrinal controversy over the question of divine grace. The merits of this seventeenth-century dispute are still a matter of debate among scholars. The antagonists in this strife were the Jesuits and another group within the Catholic Church known as the Jansenists because of their adherence to the doctrines of Cornelius Jansen, author of the *Augustinus*. Port-Royal was a Jansenist stronghold. Arnauld, Professor of Theology at the Sorbonne, embracing the Jansenist cause, argued in behalf of the *Augustinus*. Charges of heresy were brought against the theologian.

The shy and sickly Pascal, who was now more closely identified with the Jansenist group through the influence of Jacqueline, was brought by Port-Royal unostentatiously into the controversy in defense of Arnauld. Under the signature of Louis de Montalte, he addressed a series of letters supposedly to a friend in the country. The first of these, published on January 13, 1656, looks gently and humorously into the charges against Arnauld. Ingenuously and with the utmost simplicity and grace of style, Pascal released under a pseudonym the first of eighteen letters to a non-existent provincial that were ultimately to capture the world's avid interest.

Until the first letter became known, the entire controversy was confined to the councils of the Church. Laymen began to read the unknown M. de Montalte. The sensation created by the first letters was not confined to Catholic circles, but the secular world, hitherto indifferent to the quarrel, became interested.

Pascal continued to write these polemical letters, unmercifully lashing out with all the force of raillery and sarcasm. As each letter appeared, the public became more and more aroused. The world could understand a doctrinal issue at last, and it had a champion in the unidentifiable M. de Montalte, whose piety was beyond reproach and whose adherence to Rome no one could dispute. Port-Royal was no longer an obscure monastery, but the very focus of a controversy that threatened to tear the Church asunder.

The impression created by *The Provincial Letters* was without precedent. They were circulated by the thousands throughout France. After the first edition in 1656 there was an uninterrupted succession of new printings until bibliophiles lost all count. Translated into every civilized language, they were what might be called, for want of a better name, leading bestsellers for more than two centuries.

By the time the tenth letter was written, Arnauld was completely vindicated. In fact, his case was entirely forgotten in the public's enthusiasm for the eloquence, the pertinence of reasoning and the richly imaginative allusiveness in Pascal's literary shafts. The response to his declaration of independence of thought and the authority of conscience was immediate and overwhelming.

No one found out that Louis de Montalte was in reality Blaise Pascal until after the author's death. During his lifetime the greatest secrecy was maintained. Yet, because nearly everyone associated with Port-Royal was suspected of the authorship, it was only natural that fingers should also point at the mild mathematician. After the third letter was pub-

lished, Pascal left Port-Royal and lived in Paris under the
name of M. de Mons. A priest called one day upon Pascal,
in order to see Gilberte's husband, M. Perier. The priest
spoke of his suspicions concerning the authorship of the letters, but so disarming were the replies that he left without
even noticing the sheets of the seventh letter, which had
just come from the printer and were lying exposed on the
bed.

Such dramatic moments were rare in Pascal's life. The
only adventures he knew were adventures of the mind and
spirit. A meticulous writer, he achieved his simplicity and
directness of style by a painfully assiduous application to
his task. Some of his letters required twenty days for com-
position and were re-written and revised dozens of times with
the utmost pains.

The sensation the letters produced in the controversy between Jesuits and Jansenists was, at best, ephemeral; the influence upon the literature of France and the world was per-
manent, if a period of three hundred years is to be counted
as a little more than a moment in eternity. The polemical
nature of *The Provincial Letters* did not prevent them from
becoming what Boileau, the seventeenth-century classicist
critic, pronounced a work that "surpassed at once the ancients and the moderns." Voltaire, Sainte-Beuve and other
critics of every religious and literary persuasion, including
those of our own day, attest to the imperishability of *The
Provincial Letters*.

The actual time during which they were composed and
issued was between January 13, 1656, and March 24, 1657.
After the last of the letters was written, Pascal looked forward to a period of leisure in which he could devote himself
to a projected book on the Evidences of Religion. For a while
his interest in mathematics was revived, and he became absorbed in the problems of the geometry of the cycloid. Within
a very brief time he found a method for approaching the in-
tricacies of these problems and laid the groundwork by which

Newton and Leibnitz were able to bring them to final solution.

In spite of his precarious health and his unexpectedly brief return to scientific activity in the field of geometry, Pascal went back during the last year in which he was able to work to the manuscript on the Evidences of Religion. It was written in fragments, and the portions that his friends could find of it were published eight years after his death under the title, *Pensées de M. Pascal sur la Religion, et sur quelques autres sujets.*

Known and revered everywhere in the world under the briefer title, *Pensées,* it has become a kind of gospel to men of every variety of religious, aesthetic and philosophical inclination. The profundity of its thought, the lucidity of its expression and the genuine sentiment pervading its pages succeed in giving a more vivid apology for Christian faith than all the abstruse arguments of the theologians combined. Fragmentary as the thoughts are, they are integrated in their general patterns; they trace the universal search for God. Pascal is pre-eminently the religious writer who cuts across doctrine and into the very heart of the moral problem. Always persuasive, he appeals to the intellect by his passion for truth and his spiritual rectitude. But, above all, he appeals to the emotions by his almost merciless description of the plight of man without God.

As *The Provincial Letters* must be considered a masterpiece of polemical religious writing, so the *Pensées* must be regarded as a vindication and exaltation of faith. Wherever literature is treasured, this book is a living force. To Pascal, the man of science, reason alone was powerless to mitigate the human predicament. To Pascal, the man of ardent religious principles, only the power of faith and mystic revelation sufficed, for "the heart has reasons of which reason itself knows nothing."

After his sister Jacqueline, who had become sub-prioress of the Abbey of Port-Royal, died in 1661, Blaise Pascal found a home with his surviving sister, Madame Perier. In June of

1662, he was seized with a violent illness and, after lingering two months, died on August 19th at the age of thirty-nine.

The editors of the Modern Library are indeed proud to be able to offer the translation of all of Pascal's *Pensées* and *The Provincial Letters* for the first time in a single volume.

July, 1941   SAXE COMMINS

PENSÉES

THOUGHTS ON MIND AND ON STYLE

I

The difference between the mathematical and the intuitive mind.—In the one the principles are palpable, but removed from ordinary use; so that for want of habit it is difficult to turn one's mind in that direction: but if one turns it thither ever so little, one sees the principles fully, and one must have a quite inaccurate mind who reasons wrongly from principles so plain that it is almost impossible they should escape notice.

But in the intuitive mind the principles are found in common use, and are before the eyes of everybody. One has only to look, and no effort is necessary; it is only a question of good eyesight, but it must be good, for the principles are so subtle and so numerous, that it is almost impossible but that some escape notice. Now the omission of one principle leads to error; thus one must have very clear sight to see all the principles, and in the next place an accurate mind not to draw false deductions from known principles.

All mathematicians would then be intuitive if they had clear sight, for they do not reason incorrectly from principles known to them; and intuitive minds would be mathematical if they could turn their eyes to the principles of mathematics to which they are unused.

The reason, therefore, that some intuitive minds are not mathematical is that they cannot at all turn their attention to the principles of mathematics. But the reason that mathematicians are not intuitive is that they do not see what is before them, and that, accustomed to the exact and plain prin-

ciples of mathematics, and not reasoning till they have well
inspected and arranged their principles, they are lost in matters of intuition where the principles do not allow of such
arrangement. They are scarcely seen; they are felt rather
than seen; there is the greatest difficulty in making them felt
by those who do not of themselves perceive them. These principles are so fine and so numerous that a very delicate and very
clear sense is needed to perceive them, and to judge rightly
and justly when they are perceived, without for the most part
being able to demonstrate them in order as in mathematics;
because the principles are not known to us in the same way,
and because it would be an endless matter to undertake it. We
must see the matter at once, at one glance, and not by a
process of reasoning, at least to a certain degree. And thus it
is rare that mathematicians are intuitive, and that men of intuition are mathematicians, because mathematicians wish to
treat matters of intuition mathematically, and make themselves ridiculous, wishing to begin with definitions and then
with axioms, which is not the way to proceed in this kind of
reasoning. Not that the mind does not do so, but it does it
tacitly, naturally, and without technical rules; for the expression of it is beyond all men, and only a few can feel it.

Intuitive minds, on the contrary, being thus accustomed to
judge at a single glance, are so astonished when they are presented with propositions of which they understand nothing,
and the way to which is through definitions and axioms so
sterile, and which they are not accustomed to see thus in detail, that they are repelled and disheartened.

But dull minds are never either intuitive or mathematical.

Mathematicians who are only mathematicians have exact
minds, provided all things are explained to them by means of
definitions and axioms; otherwise they are inaccurate and
insufferable, for they are only right when the principles are
quite clear.

And men of intuition who are only intuitive cannot have
the patience to reach to first principles of things speculative

and conceptual, which they have never seen in the world, and which are altogether out of the common.

2

There are different kinds of right understanding; some have right understanding in a certain order of things, and not in others, where they go astray. Some draw conclusions well from a few premises, and this displays an acute judgment.

Others draw conclusions well where there are many premises.

For example, the former easily learn hydrostatics, where the premises are few, but the conclusions are so fine that only the greatest acuteness can reach them.

And in spite of that these persons would perhaps not be great mathematicians, because mathematics contain a great number of premises, and there is perhaps a kind of intellect that can search with ease a few premises to the bottom, and cannot in the least penetrate those matters in which there are many premises.

There are then two kinds of intellect: the one able to penetrate acutely and deeply into the conclusions of given premises, and this is the precise intellect; the other able to comprehend a great number of premises without confusing them, and this is the mathematical intellect. The one has force and exactness, the other comprehension. Now the one quality can exist without the other; the intellect can be strong and narrow, and can also be comprehensive and weak.

3

Those who are accustomed to judge by feeling do not understand the process of reasoning, for they would understand at first sight, and are not used to seek for principles. And others, on the contrary, who are accustomed to reason from principles, do not at all understand matters of feeling, seeking principles, and being unable to see at a glance.

4

Mathematics, intuition.—True eloquence makes light of eloquence, true morality makes light of morality; that is to say, the morality of the judgment, which has no rules, makes light of the morality of the intellect.

For it is to judgment that perception belongs, as science belongs to intellect. Intuition is the part of judgment, mathematics of intellect.

To make light of philosophy is to be a true philosopher.

5

Those who judge of a work by rule are in regard to others as those who have a watch are in regard to others. One says, "It is two hours ago"; the other says, "It is only three-quarters of an hour." I look at my watch, and say to the one, "You are weary," and to the other, "Time gallops with you"; for it is only an hour and a half ago, and I laugh at those who tell me that time goes slowly with me, and that I judge by imagination. They do not know that I judge by my watch.

6

Just as we harm the understanding, we harm the feelings also.

The understanding and the feelings are moulded by intercourse; the understanding and feelings are corrupted by intercourse. Thus good or bad society improves or corrupts them. It is, then, all-important to know how to choose in order to improve and not to corrupt them; and we cannot make this choice, if they be not already improved and not corrupted. Thus a circle is formed, and those are fortunate who escape it.

7

The greater intellect one has, the more originality one finds in men. Ordinary persons find no difference between men.

8

There are many people who listen to a sermon in the same way as they listen to vespers.

9

When we wish to correct with advantage, and to show another that he errs, we must notice from what side he views the matter, for on that side it is usually true, and admit that truth to him, but reveal to him the side on which it is false. He is satisfied with that, for he sees that he was not mistaken, and that he only failed to see all sides. Now, no one is offended at not seeing everything; but one does not like to be mistaken, and that perhaps arises from the fact that man naturally cannot see everything, and that naturally he cannot err in the side he looks at, since the perceptions of our senses are always true.

10

People are generally better persuaded by the reasons which they have themselves discovered than by those which have come into the mind of others.

11

All great amusements are dangerous to the Christian life; but among all those which the world has invented there is none more to be feared than the theatre. It is a representation of the passions so natural and so delicate that it excites them and gives birth to them in our hearts, and, above all, to that of love, principally when it is represented as very chaste and virtuous. For the more innocent it appears to innocent souls, the more they are likely to be touched by it. Its violence pleases our self-love, which immediately forms a desire to produce the same effects which are seen so well represented; and, at the same time, we make ourselves a conscience founded on the propriety of the feelings which we see there, by which the fear of pure souls is removed, since they imagine that it

cannot hurt their purity to love with a love which seems to
them so reasonable.

So we depart from the theatre with our heart so filled with
all the beauty and tenderness of love, the soul and the mind so
persuaded of its innocence, that we are quite ready to receive
its first impressions, or rather to seek an opportunity of awak-
ening them in the heart of another, in order that we may
receive the same pleasures and the same sacrifices which we
have seen so well represented in the theatre.

12

Scaramouch, who only thinks of one thing.

The doctor, who speaks for a quarter of an hour after he has
said everything, so full is he of the desire of talking.

13

One likes to see the error, the passion of Cleobuline, because she is unconscious of it. She would be displeasing, if she
were not deceived.

14

When a natural discourse paints a passion or an effect, one
feels within oneself the truth of what one reads, which was
there before, although one did not know it. Hence one is inclined to love him who makes us feel it, for he has not shown
us his own riches, but ours. And thus this benefit renders him
pleasing to us, besides that such community of intellect as we
have with him necessarily inclines the heart to love.

15

Eloquence, which persuades by sweetness, not by authority;
as a tyrant, not as a king.

16

Eloquence is an art of saying things in such a way—(1)
that those to whom we speak may listen to them without pain
and with pleasure; (2) that they feel themselves interested,

so that self-love leads them more willingly to reflection upon it.

It consists, then, in a correspondence which we seek to establish between the head and the heart of those to whom we speak, on the one hand, and, on the other, between the thoughts and the expressions which we employ. This assumes that we have studied well the heart of man so as to know all its powers, and then to find the just proportions of the discourse which we wish to adapt to them. We must put ourselves in the place of those who are to hear us, and make trial on our own heart of the turn which we give to our discourse in order to see whether one is made for the other, and whether we can assure ourselves that the hearer will be, as it were, forced to surrender. We ought to restrict ourselves, so far as possible, to the simple and natural, and not to magnify that which is little, or belittle that which is great. It is not enough that a thing be beautiful; it must be suitable to the subject, and there must be in it nothing of excess or defect.

17

Rivers are roads which move, and which carry us whither we desire to go.

18

When we do not know the truth of a thing, it is of advantage that there should exist a common error which determines the mind of man, as, for example, the moon, to which is attributed the change of seasons, the progress of diseases, etc. For the chief malady of man is restless curiosity about things which he cannot understand; and it is not so bad for him to be in error as to be curious to no purpose.

The manner in which Epictetus, Montaigne, and Salomon de Tultie wrote is the most usual, the most suggestive, the most remembered, and the oftenest quoted; because it is entirely composed of thoughts born from the common talk of life. As when we speak of the common error which exists among men that the moon is the cause of everything, we never fail to say that Salomon de Tultie says that when we do not know the truth of a thing, it is of advantage that there should exist a common error, etc.; which is the thought above.

19

The last thing one settles in writing a book is what one should put in first.

20

Order.—Why should I undertake to divide my virtues into four rather than into six? Why should I rather establish virtue in four, in two, in one? Why into *Abstine et sustine* rather than into "Follow Nature," or, "Conduct your private affairs without injustice," as Plato, or anything else? But there, you will say, everything is contained in one word. Yes, but it is useless without explanation, and when we come to explain it, as soon as we unfold this maxim which contains all the rest, they emerge in that first confusion which you desired to avoid. So, when they are all included in one, they are hidden and useless, as in a chest, and never appear save in their natural confusion. Nature has established them all without including one in the other.

21

Nature has made all her truths independent of one another. Our art makes one dependent on the other. But this is not natural. Each keeps its own place.

22

Let no one say that I have said nothing new; the arrangement of the subject is new. When we play tennis, we both play with the same ball, but one of us places it better.

I had as soon it said that I used words employed before. And in the same way if the same thoughts in a different arrangement do not form a different discourse, no more do the same words in their different arrangement form different thoughts!

23

Words differently arranged have a different meaning, and meanings differently arranged have different effects.

24

Language.—We should not turn the mind from one thing to another, except for relaxation, and that when it is necessary and the time suitable, and not otherwise. For he that relaxes out of season wearies, and he who wearies us out of season makes us languid, since we turn quite away. So much does our perverse lust like to do the contrary of what those wish to obtain from us without giving us pleasure, the coin for which we will do whatever is wanted.

25

Eloquence.—It requires the pleasant and the real; but the pleasant must itself be drawn from the true.

26

Eloquence is a painting of thought; and thus those who, after having painted it, add something more, make a picture instead of a portrait.

27

Miscellaneous. Language.—Those who make antitheses by forcing words are like those who make false windows for symmetry. Their rule is not to speak accurately, but to make apt figures of speech.

28

Symmetry is what we see at a glance; based on the fact that there is no reason for any difference, and based also on the face of man; whence it happens that symmetry is only wanted in breadth, not in height or depth.

29

When we see a natural style, we are astonished and delighted; for we expected to see an author, and we find a man.

Whereas those who have good taste, and who seeing a book expect to find a man, are quite surprised to find an author. *Plus poetice quam humane locutus es.* Those honour Nature well, who teach that she can speak on everything, even on theology.

30

We only consult the ear because the heart is wanting. The rule is uprightness.

Beauty of omission, of judgment.

31

All the false beauties which we blame in Cicero have their admirers, and in great number.

32

There is a certain standard of grace and beauty which consists in a certain relation between our nature, such as it is, weak or strong, and the thing which pleases us.

Whatever is formed according to this standard pleases us, be it house, song, discourse, verse, prose, woman, birds, rivers, trees, rooms, dress, etc. Whatever is not made according to this standard displeases those who have good taste.

And as there is a perfect relation between a song and a house which are made after a good model, because they are like this good model, though each after its kind; even so there is a perfect relation between things made after a bad model. Not that the bad model is unique, for there are many; but each bad sonnet, for example, on whatever false model it is formed, is just like a woman dressed after that model.

Nothing makes us understand better the ridiculousness of a false sonnet than to consider nature and the standard, and then to imagine a woman or a house made according to that standard.

33

Poetical beauty.—As we speak of poetical beauty, so ought we to speak of mathematical beauty and medical beauty. But we do not do so; and the reason is that we know well what is the object of mathematics, and that it consists in proofs, and what is the object of medicine, and that it consists in healing. But we do not know in what grace consists, which is the object of poetry. We do not know the natural model which we ought to imitate; and through lack of this knowledge, we have coined fantastic terms, "The golden age," "The wonder of our times," "Fatal," etc., and call this jargon poetical beauty.

But whoever imagines a woman after this model, which consists in saying little things in big words, will see a pretty girl adorned with mirrors and chains, at whom he will smile; because we know better wherein consists the charm of woman than the charm of verse. But those who are ignorant would admire her in this dress, and there are many villages in which she would be taken for the queen; hence we call sonnets made after this model "Village Queens."

34

No one passes in the world as skilled in verse unless he has put up the sign of a poet, a mathematician, etc. But educated people do not want a sign, and draw little distinction between the trade of a poet and that of an embroiderer.

People of education are not called poets or mathematicians, etc.; but they are all these, and judges of all these. No one guesses what they are. When they come into society, they talk on matters about which the rest are talking. We do not observe in them one quality rather than another, save when they have to make use of it. But then we remember it, for it is characteristic of such persons that we do not say of them that they are fine speakers, when it is not a question of oratory, and that we say of them that they are fine speakers, when it is such a question.

It is therefore false praise to give a man when we say of him, on his entry, that he is a very clever poet; and it is a bad sign when a man is not asked to give his judgment on some verses.

35

We should not be able to say of a man, "He is a mathematician," or "a preacher," or "eloquent"; but that he is "a gentleman." That universal quality alone pleases me. It is a bad sign when, on seeing a person, you remember his book. I would prefer you to see no quality till you meet it and have occasion to use it (*Ne quid nimis*), for fear some one quality prevail and designate the man. Let none think him a fine speaker, unless oratory be in question, and then let them think it.

36

Man is full of wants: he loves only those who can satisfy them all. "This one is a good mathematician," one will say. But I have nothing to do with mathematics; he would take me for a proposition. "That one is a good soldier." He would take me for a besieged town. I need, then, an upright man who can accommodate himself generally to all my wants.

37

[Since we cannot be universal and know all that is to be known of everything, we ought to know a little about everything. For it is far better to know something about everything than to know all about one thing. This universality is the best. If we can have both, still better; but if we must choose, we ought to choose the former. And the world feels this and does so; for the world is often a good judge.]

38

A poet and not an honest man.

39

If lightning fell on low places, etc., poets, and those who can only reason about things of that kind, would lack proofs.

40

If we wished to prove the examples which we take to prove other things, we should have to take those other things to be examples; for, as we always believe the difficulty is in what we wish to prove, we find the examples clearer and a help to demonstration.

Thus when we wish to demonstrate a general theorem, we must give the rule as applied to a particular case; but if we wish to demonstrate a particular case, we must begin with the general rule. For we always find the thing obscure which we wish to prove, and that clear which we use for the proof; for, when a thing is put forward to be proved, we first fill ourselves with the imagination that it is therefore obscure, and on the contrary that what is to prove it is clear, and so we understand it easily.

41

Epigrams of Martial.—Man loves malice, but not against one-eyed men nor the unfortunate, but against the fortunate and proud. People are mistaken in thinking otherwise.

For lust is the source of all our actions, and humanity, etc. We must please those who have humane and tender feelings. That epigram about two one-eyed people is worthless, for it does not console them, and only gives a point to the author's glory. All that is only for the sake of the author is worthless. *Ambitiosa recident ornamenta.*

42

To call a king "Prince" is pleasing, because it diminishes his rank.

43

Certain authors, speaking of their works, say, "My book," "My commentary," "My history," etc. They resemble middle-class people who have a house of their own, and always have "My house" on their tongue. They would do better to say,

"Our book," "Our commentary," "Our history," etc., because there is in them usually more of other people's than their own.

44

Do you wish people to believe good of you? Don't speak.

45

Languages are ciphers, wherein letters are not changed into letters, but words into words, so that an unknown language is decipherable.

46

A maker of witticisms, a bad character.

47

There are some who speak well and write badly. For the place and the audience warm them, and draw from their minds more than they think of without that warmth.

48

When we find words repeated in a discourse, and, in trying to correct them, discover that they are so appropriate that we would spoil the discourse, we must leave them alone. This is the test; and our attempt is the work of envy, which is blind, and does not see that repetition is not in this place a fault; for there is no general rule.

49

To mask nature and disguise her. No more king, pope, bishop—but *august monarch*, etc.; not Paris—*the capital of the kingdom*. There are places in which we ought to call Paris, Paris, and others in which we ought to call it the capital of the kingdom.

50

The same meaning changes with the words which express it. Meanings receive their dignity from words instead of giving it to them. Examples should be sought. . . .

"With reverence be it spoken . . ." The only thing bad is
their excuse.

59

"To extinguish the torch of sedition"; too luxuriant. "The
restlessness of his genius"; two superfluous grand words.

51

Sceptic, for obstinate.

52

No one calls another a Cartesian but he who is one himse
a pedant but a pedant, a provincial but a provincial; and
would wager it was the printer who put it on the title o
Letters to a Provincial.

53

A carriage *upset* or *overturned*, according to the meaning.
To spread abroad or *upset*, according to the meaning. (The
argument by force of M. le Maître over the friar.)

54

Miscellaneous.—A form of speech, "I should have liked to
apply myself to that."

55

The *aperitive* virtue of a key, the *attractive* virtue of a hook.

56

To guess: "The part that I take in our trouble." The Cardinal did not want to be guessed.

"My mind is disquieted." *I am disquieted* is better.

57

I always feel uncomfortable under such compliments as
these: "I have given you a great deal of trouble," "I am afraid
I am boring you," "I fear this is too long." We either carry our
audience with us, or irritate them.

58

You are ungraceful: "Excuse me, pray." Without th
excuse I would not have known there was anything an

THE MISERY OF MAN WITHOUT GOD

60

First part: Misery of man without God.

Second part: Happiness of man with God.

Or, *First part:* That nature is corrupt. Proved by nature itself.

Second part: That there is a Redeemer. Proved by Scripture.

61

Order.—I might well have taken this discourse in an order like this: to show the vanity of all conditions of men, to show the vanity of ordinary lives, and then the vanity of philosophic lives, sceptics, stoics; but the order would not have been kept. I know a little what it is, and how few people understand it. No human science can keep it. Saint Thomas did not keep it. Mathematics keep it, but they are useless on account of their depth.

62

Preface to the first part.—To speak of those who have treated of the knowledge of self; of the divisions of Charron, which sadden and weary us; of the confusion of Montaigne; that he was quite aware of his want of method, and shunned it by jumping from subject to subject; that he sought to be fashionable.

His foolish project of describing himself! And this not casually and against his maxims, since every one makes mistakes, but by his maxims themselves, and by first and chief design. For to say silly things by chance and weakness is a common misfortune; but to say them intentionally is intolerable, and to say such as that . . .

63

Montaigne.—Montaigne's faults are great. Lewd words; this is bad, notwithstanding Mademoiselle de Gournay. Credulous; *people without eyes*. Ignorant; *squaring the circle, a greater world*. His opinions on suicide, on death. He suggests an indifference about salvation, *without fear and without repentance*. As his book was not written with a religious purpose, he was not bound to mention religion; but it is always our duty not to turn men from it. One can excuse his rather free and licentious opinions on some relations of life (730,231); but one cannot excuse his thoroughly pagan views on death, for a man must renounce piety altogether, if he does not at least wish to die like a Christian. Now, through the whole of his book his only conception of death is a cowardly and effeminate one.

64

It is not in Montaigne, but in myself, that I find all that I see in him.

65

What good there is in Montaigne can only have been acquired with difficulty. The evil that is in him, I mean apart from his morality, could have been corrected in a moment, if he had been informed that he made too much of trifles and spoke too much of himself.

66

One must know oneself. If this does not serve to discover truth, it at least serves as a rule of life, and there is nothing better.

67

The vanity of the sciences.—Physical science will not console me for the ignorance of morality in the time of affliction. But the science of ethics will always console me for the ignorance of the physical sciences.

68

Men are never taught to be gentlemen, and are taught everything else; and they never plume themselves so much on the rest of their knowledge as on knowing how to be gentlemen. They only plume themselves on knowing the one thing they do not know.

69

The infinites, the mean.—When we read too fast or too slowly, we understand nothing.

70

Nature . . . —[Nature has set us so well in the centre, that if we change one side of the balance, we change the other also. *I act.* Τά ζῶα τρέχει. This makes me believe that the springs in our brain are so adjusted that he who touches one touches also its contrary.]

71

Too much and too little wine. Give him none, he cannot find truth; give him too much, the same.

72

Man's disproportion.—[This is where our innate knowledge leads us. If it be not true, there is no truth in man; and if it be true, he finds therein great cause for humiliation, being compelled to abase himself in one way or another. And since he cannot exist without this knowledge, I wish that, before entering on deeper researches into nature, he would consider her both seriously and at leisure, that he would reflect upon himself also, and knowing what proportion there is . . .] Let man then contemplate the whole of nature in her full and grand majesty, and turn his vision from the low objects which surround him. Let him gaze on that brilliant light, set like an eternal lamp to illumine the universe; let the earth appear to him a point in comparison with the vast circle described by the sun; and let him wonder at the fact that this vast circle is itself but a very fine point in comparison with that described by the stars in their revolution round the firmament. But if our view be arrested there, let our imagination pass beyond; it will sooner exhaust the power of conception than nature that of supplying material for conception. The whole visible world is only an imperceptible atom in the ample bosom of nature. No idea approaches it. We may enlarge our conceptions beyond all imaginable space; we only produce atoms in comparison with the reality of things. It is an infinite sphere, the centre of which is everywhere, the circumference nowhere. In short it is the greatest sensible mark of the almighty power of God, that imagination loses itself in that thought.

Returning to himself, let man consider what he is in comparison with all existence; let him regard himself as lost in this remote corner of nature; and from the little cell in which he finds himself lodged, I mean the universe, let him estimate at their true value the earth, kingdoms, cities, and himself. What is a man in the Infinite?

But to show him another prodigy equally astonishing, let him examine the most delicate things he knows. Let a mite be given him, with its minute body and parts incomparably more minute, limbs with their joints, veins in the limbs, blood in the veins, humours in the blood, drops in the humours, vapours in the drops. Dividing these last things again, let him exhaust his powers of conception, and let the last object at which he can arrive be now that of our discourse. Perhaps he will think that here is the smallest point in nature. I will let him see therein a new abyss. I will paint for him not only the visible universe, but all that he can conceive of nature's immensity in the womb of this abridged atom. Let him see therein an infinity of universes, each of which has its firmament, its planets, its earth, in the same proportion as in the visible world; in each earth animals, and in the last mites, in which he will find again all that the first had, finding still in these others the same thing without end and without cessation. Let him lose himself in wonders as amazing in their littleness as the others in their vastness. For who will not be astounded at the fact that our body, which a little while ago was imperceptible in the universe, itself imperceptible in the bosom of the whole, is now a colossus, a world, or rather a whole, in respect of the nothingness which we cannot reach? He who regards himself in this light will be afraid of himself, and observing himself sustained in the body given him by nature between those two abysses of the Infinite and Nothing, will tremble at the sight of these marvels; and I think that, as his curiosity changes into admiration, he will be more disposed to contemplate them in silence than to examine them with presumption.

For in fact what is man in nature? A Nothing in comparison with the Infinite, an All in comparison with the Nothing, a mean between nothing and everything. Since he is infinitely removed from comprehending the extremes, the end of things and their beginning are hopelessly hidden from him in an impenetrable secret; he is equally incapable of seeing the Nothing from which he was made, and the Infinite in which he is swallowed up.

What will he do then, but perceive the appearance of the middle of things, in an eternal despair of knowing either their beginning or their end. All things proceed from the Nothing, and are borne towards the Infinite. Who will follow these marvellous processes? The Author of these wonders understands them. None other can do so.

Through failure to contemplate these Infinites, men have rashly rushed into the examination of nature, as though they bore some proportion to her. It is strange that they have wished to understand the beginnings of things, and thence to arrive at the knowledge of the whole, with a presumption as infinite as their object. For surely this design cannot be formed without presumption or without a capacity infinite like nature.

If we are well informed, we understand that, as nature has graven her image and that of her Author on all things, they almost all partake of her double infinity. Thus we see that all the sciences are infinite in the extent of their researches. For who doubts that geometry, for instance, has an infinite infinity of problems to solve? They are also infinite in the multitude and fineness of their premises; for it is clear that those which are put forward as ultimate are not self-supporting, but are based on others which, again having others for their support, do not permit of finality. But we represent some as ultimate for reason, in the same way as in regard to material objects we call that an indivisible point beyond which our senses can no longer perceive anything, although by its nature it is infinitely divisible.

Of these two Infinites of science, that of greatness is the most palpable, and hence a few persons have pretended to know all things. "I will speak of the whole," said Democritus.

But the infinitely little is the least obvious. Philosophers have much oftener claimed to have reached it, and it is here they have all stumbled. This has given rise to such common titles as *First Principles*, *Principles of Philosophy*, and the like, as ostentatious in fact, though not in appearance, as that one which blinds us, *De omni scibili*.

We naturally believe ourselves far more capable of reaching the centre of things than of embracing their circumference. The visible extent of the world visibly exceeds us; but as we exceed little things, we think ourselves more capable of knowing them. And yet we need no less capacity for attaining the Nothing than the All. Infinite capacity is required for both, and it seems to me that whoever shall have understood the ultimate principles of being might also attain to the knowledge of the Infinite. The one depends on the other, and one leads to the other. These extremes meet and reunite by force of distance, and find each other in God, and in God alone.

Let us then take our compass; we are something, and we are

not everything. The nature of our existence hides from us the knowledge of first beginnings which are born of the Nothing; and the littleness of our being conceals from us the sight of the Infinite.

Our intellect holds the same position in the world of thought as our body occupies in the expanse of nature.

Limited as we are in every way, this state which holds the mean between two extremes is present in all our impotence. Our senses perceive no extreme. Too much sound deafens us; too much light dazzles us; too great distance or proximity hinders our view. Too great length and too great brevity of discourse tend to obscurity; too much truth is paralysing (I know some who cannot understand that to take four from nothing leaves nothing). First principles are too self-evident for us; too much pleasure disagrees with us. Too many concords are annoying in music; too many benefits irritate us; we wish to have the wherewithal to over-pay our debts. *Beneficia eo usque læta sunt dum videntur exsolvi posse; ubi multum antevenere, pro gratia odium redditur.* We feel neither extreme heat nor extreme cold. Excessive qualities are prejudicial to us and not perceptible by the senses; we do not feel but suffer them. Extreme youth and extreme age hinder the mind, as also too much and too little education. In short, extremes are for us as though they were not, and we are not within their notice. They escape us, or we them.

This is our true state; this is what makes us incapable of certain knowledge and of absolute ignorance. We sail within a vast sphere, ever drifting in uncertainty, driven from end to end. When we think to attach ourselves to any point and to fasten to it, it wavers and leaves us; and if we follow it, it eludes our grasp, slips past us, and vanishes for ever. Nothing stays for us. This is our natural condition, and yet most contrary to our inclination; we burn with desire to find solid ground and an ultimate sure foundation whereon to build a tower reaching to the Infinite. But our whole groundwork cracks, and the earth opens to abysses.

Let us therefore not look for certainty and stability. Our

reason is always deceived by fickle shadows; nothing can fix the finite between the two Infinites, which both enclose and fly from it.

If this be well understood, I think that we shall remain at rest, each in the state wherein nature has placed him. As this sphere which has fallen to us as our lot is always distant from either extreme, what matters it that man should have a little more knowledge of the universe? If he has it, he but gets a little higher. Is he not always infinitely removed from the end, and is not the duration of our life equally removed from eternity, even if it lasts ten years longer?

In comparison with these Infinites all finites are equal, and I see no reason for fixing our imagination on one more than on another. The only comparison which we make of ourselves to the finite is painful to us.

If man made himself the first object of study, he would see how incapable he is of going further. How can a part know the whole? But he may perhaps aspire to know at least the parts to which he bears some proportion. But the parts of the world are all so related and linked to one another, that I believe it impossible to know one without the other and without the whole.

Man, for instance, is related to all he knows. He needs a place wherein to abide, time through which to live, motion in order to live, elements to compose him, warmth and food to nourish him, air to breathe. He sees light; he feels bodies; in short, he is in a dependent alliance with everything. To know man, then, it is necessary to know how it happens that he needs air to live, and, to know the air, we must know how it is thus related to the life of man, etc. Flame cannot exist without air; therefore to understand the one, we must understand the other.

Since everything then is cause and effect, dependent and supporting, mediate and immediate, and all is held together by a natural though imperceptible chain, which binds together things most distant and most different, I hold it equally impossible to know the parts without knowing the whole, and to know the whole without knowing the parts in detail.

[The eternity of things in itself or in God must also astonish our brief duration. The fixed and constant immobility of nature, in comparison with the continual change which goes on within us, must have the same effect.]

And what completes our incapability of knowing things, is the fact that they are simple, and that we are composed of two opposite natures, different in kind, soul and body. For it is impossible that our rational part should be other than spiritual; and if any one maintain that we are simply corporeal, this would far more exclude us from the knowledge of things, there being nothing so inconceivable as to say that matter knows itself. It is impossible to imagine how it should know itself.

So if we are simply material, we can know nothing at all; and if we are composed of mind and matter, we cannot know perfectly things which are simple, whether spiritual or corporeal. Hence it comes that almost all philosophers have confused ideas of things, and speak of material things in spiritual terms, and of spiritual things in material terms. For they say boldly that bodies have a tendency to fall, that they seek after their centre, that they fly from destruction, that they fear the void, that they have inclinations, sympathies, antipathies, all of which attributes pertain only to mind. And in speaking of minds, they consider them as in a place, and attribute to them movement from one place to another; and these are qualities which belong only to bodies.

Instead of receiving the ideas of these things in their purity, we colour them with our own qualities, and stamp with our composite being all the simple things which we contemplate.

Who would not think, seeing us compose all things of mind and body, but that this mixture would be quite intelligible to us? Yet it is the very thing we least understand. Man is to himself the most wonderful object in nature; for he cannot conceive what the body is, still less what the mind is, and least of all how a body should be united to a mind. This is the consummation of his difficulties, and yet it is his very being. *Modus quo corporibus adhærent spiritus comprehendi ab hominibus non potest, et hoc tamen homo est.* Finally, to complete the proof of our weakness, I shall conclude with these two considerations. . . .

73

[But perhaps this subject goes beyond the capacity of reason. Let us therefore examine her solutions to problems within her powers. If there be anything to which her own interest must have made her apply herself most seriously, it is the inquiry into her own sovereign good. Let us see, then, wherein these strong and clear-sighted souls have placed it, and whether they agree.

One says that the sovereign good consists in virtue, another in pleasure, another in the knowledge of nature, another in truth, *Felix qui potuit rerum cognoscere causas,* another in total ignorance, another in indolence, others in disregarding appearances, another in wondering at nothing, *nihil admirari prope res una quæ possit facere et servare beatum,* and the true sceptics in their indifference, doubt, and perpetual suspense, and others, wiser, think to find a better definition. We are well satisfied.

To transpose after the laws to the following title.

We must see if this fine philosophy has gained nothing certain from so long and so intent study; perhaps at least the soul will know itself. Let us hear the rulers of the world on this subject. What have they thought of her substance? 394. Have they been more fortunate in locating her? 395. What have they found out about her origin, duration, and departure? 399.

Is then the soul too noble a subject for their feeble lights? Let us then abase her to matter and see if she knows whereof is made the very body which she animates, and those others which she contemplates and moves at her will. What have those great dogmatists, who are ignorant of nothing, known of this matter? *Harum sententiarum,* 393.

This would doubtless suffice, if reason were reasonable. She is reasonable enough to admit that she has been unable to find anything durable, but she does not yet despair of reaching it; she is as ardent as ever in this search, and is confident she has within her the necessary powers for this conquest. We must therefore conclude, and, after having examined her powers in their effects, observe them in themselves, and see if she has a nature and a grasp capable of laying hold of the truth.]

74

A letter *On the Foolishness of Human Knowledge and Philosophy.*

This letter before *Diversion.*

Felix qui potuit . . . Nihil admirari.

280 kinds of sovereign good in Montaigne.

75

Part I, 1, 2, c. 1, section 4.

[*Probability.*—It will not be difficult to put the case a stage lower, and make it appear ridiculous. To begin at the very beginning.] What is more absurd than to say that lifeless bodies have passions, fears, hatreds—that insensible bodies, lifeless and incapable of life, have passions which presuppose at least a sensitive soul to feel them, nay more, that the object of their dread is the void? What is there in the void that could make them afraid? Nothing is more shallow and ridiculous. This is not all; it is said that they have in themselves a source of movement to shun the void. Have they arms, legs, muscles, nerves?

76

To write against those who made too profound a study of science: Descartes.

77

I cannot forgive Descartes. In all his philosophy he would have been quite willing to dispense with God. But he had to make Him give a fillip to set the world in motion; beyond this, he has no further need of God.

78

Descartes useless and uncertain.

79

[*Descartes.*—We must say summarily: "This is made by figure and motion," for it is true. But to say what these are, and to compose the machine, is ridiculous. For it is useless, uncertain, and painful. And were it true, we do not think all philosophy is worth one hour of pain.]

80

How comes it that a cripple does not offend us, but that a fool does? Because a cripple recognises that we walk straight, whereas a fool declares that it is we who are silly; if it were not so, we should feel pity and not anger.

Epictetus asks still more strongly: "Why are we not angry if we are told that we have a headache, and why are we angry if we are told that we reason badly, or choose wrongly?" The reason is that we are quite certain that we have not a headache, or are not lame, but we are not so sure that we make a true choice. So having assurance only because we see with our whole sight, it puts us into suspense and surprise when another with his whole sight sees the opposite, and still more so when a thousand others deride our choice. For we must prefer our own lights to those of so many others, and that is bold and difficult. There is never this contradiction in the feelings towards a cripple.

81

It is natural for the mind to believe, and for the will to love; so that, for want of true objects, they must attach themselves to false.

82

Imagination.—It is that deceitful part in man, that mistress of error and falsity, the more deceptive that she is not always so; for she would be an infallible rule of truth, if she were an infallible rule of falsehood. But being most generally false, she gives no sign of her nature, impressing the same character on the true and the false.

I do not speak of fools, I speak of the wisest men; and it is among them that the imagination has the great gift of persuasion. Reason protests in vain; it cannot set a true value on things.

This arrogant power, the enemy of reason, who likes to rule and dominate it, has established in man a second nature to show how all-powerful she is. She makes men happy and sad, healthy and sick, rich and poor; she compels reason to believe, doubt, and deny; she blunts the senses, or quickens them; she has her fools and sages; and nothing vexes us more than to see that she fills her devotees with a satisfaction far more full and entire than does reason. Those who have a lively imagination are a great deal more pleased with themselves than the wise can reasonably be. They look down upon men with haughtiness; they argue with boldness and confidence, others with fear and diffidence; and this gaiety of countenance often gives them the advantage in the opinion of the hearers, such favour have the imaginary wise in the eyes of judges of like nature. Imagination cannot make fools wise; but she can make them happy, to the envy of reason which can only make its friends miserable; the one covers them with glory, the other with shame.

What but this faculty of imagination dispenses reputation, awards respect and veneration to persons, works, laws, and the great? How insufficient are all the riches of the earth without her consent!

Would you not say that this magistrate, whose venerable age commands the respect of a whole people, is governed by pure and lofty reason, and that he judges causes according to their true nature without considering those mere trifles which only affect the imagination of the weak? See him go to sermon, full of devout zeal, strengthening his reason with the ardour of his love. He is ready to listen witih exemplary respect. Let the preacher appear, and let nature have given him a hoarse

voice or a comical cast of countenance, or let his barber have
given him a bad shave, or let by chance his dress be more
dirtied than usual, then however great the truths he announces,
I wager our senator loses his gravity.

If the greatest philosopher in the world find himself upon a
plank wider than actually necessary, but hanging over a precipice, his imagination will prevail, though his reason convince
him of his safety. Many cannot bear the thought without a
cold sweat. I will not state all its effects.

Every one knows that the sight of cats or rats, the crushing
of a coal, etc., may unhinge the reason. The tone of voice
affects the wisest, and changes the force of a discourse or a
poem.

Love or hate alters the aspect of justice. How much greater
confidence has an advocate, retained with a large fee, in the
justice of his cause! How much better does his bold manner
make his case appear to the judges, deceived as they are by
appearances! How ludicrous is reason, blown with a breath in
every direction!

I should have to enumerate almost every action of men who
scarce waver save under her assaults. For reason has been
obliged to yield, and the wisest reason takes as her own principles those which the imagination of man has everywhere
rashly introduced. [He who would follow reason only would
be deemed foolish by the generality of men. We must judge by
the opinion of the majority of mankind. Because it has pleased
them, we must work all day for pleasures seen to be imaginary;
and after sleep has refreshed our tired reason, we must forthwith start up and rush after phantoms, and suffer the impressions of this mistress of the world. This is one of the sources of
error, but it is not the only one.]

Our magistrates have known well this mystery. Their red
robes, the ermine in which they wrap themselves like furry
cats, the courts in which they administer justice, the *fleurs-
de-lis*, and all such august apparel were necessary; if the physicians had not their cassocks and their mules, if the doctors
had not their square caps and their robes four times too wide,

they would never have duped the world, which cannot resist so original an appearance. If magistrates had true justice, and if physicians had the true art of healing, they would have no occasion for square caps; the majesty of these sciences would of itself be venerable enough. But having only imaginary knowledge, they must employ those silly tools that strike the imagination with which they have to deal; and thereby in fact they inspire respect. Soldiers alone are not disguised in this manner, because indeed their part is the most essential; they establish themselves by force, the others by show.

Therefore our kings seek out no disguises. They do not mask themselves in extraordinary costumes to appear such; but they are accompanied by guards and halberdiers. Those armed and red-faced puppets who have hands and power for them alone, those trumpets and drums which go before them, and those legions round about them, make the stoutest tremble They have not dress only, they have might. A very refined reason is required to regard as an ordinary man the Grand Turk, in his superb seraglio, surrounded by forty thousand janissaries.

We cannot even see an advocate in his robe and with his cap on his head, without a favourable opinion of his ability. The imagination disposes of everything; it makes beauty, justice, and happiness, which is everything in the world. I should much like to see an Italian work, of which I only know the title, which alone is worth many books, *Della opinione regina del mondo*. I approve of the book without knowing it, save the evil in it, if any. These are pretty much the effects of that deceptive faculty, which seems to have been expressly given us to lead us into necessary error. We have, however, many other sources of error.

Not only are old impressions capable of misleading us; the charms of novelty have the same power. Hence arise all the disputes of men, who taunt each other either with following the false impressions of childhood or with running rashly after the new. Who keeps the due mean? Let him appear and prove it. There is no principle, however natural to us from infancy, which may not be made to pass for a false impression either of education or of sense.

"Because," say some, "you have believed from childhood that a box was empty when you saw nothing in it, you have believed in the possibility of a vacuum. This is an illusion of your senses, strengthened by custom, which science must correct." "Because," say others, "you have been taught at school that there is no vacuum, you have perverted your common sense which clearly comprehended it, and you must correct this by returning to your first state." Which has deceived you, your senses or your education?

We have another source of error in diseases. They spoil the judgment and the senses; and if the more serious produce a sensible change, I do not doubt that slighter ills produce a proportionate impression.

Our own interest is again a marvellous instrument for nicely putting out our eyes. The justest man in the world is not allowed to be judge in his own cause; I know some who, in order not to fall into this self-love, have been perfectly unjust out of opposition. The sure way of losing a just cause has been to get it recommended to these men by their near relatives.

Justice and truth are two such subtle points, that our tools are too blunt to touch them accurately. If they reach the point, they either crush it, or lean all round, more on the false than on the true.

[Man is so happily formed that he has no . . . good of the true, and several excellent of the false. Let us now see how much . . . But the most powerful cause of error is the war existing between the senses and reason.]

83

We must thus begin the chapter on the deceptive powers. Man is only a subject full of error, natural and ineffaceable, without grace. Nothing shows him the truth. Everything deceives him. These two sources of truth, reason and the senses, besides being both wanting in sincerity, deceive each other in turn. The senses mislead the reason with false appearances, and receive from reason in their turn the same trickery which they apply to her; reason has her revenge. The passions of the soul trouble the senses, and make false impressions upon them. They rival each other in falsehood and deception.

But besides those errors which arise accidentally and through lack of intelligence, with these heterogeneous faculties . . .

84

The imagination enlarges little objects so as to fill our souls with a fantastic estimate; and, with rash insolence, it belittles the great to its own measure, as when talking of God.

85

Things which have most hold on us, as the concealment of our few possessions, are often a mere nothing. It is a nothing which our imagination magnifies into a mountain. Another turn of the imagination would make us discover this without difficulty.

86

[My fancy makes me hate a croaker, and one who pants when eating. Fancy has great weight. Shall we profit by it? Shall we yield to this weight because it is natural? No, but by resisting it . . .]

87

Næ iste magno conatu magnas nugas dixerit.
Quasi quidquam infelicius sit homini cui sua figmenta dominantur. (Plin.)

88

Children who are frightened at the face they have blackened are but children. But how shall one who is so weak in his childhood become really strong when he grows older? We only change our fancies. All that is made perfect by progress perishes also by progress. All that has been weak can never become absolutely strong. We say in vain, "He has grown, he has changed"; he is also the same.

89

Custom is our nature. He who is accustomed to the faith believes in it, can no longer fear hell, and believes in nothing else. He who is accustomed to believe that the king is terrible . . . etc. Who doubts then that our soul, being accustomed to see number, space, motion, believes that and nothing else?

90

Quod crebro videt non miratur, etiamsi cur fiat nescit; quod ante non viderit, id si evenerit, ostentum esse censet. (Cic. 583.)

91

Spongia solis.—When we see the same effect always recur, we infer a natural necessity in it, as that there will be a tomorrow, etc. But nature often deceives us, and does not subject herself to her own rules.

92

What are our natural principles but principles of custom? In children they are those which they have received from the habits of their fathers, as hunting in animals. A different custom will cause different natural principles. This is seen in experience; and if there are some natural principles ineradicable by custom, there are also some customs opposed to nature, ineradicable by nature, or by a second custom. This depends on disposition.

93

Parents fear lest the natural love of their children may fade away. What kind of nature is that which is subject to decay? Custom is a second nature which destroys the former. But what is nature? For is custom not natural? I am much afraid that nature is itself only a first custom, as custom is a second nature.

94

The nature of man is wholly natural, *omne animal.*

There is nothing he may not make natural; there is nothing natural he may not lose.

95

Memory, joy, are intuitions; and even mathematical propositions become intuitions, for education produces natural intuitions, and natural intuitions are erased by education.

96

When we are accustomed to use bad reasons for proving natural effects, we are not willing to receive good reasons when they are discovered. An example may be given from the circulation of the blood as a reason why the vein swells below the ligature.

97

The most important affair in life is the choice of a calling; chance decides it. Custom makes men masons, soldiers, slaters. "He is a good slater," says one, and, speaking of soldiers, remarks, "They are perfect fools." But others affirm, "There is nothing great but war, the rest of men are good for nothing." We choose our callings according as we hear this or that praised or despised in our childhood, for we naturally love truth and hate folly. These words move us; the only error is in their application. So great is the force of custom that out of those whom nature has only made men, are created all conditions of men. For some districts are full of masons, others of soldiers, etc. Certainly nature is not so uniform. It is custom then which does this, for it constrains nature. But sometimes nature gains the ascendancy, and preserves man's instinct, in spite of all custom, good or bad.

98

Bias leading to error.—It is a deplorable thing to see all men deliberating on means alone, and not on the end. Each thinks how he will acquit himself in his condition; but as for the choice of condition, or of country, chance gives them to us.

It is a pitiable thing to see so many Turks, heretics, and infidels follow the way of their fathers for the sole reason that each has been imbued with the prejudice that it is the best. And that fixes for each man his condition of locksmith, soldier, etc.

Hence savages care nothing for Providence.

99

There is an universal and essential difference between the actions of the will and all other actions.

The will is one of the chief factors in belief, not that it creates belief, but because things are true or false according to the aspect in which we look at them. The will, which prefers one aspect to another, turns away the mind from considering the qualities of all that it does not like to see; and thus the mind, moving in accord with the will, stops to consider the aspect which it likes, and so judges by what it sees.

100

Self-love.—The nature of self-love and of this human Ego is to love self only and consider self only. But what will man do? He cannot prevent this object that he loves from being full of faults and wants. He wants to be great, and he sees himself small. He wants to be happy, and he sees himself miserable. He wants to be perfect, and he sees himself full of imperfections. He wants to be the object of love and esteem among men, and he sees that his faults merit only their hatred and contempt. This embarrassment in which he finds himself produces in him the most unrighteous and criminal passion that can be imagined; for he conceives a mortal enmity against that truth which reproves him, and which convinces him of his faults. He would annihilate it, but, unable to destroy it in its essence, he destroys it as far as possible in his own knowledge and in that of others; that is to say, he devotes all his attention to hiding his faults both from others and from himself, and he cannot endure either that others should point them out to him, or that they should see them.

Truly it is an evil to be full of faults; but it is a still greater evil to be full of them, and to be unwilling to recognise them, since that is to add the further fault of a voluntary illusion. We do not like others to deceive us; we do not think it fair that they should be held in higher esteem by us than they deserve; it is not then fair that we should deceive them, and should wish them to esteem us more highly than we deserve.

Thus, when they discover only the imperfections and vices which we really have, it is plain they do us no wrong, since it is not they who cause them; they rather do us good, since they help us to free ourselves from an evil, namely, the ignorance of these imperfections. We ought not to be angry at their knowing our faults and despising us; it is but right that they should know us for what we are, and should despise us, if we are contemptible.

Such are the feelings that would arise in a heart full of equity and justice. What must we say then of our own heart, when we see in it a wholly different disposition? For is it not true that we hate truth and those who tell it us, and that we like them to be deceived in our favour, and prefer to be esteemed by them as being other than what we are in fact? One proof of this makes me shudder. The Catholic religion does not bind us to confess our sins indiscriminately to everybody; it allows them to remain hidden from all other men save one, to whom she bids us reveal the innermost recesses of our heart, and show ourselves as we are. There is only this one man in the world whom she orders us to undeceive, and she binds him to an inviolable secrecy, which makes this knowledge to him as if it were not. Can we imagine anything more charitable and pleasant? And yet the corruption of man is such that he finds even this law harsh; and it is one of the main reasons which has caused a great part of Europe to rebel against the Church.

How unjust and unreasonable is the heart of man, which feels it disagreeable to be obliged to do in regard to one man what in some measure it were right to do to all men! For is it right that we should deceive men?

There are different degrees in this aversion to truth; but all may perhaps be said to have it in some degree, because it is inseparable from self-love. It is this false delicacy which makes those who are under the necessity of reproving others choose so many windings and middle courses to avoid offence. They must lessen our faults, appear to excuse them, intersperse praises and evidence of love and esteem. Despite all this, the medicine does not cease to be bitter to self-love. It takes as little as it can, always with disgust, and often with a secret spite against those who administer it.

Hence it happens that if any have some interest in being loved by us, they are averse to render us a service which they know to be disagreeable. They treat us as we wish to be treated. We hate the truth, and they hide it from us. We desire flattery, and they flatter us. We like to be deceived, and they deceive us.

So each degree of good fortune which raises us in the world removes us farther from truth, because we are most afraid of wounding those whose affection is most useful and whose dislike is most dangerous. A prince may be the byword of all Europe, and he alone will know nothing of it. I am not astonished. To tell the truth is useful to those to whom it is spoken, but disadvantageous to those who tell it, because it makes them disliked. Now those who live with princes love their own interests more than that of the prince whom they serve; and so they take care not to confer on him a benefit so as to injure themselves.

This evil is no doubt greater and more common among the higher classes; but the lower are not exempt from it, since there is always some advantage in making men love us. Human life is thus only a perpetual illusion; men deceive and flatter each other. No one speaks of us in our presence as he does of us in our absence. Human society is founded on mutual deceit; few friendships would endure if each knew what his friend said of him in his absence, although he then spoke in sincerity and without passion.

Man is then only disguise, falsehood, and hypocrisy, both in himself and in regard to others. He does not wish any one to tell him the truth; he avoids telling it to others, and all these dispositions, so removed from justice and reason, have a natural root in his heart.

101

I set it down as a fact that if all men knew what each said of the other, there would not be four friends in the world. This is apparent from the quarrels which arise from the indiscreet tales told from time to time. [I say, further, all men would be . . .]

102

Some vices only lay hold of us by means of others, and these, like branches, fall on removal of the trunk.

103

The example of Alexander's chastity has not made so many continent as that of his drunkenness has made intemperate. It is not shameful not to be as virtuous as he, and it seems excusable to be no more vicious. We do not believe ourselves to be exactly sharing in the vices of the vulgar, when we see that we are sharing in those of great men; and yet we do not observe that in these matters they are ordinary men. We hold on to them by the same end by which they hold on to the rabble; for, however exalted they are, they are still united at some point to the lowest of men. They are not suspended in the air, quite removed from our society. No, no; if they are greater than we, it is because their heads are higher; but their feet are as low as ours. They are all on the same level, and rest on the same earth; and by that extremity they are as low as we are, as the meanest folk, as infants, and as the beasts.

104

When our passion leads us to do something, we forget our
duty; for example, we like a book and read it, when we ought
to be doing something else. Now, to remind ourselves of our
duty, we must set ourselves a task we dislike; we then plead
that we have something else to do, and by this means remember our duty.

105

How difficult it is to submit anything to the judgment of
another, without prejudicing his judgment by the manner in
which we submit it! If we say, "I think it beautiful," "I think
it obscure," or the like, we either entice the imagination into
that view, or irritate it to the contrary. It is better to say
nothing; and then the other judges according to what really
is, that is to say, according as it then is, and according as the
other circumstances, not of our making, have placed it. But
we at least shall have added nothing, unless it be that silence
also produces an effect, according to the turn and the interpretation which the other will be disposed to give it, or as he will
guess it from gestures or countenance, or from the tone of
the voice, if he is a physiognomist. So difficult is it not to upset
a judgment from its natural place, or, rather, so rarely is it
firm and stable!

106

By knowing each man's ruling passion, we are sure of pleasing him; and yet each has his fancies, opposed to his true
good, in the very idea which he has of the good. It is a singularly puzzling fact.

107

Lustravit lampade terras.—The weather and my mood
have little connection. I have my foggy and my fine days
within me; my prosperity or misfortune has little to do with
the matter. I sometimes struggle against luck, the glory of

mastering it makes me master it gaily; whereas I am sometimes surfeited in the midst of good fortune.

108

Although people may have no interest in what they are saying, we must not absolutely conclude from this that they are
not lying; for there are some people who lie for the mere sake
of lying.

109

When we are well we wonder what we would do if we were
ill, but when we are ill we take medicine cheerfully; the illness
persuades us to do so. We have no longer the passions and desires for amusements and promenades which health gave to us,
but which are incompatible with the necessities of illness.
Nature gives us, then, passions and desires suitable to our
present state. We are only troubled by the fears which we,
and not nature, give ourselves, for they add to the state in
which we are the passions of the state in which we are not.

As nature makes us always unhappy in every state, our
desires picture to us a happy state; because they add to the
state in which we are the pleasures of the state in which we are
not. And if we attained to these pleasures, we should not be
happy after all; because we should have other desires natural
to this new state.

We must particularise this general proposition. . . .

110

The consciousness of the falsity of present pleasures, and
the ignorance of the vanity of absent pleasures, cause inconstancy.

111

Inconstancy.—We think we are playing on ordinary organs
when playing upon man. Men are organs, it is true, but, odd,
changeable, variable [with pipes not arranged in proper or-
der]. Those who only know how to play on ordinary organs

will not produce harmonies on these. We must know where [*the keys*] are.

112

Inconstancy.—Things have different qualities, and the soul different inclinations; for nothing is simple which is presented to the soul, and the soul never presents itself simply to any object. Hence it comes that we weep and laugh at the same thing.

113

Inconstancy and oddity.—To live only by work, and to rule over the most powerful State in the world, are very opposite things. They are united in the person of the great Sultan of the Turks.

114

Variety is as abundant as all tones of the voice, all ways of walking, coughing, blowing the nose, sneezing. We distinguish vines by their fruit, and call them the Condrien, the Desargues, and such and such a stock. Is this all? Has a vine ever produced two bunches exactly the same, and has a bunch two grapes alike, etc.?

I can never judge of the same thing exactly in the same way. I cannot judge of my work, while doing it. I must do as the artists, stand at a distance, but not too far. How far, then? Guess.

115

Variety.—Theology is a science, but at the same time how many sciences? A man is a whole; but if we dissect him, will he be the head, the heart, the stomach, the veins, each vein, each portion of a vein, the blood, each humour in the blood?

A town, a country-place, is from afar a town and a country-place. But, as we draw near, there are houses, trees, tiles, leaves, grass, ants, limbs of ants, in infinity. All this is contained under the name of country-place.

116

Thoughts.—All is one, all is different. How many natures exist in man? How many vocations? And by what chance does each man ordinarily choose what he has heard praised? A well-turned heel.

117

The heel of a slipper.—"Ah! How well this is turned! Here is a clever workman! How brave is this soldier!" This is the source of our inclinations, and of the choice of conditions. "How much this man drinks! How little that one!" This makes people sober or drunk, soldiers, cowards, etc.

118

Chief talent, that which rules the rest.

119

Nature imitates herself. A seed grown in good ground brings forth fruit. A principle, instilled into a good mind, brings forth fruit. Numbers imitate space, which is of a different nature.

All is made and led by the same master, root, branches, and fruits; principles and consequences.

120

[Nature diversifies and imitates; art imitates and diversifies.]

121

Nature always begins the same things again, the years, the days, the hours; in like manner spaces and numbers follow each other from beginning to end. Thus is made a kind of infinity and eternity. Not that anything in all this is infinite and eternal, but these finite realities are infinitely multiplied. Thus it seems to me to be only the number which multiplies them that is infinite.

122

Time heals griefs and quarrels, for we change and are no longer the same persons. Neither the offender nor the offended are any more themselves. It is like a nation which we have provoked, but meet again after two generations. They are still Frenchmen, but not the same.

123

He no longer loves the person whom he loved ten years ago. I quite believe it. She is no longer the same, nor is he. He was young, and she also; she is quite different. He would perhaps love her yet, if she were what she was then.

124

We view things not only from different sides, but with different eyes; we have no wish to find them alike.

125

Contraries.—Man is naturally credulous and incredulous, timid and rash.

126

Description of man: dependency, desire of independence, need.

127

Condition of man: inconstancy, weariness, unrest.

128

The weariness which is felt by us in leaving pursuits to which we are attached. A man dwells at home with pleasure; but if he sees a woman who charms him, or if he enjoys himself in play for five or six days, he is miserable if he returns to his former way of living. Nothing is more common than that.

129

Our nature consists in motion; complete rest is death.

130

Restlessness.—If a soldier, or labourer, complain of the hardship of his lot, set him to do nothing.

131

Weariness.—Nothing is so insufferable to man as to be completely at rest, without passions, without business, without diversion, without study. He then feels his nothingness, his forlornness, his insufficiency, his dependence, his weakness, his emptiness. There will immediately arise from the depth of his heart weariness, gloom, sadness, fretfulness, vexation, despair.

132

Methinks Cæsar was too old to set about amusing himself with conquering the world. Such sport was good for Augustus or Alexander. They were still young men, and thus difficult to restrain. But Cæsar should have been more mature.

133

Two faces which resemble each other, make us laugh, when together, by their resemblance, though neither of them by itself makes us laugh.

134

How useless is painting, which attracts admiration by the resemblance of things, the originals of which we do not admire!

135

The struggle alone pleases us, not the victory. We love to see animals fighting, not the victor infuriated over the vanquished. We would only see the victorious end; and, as soon as it comes, we are satiated. It is the same in play, and the same in the search for truth. In disputes we like to see the clash of opinions, but not at all to contemplate truth when found. To observe it with pleasure, we have to see it emerge out of strife. So in the passions, there is pleasure in seeing the collision of two contraries; but when one acquires the mastery, it becomes only brutality. We never seek things for themselves, but for the search. Likewise in plays, scenes which do not rouse the emotion of fear are worthless, so are extreme and hopeless misery, brutal lust, and extreme cruelty.

136

A mere trifle consoles us, for a mere trifle distresses us.

137

Without examining every particular pursuit, it is enough to comprehend them under diversion.

138

Men naturally slaters and of all callings, save in their own rooms.

139

Diversion.—When I have occasionally set myself to consider the different distractions of men, the pains and perils to which they expose themselves at court or in war, whence arise so many quarrels, passions, bold and often bad ventures, etc., I have discovered that all the unhappiness of men arises from one single fact, that they cannot stay quietly in their own chamber. A man who has enough to live on, if he knew how to stay with pleasure at home, would not leave it to go to sea or to besiege a town. A commission in the army would not be bought so dearly, but that it is found insufferable not to budge from the town; and men only seek conversation and entering games, because they cannot remain with pleasure at home.

But on further consideration, when, after finding the cause of all our ills, I have sought to discover the reason of it, I have found that there is one very real reason, namely, the natural poverty of our feeble and mortal condition, so miserable that nothing can comfort us when we think of it closely.

Whatever condition we picture to ourselves, if we muster all the good things which it is possible to possess, royalty is the finest position in the world. Yet, when we imagine a king attended with every pleasure he can feel, if he be without diversion, and be left to consider and reflect on what he is, this feeble happiness will not sustain him; he will necessarily fall into forebodings of dangers, of revolutions which may happen, and, finally, of death and inevitable disease; so that if he be without what is called diversion, he is unhappy, and more unhappy than the least of his subjects who plays and diverts himself.

Hence it comes that play and the society of women, war, and high posts, are so sought after. Not that there is in fact any happiness in them, or that men imagine true bliss to consist in money won at play, or in the hare which they hunt; we would not take these as a gift. We do not seek that easy and peaceful lot which permits us to think of our unhappy condition, nor the dangers of war, nor the labour of office, but the bustle which averts these thoughts of ours, and amuses us.

Reasons why we like the chase better than the quarry.

Hence it comes that men so much love noise and stir; hence it comes that the prison is so horrible a punishment; hence it comes that the pleasure of solitude is a thing incomprehensible. And it is in fact the greatest source of happiness in the condition of kings, that men try incessantly to divert them, and to procure for them all kinds of pleasures.

The king is surrounded by persons whose only thought is to divert the king, and to prevent his thinking of self. For he is unhappy, king though he be, if he think of himself.

This is all that men have been able to discover to make themselves happy. And those who philosophise on the matter, and who think men unreasonable for spending a whole day in chasing a hare which they would not have bought, scarce know our nature. The hare in itself would not screen us from the sight of death and calamities; but the chase which turns away our attention from these, does screen us.

The advice given to Pyrrhus to take the rest which he was about to seek with so much labour, was full of difficulties.

[To bid a man live quietly is to bid him live happily. It is to advise him to be in a state perfectly happy, in which he can think at leisure without finding therein a cause of distress. This is to misunderstand nature.

As men who naturally understand their own condition avoid nothing so much as rest, so there is nothing they leave undone in seeking turmoil. Not that they have an instinctive knowledge of true happiness . . .

So we are wrong in blaming them. Their error does not lie in seeking excitement, if they seek it only as a diversion; the evil is that they seek it as if the possession of the objects of their quest would make them really happy. In this respect it is right to call their quest a vain one. Hence in all this both the censurers and the censured do not understand man's true nature.]

And thus, when we take the exception against them, that what they seek with such fervour cannot satisfy them, if they replied—as they should do if they considered the matter thoroughly—that they sought in it only a violent and impetuous occupation which turned their thoughts from self, and that they therefore chose an attractive object to charm and ardently attract them, they would leave their opponents without a reply. But they do not make this reply, because they do not know themselves. They do not know that it is the chase, and not the quarry, which they seek.

Dancing: We must consider rightly where to place our feet. —A gentleman sincerely believes that hunting is great and royal sport; but a beater is not of this opinion.

They imagine that if they obtained such a post, they would then rest with pleasure, and are insensible of the insatiable nature of their desire. They think they are truly seeking quiet, and they are only seeking excitement.

They have a secret instinct which impels them to seek amusement and occupation abroad, and which arises from the sense of their constant unhappiness. They have another secret instinct, a remnant of the greatness of our original nature, which teaches them that happiness in reality consists only in rest, and not in stir. And of these two contrary instincts they form within themselves a confused idea, which hides itself from their view in the depths of their soul, inciting them to aim at rest through excitement, and always to fancy that the satisfaction which they have not will come to them, if, by surmounting whatever difficulties confront them, they can thereby open the door to rest.

Thus passes away all man's life. Men seek rest in a struggle against difficulties; and when they have conquered these, rest becomes insufferable. For we think either of the misfortunes we have or of those which threaten us. And even if we should see ourselves sufficiently sheltered on all sides, weariness of its own accord would not fail to arise from the depths of the heart wherein it has its natural roots, and to fill the mind with its poison.

Thus so wretched is man that he would weary even without any cause for weariness from the peculiar state of his disposition; and so frivolous is he, that, though full of a thousand reasons for weariness, the least thing, such as playing billiards or hitting a ball, is sufficient to amuse him.

But will you say what object has he in all this? The pleasure of bragging to-morrow among his friends that he has played better than another. So others sweat in their own rooms to show to the learned that they have solved a problem in algebra, which no one had hitherto been able to solve. Many more expose themselves to extreme perils, in my opinion as foolishly, in order to boast afterwards that they have captured a town. Lastly, others wear themselves out in studying all these things, not in order to become wiser, but only in order to prove that they know them; and these are the most senseless of the band, since they are so knowingly, whereas one may suppose of the others, that if they knew it, they would no longer be foolish.

This man spends his life without weariness in playing every day for a small stake. Give him each morning the money he can win each day, on condition he does not play; you make him miserable. It will perhaps be said that he seeks the amusement of play and not the winnings. Make him then play for nothing; he will not become excited over it, and will feel bored. It is then not the amusement alone that he seeks; a languid and passionless amusement will weary him. He must get excited over it, and deceive himself by the fancy that he will be happy to win what he would not have as a gift on condition of not playing; and he must make for himself an object of passion, and excite over it his desire, his anger, his fear, to obtain his imagined end, as children are frightened at the face they have blackened.

Whence comes it that this man, who lost his only son a few months ago, or who this morning was in such trouble through being distressed by lawsuits and quarrels, now no longer thinks of them? Do not wonder; he is quite taken up in looking out for the boar which his dogs have been hunting so hotly for the last six hours. He requires nothing more. However full of sadness a man may be, he is happy for the time, if you can prevail upon him to enter into some amusement; and however happy a man may be, he will soon be discontented and wretched, if he be not diverted and occupied by some passion or pursuit which prevents weariness from overcoming him. Without amusement there is no joy; with amusement there is no sadness. And this also constitutes the happiness of persons in high position, that they have a number of people to amuse them, and have the power to keep themselves in this state.

Consider this. What is it to be superintendent, chancellor, first president, but to be in a condition wherein from early morning a large number of people come from all quarters to see them, so as not to leave them an hour in the day in which they can think of themselves? And when they are in disgrace and sent back to their country houses, where they lack neither wealth nor servants to help them on occasion, they do not fail to be wretched and desolate, because no one prevents them from thinking of themselves.

140

[How does it happen that this man, so distressed at the death of his wife and his only son, or who has some great law-

suit which annoys him, is not at this moment sad, and that he
seems so free from all painful and disquieting thoughts? We
need not wonder; for a ball has been served him, and he must
return it to his companion. He is occupied in catching it in its
fall from the roof, to win a game. How can he think of his own
affairs, pray, when he has this other matter in hand? Here is
a care worthy of occupying this great soul, and taking away
from him every other thought of the mind. This man, born to
know the universe, to judge all causes, to govern a whole state,
is altogether occupied and taken up with the business of catching a hare. And if he does not lower himself to this, and wants
always to be on the strain, he will be more foolish still, because
he would raise himself above humanity; and after all he is
only a man, that is to say capable of little and of much, of all
and of nothing; he is neither angel nor brute, but man.]

141

Men spend their time in following a ball or a hare; it is the
pleasure even of kings.

142

Diversion.—Is not the royal dignity sufficiently great in
itself to make its possessor happy by the mere contemplation
of what he is? Must he be diverted from this thought like
ordinary folk? I see well that a man is made happy by diverting him from the view of his domestic sorrows so as to occupy
all his thoughts with the care of dancing well. But will it be
the same with a king, and will he be happier in the pursuit of
these idle amusements than in the contemplation of his greatness? And what more satisfactory object could be presented
to his mind? Would it not be a deprivation of his delight for
him to occupy his soul with the thought of how to adjust his
steps to the cadence of an air, or of how to throw a [ball]
skilfully, instead of leaving it to enjoy quietly the contemplation of the majestic glory which encompasses him? Let us
make the trial; let us leave a king all alone to reflect on him-

self quite at leisure, without any gratification of the senses, without any care in his mind, without society; and we will see that a king without diversion is a man full of wretchedness. So this is carefully avoided, and near the persons of kings there never fail to be a great number of people who see to it that amusement follows business, and who watch all the time of their leisure to supply them with delights and games, so that there is no blank in it. In fact, kings are surrounded with persons who are wonderfully attentive in taking care that the king be not alone and in a state to think of himself, knowing well that he will be miserable, king though he be, if he meditate on self.

In all this I am not talking of Christian kings as Christians, but only as kings.

143

Diversion.—Men are entrusted from infancy with the care of their honour, their property, their friends, and even with the property and the honour of their friends. They are overwhelmed with business, with the study of languages, and with physical exercise; and they are made to understand that they cannot be happy unless their health, their honour, their fortune and that of their friends be in good condition, and that a single thing wanting will make them unhappy. Thus they are given cares and business which make them bustle about from break of day.—It is, you will exclaim, a strange way to make them happy! What more could be done to make them miserable?—Indeed! what could be done? We should only have to relieve them from all these cares; for then they would see themselves: they would reflect on what they are, whence they came, whither they go, and thus we cannot employ and divert them too much. And this is why, after having given them so much business, we advise them, if they have some time for relaxation, to employ it in amusement, in play, and to be always fully occupied.

How hollow and full of ribaldry is the heart of man!

144

I spent a long time in the study of the abstract sciences, and was disheartened by the small number of fellow-students in them. When I commenced the study of man, I saw that these abstract sciences are not suited to man, and that I was wandering farther from my own state in examining them, than others in not knowing them. I pardoned their little knowledge; but I thought at least to find many companions in the study of man, and that it was the true study which is suited to him. I have been deceived; still fewer study it than geometry. It is only from the want of knowing how to study this that we seek the other studies. But is it not that even here is not the knowledge which man should have, and that for the purpose of happiness it is better for him not to know himself?

145

[One thought alone occupies us; we cannot think of two things at the same time. This is lucky for us according to the world, not according to God.]

146

Man is obviously made to think. It is his whole dignity and his whole merit; and his whole duty is to think as he ought. Now, the order of thought is to begin with self, and with its Author and its end.

Now, of what does the world think? Never of this, but of dancing, playing the lute, singing, making verses, running at the ring, etc., fighting, making oneself king, without thinking what it is to be a king and what to be a man.

147

We do not content ourselves with the life we have in ourselves and in our own being; we desire to live an imaginary life in the mind of others, and for this purpose we endeavour to shine. We labour unceasingly to adorn and preserve this imaginary existence, and neglect the real. And if we possess calmness, or generosity, or truthfulness, we are eager to make it known, so as to attach these virtues to that imaginary existence. We would rather separate them from ourselves to join them to it; and we would willingly be cowards in order to acquire the reputation of being brave. A great proof of the nothingness of our being, not to be satisfied with the one without the other, and to renounce the one for the other! For he would be infamous who would not die to preserve his honour.

148

We are so presumptuous that we would wish to be known by all the world, even by people who shall come after, when we shall be no more; and we are so vain that the esteem of five or six neighbours delights and contents us.

149

We do not trouble ourselves about being esteemed in the towns through which we pass. But if we are to remain a little while there, we are so concerned. How long is necessary? A time commensurate with our vain and paltry life.

150

Vanity is so anchored in the heart of man that a soldier, a soldier's servant, a cook, a porter brags, and wishes to have his admirers. Even philosophers wish for them. Those who write against it want to have the glory of having written well; and those who read it desire the glory of having read it. I who write this have perhaps this desire, and perhaps those who will read it . . .

151

Glory.—Admiration spoils all from infancy. Ah! How well said! Ah! How well done! How well-behaved he is! etc.

The children of Port-Royal, who do not receive this stimulus of envy and glory, fall into carelessness.

152

Pride.—Curiosity is only vanity. Most frequently we wish to know but to talk. Otherwise we would not take a sea voyage in order never to talk of it, and for the sole pleasure of seeing without hope of ever communicating it.

153

Of the desire of being esteemed by those with whom we are. —Pride takes such natural possession of us in the midst of our woes, errors, etc. We even lose our life with joy, provided people talk of it.

Vanity: play, hunting, visiting, false shame, a lasting name.

154

[I have no friends to your advantage].

155

A true friend is so great an advantage, even for the greatest lords, in order that he may speak well of them, and back them in their absence, that they should do all to have one. But they should choose well; for, if they spend all their efforts in the interests of fools, it will be of no use, however well these may speak of them; and these will not even speak well of them if they find themselves on the weakest side, for they have no influence; and thus they will speak ill of them in company.

156

Ferox gens, nullam esse vitam sine armis rati.—They prefer death to peace; others prefer death to war.

Every opinion may be held preferable to life, the love of which is so strong and so natural.

157

Contradiction: contempt for our existence, to die for nothing, hatred of our existence.

158

Pursuits.—The charm of fame is so great, that we like every object to which it is attached, even death.

159

Noble deeds are most estimable when hidden. When I see some of these in history, they please me greatly. But after all they have not been quite hidden, since they have been known; and though people have done what they could to hide them, the little publication of them spoils all, for what was best in them was the wish to hide them.

160

Sneezing absorbs all the functions of the soul, as well as work does; but we do not draw therefrom the same conclusions against the greatness of man, because it is against his will. And although we bring it on ourselves, it is nevertheless against our will that we sneeze. It is not in view of the act itself; it is for another end. And thus it is not a proof of the weakness of man, and of his slavery under that action.

It is not disgraceful for man to yield to pain, and it is disgraceful to yield to pleasure. This is not because pain comes to us from without, and we ourselves seek pleasure; for it is possible to seek pain, and yield to it purposely, without this kind of baseness. Whence comes it, then, that reason thinks it honourable to succumb under stress of pain, and disgraceful to yield to the attack of pleasure? It is because pain does not tempt and attract us. It is we ourselves who choose it voluntarily, and will it to prevail over us. So that we are masters of the situation; and in this man yields to himself. But in pleasure it is man who yields to pleasure. Now only mastery and sovereignty bring glory, and only slavery brings shame.

161

Vanity.—How wonderful it is that a thing so evident as the vanity of the world is so little known, that it is a strange and surprising thing to say that it is foolish to seek greatness?

162

He who will know fully the vanity of man has only to consider the causes and effects of love. The cause is a *je ne sais quoi* (Corneille), and the effects are dreadful. This *je ne sais quoi*, so small an object that we cannot recognise it, agitates a whole country, princes, armies, the entire world.

Cleopatra's nose: had it been shorter, the whole aspect of the world would have been altered.

163

Vanity.—The cause and the effects of love: Cleopatra.

164

He who does not see the vanity of the world is himself very vain. Indeed who do not see it but youths who are absorbed in fame, diversion, and the thought of the future? But take away diversion, and you will see them dried up with weariness. They feel then their nothingness without knowing it; for it is indeed to be unhappy to be in insufferable sadness as soon as we are reduced to thinking of self, and have no diversion.

165

Thoughts.—*In omnibus requiem quæsivi.* If our condition were truly happy, we would not need diversion from thinking of it in order to make ourselves happy.

166

Diversion.—Death is easier to bear without thinking of it, than is the thought of death without peril.

167

The miseries of human life have established all this: as men have seen this, they have taken up diversion.

168

Diversion.—As men are not able to fight against death, misery, ignorance, they have taken it into their heads, in order to be happy, not to think of them at all.

169

Despite these miseries, man wishes to be happy, and only wishes to be happy, and cannot wish not to be so. But how will he set about it? To be happy he would have to make himself immortal; but, not being able to do so, it has occurred to him to prevent himself from thinking of death.

170

Diversion.—If man were happy, he would be the more so, the less he was diverted, like the Saints and God.—Yes; but is it not to be happy to have a faculty of being amused by diversion?—No; for that comes from elsewhere and from without, and thus is dependent, and therefore subject to be disturbed by a thousand accidents, which bring inevitable griefs.

171

Misery.—The only thing which consoles us for our miseries is diversion, and yet this is the greatest of our miseries. For it is this which principally hinders us from reflecting upon ourselves, and which makes us insensibly ruin ourselves. Without this we should be in a state of weariness, and this weariness would spur us to seek a more solid means of escaping from it. But diversion amuses us, and leads us unconsciously to death.

172

We do not rest satisfied with the present. We anticipate the future as too slow in coming, as if in order to hasten its course; or we recall the past, to stop its too rapid flight. So imprudent are we that we wander in the times which are not ours, and do not think of the only one which belongs to us; and so idle are we that we dream of those times which are no more, and thoughtlessly overlook that which alone exists. For the present is generally painful to us. We conceal it from our sight, because it troubles us; and if it be delightful to us, we regret to see it pass away. We try to sustain it by the future, and think of arranging matters which are not in our power, for a time which we have no certainty of reaching.

Let each one examine his thoughts, and he will find them all occupied with the past and the future. We scarcely ever think of the present; and if we think of it, it is only to take light from it to arrange the future. The present is never our end. The past and the present are our means; the future alone is our end. So we never live, but we hope to live; and, as we are always preparing to be happy, it is inevitable we should never be so.

173

They say that eclipses foretoken misfortune, because misfortunes are common, so that, as evil happens so often, they often foretell it; whereas if they said that they predict good fortune, they would often be wrong. They attribute good fortune only to rare conjunctions of the heavens; so they seldom fail in prediction.

174

Misery.—Solomon and Job have best known and best spoken of the misery of man; the former the most fortunate, and the latter the most unfortunate of men; the former knowing the vanity of pleasures from experience, the latter the reality of evils.

175

We know ourselves so little, that many think they are about to die when they are well, and many think they are well when they are near death, unconscious of approaching fever, or of the abscess ready to form itself.

176

Cromwell was about to ravage all Christendom; the royal family was undone, and his own for ever established, save for a little grain of sand which formed in his ureter. Rome herself was trembling under him; but this small piece of gravel having formed there, he is dead, his family cast down, all is peaceful, and the king is restored.

177

[Three hosts.] Would he who had possessed the friendship of the King of England, the King of Poland, and the Queen of Sweden, have believed he would lack a refuge and shelter in the world?

178

Macrobius: on the innocents slain by Herod.

179

When Augustus learnt that Herod's own son was amongst the infants under two years of age, whom he had caused to be slain, he said that it was better to be Herod's pig than his son. —Macrobius, *Sat.*, book ii, chap. 4.

180

The great and the humble have the same misfortunes, the same griefs, the same passions; but the one is at the top of the wheel, and the other near the centre, and so less disturbed by the same revolutions.

181

We are so unfortunate that we can only take pleasure in a thing on condition of being annoyed if it turn out ill, as a thousand things can do, and do every hour. He who should find the secret of rejoicing in the good, without troubling himself with its contrary evil, would have hit the mark. It is perpetual motion.

182

Those who have always good hope in the midst of misfortunes, and who are delighted with good luck, are suspected of being very pleased with the ill success of the affair, if they are not equally distressed by bad luck; and they are overjoyed to find these pretexts of hope, in order to show that they are concerned and to conceal by the joy which they feign to feel that which they have at seeing the failure of the matter.

183

We run carelessly to the precipice, after we have put something before us to prevent us seeing it.

OF THE NECESSITY OF THE WAGER

184

A letter to incite to the search after God.

And then to make people seek Him among the philosophers, sceptics, and dogmatists, who disquiet him who inquires of them.

185

The conduct of God, who disposes all things kindly, is to put religion into the mind by reason, and into the heart by grace. But to will to put it into the mind and heart by force and threats is not to put religion there, but terror, *terorrem potius quam religionem.*

186

Nisi terrerentur et non docerentur, improba quasi dominatio videretur (Aug., Ep. 48 or 49), *Contra Mendacium ad Consentium.*

187

Order.—Men despise religion; they hate it, and fear it is true. To remedy this, we must begin by showing that religion is not contrary to reason; that it is venerable, to inspire respect for it; then we must make it lovable, to make good men hope it is true; finally, we must prove it is true.

Venerable, because it has perfect knowledge of man; lovable, because it promises the true good.

64

188

In every dialogue and discourse, we must be able to say to those who take offence, "Of what do you complain?"

189

To begin by pitying unbelievers; they are wretched enough by their condition. We ought only to revile them where it is beneficial; but this does them harm.

190

To pity atheists who seek, for are they not unhappy enough? To inveigh against those who make a boast of it.

191

And will this one scoff at the other? Who ought to scoff? And yet, the latter does not scoff at the other, but pities him.

192

To reproach Milton with not being troubled, since God will reproach him.

193

Quid fiet hominibus qui minima contemnunt, majora non credunt?

194

. . . Let them at least learn what is the religion they attack, before attacking it. If this religion boasted of having a clear view of God, and of possessing it open and unveiled, it would be attacking it to say that we see nothing in the world which shows it with this clearness. But since, on the contrary, it says that men are in darkness and estranged from God, that He has hidden Himself from their knowledge, that this is in fact the name which He gives Himself in the Scriptures, *Deus absconditus;* and finally, if it endeavours equally to establish these two things: that God has set up in the Church visible signs to make Himself known to those who should seek Him sincerely, and that He has nevertheless so disguised them that He will only be perceived by those who seek Him with all their heart; what advantage can they obtain, when, in the negligence with which they make profession of being in search of the truth, they cry out that nothing reveals it to them; and since that darkness in which they are, and with which they upbraid the Church, establishes only one of the things which she affirms, without touching the other, and, very far from destroying, proves her doctrine?

In order to attack it, they should have protested that they had made every effort to seek Him everywhere, and even in that which the Church proposes for their instruction, but without satisfaction. If they talked in this manner, they would in truth be attacking one of her pretensions. But I hope here to show that no reasonable person can speak thus, and I venture even to say that no one has ever done so. We know well enough how those who are of this mind behave. They believe they have made great efforts for their instruction, when they have spent a few hours in reading some book of Scripture, and have questioned some priest on the truths of the faith. After that, they boast of having made vain search in books and among men. But, verily, I will tell them what I have often said, that this negligence is insufferable. We are not here concerned with the trifling interests of some stranger, that we should treat it in this fashion; the matter concerns ourselves and our all.

The immortality of the soul is a matter which is of so great consequence to us, and which touches us so profoundly, that we must have lost all feeling to be indifferent as to knowing what it is. All our actions and thoughts must take such different courses, according as there are or are not eternal joys to hope for, that it is impossible to take one step with sense and judgment, unless we regulate our course by our view of this point which ought to be our ultimate end.

Thus our first interest and our first duty is to enlighten ourselves on this subject, whereon depends all our conduct. Therefore among those who do not believe, I make a vast difference between those who strive with all their power to inform themselves, and those who live without troubling or thinking about it.

I can have only compassion for those who sincerely bewail their doubt, who regard it as the greatest of misfortunes, and who, sparing no effort to escape it, make of this inquiry their principal and most serious occupation.

But as for those who pass their life without thinking of this ultimate end of life, and who, for this sole reason that they do not find within themselves the lights which convince them of it, neglect to seek them elsewhere, and to examine thoroughly whether this opinion is one of those which people receive with credulous simplicity, or one of those which, although obscure in themselves, have nevertheless a solid and immovable foundation, I look upon them in a manner quite different.

This carelessness in a matter which concerns themselves, their eternity, their all, moves me more to anger than pity; it astonishes and shocks me; it is to me monstrous. I do not say this out of the pious zeal of a spiritual devotion. I expect, on the contrary, that we ought to have this feeling from principles of human interest and self-love; for this we need only see what the least enlightened persons see.

We do not require great education of the mind to understand that here is no real and lasting satisfaction; that our pleasures are only vanity; that our evils are infinite; and, lastly, that death, which threatens us every moment, must infallibly place us within a few years under the dreadful necessity of being for ever either annihilated or unhappy.

There is nothing more real than this, nothing more terrible. Be we as heroic as we like, that is the end which awaits the noblest life in the world. Let us reflect on this, and then say whether it is not beyond doubt that there is no good in this life but in the hope of another; that we are happy only in proportion as we draw near it; and that, as there are no more woes for those who have complete assurance of eternity, so there is no more happiness for those who have no insight into it.

Surely then it is a great evil thus to be in doubt, but it is at least an indispensable duty to seek when we are in such doubt; and thus the doubter who does not seek is altogether completely unhappy and completely wrong. And if besides this he is easy and content, professes to be so, and indeed boasts of it; if it is this state itself which is the subject of his joy and vanity, I have no words to describe so silly a creature.

How can people hold these opinions? What joy can we find in the expectation of nothing but hopeless misery? What reason for boasting that we are in impenetrable darkness? And how can it happen that the following argument occurs to a reasonable man?

"I know not who put me into the world, nor what the world is, nor what I myself am. I am in terrible ignorance of everything. I know not what my body is, nor my senses, nor my soul, not even that part of me which thinks what I say, which reflects on all and on itself, and knows itself no more than the rest. I see those frightful spaces of the universe which surround me, and I find myself tied to one corner of this vast expanse, without knowing why I am put in this place rather than in another, nor why the short time which is given me to live is assigned to me at this point rather than at another of the whole eternity which was before me or which shall come after me. I see nothing but infinites on all sides, which surround me as an atom, and as a shadow which endures only for an instant and returns no more. All I know is that I must soon die, but what I know least is this very death which I cannot escape.

"As I know not whence I come, so I know not whither I go. I know only that, in leaving this world, I fall for ever either into annihilation or into the hands of an angry God, without knowing to which of these two states I shall be for ever assigned. Such is my state, full of weakness and uncertainty. And from all this I conclude that I ought to spend all the days of my life without caring to inquire into what must happen to me.

Perhaps I might find some solution to my doubts, but I will not take the trouble, nor take a step to seek it; and after treating with scorn those who are concerned with this care, I will go without foresight and without fear to try the great event, and let myself be led carelessly to death, uncertain of the eternity of my future state."

Who would desire to have for a friend a man who talks in this fashion? Who would choose him out from others to tell him of his affairs? Who would have recourse to him in affliction? And indeed to what use in life could one put him?

In truth, it is the glory of religion to have for enemies men so unreasonable; and their opposition to it is so little dangerous that it serves on the contrary to establish its truths. For the Christian faith goes mainly to establish these two facts: the corruption of nature, and redemption by Jesus Christ. Now I contend that if these men do not serve to prove the truth of the redemption by the holiness of their behaviour, they at least serve admirably to show the corruption of nature by sentiments so unnatural.

Nothing is so important to man as his own state, nothing is so formidable to him as eternity; and thus it is not natural that there should be men indifferent to the loss of their existence, and to the perils of everlasting suffering. They are quite different with regard to all other things. They are afraid of mere trifles; they foresee them; they feel them. And this same man who spends so many days and nights in rage and despair for the loss of office, or for some imaginary insult to his honour, is the very one who knows without anxiety and without emotion that he will lose all by death. It is a monstrous thing to see in the same heart and at the same time this sensibility to trifles and this strange insensibility to the greatest objects. It is an incomprehensible enchantment, and a supernatural slumber, which indicates as its cause an all-powerful force.

There must be a strange confusion in the nature of man, that he should boast of being in that state in which it seems incredible that a single individual should be. However, experience has shown me so great a number of such persons that the fact would be surprising, if we did not know that the greater part of those who trouble themselves about the matter are disingenuous, and not in fact what they say. They are people who have heard it said that it is the fashion to be thus daring. It is what they call shaking off the yoke, and they try to imitate this. But it would not be difficult to make them understand how greatly they deceive themselves in thus seeking esteem. This is not the way to gain it, even I say among those men of the world who take a healthy view of things, and who know that the only way to succeed in this life is to make ourselves appear honourable, faithful, judicious, and capable of useful service to a friend; because naturally men love only what may be useful to them. Now, what do we gain by hearing it said of a man that he has now thrown off the yoke, that he does not believe there is a God who watches our actions, that he considers himself the sole master of his conduct, and that he thinks he is accountable for it only to himself? Does he think that he has thus brought us to have henceforth complete confidence in him, and to look to him for consolation, advice, and help in every need of life? Do they profess to have delighted us by telling us that they hold our soul to be only a little wind and smoke, especially by telling us this in a haughty and self-satisfied tone of voice? Is this a thing to say gaily? Is it not, on the contrary, a thing to say sadly, as the saddest thing in the world

If they thought of it seriously, they would see that this is so bad a mistake, so contrary to good sense, so opposed to decency, and so removed in every respect from that good breeding which they seek, that they would be more likely to correct than to pervert those who had an inclination to follow them. And indeed, make them give an account of their opinions, and of the reasons which they have for doubting religion, and they will say to you things so feeble and so petty, that they will persuade you of the contrary. The following is what a person one day said to such a one very appositely: "If you continue to talk in this manner, you will really make me re-

ligious." And he was right, for who would not have a horror
of holding opinions in which he would have such contemptible
persons as companions!

Thus those who only feign these opinions would be very
unhappy, if they restrained their natural feelings in order to
make themselves the most conceited of men. If, at the bottom of their heart, they are troubled at not having more light,
let them not disguise the fact; this avowal will not be shameful. The only shame is to have none. Nothing reveals more an
extreme weakness of mind than not to know the misery of a
godless man. Nothing is more indicative of a bad disposition
of heart than not to desire the truth of eternal promises.
Nothing is more dastardly than to act with bravado before
God. Let them then leave these impieties to those who are
sufficiently ill-bred to be really capable of them. Let them at
least be honest men, if they cannot be Christians. Finally, let
them recognise that there are two kinds of people one can call
reasonable; those who serve God with all their heart because
they know Him, and those who seek Him with all their heart
because they do not know Him.

But as for those who live without knowing Him and without
seeking Him, they judge themselves so little worthy of their
own care, that they are not worthy of the care of others; and
it needs all the charity of the religion which they despise, not
to despise them even to the point of leaving them to their
folly. But because this religion obliges us always to regard
them, so long as they are in this life, as capable of the grace
which can enlighten them, and to believe that they may, in a
little time, be more replenished with faith than we are, and
that, on the other hand, we may fall into the blindness wherein
they are, we must do for them what we would they should do
for us if we were in their place, and call upon them to have
pity upon themselves, and to take at least some steps in the
endeavour to find light. Let them give to reading this some
of the hours which they otherwise employ so uselessly; whatever aversion they may bring to the task, they will perhaps
gain something, and at least will not lose much. But as for

those who bring to the task perfect sincerity and a real desire to meet with truth, those I hope will be satisfied and convinced of the proofs of a religion so divine, which I have here collected, and in which I have followed somewhat after this order . . .

195

Before entering into the proofs of the Christian religion, I find it necessary to point out the sinfulness of those men who live in indifference to the search for truth in a matter which is so important to them, and which touches them so nearly.

Of all their errors, this doubtless is the one which most convicts them of foolishness and blindness, and in which it is easiest to confound them by the first glimmerings of common sense, and by natural feelings.

For it is not to be doubted that the duration of this life is but a moment; that the state of death is eternal, whatever may be its nature; and that thus all our actions and thoughts must take such different directions according to the state of that eternity, that it is impossible to take one step with sense and judgment, unless we regulate our course by the truth of that point which ought to be our ultimate end.

There is nothing clearer than this; and thus, according to the principles of reason, the conduct of men is wholly unreasonable, if they do not take another course.

On this point, therefore, we condemn those who live without thought of the ultimate end of life, who let themselves be guided by their own inclinations and their own pleasures without reflection and without concern, and, as if they could annihilate eternity by turning away their thought from it, think only of making themselves happy for the moment.

Yet this eternity exists, and death, which must open into it, and threatens them every hour, must in a little time infallibly put them under the dreadful necessity of being either annihilated or unhappy for ever, without knowing which of these eternities is for ever prepared for them.

This is a doubt of terrible consequence. They are in peril of

eternal woe and thereupon, as if the matter were not worth
the trouble, they neglect to inquire whether this is one of those
opinions which people receive with too credulous a facility, or
one of those which, obscure in themselves, have a very firm,
though hidden, foundation. Thus they know not whether
there be truth or falsity in the matter, nor whether there be
strength or weakness in the proofs. They have them before
their eyes; they refuse to look at them; and in that ignorance
they choose all that is necessary to fall into this misfortune if
it exists, to await death to make trial of it, yet to be very
content in this state, to make profession of it, and indeed to
boast of it. Can we think seriously on the importance of this
subject without being horrified at conduct so extravagant?

This resting in ignorance is a monstrous thing, and they
who pass their life in it must be made to feel its extravagance
and stupidity, by having it shown to them, so that they may
be confounded by the sight of their folly. For this is how men
reason, when they choose to live in such ignorance of what
they are, and without seeking enlightenment. "I know not,"
they say . . .

196

Men lack heart; they would not make a friend of it.

197

To be insensible to the extent of despising interesting things,
and to become insensible to the point which interests us most.

198

The sensibility of man to trifles, and his insensibility to
great things, indicates a strange inversion.

199

Let us imagine a number of men in chains, and all condemned to death, where some are killed each day in the sight
of the others, and those who remain see their own fate in that
of their fellows, and wait their turn, looking at each other

sorrowfully and without hope. It is an image of the condition of men.

200

A man in a dungeon, ignorant whether his sentence be pronounced, and having only one hour to learn it, but this hour enough, if he knew that it is pronounced, to obtain its repeal, would act unnaturally in spending that hour, not in ascertaining his sentence, but in playing piquet. So it is against nature that man, etc. It is making heavy the hand of God.

Thus not only the zeal of those who seek Him proves God, but also the blindness of those who seek Him not.

201

All the objections of this one and that one only go against themselves, and not against religion. All that infidels say . . .

202

[From those who are in despair at being without faith, we see that God does not enlighten them; but as to the rest, we see there is a God who makes them blind.]

203

Fascinatio nugacitatis.—That passion may not harm us, let us act as if we had only eight hours to live.

204

If we ought to devote eight hours of life, we ought to devote a hundred years.

205

When I consider the short duration of my life, swallowed up in the eternity before and after, the little space which I fill, and even can see, engulfed in the infinite immensity of spaces of which I am ignorant, and which know me not, I am frightened, and am astonished at being here rather than there; for there is no reason why here rather than there, why now rather than then. Who has put me here? By whose order and direction have this place and time been allotted to me? *Memoria hospitis unius diei prætereuntis.*

206

The eternal silence of these infinite spaces frightens me.

207

How many kingdoms know us not!

208

Why is my knowledge limited? Why my stature? Why my life to one hundred years rather than to a thousand? What reason has nature had for giving me such, and for choosing this number rather than another in the infinity of those from which there is no more reason to choose one than another, trying nothing else?

209

Art thou less a slave by being loved and favoured by thy master? Thou art indeed well off, slave. Thy master favours thee; he will soon beat thee.

210

The last act is tragic, however happy all the rest of the play is; at the last a little earth is thrown upon our head, and that is the end for ever.

211

We are fools to depend upon the society of our fellow-men. Wretched as we are, powerless as we are, they will not aid us; we shall die alone. We should therefore act as if we were alone, and in that case should we build fine houses, etc. We should seek the truth without hesitation; and, if we refuse it, we show that we value the esteem of men more than the search for truth.

212

Instability.—It is a horrible thing to feel all that we possess slipping away.

213

Between us and heaven or hell there is only life, which is the frailest thing in the world.

214

Injustice.—That presumption should be joined to meanness is extreme injustice.

215

To fear death without danger, and not in danger, for one must be a man.

216

Sudden death alone is feared; hence confessors stay with lords.

217

An heir finds the title-deeds of his house. Will he say, "Perhaps they are forged" and neglect to examine them?

218

Dungeon.—I approve of not examining the opinion of Copernicus; but this . . .! It concerns all our life to know whether the soul be mortal or immortal.

219

It is certain that the mortality or immortality of the soul must make an entire difference to morality. And yet philosophers have constructed their ethics independently of this: they discuss to pass an hour.

Plato, to incline to Christianity.

220

The fallacy of philosophers who have not discussed the immortality of the soul. The fallacy of their dilemma in Montaigne.

221

Atheists ought to say what is perfectly evident; now it is not perfectly evident that the soul is material.

222

Atheists.—What reason have they for saying that we cannot rise from the dead? What is more difficult, to be born or to rise again; that what has never been should be, or that what has been should be again? Is it more difficult to come into existence than to return to it? Habit makes the one appear easy to us; want of habit makes the other impossible. A popular way of thinking!

Why cannot a virgin bear a child? Does a hen not lay eggs without a cock? What distinguishes these outwardly from others? And who has told us that the hen may not form the germ as well as the cock?

223

What have they to say against the resurrection, and against the child-bearing of the Virgin? Which is the more difficult, to produce a man or an animal, or to reproduce it? And if they had never seen any species of animals, could they have conjectured whether they were produced without connection with each other?

224

How I hate these follies of not believing in the Eucharist, etc.! If the Gospel be true, if Jesus Christ be God, what difficulty is there?

225

Atheism shows strength of mind, but only to a certain degree.

226

Infidels, who profess to follow reason, ought to be exceedingly strong in reason. What say they then? "Do we not see," say they, "that the brutes live and die like men, and Turks

like Christians? They have their ceremonies, their prophets,
their doctors, their saints, their monks, like us," etc. (Is this
contrary to Scripture? Does it not say all this?)

If you care but little to know the truth, here is enough of it
to leave you in repose. But if you desire with all your heart to
know it, it is not enough; look at it in detail. This would be
sufficient for a question in philosophy; but not here, where it
concerns your all. And yet, after a trifling reflection of this
kind, we go to amuse ourselves, etc. Let us inquire of this
same religion whether it does not give a reason for this obscurity; perhaps it will teach it to us.

227

Order by dialogues.—What ought I to do? I see only darkness everywhere. Shall I believe I am nothing? Shall I believe
I am God?

"All things change and succeed each other." You are mistaken; there is . . .

228

Objection of atheists: "But we have no light."

229

This is what I see and what troubles me. I look on all sides,
and I see only darkness everywhere. Nature presents to me
nothing which is not matter of doubt and concern. If I saw
nothing there which revealed a Divinity, I would come to a
negative conclusion; if I saw everywhere the signs of a Creator, I would remain peacefully in faith. But, seeing too much
to deny and too little to be sure, I am in a state to be pitied;
wherefore I have a hundred times wished that if a God maintains nature, she should testify to Him unequivocally, and
that, if the signs she gives are deceptive, she should suppress
them altogether; that she should say everything or nothing,
that I might see which cause I ought to follow. Whereas in
my present state, ignorant of what I am or of what I ought to
do, I know neither my condition nor my duty. My heart in-

clines wholly to know where is the true good, in order to follow it; nothing would be too dear to me for eternity.

I envy those whom I see living in the faith with such carelessness, and who make such a bad use of a gift of which it
seems to me I would make such a different use.

230

It is incomprehensible that God should exist, and it is incomprehensible that He should not exist; that the soul should
be joined to the body, and that we should have no soul; that
the world should be created, and that it should not be created, etc.; that original sin should be, and that it should not
be.

231

Do you believe it to be impossible that God is infinite, without parts?—Yes. I wish therefore to show you an infinite and
indivisible thing. It is a point moving everywhere with an
infinite velocity; for it is one in all places, and is all totality
in every place.

Let this effect of nature, which previously seemed to you
impossible, make you know that there may be others of which
you are still ignorant. Do not draw this conclusion from your
experiment, that there remains nothing for you to know; but
rather that there remains an infinity for you to know.

232

Infinite movement, the point which fills everything, the
moment of rest; infinite without quantity, indivisible and
infinite.

233

Infinite—nothing.—Our soul is cast into a body, where it
finds number, time, dimension. Thereupon it reasons, and
calls this nature necessity, and can believe nothing else.

Unity joined to infinity adds nothing to it, no more than
one foot to an infinite measure. The finite is annihilated in the
presence of the infinite, and becomes a pure nothing. So our

spirit before God, so our justice before divine justice. There is not so great a disproportion between our justice and that of God, as between unity and infinity.

The justice of God must be vast like His compassion. Now justice to the outcast is less vast, and ought less to offend our feelings than mercy towards the elect.

We know that there is an infinite, and are ignorant of its nature. As we know it to be false that numbers are finite, it is therefore true that there is an infinity in number. But we do not know what it is. It is false that it is even, it is false that it is odd; for the addition of a unit can make no change in its nature. Yet it is a number, and every number is odd or even (this is certainly true of every finite number). So we may well know that there is a God without knowing what He is. Is there not one substantial truth, seeing there are so many things which are not the truth itself?

We know then the existence and nature of the finite, because we also are finite and have extension. We know the existence of the infinite, and are ignorant of its nature, because it has extension like us, but not limits like us. But we know neither the existence nor the nature of God, because He has neither extension nor limits.

But by faith we know His existence; in glory we shall know His nature. Now, I have already shown that we may well know the existence of a thing, without knowing its nature.

Let us now speak according to natural lights.

If there is a God, He is infinitely incomprehensible, since, having neither parts nor limits, He has no affinity to us. We are then incapable of knowing either what He is or if He is. This being so, who will dare to undertake the decision of the question? Not we, who have no affinity to Him.

Who then will blame Christians for not being able to give a reason for their belief, since they profess a religion for which they cannot give a reason? They declare, in expounding it to the world, that it is a foolishness, *stultitiam*; and then you complain that they do not prove it! If they proved it, they would not keep their word; it is in lacking proofs, that they are not lacking in sense. "Yes, but although this excuses those who offer it as such, and takes away from them the blame of putting it forward without reason, it does not excuse those who receive it." Let us then examine this point, and say, "God is, or He is not." But to which side shall we incline? Reason can decide nothing here. There is an infinite chaos which separated us. A game is being played at the extremity of this infinite distance where heads or tails will turn up. What will you wager? According to reason, you can do neither the one thing nor the other; according to reason, you can defend neither of the propositions.

Do not then reprove for error those who have made a choice; for you know nothing about it. "No, but I blame them for having made, not this choice, but a choice; for again both he who chooses heads and he who chooses tails are equally at fault, they are both in the wrong. The true course is not to wager at all."

Yes; but you must wager. It is not optional. You are embarked. Which will you choose then? Let us see. Since you must choose, let us see which interests you least. You have two things to lose, the true and the good; and two things to stake, your reason and your will, your knowledge and your happiness; and your nature has two things to shun, error and misery. Your reason is no more shocked in choosing one rather than the other, since you must of necessity choose. This is one point settled. But your happiness? Let us weigh the gain and the loss in wagering that God is. Let us estimate these two chances. If you gain, you gain all; if you lose, you lose nothing. Wager, then, without hesitation that He is.— "That is very fine. Yes, I must wager; but I may perhaps wager too much."—Let us see. Since there is an equal risk of gain and of loss, if you had only to gain two lives, instead of one, you might still wager. But if there were three lives to gain, you would have to play (since you are under the necessity of playing), and you would be imprudent, when you are forced to play, not to chance your life to gain three at a game where there is an equal risk of loss and gain. But there is an eternity of life and happiness. And this being so, if there were an infinity of chances, of which one only would be for you, you would still be right in wagering one to win two, and you would act stupidly, being obliged to play, by refusing to stake one life against three at a game in which out of an infinity of chances there is one for you, if there were an infinity of an infinitely happy life to gain. But there is here an infinity of an infinitely happy life to gain, a chance of gain against a finite number of chances of loss, and what you stake is finite. It is all divided; wherever the infinite is and there is not an infinity of chances of loss against that of gain, there is no time to hesitate, you must give all. And thus, when one is forced to play, he must renounce reason to preserve his life, rather than risk it for infinite gain, as likely to happen as the loss of nothingness.

For it is no use to say it is uncertain if we will gain, and it is certain that we risk, and that the infinite distance between the *certainty* of what is staked and the *uncertainty* of what will be gained, equals the finite good which is certainly staked against the uncertain infinite. It is not so, as every player stakes a certainty to gain an uncertainty, and yet he stakes a finite certainty to gain a finite uncertainty, without transgressing against reason. There is not an infinite distance between the certainty staked and the uncertainty of the gain; that is untrue. In truth, there is an infinity between the certainty of gain and the certainty of loss. But the uncertainty of the gain is proportioned to the certainty of the stake according to the proportion of the chances of gain and loss. Hence it comes that, if there are as many risks on one side as on the other, the course is to play even; and then the certainty of the stake is equal to the uncertainty of the gain, so far is it from fact that there is an infinite distance between them. And so our proposition is of infinite force, when there is the finite to stake in a game where there are equal risks of gain and of loss, and the infinite to gain. This is demonstrable; and if men are capable of any truths, this is one.

"I confess it, I admit it. But, still, is there no means of seeing the faces of the cards?"—Yes, Scripture and the rest, etc. "Yes, but I have my hands tied and my mouth closed; I am forced to wager, and am not free. I am not released, and am so made that I cannot believe. What, then, would you have me do?"

True. But at least learn your inability to believe, since reason brings you to this, and yet you cannot believe. Endeavour then to convince yourself, not by increase of proofs of God, but by the abatement of your passions. You would like to attain faith, and do not know the way; you would like to cure yourself of unbelief, and ask the remedy for it. Learn of those who have been bound like you, and who now stake all their possessions. These are people who know the way which you would follow, and who are cured of an ill of which you would be cured. Follow the way by which they began; by acting as if they believed, taking the holy water, having masses said, etc. Even this will naturally make you believe, and deaden your acuteness.—"But this is what I am afraid of."—And why? What have you to lose?

But to show you that this leads you there, it is this which will lessen the passions, which are your stumbling-blocks.

The end of this discourse.—Now, what harm will befall you in taking this side? You will be faithful, honest, humble, grateful, generous, a sincere friend, truthful. Certainly you will not have those poisonous pleasures, glory and luxury; but will you not have others? I will tell you that you will thereby gain in this life, and that, at each step you take on this road, you will see so great certainty of gain, so much nothingness in what you risk, that you will at last recognise that you have wagered for something certain and infinite, for which you have given nothing.

"Ah! This discourse transports me, charms me," etc.

If this discourse pleases you and seems impressive, know that it is made by a man who has knelt, both before and after it, in prayer to that Being, infinite and without parts, before whom he lays all he has, for you also to lay before Him all you have for your own good and for His glory, that so strength may be given to lowliness.

234

If we must not act save on a certainty, we ought not to act on religion, for it is not certain. But how many things we do on an uncertainty, sea voyages, battles! I say then we must do nothing at all, for nothing is certain, and that there is more certainty in religion than there is as to whether we may see to-morrow; for it is not certain that we may see to-morrow, and it is certainly possible that we may not see it. We cannot say as much about religion. It is not certain that it is; but who will venture to say that it is certainly possible that it is not? Now when we work for to-morrow, and so on an uncertainty, we act reasonably; for we ought to work for an uncertainty according to the doctrine of chance which was demonstrated above.

Saint Augustine has seen that we work for an uncertainty, on sea, in battle, etc. But he has not seen the doctrine of chance which proves that we should do so. Montaigne has seen that we are shocked at a fool, and that habit is all-powerful; but he has not seen the reason of this effect.

All these persons have seen the effects, but they have not seen the causes. They are, in comparison with those who have discovered the causes, as those who have only eyes are in comparison with those who have intellect. For the effects are perceptible by sense, and the causes are visible only to the intellect. And although these effects are seen by the mind, this mind is, in comparison with the mind which sees the causes, as the bodily senses are in comparison with the intellect.

235

Rem viderunt, causam non viderunt.

236

According to the doctrine of chance, you ought to put yourself to the trouble of searching for the truth; for if you die without worshipping the True Cause, you are lost.—"But," say you, "if He had wished me to worship Him, He would have left me signs of His will."—He has done so; but you neglect them. Seek them, therefore; it is well worth it.

237

Chances.—We must live differently in the world, according to these different assumptions: (1) that we could always remain in it; (2) that it is certain that we shall not remain here long, and uncertain if we shall remain here one hour. This last assumption is our condition.

238

What do you then promise me, in addition to certain troubles, but ten years of self-love (for ten years is the chance), to try hard to please without success?

239

Objection.—Those who hope for salvation are so far happy; but they have as a counterpoise the fear of hell.

Reply.—Who has most reason to fear hell: he who is in ignorance whether there is a hell, and who is certain of damnation if there is; or he who certainly believes there is a hell, and hopes to be saved if there is?

240

"I would soon have renounced pleasure," say they, "had I faith." For my part I tell you, "You would soon have faith, if you renounced pleasure." Now, it is for you to begin. If I could, I would give you faith. I cannot do so, nor therefore test the truth of what you say. But you can well renounce pleasure, and test whether what I say is true.

241

Order.—I would have far more fear of being mistaken, and of finding that the Christian religion was true, than of not being mistaken in believing it true.

OF THE MEANS OF BELIEF

242

Preface to the second part.—To speak of those who have treated of this matter.

I admire the boldness with which these persons undertake to speak of God. In addressing their argument to infidels, their first chapter is to prove Divinity from the works of nature. I should not be astonished at their enterprise, if they were addressing their argument to the faithful; for it is certain that those who have the living faith in their heart see at once that all existence is none other than the work of the God whom they adore. But for those in whom this light is extinguished, and in whom we purpose to rekindle it, persons destitute of faith and grace, who, seeking with all their light whatever they see in nature that can bring them to this knowledge, find only obscurity and darkness; to tell them that they have only to look at the smallest things which surround them, and they will see God openly, to give them, as a complete proof of this great and important matter, the course of the moon and planets, and to claim to have concluded the proof with such an argument, is to give them ground for believing that the proofs of our religion are very weak. And I see by reason and experience that nothing is more calculated to arouse their contempt.

It is not after this manner that Scripture speaks, which has a better knowledge of the things that are of God. It says, on the contrary, that God is a hidden God, and that, since the corruption of nature, He has left men in a darkness from which they can escape only through Jesus Christ, without whom all communion with God is cut off. *Nemo novit Patrem, nisi Filius, et cui voluerit Filius revelare.*

This is what Scripture points out to us, when it says in so many places that those who seek God find Him. It is not of that light, "like the noonday sun," that this is said. We do not say that those who seek the noonday sun, or water in the sea, shall find them; and hence the evidence of God must not be of this nature. So it tells us elsewhere: *Vere tu es Deus absconditus.*

243

It is an astounding fact that no canonical writer has ever made use of nature to prove God. They all strive to make us believe in Him. David, Solomon, etc., have never said, "There is no void, therefore there is a God." They must have had more knowledge than the most learned people who came after them, and who have all made use of this argument. This is worthy of attention.

244

"Why! Do you not say yourself that the heavens and birds prove God?" No. "And does your religion not say so?" No. For although it is true in a sense for some souls to whom God gives this light, yet it is false with respect to the majority of men.

245

There are three sources of belief: reason, custom, inspiration. The Christian religion, which alone has reason, does not acknowledge as her true children those who believe without inspiration. It is not that she excludes reason and custom. On the contrary, the mind must be opened to proofs, must be confirmed by custom, and offer itself in humbleness to inspirations, which alone can produce a true and saving effect. *Ne evacuetur crux Christi.*

246

Order.—After the letter *That we ought to seek God,* to write the letter *On removing obstacles*; which is the discourse on "the machine," on preparing the machine, on seeking by reason.

247

Order.—A letter of exhortation to a friend to induce him to seek. And he will reply, "But what is the use of seeking? Nothing is seen." Then to reply to him, "Do not despair." And he will answer that he would be glad to find some light, but that, according to this very religion, if he believed in it, it will be of no use to him, and that therefore he prefers not to seek. And to answer to that: The machine.

248

A letter which indicates the use of proofs by the machine.— Faith is different from proof; the one is human, the other is a gift of God. *Justus ex fide vivit.* It is this faith that God Himself puts into the heart, of which the proof is often the instrument, *fides ex auditu;* but this faith is in the heart, and makes us not say *scio,* but *credo.*

249

It is superstition to put one's hope in formalities; but it is pride to be unwilling to submit to them.

250

The external must be joined to the internal to obtain anything from God, that is to say, we must kneel, pray with the lips, etc., in order that proud man, who would not submit himself to God, may be now subject to the creature. To expect help from these externals is superstition; to refuse to join them to the internal is pride.

251

Other religions, as the pagan, are more popular, for they consist in externals. But they are not for educated people. A purely intellectual religion would be more suited to the learned, but it would be of no use to the common people. The Christian religion alone is adapted to all, being composed of externals and internals. It raises the common people to the internal, and humbles the proud to the external; it is not perfect without the two, for the people must understand the spirit of the letter, and the learned must submit their spirit to the letter.

252

For we must not misunderstand ourselves; we are as much automatic as intellectual; and hence it comes that the instrument by which conviction is attained is not demonstrated alone. How few things are demonstrated! Proofs only convince the mind. Custom is the source of our strongest and most believed proofs. It bends the automaton, which persuades the mind without its thinking about the matter. Who has demonstrated that there will be a to-morrow, and that we shall die? And what is more believed? It is, then, custom which persuades us of it; it is custom that makes so many men Christians; custom that makes them Turks, heathens, artisans, soldiers, etc. (Faith in baptism is more received among Christians than among Turks.) Finally, we must have recourse to it when once the mind has seen where the truth is, in order to quench our thirst, and steep ourselves in that belief, which escapes us at every hour; for always to have proofs ready is too much trouble. We must get an easier belief, which is that of custom, which, without violence, without art, without argument, makes us believe things, and inclines all our powers to this belief, so that our soul falls naturally into it. It is not enough to believe only by force of conviction, when the automaton is inclined to believe the contrary. Both our parts must be made to believe, the mind by reasons which it is sufficient to have seen once in a lifetime, and the automaton by custom, and by not allowing it to incline to the contrary. *Inclina cor meum, Deus.*

The reason acts slowly, with so many examinations, and

on so many principles, which must be always present, that at every hour it falls asleep, or wanders, through want of having all its principles present. Feeling does not act thus; it acts in a moment, and is always ready to act. We must then put our faith in feeling; otherwise it will be always vacillating.

253

Two extremes: to exclude reason, to admit reason only.

254

It is not a rare thing to have to reprove the world for too much docility. It is a natural vice like credulity, and as pernicious. Superstition.

255

Piety is different from superstition.

To carry piety as far as superstition is to destroy it.

The heretics reproach us for this superstitious submission. This is to do what they reproach us for . . .

Infidelity, not to believe in the Eucharist, because it is not seen.

Superstition to believe propositions. Faith, etc.

256

I say there are few true Christians, even as regards faith. There are many who believe but from superstition. There are many who do not believe solely from wickedness. Few are between the two.

In this I do not include those who are of truly pious character, nor all those who believe from a feeling in their heart.

257

There are only three kinds of persons; those who serve God, having found Him; others who are occupied in seeking Him, not having found Him; while the remainder live without seeking Him, and without having found Him. The first are reasonable and happy, the last are foolish and unhappy; those between are unhappy and reasonable.

258

Unusquisque sibi Deum fingit.
Disgust.

259

Ordinary people have the power of not thinking of that about which they do not wish to think. "Do not meditate on the passages about the Messiah," said the Jew to his son. Thus our people often act. Thus are false religions preserved, and even the true one, in regard to many persons.

But there are some who have not the power of thus preventing thought, and who think so much the more as they are forbidden. These undo false religions, and even the true one, if they do not find solid arguments.

260

They hide themselves in the press, and call numbers to their rescue. Tumult.

Authority.—So far from making it a rule to believe a thing because you have heard it, you ought to believe nothing without putting yourself into the position as if you had never heard it.

It is your own assent to yourself, and the constant voice of your own reason, and not of others, that should make you believe.

Belief is so important! A hundred contradictions might be true. If antiquity were the rule of belief, men of ancient time would then be without rule. If general consent, if men had perished?

False humanity, pride.

Lift the curtain. You try in vain; if you must either believe, or deny, or doubt. Shall we then have no rule? We judge that animals do well what they do. Is there no rule whereby to judge men?

To deny, to believe, and to doubt well, are to a man what the race is to a horse.

Punishment of those who sin, error.

261

Those who do not love the truth take as a pretext that it is disputed, and that a multitude deny it. And so their error arises only from this, that they do not love either truth or charity. Thus they are without excuse.

262

Superstition and lust. Scruples, evil desires. Evil fear; fear, not such as comes from a belief in God, but such as comes from a doubt whether He exists or not. True fear comes from faith; false fear comes from doubt. True fear is joined to hope, because it is born of faith, and because men hope in the God in whom they believe. False fear is joined to despair, because men fear the God in whom they have no belief. The former fear to lose Him; the latter fear to find Him.

263

"A miracle," says one, "would strengthen my faith." He says so when he does not see one. Reasons, seen from afar, appear to limit our view; but when they are reached, we begin to see beyond. Nothing stops the nimbleness of our mind. There is no rule, say we, which has not some exceptions, no truth so general which has not some aspect in which it fails. It is sufficient that it be not absolutely universal to give us a pretext for applying the exceptions to the present subject, and for saying, "This is not always true; there are therefore cases where it is not so." It only remains to show that this is one of them; and that is why we are very awkward or unlucky, if we do not find one some day.

264

We do not weary of eating and sleeping every day, for hunger and sleepiness recur. Without that we should weary of them. So, without the hunger for spiritual things, we weary of them. Hunger after righteousness, the eighth beautitude.

265

Faith indeed tells what the senses do not tell, but not the contrary of what they see. It is above them and not contrary to them.

266

How many stars have telescopes revealed to us which did not exist for our philosophers of old! We freely attack Holy Scripture on the great number of stars, saying, "There are only one thousand and twenty-eight, we know it." There is grass on the earth, we see it—from the moon we would not see it—and on the grass are leaves, and in these leaves are small animals; but after that no more.—O presumptuous man!—The compounds are composed of elements, and the elements not.—O presumptuous man! Here is a fine reflection.—We must not say that there is anything which we do not see.—We must then talk like others, but not think like them.

267

The last proceeding of reason is to recognise that there is an infinity of things which are beyond it. It is but feeble if it does not see so far as to know this. But if natural things are beyond it, what will be said of supernatural?

268

Submission.—We must know where to doubt, where to feel certain, where to submit. He who does not do so, understands not the force of reason. There are some who offend against these three rules, either by affirming everything as demonstrative, from want of knowing what demonstration is; or by doubting everything, from want of knowing where to submit; or by submitting in everything, from want of knowing where they must judge.

269

Submission is the use of reason in which consists true Christianity.

270

Saint Augustine.—Reason would never submit, if it did not judge that there are some occasions on which it ought to submit. It is then right for it to submit, when it judges that it ought to submit.

271

Wisdom sends us to childhood. *Nisi efficiamini sicut parvuli.*

272

There is nothing so conformable to reason as this disavowal of reason.

273

If we submit everything to reason, our religion will have no mysterious and supernatural element. If we offend the principles of reason, our religion will be absurd and ridiculous.

274

All our reasoning reduces itself to yielding to feeling.

But fancy is like, though contrary to feeling, so that we cannot distinguish between these contraries. One person says that my feeling is fancy, another that his fancy is feeling. We should have a rule. Reason offers itself; but it is pliable in every sense; and thus there is no rule.

275

Men often take their imagination for their heart; and they believe they are converted as soon as they think of being converted.

276

M. de Roannez said: "Reasons come to me afterwards, but at first a thing pleases or shocks me without my knowing the reason, and yet it shocks me for that reason which I only discover afterwards." But I believe, not that it shocked him for the reasons which were found afterwards, but that these reasons were only found because it shocks him.

277

The heart has its reasons, which reason does not know. We feel it in a thousand things. I say that the heart naturally loves the Universal Being, and also itself naturally, according as it gives itself to them; and it hardens itself against one or the other at its will. You have rejected the one, and kept the other. Is it by reason that you love yourself?

278

It is the heart which experiences God, and not the reason. This, then, is faith: God felt by the heart, not by the reason. Faith is a gift of God; do not believe that we said it was a gift of reasoning. Other religions do not say this of their faith. They only give reasoning in order to arrive at it, and yet it does not bring them to it.

279

Faith is a gift of God; do not believe that we said it was a gift of reasoning. Other religions do not say this of their faith. They only gave reasoning in order to arrive at it, and yet it does not bring them to it.

280

The knowledge of God is very far from the love of Him.

281

Heart, instinct, principles.

282

We know truth, not only by the reason, but also by the heart, and it is in this last way that we know first principles; and reason, which has no part in it, tries in vain to impugn them. The sceptics, who have only this for their object, labour to no purpose. We know that we do not dream, and however impossible it is for us to prove it by reason, this inability demonstrates only the weakness of our reason, but not, as they affirm, the uncertainty of all our knowledge. For the knowledge of first principles, as space, time, motion, number, is as sure as any of those which we get from reasoning. And reason must trust these intuitions of the heart, and must base them on every argument. (We have intuitive knowledge of the tri-dimensional nature of space, and of the infinity of number, and reason then shows that there are no two square numbers one of which is double of the other. Principles are intuited, propositions are inferred, all with certainty, though in different ways.) And it is as useless and absurd for reason to demand from the heart proofs of her first principles, before admitting them, as it would be for the heart to demand from reason an intuition of all demonstrated propositions before accepting them.

This inability ought, then, to serve only to humble reason, which would judge all, but not to impugn our certainty, as if only reason were capable of instructing us. Would to God, on the contrary, that we had never need of it, and that we knew everything by instinct and intuition! But nature has refused us this boon. On the contrary, she has given us but very little knowledge of this kind; and all the rest can be acquired only by reasoning.

Therefore, those to whom God has imparted religion by intuition are very fortunate, and justly convinced. But to those who do not have it, we can give it only by reasoning, waiting for God to give them spiritual insight, without which faith is only human, and useless for salvation.

283

Order.—Against the objection that Scripture has no order.
The heart has its own order; the intellect has its own, which is by principle and demonstration. The heart has another. We do not prove that we ought to be loved by enumerating in order the causes of love; that would be ridiculous.

Jesus Christ and Saint Paul employ the rule of love, not of intellect; for they would warm, not instruct. It is the same with Saint Augustine. This order consists chiefly in digressions on each point to indicate the end, and keep it always in sight.

284

Do not wonder to see simple people believe without reasoning. God imparts to them love of Him and hatred of self. He inclines their heart to believe. Men will never believe with a saving and real faith, unless God inclines their heart; and they will believe as soon as He inclines it. And this is what David knew well, when he said: *Inclina cor meum, Deus, in* . . .

285

Religion is suited to all kinds of minds. Some pay attention only to its establishment, and this religion is such that its very establishment suffices to prove its truth. Others trace it even to the apostles. The more learned go back to the beginning of the world. The angels see it better still, and from a more distant time.

286

Those who believe without having read the Testaments, do so because they have an inward disposition entirely holy, and all that they hear of our religion conforms to it. They feel that a God has made them; they desire only to love God; they desire to hate themselves only. They feel that they have no strength in themselves; that they are incapable of coming to God; and that if God does not come to them, they can have no communion with Him. And they hear our religion say that men must love God only, and hate self only; but that all being corrupt and unworthy of God, God made Himself man to unite Himself to us. No more is required to persuade men who have this disposition in their heart, and who have this knowledge of their duty and of their inefficiency.

287

Those whom we see to be Christians without the knowledge of the prophets and evidences, nevertheless judge of their religion as well as those who have that knowledge. They judge of it by the heart, as others judge of it by the intellect. God Himself inclines them to believe, and thus they are most effectively convinced.

I confess indeed that one of those Christians who believe without proofs will not perhaps be capable of convincing an infidel who will say the same of himself. But those who know the proofs of religion will prove without difficulty that such a believer is truly inspired by God, though he cannot prove it himself.

For God having said in His prophecies (which are undoubtedly prophecies), that in the reign of Jesus Christ He would spread His spirit abroad among nations, and that the youths and maidens and children of the Church would prophesy; it is certain that the Spirit of God is in these, and not in the others.

288

Instead of complaining that God had hidden Himself, you will give Him thanks for having revealed so much of Himself; and you will also give Him thanks for not having revealed Himself to haughty sages, unworthy to know so holy a God.

Two kinds of persons know Him: those who have a humble heart, and who love lowliness, whatever kind of intellect they may have, high or low; and those who have sufficient understanding to see the truth, whatever opposition they may have to it.

289

Proof.—1. The Christian religion, by its establishment, having established itself so strongly, so gently, whilst so contrary to nature.—2. The sanctity, the dignity, and the humility of a Christian soul.—3. The miracles of Holy Scripture.—4. Jesus Christ in particular.—5. The apostles in

particular.—6. Moses and the prophets in particular.—7.
The Jewish people.—8. The prophecies.—9. Perpetuity; no
religion has perpetuity.—10. The doctrine which gives a
reason for everything.—11. The sanctity of this law.—12.
By the course of the world.

Surely, after considering what is life and what is religion,
we should not refuse to obey the inclination to follow it, if it
comes into our heart; and it is certain that there is no ground
for laughing at those who follow it.

290

Proofs of religion.—Morality, Doctrine, Miracles, Prophecies, Types.

SECTION V

JUSTICE AND THE REASON OF EFFECTS

291

In the letter *On Injustice* can come the ridiculousness of the law that the elder gets all. "My friend, you were born on this side of the mountain, it is therefore just that your elder brother gets everything."

"Why do you kill me?"

292

He lives on the other side of the water.

293

"Why do you kill me? What! do you not live on the other side of the water? If you lived on this side, my friend, I should be an assassin, and it would be unjust to slay you in this manner. But since you live on the other side, I am a hero, and it is just."

294

On what shall man found the order of the world which he would govern? Shall it be on the caprice of each individual? What confusion! Shall it be on justice? Man is ignorant of it.

Certainly had he known it, he would not have established this maxim, the most general of all that obtain among men, that each should follow the custom of his own country. The glory of true equity would have brought all nations under subjection, and legislators would not have taken as their model the fancies and caprice of Persians and Germans instead of this unchanging justice. We would have seen it set up in all the States on earth and in all times; whereas we see neither justice nor injustice which does not change its nature with change in climate. Three degrees of latitude reverse all jurisprudence; a meridian decides the truth. Fundamental laws change after a few years of possession; right has its epochs; the entry of Saturn into the Lion marks to us the origin of such and such a crime. A strange justice that is bounded by a river! Truth on this side of the Pyrenees, error on the other side.

Men admit that justice does not consist in these customs, but that it resides in natural laws, common to every country. They would certainly maintain it obstinately, if reckless chance which has distributed human laws had encountered even one which was universal; but the farce is that the caprice of men has so many vagaries that there is no such law.

Theft, incest, infanticide, parricide, have all had a place among virtuous actions. Can anything be more ridiculous than that a man should have the right to kill me because he lives on the other side of the water, and because his ruler has a quarrel with mine, though I have none with him?

Doubtless there are natural laws; but good reason once corrupted has corrupted all. *Nihil amplius nostrum est; quod nostrum dicimus, artis est. Ex senatus—consultis et plebiscitis crimina exercentur. Ut olim vitiis, sic nunc legibus laboramus.*

The result of this confusion is that one affirms the essence of justice to be the authority of the legislator; another, the interest of the sovereign; another, present custom, and this is the most sure. Nothing, according to reason alone, is just in itself; all changes with time. Custom creates the whole of equity, for the simple reason that it is accepted. It is the mystical foundation of its authority; whoever carries it back to first principles destroys it. Nothing is so faulty as those laws which correct faults. He who obeys them because they are just, obeys a justice which is imaginary, and not the essence of law; it is quite self-contained, it is law and nothing more. He who will examine its motive will find it so feeble and so trifling that if he be not accustomed to contemplate the wonders of human imagination, he will marvel that one century has gained for it so much pomp and reverence. The art of opposition and of revolution is to unsettle established customs, sounding them even to their source, to point out their want of authority and justice. We must, it is said, get back to the natural and fundamental laws of the State, which an unjust custom has abolished. It is a game certain to result in the loss of all; nothing will be just on the balance. Yet people readily lend their ear to such arguments. They shake off the yoke as soon as they recognise it; and the great profit by their ruin, and by that of these curious investigators of accepted customs. But from a contrary mistake men sometimes think they can justly do everything which is not without an example. That is why the wisest of legislators said that it was necessary to deceive men for their own good; and another, a good politician, *Cum veritatem qua liberetur ignoret, expedit quod fallatur.* We must not see the fact of usurpation; law was once introduced without reason, and has become reasonable. We must make it regarded as authoritative, eternal, and conceal its origin, if we do not wish that it should soon come to an end.

295

Mine, thine.—"This dog is mine," said those poor children; "that is my place in the sun." Here is the beginning and the image of the usurpation of all the earth.

296

When the question for consideration is whether we ought to make war, and kill so many men—condemn so many Spaniards to death—only one man is judge, and he is an interested party. There should be a third, who is disinterested.

297

Veri juris.—We have it no more; if we had it, we should take conformity to the customs of a country as the rule of justice. It is here that, not finding justice, we have found force, etc.

298

Justice, might.—It is right that what is just should be obeyed; it is necessary that what is strongest should be obeyed. Justice without might is helpless; might without justice is tyrannical. Justice without might is gainsaid, because there are always offenders; might without justice is condemned. We must then combine justice and might, and for this end make what is just strong, or what is strong just.

Justice is subject to dispute; might is easily recognised and is not disputed. So we cannot give might to justice, because might has gainsaid justice, and has declared that it is she herself who is just. And thus being unable to make what is just strong, we have made what is strong just.

299

The only universal rules are the laws of the country in ordinary affairs, and of the majority in others. Whence comes this? From the might which is in them. Hence it comes that kings, who have power of a different kind, do not follow the majority of their ministers.

No doubt equality of goods is just; but, being unable to cause might to obey justice, men have made it just to obey might. Unable to strengthen justice, they have justified might; so that the just and the strong should unite, and there should be peace, which is the sovereign good.

300

"When a strong man armed keepeth his goods, his goods are in peace."

301

Why do we follow the majority? Is it because they have more reason? No, because they have more power.

Why do we follow the ancient laws and opinions? Is it

because they are more sound? No, but because they are
unique, and remove from us the root of difference.

302

. . . It is the effect of might, not of custom. For those who
are capable of originality are few; the greater number will
only follow, and refuse glory to those inventors who seek it by
their inventions. And if these are obstinate in their wish to
obtain glory, and despise those who do not invent, the latter
will call them ridiculous names, and will beat them with a
stick. Let no one then boast of his subtlety, or let him keep
his complacency to himself.

303

Might is the sovereign of the world, and not opinion.—But
opinion makes use of might.—It is might that makes opinion.
Gentleness is beautiful in our opinion. Why? Because he who
will dance on a rope will be alone, and I will gather a stronger
mob of people who will say that it is unbecoming.

304

The cords which bind the respect of men to each other are
in general cords of necessity; for there must be different degrees, all men wishing to rule, and not all being able to do so,
but some being able.

Let us then imagine we see society in the process of formation. Men will doubtless fight till the stronger party over-
comes the weaker, and a dominant party is established. But
when this is once determined, the masters, who do not desire
the continuation of strife, then decree that the power which
is in their hands shall be transmitted as they please. Some
place it in election by the people, others in hereditary succession, etc.

And this is the point where imagination begins to play its
part. Till now power makes fact; now power is sustained by
imagination in a certain party, in France in the nobility, in
Switzerland in the burgesses, etc.

These cords which bind the respect of men to such and such an individual are therefore the cords of imagination.

305

The Swiss are offended by being called gentlemen, and prove themselves true plebeians in order to be thought worthy of great office.

306

As duchies, kingships, and magistracies are real and necessary, because might rules all, they exist everywhere and always. But since only caprice makes such and such a one a ruler, the principle is not constant, but subject to variation, etc.

307

The chancellor is grave, and clothed with ornaments, for his position is unreal. Not so the king, he has power, and has nothing to do with the imagination. Judges, physicians, etc., appeal only to the imagination.

308

The habit of seeing kings accompanied by guards, drums, officers, and all the paraphernalia which mechanically inspire respect and awe, makes their countenance, when sometimes seen alone without these accompaniments, impress respect and awe on their subjects; because we cannot separate in thought their persons from the surroundings with which we see them usually joined. And the world, which knows not that this effect is the result of habit, believes that it arises by a natural force, whence come these words, "The character of Divinity is stamped on his countenance," etc.

309

Justice.—As custom determines what is agreeable, so also does it determine justice.

310

King and tyrant.—I, too, will keep my thoughts secret.

I will take care on every journey.

Greatness of establishment, respect for establishment.

The pleasure of the great is the power to make people happy.

The property of riches is to be given liberally.

The property of each thing must be sought. The property of power is to protect.

When force attacks humbug, when a private soldier takes the square cap off a first president, and throws it out of the window.

311

The government founded on opinion and imagination reigns for some time, and this government is pleasant and voluntary; that founded on might lasts for ever. Thus opinion is the queen of the world, but might is its tyrant.

312

Justice is what is established; and thus all our established laws will necessarily be regarded as just without examination, since they are established.

313

Sound opinions of the people.—Civil wars are the greatest of evils. They are inevitable, if we wish to reward desert; for all will say they are deserving. The evil we have to fear from a fool who succeeds by right of birth, is neither so great nor so sure.

314

God has created all for Himself. He has bestowed upon Himself the power of pain and pleasure.

You can apply it to God, or to yourself. If to God, the Gospel is the rule. If to yourself, you will take the place of

God. As God is surrounded by persons full of charity, who ask of Him the blessings of charity that are in His power, so . . . Recognise, then, and learn that you are only a king of lust, and take the ways of lust.

315

The reason of effects.—It is wonderful that men would not have me honour a man clothed in brocade, and followed by seven or eight lackeys! Why! He will have me thrashed, if I do not salute him. This custom is a farce. It is the same with a horse in fine trappings in comparison with another! Montaigne is a fool not to see what difference there is, to wonder at our finding any, and to ask the reason. "Indeed," says he, "how comes it," etc. . . .

316

Sound opinions of the people.—To be spruce is not altogether foolish, for it proves that a great number of people work for one. It shows by one's hair, that one has a valet, a perfumer, etc., by one's band, thread, lace, . . . etc. Now it is not merely superficial nor merely outward show to have many arms at command. The more arms one has, the more powerful one is. To be spruce is to show one's power.

317

Deference means, "Put yourself to inconvenience." This is apparently silly, but is quite right. For it is to say, "I would indeed put myself to inconvenience if you required it, since indeed I do so when it is of no service to you." Deference further serves to distinguish the great. Now if deference was displayed by sitting in an arm-chair, we should show deference to everybody, and so no distinction would be made; but, being put to inconvenience, we distinguish very well.

318

He has four lackeys.

319

How rightly do we distinguish men by external appearances rather than by internal qualities! Which of us two shall have precedence? Who will give place to the other? The least clever. But I am as clever as he. We should have to fight over this. He has four lackeys, and I have only one. This can be seen; we have only to count. It falls to me to yield, and I am a fool if I contest the matter. By this means we are at peace, which is the greatest of boons.

320

The most unreasonable things in the world become most reasonable, because of the unruliness of men. What is less reasonable than to choose the eldest son of a queen to rule a State? We do not choose as captain of a ship the passenger who is of the best family.

This law would be absurd and unjust; but because men are so themselves, and always will be so, it becomes reasonable and just. For whom will men choose, as the most virtuous and able? We at once come to blows, as each claims to be the most virtuous and able. Let us then attach this quality to something indisputable. This is the king's eldest son. That is clear, and there is no dispute. Reason can do no better, for civil war is the greatest of evils.

321

Children are astonished to see their comrades respected.

322

To be of noble birth is a great advantage. In eighteen years it places a man within the select circle, known and respected, as another would have merited in fifty years. It is a gain of thirty years without trouble.

323

What is the Ego?

Suppose a man puts himself at a window to see those who

pass by. If I pass by, can I say that he placed himself there to see me? No; for he does not think of me in particular. But does he who loves someone on account of beauty really love that person? No; for the small-pox, which will kill beauty without killing the person, will cause him to love her no more.

And if one loves me for my judgment, memory, he does not love *me*, for I can lose these qualities without losing myself. Where, then, is this Ego, if it be neither in the body nor in the soul? And how love the body or the soul, except for these qualities which do not constitute *me*, since they are perishable? For it is impossible and would be unjust to love the soul of a person in the abstract, and whatever qualities might be therein. We never, then, love a person, but only qualities.

Let us, then, jeer no more at those who are honoured on account of rank and office; for we love a person only on account of borrowed qualities.

324

The people have very sound opinions, for example:

1. In having preferred diversion and hunting to poetry. The half-learned laugh at it, and glory in being above the folly of the world; but the people are right for a reason which these do not fathom.

2. In having distinguished men by external marks, as birth or wealth. The world again exults in showing how unreasonable this is; but it is very reasonable. Savages laugh at an infant king.

3. In being offended at a blow, or in desiring glory so much. But it is very desirable on account of the other essential goods which are joined to it; and a man who has received a blow, without resenting it, is overwhelmed with taunts and indignities.

4. In working for the uncertain; in sailing on the sea; in walking over a plank.

325

Montaigne is wrong. Custom should be followed only because it is custom, and not because it is reasonable or just.

But people follow it for this sole reason, that they think it just. Otherwise they would follow it no longer, although it were the custom; for they will only submit to reason or justice. Custom without this would pass for tyranny; but the sovereignty of reason and justice is no more tyrannical than that of desire. They are principles natural to man.

It would therefore be right to obey laws and customs, because they are laws; but we should know that there is neither truth nor justice to introduce into them, that we know nothing of these, and so must follow what is accepted. By this means we would never depart from them. But people cannot accept this doctrine; and, as they believe that truth can be found, and that it exists in law and custom, they believe them, and take their antiquity as a proof of their truth, and not simply of their authority apart from truth. Thus they obey laws, but they are liable to revolt when these are proved to be valueless; and this can be shown of all, looked at from a certain aspect.

326

Injustice.—It is dangerous to tell the people that the laws are unjust; for they obey them only because they think them just. Therefore it is necessary to tell them at the same time that they must obey them because they are laws, just as they must obey superiors, not because they are just, but because they are superiors. In this way all sedition is prevented, if this can be made intelligible, and it be understood what is the proper definition of justice.

327

The world is a good judge of things, for it is in natural ignorance, which is man's true state. The sciences have two extremes which meet. The first is the pure natural ignorance in which all men find themselves at birth. The other extreme is that reached by great intellects, who, having run through all that men can know, find they know nothing, and come back again to that same ignorance from which they set out; but this is a learned ignorance which is conscious of itself.

Those between the two, who have departed from natural ignorance and not been able to reach the other, have some smattering of this vain knowledge, and pretend to be wise. These trouble the world, and are bad judges of everything. The people and the wise constitute the world; these despise it, and are despised. They judge badly of everything, and the world judges rightly of them.

328

The reason of effects.—Continual alternation of pro and con.

We have then shown that man is foolish, by the estimation he makes of things which are not essential; and all these opinions are destroyed. We have next shown that all these opinions are very sound, and that thus, since all these vanities are well founded, the people are not so foolish as is said. And so we have destroyed the opinion which destroyed that of the people.

But we must now destroy this last proposition, and show that it remains always true that the people are foolish, though their opinions are sound; because they do not perceive the truth where it is, and, as they place it where it is not, their opinions are always very false and very unsound.

329

The reason of effects.—The weakness of man is the reason why so many things are considered fine, as to be good at play-ing the lute. It is only an evil because of our weakness.

330

The power of kings is founded on the reason and on the folly of the people, and specially on their folly. The greatest and most important thing in the world has weakness for its foundation, and this foundation is wonderfully sure; for there is nothing more sure than this, that the people will be weak. What is based on sound reason is very ill-founded, as the estimate of wisdom.

331

We can only think of Plato and Aristotle in grand academic robes. They were honest men, like others, laughing with their friends, and when they diverted themselves with writing their *Laws* and the *Politics*, they did it as an amusement. That part of their life was the least philosophic and the least serious; the most philosophic was to live simply and quietly. If they wrote on politics, it was as if laying down rules for a lunatic asylum; and if they presented the appearance of speaking of a great matter, it was because they knew that the madmen, to whom they spoke, thought they were kings and emperors. They entered into their principles in order to make their madness as little harmful as possible.

332

Tyranny consists in the desire of universal power beyond its scope.

There are different assemblies of the strong, the fair, the sensible, the pious, in which each man rules at home, not elsewhere. And sometimes they meet, and the strong and the fair foolishly fight as to who shall be master, for their mastery is of different kinds. They do not understand one another, and their fault is the desire to rule everywhere. Nothing can effect this, not even might, which is of no use in the kingdom of the wise, and is only mistress of external actions.

Tyranny— . . . So these expressions are false and tyrannical: "I am fair, therefore I must be feared. I am strong, therefore I must be loved. I am . . ."

Tyranny is the wish to have in one way what can only be had in another. We render different duties to different merits; the duty of love to the pleasant; the duty of fear to the strong; duty of belief to the learned.

We must render these duties; it is unjust to refuse them, and unjust to ask others. And so it is false and tyrannical to say, "He is not strong, therefore I will not esteem him; he is not able, therefore I will not fear him."

333

Have you never seen people who, in order to complain of the little fuss you make about them, parade before you the example of great men who esteem them? In answer I reply to them, "Show me the merit whereby you have charmed these persons, and I also will esteem you."

334

The reason of effects.—Lust and force are the source of all our actions; lust causes voluntary actions, force involuntary ones.

335

The reason of effects.—It is then true to say that all the world is under a delusion; for, although the opinions of the people are sound, they are not so as conceived by them, since they think the truth to be where it is not. Truth is indeed in their opinions, but not at the point where they imagine it. [Thus] it is true that we must honour noblemen, but not because noble birth is real superiority, etc.

336

The reason of effects.—We must keep our thought secret, and judge everything by it, while talking like the people.

337

The reason of effects. Degrees. The people honour persons of high birth. The semi-learned despise them, saying that birth is not a personal, but a chance superiority. The learned honour them, not for popular reasons, but for secret reasons. Devout persons, who have more zeal than knowledge, despise them, in spite of that consideration which makes them honoured by the learned, because they judge them by a new light which piety gives them. But perfect Christians honour them by another and higher light. So arise a succession of opinions for and against, according to the light one has.

338

True Christians nevertheless comply with folly, not because they respect folly, but the command of God, who for the punishment of men has made them subject to these follies. *Omnis creatura subjecta est vanitati. Liberabitur.* Thus Saint Thomas explains the passage in Saint James on giving place to the rich, that if they do it not in the sight of God, they depart from the command of religion.

THE PHILOSOPHERS

339

I can well conceive a man without hands, feet, head (for it is only experience which teaches us that the head is more necessary than feet). But I cannot conceive man without thought; he would be a stone or a brute.

340

The arithmetical machine produces effects which approach nearer to thought than all the actions of animals. But it does nothing which would enable us to attribute will to it, as to the animals.

341

The account of the pike and frog of Liancourt. They do it always, and never otherwise, nor any other thing showing mind.

342

If an animal did by mind what it does by instinct, and if it spoke by mind what it speaks by instinct, in hunting, and in warning its mates that the prey is found or lost; it would indeed also speak in regard to those things which affect it closer, as example, "Gnaw me this cord which is wounding me, and which I cannot reach."

343

The beak of the parrot, which it wipes, although it is clean.

344

Instinct and reason, marks of two natures.

345

Reason commands us far more imperiously than a master;
for in disobeying the one we are unfortunate, and in disobeying the other we are fools.

346

Thought constitutes the greatness of man.

347

Man is but a reed, the most feeble thing in nature; but he
is a thinking reed. The entire universe need not arm itself to
crush him. A vapour, a drop of water suffices to kill him. But,
if the universe were to crush him, man would still be more
noble than that which killed him, because he knows that he
dies and the advantage which the universe has over him; the
universe knows nothing of this.

All our dignity consists, then, in thought. By it we must
elevate ourselves, and not by space and time which we cannot
fill. Let us endeavour, then, to think well; this is the principle
of morality.

348

A thinking reed.—It is not from space that I must seek my
dignity, but from the government of my thought. I shall have
no more if I possess worlds. By space the universe encompasses and swallows me up like an atom; by thought I comprehend the world.

349

Immateriality of the soul.—Philosophers who have mastered their passions. What matter could do that?

350

The Stoics.—They conclude that what has been done once can be done always, and that since the desire of glory imparts some power to those whom it possesses, others can do likewise. There are feverish movements which health cannot imitate.

Epictetus concludes that since there are consistent Christians, every man can easily be so.

351

Those great spiritual efforts, which the soul sometimes assays, are things on which it does not lay hold. It only leaps to them, not as upon a throne, for ever, but merely for an instant.

352

The strength of a man's virtue must not be measured by his efforts, but by his ordinary life.

353

I do not admire the excess of a virtue as of valour, except I see at the same time the excess of the opposite virtue, as in Epaminondas, who had the greatest valour and the greatest kindness. For otherwise it is not to rise, it is to fall. We do not display greatness by going to one extreme, but in touching both at once, and filling all the intervening space. But perhaps this is only a sudden movement of the soul from one to the other extreme, and in fact it is ever at one point only, as in the case of a firebrand. Be it so, but at least this indicates agility if not expanse of soul.

354

Man's nature is not always to advance; it has its advances and retreats.

Fever has its cold and hot fits; and the cold proves as well as the hot the greatness of the fire of fever.

The discoveries of men from age to age turn out the same.

The kindness and the malice of the world in general are the same. *Plerumque gratæ principibus vices.*

355

Continuous eloquence wearies.

Princes and kings sometimes play. They are not always on their thrones. They weary there. Grandeur must be abandoned to be appreciated. Continuity in everything is unpleasant. Cold is agreeable, that we may get warm.

Nature acts by progress, *itus et reditus*. It goes and returns, then advances further, then twice as much backwards, then more forward than ever, etc.

The tide of the sea behaves in the same manner; and so apparently does the sun in its course.

356

The nourishment of the body is little by little. Fullness of nourishment and smallness of substance.

357

When we would pursue virtues to their extremes on either side, vices present themselves, which insinuate themselves insensibly there, in their insensible journey towards the infinitely little; and vices present themselves in a crowd towards the infinitely great, so that we lose ourselves in them, and no longer see virtues. We find fault with perfection itself.

358

Man is neither angel nor brute, and the unfortunate thing is that he who would act the angel acts the brute.

359

We do not sustain ourselves in virtue by our own strength, but by the balancing of two opposed vices, just as we remain upright amidst two contrary gales. Remove one of the vices, and we fall into the other.

360

What the Stoics propose is so difficult and foolish!

The Stoics lay down that all those who are not at the high degree of wisdom are equally foolish and vicious, as those who are two inches under water.

361

*The sovereign good. Dispute about the sovereign good.—
Ut sis contentus temetipso et ex te nascentibus bonis.* There is a contradiction, for in the end they advise suicide. Oh! What a happy life, from which we are to free ourselves as from the plague!

362

Ex senatus-consultis et plebiscitis . . .
To ask like passages.

363

Ex senatus-consultis et plebiscitis scelera exercentur. Sen. 588.

Nihil tam absurde dici potest quod non dicatur ab aliquo philosophorum. Divin.

Quibusdam destinatis sententiis consecrati quæ non probant coguntur defendere. Cic.

Ut omnium rerum sic litterarum quoque intemperantia laboramus. Senec.

Id maxime quemque decet, quod est cujusque suum maxime.

Hos natura modos primum dedit. Georg.

Paucis opus est litteris ad bonam mentem.

Si quando turpe non sit, tamen non est non turpe quum id a multitudine laudetur.

Mihi sic usus est, tibi ut opus est facto, fac. Ter.

364

Rarum est enim ut satis se quisque vereatur.
Tot circa unum caput tumultuantes deos.

Nihil turpius quam cognitioni assertionem præcurrere. Cic.
Nec me pudet, ut istos, fateri nescire quid nesciam.
Melius non incipient.

365

Thought.—All the dignity of man consists in thought. Thought is therefore by its nature a wonderful and incomparable thing. It must have strange defects to be contemptible. But it has such, so that nothing is more ridiculous. How great it is in its nature! How vile it is in its defects!

But what is this thought? How foolish it is!

366

The mind of this sovereign judge of the world is not so independent that it is not liable to be disturbed by the first din about it. The noise of a cannon is not necessary to hinder its thoughts; it needs only the creaking of a weathercock or a pulley. Do not wonder if at present it does not reason well; a fly is buzzing in its ears; that is enough to render it incapable of good judgment. If you wish it to be able to reach the truth, chase away that animal which holds its reason in check and disturbs that powerful intellect which rules towns and kingdoms. Here is a comical god! *O ridicolosissimo eroe!*

367

The power of flies; they win battles, hinder our soul from acting, eat our body.

368

When it is said that heat is only the motions of certain molecules, and light the *conatus recedendi* which we feel, it astonishes us. What! Is pleasure only the ballet of our spirits? We have conceived so different an idea of it! And these sensations seem so removed from those others which we say are the same as those with which we compare them! The sensation from the fire, that warmth which affects us in a manner wholly different from touch, the reception of sound and light, all this appears to us mysterious, and yet it is material like the blow of a stone. It is true that the smallness of the spirits which enter into the pores touches other nerves, but there are always some nerves touched.

369

Memory is necessary for all the operations of reason.

370

[Chance gives rise to thoughts, and chance removes them; no art can keep or acquire them.

A thought has escaped me. I wanted to write it down. I write instead that it has escaped me.]

371

[When I was small, I hugged my book; and because it sometimes happened to me to . . . in believing I hugged it, I doubted. . . .]

372

In writing down my thought, it sometimes escapes me; but this makes me remember my weakness, that I constantly forget. This is as instructive to me as my forgotten thought; for I strive only to know my nothingness.

373

Scepticism.—I shall here write my thoughts without order, and not perhaps in unintentional confusion; that is true order, which will always indicate my object by its very disorder. I should do too much honour to my subject, if I treated it with order, since I want to show that it is incapable of it.

374

What astonishes me most is to see that all the world is not astonished at its own weakness. Men act seriously, and each follows his own mode of life, not because it is in fact good to follow since it is the custom, but as if each man knew certainly

where reason and justice are. They find themselves continually deceived, and by a comical humility think it is their own
fault, and not that of the art which they claim always to
possess. But it is well there are so many such people in the
world, who are not sceptics for the glory of scepticism, in order
to show that man is quite capable of the most extravagant
opinions, since he is capable of believing that he is not in a
state of natural and inevitable weakness, but, on the contrary,
of natural wisdom.

Nothing fortifies scepticism more than that there are some
who are not sceptics; if all were so, they would be wrong.

375

[I have passed a great part of my life believing that there
was justice, and in this I was not mistaken; for there is justice
according as God has willed to reveal it to us. But I did not
take it so, and this is where I made a mistake; for I believed
that our justice was essentially just, and that I had that
whereby to know and judge of it. But I have so often found
my right judgment at fault, that at last I have come to distrust
myself, and then others. I have seen changes in all nations and
men, and thus after many changes of judgment regarding
true justice, I have recognised that our nature was but in continual change, and I have not changed since; and if I changed,
I would confirm my opinion.

The sceptic Arcesilaus, who became a dogmatist.]

376

This sect derives more strength from its enemies than from
its friends; for the weakness of man is far more evident in
those who know it not than in those who know it.

377

Discourses on humility are a source of pride in the vain, and
of humility in the humble. So those on scepticism cause believers to affirm. Few men speak humbly of humility, chastely
of chastity, few doubtingly of scepticism. We are only false-

hood, duplicity, contradiction; we both conceal and disguise ourselves from ourselves.

378

Scepticism.—Excess, like defect of intellect, is accused of madness. Nothing is good but mediocrity. The majority has settled that, and finds fault with him who escapes it at whichever end. I will not oppose it. I quite consent to put myself there, and refuse to be at the lower end, not because it is low, but because it is an end; for I would likewise refuse to be placed at the top. To leave the mean is to abandon humanity. The greatness of the human soul consists in knowing how to preserve the mean. So far from greatness consisting in leaving it, it consists in not leaving it.

379

It is not good to have too much liberty. It is not good to have all one wants.

380

All good maxims are in the world. We only need to apply them. For instance, we do not doubt that we ought to risk our lives in defence of the public good; but for religion, no.

It is true there must be inequality among men; but if this be conceded, the door is opened not only to the highest power, but to the highest tyranny.

We must relax our minds a little; but this opens the door to the greatest debauchery. Let us mark the limits. There are no limits in things. Laws would put them there, and the mind cannot suffer it.

381

When we are too young, we do not judge well; so, also, when we are too old. If we do not think enough, or if we think too much on any matter, we get obstinate and infatuated with it. If one considers one's work immediately after having done it, one is entirely prepossessed in its favour; by delaying too long, one can no longer enter into the spirit of it. So with pictures seen from too far or too near; there is but one exact point which is the true place wherefrom to look at them: the rest are too near, too far, too high, or too low. Perspective determines that point in the art of painting. But who shall determine it in truth and morality?

382

When all is equally agitated, nothing appears to be agitated, as in a ship. When all tend to debauchery, none appears to do so. He who stops draws attention to the excess of others, like a fixed point.

383

The licentious tell men of orderly lives that they stray from nature's path, while they themselves follow it; as people in a ship think those move who are on the shore. On all sides the language is similar. We must have a fixed point in order to judge. The harbour decides for those who are in a ship; but where shall we find a harbour in morality?

384

Contradiction is a bad sign of truth; several things which are certain are contradicted; several things which are false pass without contradiction. Contradiction is not a sign of falsity, nor the want of contradiction a sign of truth.

385

Scepticism.—Each thing here is partly true and partly false. Essential truth is not so; it is altogether pure and altogether true. This mixture dishonours and annihilates it. Nothing is purely true, and thus nothing is true, meaning by that pure truth. You will say it is true that homicide is wrong. Yes; for we know well the wrong and the false. But what will you say is good? Chastity? I say no; for the world would come to an end. Marriage? No; continence is better. Not to kill? No; for lawlessness would be horrible, and the wicked would kill all the good. To kill? No; for that destroys nature. We possess truth and goodness only in part, and mingled with falsehood and evil.

386

If we dreamt the same thing every night, it would affect us as much as the objects we see every day. And if an artisan were sure to dream every night for twelve hours' duration that he was a king, I believe he would be almost as happy as a king, who should dream every night for twelve hours on end that he was an artisan.

If we were to dream every night that we were pursued by enemies, and harassed by these painful phantoms, or that we passed every day in different occupations, as in making a voyage, we should suffer almost as much as if it were real, and should fear to sleep, as we fear to wake when we dread in fact to enter on such mishaps. And, indeed, it would cause pretty nearly the same discomforts as the reality.

But since dreams are all different, and each single one is diversified, what is seen in them affects us much less than what we see when awake, because of its continuity, which is not, however, so continuous and level as not to change too; but it changes less abruptly, except rarely, as when we travel, and then we say, "It seems to me I am dreaming." For life is a dream a little less inconstant.

387

[It may be that there are true demonstrations; but this is not certain. Thus, this proves nothing else but that it is not certain that all is uncertain, to the glory of scepticism.]

388

Good sense.—They are compelled to say, "You are not acting in good faith; we are not asleep," etc. How I love to see this proud reason humiliated and suppliant! For this is not the language of a man whose right is disputed, and who defends it with the power of armed hands. He is not foolish

enough to declare that men are not acting in good faith, but
he punishes this bad faith with force.

389

Ecclesiastes shows that man without God is in total ignorance and inevitable misery. For it is wretched to have the
wish, but not the power. Now he would be happy and assured
of some truth, and yet he can neither know, nor desire not to
know. He cannot even doubt.

390

My God! How foolish this talk is! "Would God have made
the world to damn it? Would He ask so much from persons so
weak?" etc. Scepticism is the cure for this evil, and will take
down this vanity.

391

Conversation.—Great words: Religion, I deny it.
Conversation.—Scepticism helps religion.

392

Against Scepticism.—[. . . It is, then, a strange fact that
we cannot define these things without obscuring them, while
we speak of them with all assurance.] We assume that all conceive of them in the same way; but we assume it quite gratui-
tously, for we have no proof of it. I see, in truth, that the same
words are applied on the same occasions, and that every time
two men see a body change its place, they both express their
view of this same fact by the same word, both saying that it
has moved; and from this conformity of application we derive
a strong conviction of a conformity of ideas. But this is not
absolutely or finally convincing, though there is enough to
support a bet on the affirmative, since we know that we often
draw the same conclusions from different premises.

This is enough, at least, to obscure the matter; not that it
completely extinguishes the natural light which assures us of
these things. The academicians would have won. But this

dulls it, and troubles the dogmatists to the glory of the sceptical crowd, which consists in this doubtful ambiguity, and in a certain doubtful dimness from which our doubts cannot take away all the clearness, nor our own natural lights chase away all the darkness.

393

It is a singular thing to consider that there are people in the world who, having renounced all the laws of God and nature, have made laws for themselves which they strictly obey, as, for instance, the soldiers of Mahomet, robbers, heretics, etc. It is the same with logicians. It seems that their license must be without any limits or barriers, since they have broken through so many that are so just and sacred.

394

All the principles of sceptics, stoics, atheists, etc., are true. But their conclusions are false, because the opposite principles are also true.

395

Instinct, reason.—We have an incapacity of proof, insurmountable by all dogmatism. We have an idea of truth, invincible to all scepticism.

396

Two things instruct man about his whole nature; instinct and experience.

397

The greatness of man is great in that he knows himself to be miserable. A tree does not know itself to be miserable. It is then being miserable to know oneself to be miserable; but it is also being great to know that one is miserable.

398

All these same miseries prove man's greatness. They are the miseries of a great lord, of a deposed king.

399

We are not miserable without feeling it. A ruined house is not miserable. Man only is miserable. *Ego vir videns.*

400

The greatness of man.—We have so great an idea of the soul of man that we cannot endure being despised, or not being esteemed by any soul; and all the happiness of men consists in this esteem.

401

Glory.—The brutes do not admire each other. A horse does not admire his companion. Not that there is no rivalry between them in a race, but that is of no consequence; for, when in the stable, the heaviest and most ill-formed does not give up his oats to another, as men would have others do to them. Their virtue is satisfied with itself.

402

The greatness of man even in his lust, to have known how to extract from it a wonderful code, and to have drawn from it a picture of benevolence.

403

Greatness.—The reasons of effects indicate the greatness of man, in having extracted so fair an order from lust.

404

The greatest baseness of man is the pursuit of glory. But it is also the greatest mark of his excellence; for whatever possessions he may have on earth, whatever health and essential comfort, he is not satisfied if he has not the esteem of men. He values human reason so highly that, whatever advantages he may have on earth, he is not content if he is not also ranked highly in the judgment of man. This is the finest position in the world. Nothing can turn him from that desire, which is the most indelible quality of man's heart.

And those who most despise men, and put them on a level with the brutes, yet wish to be admired and believed by men, and contradict themselves by their own feelings; their nature, which is stronger than all, convincing them of the greatness of man more forcibly than reason convinces them of their baseness.

405

Contradiction.—Pride counterbalancing all miseries. Man either hides his miseries, or, if he disclose them, glories in knowing them.

406

Pride counterbalances and takes away all miseries. Here is a strange monster, and a very plain aberration. He is fallen from his place, and is anxiously seeking it. This is what all men do. Let us see who will have found it.

407

When malice has reason on its side it becomes proud, and parades reason in all its splendour. When austerity or stern choice has not arrived at the true good, and must needs return to follow nature, it becomes proud by reason of this return.

408

Evil is easy, and has infinite forms; good is almost unique. But a certain kind of evil is as difficult to find as what we call good; and often on this account such particular evil gets passed off as good. An extraordinary greatness of soul is needed in order to attain to it as well as to good.

409

The greatness of man.—The greatness of man is so evident, that it is even proved by his wretchedness. For what in animals is nature we call in man wretchedness; by which we recognise that, his nature being now like that of animals, he has fallen from a better nature which once was his.

For who is unhappy at not being a king, except a deposed king? Was Paulus Æmilius unhappy at being no longer con-sul? On the contrary, everybody thought him happy in having been consul, because the office could only be held for a time. But men thought Perseus so unhappy in being no longer king, because the condition of kingship implied his being always king, that they thought it strange that he endured life. Who is unhappy at having only one mouth? And who is not unhappy at having only one eye? Probably no man ever ventured to mourn at not having three eyes. But any one is inconsolable at having none.

410

Perseus, King of Macedon.—Paulus Æmilius reproached Perseus for not killing himself.

411

Notwithstanding the sight of all our miseries, which press upon us and take us by the throat, we have an instinct which we cannot repress, and which lifts us up.

412

There is internal war in man between reason and the pas-sions.

If he had only reason without passions . . .

If he had only passions without reason . . .

But having both, he cannot be without strife, being unable to be at peace with the one without being at war with the other. Thus he is always divided against, and opposed to himself.

413

This internal war of reason against the passions has made a division of those who would have peace into two sects. The first would renounce their passions, and become gods; the others would renounce reason, and become brute beasts. (Des Barreaux.) But neither can do so, and reason still remains, to condemn the vileness and injustice of the passions, and to trouble the repose of those who abandon themselves to them; and the passions keep always alive in those who would renounce them.

414

Men are so necessarily mad, that not to be mad would amount to another form of madness.

415

The nature of man may be viewed in two ways: the one according to its end, and then he is great and incomparable; the other according to the multitude, just as we judge of the nature of the horse and the dog, popularly, by seeing its fleetness, *et animum arcendi*; and then man is abject and vile. These are the two ways which make us judge of him differently, and which occasion such disputes among philosophers. For one denies the assumption of the other. One says, "He is not born for this end, for all his actions are repugnant to it." The other says, "He forsakes his end, when he does these base actions."

416

For Port-Royal. Greatness and wretchedness.—Wretchedness being deduced from greatness, and greatness from wretchedness, some have inferred man's wretchedness all the more because they have taken his greatness as a proof of it, and others have inferred his greatness with all the more force, because they have inferred it from his very wretchedness. All that the one party has been able to say in proof of his greatness has only served as an argument of his wretchedness to the others, because the greater our fall, the more wretched we are, and *vice versa*. The one party is brought back to the other in an endless circle, it being certain that in proportion as men possess light they discover both the greatness and the wretchedness of man. In a word, man knows that he is wretched. He is therefore wretched, because he is so; but he is really great because he knows it.

417

This twofold nature of man is so evident that some have thought that we had two souls. A single subject seemed to them incapable of such sudden variations from unmeasured presumption to a dreadful dejection of heart.

418

It is dangerous to make man see too clearly his equality with the brutes without showing him his greatness. It is also dangerous to make him see his greatness too clearly, apart from his vileness. It is still more dangerous to leave him in ignorance of both. But it is very advantageous to show him both. Man must not think that he is on a level either with the brutes or with the angels, nor must he be ignorant of both sides of his nature; but he must know both.

419

I will not allow man to depend upon himself, or upon another, to the end that being without a resting-place and without repose . . .

420

If he exalt himself, I humble him; if he humble himself, I exalt him; and I always contradict him, till he understands that he is an incomprehensible monster.

421

I blame equally those who choose to praise man, those who choose to blame him, and those who choose to amuse themselves; and I can only approve of those who seek with lamentation.

422

It is good to be tired and wearied by the vain search after the true good, that we may stretch out our arms to the Redeemer.

423

*Contraries. After having shown the vileness and the great-
ness of man.*—Let man now know his value. Let him love himself, for there is in him a nature capable of good; but let him
not for this reason love the vileness which is in him. Let him
despise himself, for this capacity is barren; but let him not
therefore despise this natural capacity. Let him hate himself,
let him love himself; he has within him the capacity of knowing the truth and of being happy, but he possesses no truth,
either constant or satisfactory.

I would then lead man to the desire of finding truth; to be
free from passions, and ready to follow it where he may find it,
knowing how much his knowledge is obscured by the passions.
I would indeed that he should hate in himself the lust which
determined his will by itself, so that it may not blind him in
making his choice, and may not hinder him when he has
chosen.

424

All these contradictions, which seem most to keep me from
the knowledge of religion, have led me most quickly to the
true one.

MORALITY AND DOCTRINE

425

Second part.—That man without faith cannot know the true good, nor justice.

All men seek happiness. This is without exception. Whatever different means they employ, they all tend to this end. The cause of some going to war, and of others avoiding it, is the same desire in both, attended with different views. The will never takes the least step but to this object. This is the motive of every action of every man, even of those who hang themselves.

And yet after such a great number of years, no one without faith has reached the point to which all continually look. All complain, princes and subjects, noblemen and commoners, old and young, strong and weak, learned and ignorant, healthy and sick, of all countries, all times, all ages, and all conditions.

A trial so long, so continuous, and so uniform, should certainly convince us of our inability to reach the good by our own efforts. But example teaches us little. No resemblance is ever so perfect that there is not some slight difference; and hence we expect that our hope will not be deceived on this occasion as before. And thus, while the present never satisfies us, experience dupes us, and from misfortune to misfortune leads us to death, their eternal crown.

What is it then that this desire and this inability proclaim to us, but that there was once in man a true happiness of which there now remain to him only the mark and empty trace, which he in vain tries to fill from all his surroundings, seeking from things absent the help he does not obtain in things present? But these are all inadequate, because the infinite abyss can only be filled by an infinite and immutable object, that is to say, only by God Himself.

He only is our true good, and since we have forsaken Him, it is a strange thing that there is nothing in nature which has not been serviceable in taking His place; the stars, the heavens, earth, the elements, plants, cabbages, leeks, animals, insects, calves, serpents, fever, pestilence, war, famine, vices, adultery, incest. And since man has lost the true good, everything can appear equally good to him, even his own destruction, though so opposed to God, to reason, and to the whole course of nature.

Some seek good in authority, others in scientific research, others in pleasure. Others, who are in fact nearer the truth, have considered it necessary that the universal good, which all men desire, should not consist in any of the particular things which can only be possessed by one man, and which, when shared, afflict their possessors more by the want of the part he has not, than they please him by the possession of what he has. They have learned that the true good should be such as all can possess at once, without diminution, and without envy, and which no one can lose against his will. And their reason is that this desire being natural to man, since it is necessarily in all, and that it is impossible not to have it, they infer from it . . .

426

True nature being lost, everything becomes its own nature; as the true good being lost, everything becomes its own true good.

427

Man does not know in what rank to place himself. He has plainly gone astray, and fallen from his true place without being able to find it again. He seeks it anxiously and unsuccessfully everywhere in impenetrable darkness.

428

If it is a sign of weakness to prove God by nature, do not despise Scripture; if it is a sign of strength to have known these contradictions, esteem Scripture.

429

The vileness of man in submitting himself to the brutes, and in even worshipping them.

430

For Port-Royal. The beginning, after having explained the incomprehensibility.—The greatness and the wretchedness of man are so evident that the true religion must necessarily teach us both that there is in man some great source of greatness, and a great source of wretchedness. It must then give us a reason for these astonishing contradictions.

In order to make man happy, it must prove to him that there is a God; that we ought to love Him; that our true happiness is to be in Him, and our sole evil to be separated from Him; it must recognise that we are full of darkness which hinders us from knowing and loving Him; and that thus, as our duties compel us to love God, and our lusts turn us away from Him, we are full of unrighteousness. It must give us an explanation of our opposition to God and to our own good. It must teach us the remedies for these infirmities, and the means of obtaining these remedies. Let us therefore examine all the religions of the world, and see if there be any other than the Christian which is sufficient for this purpose.

Shall it be that of the philosophers, who put forward as the chief good, the good which is in ourselves? Is this the true good? Have they found the remedy for our ills? Is man's pride cured by placing him on an equality with God? Have those who have made us equal to the brutes, or the Mahommedans who have offered us earthly pleasures as the chief good even in eternity, produced the remedy for our lusts? What religion, then, will teach us to cure pride and lust? What religion will in fact teach us our good, our duties, the weakness which turns us from them, the cause of this weakness, the remedies which can cure it, and the means of obtaining these remedies?

All other religions have not been able to do so. Let us see what the wisdom of God will do.

"Expect neither truth," she says, "nor consolation from men. I am she who formed you, and who alone can teach you what you are. But you are now no longer in the state in which I formed you. I created man holy, innocent, perfect. I filled him with light and intelligence. I communicated to him my glory and my wonders. The eye of man saw then the majesty of God. He was not then in the darkness which blinds him, nor subject to mortality and the woes which afflict him. But he has not been able to sustain so great glory without falling into pride. He wanted to make himself his own centre, and independent of my help. He withdrew himself from my rule; and, on his making himself equal to me by the desire of finding his happiness in himself, I abandoned him to himself. And setting in revolt the creatures that were subject to him, I made them his enemies; so that man is now become like the brutes, and so estranged from me that there scarce remains to him a dim vision of his Author. So far has all his knowledge been extinguished or disturbed! The senses, independent of reason, and often the masters of reason, have led him into pursuit of pleasure. All creatures either torment or tempt him, and domineer over him, either subduing him by their strength, or fascinating him by their charms, a tyranny more awful and more imperious.

"Such is the state in which men now are. There remains to them some feeble instinct of the happiness of their former state; and they are plunged in the evils of their blindness and their lust, which have become their second nature.

"From this principle which I disclose to you, you can recognise the cause of those contradictions which have astonished all men, and have divided them into parties holding so different views. Observe, now, all the feelings of greatness and glory

which the experience of so many woes cannot stifle, and see
if the cause of them must not be in another nature."

For Port-Royal to-morrow (*Prosopopœa*).—"It is in vain,
O men, that you seek within yourselves the remedy for your
ills. All your light can only reach the knowledge that not in
yourselves will you find truth or good. The philosophers have
promised you that, and you have been unable to do it. They
neither know what is your true good, nor what is your true
state. How could they have given remedies for your ills, when
they did not even know them? Your chief maladies are pride,
which takes you away from God, and lust, which binds you
to earth; and they have done nothing else but cherish one or
other of these diseases. If they gave you God as an end, it was
only to administer to your pride; they made you think that
you are by nature like Him, and conformed to Him. And those
who saw the absurdity of this claim put you on another precipice, by making you understand that your nature was like
that of the brutes, and led you to seek your good in the lusts
which are shared by the animals. This is not the way to cure
you of your unrighteousness, which these wise men never
knew. I alone can make you understand who you are. . . ."

Adam, Jesus Christ.

If you are united to God, it is by grace, not by nature. If
you are humbled, it is by penitence, not by nature.

Thus this double capacity . . .

You are not in the state of your creation.

As these two states are open, it is impossible for you not to
recognise them. Follow your own feelings, observe yourselves,
and see if you do not find the lively characteristics of these
two natures. Could so many contradictions be found in a
simple subject?

—Incomprehensible.—Not all that is incomprehensible
ceases to exist. Infinite number. An infinite space equal to a
finite.

—Incredible that God should unite Himself to us.—This
consideration is drawn only from the sight of our vileness.
But if you are quite sincere over it, follow it as far as I have

done, and recognise that we are indeed so vile that we are incapable in ourselves of knowing if His mercy cannot make us capable of Him. For I would know how this animal, who knows himself to be so weak, has the right to measure the mercy of God, and set limits to it, suggested by his own fancy. He has so little knowledge of what God is, that he does not know what he himself is, and, completely disturbed at the sight of his own state, dares to say that God cannot make him capable of communion with Him.

But I would ask him if God demands anything else from him than the knowledge and love of Him, and why, since his nature is capable of love and knowledge, he believes that God cannot make Himself known and loved by him. Doubtless he knows at least that he exists, and that he loves something. Therefore, if he sees anything in the darkness wherein he is, and if he finds some object of his love among the things on earth, why, if God impart to him some ray of His essence, will he not be capable of knowing and of loving Him in the manner in which it shall please Him to communicate Himself to us? There must then be certainly an intolerable presumption in arguments of this sort, although they seem founded on an apparent humility, which is neither sincere nor reasonable, if it does not make us admit that, not knowing of ourselves what we are, we can only learn it from God.

"I do not mean that you should submit your belief to me without reason, and I do not aspire to overcome you by tyranny. In fact, I do not claim to give you a reason for everything. And to reconcile these contradictions, I intend to make you see clearly, by convincing proofs, those divine signs in me, which may convince you of what I am, and may gain authority for me by wonders and proofs which you cannot reject; so that you may then believe without . . . the things which I teach you, since you will find no other ground for rejecting them, except that you cannot know of yourselves if they are true or not.

"God has willed to redeem men, and to open salvation to those who seek it. But men render themselves so unworthy of it, that it is right that God should refuse to some, because of their obduracy, what He grants to others from a compassion which is not due to them. If He had willed to overcome the obstinacy of the most hardened, He could have done so by revealing Himself so manifestly to them that they could not have doubted of the truth of His essence; as it will appear at the last day, with such thunders and such a convulsion of nature, that the dead will rise again, and the blindest will see Him.

"It is not in this manner that He has willed to appear in His advent of mercy, because, as so many make themselves unworthy of His mercy, He has willed to leave them in the loss of the good which they do not want. It was not then right that He should appear in a manner manifestly divine, and completely capable of convincing all men; but it was also not right that He should come in so hidden a manner that He could not be known by those who should sincerely seek Him. He has willed to make Himself quite recognisable by those; and thus, willing to appear openly to those who seek Him with all their heart, and to be hidden from those who flee from Him with all their heart, He so regulates the knowledge of Himself that He has given signs of Himself, visible to those who seek Him, and not to those who seek Him not. There is enough light for those who only desire to see, and enough obscurity for those who have a contrary disposition."

431

No other religion has recognised that man is the most excellent creature. Some, which have quite recognised the reality of his excellence, have considered as mean and ungrateful the low opinions which men naturally have of themselves; and others, which have thoroughly recognised how real is this vileness, have treated with proud ridicule those feelings of greatness, which are equally natural to man.

"Lift your eyes to God," say the first; "see Him whom you resemble, and who has created you to worship Him. You can make yourselves like unto Him; wisdom will make you equal to Him, if you will follow it." "Raise your heads, free men," says Epictetus. And others say, "Bend your eyes to the earth, wretched worm that you are, and consider the brutes whose companion you are."

What, then, will man become? Will he be equal to God or the brutes? What a frightful difference! What, then, shall we be? Who does not see from all this that man has gone astray, that he has fallen from his place, that he anxiously seeks it, that he cannot find it again? And who shall then direct him to it? The greatest men have failed.

432

Scepticism is true; for, after all, men before Jesus Christ did not know where they were, nor whether they were great or small. And those who have said the one or the other, knew nothing about it, and guessed without reason and by chance. They also erred always in excluding the one or the other.

Quod ergo ignorantes, quæritis, religio annuntiat vobis.

433

After having understood the whole nature of man.—That a religion may be true, it must have knowledge of our nature. It ought to know its greatness and littleness, and the reason of both. What religion but the Christian has known this?

434

The chief arguments of the sceptics—I pass over the lesser ones—are that we have no certainty of the truth of these principles apart from faith and revelation, except in so far as we naturally perceive them in ourselves. Now this natural intuition is not a convincing proof of their truth; since, having no certainty, apart from faith, whether man was created by a good God, or by a wicked demon, or by chance, it is doubtful whether these principles given to us are true, or false, or uncertain, according to our origin. Again, no person is certain, apart from faith, whether he is awake or sleeps, seeing that during sleep we believe that we are awake as firmly as we do when we *are* awake; we believe that we see space, figure, and motion; we are aware of the passage of time, we measure it; and in fact we act as if we were awake. So that half of our life being passed in sleep, we have on our own admission no idea of truth, whatever we may imagine. As all our intuitions are then illusions, who knows whether the other half of our life, in which we think we are awake, is not another sleep a little different from the former, from which we awake when we suppose ourselves asleep?

[And who doubts that, if we dreamt in company, and the dreams chanced to agree, which is common enough, and if we were always alone when awake, we should believe that matters were reversed? In short, as we often dream that we dream, heaping dream upon dream, may it not be that this half of our life, wherein we think ourselves awake, is itself only a dream on which the others are grafted, from which we wake at death, during which we have as few principles of truth and good as during natural sleep, these different thoughts which disturb us being perhaps only illusions like the flight of time and the vain fancies of our dreams?]

These are the chief arguments on one side and the other.

I omit minor ones, such as the sceptical talk against the impressions of custom, education, manners, country, and the like. Though these influence the majority of common folk, who dogmatise only on shallow foundations, they are upset by the least breath of the sceptics. We have only to see their books if we are not sufficiently convinced of this, and we shall very quickly become so, perhaps too much.

I notice the only strong point of the dogmatists, namely, that, speaking in good faith and sincerely, we cannot doubt natural principles. Against this the sceptics set up in one word the uncertainty of our origin, which includes that of our nature. The dogmatists have been trying to answer this objection ever since the world began.

So there is open war among men, in which each must take a part, and side either with dogmatism or scepticism. For he who thinks to remain neutral is above all a sceptic. This neutrality is the essence of the sect; he who is not against them is essentially for them. [In this appears their advantage.] They are not for themselves; they are neutral, indifferent, in suspense as to all things, even themselves being no exception.

What then shall man do in this state? Shall he doubt everything? Shall he doubt whether he is awake, whether he is being pinched, or whether he is being burned? Shall he doubt whether he doubts? Shall he doubt whether he exists? We cannot go so far as that; and I lay it down as a fact that there never has been a real complete sceptic. Nature sustains our feeble reason, and prevents it raving to this extent.

Shall he then say, on the contrary, that he certainly possesses truth—he who, when pressed ever so little, can show no title to it, and is forced to let go his hold?

What a chimera then is man! What a novelty! What a monster, what a chaos, what a contradiction, what a prodigy! Judge of all things, imbecile worm of the earth; depositary of truth, a sink of uncertainty and error; the pride and refuse of the universe!

Who will unravel this tangle? Nature confutes the sceptics, and reason confutes the dogmatists. What then will you become, O men! who try to find out by your natural reason what is your true condition? You cannot avoid one of these sects, nor adhere to one of them.

Know then, proud man, what a paradox you are to yourself. Humble yourself, weak reason; be silent, foolish nature; learn that man infinitely transcends man, and learn from your Master your true condition, of which you are ignorant. Hear God.

For in fact, if man had never been corrupt, he would enjoy in his innocence both truth and happiness with assurance; and if man had always been corrupt, he would have no idea of truth or bliss. But, wretched as we are, and more so than if there were no greatness in our condition, we have an idea of happiness, and cannot reach it. We perceive an image of truth, and possess only a lie. Incapable of absolute ignorance and of certain knowledge, we have thus been manifestly in a degree of perfection from which we have unhappily fallen.

It is, however, an astonishing thing that the mystery furthest removed from our knowledge, namely, that of the transmission of sin, should be a fact without which we can have no knowledge of ourselves. For it is beyond doubt that there is nothing which more shocks our reason than to say that the sin of the first man has rendered guilty those, who, being so removed from this source, seem incapable of participation in it. This transmission does not only seem to us impossible, it seems also very unjust. For what is more contrary to the rules of our miserable justice than to damn eternally an infant incapable of will, for a sin wherein he seems to have so little a share, that it was committed six thousand years before he was in existence? Certainly nothing offends us more rudely than this doctrine; and yet, without this mystery, the most incomprehensible of all, we are incomprehensible to ourselves. The knot of our condition takes its twists and turns in this abyss, so that man is more inconceivable without this mystery than this mystery is inconceivable to man.

[Whence it seems that God, willing to render the difficulty of our existence unintelligible to ourselves, has concealed the knot so high, or, better speaking, so low, that we are quite incapable of reaching it; so that it is not by the proud exertions of our reason, but by the simple submissions of reason, that we can truly know ourselves.

These foundations, solidly established on the inviolable authority of religion, make us know that there are two truths of faith equally certain: the one, that man, in the state of creation, or in that of grace, is raised above all nature, made like unto God and sharing in His divinity; the other, that in the state of corruption and sin, he is fallen from this state and made like unto the beasts.

These two propositions are equally sound and certain. Scripture manifestly declares this to us, when it says in some places: *Deliciæ meæ esse cum filiis hominum. Effundam spiritum meum super omnem carnem. Dii estis*, etc.; and in other places, *Omnis caro fænum. Homo assimilatus est jumentis insipientibus, et similis factus est illis. Dixi in corde meo de filiis hominum.* Eccles. iii.

Whence it clearly seems that man by grace is made like unto God, and a partaker in His divinity, and that without grace he is like unto the brute beasts.]

435

Without this divine knowledge what could men do but either become elated by the inner feeling of their past greatness which still remains to them, or become despondent at the sight of their present weakness? For, not seeing the whole truth, they could not attain to perfect virtue. Some considering nature as incorrupt, others as incurable, they could not escape either pride or sloth, the two sources of all vice; since they cannot but either abandon themselves to it through cowardice, or escape it by pride. For if they knew the excellence of man, they were ignorant of his corruption; so that they easily avoided sloth, but fell into pride. And if they recognised the infirmity of nature, they were ignorant of its dignity; so that they could easily avoid vanity, but it was to fall into despair. Thence arise the different schools of the Stoics and Epicureans, the Dogmatists, Academicians, etc.

The Christian religion alone has been able to cure these two vices, not by expelling the one through means of the other according to the wisdom of the world, but by expelling both according to the simplicity of the Gospel. For it teaches the righteous that it raises them even to a participation in divinity itself; that in this lofty state they still carry the source of all corruption, which renders them during all their life subject to error, misery, death, and sin; and it proclaims to the most ungodly that they are capable of the grace of their Redeemer. So making those tremble whom it justifies, and consoling those whom it condemns, religion so justly tempers fear with hope through that double capacity of grace and of sin, common to all, that it humbles infinitely more than reason alone can do, but without despair; and it exalts infinitely more than natural pride, but without inflating; thus making it evident that alone being exempt from error and vice, it alone fulfils the duty of instructing and correcting men.

Who then can refuse to believe and adore this heavenly light? For is it not clearer than day that we perceive within ourselves ineffaceable marks of excellence? And is it not equally true that we experience every hour the results of our deplorable condition? What does this chaos and monstrous confusion proclaim to us but the truth of these two states, with a voice so powerful that it is impossible to resist it?

436

Weakness.—Every pursuit of men is to get wealth; and they cannot have a title to show that they possess it justly, for they have only that of human caprice; nor have they strength to hold it securely. It is the same with knowledge, for disease takes it away. We are incapable both of truth and goodness.

437

We desire truth, and find within ourselves only uncertainty. We seek happiness, and find only misery and death.

We cannot but desire truth and happiness, and are incapable of certainty or happiness. This desire is left to us, partly to punish us, partly to make us perceive wherefrom we are fallen.

438

If man is not made for God, why is he only happy in God? If man is made for God, why is he so opposed to God?

439

Nature corrupted.—Man does not act by reason, which constitutes his being.

440

The corruption of reason is shown by the existence of so many different and extravagant customs. It was necessary that truth should come, in order that man should no longer dwell within himself.

441

For myself, I confess that so soon as the Christian religion reveals the principle that human nature is corrupt and fallen from God, that opens my eyes to see everywhere the mark of this truth: for nature is such that she testifies everywhere, both within man and without him, to a lost God and a corrupt nature.

442

Man's true nature, his true good, true virtue, and true religion, are things of which the knowledge is inseparable.

443

Greatness, wretchedness.—The more light we have, the more greatness and the more baseness we discover in man. Ordinary men—those who are more educated: philosophers, they astonish ordinary men—Christians, they astonish philosophers.

Who will then be surprised to see that religion only makes us know profoundly what we already know in proportion to our light?

444

This religion taught to her children what men have only been able to discover by their greatest knowledge.

445

Original sin is foolishness to men, but it is admitted to be such. You must not then reproach me for the want of reason in this doctrine, since I admit it to be without reason. But this foolishness is wiser than all the wisdom of men, *sapientius est hominibus*. For without this, what can we say that man is? His whole state depends on this imperceptible point. And how should it be perceived by his reason, since it is a thing against reason, and since reason, far from finding it out by her own ways, is averse to it when it is presented to her?

446

Of original sin. Ample tradition of original sin according to the Jews.

On the saying in Genesis viii, 21: "The imagination of man's heart is evil from his youth."

R. Moses Haddarschan: This evil leaven is placed in man from the time that he is formed.

Massechet Succa: This evil leaven has seven names in Scripture. It is called *evil, the foreskin, uncleanness, an enemy, a scandal, a heart of stone, the north wind;* all this signifies the malignity which is concealed and impressed in the heart of man.

Midrasch Tillim says the same thing, and that God will deliver the good nature of man from the evil.

This malignity is renewed every day against man, as it is written, Psalm xxxvii, 32: "The wicked watcheth the righteous, and seeketh to slay him"; but God will not abandon him. This malignity tries the heart of man in this life, and will accuse him in the other. All this is found in the Talmud.

Midrasch Tillim on Psalm iv, 4: "Stand in awe and sin not." Stand in awe and be afraid of your lust, and it will not lead you into sin. And on Psalm xxxvi, 1: "The wicked has said within his own heart, Let not the fear of God be before me." That is to say that the malignity natural to man has said that to the wicked.

Midrasch el Kohelet: "Better is a poor and wise child than an old and foolish king who cannot foresee the future." The child is virtue, and the king is the malignity of man. It is called king because all the members obey it, and old because it is in the human heart from infancy to old age, and foolish because it leads man in the way of [*perdition*], which he does not foresee. The same thing is in *Midrasch Tillim.*

Bereschist Rabba on Psalm xxxv, 10: "Lord, all my bones shall bless Thee, which deliverest the poor from the tyrant." And is there a greater tyrant than the evil leaven? And on

Proverbs xxv, 21: "If thine enemy be hungry, give him bread to eat." That is to say, if the evil leaven hunger, give him the bread of wisdom of which it is spoken in Proverbs ix., and if he be thirsty, give him the water of which it is spoken in Isaiah lv.

Midrasch Tillim says the same thing, and that Scripture in that passage, speaking of the enemy, means the evil leaven; and that, in [*giving*] him that bread and that water, we heap coals of fire on his head.

Midrasch el Kohelet on Ecclesiastes ix, 14: "A great king besieged a little city." This great king is the evil leaven; the great bulwarks built against it are temptations; and there has been found a poor wise man who has delivered it—that is to say, virtue.

And on Psalm xli, 1: "Blessed is he that considereth the poor."

And on Psalm lxxviii, 39: "The spirit passeth away, and cometh not again"; whence some have erroneously argued against the immortality of the soul. But the sense is that this spirit is the evil leaven, which accompanies man till death, and will not return at the resurrection.

And on Psalm ciii the same thing.

And on Psalm xvi.

Principles of Rabbinism: two Messiahs.

447

Will it be said that, as men have declared that righteousness has departed the earth, they therefore knew of original sin?—*Nemo ante obitum beatus est*—that is to say, they knew death to be the beginning of eternal and essential happiness?

448

[*Milton*] sees well that nature is corrupt, and that men are averse to virtue; but he does not know why they cannot fly higher.

449

Order.—After *Corruption* to say: "It is right that all those who are in that state should know it, both those who are content with it, and those who are not content with it; but it is not right that all should see Redemption."

450

If we do not know ourselves to be full of pride, ambition, lust, weakness, misery, and injustice, we are indeed blind. And if, knowing this, we do not desire deliverance, what can we say of a man . . .?

What, then, can we have but esteem for a religion which knows so well the defects of man, and desire for the truth of a religion which promises remedies so desirable?

451

All men naturally hate one another. They employ lust as far as possible in the service of the public weal. But this is only a [*pretence*] and a false image of love; for at bottom it is only hate.

452

To pity the unfortunate is not contrary to lust. On the contrary, we can quite well give such evidence of friendship, and acquire the reputation of kindly feeling, without giving anything.

453

From lust men have found and extracted excellent rules of policy, morality, and justice; but in reality this vile root of man, this *figmentum malum,* is only covered, it is not taken away.

454

Injustice.—They have not found any other means of satisfying lust without doing injury to others.

455

Self is hateful. You, Milton, conceal it; you do not for that reason destroy it; you are, then, always hateful.

—No; for in acting as we do to oblige everybody, we give no more occasion for hatred of us.—That is true, if we only hated in Self the vexation which comes to us from it. But if I hate it because it is unjust, and because it makes itself the centre of everything, I shall always hate it.

In a word, the Self has two qualities: it is unjust in itself since it makes itself the centre of everything; it is inconvenient to others since it would enslave them; for each Self is the enemy, and would like to be the tyrant of all others. You take away its inconvenience, but not its injustice, and so you do not render it lovable to those who hate injustice; you render it lovable only to the unjust, who do not any longer find in it an enemy. And thus you remain unjust, and can please only the unjust.

456

It is a perverted judgment that makes every one place himself above the rest of the world, and prefer his own good, and the continuance of his own good fortune and life, to that of the rest of the world!

457

Each one is all in all to himself; for he being dead, all is dead to him. Hence it comes that each believes himself to be all in all to everybody. We must not judge of nature by ourselves, but by it.

458

"All that is in the world is the lust of the flesh, or the lust of the eyes, or the pride of life; *libido sentiendi, libido sciendi, libido dominandi.*" Wretched is the cursed land which these three rivers of fire enflame rather than water! Happy they who, on these rivers, are not overwhelmed nor carried away,

but are immovably fixed, not standing but seated on a low and
secure base, whence they do not rise before the light, but,
having rested in peace, stretch out their hands to Him, who
must lift them up, and make them stand upright and firm in
the porches of the holy Jerusalem! There pride can no longer
assail them nor cast them down; and yet they weep, not to see
all those perishable things swept away by the torrents, but at
the remembrance of their loved country, the heavenly Jerusalem, which they remember without ceasing during their pro-
longed exile.

459

The rivers of Babylon rush and fall and sweep away.

O holy Zion, where all is firm and nothing falls!

We must sit upon the waters, not under them or in them,
but on them; and not standing but seated; being seated to be
humble, and being above them to be secure. But we shall
stand in the porches of Jerusalem.

Let us see if this pleasure is stable or transitory; if it pass
away, it is a river of Babylon.

460

The lust of the flesh, the lust of the eyes, pride, etc.—There
are three orders of things: the flesh, the spirit, and the will.
The carnal are the rich and kings; they have the body as their
object. Inquirers and scientists; they have the mind as their
object. The wise; they have righteousness as their object.

God must reign over all, and all men must be brought back
to Him. In things of the flesh lust reigns specially; in intellectual matters, inquiry specially; in wisdom, pride specially.
Not that a man cannot boast of wealth or knowledge, but it is
not the place for pride; for in granting to a man that he is
learned, it is easy to convince him that he is wrong to be proud.
The proper place for pride is in wisdom, for it cannot be
granted to a man that he has made himself wise, and that he is
wrong to be proud; for that is right. Now God alone gives
wisdom, and that is why *Qui gloriatur, in Domino glorietur.*

461

The three lusts have made three sects; and the philosophers have done no other thing than follow one of the three lusts.

462

Search for the true good.—Ordinary men place the good in fortune and external goods, or at least in amusement. Philosophers have shown the vanity of all this, and have placed it where they could.

463

[*Against the philosophers who believe in God without Jesus Christ.*]

Philosophers.—They believe that God alone is worthy to be loved and admired; and they have desired to be loved and admired of men, and do not know their own corruption. If they feel full of feelings of love and admiration, and find therein their chief delight, very well, let them think themselves good. But if they find themselves averse to Him, if they have no inclination but the desire to establish themselves in the esteem of men, and if their whole perfection consists only in making men—but without constraint—find their happiness in loving them, I declare that this perfection is horrible. What! they have known God, and have not desired solely that men should love Him, but that men should stop short at them! They have wanted to be the object of the voluntary delight of men.

464

Philosophers.—We are full of things which take us out of ourselves.

Our instinct makes us feel that we must seek our happiness outside ourselves. Our passions impel us outside, even when no objects present themselves to excite them. External objects tempt us of themselves, and call to us, even when we are not thinking of them. And thus philosophers have said in vain,

"Retire within yourselves, you will find your good there."
We do not believe them, and those who believe them are the
most empty and the most foolish.

465

The Stoics say, "Retire within yourselves; it is there you
will find your rest." And that is not true.

Others say, "Go out of yourselves; seek happiness in
amusement." And this is not true. Illness comes.

Happiness is neither without us nor within us. It is in God,
both without us and within us.

466

Had Epictetus seen the way perfectly, he would have said
to men, "You follow a wrong road"; he shows that there is another, but he does not lead to it. It is the way of willing what
God wills. Jesus Christ alone leads to it: *Via, veritas*.

The vices of Zeno himself.

467

The reason of effects.—Epictetus. Those who say, "You
have a headache"; this is not the same thing. We are assured of health, and not of justice; and in fact his own was
nonsense.

And yet he believed it demonstrable, when he said, "It is
either in our power or it is not." But he did not perceive that
it is not in our power to regulate the heart, and he was wrong
to infer from this the fact that there were some Christians.

468

No other religion has proposed to men to hate themselves.
No other religion then can please those who hate themselves,
and who seek a Being truly lovable. And these, if they had
never heard of the religion of a God humiliated, would embrace it at once.

469

I feel that I might not have been; for the Ego consists in my thoughts. Therefore I, who think, would not have been, if my mother had been killed before I had life. I am not then a necessary being. In the same way I am not eternal or infinite; but I see plainly that there exists in nature a necessary Being, eternal and infinite.

470

"Had I seen a miracle," say men, "I should become converted." How can they be sure they would do a thing of the nature of which they are ignorant? They imagine that this conversion consists in a worship of God which is like commerce, and in a communion such as they picture to themselves. True religion consists in annihilating self before that Universal Being, whom we have so often provoked, and who can justly destroy us at any time; in recognising that we can do nothing without Him, and have deserved nothing from Him but His displeasure. It consists in knowing that there is an unconquerable opposition between us and God, and that without a mediator there can be no communion with Him.

471

It is unjust that men should attach themselves to me, even though they do it with pleasure and voluntarily. I should deceive those in whom I had created this desire; for I am not the end of any, and I have not the wherewithal to satisfy them. Am I not about to die? And thus the object of their attachment will die. Therefore, as I would be blamable in causing a falsehood to be believed, though I should employ gentle persuasion, though it should be believed with pleasure, and though it should give me pleasure; even so I am blamable in making myself loved, and if I attract persons to attach themselves to me. I ought to warn those who are ready to consent to a lie, that they ought not to believe it, whatever advantage comes to me from it; and likewise that they ought not to attach themselves to me; for they ought to spend their life and their care in pleasing God, or in seeking Him.

472

Self-will will never be satisfied, though it should have command of all it would; but we are satisfied from the moment we renounce it. Without it we cannot be discontented; with it we cannot be content.

473

Let us imagine a body full of thinking members.

474

Members. To commence with that.—To regulate the love which we owe to ourselves, we must imagine a body full of thinking members, for we are members of the whole, and must see how each member should love itself, etc. . . .

475

If the feet and the hands had a will of their own, they could only be in their order in submitting this particular will to the primary will which governs the whole body. Apart from that, they are in disorder and mischief; but in willing only the good of the body, they accomplish their own good.

476

We must love God only and hate self only.

If the foot had always been ignorant that it belonged to the body, and that there was a body on which it depended, if it had only had the knowledge and the love of self, and if it came to know that it belonged to a body on which it depended, what regret, what shame for its past life, for having been useless to the body which inspired its life, which would have annihilated it if it had rejected it and separated it from itself, as it kept itself apart from the body! What prayers for its preservation in it! And with what submission would it allow itself to be governed by the will which rules the body, even to consenting, if necessary, to be cut off, or it would lose its character as member! For every member must be quite willing to perish for the body, for which alone the whole is.

477

It is false that we are worthy of the love of others; it is unfair that we should desire it. If we were born reasonable and impartial, knowing ourselves and others, we should not give this bias to our will. However, we are born with it; therefore born unjust, for all tends to self. This is contrary to all order. We must consider the general good; and the propensity to self is the beginning of all disorder, in war, in politics, in economy, and in the particular body of man. The will is therefore depraved.

If the members of natural and civil communities tend towards the weal of the body, the communities themselves ought to look to another more general body of which they are members. We ought therefore to look to the whole. We are therefore born unjust and depraved.

478

When we want to think of God, is there nothing which turns us away, and tempts us to think of something else? All this is bad, and is born in us.

479

If there is a God, we must love Him only, and not the creatures of a day. The reasoning of the ungodly in the Book of Wisdom is only based upon the non-existence of God. "On that supposition," say they, "let us take delight in the creatures." That is the worst that can happen. But if there were a God to love, they would not have come to this conclusion, but to quite the contrary. And this is the conclusion of the wise: "There is a God, let us therefore not take delight in the creatures."

Therefore all that incites us to attach ourselves to the creatures is bad; since it prevents us from serving God if we know

Him, or from seeking Him if we know Him not. Now we are full of lust. Therefore we are full of evil; therefore we ought to hate ourselves and all that excited us to attach ourselves to any other object than God only.

480

To make the members happy, they must have one will, and submit it to the body.

481

The examples of the noble deaths of the Lacedæmonians and others scarce touch us. For what good is it to us? But the example of the death of the martyrs touches us; for they are "our members." We have a common tie with them. Their resolution can form ours, not only by example, but because it has perhaps deserved ours. There is nothing of this in the examples of the heathen. We have no tie with them; as we do not become rich by seeing a stranger who is so, but in fact by seeing a father or a husband who is so.

482

Morality.—God having made the heavens and the earth, which do not feel the happiness of their being, He has willed to make beings who should know it, and who should compose a body of thinking members. For our members do not feel the happiness of their union, of their wonderful intelligence, of the care which has been taken to infuse into them minds, and to make them grow and endure. How happy they would be if they saw and felt it! But for this they would need to have intelligence to know it, and good-will to consent to that of the universal soul. But if, having received intelligence, they employed it to retain nourishment for themselves without allowing it to pass to the other members, they would be not only unjust, but also miserable, and would hate rather than love themselves; their blessedness, as well as their duty, consisting in their consent to the guidance of the whole soul to which they belong, which loves them better than they love themselves.

483

To be a member is to have neither life, being, nor movement, except through the spirit of the body, and for the body.

The separate member, seeing no longer the body to which it belongs, has only a perishing and dying existence. Yet it believes it is a whole, and seeing not the body on which it depends, it believes it depends only on self, and desires to make itself both centre and body. But not having in itself a principle of life, it only goes astray, and is astonished in the uncertainty of its being; perceiving in fact that it is not a body, and still not seeing that it is a member of a body. In short, when it comes to know itself, it has returned as it were to its own home, and loves itself only for the body. It deplores its past wanderings.

It cannot by its nature love any other thing, except for itself and to subject it to self, because each thing loves itself more than all. But in loving the body, it loves itself, because it only exists in it, by it, and for it. *Qui adhæret Deo unus spiritus est.*

The body loves the hand; and the hand, if it had a will, should love itself in the same way as it is loved by the soul. All love which goes beyond this is unfair.

Adhærens Deo unus spiritus est. We love ourselves, because we are members of Jesus Christ. We love Jesus Christ, because He is the body of which we are members. All is one, one is in the other, like the Three Persons.

484

Two laws suffice to rule the whole Christian Republic better than all the laws of statecraft.

485

The true and only virtue, then, is to hate self (for we are hateful on account of lust), and to seek a truly lovable being to love. But as we cannot love what is outside ourselves, we must love a being who is in us, and is not ourselves; and that is true of each and all men. Now, only the Universal Being is such. The kingdom of God is within us; the universal good is within us, is ourselves—and not ourselves.

486

The dignity of man in his innocence consisted in using and having dominion over the creatures, but now in separating himself from them, and subjecting himself to them.

487

Every religion is false, which as to its faith does not worship one God as the origin of everything, and which as to its morality does not love one only God as the object of everything.

488

. . . But it is impossible that God should ever be the end, if He is not the beginning. We lift our eyes on high, but lean upon the sand; and the earth will dissolve, and we shall fall whilst looking at the heavens.

489

If there is one sole source of everything, there is one sole end of everything; everything through Him, everything for Him. The true religion, then, must teach us to worship Him only, and to love Him only. But as we find ourselves unable to worship what we know not, and to love any other object but ourselves, the religion which instructs us in these duties must instruct us also of this inability, and teach us also the remedies for it. It teaches us that by one man all was lost, and the bond broken between God and us, and that by one man the bond is renewed.

We are born so averse to this love of God, and it is so necessary that we must be born guilty, or God would be unjust.

490

Men, not being accustomed to form merit, but only to recompense it where they find it formed, judge of God by themselves.

491

The true religion must have as a characteristic the obligation to love God. This is very just, and yet no other religion has commanded this; ours has done so. It must also be aware of human lust and weakness; ours is so. It must have adduced remedies for this; one is prayer. No other religion has asked of God to love and follow Him.

492

He who hates not in himself his self-love, and that instinct which leads him to make himself God, is indeed blinded. Who does not see that there is nothing so opposed to justice and truth? For it is false that we deserve this, and it is unfair and impossible to attain it, since all demand the same thing. It is, then, a manifest injustice which is innate in us, of which we cannot get rid, and of which we must get rid.

Yet no religion has indicated that this was a sin; or that we were born in it; or that we were obliged to resist it; or has thought of giving us remedies for it.

493

The true religion teaches our duties; our weaknesses, pride, and lust; and the remedies, humility and mortification.

494

The true religion must teach greatness and misery; must lead to the esteem and contempt of self, to love and to hate.

495

If it is an extraordinary blindness to live without investigating what we are, it is a terrible one to live an evil life, while believing in God.

496

Experience makes us see an enormous difference between piety and goodness.

497

*Against those who, trusting to the mercy of God, live heed-
lessly, without doing good works.*—As the two sources of our
sins are pride and sloth, God has revealed to us two of His
attributes to cure them, mercy and justice. The property of
justice is to humble pride, however holy may be our works,
et non intres in judicium, etc.; and the property of mercy is to
combat sloth by exhorting to good works, according to that
passage: "The goodness of God leadeth to repentance," and
that other of the Ninevites: "Let us do penance to see if per-
adventure He will pity us." And thus mercy is so far from
authorising slackness, that it is on the contrary the quality
which formally attacks it; so that instead of saying, "If there
were no mercy in God we should have to make every kind of
effort after virtue," we must say, on the contrary, that it is
because there is mercy in God, that we must make every kind
of effort.

498

It is true there is difficulty in entering into godliness. But
this difficulty does not arise from the religion which begins in
us, but from the irreligion which is still there. If our senses
were not opposed to penitence, and if our corruption were
not opposed to the purity of God, there would be nothing in
this painful to us. We suffer only in proportion as the vice
which is natural to us resists supernatural grace. Our heart
feels torn asunder between these opposed efforts. But it would
be very unfair to impute this violence to God, who is drawing
us on, instead of to the world, which is holding us back. It is as
a child, which a mother tears from the arms of robbers, in the
pain it suffers, should love the loving and legitimate violence
of her who procures its liberty, and detest only the impetuous
and tyrannical violence of those who detain it unjustly. The
most cruel war which God can make with men in this life is to
leave them without that war which He came to bring. "I
came to send war," He says, "and to teach them of this war.

I came to bring fire and the sword." Before Him the world
lived in this false peace.

499

External works.—There is nothing so perilous as what
pleases God and man. For those states, which please God and
man, have one property which pleases God, and another
which pleases men; as the greatness of Saint Teresa. What
pleased God was her deep humility in the midst of her revelations; what pleased men was her light. And so we torment
ourselves to imitate her discourses, thinking to imitate her
conditions, and not so much to love what God loves, and to
put ourselves in the state which God loves.

It is better not to fast, and be thereby humbled, than to
fast and be self-satisfied therewith. The Pharisee and the
Publican.

What use will memory be to me, if it can alike hurt and
help me, and all depends upon the blessing of God, who gives
only to things done for Him, according to His rules and in His
ways, the manner being thus as important as the thing, and
perhaps more; since God can bring forth good out of evil, and
without God we bring forth evil out of good?

500

The meaning of the words, good and evil.

501

First step: to be blamed for doing evil, and praised for
doing good.

Second step: to be neither praised, nor blamed.

502

Abraham took nothing for himself, but only for his servants.
So the righteous man takes for himself nothing of the world,
nor of the applause of the world, but only for his passions,
which he uses as their master, saying to the one, "Go," and to
another, "Come." *Sub te erit appetitus tuus.* The passions
thus subdued are virtues. Even God attributes to Himself

avarice, jealousy, anger; and these are virtues as well as kindness, pity, constancy, which are also passions. We must employ them as slaves, and, leaving to them their food, prevent the soul from taking any of it. For, when the passions become masters, they are vices; and they give their nutriment to the soul, and the soul nourishes itself upon it, and is poisoned.

503

Philosophers have consecrated the vices by placing them in God Himself. Christians have consecrated the virtues.

504

The just man acts by faith in the least things; when he reproves his servants, he desires their conversion by the Spirit of God, and prays God to correct them; and he expects as much from God as from his own reproofs, and prays God to bless his corrections. And so in all his other actions he proceeds with the Spirit of God; and his actions deceive us by reason of the . . . or suspension of the Spirit of God in him; and he repents in his affliction.

505

All things can be deadly to us, even the things made to serve us; as in nature walls can kill us, and stairs can kill us, if we do not walk circumspectly.

The least movement affects all nature; the entire sea changes because of a rock. Thus in grace, the least action affects everything by its consequences; therefore everything is important.

In each action we must look beyond the action at our past, present, and future state, and at others whom it affects, and see the relations of all those things. And then we shall be very cautious.

506

Let God not impute to us our sins, that is to say, all the consequences and results of our sins, which are dreadful, even those of the smallest faults, if we wish to follow them out mercilessly!

507

The spirit of grace; the hardness of the heart; external circumstances.

508

Grace is indeed needed to turn a man into a saint; and he who doubts it does not know what a saint or a man is.

509

Philosophers.—A fine thing to cry to a man who does not know himself, that he should come of himself to God! And a fine thing to say so to a man who does know himself!

510

Man is not worthy of God, but he is not incapable of being made worthy.

It is unworthy of God to unite Himself to wretched man; but it is not unworthy of God to pull him out of his misery.

511

If we would say that man is too insignificant to deserve communion with God, we must indeed be very great to judge of it.

512

It is, in peculiar phraseology, wholly the body of Jesus Christ, but it cannot be said to be the whole body of Jesus Christ. The union of two things without change does not enable us to say that one becomes the other; the soul thus being united to the body, the fire to the timber, without change. But change is necessary to make the form of the one become the form of the other; thus the union of the Word to man. Because my body without my soul would not make the body of a man; therefore my soul united to any matter whatsoever will make my body. It does not distinguish the necessary condition from the sufficient condition; the union is necessary, but not sufficient. The left arm is not the right.

Impenetrability is a property of matter.

Identity *de numers* in regard to the same time requires the identity of matter.

Thus if God united my soul to a body in China, the same body, *idem numero*, would be in China.

The same river which runs there is *idem numero* as that which runs at the same time in China.

513

Why God has established prayer.

1. To communicate to His creatures the dignity of causality.

2. To teach us from whom our virtue comes.

3. To make us deserve other virtues by work.

(But to keep His own pre-eminence, He grants prayer to whom He pleases.)

Objection: But we believe that we hold prayer of ourselves.

This is absurd; for since, though having faith, we cannot have virtues, how should we have faith? Is there a greater distance between infidelity and faith than between faith and virtue?

Merit. This word is ambiguous.

Meruit habere Redemptorem.

Meruit tam sacra membra tangere.

Digno tam sacra membra tangere.

Non sum dignus.

Qui manducat indignus.

Dignus est accipere.

Dignare me.

God is only bound according to His promises. He has promised to grant justice to prayers; He has never promised prayer only to the children of promise.

Saint Augustine has distinctly said that strength would be taken away from the righteous. But it is by chance that he

said it; for it might have happened that the occasion of saying it did not present itself. But his principles make us see
that when the occasion for it presented itself, it was impossible that he should not say it, or that he should say anything
to the contrary. It is then rather that he was forced to say it,
when the occasion presented itself, than that he said it, when
the occasion presented itself, the one being of necessity, the
other of chance. But the two are all that we can ask.

514

The elect will be ignorant of their virtues, and the outcast
of the greatness of their sins: "Lord, when saw we Thee an
hungered, thirsty?" etc.

515

Romans iii, 27. Boasting is excluded. By what law? Of
works? Nay, but by faith. Then faith is not within our power
like the deeds of the law, and it is given to us in another way.

516

Comfort yourselves. It is not from yourselves that you
should expect grace; but, on the contrary, it is in expecting
nothing from yourselves, that you must hope for it.

517

Every condition, and even the martyrs, have to fear, according to Scripture.

The greatest pain of purgatory is the uncertainty of the
judgment. *Deus absconditus*.

518

John viii. *Multi crediderunt in eum. Dicebat ergo Jesus:
"Si manseritis . . . VERE mei discipuli eritis, et VERITAS
LIBERABIT VOS." Responderunt: "Semen Abrahæ sumus,
et nemini servimus unquam."*

There is a great difference between disciples and true disciples. We recognise them by telling them that the truth will

make them free; for if they answer that they are free, and that it is in their power to come out of slavery to the devil, they are indeed disciples, but not true disciples.

519

The law has not destroyed nature, but has instructed it; grace has not destroyed the law, but has made it act. Faith received at baptism is the source of the whole life of Christians and of the converted.

520

Grace will always be in the world, and nature also; so that the former is in some sort natural. And thus there will always be Pelagians, and always Catholics, and always strife; because the first birth makes the one, and the grace of the second birth the other.

521

The law imposed what it did not give. Grace gives what it imposes.

522

All faith consists in Jesus Christ and in Adam, and all morality in lust and in grace.

523

There is no doctrine more appropriate to man than this, which teaches him his double capacity of receiving and of losing grace, because of the double peril to which he is exposed, of despair or of pride.

524

The philosophers did not prescribe feelings suitable to the two states.

They inspired feelings of pure greatness, and that is not man's state.

They inspired feelings of pure littleness, and that is not man's state.

There must be feelings of humility, not from nature, but from penitence, not to rest in them, but to go on to greatness. There must be feelings of greatness, not from merit, but from grace, and after having passed through humiliation.

525

Misery induces despair, pride induces presumption. The Incarnation shows man the greatness of his misery by the greatness of the remedy which he required.

526

The knowledge of God without that of man's misery causes pride. The knowledge of man's misery without that of God causes despair. The knowledge of Jesus Christ constitutes the middle course, because in Him we find both God and our misery.

527

Jesus Christ is a God whom we approach without pride, and before whom we humble ourselves without despair.

528

. . . Not a degradation which renders us incapable of good, nor a holiness exempt from evil.

529

A person told me one day that on coming from confession he felt great joy and confidence. Another told me that he remained in fear. Whereupon I thought that these two together would make one good man, and that each was wanting in that he had not the feeling of the other. The same often happens in other things.

530

He who knows the will of his master will be beaten with more blows, because of the power he has by his knowledge. *Qui justus est, justificetur adhuc,* because of the power he has by justice. From him who has received most, will the greatest reckoning be demanded, because of the power he has by this help.

531

Scripture has provided passages of consolation and of warning for all conditions.

Nature seems to have done the same thing by her two infinities, natural and moral; for we shall always have the higher and the lower, the more clever and the less clever, the most exalted and the meanest, in order to humble our pride, and exalt our humility.

532

Comminutum cor (Saint Paul). This is the Christian character. *Alba has named you, I know you no more* (Corneille). That is the inhuman character. The human character is the opposite.

533

There are only two kinds of men: the righteous who believe themselves sinners; the rest, sinners, who believe themselves righteous.

534

We owe a great debt to those who point out faults. For they mortify us. They teach us that we have been despised. They do not prevent our being so in the future; for we have many other faults for which we may be despised. They prepare for us the exercise of correction and freedom from fault.

535

Man is so made that by continually telling him he is a fool he believes it, and by continually telling it to himself he makes himself believe it. For man holds an inward talk with his self alone, which it behoves him to regulate well: *Corrumpunt bonos mores colloquia prava*. We must keep silent as much as possible and talk with ourselves only of God, whom we know to be true; and thus we convince ourselves of the truth.

536

Christianity is strange. It bids man recognise that he is vile, even abominable, and bids him desire to be like God. Without such a counterpoise, this dignity would make him horribly vain, or this humiliation would make him terribly abject.

537

With how little pride does a Christian believe himself united to God! With how little humiliation does he place himself on a level with the worms of earth!

A glorious manner to welcome life and death, good and evil!

538

What difference in point of obedience is there between a soldier and a Carthusian monk? For both are equally under obedience and dependent, both engaged in equally painful exercises. But the soldier always hopes to command, and never attains this, for even captains and princes are ever slaves and dependants; still he ever hopes and ever works to attain this. Whereas the Carthusian monk makes a vow to be always dependent. So they do not differ in their perpetual thraldom, in which both of them always exist, but in the hope, which one always has, and the other never.

539

The hope which Christians have of possessing an infinite good is mingled with real enjoyment as well as with fear; for it is not as with those who should hope for a kingdom, of which they, being subjects, would have nothing; but they hope for holiness, for freedom from injustice, and they have something of this.

540

None is so happy as a true Christian, nor so reasonable, virtuous, or amiable.

541

The Christian religion alone makes man altogether *lovable and happy*. In honesty, we cannot perhaps be altogether lovable and happy.

542

Preface.—The metaphysical proofs of God are so remote from the reasoning of men, and so complicated, that they make little impression; and if they should be of service to some, it would be only during the moment that they see such demonstration; but an hour afterwards they fear they have been mistaken.

Quod curiositate cognoverunt superbia amiserunt.

This is the result of the knowledge of God obtained without Jesus Christ; it is communion without a mediator with the God whom they have known without a mediator. Whereas those who have known God by a mediator know their own wretchedness.

543

The God of the Christians is a God who makes the soul feel that He is her only good, that her only rest is in Him, that her only delight is in loving Him; and who makes her at the same time abhor the obstacles which keep her back, and prevent her from loving God with all her strength. Self-love and lust, which hinder us, are unbearable to her. Thus God makes her feel that she has this root of self-love which destroys her, and which He alone can cure.

544

Jesus Christ did nothing but teach men that they loved themselves, that they were slaves, blind, sick, wretched, and sinners; that He must deliver them, enlighten, bless, and heal them; that this would be effected by hating self, and by following Him through suffering and the death on the cross.

545

Without Jesus Christ man must be in vice and misery; with Jesus Christ man is free from vice and misery; in Him is all our virtue and all our happiness. Apart from Him there is but vice, misery, darkness, death, despair.

546

We know God only by Jesus Christ. Without this mediator all communion with God is taken away; through Jesus Christ we know God. All those who have claimed to know God, and to prove Him without Jesus Christ, have had only weak proofs. But in proof of Jesus Christ we have the prophecies, which are solid and palpable proofs. And these prophecies, being accomplished and proved true by the event, mark the certainty of these truths, and therefore the divinity of Christ. In Him then, and through Him, we know God. Apart from Him, and without the Scripture, without original sin, without a necessary mediator promised and come, we cannot absolutely prove God, nor teach right doctrine and right morality. But through Jesus Christ, and in Jesus Christ, we prove God, and teach morality and doctrine. Jesus Christ is then the true God of men.

But we know at the same time our wretchedness; for this God is none other than the Saviour of our wretchedness. So we can only know God well by knowing our iniquities. Therefore those who have known God, without knowing their wretchedness, have not glorified Him, but have glorified themselves. *Quia . . . non cognovit per sapientiam . . . placuit Deo per stultitiam prædicationis salvos facere.*

547

Not only do we know God by Jesus Christ alone, but we know ourselves only by Jesus Christ. We know life and death only through Jesus Christ. Apart from Jesus Christ, we do not know what is our life, nor our death, nor God, nor ourselves.

Thus without the Scripture, which has Jesus Christ alone for its object, we know nothing, and see only darkness and confusion in the nature of God, and in our own nature.

548

It is not only impossible but useless to know God without Jesus Christ. They have not departed from Him, but approached; they have not humbled themselves, but . . .

Quo quisque optimus est, pessimus, si hoc ipsum, quod optimus est, adscribat sibi.

549

I love poverty because He loved it. I love riches because they afford me the means of helping the very poor. I keep faith with everybody; I do not render evil to those who wrong me, but I wish them a lot like mine, in which I receive neither evil nor good from men. I try to be just, true, sincere, and faithful to all men; I have a tender heart for those to whom God has more closely united me; and whether I am alone, or seen of men, I do all my actions in the sight of God, who must judge of them, and to whom I have consecrated them all.

These are my sentiments; and every day of my life I bless my Redeemer, who has implanted them in me, and who, of a man full of weakness, of miseries, of lust, of pride, and of ambition, has made a man free from all these evils by the power of His grace, to which all the glory of it is due, as of myself I have only misery and error.

550

Dignior plagis quam osculis non timeo quia amo.

551

The Sepulchre of Jesus Christ.—Jesus Christ was dead, but seen on the Cross. He was dead, and hidden in the Sepulchre. Jesus Christ was buried by the saints alone.

Jesus Christ wrought no miracle at the Sepulchre.

Only the saints entered it.

It is there, not on the Cross, that Jesus Christ takes a new life.

It is the last mystery of the Passion and the Redemption.

Jesus Christ had nowhere to rest on earth but in the Sepulchre. His enemies only ceased to persecute Him at the Sepulchre.

552

The Mystery of Jesus.—Jesus suffers in His passions the torments which men inflict upon Him; but in His agony He suffers the torments which He inflicts on Himself; *turbare semetipsum.* This is a suffering from no human, but an almighty hand, for He must be almighty to bear it.

Jesus seeks some comfort at least in His three dearest friends, and they are asleep. He prays them to bear with Him for a little, and they leave Him with entire indifference, having so little compassion that it could not prevent their sleeping even for a moment. And thus Jesus was left alone to the wrath of God.

Jesus is alone on the earth, without any one not only to feel and share His suffering, but even to know of it; He and Heaven were alone in that knowledge.

Jesus is in a garden, not of delight as the first Adam, where he lost himself and the whole human race, but in one of agony, where He saved Himself and the whole human race.

He suffers this affliction and this desertion in the horror of night.

I believe that Jesus never complained but on this single occasion; but then He complained as if he could no longer bear His extreme suffering. "My soul is sorrowful, even unto death."

Jesus seeks companionship and comfort from men. This is the sole occasion in all His life, as it seems to me. But He receives it not, for His disciples are asleep.

Jesus will be in agony even to the end of the world. We must not sleep during that time.

Jesus, in the midst of this universal desertion, including that of His own friends chosen to watch with Him, finding them asleep, is vexed because of the danger to which they expose, not Him, but themselves; He cautions them for their own safety and their own good, with a sincere tenderness for them during their ingratitude, and warns them that the spirit is willing and the flesh weak.

Jesus, finding them still asleep, without being restrained by any consideration for themselves or for Him, has the kindness not to waken them, and leaves them in repose.

Jesus prays, uncertain of the will of His Father, and fears death; but, when He knows it, He goes forward to offer Himself to death. *Eamus. Processit* (John).

Jesus asked of men and was not heard.

Jesus, while His disciples slept, wrought their salvation. He has wrought that of each of the righteous while they slept, both in their nothingness before their birth, and in their sins after their birth.

He prays only once that the cup pass away, and then with submission; and twice that it come if necessary.

Jesus is weary.

Jesus, seeing all His friends asleep and all His enemies wakeful, commits Himself entirely to His Father.

Jesus does not regard in Judas his enmity, but the order of God, which He loves and admits, since He calls him friend.

Jesus tears Himself away from His disciples to enter into His agony; we must tear ourselves away from our nearest and dearest to imitate Him.

Jesus being in agony and in the greatest affliction, let us pray longer.

We implore the mercy of God, not that He may leave us at peace in our vices, but that He may deliver us from them.

If God gave us masters by His own hand, oh! how necessary for us to obey them with a good heart! Necessity and events follow infallibly.

—"Console thyself, thou wouldst not seek Me, if thou hadst not found Me.

"I thought of thee in Mine agony, I have sweated such drops of blood for thee.

"It is tempting Me rather than proving thyself, to think if thou wouldst do such and such a thing on an occasion which has not happened; I shall act in thee if it occur.

"Let thyself be guided by My rules; see how well I have led the Virgin and the saints who have let Me act in them.

"The Father loves all that I do.

"Dost thou wish that it always cost Me the blood of My humanity, without thy shedding tears?

"Thy conversion is My affair; fear not, and pray with confidence as for Me.

"I am present with thee by My Word in scripture, by My Spirit in the Church and by inspiration, by My power in the priests, by My prayer in the faithful.

"Physicians will not heal thee, for thou wilt die at last. But it is I who heal thee, and make the body immortal.

"Suffer bodily chains and servitude, I deliver thee at present only from spiritual servitude.

"I am more a friend to thee than such and such an one, for I have done for thee more than they; they would not have suffered what I have suffered from thee, and they would not have died for thee as I have done in the time of thine infidelities and cruelties, and as I am ready to do, and do, among My elect and at the Holy Sacrament."

"If thou knewest thy sins, thou wouldst lose heart."

—I shall lose it then, Lord, for on Thy assurance I believe their malice.

—"No, for I, by whom thou learnest, can heal thee of them, and what I say to thee is a sign that I will heal thee. In proportion to thy expiation of them, thou wilt know them, and it will be said to thee: 'Behold, thy sins are forgiven thee.' Repent, then, for thy hidden sins, and for the secret malice of those which thou knowest."

—Lord, I give Thee all.

—"I love thee more ardently than thou hast loved thine abominations, *ut immundus pro luto.*

"To Me be the glory, not to thee, worm of the earth.

"Ask thy confessor, when My own words are to thee occasion of evil, vanity, or curiosity."

—I see in me depths of pride, curiosity, and lust. There is no relation between me and God, nor Jesus Christ the Righteous. But He has been made sin for me; all Thy scourges are fallen upon Him. He is more abominable than I, and, far from abhorring me, He holds Himself honoured that I go to Him and succour Him.

But He has healed Himself, and still more so will He heal me.

I must add my wounds to His, and join myself to Him; and He will save me in saving Himself. But this must not be postponed to the future.

Eritis sicut dii scientes bonum et malum. Each one creates his god, when judging, "This is good or bad"; and men mourn or rejoice too much at events.

Do little things as though they were great, because of the majesty of Jesus Christ who does them in us, and who lives our life; and do the greatest things as though they were little and easy, because of His omnipotence.

553

It seems to me that Jesus Christ only allowed His wounds to be touched after His resurrection: *Noli me tangere.* We must unite ourselves only to His sufferings.

At the Last Supper He gave Himself in communion as about to die; to the disciples at Emmaus as risen from the dead; to the whole Church as ascended into heaven.

554

"Compare not thyself with others, but with Me. If thou dost not find Me in those with whom thou comparest thyself, thou comparest thyself to one who is abominable. If thou findest Me in them, compare thyself to Me. But whom wilt thou compare? Thyself, or Me in thee? If it is thyself, it is one who is abominable. If it is I, thou comparest Me to Myself. Now I am God in all.

"I speak to thee, and often counsel thee, because thy director cannot speak to thee, for I do not want thee to lack a guide.

"And perhaps I do so at his prayers, and thus he leads thee without thy seeing it. Thou wouldst not seek Me, if thou didst not possess Me.

"Be not therefore troubled."

THE FUNDAMENTALS OF THE CHRISTIAN RELIGION

555

. . . Men blaspheme what they do not know. The Christian religion consists in two points. It is of equal concern to men to know them, and it is equally dangerous to be ignorant of them. And it is equally of God's mercy that He has given indications of both.

And yet they take occasion to conclude that one of these points does not exist, from that which should have caused them to infer the other. The sages who have said there is only one God have been persecuted, the Jews were hated, and still more the Christians. They have seen by the light of nature that if there be a true religion on earth, the course of all things must tend to it as to a centre.

The whole course of things must have for its object the establishment and the greatness of religion. Men must have within them feelings suited to what religion teaches us. And, finally, religion must so be the object and centre to which all things tend, that whoever knows the principles of religion can give an explanation both of the whole nature of man in particular, and of the whole course of the world in general.

And on this ground they take occasion to revile the Christian religion, because they misunderstand it. They imagine that it consists simply in the worship of a God considered as great, powerful, and eternal; which is strictly deism, almost as far removed from the Christian religion as atheism, which is its exact opposite. And thence they conclude that this religion is not true, because they do not see that all things concur to the establishment of this point, that God does not manifest Himself to men with all the evidence which He could show.

But let them conclude what they will against deism, they will conclude nothing against the Christian religion, which properly consists in the mystery of the Redeemer, who, uniting in Himself the two natures, human and divine, has redeemed men from the corruption of sin in order to reconcile them in His divine person to God.

The Christian religion, then, teaches men these two truths; that there is a God whom men can know, and that there is a corruption in their nature which renders them unworthy of Him. It is equally important to men to know both these points; and it is equally dangerous for man to know God without knowing his own wretchedness, and to know his own wretchedness without knowing the Redeemer who can free him from it. The knowledge of only one of these points gives rise either to the pride of philosophers, who have known God, and not their own wretchedness, or to the despair of atheists, who know their own wretchedness, but not the Redeemer.

And, as it is alike necessary to man to know these two points, so is it alike merciful of God to have made us know them. The Christian religion does this; it is in this that it consists.

Let us herein examine the order of the world, and see if all things do not tend to establish these two chief points of this religion: Jesus Christ is the end of all, and the centre to which all tends. Whoever knows Him knows the reason of everything.

Those who fall into error err only through failure to see one of these two things. We can then have an excellent knowledge of God without that of our own wretchedness, and of our own wretchedness without that of God. But we cannot know Jesus Christ without knowing at the same time both God and our own wretchedness.

Therefore I shall not undertake here to prove by natural

reasons either the existence of God, or the Trinity, or the immortality of the soul, or anything of that nature; not only because I should not feel myself sufficiently able to find in nature arguments to convince hardened atheists, but also because such knowledge without Jesus Christ is useless and barren. Though a man should be convinced that numerical proportions are immaterial truths, eternal and dependent on a first truth, in which they subsist, and which is called God, I should not think him far advanced towards his own salvation.

The God of Christians is not a God who is simply the author of mathematical truths, or of the order of the elements; that is the view of heathens and Epicureans. He is not merely a God who exercises His providence over the life and fortunes of men, to bestow on those who worship Him a long and happy life. That was the portion of the Jews. But the God of Abraham, the God of Isaac, the God of Jacob, the God of Christians, is a God of love and of comfort, a God who fills the soul and heart of those whom He possesses, a God who makes them conscious of their inward wretchedness, and His infinite mercy, who unites Himself to their inmost soul, who fills it with humility and joy, with confidence and love, who renders them incapable of any other end than Himself.

All who seek God without Jesus Christ, and who rest in nature, either find no light to satisfy them, or come to form for themselves a means of knowing God and serving Him without a mediator. Thereby they fall either into atheism, or into deism, two things which the Christian religion abhors almost equally.

Without Jesus Christ the world would not exist; for it should needs be either that it would be destroyed or be a hell.

If the world existed to instruct man of God, His divinity would shine through every part in it in an indisputable manner; but as it exists only by Jesus Christ, and for Jesus Christ, and to teach men both their corruption and their redemption, all displays the proofs of these two truths.

All appearance indicates neither a total exclusion nor a manifest presence of divinity, but the presence of a God who hides Himself. Everything bears this character.

. . . Shall he alone who knows his nature know it only to be miserable? Shall he alone who knows it be alone unhappy?

. . . He must not see nothing at all, nor must he see sufficient for him to believe he possesses it; but he must see enough to know that he has lost it. For to know of his loss, he must see and not see; and that is exactly the state in which he naturally is.

. . . Whatever part he takes, I shall not leave him at rest . . .

556

. . . It is then true that everything teaches man his condition, but he must understand this well. For it is not true that all reveals God, and it is not true that all conceals God. But it is at the same time true that He hides Himself from those who tempt Him, and that He reveals Himself to those who seek Him, because men are both unworthy and capable of God; unworthy by their corruption, capable by their original nature.

557

What shall we conclude from all our darkness, but our unworthiness?

558

If there never had been any appearance of God, this eternal deprivation would have been equivocal, and might have as well corresponded with the absence of all divinity, as with the unworthiness of men to know Him; but His occasional, though not continual, appearances remove the ambiguity. If He appeared once, He exists always; and thus we cannot but conclude both that there is a God, and that men are unworthy of Him.

559

We do not understand the glorious state of Adam, nor the nature of his sin, nor the transmission of it to us. These are matters which took place under conditions of a nature altogether different from our own, and which transcend our present understanding.

The knowledge of all this is useless to us as a means of escape from it; and all that we are concerned to know, is that we are miserable, corrupt, separated from God, but ransomed by Jesus Christ, whereof we have wonderful proofs on earth.

So the two proofs of corruption and redemption are drawn from the ungodly, who live in indifference to religion, and from the Jews who are irreconcilable enemies.

560

There are two ways of proving the truths of our religion; one by the power of reason, the other by the authority of him who speaks.

We do not make use of the latter, but of the former. We do not say, "This must be believed, for Scripture, which says it, is divine." But we say that it must be believed for such and such a reason, which are feeble arguments, as reason may be bent to everything.

561

There is nothing on earth that does not show either the wretchedness of man, or the mercy of God; either the weakness of man without God, or the strength of man with God.

562

It will be one of the confusions of the damned to see that they are condemned by their own reason, by which they claimed to condemn the Christian religion.

563

The prophecies, the very miracles and proofs of our religion, are not of such a nature that they can be said to be absolutely convincing. But they are also of such a kind that it cannot be said that it is unreasonable to believe them. Thus there is both evidence and obscurity to enlighten some and confuse others. But the evidence is such that it surpasses, or at least equals, the evidence to the contrary; so that it is not reason which can determine men not to follow it, and thus it can only be lust or malice of heart. And by this means there is sufficient evidence to condemn, and insufficient to convince; so that it appears in those who follow it, that it is grace, and not reason, which makes them follow it; and in those who shun it, that it is lust, not reason, which makes them shun it.

Vere discipuli, vere Israëlita, vere liberi, vere cibus.

564

Recognise, then, the truth of religion in the very obscurity of religion, in the little light we have of it, and in the indifference which we have to knowing it.

565

We understand nothing of the works of God, if we do not take as a principle that He has willed to blind some, and enlighten others.

566

The two contrary reasons. We must begin with that; without that we understand nothing, and all is heretical; and we must even add at the end of each truth that the opposite truth is to be remembered.

567

Objection. The Scripture is plainly full of matters not dictated by the Holy Spirit.—*Answer.* Then they do not harm faith.—*Objection.* But the Church has decided that all is of the Holy Spirit.—*Answer.* I answer two things: first, the Church has not so decided; secondly, if she should so decide, it could be maintained.

Do you think that the prophecies cited in the Gospel are related to make you believe? No, it is to keep you from believing.

568

Canonical.—The heretical books in the beginning of the Church serve to prove the canonical.

569

To the chapter on the *Fundamentals* must be added that on *Typology* touching the reason of types: why Jesus Christ was prophesied as to His first coming; why prophesied obscurely as to the manner.

570

The reason why. Types.—[They had to deal with a carnal people and to render them the depositary of the spiritual covenant.] To give faith to the Messiah, it was necessary there should have been precedent prophesies, and that these should be conveyed by persons above suspicion, diligent, faithful, unusually zealous, and known to all the world.

To accomplish all this, God chose this carnal people, to whom He entrusted the prophecies which foretell the Messiah as a deliverer, and as a dispenser of those carnal goods which this people loved. And thus they have had an extraordinary passion for their prophets, and, in sight of the whole world, have had charge of these books which foretell their Messiah, assuring all nations that He should come, and in the way foretold in the books, which they held open to the whole world. Yet this people, deceived by the poor and ignominious advent of the Messiah, have been His most cruel enemies. So that they, the people least open to suspicion in the world of favouring us, the most strict and most zealous that can be named for their law and their prophets, have kept the books incorrupt. Hence those who have rejected and crucified Jesus Christ, who has been to them an offence, are those who have charge of the books which testify of Him, and state that He will be an offence and rejected. Therefore they have shown it was He by rejecting Him, and He has been alike proved both by the righteous Jews who received Him, and by the unrighteous who rejected Him, both facts having been foretold.

Wherefore the prophecies have a hidden and spiritual meaning to which this people were hostile, under the carnal meaning which they loved. If the spiritual meaning had been revealed, they would not have loved it, and, unable to bear it, they would not have been zealous of the preservation of their books and their ceremonies; and if they had loved these spiritual promises, and had preserved them incorrupt till the time of the Messiah, their testimony would have had no force, because they had been his friends.

Therefore it was well that the spiritual meaning should be concealed; but, on the other hand, if this meaning had been so hidden as not to appear at all, it could not have served as a proof of the Messiah. What then was done? In a crowd of passages it has been hidden under the temporal meaning, and in a few has been clearly revealed; besides that the time and the state of the world have been so clearly foretold that it is clearer than the sun. And in some places this spiritual meaning is so clearly expressed, that it would require a blindness like that which the flesh imposes on the spirit when it is subdued by it, not to recognise it.

See, then, what has been the prudence of God. This meaning is concealed under another in an infinite number of passages, and in some, though rarely, it is revealed; but yet so that the passages in which it is concealed are equivocal, and can suit both meanings; whereas the passages where it is disclosed are unequivocal, and can only suit the spiritual meaning.

So that this cannot lead us into error, and could only be misunderstood by so carnal a people.

For when blessings are promised in abundance, what was to prevent them from understanding the true blessings, but their covetousness, which limited the meaning to worldly goods? But those whose only good was in God referred them to God alone. For there are two principles, which divide the wills of men, covetousness and charity. Not that covetousness cannot exist along with faith in God, nor charity with worldly riches; but covetousness uses God, and enjoys the world, and charity is the opposite.

Now the ultimate end gives names to things. All which prevents us from attaining it, is called an enemy to us. Thus the creatures, however good, are the enemies of the righteous, when they turn them away from God, and God Himself is the enemy of those whose covetousness He confounds.

Thus as the significance of the word "enemy" is dependent on the ultimate end, the righteous understood by it their passions, and the carnal the Babylonians; and so these terms were obscure only for the unrighteous. And this is what Isaiah says: *Signa legem in electis meis,* and that Jesus Christ shall be a stone of stumbling. But, "Blessed are they who shall not be offended in him." Hosea, *ult.,* says excellently, "Where is the wise? and he shall understand what I say. The righteous shall know them, for the ways of God are right; but the transgressors shall fall therein."

571

Hypothesis that the apostles were impostors.—The time clearly, the manner obscurely.—Five typical proofs.

$$2000 \begin{cases} 1600 \text{ prophets.} \\ 400 \text{ scattered.} \end{cases}$$

572

Blindness of Scripture.—"The Scripture," said the Jews, "says that we shall not know whence Christ will come (John vii, 27, and xii, 34). The Scripture says that Christ abideth for ever, and He said that He should die." Therefore, says Saint John, they believed not, though He had done so many miracles, that the word of Isaiah might be fulfilled: "He hath blinded them," etc.

573

Greatness.—Religion is so great a thing that it is right that those who will not take the trouble to seek it, if it be obscure, should be deprived of it. Why, then, do any complain, if it be such as can be found by seeking?

574

All things work together for good to the elect, even the obscurities of Scripture; for they honour them because of what is divinely clear. And all things work together for evil to the rest of the world, even what is clear; for they revile such, because of the obscurities which they do not understand.

575

The general conduct of the world towards the Church: God willing to blind and to enlighten.—The event having proved the divinity of these prophecies, the rest ought to be believed. And thereby we see the order of the world to be of this kind. The miracles of the Creation and the Deluge being forgotten, God sends the law and the miracles of Moses, the prophets who prophesied particular things; and to prepare a lasting miracle, He prepares prophecies and their fulfilment; but, as the prophecies could be suspected, He desires to make them above suspicion, etc.

576

God has made the blindness of this people subservient to the good of the elect.

577

There is sufficient clearness to enlighten the elect, and sufficient obscurity to humble them. There is sufficient obscurity to blind the reprobate, and sufficient clearness to condemn them, and make them inexcusable.—Saint Augustine, Montaigne, Sébond.

The genealogy of Jesus Christ in the Old Testament is in-

termingled with so many others that are useless, that it cannot
be distinguished. If Moses had kept only the record of the
ancestors of Christ, that might have been too plain. If he
had not noted that of Jesus Christ, it might not have been
sufficiently plain. But, after all, whoever looks closely sees
that of Jesus Christ expressly traced through Tamar, Ruth,
etc.

Those who ordained these sacrifices, knew their uselessness; those who have declared their uselessness, have not
ceased to practise them.

If God had permitted only one religion, it has been too
easily known; but when we look at it closely, we clearly discern the truth amidst this confusion.

The premiss.—Moses was a clever man. If, then, he ruled
himself by his reason, he would say nothing clearly which
was directly against reason.

Thus all the very apparent weaknesses are strength. Example; the two genealogies in Saint Matthew and Saint Luke.
What can be clearer than that this was not concerted?

578

God (and the Apostles), foreseeing that the seeds of pride
would make heresies spring up, and being unwilling to give
them occasion to arise from correct expressions, has put in
Scripture and the prayers of the Church contrary words and
sentences to produce their fruit in time.

So in morals He gives charity, which produces fruits contrary to lust.

579

Nature has some perfections to show that she is the image
of God, and some defects to show that she is only His image.

580

God prefers rather to incline the will than the intellect.
Perfect clearness would be of use to the intellect, and would
harm the will. To humble pride.

581

We make an idol of truth itself; for truth apart from charity is not God, but His image and idol, which we must neither love nor worship; and still less must we love or worship its opposite, namely, falsehood.

I can easily love total darkness; but if God keeps me in a state of semi-darkness, such partial darkness displeases me, and, because I do not see therein the advantage of total darkness, it is unpleasant to me. This is a fault, and a sign that I make for myself an idol of darkness, apart from the order of God. Now only His order must be worshipped.

582

The feeble-minded are people who know the truth, but only affirm it so far as consistent with their own interest. But, apart from that, they renounce it.

583

The world exists for the exercise of mercy and judgment, not as if men were placed in it out of the hands of God, but as hostile to God; and to them He grants by grace sufficient light, that they may return to Him, if they desire to seek and follow Him; and also that they may be punished, if they refuse to seek or follow Him.

584

That God has willed to hide Himself.—If there were only one religion, God would indeed be manifest. The same would be the case, if there were no martyrs but in our religion.

God being thus hidden, every religion which does not affirm that God is hidden, is not true; and every religion which does not give the reason of it, is not instructive. Our religion does all this: *Vere tu es Deus absconditus.*

585

If there were no obscurity, man would not be sensible of his corruption; if there were no light, man would not hope for a remedy. Thus, it is not only fair, but advantageous to us, that God be partly hidden and partly revealed; since it is equally dangerous to man to know God without knowing his own wretchedness, and to know his own wretchedness without knowing God.

586

This religion, so great in miracles, saints, blameless Fathers, learned and great witnesses, martyrs, established kings as David, and Isaiah, a prince of the blood, and so great in science, after having displayed all her miracles and all her wisdom, rejects all this, and declares that she has neither wisdom nor signs, but only the cross and foolishness.

For those, who, by these signs and that wisdom, have deserved your belief, and who have proved to you their character, declare to you that nothing of all this can change you, and render you capable of knowing and loving God, but the power of the foolishness of the cross without wisdom and signs, and not the signs without this power. Thus our religion is foolish in respect to the effective cause, and wise in respect to the wisdom which prepares it.

587

Our religion is wise and foolish. Wise, because it is the most learned, and the most founded on miracles, prophecies, etc. Foolish, because it is not all this which makes us belong to it. This makes us indeed condemn those who do not belong to it; but it does not cause belief in those who do belong to it. It is the cross that makes them believe, *ne evacuata sit crux*. And so Saint Paul, who came with wisdom and signs, says that he has come neither with wisdom nor with signs; for he came to convert. But those who come only to convince, can say that they come with wisdom and with signs.

PERPETUITY

588

On the fact that the Christian religion is not the only religion.—So far is this from being a reason for believing that it is not the true one, that, on the contrary, it makes us see that it is so.

589

Men must be sincere in all religions; true heathens, true Jews, true Christians.

590

J. C.

Heathens | Mahomet

Ignorance
of God.

591

The falseness of other religions.—They have no witnesses. Jews have. God defies other religions to produce such signs: Isaiah xliii, 9; xliv, 8.

592

History of China.—I believe only the histories, whose witnesses got themselves killed.

[Which is the more credible of the two, Moses or China?]

It is not a question of seeing this summarily. I tell you there is in it something to blind, and something to enlighten.

By this one word I destroy all your reasoning. "But China

obscures," say you; and I answer, "China obscures, but there is clearness to be found; seek it."

Thus all that you say makes for one of the views, and not at all against the other. So this serves, and does no harm.

We must then see this in detail; we must put the papers on the table.

593

Against the history of China. The historians of Mexico, the five suns, of which the last is only eight hundred years old.

The difference between a book accepted by a nation, and one which makes a nation.

594

Mahomet was without authority. His reasons then should have been very strong, having only their own force. What does he say then, that we must believe him?

595

The Psalms are chanted throughout the whole world.

Who renders testimony to Mahomet? Himself. Jesus Christ desires His own testimony to be as nothing.

The quality of witnesses necessitates their existence always and everywhere; and he, miserable creature, is alone.

596

Against Mahomet.—The Koran is not more of Mahomet than the Gospel is of Saint Matthew, for it is cited by many authors from age to age. Even its very enemies, Celsus and Porphyry, never denied it.

The Koran says Saint Matthew was an honest man. Therefore Mahomet was a false prophet for calling honest men wicked, or for not agreeing with what they have said of Jesus Christ.

597

It is not by that which is obscure in Mahomet, and which may be interpreted in a mysterious sense, that I would have him judged, but by what is clear, as his paradise and the rest. In that he is ridiculous. And since what is clear is ridiculous, it is not right to take his obscurities for mysteries.

It is not the same with the Scripture. I agree that there are in it obscurities as strange as those of Mahomet; but there are admirably clear passages, and the prophecies are manifestly fulfilled. The cases are therefore not on a par. We must not confound, and put on one level things which only resemble each other in their obscurity, and not in the clearness, which requires us to reverence the obscurities.

598

The difference between Jesus Christ and Mahomet.— Mahomet was not foretold; Jesus Christ was foretold.

Mahomet slew; Jesus Christ caused His own to be slain.

Mahomet forbade reading; the Apostles ordered reading.

In fact the two are so opposed, that if Mahomet took the way to succeed from a worldly point of view, Jesus Christ, from the same point of view, took the way to perish. And instead of concluding that, since Mahomet succeeded, Jesus Christ might well have succeeded, we ought to say that since Mahomet succeeded, Jesus Christ should have failed.

599

Any man can do what Mahomet has done; for he performed no miracles, he was not foretold. No man can do what Christ has done.

600

The heathen religion has no foundation [at the present day. It is said once to have had a foundation by the oracles which spoke. But what are the books which assure us of this? Are they so worthy of belief on account of the virtue of their authors? Have they been preserved with such care that we can be sure that they have not been meddled with?]

The Mahometan religion has for a foundation the Koran

and Mahomet. But has this prophet, who was to be the last hope of the world, been foretold? What sign has he that every other man has not, who chooses to call himself a prophet? What miracles does he himself say that he has done? What mysteries has he taught, even according to his own tradition? What was the morality, what the happiness held out by him?

The Jewish religion must be differently regarded in the tradition of the Holy Bible, and in the tradition of the people. Its morality and happiness are absurd in the tradition of the people, but are admirable in that of the Holy Bible. (And all religion is the same; for the Christian religion is very different in the Holy Bible and in the casuists.) The foundation is admirable; it is the most ancient book in the world, and the most authentic; and whereas Mahomet, in order to make his own book continue in existence, forbade men to read it, Moses, for the same reason, ordered every one to read his.

Our religion is so divine that another divine religion has only been the foundation of it.

601

Order.—To see what is clear and indisputable in the whole state of the Jews.

602

The Jewish religion is wholly divine in its authority, its duration, its perpetuity, its morality, its doctrine, and its effects.

603

The only science contrary to common sense and human nature is that alone which has always existed among men.

604

The only religion contrary to nature, to common sense, and to our pleasure, is that alone which has always existed.

605

No religion but our own has taught that man is born in sin. No sect of philosophers has said this. Therefore none have declared the truth.

No sect or religion has always existed on earth, but the Christian religion.

606

Whoever judges of the Jewish religion by its coarser forms will misunderstand it. It is to be seen in the Holy Bible, and in the tradition of the prophets, who have made it plain enough that they did not interpret the law according to the letter. So our religion is divine in the Gospel, in the Apostles, and in tradition; but it is absurd in those who tamper with it.

The Messiah, according to the carnal Jews, was to be a great temporal prince. Jesus Christ, according to carnal Christians, has come to dispense us from the love of God, and to give us sacraments which shall do everything without our help. Such is not the Christian religion, nor the Jewish. True Jews and true Christians have always expected a Messiah who should make them love God, and by that love triumph over their enemies.

607

The carnal Jews hold a midway place between Christians and heathens. The heathens know not God, and love the world only. The Jews know the true God, and love the world only. The Christians know the true God, and love not the world. Jews and heathens love the same good. Jews and Christians know the same God.

The Jews were of two kinds; the first had only heathen affections, the other had Christian affections.

608

There are two kinds of men in each religion: among the heathen, worshippers of beasts, and the worshippers of the one only God of natural religion; among the Jews, the carnal, and the spiritual, who were the Christians of the old law; among Christians, the coarser-minded, who are the Jews of the new law. The carnal Jews looked for a carnal Messiah; the coarser Christians believe that the Messiah has dispensed them from the love of God; true Jews and true Christians worship a Messiah who makes them love God.

609

To show that the true Jews and the true Christians have but the same religion.—The religion of the Jews seemed to consist essentially in the fatherhood of Abraham, in circumcision, in sacrifices, in ceremonies, in the Ark, in the temple, in Jerusalem, and, finally, in the law, and in the covenant with Moses.

I say that it consisted in none of those things, but only in the love of God, and that God disregarded all the other things.

That God did not accept the posterity of Abraham.

That the Jews were to be punished like strangers, if they transgressed. *Deut.* viii, 19; "If thou do at all forget the Lord thy God, and walk after other gods, I testify against you this day that ye shall surely perish, as the nations which the Lord destroyeth before your face."

That strangers, if they loved God, were to be received by Him as the Jews. *Isaiah* lvi, 3: "Let not the stranger say, 'The Lord will not receive me.' The strangers who join themselves unto the Lord to serve Him and love Him, will I bring unto my holy mountain, and accept therein sacrifices, for mine house is a house of prayer."

That the true Jews considered their merit to be from God only, and not from Abraham. *Isaiah* lxiii, 16; "Doubtless thou art our Father, though Abraham be ignorant of us, and Israel acknowledge us not. Thou art our Father and our Redeemer."

Moses himself told them that God would not accept persons. *Deut.* x, 17: "God," said he, "regardeth neither persons nor sacrifices."

The Sabbath was only a sign, *Exod.* xxxi, 13; and in memory of the escape from Egypt, *Deut.* v, 19. Therefore it is no longer necessary, since Egypt must be forgotten.

Circumcision was only a sign, *Gen.* xvii, 11. And thence it came to pass that, being in the desert, they were not circumcised, because they could not be confounded with other peoples; and after Jesus Christ came, it was no longer necessary.

That the circumcision of the heart is commanded. *Deut.* x, 16; *Jeremiah* iv, 4: "Be ye circumcised in heart; take away the superfluities of your heart, and harden yourselves not. For your God is a mighty God, strong and terrible, who accepteth not persons."

That God said He would one day do it. *Deut.* xxx, 6; "God will circumcise thine heart, and the heart of thy seed, that thou mayest love Him with all thine heart."

That the uncircumcised in heart shall be judged. *Jeremiah* ix, 26: For God will judge the uncircumcised peoples, and all the people of Israel, because he is "uncircumcised in heart."

That the external is of no avail apart from the internal. *Joel* ii, 13: *Scindite corda vestra,* etc.; *Isaiah* lviii, 3, 4, etc.

The love of God is enjoined in the whole of Deuteronomy. *Deut.* xxx, 19: "I call heaven and earth to record that I have set before you life and death, that you should choose life, and love God, and obey Him, for God is your life."

That the Jews, for lack of that love, should be rejected for their offences, and the heathen chosen in their stead. *Hosea* i, 10; *Deut.* xxxii, 20. "I will hide myself from them in view of their latter sins, for they are a froward generation without faith. They have moved me to jealousy with that which is not God, and I will move them to jealousy with those which are not a people, and with an ignorant and foolish nation." *Isaiah* lxv, 1.

That temporal goods are false, and that the true good is to be united to God. *Psalm* cxliii, 15.

That their feasts are displeasing to God. *Amos* v, 21.

That the sacrifices of the Jews displeased God. *Isaiah* lxvi. 1—3; i, 11; *Jer.* vi, 20; David, *Miserere.*—Even on the part of the good, *Expectavi. Psalm* xlix, 8, 9, 10, 11, 12, 13 and 14.

That He has established them only for their hardness. *Micah,* admirably, vi; 1 *Kings* xv, 22; *Hosea* vi, 6.

That the sacrifices of the Gentiles will be accepted of God, and that God will take no pleasure in the sacrifices of the Jews. *Malachi* i, 11.

That God will make a new covenant with the Messiah, and the old will be annulled. *Jer.* xxxi, 31. *Mandata non bona. Ezek.*

That the old things will be forgotten. *Isaiah* xliii, 18, 19; lxv, 17, 10.

That the Ark will no longer be remembered. *Jer.* iii, 15, 16.

That the temple should be rejected. *Jer.* vii, 12, 13, 14.

That the sacrifices should be rejected, and other pure sacrifices established. *Malachi* i, 11.

That the order of Aaron's priesthood should be rejected, and that of Melchizedek introduced by the Messiah. *Ps. Dixit Dominus.*

That this priesthood should be eternal. *Ibid.*

That Jerusalem should be rejected, and Rome admitted. *Ps. Dixit Dominus.*

That the name of the Jews should be rejected, and a new name given. *Isaiah* lxv, 15.

That this last name should be more excellent than that of the Jews, and eternal. *Isaiah* lvi, 5.

That the Jews should be without prophets (Amos), without a king, without princes, without sacrifice, without an idol.

That the Jews should nevertheless always remain a people. *Jer.* xxxi, 36.

610

Republic.—The Christian republic—and even the Jewish —has only had God for ruler, as Philo the Jew notices, *On Monarchy.*

When they fought, it was for God only; their chief hope

was in God only; they considered their towns as belonging
to God only, and kept them for God. 1 *Chron.* xix, 13.

611

Gen. xvii, 7. *Statuam pactum meum inter me et te fœdere
sempiterno . . . ut sim Deus tuus . . .*
  Et tu ergo custodies pactum meum.

612

Perpetuity.—That religion has always existed on earth,
which consists in believing that man has fallen from a state
of glory and of communion with God into a state of sorrow,
penitence, and estrangement from God, but that after this
life we shall be restored by a Messiah who should have come.
All things have passed away, and this has endured, for which
all things are.

Men have in the first age of the world been carried away
into every kind of debauchery, and yet there were saints, as
Enoch, Lamech, and others, who waited patiently for the
Christ promised from the beginning of the world. Noah saw
the wickedness of men at its height; and he was held worthy
to save the world in his person, by the hope of the Messiah
of whom he was the type. Abraham was surrounded by idolaters, when God made known to him the mystery of the Messiah, whom he welcomed from afar. In the time of Isaac and
Jacob abomination was spread over all the earth; but these
saints lived in faith; and Jacob, dying and blessing his children, cried in a transport which made him break off his discourse, "I await, O my God, the Saviour whom Thou hast
promised. *Salutare tuum expectabo, Domine.*" The Egyptians
were infected both with idolatry and magic; the very people
of God were led astray by their example. Yet Moses and
others believed Him whom they saw not, and worshipped
Him, looking to the eternal gifts which He was preparing for
them.

The Greeks and Latins then set up false deities; the poets

made a hundred different theologies, while the philosophers separated into a thousand different sects; and yet in the heart of Judæa there were always chosen men who foretold the coming of this Messiah, which was known to them alone.

He came at length in the fullness of time, and time has since witnessed the birth of so many schisms and heresies, so many political revolutions, so many changes in all things; yet this Church, which worships Him who has always been worshipped, has endured uninterruptedly. It is a wonderful, incomparable, and altogether divine fact that this religion, which has always endured, has always been attacked. It has been a thousand times on the eve of universal destruction, and every time it has been in that state, God has restored it by extraordinary acts of His power. This is astonishing, as also that it has preserved itself without yielding to the will of tyrants. For it is not strange that a State endures, when its laws are sometimes made to give way to necessity, but that . . . (See the passage indicated in Montaigne.)

613

States would perish if they did not often make their laws give way to necessity. But religion has never suffered this, or practised it. Indeed, there must be these compromises, or miracles. It is not strange to be saved by yieldings, and this is not strictly self-preservation; besides, in the end they perish entirely. None has endured a thousand years. But the fact that this religion has always maintained itself, inflexible as it is, proves its divinity.

614

Whatever may be said, it must be admitted that the Christian religion has something astonishing in it. Some will say, "This is because you were born in it." Far from it; I stiffen myself against it for this very reason, for fear this prejudice bias me. But although I am born in it, I cannot help finding it so.

615

Perpetuity.—The Messiah has always been believed in. The tradition from Adam was fresh in Noah and in Moses. Since then the prophets have foretold him, while at the same time foretelling other things, which, being from time to time fulfilled in the sight of men, showed the truth of their mission, and consequently that of their promises touching the Messiah. Jesus Christ performed miracles, and the Apostles also, who converted all the heathen; and all the prophecies being thereby fulfilled, the Messiah is for ever proved.

616

Perpetuity.—Let us consider that since the beginning of the world the expectation of worship of the Messiah has existed uninterruptedly; that there have been found men, who said that God had revealed to them that a Redeemer was to be born, who should save His people; that Abraham came afterwards, saying that he had had a revelation that the Messiah was to spring from him by a son, whom he should have; that Jacob declared that, of his twelve sons, the Messiah would spring from Judah; that Moses and the prophets then came to declare the time and the manner of His coming; that they said their law was only temporary till that of the Messiah, that it should endure till then, but that the other should last for ever; that thus either their law, or that of the Messiah, of which it was the promise, would be always upon the earth; that, in fact, it has always endured; that at last Jesus Christ came with all the circumstances foretold. This is wonderful.

617

This is positive fact. While all philosophers separate into different sects, there is found in one corner of the world the most ancient people in it, declaring that all the world is in error, that God has revealed to them the truth, that they will always exist on the earth. In fact, all other sects come to an end, this one still endures, and has done so for four thousand years.

They declare that they hold from their ancestors that man has fallen from communion with God, and is entirely estranged from God, but that He has promised to redeem them; that this doctrine shall always exist on the earth; that their law has a double signification; that during sixteen hundred years they have had people, whom they believed prophets, foretelling both the time and the manner; that four hundred years after they were scattered everywhere, because Jesus Christ was to be everywhere announced; that Jesus Christ came in the manner, and at the time foretold; that the Jews have since been scattered abroad under a curse, and nevertheless still exist.

618

I see the Christian religion founded upon a preceding religion, and this is what I find as a fact.

I do not here speak of the miracles of Moses, of Jesus Christ, and of the Apostles, because they do not at first seem convincing, and because I only wish here to put in evidence all those foundations of the Christian religion which are beyond doubt, and which cannot be called in question by any person whatsoever. It is certain that we see in many places of the world a peculiar people, separated from all other peoples of the world, and called the Jewish people.

I see then a crowd of religions in many parts of the world and in all times; but their morality cannot please me, nor can their proofs convince me. Thus I should equally have rejected the religion of Mahomet and of China, of the ancient Romans and of the Egyptians, for the sole reason, that none having more marks of truth than another, nor anything which should necessarily persuade me, reason cannot incline to one rather than the other.

But, in thus considering this changeable and singular variety of morals and beliefs at different times, I find in one corner of the world a peculiar people, separated from all other peoples on earth, the most ancient of all, and whose histories are earlier by many generations than the most ancient which we possess.

I find, then, this great and numerous people, sprung from a single man, who worship one God, and guide themselves by a law which they say that they obtained from His own hand. They maintain that they are the only people in the world to whom God has revealed His mysteries; that all men are corrupt and in disgrace with God; that they are all abandoned to their senses and their own imagination, whence come the strange errors and continual changes which happen among them, both of religions and of morals, whereas they themselves remain firm in their conduct; but that God will not leave other nations in this darkness for ever; that there will come a Saviour for all; that they are in the world to announce Him to men; that they are expressly formed to be forerunners and heralds of this great event, and to summon all nations to join with them in the expectation of this Saviour.

To meet with this people is astonishing to me, and seems to me worthy of attention. I look at the law which they boast of having obtained from God, and I find it admirable. It is the first law of all, and is of such a kind that, even before the term *law* was in currency among the Greeks, it had, for nearly a thousand years earlier, been uninterruptedly accepted and observed by the Jews. I likewise think it strange that the first law of the world happens to be the most perfect; so that the greatest legislators have borrowed their laws from it, as is apparent from the law of the Twelve Tables at Athens, afterwards taken by the Romans, and as it would be easy to prove, if Josephus and others had not sufficiently dealt with this subject.

619

Advantages of the Jewish people.—In this search the Jewish people at once attracts my attention by the number of wonderful and singular facts which appear about them.

I first see that they are a people wholly composed of

brethren, and whereas all others are formed by the assemblage of an infinity of families, this, though so wonderfully fruitful, has all sprung from one man alone, and, being thus all one flesh, and members one of another, they constitute a powerful state of one family. This is unique.

This family, or people, is the most ancient within human knowledge, a fact which seems to me to inspire a peculiar veneration for it, especially in view of our present inquiry; since if God had from all time revealed Himself to men, it is to these we must turn for knowledge of the tradition.

This people are not eminent solely by their antiquity, but are also singular by their duration, which has always continued from their origin till now. For whereas the nations of Greece and of Italy, of Lacedæmon, of Athens and of Rome, and others who came long after, have long since perished, these ever remain, and in spite of the endeavours of many powerful kings who have a hundred times tried to destroy them, as their historians testify, and as it is easy to conjecture from the natural order of things during so long a space of years, they have nevertheless been preserved (and this preservation has been foretold); and extending from the earliest times to the latest, their history comprehends in its duration all our histories [which it preceded by a long time].

The law by which this people is governed is at once the most ancient law in the world, the most perfect, and the only one which has been always observed without a break in a state. This is what Josephus admirably proves, *against Apion*, and also Philo the Jew, in different places, where they point out that it is so ancient that the very name of *law* was only known by the oldest nation more than a thousand years afterwards; so that Homer, who has written the history of so many states, has never used the term. And it is easy to judge of its perfection by simply reading it; for we see that it has provided for all things with so great wisdom, equity, and judgment, that the most ancient legislators, Greek and Roman, having had some knowledge of it, have borrowed from it their principal laws; this is evident from what are called the Twelve Tables, and from the other proofs which Josephus gives.

But this law is at the same time the severest and strictest of all in respect to their religious worship, imposing on this people, in order to keep them to their duty, a thousand peculiar and painful observances, on pain of death. Whence it is very astonishing that it has been constantly preserved during many centuries by a people, rebellious and impatient as this one was; while all other states have changed their laws from time to time, although these were far more lenient.

The book which contains this law, the first of all, is itself the most ancient book in the world, those of Homer, Hesiod, and others, being six or seven hundred years later.

620

The creation and the deluge being past, and God no longer requiring to destroy the world, nor to create it anew, nor to give such great signs of Himself, He began to establish a people on the earth, purposely formed, who were to last until the coming of the people whom the Messiah should fashion by His spirit.

621

The creation of the world beginning to be distant, God provided a single contemporary historian, and appointed a whole people as guardians of this book, in order that this history might be the most authentic in the world, and that all men might thereby learn a fact so necessary to know, and which could only be known through that means.

622

[Japhet begins the genealogy.]
Joseph folds his arms, and prefers the younger.

623

Why should Moses make the lives of men so long, and their generations so few?

Because it is not the length of years, but the multitude of generations, which renders things obscure. For truth is perverted only by the change of men. And yet he puts two things, the most memorable that were ever imagined, namely, the creation and the deluge, so near that we reach from one to the other.

624

Shem, who saw Lamech, who saw Adam, saw also Jacob, who saw those who saw Moses; therefore the deluge and the creation are true. This is conclusive among certain people who understand it rightly.

625

The longevity of the patriarchs, instead of causing the loss of past history, conduced, on the contrary, to its preservation. For the reason why we are sometimes insufficiently instructed in the history of our ancestors, is that we have never lived long with them, and that they are often dead before we have attained the age of reason. Now, when men lived so long, children lived long with their parents. They conversed long with them. But what else could be the subject of their talk save the history of their ancestors, since to that all history was reduced, and men did not study science or art, which now form a large part of daily conversation? We see also that in these days tribes took particular care to preserve their genealogies.

626

I believe that Joshua was the first of God's people to have this name, as Jesus Christ was the last of God's people.

627

Antiquity of the Jews.—What a difference there is between one book and another! I am not astonished that the Greeks made the Iliad, nor the Egyptians and the Chinese their histories.

We have only to see how this originates. These fabulous historians are not contemporaneous with the facts about which they write. Homer composes a romance, which he gives out as such, and which is received as such; for nobody doubted that Troy and Agamemnon no more existed than did the golden apple. Accordingly he did not think of making a history, but solely a book to amuse; he is the only writer of his time; the beauty of the work has made it last, every one learns it and talks of it, it is necessary to know it, and each one knows it by heart. Four hundred years afterwards the witnesses of these facts are no longer alive, no one knows of his own knowledge if it be a fable or a history; one has only learnt it from his ancestors, and this can pass for truth.

Every history which is not contemporaneous, as the books of the Sibyls and Trismegistus, and so many others which have been believed by the world, are false, and found to be false in the course of time. It is not so with contemporaneous writers.

There is a great difference between a book which an individual writes, and publishes to a nation, and a book which itself creates a nation. We cannot doubt that the book is as old as the people.

628

Josephus hides the shame of his nation.
Moses does not hide his own shame.
Quis mihi det ut omnes prophetent?
He was weary of the multitude.

629

The sincerity of the Jews.—Maccabees, after they had no more prophets; the Masorah, since Jesus Christ.
This book will be a testimony for you.
Defective and final letters.
Sincere against their honour, and dying for it; this has no example in the world, and no root in nature.

630

Sincerity of the Jews.—They preserve lovingly and carefully the book in which Moses declares that they have been all their life ungrateful to God, and that he knows they will be still more so after his death; but that he calls heaven and earth to witness against them, and that he has [*taught*] them enough.

He declares that God, being angry with them, shall at last scatter them among all the nations of the earth; that as they have offended Him by worshipping gods who were not their God, so He will provoke them by calling a people who are not His people; that He desires that all His words be preserved for ever, and that His book be placed in the Ark of the Covenant to serve for ever as a witness against them.

Isaiah says the same thing, xxx.

631

On Esdras.—The story that the books were burnt with the temple proved false by Maccabees: "Jeremiah gave them the law."

The story that he recited the whole by heart. Josephus and Esdras point out *that he read the book*. Baronius, *Ann.*, p. 180: *Nullus penitus Hebræorum antiquorum reperitur qui tradiderit libros periisse et per Esdram esse restitutos, nisi in IV Esdræ.*

The story that he changed the letters.

Philo, *in Vita Moysis: Illa lingua ac character quo antiquitus scripta est lex sic permansit usque ad LXX.*

Josephus says that the Law was in Hebrew when it was translated by the Seventy.

Under Antiochus and Vespasian, when they wanted to abolish the books, and when there was no prophet, they could not do so. And under the Babylonians, when no persecution had been made, and when there were so many prophets, would they have let them be burnt?

Josephus laughs at the Greeks who would not hear . . .

Tertullian.—*Perinde potuit abolefactam eam violentia ca-taclysmi in spiritu rursus reformare, quemadmodum et Hiero-solymis Babylonia expugnatione deletis, omne instrumentum Judaicæ literaturæ per Esdram constat restauratum.*

He says that Noah could as easily have restored in spirit the book of Enoch, destroyed by the Deluge, as Esdras could have restored the Scriptures lost during the Captivity.

(Θεὸς) ἐν τῇ ἐπὶ Ναβουχοδόνοσορ αἰχμαλωσίᾳ τοῦ λαοῦ, διαφθαρεισῶν τῶν Γραφῶν . . . ἐνέπνευσε Ἐσδρᾷ τῷ ἱερεῖ, ἐκ τῆς φυλῆς Λευὶ τοὺς τῶν προγεγονότων προφητῶν πάντας ἀνατάξασθαι λόγους, καὶ ἀποκαταστῆσαι τῷ λαῷ τὴν διὰ Μωυσέως νομοθεσίαν. He alleges this to prove that it is not incredible that the Seventy may have explained the Holy Scriptures with that uniformity which we admire in them. And he took that from Saint Irenæus.

Saint Hilary, in his preface to the Psalms, says that Esdras arranged the Psalms in order.

The origin of this tradition comes from the 14th chapter of the fourth book of Esdras. *Deus glorificatus est, et Scripturæ vere divinæ creditæ sunt, omnibus eandem et eisdem verbis et eisdem nominibus recitantibus ab initio usque ad finem, uti et præsentes gentes cognoscerent quoniam per inspirationem Dei interpretatæ sunt Scripturæ, et non esset mirabile Deum hoc in eis operatum: quando in ea captivitate populi quæ facta est a Nabuchodonosor, corruptis scripturis et post 70 annos Judæis descendentibus in regionem suam, et post deinde temporibus Artaxerxis Persarum regis, inspiravit Es-dræ sacerdoti tribus Levi præteritorum prophetarum omnes rememorare sermones, et restituere populo eam legem quæ data est per Moysen.*

632

Against the story in Esdras, 2 *Maccab.* ii;—Josephus, *Antiquities,* II, i—Cyrus took occasion from the prophecy of Isaiah to release the people. The Jews held their property in peace under Cyrus in Babylon; hence they could well have the Law.

Josephus, in the whole history of Esdras, does not say one word about this restoration.—2 Kings xvii, 27.

633

If the story in Esdras is credible, then it must be believed that the Scripture is Holy Scripture; for this story is based only on the authority of those who assert that of the Seventy, which shows that the Scripture is holy.

Therefore if this account be true, we have what we want therein; if not, we have it elsewhere. And thus those who would ruin the truth of our religion, founded on Moses, establish it by the same authority by which they attack it. So by this providence it still exists.

634

Chronology of Rabbinism. (The citations of pages are from the book *Pugio.*)

Page 27. R. Hakadosch (*anno* 200), author of the *Mischna,* or vocal law, or second law.

Commentaries on the *Mischna* (*anno* 340):
- The one *Siphra.*
- *Barajetot.*
- *Talmud Hierosol.*
- *Tosiphtot.*

Bereschit Rabah, by R. Osaiah Rabah, commentary on the *Mischna.*

Bereschit Rabah, Bar Naconi, are subtle and pleasant discourses, historical and theological. This same author wrote the books called *Rabot.*

A hundred years after the *Talmud Hierosol* was composed the *Babylonian Talmud,* by R. Ase, A.D. 440, by the universal consent of all the Jews, who are necessarily obliged to observe all that is contained therein.

The addition of R. Ase is called the *Gemara,* that is to say, the "commentary" on the *Mischna.*

And the Talmud includes together the *Mischna* and the *Gemara.*

635

If does not indicate indifference: Malachi, Isaiah.
Is., *Si volumus*, etc.
In quacumque die.

636

Prophecies.—The sceptre was not interrupted by the captivity in Babylon, because the return was promised and foretold.

637

Proofs of Jesus Christ.—Captivity, with the assurance of deliverance within seventy years, was not real captivity. But now they are captives without any hope.

God has promised them that even though He should scatter them to the ends of the earth, nevertheless if they were faithful to His law, He would assemble them together again. They are very faithful to it, and remain oppressed.

638

When Nebuchadnezzar carried away the people, for fear they should believe that the sceptre had departed from Judah, they were told beforehand that they would be there for a short time, and that they would be restored. They were always consoled by the prophets; and their kings continued. But the second destruction is without promise of restoration, without prophets, without kings, without consolation, without hope, because the sceptre is taken away for ever.

639

It is a wonderful thing, and worthy of particular attention, to see this Jewish people existing so many years in perpetual misery, it being necessary as a proof of Jesus Christ, both that they should exist to prove Him, and that they should be miserable because they crucified Him; and though to be miserable and to exist are contradictory, they nevertheless still exist in spite of their misery.

640

They are visibly a people expressly created to serve as a witness to the Messiah (Isaiah, xliii, 9; xliv, 8). They keep the books, and love them, and do not understand them. And all this was foretold; that God's judgments are entrusted to them, but as a sealed book.

SECTION X

TYPOLOGY

641

Proof of the two Testaments at once.—To prove the two at one stroke, we need only see if the prophecies in one are fulfilled in the other. To examine the prophecies, we must understand them. For if we believe they have only one meaning, it is certain that the Messiah has not come; but if they have two meanings, it is certain that He has come in Jesus Christ.

The whole problem then is to know if they have two meanings.

That the Scripture has two meanings, which Jesus Christ and the Apostles have given, is shown by the following proofs:

1. Proof by Scripture itself.

2. Proof by the Rabbis. Moses Maimonides says that it has two aspects, and that the prophets have prophesied Jesus Christ only.

3. Proof by the Kabbala.

4. Proof by the mystical interpretation which the Rabbis themselves give to Scripture.

5. Proof by the principles of the Rabbis, that there are two meanings; that there are two advents of the Messiah, a glorious and an humiliating one, according to their desert; that the prophets have prophesied of the Messiah only—the Law is not eternal, but must change at the coming of the Messiah—that then they shall no more remember the Red Sea; that the Jews and the Gentiles shall be mingled.

[6. Proof by the key which Jesus Christ and the Apostles give us.]

215

642

Isaiah, li. The Red Sea an image of the Redemption. *Ut sciatis quod filius hominis habet potestatem remittendi peccata, tibi dico: Surge.* God, wishing to show that He could form a people holy with an invisible holiness, and fill them with an eternal glory, made visible things. As nature is an image of grace, He has done in the bounties of nature what He would do in those of grace, in order that we might judge that He could make the invisible, since He made the visible excellently.

Therefore He saved this people from the deluge; He has raised them up from Abraham, redeemed them from their enemies, and set them at rest.

The object of God was not to save them from the deluge, and raise up a whole people from Abraham, only in order to bring them into a rich land.

And even grace is only the type of glory, for it is not the ultimate end. It has been symbolised by the law, and itself symbolises [*glory*]. But it is the type of it, and the origin or cause.

The ordinary life of men is like that of the saints. They all seek their satisfaction, and differ only in the object in which they place it; they call those their enemies who hinder them, etc. God has then shown the power which He has of giving invisible blessings, by that which He has shown Himself to have over things visible.

643

Types.—God, wishing to form for Himself an holy people, whom He should separate from all other nations, whom He should deliver from their enemies, and should put into a place of rest, has promised to do so, and has foretold by His prophets the time and the manner of His coming. And yet, to confirm the hope of His elect, He has made them see in it an image through all time, without leaving them devoid of assurances of His power and of His will to save them. For, at the creation of man, Adam was the witness, and guardian of the promise of a Saviour, who should be born of woman, when men were still so near the creation that they could not have forgotten their creation and their fall. When those who had seen Adam were no longer in the world, God sent Noah whom He saved, and drowned the whole earth by a miracle which sufficiently indicated the power which He had to save the world, and the will which He had to do so, and to raise up from the seed of woman Him whom He had promised. This miracle was enough to confirm the hope of men.

The memory of the deluge being so fresh among men, while Noah was still alive, God made promises to Abraham, and, while Shem was still living, sent Moses, etc. . . .

644

Types.—God, willing to deprive His own of perishable blessings, created the Jewish people in order to show that this was not owing to lack of power.

645

The Synagogue did not perish, because it was a type. But because it was only a type, it fell into servitude. The type existed till the truth came, in order that the Church should be always visible, either in the sign which promised it, or in substance.

646

That the law was figurative.

647

Two errors: 1. To take everything literally. 2. To take everything spiritually.

648

To speak against too greatly figurative language.

649

There are some types clear and demonstrative, but others which seem somewhat far-fetched, and which convince only

those who are already persuaded. These are like the Apocalyptics. But the difference is that they have none which are
certain, so that nothing is so unjust as to claim that theirs are
as well founded as some of ours; for they have none so demonstrative as some of ours. The comparison is unfair. We must
not put on the same level, and confound things, because they
seem to agree in one point, while they are so different in another. The clearness in divine things requires us to revere the
obscurities in them.

[It is like men, who employ a certain obscure language
among themselves. Those who should not understand it,
would understand only a foolish meaning.]

650

*Extravagances of the Apocalyptics, Preadamites, Millena-
rians, etc.*—He who would base extravagant opinions on
Scripture, will, for example, base them on this. It is said that
"this generation shall not pass till all these things be fulfilled."
Upon that I will say that after that generation will come
another generation, and so on ever in succession.

Solomon and the King are spoken of in the second book of
Chronicles, as if they were two different persons. I will say
that they were two.

651

Particular Types.—A double law, double tables of the law,
a double temple, a double captivity.

652

Types.—The prophets prophesied by symbols of a girdle,
a beard and burnt hair, etc.

653

Difference between dinner and supper.

In God the word does not differ from the intention, for He is
true; nor the word from the effect, for He is powerful; nor the
means from the effect, for He is wise. Bern., *Ult. Sermo in
Missam.*

Augustine, *De Civit. Dei*, v, 10. This rule is general. God can do everything, except those things, which if He could do, He would not be almighty, as dying, being deceived, lying, etc.

Several Evangelists for the confirmation of the truth; their difference useful.

The Eucharist after Lord's Supper. Truth after the type.

The ruin of Jerusalem, a type of the ruin of the world, forty years after the death of Jesus. "I know not," as a man, or as an ambassador (Mark xiii, 32). (Matthew xxiv, 36.)

Jesus condemned by the Jews and the Gentiles.

The Jews and the Gentiles typified by the two sons. Aug., *De Civ.* xx, 29.

654

The six ages, the six Fathers of the six ages, the six wonders at the beginning of the six ages, the six mornings at the beginning of the six ages.

655

Adam *forma futuri*. The six days to form the one, the six ages to form the other. The six days, which Moses represents for the formation of Adam, are only the picture of the six ages to form Jesus Christ and the Church. If Adam had not sinned, and Jesus Christ had not come, there had been only one covenant, only one age of men, and the creation would have been represented as accomplished at one single time.

656

Types.—The Jewish and Egyptian peoples were plainly foretold by the two individuals whom Moses met; the Egyptian beating the Jew, Moses avenging him and killing the Egyptian, and the Jew being ungrateful.

657

The symbols of the Gospel for the state of the sick soul are sick bodies; but because one body cannot be sick enough to express it well, several have been needed. Thus there are the deaf, the dumb, the blind, the paralytic, the dead Lazarus, the possessed. All this crowd is in the sick soul.

658

Types.—To show that the Old Testament is only figurative, and that the prophets understood by temporal blessings other blessings, this is the proof:

First, that this would be unworthy of God.

Secondly, that their discourses express very clearly the promise of temporal blessings, and that they say nevertheless that their discourses are obscure, and that their meaning will not be understood. Whence it appears that this secret meaning was not that which they openly expressed, and that consequently they meant to speak of other sacrifices, of another deliverer, etc. They say that they will be understood only in the fullness of time (Jer. xxx, *ult.*).

The third proof is that their discourses are contradictory, and neutralise each other; so that if we think that they did not mean by the words "law" and "sacrifice" anything else than that of Moses, there is a plain and gross contradiction. Therefore they meant something else, sometimes contradicting themselves in the same chapter. Now, to understand the meaning of an author . . .

659

Lust has become natural to us, and has made our second nature. Thus there are two natures in us—the one good, the other bad. Where is God? Where you are not, and the kingdom of God is within you. The Rabbis.

660

Penitence, alone of all these mysteries, has been manifestly declared to the Jews, and by Saint John, the Forerunner; and then the other mysteries; to indicate that in each man, as in the entire world, this order must be observed.

661

The carnal Jews understood neither the greatness nor the humiliation of the Messiah foretold in their prophecies. They misunderstood Him in His foretold greatness, as when He said that the Messiah should be lord of David, though his son, and that He was before Abraham, who had seen Him. They did not believe Him so great as to be eternal, and they likewise misunderstood Him in His humiliation and in His death. "The Messiah," said they, "abideth for ever, and this man says that he shall die." Therefore they believed Him neither mortal nor eternal; they only sought in Him for a carnal greatness.

662

Typical.—Nothing is so like charity as covetousness, and nothing is so opposed to it. Thus the Jews, full of possessions which flattered their covetousness, were very like Christians, and very contrary. And by this means they had the two qualities which it was necessary they should have, to be very like the Messiah to typify Him, and very contrary not to be suspected witnesses.

663

Typical.—God made use of the lust of the Jews to make them minister to Jesus Christ, [who brought the remedy for their lust].

664

Charity is not a figurative precept. It is dreadful to say that Jesus Christ, who came to take away types in order to establish the truth, came only to establish the type of charity, in order to take away the existing reality which was there before.

"If the light be darkness, how great is that darkness!"

665

Fascination. *Somnum suum. Figura hujus mundi.*
The Eucharist. *Comedes panem tuum. Panem nostrum.*

Inimici Dei terram lingent. Sinners lick the dust, that is to say, love earthly pleasures.

The Old Testament contains the types of future joy, and the New contains the means of arriving at it. The types were of joy; the means of penitence; and nevertheless the Paschal Lamb was eaten with bitter herbs, *cum amaritudinibus.*

Singularis sum ego donec transeam.—Jesus Christ before His death was almost the only martyr.

666

Typical.—The expressions, sword, shield. *Potentissime.*

667

We are estranged, only by departing from charity. Our prayers and our virtues are abominable before God, if they are not the prayers and the virtues of Jesus Christ. And our sins will never be the object of [*mercy*], but of the justice of God, if they are not [*those of*] Jesus Christ. He has adopted our sins, and has [*admitted*] us into union [*with Him*], for virtues are [*His own, and*] sins are foreign to Him; while virtues [*are*] foreign to us, and our sins are our own.

Let us change the rule which we have hitherto chosen for judging what is good. We had our own will as our rule. Let us now take the will of [*God*]; all that He wills is good and right to us, all that He does not will is [*bad*].

All that God does not permit is forbidden. Sins are forbidden by the general declaration that God has made, that He did not allow them. Other things which He has left without general prohibition, and which for that reason are said to be permitted, are nevertheless not always permitted. For when God removed some one of them from us, and when, by the event, which is a manifestation of the will of God, it appears that God does not will that we should have a thing, that is then forbidden to us as sin; since the will of God is that we should not have one more than another. There is this sole difference between these two things, that it is certain that God will never allow sin, while it is not certain that He will never allow the other. But so long as God does not permit it, we ought to regard it as sin; so long as the absence of God's will, which alone is all goodness and all justice, renders it unjust and wrong.

668

To change the type, because of our weakness.

669

Types.—The Jews had grown old in these earthly thoughts, that God loved their father Abraham, his flesh and what sprung from it; that on account of this He had multiplied them, and distinguished them from all other nations, without allowing them to intermingle; that when they were languishing in Egypt, He brought them out with all these great signs in their favour; that He fed them with manna in the desert, and led them into a very rich land; that He gave them kings and a well-built temple, in order to offer up beasts before Him, by the shedding of whose blood they should be purified; and that at last He was to send them the Messiah to make them masters of all the world, and foretold the time of His coming.

The world having grown old in these carnal errors, Jesus Christ came at the time foretold, but not with the expected glory; and thus men did not think it was He. After His death, Saint Paul came to teach men that all these things had happened in allegory; that the kingdom of God did not consist in the flesh, but in the spirit; that the enemies of men were not the Babylonians, but the passions; that God delighted not in temples made with hands, but in a pure and contrite heart; that the circumcision of the body was unprofitable, but that of the heart was needed; that Moses had not given them the bread from heaven, etc.

But God, not having desired to reveal these things to this people who were unworthy of them, and having nevertheless desired to foretell them, in order that they might be believed, foretold the time clearly, and expressed the things sometimes clearly, but very often in figures, in order that those who loved symbols might consider them, and those who loved what was symbolised might see it therein.

All that tends not to charity is figurative.

The sole aim of the Scripture is charity.

All which tends not to the sole end is the type of it. For since there is only one end, all which does not lead to it in express terms is figurative.

God thus varies that sole precept of charity to satisfy our curiosity, which seeks for variety, by that variety which still leads us to the one thing needful. For one thing alone is needful, and we love variety; and God satisfies both by these varieties, which lead to the one thing needful.

The Jews have so much loved the shadows, and have so strictly expected them, that they have misunderstood the reality, when it came in the time and manner foretold.

The Rabbis take the breasts of the Spouse for types, and all that does not express the only end they have, namely, temporal good.

And Christians take even the Eucharist as a type of the glory at which they aim.

670

The Jews, who have been called to subdue nations and kings, have been the slaves of sin; and the Christians, whose calling has been to be servants and subjects, are free children.

671

A formal point.—When Saint Peter and the Apostles deliberated about abolishing circumcision, where it was a question of acting against the law of God, they did not heed the prophets, but simply the reception of the Holy Spirit in the persons uncircumcised.

They thought it more certain that God approved of those whom He filled with His Spirit, than it was that the law must be obeyed. They knew that the end of the law was only the Holy Spirit; and that thus, as men certainly had this without circumcision, it was not necessary.

672

Fac secundum exemplar quod tibi ostensum est in monte.—
The Jewish religion then has been formed on its likeness to
the truth of the Messiah; and the truth of the Messiah has
been recognised by the Jewish religion, which was the type of
it.

Among the Jews the truth was only typified; in heaven it
is revealed.

In the Church it is hidden, and recognised by its resemblance to the type.

The type has been made according to the truth, and the
truth has been recognised according to the type.

Saint Paul says himself that people will forbid to marry,
and he himself speaks of it to the Corinthians in a way which
is a snare. For if a prophet had said the one, and Saint Paul
had then said the other, he would have been accused.

673

Typical.—"Do all things according to the pattern which
has been shown thee on the mount." On which Saint Paul
says that the Jews have shadowed forth heavenly things.

674

. . . And yet this Covenant, made to blind some and enlighten others, indicated in those very persons, whom it
blinded, the truth which should be recognised by others. For
the visible blessings which they received from God were so
great and so divine, that He indeed appeared able to give
them those that are invisible, and a Messiah.

For nature is an image of Grace, and visible miracles are
images of the invisible. *Ut sciatis . . . tibi dico: Surge.*

Isaiah says that Redemption will be as the passage of the
Red Sea.

God has then shown by the deliverance from Egypt, and
from the sea, by the defeat of kings, by the manna, by the
whole genealogy of Abraham, that He was able to save, to

send down bread from heaven, etc.; so that the people hostile to Him are the type and the representation of the very Messiah whom they know not, etc.

He has then taught us at last that all these things were only types, and what is "true freedom," a "true Israelite," "true circumcision," "true bread from heaven," etc.

In these promises each one finds what he has most at heart, temporal benefits or spiritual, God or the creatures; but with this difference, that those who therein seek the creatures find them, but with many contradictions, with a prohibition against loving them, with the command to worship God only, and to love Him only, which is the same thing, and, finally, that the Messiah came not for them; whereas those who therein seek God find Him, without any contradiction, with the command to love Him only, and that the Messiah came in the time foretold, to give them the blessings which they ask.

Thus the Jews had miracles and prophecies, which they saw fulfilled, and the teaching of their law was to worship and love God only; it was also perpetual. Thus it had all the marks of the true religion; and so it was. But the Jewish teaching must be distinguished from the teaching of the Jewish law. Now the Jewish teaching was not true, although it had miracles and prophecy and perpetuity, because it had not this other point of worshipping and loving God only.

675

The veil, which is upon these books for the Jews, is there also for evil Christians, and for all who do not hate themselves.

But how well disposed men are to understand them and to know Jesus Christ, when they truly hate themselves!

676

A type conveys absence and presence, pleasure and pain.

A cipher has a double meaning, one clear, and one in which it is said that the meaning is hidden.

677

Types.—A portrait conveys absence and presence, pleasure and pain. The reality excludes absence and pain.

To know if the law and the sacrifices are a reality or a type, we must see if the prophets, in speaking of these things, confined their view and their thought to them, so that they saw only the old covenant; or if they saw therein something else of which they were the representation, for in a portrait we see the thing figured. For this we need only examine what they say of them.

When they say that it will be eternal, do they mean to speak of that covenant which they say will be changed; and so of the sacrifices, etc.?

A cipher has two meanings. When we find out an important letter in which we discover a clear meaning, and in which it is nevertheless said that the meaning is veiled and obscure, that it is hidden, so that we might read the letter without seeing it, and interpret it without understanding it, what must we think but that here is a cipher with a double meaning, and the more so if we find obvious contradictions in the literal meaning? The prophets have clearly said that Israel would be always loved by God, and that the law would be eternal; and they have said that their meaning would not be understood, and that it was veiled.

How greatly then ought we to value those who interpret the cipher, and teach us to understand the hidden meaning, especially if the principles which they educe are perfectly clear and natural! This is what Jesus Christ did, and the Apostles. They broke the seal; He rent the veil, and revealed the spirit. They have taught us through this that the enemies of man are his passions; that the Redeemer would be spiritual, and His reign spiritual; that there would be two advents, one in lowliness to humble the proud, the other in glory to exalt the humble; that Jesus Christ would be both God and man.

678

Types.—Jesus Christ opened their mind to understand the Scriptures.

Two great revelations are these. (1) All things happened to them in types: *vere Israëlitæ, vere liberi,* true bread from Heaven. (2) A God humbled to the Cross. It was necessary that Christ should suffer in order to enter into glory, "that He should destroy death through death." Two advents.

679

Types.—When once this secret is disclosed, it is impossible not to see it. Let us read the Old Testament in this light, and let us see if the sacrifices were real; if the fatherhood of Abraham was the true cause of the friendship of God; and if the promised land was the true place of rest. No. They are therefore types. Let us in the same way examine all those ordained ceremonies, all those commandments which are not of charity, and we shall see that they are types.

All these sacrifices and ceremonies were then either types or nonsense. Now these are things too clear, and too lofty, to be thought nonsense.

To know if the prophets confined their view in the Old Testament, or saw therein other things.

680

Typical.—The key of the cipher. *Veri adoratores.*—*Ecce agnus Dei qui tollit peccata mundi.*

681

Is. i, 21. Change of good into evil, and the vengeance of God. Is. x, 1; xxvi, 20; xxviii, 1. Miracles: Is. xxxiii, 9; xl, 17; xli, 26; xliii, 13.

Jer. xi, 21; xv, 12; xvii, 9. *Pravum est cor omnium et incrustabile; quis cognoscet illud?* that is to say, Who can know all its evil? For it is already known to be wicked. *Ego dominus,* etc.—vii, 14, *Faciam domui huic,* etc. Trust in external sacrifices—vii, 22, *Quia non sum locutus,* etc. Outward sacrifice is not the essential point—xi, 13, *Secundum nume-rum,* etc. A multitude of doctrines.

Is. xliv, 20–24; liv, 8; lxiii, 12–17; lxvi, 17. Jer. ii, 35; iv, 22–24; v, 4, 29–31; vi, 16; xxiii, 15–17.

682

Types.—The letter kills. All happened in types. Here is the cipher which Saint Paul gives us. Christ must suffer. An humiliated God. Circumcision of the heart, true fasting, true sacrifice, a true temple. The prophets have shown that all these must be spiritual.

Not the meat which perishes, but that which does not perish.

"Ye shall be free indeed." Then the other freedom was only a type of freedom.

"I am the true bread from Heaven."

683

Contradiction.—We can only describe a good character by reconciling all contrary qualities, and it is not enough to keep up a series of harmonious qualities, without reconciling contradictory ones. To understand the meaning of an author, we must make all the contrary passages agree.

Thus, to understand Scripture, we must have a meaning in which all the contrary passages are reconciled. It is not enough to have one which suits many concurring passages; but it is necessary to have one which reconciles even contradictory passages.

Every author has a meaning in which all the contradictory passages agree, or he has no meaning at all. We cannot affirm the latter of Scripture and the prophets; they undoubtedly are full of good sense. We must then seek for a meaning which reconciles all discrepancies.

The true meaning then is not that of the Jews; but in Jesus Christ all the contradictions are reconciled.

The Jews could not reconcile the cessation of the royalty

and principality, foretold by Hosea, with the prophecy of Jacob.

If we take the law, the sacrifices, and the kingdom as realities, we cannot reconcile all the passages. They must then necessarily be only types. We cannot even reconcile the passages of the same author, nor of the same book, nor sometimes of the same chapter, which indicates copiously what was the meaning of the author. As when Ezekiel, chap. xx, says that man will not live by the commandments of God and will live by them.

684

Types.—If the law and the sacrifices are the truth, it must please God, and must not displease Him. If they are types, they must be both pleasing and displeasing.

Now in all the Scripture they are both pleasing and displeasing. It is said that the law shall be changed; that the sacrifice shall be changed; that they shall be without law, without a prince, and without a sacrifice; that a new covenant shall be made; that the law shall be renewed; that the precepts which they have received are not good; that their sacrifices are abominable; that God has demanded none of them.

It is said, on the contrary, that the law shall abide for ever; that this covenant shall be for ever; that sacrifice shall be eternal; that the sceptre shall never depart from among them, because it shall not depart from them till the eternal King comes.

Do all these passages indicate what is real? No. Do they then indicate what is typical? No, but what is either real or typical. But the first passages, excluding as they do reality, indicate that all this is only typical.

All these passages together cannot be applied to reality; all can be said to be typical; therefore they are not spoken of reality, but of the type.

Agnus occisus est ab origine mundi. A sacrificing judge.

685

Contradictions.—The sceptre till the Messiah—without king or prince.

The eternal law—changed.

The eternal covenant—a new covenant.

Good laws—bad precepts. Ezekiel.

686

Types.—When the word of God, which is really true, is false literally, it is true spiritually. *Sede a dextris meis:* this is false literally, therefore it is true spiritually.

In these expressions, God is spoken of after the manner of men; and this means nothing else but that the intention which men have in giving a seat at their right hand, God will have also. It is then an indication of the intention of God, not of His manner of carrying it out.

Thus when it is said, "God has received the odour of your incense, and will in recompense give you a rich land," that is equivalent to saying that the same intention which a man would have, who, pleased with your perfumes, should in recompense give you a rich land, God will have towards you, because you have had the same intention as a man has towards him to whom he presents perfumes. So *iratus est,* a "jealous God," etc. For, the things of God being inexpressible, they cannot be spoken of otherwise, and the Church makes use of them even to-day: *Quia confortavit seras,* etc.

It is not allowable to attribute to Scripture the meaning which is not revealed to us that it has. Thus, to say that the closed *mem* of Isaiah signifies six hundred, has not been revealed. It might be said that the final *tsade* and *he deficientes* may signify mysteries. But it is not allowable to say so, and still less to say this is the way of the philosopher's stone. But we say that the literal meaning is not the true meaning, because the prophets have themselves said so.

687

I do not say that the *mem* is mystical.

688

Moses (Deut. xxx) promises that God will circumcise their heart to render them capable of loving Him.

689

One saying of David, or of Moses, as for instance that "God will circumcise the heart," enables us to judge of their spirit. If all their other expressions were ambiguous, and left us in doubt whether they were philosophers or Christians, one saying of this kind would in fact determine all the rest, as one sentence of Epictetus decides the meaning of all the rest to be the opposite. So far ambiguity exists, but not afterwards.

690

If one of two persons, who are telling silly stories, uses language with a double meaning, understood in his own circle, while the other uses it with only one meaning, any one not in the secret, who hears them both talk in this manner, will pass upon them the same judgment. But if afterwards, in the rest of their conversation one says angelic things, and the other always dull commonplaces, he will judge that the one spoke in mysteries, and not the other; the one having sufficiently shown that he is incapable of such foolishness, and capable of being mysterious; and the other that he is incapable of mystery, and capable of foolishness.

The Old Testament is a cipher.

691

There are some that see clearly that man has no other enemy than lust, which turns him from God, and not God; and that he has no other good than God, and not a rich land. Let those who believe that the good of man is in the flesh, and evil in what turns him away from sensual pleasures, [*satiate*] themselves with them, and [*die*] in them. But let those who seek God with all their heart, who are only troubled at not

seeing Him, who desire only to possess Him, and have as
enemies only those who turn them away from Him, who are
grieved at seeing themselves surrounded and overwhelmed
with such enemies, take comfort. I proclaim to them happy
news. There exists a Redeemer for them. I shall show Him to
them. I shall show that there is a God for them. I shall not
show Him to others. I shall make them see that a Messiah has
been promised, who should deliver them from their enemies,
and that One has come to free them from their iniquities, but
not from their enemies.

When David foretold that the Messiah would deliver His
people from their enemies, one can believe that in the flesh
these would be the Egyptians; and then I cannot show that
the prophecy was fulfilled. But one can well believe also that
the enemies would be their sins; for indeed the Egyptians
were not their enemies, but their sins were so. This word,
enemies, is therefore ambiguous. But if he says elsewhere, as
he does, that He will deliver His people from their sins, as
indeed do Isaiah and others, the ambiguity is removed, and
the double meaning of enemies is reduced to the simple
meaning of iniquities. For if he had sins in his mind, he could
well denote them as enemies; but if he thought of enemies,
he could not designate them as iniquities.

Now Moses, David, and Isaiah used the same terms. Who
will say then that they have not the same meaning, and that
David's meaning, which is plainly iniquities when he spoke of
enemies, was not the same as [that of] Moses when speaking
of enemies?

Daniel (ix) prays for the deliverance of the people from
the captivity of their enemies. But he was thinking of sins,
and, to show this, he says that Gabriel came to tell him that
his prayer was heard, and that there were only seventy weeks
to wait, after which the people would be freed from iniquity,
sin would have an end, and the Redeemer, the Holy of Holies,
would bring *eternal* justice, not legal, but eternal.

THE PROPHECIES

692

When I see the blindness and the wretchedness of man, when I regard the whole silent universe, and man without light, left to himself, and, as it were, lost in this corner of the universe, without knowing who has put him there, what he has come to do, what will become of him at death, and incapable of all knowledge, I become terrified, like a man who should be carried in his sleep to a dreadful desert island, and should awake without knowing where he is, and without means of escape. And thereupon I wonder how people in a condition so wretched do not fall into despair. I see other persons around me of a like nature. I ask them if they are better informed than I am. They tell me that they are not. And thereupon these wretched and lost beings, having looked around them, and seen some pleasing objects, have given and attached themselves to them. For my own part, I have not been able to attach myself to them, and, considering how strongly it appears that there is something else than what I see, I have examined whether this God has not left some sign of Himself.

I see many contradictory religions, and consequently all false save one. Each wants to be believed on its own authority, and threatens unbelievers. I do not therefore believe them. Every one can say this; every one can call himself a prophet. But I see that Christian religion wherein prophecies are fulfilled; and that is what every one cannot do.

693

And what crowns all this is prediction, so that it should not be said that it is chance which has done it.

Whosoever, having only a week to live, will not find out that it is expedient to believe that all this is not a stroke of chance . . .

Now, if the passions had no hold on us, a week and a hundred years would amount to the same thing.

694

Prophecies.—Great Pan is dead.

695

Susceperunt verbum cum omni aviditate, scrutantes Scripturas, si ita se haberent.

696

Prodita lege.—Impleta cerne.—Implenda collige.

697

We understand the prophecies only when we see the events happen. Thus the proofs of retreat, discretion, silence, etc. are proofs only to those who know and believe them.

Joseph so internal in a law so external.

Outward penances dispose to inward, as humiliations to humility. Thus the . . .

698

The synagogue has preceded the church; the Jews, the Christians. The prophets have foretold the Christians; Saint John, Jesus Christ.

699

It is glorious to see with the eyes of faith the history of Herod and of Cæsar.

700

The zeal of the Jews for their law and their temple (Josephus, and Philo the Jew, *Ad Caïum*). What other people had such a zeal? It was necessary they should have it.

Jesus Christ foretold as to the time and the state of the world. The ruler taken from the thigh, and the fourth monarchy. How lucky we are to see this light amidst this darkness!

How fine it is to see, with the eyes of faith, Darius and Cyrus, Alexander, the Romans, Pompey and Herod working, without knowing it, for the glory of the Gospel!

701

Zeal of the Jewish people for the law, especially after there were no more prophets.

702

While the prophets were for maintaining the law, the people were indifferent. But since there have been no more prophets, zeal has succeeded them.

703

The devil troubled the zeal of the Jews before Jesus Christ, because he would have been their salvation, but not since.

The Jewish people scorned by the Gentiles; the Christian people persecuted.

704

Proof.—Prophecies with their fulfilment; what has preceded and what has followed Jesus Christ.

705

The prophecies are the strongest proof of Jesus Christ. It is for them also that God has made most provision; for the event which has fulfilled them is a miracle existing since the birth of the Church to the end. So God has raised up prophets during sixteen hundred years, and, during four hundred years afterwards, He has scattered all these prophecies among all the Jews, who carried them into all parts of the world. Such was the preparation for the birth of Jesus Christ, and, as His Gospel was to be believed by all the world, it was not only necessary that there should be prophecies to make it believed, but that these prophecies should exist throughout the whole world, in order to make it embraced by the whole world.

706

But it was not enough that the prophecies should exist. It was necessary that they should be distributed throughout all places, and preserved throughout all times. And in order that this agreement might not be taken for an effect of chance, it was necessary that this should be foretold.

It is far more glorious for the Messiah that the Jews should be the spectators, and even the instruments of His glory, besides that God had reserved them.

707

Prophecies.—The time foretold by the state of the Jewish people, by the state of the heathen, by the state of the temple, by the number of years.

708

One must be bold to predict the same thing in so many ways. It was necessary that the four idolatrous or pagan monarchies, the end of the kingdom of Judah, and the seventy weeks, should happen at the same time, and all this before the second temple was destroyed.

709

Prophecies.—If one man alone had made a book of predictions about Jesus Christ, as to the time and the manner, and Jesus Christ had come in conformity to these prophecies, this fact would have infinite weight.

But there is much more here. Here is a succession of men

during four thousand years, who, consequently and without variation, come, one after another, to foretell this same event. Here is a whole people who announce it, and who have existed for four thousand years, in order to give corporate testimony of the assurances which they have, and from which they cannot be diverted by whatever threats and persecutions people may make against them. This is far more important.

710

Predictions of particular things.—They were strangers in Egypt, without any private property, either in that country or elsewhere. [There was not the least appearance, either of the royalty which had previously existed so long, or of that supreme council of seventy judges which they called the *Sanhedrin,* and which, having been instituted by Moses, lasted to the time of Jesus Christ. All these things were as far removed from their state at that time as they could be], when Jacob, dying, and blessing his twelve children, declared to them, that they would be proprietors of a great land, and foretold in particular to the family of Judah, that the kings, who would one day rule them, should be of his race; and that all his brethren should be their subjects; [and that even the Messiah, who was to be the expectation of nations, should spring from him; and that the kingship should not be taken away from Judah, nor the ruler and law-giver of his descendants, till the expected Messiah should arrive in his family].

This same Jacob, disposing of this future land as though he had been its ruler, gave a portion to Joseph more than to the others. "I give you," said he, "one part more than to your brothers." And blessing his two children, Ephraim and Manasseh, whom Joseph had presented to him, the elder, Manasseh, on his right, and the young Ephraim on his left, he put his arms crosswise, and placing his right hand on the head of Ephraim, and his left on Manasseh, he blessed them in this manner. And, upon Joseph's representing to him that he was preferring the younger, he replied to him with admirable resolution: "I know it well, my son; but Ephraim

will increase more than Manasseh." This has been indeed so
true in the result, that, being alone almost as fruitful as the
two entire lines which composed a whole kingdom, they have
been usually called by the name of Ephraim alone.

This same Joseph, when dying, bade his children carry his
bones with them when they should go into that land, to which
they only came two hundred years afterwards.

Moses, who wrote all these things so long before they happened, himself assigned to each family portions of that land
before they entered it, as though he had been its ruler. [In
fact he declared that God was to raise up from their nation
and their race a prophet, of whom he was the type; and he
foretold them exactly all that was to happen to them in the
land which they were to enter after his death, the victories
which God would give them, their ingratitude towards God,
the punishments which they would receive for it, and the rest
of their adventures.] He gave them judges who should make
the division. He prescribed the entire form of political government which they should observe, the cities of refuge which
they should build, and . . .

711

The prophecies about particular things are mingled with
those about the Messiah, so that the prophecies of the Messiah should not be without proofs, nor the special prophecies
without fruit.

712

Perpetual captivity of the Jews.—Jer. xi, 11: "I will bring
evil upon Judah from which they shall not be able to escape."

Types.—Is. v: "The Lord had a vineyard, from which He
looked for grapes; and it brought forth only wild grapes. I
will therefore lay it waste, and destroy it; the earth shall only
bring forth thorns, and I will forbid the clouds from [*raining*]
upon it. The vineyard of the Lord is the house of Israel, and
the men of Judah His pleasant plant. I looked that they
should do justice, and they bring forth only iniquities."

Is. viii: "Sanctify the Lord with fear and trembling; let Him be your only dread, and He shall be to you for a sanctuary, but for a stone of stumbling and a rock of offence to both the houses of Israel, for a gin and for a snare to the inhabitants of Jerusalem; and many among them shall stumble against that stone, and fall, and be broken, and be snared, and perish. Hide my words, and cover my law for my disciples.

"I will then wait in patience upon the Lord that hideth and concealeth Himself from the house of Jacob."

Is. xxix: "Be amazed and wonder, people of Israel; stagger and stumble, and be drunken, but not with wine; stagger, but not with strong drink. For the Lord hath poured out upon you the spirit of deep sleep. He will close your eyes; He will cover your princes and your prophets that have visions." (Daniel xii: "The wicked shall not understand, but the wise shall understand." Hosea, the last chapter, the last verse, after many temporal blessings, says: "Who is wise, and he shall understand these things, etc.?") "And the visions of all the prophets are become unto you as a sealed book, which men deliver to one that is learned, and who can read; and he saith, I cannot read it, for it is sealed. And when the book is delivered to them that are not learned, they say, I am not learned.

"Wherefore the Lord said, Forasmuch as this people with their lips do honour me, but have removed their heart far from me,"—there is the reason and the cause of it; for if they adored God in their hearts, they would understand the prophecies,—"and their fear towards me is taught by the precept of man. Therefore, behold, I will proceed to do a marvellous work among this people, even a marvellous work and a wonder; for the wisdom of their wise men shall perish, and their understanding shall be [hid]."

Prophecies. Proofs of Divinity.—Is. xli: "Shew the things that are to come hereafter, that we may know that ye are gods: we will incline our heart unto your words. Teach us the things that have been at the beginning, and declare us things for to come.

"By this we shall know that ye are gods. Yea, do good or do evil, if you can. Let us then behold it and reason together. Behold, ye are of nothing, and only an abomination, etc. Who," (among contemporary writers), "hath declared from the beginning that we may know of the things done from the beginning and origin? that we may say, You are righteous. There is none that teacheth us, yea, there is none that declareth the future."

Is. xlii: "I am the Lord, and my glory will I not give to another. I have foretold the things which have come to pass, and things that are to come do I declare. Sing unto God a new song in all the earth.

"Bring forth the blind people that have eyes and see not, and the deaf that have ears and hear not. Let all the nations be gathered together. Who among them can declare this, and shew us former things, and things to come? Let them bring forth their witnesses, that they may be justified; or let them hear, and say, It is truth.

"Ye are my witnesses, saith the Lord, and my servant whom I have chosen; that ye may know and believe me, and understand that I am He.

"I have declared, and have saved, and I alone have done wonders before your eyes: ye are my witnesses, said the Lord, that I am God.

"For your sake I have brought down the forces of the Babylonians. I am the Lord, your Holy One and Creator.

"I have made a way in the sea, and a path in the mighty waters. I am He that drowned and destroyed for ever the mighty enemies that have resisted you.

"Remember ye not the former things, neither consider the things of old.

"Behold, I will do a new thing; now it shall spring forth; shall ye not know it? I will even make a way in the wilderness, and rivers in the desert.

"This people have I formed for myself; I have established them to shew forth my praise, etc.

"I, even I, am He that blotteth out thy transgressions for mine own sake, and will not remember thy sins. Put in remembrance your ingratitude: see thou, if thou mayest be justified. Thy first father hath sinned, and thy teachers have transgressed against me."

Is. xliv: "I am the first, and I am the last, saith the Lord. Let him who will equal himself to me, declare the order of things since I appointed the ancient people, and the things that are coming. Fear ye not: have I not told you all these things? Ye are my witnesses."

Prophecy of Cyrus.—Is. xlv, 4: "For Jacob's sake, mine elect, I have called thee by thy name."

Is. xlv, 21: "Come and let us reason together. Who hath declared this from ancient time? Who hath told it from that time? Have not I, the Lord?"

Is. xlvi: "Remember the former things of old, and know there is none like me, declaring the end from the beginning, and from ancient times the things that are not yet done, saying, My counsel shall stand, and I will do all my pleasure."

Is. xlii: "Behold, the former things are come to pass, and new things do I declare; before they spring forth I tell you of them."

Is. xlviii, 3: "I have declared the former things from the beginning; I did them suddenly; and they came to pass. Because I know that thou art obstinate, that thy spirit is rebellious, and thy brow brass; I have even declared it to thee before it came to pass: lest thou shouldst say that it was the work of thy gods, and the effect of their commands.

"Thou hast seen all this; and will not ye declare it? I have shewed thee new things from this time, even hidden things, and thou didst not know them. They are created now, and not from the beginning; I have kept them hidden from thee; lest thou shouldst say, Behold, I knew them.

"Yea, thou knewest not; yea, thou heardest not; yea, from that time that thine ear was not opened: for I knew that thou couldst deal very treacherously, and wast called a transgressor from the womb."

Reprobation of the Jews and conversion of the Gentiles.—
Is. lxv: "I am sought of them that asked not for me; I am
found of them that sought me not; I said, Behold me, behold
me, behold me, unto a nation that did not call upon my name.

"I have spread out my hands all the day unto an unbelieving people, which walketh in a way that was not good, after
their own thoughts; a people that provoketh me to anger continually by the sins they commit in my face; that sacrificeth
to idols, etc.

"These shall be scattered like smoke in the day of my
wrath, etc.

"Your iniquities, and the iniquities of your fathers, will I
assemble together, and will recompense you for all according
to your works.

"Thus saith the Lord, As the new wine is found in the clus-
ter, and one saith, Destroy it not, for a blessing is in it [and
the promise of fruit]: for my servants' sake I will not destroy
all Israel.

"Thus I will bring forth a seed out of Jacob and out of
Judah, an inheritor of my mountains, and mine elect and my
servants shall inherit it, and my fertile and abundant plains;
but I will destroy all others, because you have forgotten your
God to serve strange gods. I called, and ye did not answer; I
spake, and ye did not hear; and ye did choose the thing which
I forbade.

"Therefore thus saith the Lord, Behold, my servants shall
eat, but ye shall be hungry; my servants shall rejoice, but ye
shall be ashamed; my servants shall sing for joy of heart, but
ye shall cry and howl for vexation of spirit.

"And ye shall leave your name for a curse unto my chosen:
for the Lord shall slay thee, and call His servants by another
name, that he who blesseth himself in the earth shall bless
himself in God, etc., because the former troubles are forgotten.

"For, behold, I create new heavens and a new earth; and
the former things shall not be remembered, nor come into
mind.

"But be ye glad and rejoice for ever in that which I create;

for, behold, I create Jerusalem a rejoicing, and her people a joy.

"And I will rejoice in Jerusalem and joy in my people; and the voice of weeping shall no more be heard in her, nor the voice of crying.

"Before they call, I will answer; and while they are yet speaking, I will hear. The wolf and the lamb shall feed together, and the lion shall eat straw like the bullock; and dust shall be the serpent's meat. They shall not hurt nor destroy in all my holy mountain."

Is. lvi, 3: "Thus saith the Lord, Keep ye judgment, and do justice: for my salvation is near to come, and my righteousness to be revealed.

"Blessed is the man that doeth this, that keepeth the Sabbath, and keepeth his hand from doing any evil.

"Neither let the strangers that have joined themselves to me, say, God will separate me from His people. For thus saith the Lord: Whoever will keep my Sabbath, and choose the things that please me, and take hold of my covenant; even unto them will I give in mine house a place and a name better than that of sons and of daughters: I will give them an everlasting name, that shall not be cut off."

Is. lix, 9: "Therefore for our iniquities is justice far from us: we wait for light, but behold obscurity; for brightness, but we walk in darkness. We grope for the wall like the blind; we stumble at noonday as in the night: we are in desolate places as dead men.

"We roar all like bears, and mourn sore like doves; we look for judgment, but there is none; for salvation, but it is far from us."

Is. lxvi, 18: "But I know their works and their thoughts; it shall come that I will gather all nations and tongues, and they shall see my glory.

"And I will set a sign among them, and I will send those that escape of them unto the nations, to Africa, to Lydia, to Italy, to Greece, and to the people that have not heard my fame, neither have seen my glory. And they shall bring your brethren."

Jer. vii. *Reprobation of the Temple:* "Go ye unto Shiloth, where I set my name at the first, and see what I did to it for the wickedness of my people. And now, because ye have done all these works, saith the Lord, I will do unto this house, wherein my name is called upon, wherein ye trust, and unto the place which I gave to your priests, as I have done to Shiloth." (For I have rejected it, and made myself a temple elsewhere.)

"And I will cast you out of my sight, as I have cast out all your brethren, even the seed of Ephraim." (Rejected for ever.) "Therefore pray not for this people."

Jer. vii, 22: "What avails it you to add sacrifice to sacrifice? For I spake not unto your fathers, when I brought them out of the land of Egypt, concerning burnt offerings or sacrifices. But this thing commanded I them, saying, Obey and be faithful to my commandments, and I will be your God, and ye shall be my people." (It was only after they had sacrificed to the golden calf that I gave myself sacrifices to turn into good an evil custom.)

Jer. vii, 4: "Trust ye not in lying words, saying, The temple of the Lord, the temple of the Lord, the temple of the Lord, are these."

713

The Jews witnesses for God. Is. xliii, 9; xliv, 8.

Prophecies fulfilled.—1 Kings xiii, 2.—1 Kings xxiii, 16.—Joshua vi, 26.—1 Kings xvi, 34.—Deut. xxiii.

Malachi i, 11. The sacrifice of the Jews rejected, and the sacrifice of the heathen, (even out of Jerusalem,) and in all places.

Moses, before dying, foretold the calling of the Gentiles, Deut. xxxii, 21, and the reprobation of the Jews.

Moses foretold what would happen to each tribe.

Prophecy.—"Your name shall be a curse unto mine elect, and I will give them another name."

"Make their heart fat," and how? by flattering their lust and making them hope to satisfy it.

714

Prophecy.—Amos and Zechariah. They have sold the just one, and therefore will not be recalled.—Jesus Christ betrayed.

They shall no more remember Egypt. See Is. xliii, 16, 17, 18, 19. Jer. xxiii, 6, 7.

Prophecy.—The Jews shall be scattered abroad. Is. xxvii, 6. —A new law, Jerem. xxxi, 32.

Malachi. *Grotius.*—The second temple glorious.—Jesus Christ will come. Haggai ii, 7, 8, 9, 10.

The calling of the Gentiles. Joel ii, 28. Hosea ii, 24. Deut. xxxii, 21. Malachi i, 11.

715

Hosea iii.—Is. xlii, xlviii, liv, lx, lxi, last verse. "I foretold it long since that they might know that it is I." Jaddus to Alexander.

716

[*Prophecies.*—The promise that David will always have descendants. Jer. xiii, 13.]

717

The eternal reign of the race of David, 2 Chron., by all the prophecies, and with an oath. And it was not temporally fulfilled. Jer. xxiii, 20.

718

We might perhaps think that, when the prophets foretold that the sceptre should not depart from Judah until the eternal King came, they spoke to flatter the people, and that their prophecy was proved false by Herod. But to show that this was not their meaning, and that, on the contrary, they knew well that this temporal kingdom should cease, they said that they would be without a king and without a prince, and for a long time. Hosea iii, 4.

719

Non habemus regem nisi Cæsarem. Therefore Jesus Christ was the Messiah, since they had no longer any king but a stranger, and would have no other.

720

We have no king but Cæsar.

721

Daniel ii: "All thy soothsayers and wise men cannot shew unto thee the secret which thou hast demanded. But there is a God in heaven who can do so, and that hath revealed to thee in thy dream what shall be in the latter days." (This dream must have caused him much misgiving.)

"And it is not by my own wisdom that I have knowledge of this secret, but by the revelation of this same God, that hath revealed it to me, to make it manifest in thy presence.

"Thy dream was then of this kind. Thou sawest a great image, high and terrible, which stood before thee. His head was of gold, his breast and arms of silver, his belly and his thighs of brass, his legs of iron, his feet part of iron and part of clay. Thus thou sawest till that a stone was cut out without hands, which smote the image upon his feet, that were of iron and of clay, and brake them to pieces.

"Then was the iron, the clay, the brass, the silver, and the gold broken to pieces together, and the wind carried them away; but this stone that smote the image became a great mountain, and filled the whole earth. This is the dream, and now I will give thee the interpretation thereof.

"Thou who art the greatest of kings, and to whom God hath given a power so vast that thou art renowned among all peoples, art the head of gold which thou hast seen. But after thee shall arise another kingdom inferior to thee, and another third kingdom of brass, which shall bear rule over all the earth.

"But the fourth kingdom shall be strong as iron, and even as iron breaketh in pieces and subdueth all things, so shall this empire break in pieces and bruise all.

"And whereas thou sawest the feet and toes, part of clay and part of iron, the kingdom shall be divided; but there shall be in it of the strength of iron and of the weakness of clay.

"But as iron cannot be firmly mixed with clay, so they who are represented by the iron and by the clay, shall not cleave one to another though united by marriage.

"Now in the days of these kings shall God set up a kingdom, which shall never be destroyed, nor ever be delivered up to other people. It shall break in pieces and consume all these kingdoms, and it shall stand for ever, according as thou sawest that the stone was cut out of the mountain without hands, and that it fell from the mountain, and brake in pieces the iron, the clay, the silver, and the gold. God hath made known to thee what shall come to pass hereafter. This dream is certain, and the interpretation thereof sure.

"Then Nebuchadnezzar fell upon his face towards the earth," etc.

Daniel viii, 8. "Daniel having seen the combat of the ram and of the he-goat, who vanquished him and ruled over the earth, whereof the principal horn being broken four others came up toward the four winds of heaven, and out of one of them came forth a little horn, which waxed exceedingly great toward the south, and toward the east, and toward the land of Israel, and it waxed great even to the host of heaven; and it cast down some of the stars, and stamped upon them, and at last overthrew the prince, and by him the daily sacrifice was taken away, and the place of his sanctuary was cast down.

"This is what Daniel saw. He sought the meaning of it, and a voice cried in this manner, 'Gabriel, make this man to understand the vision.' And Gabriel said:

"The ram which thou sawest is the king of the Medes and Persians, and the he-goat is the king of Greece, and the great horn that is between his eyes is the first king of this monarchy.

"Now that being broken, whereas four stood up for it, four

kingdoms shall stand up out of the nation, but not in his power.

"And in the latter time of their kingdom, when iniquities are come to the full, there shall arise a king, insolent and strong, but not by his own power, to whom all things shall succeed after his own will; and he shall destroy the holy people, and through his policy also he shall cause craft to prosper in his hand, and he shall destroy many. He shall also stand up against the Prince of princes, but he shall perish miserably, and nevertheless by a violent hand."

Daniel ix, 20. "Whilst I was praying with all my heart, and confessing my sin and the sin of all my people, and prostrating myself before my God, even Gabriel, whom I had seen in the vision at the beginning, came to me and touched me about the time of the evening oblation, and he informed me and said, O Daniel, I am now come forth to give thee the knowledge of things. At the beginning of thy supplications I came to shew that which thou didst desire, for thou are greatly beloved: therefore understand the matter, and consider the vision. Seventy weeks are determined upon thy people, and upon thy holy city, to finish the transgression, and to make an end of sins, and to abolish iniquity, and to bring in everlasting righteousness; to accomplish the vision and the prophecies, and to anoint the Most Holy. (After which this people shall be no more thy people, nor this city the holy city. The times of wrath shall be passed, and the years of grace shall come for ever.)

"Know therefore, and understand, that, from the going forth of the commandment to restore and to build Jerusalem unto the Messiah the Prince, shall be seven weeks, and three score and two weeks." (The Hebrews were accustomed to divide numbers, and to place the small first. Thus, 7 and 62 make 69. Of this 70 there will then remain the 70th, that is to say, the 7 last years of which he will speak next.)

"The street shall be built again, and the wall, even in troublous times. And after three score and two weeks," (which have followed the first seven. Christ will then be killed after the sixty-nine weeks, that is to say, in the last week), "the Christ shall be cut off, and a people of the prince that shall come shall destroy the city and the sanctuary, and overwhelm all, and the end of that war shall accomplish the desolation."

"Now one week," (which is the seventieth, which remains), "shall confirm the covenant with many, and in the midst of the week," (that is to say, the last three and a half years), "he shall cause the sacrifice and the oblation to cease, and for the overspreading of abominations he shall make it desolate, even until the consummation, and that determined shall be poured upon the desolate."

Daniel xi. "The angel said to Daniel: There shall stand up yet," (after Cyrus, under whom this still is), "three kings in Persia," (Cambyses, Smerdis, Darius); "and the fourth who shall then come," (Xerxes) "shall be far richer than they all, and far stronger, and shall stir up all his people against the Greeks.

"But a mighty king shall stand up," (Alexander), "that shall rule with great dominion, and do according to his will. And when he shall stand up, his kingdom shall be broken, and shall be divided in four parts toward the four winds of heaven," (as he had said above, vii, 6; viii, 8), "but not his posterity; and his successors shall not equal his power, for his kingdom shall be plucked up, even for others besides these," (his four chief successors).

"And the king of the south," (Ptolemy, son of Lagos, Egypt), "shall be strong; but one of his princes shall be strong above him, and his dominion shall be a great dominion," (Seleucus, King of Syria. Appian says that he was the most powerful of Alexander's successors).

"And in the end of years they shall join themselves together, and the king's daughter of the south," (Berenice, daughter of Ptolemy Philadelphus, son of the other Ptolemy), "shall come to the king of the north," (to Antiochus Deus, King of Syria and of Asia, son of Seleucus Lagidas), "to make peace between these princes.

"But neither she nor her seed shall have a long authority;

for she and they that brought her, and her children, and her friends, shall be delivered to death." (Berenice and her son were killed by Seleucus Callinicus.)

"But out of a branch of her roots shall one stand up," (Ptolemy Euergetes was the issue of the same father as Berenice), "which shall come with a mighty army into the land of the king of the north, where he shall put all under subjection, and he shall also carry captive into Egypt their gods, their princes, their gold, their silver, and all their precious spoils," (if he had not been called into Egypt by domestic reasons, says Justin, he would have entirely stripped Seleucus); "and he shall continue several years when the king of the north can do nought against him.

"And so he shall return into his kingdom. But his sons shall be stirred up, and shall assemble a multitude of great forces," (Seleucus Ceraunus, Antiochus the Great). "And their army shall come and overthrow all; wherefore the king of the south shall be moved with choler, and shall also form a great army, and fight him," (Ptolemy Philopator against Antiochus the Great at Raphia), "and conquer; and his troops shall become insolent, and his heart shall be lifted up," (this Ptolemy desecrated the temple; Josephus): "he shall cast down many ten thousands, but he shall not be strengthened by it. For the king of the north," (Antiochus the Great), "shall return with a greater multitude than before, and in those times also a great number of enemies shall stand up against the king of the south," (during the reign of the young Ptolemy Epiphanes); "also the apostates and robbers of thy people shall exalt themselves to establish the vision; but they shall fall." (Those who abandon their religion to please Euergetes, when he will send his troops to Scopas; for Antiochus will again take Scopas, and conquer them.) "And the king of the north shall destroy the fenced cities, and the arms of the south shall not withstand, and all shall yield to his will; he shall stand in the land of Israel, and it shall yield to him. And thus he shall think to make himself master of all the empire of Egypt," (despising the youth of Epiphanes, says Justin).

"And for that he shall make alliance with him, and give his daughter" (Cleopatra, in order that she may betray her husband. On which Appian says that doubting his ability to make himself master of Egypt by force, because of the protection of the Romans, he wished to attempt it by cunning). "He shall wish to corrupt her, but she shall not stand on his side, neither be for him. Then he shall turn his face to other designs, and shall think to make himself master of some isles," (that is to say, seaports), "and shall take many," (as Appian says).

"But a prince shall oppose his conquests," (Scipio Africanus, who stopped the progress of Antiochus the Great, because he offended the Romans in the person of their allies), "and shall cause the reproach offered by him to cease. He shall then return into his kingdom and there perish, and be no more." (He was slain by his soldiers.)

"And he who shall stand up in his estate," (Seleucus Philopator or Soter, the son of Antiochus the Great), "shall be a tyrant, a raiser of taxes in the glory of the kingdom," (which means the people), "but within a few days he shall be destroyed, neither in anger nor in battle. And in his place shall stand up a vile person, unworthy of the honour of the kingdom, but he shall come in cleverly by flatteries. All armies shall bend before him; he shall conquer them, and even the prince with whom he has made a covenant. For having renewed the league with him, he shall work deceitfully, and enter with a small people into his province, peaceably and without fear. He shall take the fattest places, and shall do that which his fathers have not done, and ravage on all sides. He shall forecast great devices during his time."

722

Prophecies.—The seventy weeks of Daniel are ambiguous as regards the term of commencement, because of the terms of the prophecy; and as regards the term of conclusion, because of the differences among chronologists. But all this difference extends only to two hundred years.

723

Predictions.—That in the fourth monarchy, before the destruction of the second temple, before the dominion of the Jews was taken away, in the seventieth week of Daniel, during the continuance of the second temple, the heathen should be instructed, and brought to the knowledge of the God worshipped by the Jews; that those who loved Him should be delivered from their enemies, and filled with His fear and love.

And it happened that in the fourth monarchy, before the destruction of the second temple, etc., the heathen in great number worshipped God, and led an angelic life. Maidens dedicated their virginity and their life to God. Men renounced their pleasures. What Plato could only make acceptable to a few men, specially chosen and instructed, a secret influence imparted by the power of a few words, to a hundred million ignorant men.

The rich left their wealth. Children left the dainty homes of their parents to go into the rough desert. (See Philo the Jew.) All this was foretold a great while ago. For two thousand years no heathen had worshipped the God of the Jews; and at the time foretold, a great number of the heathen worshipped this only God. The temples were destroyed. The very kings made submission to the cross. All this was due to the Spirit of God, which was spread abroad upon the earth.

No heathen, since Moses until Jesus Christ, believed according to the very Rabbis. A great number of the heathen, after Jesus Christ, believed in the books of Moses, kept them in substance and spirit, and only rejected what was useless.

724

Prophecies.—The conversion of the Egyptians (Isaiah xix, 19); an altar in Egypt to the true God.

725

Prophecies.—*In Egypt.*—*Pugio Fidei,* p. 659. *Talmud.*
"It is a tradition among us, that, when the Messiah shall

come, the house of God, destined for the dispensation of His Word, shall be full of filth and impurity; and that the wisdom of the scribes shall be corrupt and rotten. Those who shall be afraid to sin, shall be rejected by the people, and treated as senseless fools."

Is. xlix: "Listen, O isles, unto me, and hearken, ye people, from afar: The Lord hath called me by my name from the womb of my mother; in the shadow of His hand hath He hid me, and hath made my words like a sharp sword, and said unto me, Thou art my servant in whom I will be glorified. Then I said, Lord, have I laboured in vain? have I spent my strength for nought? yet surely my judgment is with Thee, O Lord, and my work with Thee. And now, saith the Lord, that formed me from the womb to be His servant, to bring Jacob and Israel again to Him, Thou shalt be glorious in my sight, and I will be thy strength. It is a light thing that thou shouldst convert the tribes of Jacob; I have raised thee up for a light to the Gentiles, that thou mayest be my salvation unto the ends of the earth. Thus saith the Lord to him whom man despiseth, to him whom the nation abhorreth, to a servant of rulers, Princes and kings shall worship thee, because the Lord is faithful that hath chosen thee.

"Again saith the Lord unto me, I have heard thee in the days of salvation and of mercy, and I will preserve thee for a covenant of the people, to cause to inherit the desolate nations, that thou mayest say to the prisoners: Go forth; to them that are in darkness show yourselves, and possess these abundant and fertile lands. They shall not hunger nor thirst, neither shall the heat nor sun smite them; for he that hath mercy upon them shall lead them, even by the springs of waters shall he guide them, and make the mountains a way before them. Behold, the peoples shall come from all parts, from the east and from the west, from the north and from the south. Let the heavens give glory to God; let the earth be joyful; for it hath pleased the Lord to comfort His people, and He will have mercy upon the poor who hope in Him.

"Yet Zion dared to say: The Lord hath forsaken me, and

hath forgotten me. Can a woman forget her child, that she should not have compassion on the son of her womb? but if she forget, yet will not I forget thee, O Sion. I will bear thee always between my hands, and thy walls are continually before me. They that shall build thee are come, and thy destroyers shall go forth of thee. Lift up thine eyes round about, and behold; all these gather themselves together, and come to thee. As I live, saith the Lord, thou shalt surely clothe thee with them all, as with an ornament. Thy waste and thy desolate places, and the land of thy destruction, shall even now be too narrow by reason of the inhabitants, and the children thou shalt have after thy barrenness shall say again in thy ears: The place is too strait for me: give place to me that I may dwell. Then shalt thou say in thy heart: Who hath begotten me these, seeing I have lost my children, and am desolate, a captive, and removing to and fro? and who brought up these? Behold, I was left alone; these, where had they been? And the Lord shall say to thee: Behold, I will lift up mine hand to the Gentiles, and set up my standard to the people; and they shall bring thy sons in their arms and in their bosoms. And kings shall be their nursing fathers, and queens their nursing mothers; they shall bow down to thee with their face toward the earth, and lick up the dust of thy feet; and thou shalt know that I am the Lord; for they shall not be ashamed that wait for me. Shall the prey be taken from the mighty? But even if the captives be taken away from the strong, nothing shall hinder me from saving thy children, and from destroying thy enemies; and all flesh shall know that I am the Lord, thy Saviour and thy Redeemer, the mighty One of Jacob.

"Thus saith the Lord: What is the bill of this divorcement, wherewith I have put away the synagogue? and why have I delivered it into the hand of your enemies? Is it not for your iniquities and for your transgressions that I have put it away?

"For I came, and no man received me; I called and there was none to hear. Is my arm shortened, that I cannot redeem?

"Therefore I will show the tokens of mine anger; I will clothe the heavens with darkness, and make sackcloth their covering.

"The Lord hath given me the tongue of the learned that I should know how to speak a word in season to him that is weary. He hath opened mine ear, and I have listened to Him as a master.

"The Lord hath revealed His will, and I was not rebellious.

"I gave my body to the smiters, and my cheeks to outrage; I hid not my face from shame and spitting. But the Lord hath helped me; therefore I have not been confounded.

"He is near that justifieth me; who will contend with me? who will be mine adversary, and accuse me of sin, God himself being my protector?

"All men shall pass away, and be consumed by time; let those that fear God hearken to the voice of His servant; let him that languisheth in darkness put his trust in the Lord. But as for you, ye do but kindle the wrath of God upon you; ye walk in the light of your fire and in the sparks that ye have kindled. This shall ye have of mine hand; ye shall lie down in sorrow.

"Hearken to me, ye that follow after righteousness, ye that seek the Lord: look unto the rock whence ye are hewn, and to the hole of the pit whence ye are digged. Look unto Abraham, your father, and unto Sarah that bare you: for I called him alone, when childless, and increased him. Behold, I have comforted Zion, and heaped upon her blessings and consolations.

"Hearken unto me, my people, and give ear unto me; for a law shall proceed from me, and I will make my judgment to rest for a light of the Gentiles."

Amos viii. The prophet, having enumerated the sins of Israel, said that God had sworn to take vengeance on them.

He says this: "And it shall come to pass in that day, saith the Lord, that I will cause the sun to go down at noon, and I will darken the earth in the clear day; and I will turn your feasts into mourning, and all your songs into lamentation.

"You all shall have sorrow and suffering, and I will make this nation mourn as for an only son, and the end therefore as a bitter day. Behold, the days come, saith the Lord, that I will send a famine in the land, not a famine of bread, nor a thirst for water, but of hearing the words of the Lord. And they shall wander from sea to sea, and from the north even to the east; they shall run to and fro to seek the word of the Lord, and shall not find it.

"In that day shall the fair virgins and young men faint for thirst. They that have followed the idols of Samaria, and sworn by the god of Dan, and followed the manner of Beer-sheba, shall fall, and never rise up again."

Amos iii, 2: "Ye only have I known of all the families of the earth for my people."

Daniel xii, 7. Having described all the extent of the reign of the Messiah, he says: "All these things shall be finished, when the scattering of the people of Israel shall be accomplished."

Haggai ii, 4: "Ye who, comparing this second house with the glory of the first, despise it, be strong, saith the Lord, be strong, O Zerubbabel, and O Jesus, the high priest, be strong, all ye people of the land, and work. For I am with you, saith the Lord of hosts; according to the word that I covenanted with you when ye came out of Egypt, so my spirit remaineth among you. Fear ye not. For thus saith the Lord of hosts: Yet one little while, and I will shake the heavens, and the earth, and the sea, and the dry land," (a way of speaking to indicate a great and an extraordinary change); "and I will shake all nations, and the desire of all the Gentiles shall come; and I will fill this house with glory, saith the Lord.

"The silver is mine, and the gold is mine, saith the Lord," (that is to say, it is not by that that I wish to be honoured; as it is said elsewhere: All the beasts of the field are mine, what advantages me that they are offered me in sacrifice?). "The glory of this latter house shall be greater than of the former, saith the Lord of hosts; and in this place will I establish my house, saith the Lord.

"According to all that thou desiredst in Horeb in the day of the assembly, saying, Let us not hear again the voice of the Lord, neither let us see this fire any more, that we die not. And the Lord said unto me, Their prayer is just. I will raise them up a prophet from among their brethren, like unto thee, and will put my words in his mouth; and he shall speak unto them all that I shall command him. And it shall come to pass, that whosoever will not hearken unto my words which he will speak in my name, I will require it of him."

Genesis xlix: "Judah, thou art he whom thy brethren shall praise, and thou shalt conquer thine enemies; thy father's children shall bow down before thee. Judah is a lion's whelp: from the prey, my son, thou art gone up, and art couched as a lion, and as a lioness that shall be roused up.

"The sceptre shall not depart from Judah, nor a lawgiver from between his feet, until Shiloh come; and unto him shall the gathering of the people be."

726

During the life of the Messiah.—Ænigmatis.—Ezek. xvii.

His forerunner. Malachi iii.

He will be born an infant. Is. ix.

He will be born in the village of Bethlehem. Micah v. He will appear chiefly in Jerusalem, and will be a descendant of the family of Judah and of David.

He is to blind the learned and the wise, Is. vi, viii, xxix, etc.; and to preach the Gospel to the lowly, Is. xxix; to open the eyes of the blind, give health to the sick, and bring light to those that languish in darkness. Is. lxi.

He is to show the perfect way, and be the teacher of the Gentiles. Is. lv; xlii, 1—7.

The prophecies are to be unintelligible to the wicked, Dan. xii; Hosea xiv, 10; but they are to be intelligible to those who are well informed.

The prophecies, which represent Him as poor, represent Him as master of the nations. Is. lii, 14, etc.; liii; Zech. ix, 9.

The prophecies, which foretell the time, foretell Him only

as master of the nations and suffering, and not as in the clouds nor as judge. And those, which represent Him thus as judge and in glory, do not mention the time. When the Messiah is spoken of as great and glorious, it is as the judge of the world, and not its Redeemer.

He is to be the victim for the sins of the world. Is. xxxix, liii, etc.

He is to be the precious corner-stone. Is. xxviii, 16.

He is to be a stone of stumbling and offence. Is. viii. Jerusalem is to dash against this stone.

The builders are to reject this stone. Ps. cxvii, 22.

God is to make this stone the chief corner-stone.

And this stone is to grow into a huge mountain, and fill the whole earth. Dan. ii.

So He is to be rejected, despised, betrayed (Ps. cviii, 8), sold (Zech. xi, 12), spit upon, buffeted, mocked, afflicted in innumerable ways, given gall to drink (Ps. lxviii), pierced (Zech. xii), His feet and His hands pierced, slain, and lots cast for His raiment.

He will rise again (Ps. xv) the third day (Hosea vi, 3).

He will ascend to heaven to sit on the right hand. Ps. cx.

The kings will arm themselves against Him. Ps. ii.

Being on the right hand of the Father, He will be victorious over His enemies.

The kings of the earth and all nations will worship Him. Is. lx.

The Jews will continue as a nation. Jeremiah.

They will wander, without kings, etc. (Hosea iii), without prophets (Amos), looking for salvation and finding it not (Isaiah).

Calling of the Gentiles by Jesus Christ. Is. lii, 15; lv, 5; lx, etc. Ps. lxxxi.

Hosea i, 9: "Ye are not my people, and I will not be your God, when ye are multiplied after the dispersion. In the places where it was said, Ye are not my people, I will call them my people."

727

It was not lawful to sacrifice outside of Jerusalem, which was the place that the Lord had chosen, nor even to eat the tithes elsewhere. Deut. xii, 5, etc.; Deut. xiv, 23, etc.; xv, 20; xvi, 2, 7, 11, 15.

Hosea foretold that they should be without a king, without a prince, without a sacrifice, and without an idol; and this prophecy is now fulfilled, as they cannot make a lawful sacrifice out of Jerusalem.

728

Predictions.—It was foretold that, in the time of the Messiah, He should come to establish a new covenant, which should make them forget the escape from Egypt (Jer. xxiii, 5; Is. xliii, 10); that He should place His law not in externals, but in the heart; that He should put His fear, which had only been from without, in the midst of the heart. Who does not see the Christian law in all this?

729

. . . That then idolatry would be overthrown; that this Messiah would cast down all idols, and bring men into the worship of the true God.

That the temples of the idols would be cast down, and that among all nations, and in all places of the earth. He would be offered a pure sacrifice, not of beasts.

That He would be king of the Jews and Gentiles. And we see this king of the Jews and Gentiles oppressed by both, who conspire His death; and ruler of both, destroying the worship of Moses in Jerusalem, which was its centre, where He made His first Church; and also the worship of idols in Rome, the centre of it, where He made His chief Church.

730

Prophecies.—That Jesus Christ will sit on the right hand, till God has subdued His enemies.

Therefore He will not subdue them Himself.

731

". . . Then they shall teach no more every man his neighbour, saying, Here is the Lord, *for God shall make Himself known to all.*"

". . . Your sons shall prophesy." "I will put my spirit and my fear *in your heart.*"

All that is the same thing. To prophesy is to speak of God, not from outward proofs, but from an inward and immediate feeling.

732

That He would teach men the perfect way.

And there has never come, before Him nor after Him, any man who has taught anything divine approaching to this.

733

. . . That Jesus Christ would be small in His beginning, and would then increase. The little stone of Daniel.

If I had in no wise heard of the Messiah, nevertheless, after such wonderful predictions of the course of the world which I see fulfilled, I see that He is divine. And if I knew that these same books foretold a Messiah, I should be sure that He would come; and seeing that they place His time before the destruction of the second temple, I should say that He had come.

734

Prophecies.—That the Jews would reject Jesus Christ, and would be rejected of God, for this reason, that the chosen vine brought forth only wild grapes. That the chosen people would be fruitless, ungrateful, and unbelieving, *populum non credentem et contradicentem.* That God would strike them with blindness, and in full noon they would grope like the blind; and that a forerunner would go before Him.

735

Transfixerunt. Zech. xii, 10.

That a deliverer should come, who would crush the demon's

head, and free His people from their sins, *ex omnibus iniqui-tatibus*; that there should be a New Covenant, which would be eternal; that there should be another priesthood after the order of Melchisedek, and it should be eternal; that the Christ should be glorious, mighty, strong, and yet so poor that He would not be recognised, nor taken for what He is, but rejected and slain; that His people who denied Him should no longer be His people; that the idolaters should receive Him, and take refuge in Him; that He should leave Zion to reign in the centre of idolatry; that nevertheless the Jews should continue for ever; that He should be of Judah, and when there should be no longer a king.

PROOFS OF JESUS CHRIST

736

Therefore I reject all other religions. In that way I find an answer to all objections. It is right that a God so pure should only reveal Himself to those whose hearts are purified. Hence this religion is lovable to me, and I find it now sufficiently justified by so divine a morality. But I find more in it.

I find it convincing that, since the memory of man has lasted, it was constantly announced to men that they were universally corrupt, but that a Redeemer should come; that it was not one man who said it, but innumerable men, and a whole nation expressly made for the purpose, and prophesying for four thousand years. This is a nation which is more ancient than every other nation. Their books, scattered abroad, are four thousand years old.

The more I examine them, the more truths I find in them: an entire nation foretell Him before His advent, and an entire nation worship Him after His advent; what has preceded and what has followed; in short, people without idols and kings, this synagogue which was foretold, and these wretches who frequent it, and who, being our enemies, are admirable witnesses of the truth of these prophecies, wherein their wretchedness and even their blindness are foretold.

I find this succession, this religion, wholly divine in its authority, in its duration, in its perpetuity, in its morality, in its conduct, in its doctrine, in its effects. The frightful darkness of the Jews was foretold. *Eris palpans in meridie. Dabitur liber scienti literas, et dicet: Non possum legere.* While the sceptre was still in the hands of the first foreign usurper, there is the report of the coming of Jesus Christ.

So I hold out my arms to my *Redeemer*, who, having been foretold for four thousand years, has come to suffer and to die for me on earth, at the time and under all the circumstances foretold. By His grace, I await death in peace, in the hope of being eternally united to Him. Yet I live with joy, whether in the prosperity which it pleases Him to bestow upon me, or in the adversity which He sends for my good, and which He has taught me to bear by His example.

737

The prophecies having given different signs which should all happen at the advent of the Messiah, it was necessary that all these signs should occur at the same time. So it was necessary that the fourth monarchy should have come, when the seventy weeks of Daniel were ended; and that the sceptre should have then departed from Judah. And all this happened without any difficulty. Then it was necessary that the Messiah should come; and Jesus Christ then came, who was called the Messiah. And all this again was without difficulty. This indeed shows the truth of the prophecies.

738

The prophets foretold, and were not foretold. The saints again were foretold, but did not foretell. Jesus Christ both foretold and was foretold.

739

Jesus Christ, whom the two Testaments regard, the Old as its hope, the New as its model, and both as their centre.

740

The two oldest books in the world are those of Moses and Job, the one a Jew and the other a Gentile. Both of them look upon Jesus Christ as their common centre and object: Moses in relating the promises of God to Abraham, Jacob, etc., and his prophecies; and Job, *Quis mihi det ut,* etc. *Scio enim quod redemptor meus vivit,* etc.

741

The Gospel only speaks of the virginity of the Virgin up to the time of the birth of Jesus Christ. All with reference to Jesus Christ.

742

Proofs of Jesus Christ.

Why was the book of Ruth preserved?

Why the story of Tamar?

743

"Pray that ye enter not into temptation." It is dangerous to be tempted; and people are tempted because they do not pray.

Et tu conversus confirma fratres tuos. But before, *conversus Jesus respexit Petrum.*

Saint Peter asks permission to strike Malchus, and strikes before hearing the answer. Jesus Christ replies afterwards.

The word, *Galilee,* which the Jewish mob pronounced as if by chance, in accusing Jesus Christ before Pilate, afforded Pilate a reason for sending Jesus Christ to Herod. And thereby the mystery was accomplished, that He should be judged by Jews and Gentiles. Chance was apparently the cause of the accomplishment of the mystery.

744

Those who have a difficulty in believing seek a reason in the fact that the Jews do not believe. "Were this so clear," say they, "why did the Jews not believe?" And they almost wish that they had believed, so as not to be kept back by the example of their refusal. But it is their very refusal that is the foundation of our faith. We should be much less disposed to the faith, if they were on our side. We should then have a more ample pretext. The wonderful thing is to have made the

Jews great lovers of the things foretold, and great enemies of their fulfilment.

745

The Jews were accustomed to great and striking miracles, and so, having had the great miracles of the Red Sea and of the land of Canaan as an epitome of the great deeds of their Messiah, they therefore looked for more striking miracles, of which those of Moses were only the patterns.

746

The carnal Jews and the heathen have their calamities, and Christians also. There is no Redeemer for the heathen, for they do not so much as hope for one. There is no Redeemer for the Jews; they hope for Him in vain. There is a Redeemer only for Christians. (See *Perpetuity*.)

747

In the time of the Messiah the people divided themselves. The spiritual embraced the Messiah, and the coarser-minded remained to serve as witnesses of Him.

748

"If this was clearly foretold to the Jews, how did they not believe it, or why were they not destroyed for resisting a fact so clear?"

I reply: in the first place, it was foretold both that they would not believe a thing so clear, and that they would not be destroyed. And nothing is more to the glory of the Messiah; for it was not enough that there should be prophets; their prophets must be kept above suspicion. Now, etc.

749

If the Jews had all been converted by Jesus Christ, we should have none but questionable witnesses. And if they had been entirely destroyed, we should have no witnesses at all.

750

What do the prophets say of Jesus Christ? That He will be clearly God? No; but that He is a God truly hidden; that He will be slighted; that none will think that it is He; that He will be a stone of stumbling, upon which many will stumble, etc. Let people then reproach us no longer for want of clearness, since we make profession of it.

But, it is said, there are obscurities.—And without that, no one would have stumbled over Jesus Christ, and this is one of the formal pronouncements of the prophets: *Excæca* . . .

751

Moses first teaches the Trinity, original sin, the Messiah.

David: a great witness; a king, good, merciful, a beautiful soul, a sound mind, powerful. He prophesies, and his wonder comes to pass. This is infinite.

He had only to say that he was the Messiah. if he had been vain; for the prophecies are clearer about him than about Jesus Christ. And the same with Saint John.

752

Herod was believed to be the Messiah. He had taken away the sceptre from Judah, but he was not of Judah. This gave rise to a considerable sect.

Curse of the Greeks upon those who count three periods of time.

In what way should the Messiah come, seeing that through Him the sceptre was to be eternally in Judah, and at His coming the sceptre was to be taken away from Judah?

In order to effect that seeing they should not see, and hearing they should not understand, nothing could be better done.

753

Homo existens te Deum facit.
Scriptum est, Dii estis, et non potest solvi Scriptura.
Hæc infirmitas non est ad vitam et est ad mortem.
Lazarus dormit, et deinde dixit: Lazarus mortuus est.

754

The apparent discrepancy of the Gospels.

755

What can we have but reverence for a man who foretells plainly things which come to pass, and who declares his intention both to blind and to enlighten, and who intersperses obscurities among the clear things which come to pass?

756

The time of the first advent was foretold; the time of the second is not so; because the first was to be obscure, and the second is to be brilliant, and so manifest that even His enemies will recognise it. But, as He was first to come only in obscurity, and to be known only of those who searched the Scriptures . . .

757

God, in order to cause the Messiah to be known by the good and not to be known by the wicked, made Him to be foretold in this manner. If the manner of the Messiah had been clearly foretold, there would have been no obscurity, even for the wicked. If the time had been obscurely foretold, there would have been obscurity, even for the good. For their [goodness of heart] would not have made them understand, for instance, that the closed *mem* signifies six hundred years. But that time has been clearly foretold, and the manner in types.

By this means, the wicked, taking the promised blessings for material blessings, have fallen into error, in spite of the clear prediction of the time; and the good have not fallen in error. For the understanding of the promised blessings depends on the heart, which calls "good" that which it loves; but the understanding of the promised time does not depend on the heart. And thus the clear prediction of the time, and the obscure prediction of the blessings, deceive the wicked alone.

758

[Either the Jews or the Christians must be wicked.]

759

The Jews reject Him, but not all. The saints receive Him,
and not the carnal-minded. And so far is this from being
against His glory, that it is the last touch which crowns it.
For their argument, the only one found in all their writings, in
the Talmud and in the Rabbinical writings, amounts only to
this, that Jesus Christ has not subdued the nations with sword
in hand, *gladiumt uum, potentissime.* (Is this all they have to
say? Jesus Christ has been slain, say they. He has failed. He
has not subdued the heathen with His might. He has not
bestowed upon us their spoil. He does not give riches. Is this
all they have to say? It is in this respect that He is lovable to
me. I would not desire Him whom they fancy.) It is evident
that it is only His life which has prevented them from accepting Him; and through this rejection they are irreproachable
witnesses, and, what is more, they thereby accomplish the
prophecies.

[By means of the fact that this people have not accepted
Him, this miracle here has happened. The prophecies were
the only lasting miracles which could be wrought, but they
were liable to be denied.]

760

The Jews, in slaying Him in order not to receive Him as the
Messiah, have given Him the final proof of being the Messiah.

And in continuing not to recognise Him, they made themselves irreproachable witnesses. Both in slaying Him, and
in continuing to deny Him, they have fulfilled the prophecies
(Isa. lx; Ps. lxxi).

761

What could the Jews, His enemies, do? If they receive Him,
they give proof of Him by their reception; for then the guar-

dians of the expectation of the Messiah receive Him. If they reject Him, they give proof of Him by their rejection.

762

The Jews, in testing if He were God, have shown that He was man.

763

The Church has had as much difficulty in showing that Jesus Christ was man, against those who denied it, as in showing that He was God; and the probabilities were equally great.

764

Source of contradictions.—A God humiliated, even to the death on the cross; a Messiah triumphing over death by his own death. Two natures in Jesus Christ, two advents, two states of man's nature.

765

Types.—Saviour, father, sacrificer, offering, food, king, wise, law-giver, afflicted, poor, having to create a people whom He must lead and nourish, and bring into His land . . .

Jesus Christ. Offices.—He alone had to create a great people, elect, holy, and chosen; to lead, nourish, and bring it into the place of rest and holiness; to make it holy to God; to make it the temple of God; to reconcile it to, and save it from, the wrath of God; to free it from the slavery of sin, which visibly reigns in man; to give laws to this people, and engrave these laws on their heart; to offer Himself to God for them, and sacrifice Himself for them; to be a victim without blemish, and Himself the sacrificer, having to offer Himself, His body, and His blood, and yet to offer bread and wine to God . . .

Ingrediens mundum.

"Stone upon stone."

What preceded and what followed. All the Jews exist still, and are wanderers.

766

Of all that is on earth, He partakes only of the sorrows, not of the joys. He loves His neighbours, but His love does not confine itself within these bounds, and overflows to His own enemies, and then to those of God.

767

Jesus Christ typified by Joseph, the beloved of his father, sent by his father to see his brethren, etc., innocent, sold by his brethren for twenty pieces of silver, and thereby becoming their lord, their saviour, the saviour of strangers, and the saviour of the world; which had not been but for their plot to destroy him, their sale and their rejection of him.

In prison Joseph innocent between two criminals; Jesus Christ on the cross between two thieves. Joseph foretells freedom to the one, and death to the other, from the same omens. Jesus Christ saves the elect, and condemns the outcast for the same sins. Joseph foretells only; Jesus Christ acts. Joseph asks him who will be saved to remember him, when he comes into his glory; and he whom Jesus Christ saves asks that He will remember him, when He comes into His kingdom.

768

The conversion of the heathen was only reserved for the grace of the Messiah. The Jews have been so long in opposition to them without success; all that Solomon and the prophets said has been useless. Sages, like Plato and Socrates, have not been able to persuade them.

769

After many persons had gone before, Jesus Christ at last came to say: "Here am I, and this is the time. That which the prophets have said was to come in the fullness of time, I tell you my apostles will do. The Jews shall be cast out. Jerusalem shall be soon destroyed. And the heathen shall enter into the knowledge of God. My apostles shall do this after you have slain the heir of the vineyard."

Then the apostles said to the Jews: "You shall be accursed," (*Celsus laughed at it*); and to the heathen, "You shall enter into the knowledge of God." And this then came to pass.

770

Jesus Christ came to blind those who saw clearly, and to give sight to the blind; to heal the sick, and leave the healthy to die; to call to repentance, and to justify sinners, and to leave the righteous in their sins; to fill the needy, and leave the rich empty.

771

Holiness.—Effundam spiritum meum. All nations were in unbelief and lust. The whole world now became fervent with love. Princes abandoned their pomp; maidens suffered martyrdom. Whence came this influence? The Messiah was come. These were the effect and sign of His coming.

772

Destruction of the Jews and heathen by Jesus Christ: *Omnes gentes venient et adorabunt eum. Parum est ut*, etc. *Postula a me. Adorabunt eum omnes reges. Testes iniqui. Dabit maxillam percutienti. Dederunt fel in escam.*

773

Jesus Christ for all, Moses for a nation.

The Jews blessed in Abraham: "I will bless those that bless thee." But: "All nations blessed in his seed." *Parum est ut*, etc.

Lumen ad revelationem gentium.

Non fecit taliter omni nationi, said David, in speaking of the Law. But, in speaking of Jesus Christ, we must say: *Fecit taliter omni nationi. Parum est ut*, etc., Isaiah. So it belongs to Jesus Christ to be universal. Even the Church offers sacri-

fice only for the faithful. Jesus Christ offered that of the cross
for all.

774

There is heresy in always explaining *omnes* by "all," and
heresy is not explaining it sometimes by "all." *Bibite ex hoc
omnes*; The Huguenots are heretics in explaining it by "all."
In quo omnes peccaverunt; the Huguenots are heretics in excepting the children of true believers. We must then follow
the Fathers and tradition in order to know when to do so,
since there is heresy to be feared on both sides.

775

*Ne timeas pusillus grex. Timore et tremore.—Quid ergo?
Ne timeas [modo] timeas.* Fear not, provided you fear; but
if you fear not, then fear.
Qui me recipit, non me recipit, sed eum qui me misit.
Nemo scit, neque Filius.
Nubes lucida obumbravit.
Saint John was to turn the hearts of the fathers to the
children, and Jesus Christ to plant division. There is not con-
tradiction.

776

The effects *in communi* and *in particulari*. The semi-
Pelagians err in saying of *in communi* what is true only *in
particulari*; and the Calvinists in saying *in particulari* what is
true *in communi*. (Such is my opinion.)

777

*Omnis Judæa regio, et Jerosolomymi universi, et baptiza-
bantur.* Because of all the conditions of men who came there.
From these stones there *can* come children unto Abraham.

778

If men knew themselves, God would heal and pardon them.
Ne convertantur et sanem eos, et dimittantur eis peccata.

779

Jesus Christ never condemned without hearing. To Judas: *Amice, ad quid venisti?* To him that had not on the wedding garment, the same.

780

The types of the completeness of the Redemption, as that the sun gives light to all, indicate only completeness; but [*the types*] of exclusions, as of the Jews elected to the exclusion of the Gentiles, indicate exclusion.

"Jesus Christ the Redeemer of all."—Yes, for He has offered, like a man who has ransomed all those who were willing to come to Him. If any die on the way, it is their misfortune; but, so far as He was concerned, He offered them redemption.—That holds good in this example, where he who ransoms and he who prevents death are two persons, but not of Jesus Christ, who does both these things.—No, for Jesus Christ, in the quality of Redeemer, is not perhaps Master of all; and thus, in so far as it is in Him, He is the Redeemer of all.

When it is said that Jesus Christ did not die for all, you take undue advantage of a fault in men who at once apply this exception to themselves; and this is to favour despair, instead of turning them from it to favour hope. For men thus accustom themselves in inward virtues by outward customs.

781

The victory over death. "What is a man advantaged if he gain the whole world and lose his own soul? Whosoever will save his soul, shall lose it."

"I am not come to destroy the law, but to fulfil."

"Lambs took not away the sins of the world, but I am the lamb which taketh away the sins."

"Moses hath not led you out of captivity, and made you truly free."

782

. . . Then Jesus Christ comes to tell men that they have no other enemies but themselves; that it is their passions which keep them apart from God; that He comes to destroy these, and give them His grace, so as to make of them all one Holy Church; that He comes to bring back into this Church the heathen and Jews; that He comes to destroy the idols of the former and the superstition of the latter. To this all men are opposed, not only from the natural opposition of lust; but, above all, the kings of the earth, as had been foretold, join together to destroy this religion at its birth. (*Proph.: Quare fremuerunt gentes . . . reges terræ . . . adversus Christum.*)

All that is great on earth is united together; the learned, the wise, the kings. The first write; the second condemn; the last kill. And notwithstanding all these oppositions, these men, simple and weak, resist all these powers, subdue even these kings, these learned men and these sages, and remove idolatry from all the earth. And all this is done by the power which had foretold it.

783

Jesus Christ would not have the testimony of devils, nor of those who were not called, but of God and John the Baptist.

784

I consider Jesus Christ in all persons and in ourselves: Jesus Christ as a Father in His Father, Jesus Christ as a Brother in His Brethren, Jesus Christ as poor in the poor, Jesus Christ as rich in the rich, Jesus Christ as Doctor and Priest in priests, Jesus Christ as Sovereign in princes, etc. For by His glory He is all that is great, being God; and by His mortal life He is all that is poor and abject. Therefore He has taken this unhappy condition, so that He could be in all persons, and the model of all conditions.

785

Jesus Christ is an obscurity (according to what the world calls obscurity), such that historians, writing only of important matters of states, have hardly noticed Him.

786

On the fact that neither Josephus, nor Tacitus, nor other historians have spoken of Jesus Christ.—So far is this from telling against Christianity, that on the contrary it tells for it. For it is certain that Jesus Christ has existed; that His religion has made a great talk; and that these persons were not ignorant of it. Thus it is plain that they purposely concealed it, or that, if they did speak of it, their account has been suppressed or changed.

787

"I have reserved me seven thousand." I love the worshippers unknown to the world and to the very prophets.

788

As Jesus Christ remained unknown among men, so His truth remains among common opinions without external difference. Thus the Eucharist among ordinary bread.

789

Jesus would not be slain without the forms of justice; for it is far more ignominious to die by justice than by an unjust sedition.

790

The false justice of Pilate only serves to make Jesus Christ suffer; for he causes Him to be scourged by his false justice, and afterwards puts Him to death. It would have been better to have put Him to death at once. Thus it is with the falsely just. They do good and evil works to please the world, and to show that they are not altogether of Jesus Christ; for they are ashamed of Him. And at last, under great temptation and on great occasions, they kill Him.

791

What man ever had more renown? The whole Jewish people foretell Him before His coming. The Gentile people worship

Him after His coming. The two peoples, Gentile and Jewish, regard Him as their centre.

And yet what man enjoys this renown less? Of thirty-three years, He lives thirty without appearing. For three years He passes as an impostor; the priests and the chief people reject Him; His friends and His nearest relatives despise Him. Finally, He dies, betrayed by one of His own disciples, denied by another, and abandoned by all.

What part, then, has He in this renown? Never had man so much renown; never had man more ignominy. All that renown has served only for us, to render us capable of recognising Him; and He had none of it for Himself.

792

The infinite distance between body and mind is a symbol of the infinitely more infinite distance between mind and charity; for charity is supernatural.

All the glory of greatness has no lustre for people who are in search of understanding.

The greatness of clever men is invisible to kings, to the rich, to chiefs, and to all the worldly great.

The greatness of wisdom, which is nothing if not of God, is invisible to the carnal-minded and to the clever. These are three orders differing in kind.

Great geniuses have their power, their glory, their greatness, their victory, their lustre, and have no need of worldly greatness, with which they are not in keeping. They are seen, not by the eye, but by the mind; this is sufficient.

The saints have their power, their glory, their victory, their lustre, and need no worldly or intellectual greatness, with which they have no affinity; for these neither add anything to them, nor take away anything from them. They are seen of God and the angels, and not of the body, nor of the curious mind. God is enough for them.

Archimedes, apart from his rank, would have the same veneration. He fought no battles for the eyes to feast upon; but he has given his discoveries to all men. Oh! how brilliant he was to the mind!

Jesus Christ, without riches, and without any external exhibition of knowledge, is in His own order of holiness. He did not invent; He did not reign. But He was humble, patient, holy, holy to God, terrible to devils, without any sin. Oh! in what great pomp and in what wonderful splendour, He is come to the eyes of the heart, which perceive wisdom!

It would have been useless for Archimedes to have acted the prince in his books on geometry, although he was a prince.

It would have been useless for our Lord Jesus Christ to come like a king, in order to shine forth in His kingdom of holiness. But He came there appropriately in the glory of His own order.

It is most absurd to take offence at the lowliness of Jesus Christ, as if His lowliness were in the same order as the greatness which He came to manifest. If we consider this greatness in His life, in His passion, in His obscurity, in His death, in the choice of His disciples, in their desertion, in His secret resurrection, and the rest, we shall see it to be so immense, that we shall have no reason for being offended at a lowliness which is not of that order.

But there are some who can only admire worldly greatness, as though there were no intellectual greatness; and others who only admire intellectual greatness, as though there were not infinitely higher things in wisdom.

All bodies, the firmament, the stars, the earth and its kingdoms, are not equal to the lowest mind; for mind knows all these and itself; and these bodies nothing.

All bodies together, and all minds together, and all their products, are not equal to the least feeling of charity. This is of an order infinitely more exalted.

From all bodies together, we cannot obtain one little thought; this is impossible, and of another order. From all bodies and minds, we cannot produce a feeling of true charity; this is impossible, and of another and supernatural order.

793

Why did Jesus Christ not come in a visible manner, instead of obtaining testimony of Himself from preceding prophecies? Why did He cause Himself to be foretold in types?

794

If Jesus Christ had only come to sanctify, all Scripture and all things would tend to that end; and it would be quite easy to convince unbelievers. If Jesus Christ had only come to blind, all His conduct would be confused; and we would have no means of convincing unbelievers. But as He came *in sanctificationem et in scandalum*, as Isaiah says, we cannot convince unbelievers, and they cannot convince us. But by this very fact we convince them; since we say that in His whole conduct there is no convincing proof on one side or the other.

795

Jesus Christ does not say that He is not of Nazareth, in order to leave the wicked in their blindness; nor that He is not Joseph's son.

796

Proofs of Jesus Christ.—Jesus Christ said great things so simply, that it seems as though He had not thought them great; and yet so clearly that we easily see what He thought of them. This clearness, joined to this simplicity, is wonderful.

797

The style of the gospel is admirable in so many ways, and among the rest in hurling no invectives against the persecutors and enemies of Jesus Christ. For there is no such invective in any of the historians against Judas, Pilate, or any of the Jews.

If this moderation of the writers of the Gospels had been assumed, as well as many other traits of so beautiful a character, and they had only assumed it to attract notice, even if they had not dared to draw attention to it themselves, they would not have failed to secure friends, who would have made such remarks to their advantage. But as they acted thus without pretence, and from wholly disinterested motives, they did not point it out to any one; and I believe that many such facts have not been noticed till now, which is evidence of the natural disinterestedness with which the thing has been done.

798

An artisan who speaks of wealth, a lawyer who speaks of war, of royalty, etc.; but the rich man rightly speaks of wealth, a king speaks indifferently of a great gift he has just made, and God rightly speaks of God.

799

Who has taught the evangelists the qualities of a perfectly heroic soul, that they paint it so perfectly in Jesus Christ? Why do they make Him weak in His agony? Do they not know how to paint a resolute death? Yes, for the same Saint Luke paints the death of Saint Stephen as braver than that of Jesus Christ.

They make Him therefore capable of fear, before the necessity of dying has come, and then altogether brave.

But when they make Him so troubled, it is when He afflicts Himself; and when men afflict Him, He is altogether strong.

800

Proof of Jesus Christ.—The supposition that the apostles were impostors is very absurd. Let us think it out. Let us imagine those twelve men, assembled after the death of Jesus Christ, plotting to say that He was risen. By this they attack all the powers. The heart of man is strangely inclined to fickleness, to change, to promises, to gain. However little any of them might have been led astray by all these attractions, nay more, by the fear of prisons, tortures, and death, they were lost. Let us follow up this thought.

801

The apostles were either deceived or deceivers. Either supposition has difficulties; for it is not possible to mistake a man raised from the dead . . .

While Jesus Christ was with them, He could sustain them But, after that, if He did not appear to them, who inspired them to act?

THE MIRACLES

802

The beginning.—Miracles enable us to judge of doctrine, and doctrine enables us to judge of miracles.

There are false miracles and true. There must be a distinction, in order to know them; otherwise they would be useless. Now they are not useless; on the contrary, they are fundamental. Now the rule which is given to us must be such, that it does not destroy the proof which the true miracles give of the truth, which is the chief end of the miracles.

Moses has given two rules: that the prediction does not come to pass (Deut. xviii), and that they do not lead to idolatry (Deut. xiii); and Jesus Christ one.

If doctrine regulates miracles, miracles are useless for doctrine.

If miracles regulate . . .

Objection to the rule.—The distinction of the times. One rule during the time of Moses, another at present.

803

Miracle.—It is an effect, which exceeds the natural power of the means which are employed for it; and what is not a miracle is an effect, which does not exceed the natural power of the means which are employed for it. Thus, those who heal by invocation of the devil do not work a miracle; for that does not exceed the natural power of the devil. But . . .

804

The two fundamentals; one inward, the other outward; grace and miracles; both supernatural.

805

Miracles and truth are necessary, because it is necessary to convince the entire man, in body and soul.

806

In all times, either men have spoken of the true God, or the true God has spoken to men.

807

Jesus Christ has verified that He was the Messiah, never in verifying His doctrine by Scripture and the prophecies, but always by His miracles.

He proves by a miracle that He remits sins.

Rejoice not in your miracles, said Jesus Christ, but because your names are written in heaven.

If they believe not Moses, neither will they believe one risen from the dead.

Nicodemus recognises by His miracles that His teaching is of God. *Scimus quia venisti a Deo magister; nemo enim potest hæc signa facere quæ tu facis nisi Deus fuerit cum eo.* He does not judge of the miracles by the teaching, but of the teaching by the miracles.

The Jews had a doctrine of God as we have one of Jesus Christ, and confirmed by miracles. They were forbidden to believe every worker of miracles; and they were further commanded to have recourse to the chief priests, and to rely on them.

And thus, in regard to their prophets, they had all those reasons which we have for refusing to believe the workers of miracles.

And yet they were very sinful in rejecting the prophets, and Jesus Christ, because of their miracles; and they would not have been culpable, if they had not seen the miracles. *Nisi fecissem . . . peccatum non haberent.* Therefore all belief rests upon miracles.

Prophecy is not called miracle; as Saint John speaks of the first miracle in Cana, and then of what Jesus Christ says to the woman of Samaria, when He reveals to her all her hidden life. Then He heals the centurion's son; and Saint John calls this "the second miracle."

808

The combinations of miracles.

809

The second miracle can suppose the first, but the first cannot suppose the second.

810

Had it not been for the miracles, there would have been no sin in not believing in Jesus Christ.

811

I should not be a Christian, but for the miracles, said Saint Augustine.

812

Miracles.—How I hate those who make men doubt of miracles! Montaigne speaks of them as he should in two places. In one, we see how careful he is; and yet, in the other, he believes, and makes sport of unbelievers.

However it may be, the Church is without proofs if they are right.

813

Montaigne against miracles.
Montaigne for miracles.

814

It is not possible to have a reasonable belief against miracles.

815

Unbelievers the most credulous. They believe the miracles of Vespasian, in order not to believe those of Moses.

816

Title: How it happens that men believe so many liars, who say that they have seen miracles, and do not believe any of those who say that they have secrets to make men immortal, or restore youth to them.—Having considered how it happens that so great credence is given to so many impostors, who say they have remedies, often to the length of men putting their lives into their hands, it has appeared to me that the true cause is that there are true remedies. For it would not be possible that there should be so many false remedies, and that so much faith should be placed in them, if there were none true. If there had never been any remedy for any ill, and all ills had been incurable, it is impossible that men should have imagined that they could give remedies, and still more impossible that so many others should have believed those who boasted of having remedies; in the same way as did a man boast of preventing death, no one would believe him, because there is no example of this. But as there were a number of remedies found to be true by the very knowledge of the greatest men, the belief of men is thereby induced; and, this being known to be possible, it has been therefore concluded that it was. For people commonly reason thus: "A thing is possible, therefore it is"; because the thing cannot be denied generally, since there are particular effects which are true, the people, who cannot distinguish which among these particular effects are true, believe them all. In the same way, the reason why so many false effects are credited to the moon, is that there are some true, as the tide.

It is the same with prophecies, miracles, divination by dreams, sorceries, etc. For if there had been nothing true in all this, men would have believed nothing of them; and thus,

instead of concluding that there are no true miracles because
there are so many false, we must, on the contrary, say that
there certainly are true miracles, since there are false, and
that there are false miracles only because some are true. We
must reason in the same way about religion; for it would not not
be possible that men should have imagined so many false religions, if there had not been a true one. The objection to
this is that savages have a religion; but the answer is that
they have heard the true spoken of, as appears by the deluge,
circumcision, the cross of Saint Andrew, etc.

817

Having considered how it comes that there are so many
false miracles, false revelations, sorceries, etc., it has seemed
to me that the true cause is that there are some true; for it
would not be possible that there should be so many false
miracles, if there were none true, nor so many false revelations, if there were none true, nor so many false religions, if
there were not one true. For if there had never been all this,
it is almost impossible that men should have imagined it, and
still more impossible that so many others should have believed it. But as there have been very great things true, and
as they have been believed by great men, this impression has
been the cause that nearly everybody is rendered capable of
believing also the false. And thus, instead of concluding that
there are no true miracles, since there are so many false, it
must be said, on the contrary, that there are true miracles,
since there are so many false; and that there are false ones
only because there are true; and that in the same way there are
false religions because there is one true.—Objection to this:
savages have a religion. But this is because they have heard
the true spoken of, as appears by the cross of Saint Andrew,
the deluge, circumcision, etc.—This arises from the fact that
the human mind, finding itself inclined to that side by the
truth, becomes thereby susceptible of all the falsehoods of
this . . .

818

Jeremiah xxiii, 32. The *miracles* of the false prophets. In the Hebrew and Vatable they are the *tricks*.

Miracle does not always signify miracle. 1 Sam. xiv, 15; *miracle* signifies *fear*, and is so in the Hebrew. The same evidently in Job xxxiii, 7; and also Isaiah xxi, 4; Jeremiah xliv, 12. *Portentum* signifies *simulacrum*, Jeremiah l, 38; and it is so in the Hebrew and Vatable. Isaiah viii, 18. Jesus Christ says that He and His will be in *miracles*.

819

If the devil favoured the doctrine which destroys him, he would be divided against himself, as Jesus Christ said. If God favoured the doctrine which destroys the Church, He would be divided against Himself. *Omne regnum divisum.* For Jesus Christ wrought against the devil, and destroyed his power over the heart, of which exorcism is the symbolisation, in order to establish the kingdom of God. And thus He adds, *Si in digito Dei . . . regnum Dei ad vos.*

820

There is a great difference between tempting and leading into error. God tempts, but He does not lead into error. To tempt is to afford opportunities, which impose no necessity; if men do not love God, they will do a certain thing. To lead into error is to place a man under the necessity of inferring and following out what is untrue.

821

Abraham and Gideon are above revelation. The Jews blinded themselves in judging of miracles by the Scripture. God has never abandoned His true worshippers.

I prefer to follow Jesus Christ than any other, because He has miracle, prophecy, doctrine, perpetuity, etc.

The Donatists. No miracle which obliges them to say it is the devil.

The more we particularise God, Jesus Christ, the Church . . .

822

If there were no false miracles, there would be certainty. If there were no rule to judge of them, miracles would be useles and there would be no reason for believing.

Now there is, humanly speaking, no human certainty, but we have reason.

823

Either God has confounded the false miracles, or He has foretold them; and in both ways He has raised Himself above what is supernatural with respect to us, and has raised us to it.

824

Miracles serve not to convert, but to condemn. (Q. 113, A. 10, *Ad.* 2.)

825

Reasons why we do not believe.

John xii, 37. *Cum autem tanta signa fecisset, non credebant in eum, ut sermo Isayæ impleretur. Excæcavit,* etc.

Hæc dixit Isaias, quando vidit gloriam ejus et locutus est de eo.

Judæi signa petunt et Græci sapientiam quærunt, nos autem Jesum crucifixum. Sed plenum signis, sed plenum sapientia; vos autem Christum non crucifixum et religionem sine miraculis et sine sapientia.

What makes us not believe in the true miracles, is want of love. John: *Sed vos non creditis, quia non estis ex ovibus.* What makes us believe the false is want of love. II Thess. ii.

The foundation of religion. It is the miracles. What then? Does God speak against miracles, against the foundations of the faith which we have in Him?

If there is a God, faith in God must exist on earth. Now the miracles of Jesus Christ are not foretold by Antichrist, but the miracles of Antichrist are foretold by Jesus Christ. And so if Jesus Christ were not the Messiah, He would have indeed led into error. When Jesus Christ foretold the miracles of Antichrist, did He think of destroying faith in His own miracles?

Moses foretold Jesus Christ, and bade to follow Him. Jesus Christ foretold Antichrist, and forbade to follow him.

It was impossible that in the time of Moses men should keep their faith for Antichrist, who was unknown to them. But it is quite easy, in the time of Antichrist, to believe in Jesus Christ, already known.

There is no reason for believing in Antichrist, which there is not for believing in Jesus Christ. But there are reasons for believing in Jesus Christ, which there are not for believing in the other.

826

Judges xiii, 23: "If the Lord were pleased to kill us, He would not have shewed us all these things."

Hezekiah, Sennacherib.

Jeremiah. Hananiah, the false prophet, dies in seven months.

2 Macc. iii. The temple, ready for pillage, miraculously succoured.—2 Macc. xv.

1 Kings xvii. The widow to Elijah, who had restored her son, "By this I know that thy words are true."

1 Kings xviii. Elijah with the prophets of Baal.

In the dispute concerning the true God and the truth of religion, there has never happened any miracle on the side of error, and not of truth.

827

Opposition.—Abel, Cain; Moses, the Magicians; Elijah, the false prophets: Jeremiah, Hananiah; Micaiah, the false prophets; Jesus Christ, the Pharisees; Saint Paul, Bar-jesus; the Apostles, the Exorcists; Christians, unbelievers; Catholics, heretics; Elijah, Enoch, Antichrist.

828

Jesus Christ says that the Scriptures testify of Him. But He does not point out in what respect.

Even the prophecies could not prove Jesus Christ during His life; and so, men would not have been culpable for not believing in Him before His death, had the miracles not sufficed without doctrine. Now those who did not believe in Him, when He was still alive, were sinners, as He said Himself, and without excuse. Therefore they must have had proof beyond doubt, which they resisted. Now, they had not the prophecies, but only the miracles. Therefore the latter suffice, when the doctrine is not inconsistent with them; and they ought to be believed.

John vii, 40. *Dispute among the Jews as among the Christians of to-day.* Some believed in Jesus Christ; others believed Him not, because of the prophecies which said that He should be born in Bethlehem. They should have considered more carefully whether He was not. For His miracles being convincing, they should have been quite sure of these supposed contradictions of His teaching to Scripture; and this obscurity did not excuse, but blinded them. Thus those who refuse to believe in the miracles in the present day on account of a supposed contradiction, which is unreal, are not excused.

The Pharisees said to the people, who believed in Him, because of His miracles: "This people who knoweth not the law are cursed. But have any of the rulers or of the Pharisees believed in him? For we know that out of Galilee ariseth no prophet." Nicodemus answered: "Doth our law judge any man before it hear him, [and specially, such a man who works such miracles]?"

829

The prophecies were ambiguous; they are no longer so.

830

The five propositions were ambiguous; they are no longer so.

831

Miracles are no longer necessary, because we have had
them already. But when tradition is no longer minded; when
the Pope alone is offered to us; when he has been imposed
upon; and when the true source of truth, which is tradition,
is thus excluded; and the Pope, who is its guardian, is biased;
the truth is no longer free to appear. Then, as men speak no
longer of truth, truth itself must speak to men. This is what
happened in the time of Arius. (Miracles under Diocletian
and under Arius.)

832

Miracle.—The people concluded this of themselves; but if
the reason of it must be given to you . . .

It is unfortunate to be in exception to the rule. The same
must be strict, and opposed to exception. But yet, as it is
certain that there are exceptions to a rule, our judgment
must though strict, be just.

833

John vi, 26: *Non quia vidisti signum, sed quia saturati
estis.*

Those who follow Jesus Christ because of His miracles
honour His power in all the miracles which it produces. But
those who, making profession to follow Him because of His
miracles, follow Him in fact only because He comforts them
and satisfies them with worldly blessings, discredit His miracles, when they are opposed to their own comforts.

John ix: *Non est hic homo a Deo, quia sabbatum non cus-
todit. Alii: Quomodo potest homo peccator hæc signa facere?*

Which is the most clear?

This house is not of God; for they do not there believe that
the five propositions are in Jansenius. Others: This house is
of God; for in it there are wrought strange miracles.

Which is the most clear?

*Tu quid dicis? Dico quia propheta est. Nisi esset hic a
Deo, non poterat facere quidquam.*

834

In the Old Testament, when they will turn you from God. In the New, when they will turn you from Jesus Christ. These are the occasions for excluding particular miracles from belief. No others need be excluded.

Does it therefore follow that they would have the right to exclude all the prophets who came to them? No; they would have sinned in not excluding those who denied God, and would have sinned in excluding those who did not deny God.

So soon, then, as we see a miracle, we must either assent to it, or have striking proofs to the contrary. We must see if it denies a God, or Jesus Christ, or the Church.

835

There is a great difference between not being for Jesus Christ and saying so, and not being for Jesus Christ and pretending to be so. The one party can do miracles, not the others. For it is clear of the one party, that they are opposed to the truth, but not of the others; and thus miracles are clearer.

836

That we must love one God only is a thing so evident, that it does not require miracles to prove it.

837

Jesus Christ performed miracles, then the apostles, and the first saints in great number; because the prophecies not being yet accomplished, but in the process of being accomplished by them, the miracles alone bore witness to them. It was foretold that the Messiah should convert the nations. How could this prophecy be fulfilled without the conversion of the nations? And how could the nations be converted to the Messiah, if they did not see this final effect of the prophecies which prove Him? Therefore, till He had died, risen again, and converted the nations, all was not accomplished;

and so miracles were needed during all this time. Now they
are no longer needed against the Jews; for the accomplished
prophecies constitute a lasting miracle.

838

"Though ye believe not Me, believe at least the works."
He refers them, as it were, to the strongest proof.

It had been told to the Jews, as well as to Christians, that
they should not always believe the prophets; but yet the
Pharisees and Scribes are greatly concerned about His miracles, and try to show that they are false, or wrought by the
devil. For they must needs be convinced, if they acknowledge
that they are of God.

At the present day we are not troubled to make this distinction. Still it is very easy to do: those who deny neither
God nor Jesus Christ do no miracles which are not certain.
*Nemo facit virtutem in nomine meo, et cito possit de me male
loqui.*

But we have not to draw this distinction. Here is a sacred
relic. Here is a thorn from the crown of the Saviour of the
world, over whom the prince of this world has no power, which
works miracles by the peculiar power of the blood shed for us.
Now God Himself chooses this house in order to display con-
spicuously therein His power.

These are not men who do miracles by an unknown and
doubtful virtue, which makes a decision difficult for us. It is
God Himself. It is the instrument of the Passion of His only
Son, who, being in many places, chooses this, and makes men
come from all quarters there to receive these miraculous
alleviations in their weaknesses.

839

The Church has three kinds of enemies: the Jews, who
have never been of her body; the heretics, who have with-
drawn from it; and the evil Christians, who rend her from
within.

These three kinds of different adversaries usually attack

her in different ways. But here they attack her in one and the same way. As they are all without miracles, and as the Church has always had miracles against them, they have all had the same interest in evading them; and they all make use of this excuse, that doctrine must not be judged by miracles, but miracles by doctrine. There were two parties among those who heard Jesus Christ: those who followed His teaching on account of His miracles; others who said . . . There were two parties in the time of Calvin . . . There are now the Jesuits, etc.

840

Miracles furnish the test in matters of doubt, between Jews and heathens, Jews and Christians, Catholics and heretics, the slandered and slanderers, between the two crosses.

But miracles would be useless to heretics; for the Church, authorised by miracles which have already obtained belief, tells us that they have not the true faith. There is no doubt that they are not in it, since the first miracles of the Church exclude belief of theirs. Thus there is miracle against miracle, both the first and greatest being on the side of the Church.

These nuns, astonished at what is said, that they are in the way of perdition; that their confessors are leading them to Geneva; that they suggest to them that Jesus Christ is not in the Eucharist, nor on the right hand of the Father; know that all this is false, and therefore offer themselves to God in this state. *Vide si via iniquitatis in me est.* What happens thereupon? This place, which is said to be the temple of the devil, God makes His own temple. It is said that the children must be taken away from it. God heals them there. It is said that it is the arsenal of hell. God makes of it the sanctuary of His grace. Lastly, they are threatened with all the fury and vengeance of heaven; and God overwhelms them with favours. A man would need to have lost his senses to conclude from this that they are therefore in the way of perdition.

(We have without doubt the same signs as Saint Athanasius.)

841

Si tu es Christus, dic nobis.

Opera quæ ego facio in nomine patris mei, hæc testimonium perhibent de me. Sed vos non creditis quia non estis ex ovibus meis. Oves meæ vocem meam audiunt.

John vi, 30. *Quod ergo tu facis signum ut videamus et credamus tibi?—Non dicunt: Quam doctrinam prædicas?*

Nemo potest facere signa quæ tu facis nisi Deus.

2 Macc. xiv, 15. *Deus qui signis evidentibus suam portionem protegit.*

Volumus signum videre de cœlo, tentantes eum. Luke xi, 16. *Generatio prava signum quærit; et non dabitur.*

Et ingemiscens ait: Quid generatio ista signum quærit? (Mark viii, 12.) They asked a sign with an evil intention.

Et non poterat facere. And yet he promises them the sign of Jonah, the great and wonderful miracle of his resurrection.

Nisi videritis, non creditis. He does not blame them for not believing unless there are miracles, but for not believing unless they are themselves spectators of them.

Antichrist *in signis mendacibus,* says Saint Paul, 2 Thess. ii.

Secundum operationem Satanæ, in seductione iis qui pereunt eo quod charitatem veritatis non receperunt ut salvi fierent, ideo mittet illis Deus optationes erroris ut credant mendacio.

As in the passage of Moses: *Tentat enim vos Deus, utrum diligatis eum.*

Ecce prædixi vobis: vos ergo videte.

842

Here is not the country of truth. She wanders unknown amongst men. God has covered her with a veil, which leaves her unrecognised by those who do not hear her voice. Room is opened for blasphemy, even against the truths that are at least very likely. If the truths of the Gospel are published, the contrary is published too, and the questions are obscured, so that the people cannot distinguish. And they ask, "What have you to make you believed rather than others? What sign do you give? You have only words, and so have we. If you had miracles, good and well." That doctrine ought to be supported by miracles is a truth, which they misuse in order to revile doctrine. And if miracles happen, it is said that miracles are not enough without doctrine; and this is another truth, which they misuse in order to revile miracles.

Jesus Christ cured the man born blind, and performed a number of miracles on the Sabbath day. In this way He blinded the Pharisees, who said that miracles must be judged by doctrine.

"We have Moses: but, as for this fellow, we know not from whence he is." It is wonderful that you know not whence He is, and yet He does such miracles.

Jesus Christ spoke neither against God, nor against Moses.

Antichrist and the false prophets, foretold by both Testaments, will speak openly against God and against Jesus Christ. Who is not hidden . . . God would not allow him, who would be a secret enemy, to do miracles openly.

In a public dispute where the two parties profess to be for God, for Jesus Christ, for the Church, miracles have never been on the side of the false Christians, and the other side has never been without a miracle.

"He hath a devil." John x, 21. And others said, "Can a devil open the eyes of the blind?"

The proofs which Jesus Christ and the apostles draw from Scripture are not conclusive; for they say only that Moses foretold that a prophet should come. But they do not thereby prove that this is He; and that is the whole question. These passages therefore serve only to show that they are not contrary to Scripture, and that there appears no inconsistency, but not that there is agreement. Now this is enough, namely, exclusion of inconsistency, along with miracles.

There is a mutual duty between God and men. We must pardon Him this saying: *Quid debui?* "Accuse me," said God in Isaiah.

"God must fulfil His promises," etc.

Men owe it to God to accept the religion which He sends. God owes it to men not to lead them into error. Now, they would be led into error, if the workers of miracles announced a doctrine which should not appear evidently false to the light of common sense, and if a greater worker of miracles had not already warned men not to believe them.

Thus, if there were divisions in the Church, and the Arians, for example, who declared themselves founded on Scripture just as the Catholics, had done miracles, and not the Catholics, men should have been led into error.

For, as a man, who announces to us the secrets of God, is not worthy to be believed on his private authority, and that is why the ungodly doubt him; so when a man, as a token of the communion which he has with God, raises the dead, foretells the future, removes the seas, heals the sick, there is none so wicked as not to bow to him, and the incredulity of Pharaoh and the Pharisees is the effect of a supernatural obduracy.

When, therefore, we see miracles and a doctrine not suspicious, both on one side, there is no difficulty. But when we see miracles and suspicious doctrine on the same side, we must then see which is the clearest. Jesus Christ was suspected.

Bar-jesus blinded. The power of God surpasses that of His enemies.

The Jewish exorcists beaten by the devils, saying, "Jesus I know, and Paul I know; but who are ye?"

Miracles are for doctrine, and not doctrine for miracles.

If the miracles are true, shall we be able to persuade men of all doctrine? No; for this will not come to pass. *Si angelus* . . .

Rule: we must judge of doctrine by miracles; we must judge of miracles by doctrine. All this is true, but contains no contradiction.

For we must distinguish the times.

How glad you are to know the general rules, thinking

thereby to set up dissension, and render all useless! We shall prevent you, my father; truth is one and constant.

It is impossible, from the duty of God to men, that a man, hiding his evil teaching, and only showing the good, saying that he conforms to God and the Church, should do miracles so as to instil insensibly a false and subtle doctrine. This cannot happen.

And still less, that God, who knows the heart, should perform miracles in favour of such a one.

843

The three marks of religion: perpetuity, a good life, miracles. They destroy perpetuity by their doctrine of probability; a good life by their morals; miracles by destroying either their truth or the conclusions to be drawn from them.

If we believe them, the Church will have nothing to do with perpetuity, holiness, and miracles. The heretics deny them, or deny the conclusions to be drawn from them; they do the same. But one would need to have no sincerity in order to deny them, or again to lose one's senses in order to deny the conclusions to be drawn from them.

Nobody has ever suffered martyrdom for the miracles which he says he has seen; for the folly of men goes perhaps to the length of martyrdom, for those which the Turks believe by tradition, but not for those which they have seen.

844

The heretics have always attacked these three marks, which they have not.

845

First objection: "An angel from heaven. We must not judge of truth by miracles, but of miracles by truth. Therefore the miracles are useless."

Now they are of use, and they must not be in opposition to the truth. Therefore what Father Lingende has said, that "God will not permit that a miracle may lead into error . . ."

When there shall be a controversy in the same Church, miracle will decide.

Second objection: "But Antichrist will do miracles."

The magicians of Pharaoh did not entice to error. Thus we cannot say to Jesus respecting Antichrist, "You have led me into error." For Antichrist will do them against Jesus Christ, and so they cannot lead into error. Either God will not permit false miracles, or He will procure greater.

[Jesus Christ has existed since the beginning of the world: this is more impressive than all the miracles of Antichrist.]

If in the same Church there should happen a miracle on the side of those in error, men would be led into error. Schism is visible; a miracle is visible. But schism is more a sign of error than a miracle is a sign of truth. Therefore a miracle cannot lead into error.

But apart from schism, error is not so obvious as a miracle is obvious. Therefore a miracle could lead into error.

Ubi est Deus tuus? Miracles show Him, and are a light.

846

One of the anthems for Vespers at Christmas: *Exortum est in tenebris lumen rectis corde.*

847

If the compassion of God is so great that He instructs us to our benefit, even when He hides Himself, what light ought we not to expect from Him when He reveals Himself?

848

Will *Est et non est* be received in faith itself as well as in miracles? And if it is inseparable in the others . . .

When Saint Xavier works miracles.—[Saint Hilary. "Ye wretches, who oblige us to speak of miracles."]

Unjust judges, make not your own laws on the moment; judge by those which are established, and by yourselves. *Væ qui conditis leges iniquas.*

Miracles endless, false.

In order to weaken your adversaries, you disarm the whole Church.

If they say that our salvation depends upon God, they are "heretics." If they say that they are obedient to the Pope, that is "hypocrisy." If they are ready to subscribe to all the articles, that is not enough. If they say that a man must not be killed for an apple, "they attack the morality of Catholics." If miracles are done among them, it is not a sign of holiness, and is, on the contrary, a symptom of heresy.

This way in which the Church has existed is that truth has been without dispute, or, if it has been contested, there has been the Pope, or, failing him, there has been the Church.

849

The five propositions condemned, but no miracle; for the truth was not attacked. But the Sorbonne . . . but the bull . . .

It is impossible that those who love God with all their heart should fail to recognise the Church; so evident is she.—It is impossible that those who do not love God should be convinced of the Church.

Miracles have such influence that it was necessary that God should warn men not to believe in them in opposition to Him, all clear as it is that there is a God. Without this they would have been able to disturb men.

And thus so far from these passages, Deut. xiii, making against the authority of the miracles, nothing more indicates their influence. And the same in respect of Antichrist. "To seduce, if it were possible, even the elect."

850

The history of the man born blind.

What says Saint Paul? Does he continually speak of the evidence of the prophecies? No, but of his own miracle. What says Jesus Christ? Does He speak of the evidence of the prophecies? No; His death had not fulfilled them. But he says, *Si non fecissem*. Believe the works.

Two supernatural foundations of our wholly supernatural

religion; one visible, the other invisible; miracles with grace, miracles without grace.

The synagogue, which had been treated with love as a type of the Church, and with hatred, because it was only the type, has been restored, being on the point of falling when it was well with God, and thus a type.

Miracles prove the power which God has over hearts, by that which He exercises over bodies.

The Church has never approved a miracle among heretics.

Miracles a support of religion: they have been the test of Jews; they have been the test of Christians, saints, innocents, and true believers.

A miracle among schismatics is not so much to be feared; for schism, which is more obvious than a miracle, visibly indicates their error. But when there is no schism, and error is in question, miracle decides.

Si non fecissem quæ alius non fecit. The wretches who have obliged us to speak of miracles.

Abraham and Gideon confirm faith by miracles.

Judith. God speaks at last in their greatest oppression.

If the cooling of love leaves the Church almost without believers, miracles will rouse them. This is one of the last effects of grace.

If one miracle were wrought among the Jesuits!

When a miracle disappoints the expectation of those in whose presence it happens, and there is a disproportion between the state of their faith and the instrument of the miracle, it ought then to induce them to change. But with you it is otherwise. There would be as much reason in saying that, if the Eucharist raised a dead man, it would be necessary for one to turn a Calvinist rather than remain a Catholic. But when it crowns the expectation, and those, who hoped that God would bless the remedies, see themselves healed without remedies . . .

The ungodly.—No sign has ever happened on the part of the devil without a stronger sign on the part of God, or even without it having been foretold that such would happen.

851

Unjust persecutors of those whom God visibly protects. If they reproach you with your excesses, "they speak as the heretics." If they say that the grace of Jesus Christ distinguishes us, "they are heretics." If they do miracles, "it is the mark of their heresy."

Ezekiel.—They say: These are the people of God who speak thus.

It is said, "Believe in the Church"; but it is not said, "Believe in miracles"; because the last is natural, and not the first. The one had need of a precept, not the other. Hezekiah.

The synagogue was only a type, and thus it did not perish; and it was only a type, and so it is decayed. It was a type which contained the truth, and thus it has lasted until it no longer contained the truth.

My reverend father, all this happened in types. Other religions perish; this one perishes not.

Miracles are more important than you think. They have served for the foundation, and will serve for the continuation of the Church till Antichrist, till the end.

The two witnesses.

In the Old Testament and the New, miracles are performed in connection with types. Salvation, or a useless thing, if not to show that we must submit to the Scriptures: type of the sacrament.

852

[We must judge soberly of divine ordinances, my father. Saint Paul in the isle of Malta.]

853

The hardness of the Jesuits, then, surpasses that of the Jews, since those refused to believe Jesus Christ innocent only because they doubted if His miracles were of God. Whereas the Jesuits, though unable to doubt that the miracles of Port-Royal are of God, do not cease to doubt still the innocence of that house.

854

I suppose that men believe miracles. You corrupt religion either in favour of your friends, or against your enemies. You arrange it at your will.

855

On the miracle.—As God has made no family more happy, let it also be the case that He find none more thankful.

APPENDIX: POLEMICAL FRAGMENTS

856

Clearness, obscurity.—There would be too great darkness, if truth had not visible signs. This is a wonderful one, that it has always been preserved in one Church and one visible assembly [of men]. There would be too great clearness, if there were only one opinion in this Church. But in order to recognise what is true, one has only to look at what has always existed; for it is certain that truth has always existed, and that nothing false has always existed.

857

The history of the Church ought properly to be called the history of truth.

858

There is a pleasure in being in a ship beaten about by a storm, when we are sure that it will not founder. The persecutions which harass the Church are of this nature.

859

In addition to so many other signs of piety, they are also persecuted, which is the best sign of piety.

860

The Church is in an excellent state, when it is sustained by God only.

861

The Church has always been attacked by opposite errors, but perhaps never at the same time, as now. And if she suffer more because of the multiplicity of errors, she derives this advantage from it, that they destroy each other.

She complains of both, but far more of the Calvinists, because of the schism.

It is certain that many of the two opposite sects are deceived. They must be disillusioned.

Faith embraces many truths which seem to contradict each other. *There is a time to laugh, and a time to weep,* etc. *Responde. Ne respondeas,* etc.

The source of this is the union of the two natures in Jesus Christ; and also the two worlds (the creation of a new heaven and a new earth; a new life and a new death; all things double, and the same names remaining); and finally the two natures that are in the righteous, (for they are the two worlds, and a member and image of Jesus Christ. And thus all the names suit them: righteous, yet sinners; dead, yet living; living, yet dead; elect, yet outcast, etc.).

There are then a great number of truths, both of faith and of morality, which seem contradictory, and which all hold good together in a wonderful system. The source of all heresies is the exclusion of some of these truths; and the source of all the objections which the heretics make against us is the ignorance of some of our truths. And it generally happens that, unable to conceive the connection of two opposite truths, and believing that the admission of one involves the exclusion of the other, they adhere to the one, exclude the other, and think of us as opposed to them. Now exclusion is the cause of their heresy; and ignorance that we hold the other truth causes their objections.

1st example: Jesus Christ is God and man. The Arians, unable to reconcile these things, which they believe incompatible, say that He is man; in this they are Catholics. But they deny that He is God; in this they are heretics. They allege that we deny His humanity; in this they are ignorant.

2nd example: On the subject of the Holy Sacrament. We believe that, the substance of the bread being changed, and being consubstantial with that of the body of our Lord, Jesus Christ is therein really present. That is one truth. Another is that this Sacrament is also a type of the cross and of glory, and a commemoration of the two. That is the Catholic faith, which comprehends these two truths which seem opposed.

The heresy of to-day, not conceiving that this Sacrament contains at the same time both the presence of Jesus Christ and a type of Him, and that it is a sacrifice and a commemoration of a sacrifice, believes that neither of these truths can be admitted without excluding the other for this reason.

They fasten to this point alone, that this Sacrament is typical; and in this they are not heretics. They think that we exclude this truth; hence it comes that they raise so many objections to us out of the passages of the Fathers which assert it. Finally, they deny the presence; and in this they are heretics.

3rd example: Indulgences.

The shortest way, therefore, to prevent heresies is to instruct in all truths; and the surest way to refute them is to declare them all. For what will the heretics say?

In order to know whether an opinion is a Father's . . .

862

All err the more dangerously, as they each follow a truth. Their fault is not in following a falsehood, but in not following another truth.

863

Truth is so obscure in these times, and falsehood so established, that unless we love the truth, we cannot know it.

864

If there is ever a time in which we must make profession of two opposite truths, it is when we are reproached for omitting

one. Therefore the Jesuits and Jansenists are wrong in concealing them, but the Jansenists more so, for the Jesuits have
better made profession of the two.

865

Two kinds of people make things equal to one another, as
feasts to working days, Christians to priests, all things among
them, etc. And hence the one party conclude that what is
then bad for priests is also so for Christians, and the other
that what is not bad for Christians is lawful for priests.

866

If the ancient Church was in error, the Church is fallen. If
she should be in error to-day, it is not the same thing; for she
has always the superior maxim of tradition from the hand of
the ancient Church; and so this submission and this conformity to the ancient Church prevail and correct all. But
the ancient Church did not assume the future Church, and
did not consider her, as we assume and consider the ancient.

867

That which hinders us in comparing what formerly occurred in the Church with what we see there now, is that we
generally look upon Saint Athanasius, Saint Theresa, and the
rest, as crowned with glory, and acting towards us as gods.
Now that time has cleared up things, it does so appear. But
at the time when he was persecuted, this great saint was a man
called Athanasius; and Saint Theresa was a nun. "Elias was
a man subject to like passions as we are," says Saint James,
to disabuse Christians of that false idea which makes us reject the example of the saints, as disproportioned to our state.
"They were saints," say we, "they are not like us." What
then actually happened? Saint Athanasius was a man called
Athanasius, accused of many crimes, condemned by such and
such a council for such and such a crime. All the bishops
assented to it, and finally the Pope. What said they to those

who opposed this? That they disturbed the peace, that they created schism, etc.

Zeal, light. Four kinds of persons: zeal without knowledge; knowledge without zeal; neither knowledge nor zeal; both zeal and knowledge. The first three condemned him. The last acquitted him, were excommunicated by the Church, and yet saved the Church.

868

If Saint Augustine came at the present time, and was as little authorised as his defenders, he would accomplish nothing. God directs His Church well, by having sent him before with authority.

869

God has not wanted to absolve without the Church. As she has part in the offence, He desires her to have part in the pardon. He associates her with this power, as kings their parliaments. But if she absolves or binds without God, she is no longer the Church. For, as in the case of parliament, even if the king have pardoned a man, it must be ratified; but if parliament ratifies without the king, or refuses to ratify on the order of the king, it is no longer the parliament of the king, but a rebellious assembly.

870

The Church, the Pope. Unity, plurality.—Considering the Church as a unity, the Pope, who is its head, is as the whole. Considering it as a plurality, the Pope is only a part of it. The Fathers have considered the Church now in the one way, now in the other. And thus they have spoken differently of the Pope. (Saint Cyprian: *Sacerdos Dei.*) But in establishing one of these truths, they have not excluded the other. Plurality which is not reduced to unity is confusion; unity which does not depend on plurality is tyranny. There is scarcely any other country than France in which it is permissible to say that the Council is above the Pope.

871

The Pope is head. Who else is known of all? Who else is recognised by all, having power to insinuate himself into all the body, because he holds the principal shoot, which insinuates itself everywhere? How easy it was to make this degenerate into tyranny! That is why Christ has laid down for them this precept: *Vos autem non sic.*

872

The Pope hates and fears the learned, who do not submit to him at will.

873

We must not judge of what the Pope is by some words of the Fathers—as the Greeks said in a council, important rules —but by the acts of the Church and the Fathers, and by the canons.

Duo aut tres in unum. Unity and plurality. It is an error to exclude one of the two, as the papists do who exclude plurality, or the Huguenots who exclude unity.

874

Would the Pope be dishonoured by having his knowledge from God and tradition; and is it not dishonouring him to separate him from this holy union?

875

God does not perform miracles in the ordinary conduct of His Church. It would be a strange miracle if infallibility existed in one man. But it appears so natural for it to reside in a multitude, since the conduct of God is hidden under nature, as in all His other works.

876

Kings dispose of their own power; but the Popes cannot dispose of theirs.

877

Summum jus, summa injuria.

The majority is the best way, because it is visible, and has strength to make itself obeyed. Yet it is the opinion of the least able.

If men could have done it, they would have placed might in the hands of justice. But as might does not allow itself to be managed as men want, because it is a palpable quality, whereas justice is a spiritual quality of which men dispose as they please, they have placed justice in the hands of might. And thus that is called just which men are forced to obey.

Hence comes the right of the sword, for the sword gives a true right. Otherwise we should see violence on one side and justice on the other (end of the twelfth *Provincial*). Hence comes the injustice of the Fronde, which raises its alleged justice against power. It is not the same in the Church, for there is a true justice and no violence.

878

Injustice.—Jurisdiction is not given for the sake of the judge, but for that of the litigant. It is dangerous to tell this to the people. But the people have too much faith in you; it will not harm them, and may serve you. It should therefore be made known. *Pasce oves meas, non tuas.* You owe me pasturage.

879

Men like certainty. They like the Pope to be infallible in faith, and grave doctors to be infallible in morals, so as to have certainty.

880

The Church teaches, and God inspires, both infallibly. The work of the Church is of use only as a preparation for grace or condemnation. What it does is enough for condemnation, not for inspiration.

881

Every time the Jesuits may impose upon the Pope, they will make all Christendom perjured.

The Pope is very easily imposed upon, because of his occupations, and the confidence which he has in the Jesuits; and the Jesuits are very capable of imposing upon him by means of calumny.

882

The wretches who have obliged me to speak of the basis of religion.

883

Sinners purified without penitence; the righteous justified without love; all Christians without the grace of Jesus Christ; God without power over the will of men; a predestination without mystery; a redemption without certitude!

884

Any one is made a priest, who wants to be so, as under Jeroboam.

It is a horrible thing that they propound to us the discipline of the Church of to-day as so good, that it is made a crime to desire to change it. Formerly it was infallibly good, and it was thought that it could be changed without sin; and now, such as it is, we cannot wish it changed! It has indeed been permitted to change the custom of not making priests without such great circumspection, that there were hardly any who were worthy; and it is not allowed to complain of the custom which makes so many who are unworthy!

885

Heretics.—Ezekiel. All the heathen, and also the Prophet, spoke evil of Israel. But the Israelites were so far from having the right to say to him, "You speak like the heathen," that he is most forcible upon this, that the heathen say the same as he.

886

The Jansenists are like the heretics in the reformation of morality; but you are like them in evil.

887

You are ignorant of the prophecies, if you do not know that all this must happen; princes, prophets, Pope, and even the priests. And yet the Church is to abide. By the grace of God we have not come to that. Woe to these priests! But we hope that God will bestow His mercy upon us that we shall not be of them.

Saint Peter, ii: false prophets in the past, the image of future ones.

888

. . . So that if it is true, on the one hand, that some lax monks, and some corrupt casuists, who are not members of the hierarchy, are steeped in these corruptions, it is, on the other hand, certain that the true pastors of the Church, who are the true guardians of the Divine Word, have preserved it unchangeably against the efforts of those who have attempted to destroy it.

And thus true believers have no pretext to follow that laxity, which is only offered to them by the strange hands of these casuists, instead of the sound doctrine which is presented to them by the fatherly hands of their own pastors. And the ungodly and heretics have no ground for publishing these abuses as evidence of imperfection in the providence of God over His Church; since, the Church consisting properly in the body of the hierarchy, we are so far from being able to conclude from the present state of matters that God has abandoned her to corruption, that it has never been more apparent than at the present time that God visibly protects her from corruption.

For if some of these men, who, by an extraordinary vocation, have made profession of withdrawing from the world and adopting the monks' dress, in order to live in a more perfect state than ordinary Christians, have fallen into excesses which horrify ordinary Christians, and have become to us what the false prophets were among the Jews; this is a private and personal misfortune, which must indeed be deplored, but from which nothing can be inferred against the care which God takes of His Church; since all these things are so clearly foretold, and it has been so long since announced that these temptations would arise from people of this kind; so that when we are well instructed, we see in this rather evidence of the care of God than of His forgetfulness in regard to us.

889

Tertullian: *Nunquam Ecclesia reformabitur.*

890

Heretics, who take advantage of the doctrine of the Jesuits, must be made to know that it is not that of the Church [*the doctrine of the Church*], and that our divisions do not separate us from the altar.

891

If in differing we condemned, you would be right. Uniformity without diversity is useless to others; diversity without uniformity is ruinous for us. The one is harmful outwardly; the other inwardly.

892

By showing the truth, we cause it to be believed; but by showing the injustice of ministers, we do not correct it. Our mind is assured by a proof of falsehood; our purse is not made secure by proof of injustice.

893

Those who love the Church lament to see the corruption of morals; but laws at least exist. But these corrupt the laws. The model is damaged.

894

Men never do evil so completely and cheerfully as when they do it from religious conviction.

895

It is in vain that the Church has established these words, anathemas, heresies, etc. They are used against her.

896

The servant knoweth not what his lord doeth, for the master tells him only the act and not the intention. And this is why he often obeys slavishly, and defeats the intention. But Jesus Christ has told us the object. And you defeat that object.

897

They cannot have perpetuity, and they seek universality; and therefore they make the whole Church corrupt, that they may be saints.

898

Against those who misuse passages of Scripture, and who pride themselves in finding one which seems to favour their error.—The chapter for Vespers, Passion Sunday, the prayer for the king.

Explanation of these words: "He that is not with me is against me." And of these others: "He that is not against you is for you." A person who says: "I am neither for nor against"; we ought to reply to him . . .

899

He who will give the meaning of Scripture, and does not take it from Scripture, is an enemy of Scripture. (Aug., *De Doct. Christ.*)

900

Humilibus dat gratiam; an ideo non dedit humilitatem?
Sui eum non receperunt; quotquot autem non receperunt an non erant sui?

901

"It must indeed be," says Feuillant, "that this is not so certain; for controversy indicates uncertainty (Saint Athanasius, Saint Chrysostom, morals, unbelievers)."

The Jesuits have not made the truth uncertain, but they have made their own ungodliness certain.

Contradiction has always been permitted, in order to blind the wicked; for all that offends truth or love is evil. This is the true principle.

902

All religions and sects in the world have had natural reason for a guide. Christians alone have been constrained to take their rules from without themselves, and to acquaint themselves with those which Jesus Christ bequeathed to men of old to be handed down to true believers. This constraint wearies these good Fathers. They desire, like other people, to have liberty to follow their own imaginations. It is in vain that we cry to them, as the prophets said to the Jews of old: "Enter into the Church; acquaint yourselves with the precepts which the men of old left to her, and follow those paths." They have answered like the Jews: "We will not walk in them; but we will follow the thoughts of our hearts"; and they have said, "We will be as the other nations."

903

They make a rule of exception.

Have the men of old given absolution before penance? Do this as exceptional. But of the exception you make a rule without exception, so that you do not even want the rule to be exceptional.

904

On confessions and absolutions without signs of regret.

God regards only the inward; the Church judges only by the outward. God absolves as soon as He sees penitence in the heart; the Church when she sees it in works. God will make a Church pure within, which confounds, by its inward and entirely spiritual holiness, the inward impiety of proud sages and Pharisees; and the Church will make an assembly of men whose external manners are so pure as to confound the manners of the heathen. If there are hypocrites among them, but so well disguised that she does not discover their venom, she tolerates them; for, though they are not accepted of God, whom they cannot deceive, they are of men, whom they do deceive. And thus she is not dishonoured by their conduct, which appears holy. But you want the Church to judge neither of the inward, because that belongs to God alone, nor of the outward, because God dwells only upon the inward; and thus, taking away from her all choice of men, you retain in the Church the most dissolute, and those who dishonour her so greatly, that the synagogues of the Jews and sects of philosophers would have banished them as unworthy, and have abhorred them as impious.

905

The easiest conditions to live in according to the world are the most difficult to live in according to God, and vice versa. Nothing is so difficult according to the world as the religious life; nothing is easier than to live it according to God. Nothing is easier, according to the world, than to live in high office and great wealth; nothing is more difficult than to live in them according to God, and without acquiring an interest in them and a liking for them.

906

The casuists submit the decision to the corrupt reason, and the choice of decisions to the corrupt will, in order that all that is corrupt in the nature of man may contribute to his conduct.

907

But is it *probable* that *probability* gives assurance?

Difference between rest and security of conscience. Nothing

gives certainty but truth; nothing gives rest but the sincere
search for truth.

908

The whole society itself of their casuists cannot give assurance to a conscience in error, and that is why it is important
to choose good guides.

Thus they will be doubly culpable, both in having followed
ways which they should not have followed, and in having
listened to teachers to whom they should not have listened.

909

Can it be anything but compliance with the world which
makes you find things probable? Will you make us believe
that it is truth, and that if duelling were not the fashion, you
would find it probable that they might fight, considering the
matter in itself?

910

Must we kill to prevent there being any wicked? This is to
make both parties wicked instead of one. *Vince in bono malum.*
(Saint Augustine.)

911

Universal.—Ethics and language are special, but universal
sciences.

912

Probability.—Each one can employ it; no one can take it
away.

913

They allow lust to act, and check scruples; whereas they
should do the contrary.

914

Montalte.—Lax opinions please men so much, that it is
strange that theirs displease. It is because they have exceeded
all bounds. Again, there are many people who see the truth,

and who cannot attain to it; but there are few who do not know that the purity of religion is opposed to our corruptions. It is absurd to say that an eternal recompense is offered to the morality of Escobar.

915

Probability.—They have some true principles; but they misuse them. Now, the abuse of truth ought to be as much punished as the introduction of falsehood.

As if there were two hells, one for sins against love, the other for those against justice!

916

Probability.—The earnestness of the saints in seeking the truth was useless, if the probable is trustworthy. The fear of the saints who have always followed the surest way (Saint Theresa having always followed her confessor).

917

Take away *probability*, and you can no longer please the world; give *probability*, and you can no longer displease it.

918

These are the effects of the sins of the peoples and of the Jesuits. The great have wished to be flattered. The Jesuits have wished to be loved by the great. They have all been worthy to be abandoned to the spirit of lying, the one party to deceive, the others to be deceived. They have been avaricious, ambitious, voluptuous. *Coacervabunt tibi magistros.* Worthy disciples of such masters, they have sought flatterers, and have found them.

919

If they do not renounce their doctrine of probability, their good maxims are as little holy as the bad, for they are founded on human authority; and thus, if they are more just, they will be more reasonable, but not more holy. They take after the wild stem on which they are grafted.

If what I say does not serve to enlighten you, it will be of use to the people.

If these are silent, the stones will speak.

Silence is the greatest persecution; the saints were never silent. It is true that a call is necessary; but it is not from the decrees of the Council that we must learn whether we are called, it is from the necessity of speaking. Now, after Rome has spoken, and we think that she has condemned the truth, and that they have written it, and after the books which have said the contrary are censured; we must cry out so much the louder, the more unjustly we are censured, and the more violently they would stifle speech, until there come a Pope who hears both parties, and who consults antiquity to do justice. So the good Popes will find the Church still in outcry.

The Inquisition and the Society are the two scourges of the truth.

Why do you not accuse them of Arianism? For, though they have said that Jesus Christ is God, perhaps they mean by it not the natural interpretation, but as it is said, *Dii estis*.

If my Letters are condemned at Rome, that which I condemn in them is condemned in heaven. *Ad tuum, Domine Jesu, tribunal appello.*

You yourselves are corruptible.

I feared that I had written ill, seeing myself condemned; but the example of so many pious writings makes me believe the contrary. It is no longer allowable to write well, so corrupt or ignorant is the Inquisition!

"It is better to obey God than men."

I fear nothing; I hope for nothing. It is not so with the bishops. Port-Royal fears, and it is bad policy to disperse them; for they will fear no longer and will cause greater fear. I do not even fear your like censures, if they are not founded on those of tradition. Do you censure all? What! Even my respect? No. Say then what, or you will do nothing, if you do not point out the evil, and why it is evil. And this is what they will have great difficulty in doing.

Probability.—They have given a ridiculous explanation of certitude; for, after having established that all their ways are sure, they have no longer called that sure which leads to heaven without danger of not arriving there by it, but that which leads there without danger of going out of that road.

920

. . . The saints indulge in subtleties in order to think themselves criminals, and impeach their better actions. And these indulge in subtleties in order to excuse the most wicked.

The heathen sages erected a structure equally fine outside, but upon a bad foundation; and the devil deceived men by this apparent resemblance based upon the most different foundation.

Man never had so good a cause as I; and others have never furnished so good a capture as you . . .

The more they point out weakness in my person, the more they authorise my cause.

You say that I am a heretic. Is that lawful? And if you do not fear that men do justice, do you not fear that God does justice?

You will feel the force of the truth, and you will yield to it . . .

There is something supernatural in such a blindness. *Digna necessitas. Mentiris impudentissime* . . .

Doctrina sua noscitur vir . . .

False piety, a double sin.

I am alone against thirty thousand. No. Protect, you, the court; protect, you, deception; let me protect the truth. It is all my strength. If I lose it, I am undone. I shall not lack accusations, and persecutions. But I possess the truth, and we shall see who will take it away.

I do not need to defend religion, but you do not need to defend error and injustice. Let God, out of His compassion, having no regard to the evil which is in me, and having regard

to the good which is in you, grant us all grace that truth may
not be overcome in my hands, and that falsehood . . .

921

Probable.—Let us see if we seek God sincerely, by comparison of the things which we love. It is *probable* that this food
will not poison me. It is *probable* that I shall not lose my
action by not prosecuting it . . .

922

It is not absolution only which remits sins by the sacrament
of penance, but contrition, which is not real if it does not
seek the sacrament.

923

People who do not keep their word, without faith, without
honour, without truth, deceitful in heart, deceitful in speech;
for which that amphibious animal in fable was once reproached, which held itself in a doubtful position between the
fish and the birds . . .

It is important to kings and princes to be considered pious;
and therefore they must confess themselves to you.

THE PROVINCIAL LETTERS

*Disputes in the Sorbonne, and the invention of proximate power—
a term employed by the Jesuits to procure the censure of
M. Arnauld*

Paris, January 23, 1656

SIR,—We were entirely mistaken. It was only yesterday
that I was undeceived. Until that time I had labored under
the impression that the disputes in the Sorbonne were vastly
important, and deeply affected the interests of religion. The
frequent convocations of an assembly so illustrious as that of
the Theological Faculty of Paris, attended by so many extraordinary and unprecedented circumstances, led one to form
such high expectations, that it was impossible to help coming
to the conclusion that the subject was most extraordinary.
You will be greatly surprised, however, when you learn from
the following account, the issue of this grand demonstration,
which, having made myself perfectly master of the subject,
I shall be able to tell you in very few words.

Two questions, then, were brought under examination; the
one a question of fact, the other a question of right.

The question of fact consisted in ascertaining whether M.
Arnauld was guilty of presumption, for having asserted in
his second letter that he had carefully perused the book of
Jansenius, and that he had not discovered the propositions
condemned by the late pope; but that, nevertheless, as he condemned these propositions wherever they might occur, he
condemned them in Jansenius, if they were really contained
in that work.

The question here was, if he could, without presumption, entertain a doubt that these propositions were in Jansenius, after the bishops had declared that they were.

The matter having been brought before the Sorbonne, seventy-one doctors undertook his defence, maintaining that the only reply he could possibly give to the demands made upon him in so many publications, calling on him to say if he held that these propositions were in that book, was, that he had not been able to find them, but that if they were in the book, he condemned them in the book.

Some even went a step farther, and protested that, after all the search they had made into the book, they had never stumbled upon these propositions, and that they had, on the contrary, found sentiments entirely at variance with them. They then earnestly begged that, if any doctor present had discovered them, he would have the goodness to point them out; adding, that what was so easy could not reasonably be refused, as this would be the surest way to silence the whole of them, M. Arnauld included; but this proposal has been uniformly declined. So much for the one side.

On the other side are eighty secular doctors, and some forty mendicant friars, who have condemned M. Arnauld's proposition, without choosing to examine whether he has spoken truly or falsely—who, in fact, have declared, that they have nothing to do with the veracity of his proposition, but simply with its temerity.

Besides these, there were fifteen who were not in favor of the censure, and who are called Neutrals.

Such was the issue of the question of fact, regarding which, I must say, I give myself very little concern. It does not affect my conscience in the least whether M. Arnauld is presumptuous, or the reverse; and should I be tempted, from curiosity, to ascertain whether these propositions are contained in Jansenius, his book is neither so very rare nor so very large as to hinder me from reading it over from beginning to end, for my own satisfaction, without consulting the Sorbonne on the matter.

Were it not, however, for the dread of being presumptuous myself, I really think that I would be disposed to adopt the opinion which has been formed by the most of my acquaintances, who, though they have believed hitherto on common report that the propositions were in Jansenius, begin now to suspect the contrary, owing to this strange refusal to point them out—a refusal, the more extraordinary to me, as I have not yet met with a single individual who can say that he has discovered them in that work. I am afraid, therefore, that this censure will do more harm than good, and that the impression which it will leave on the minds of all who know its history will be just the reverse of the conclusion that has been come to. The truth is, the world has become sceptical of late, and will not believe things till it sees them. But, as I said before, this point is of very little moment, as it has no concern with religion.

The question of right, from its affecting the faith, appears much more important, and, accordingly, I took particular pains in examining it. You will be relieved, however, to find that it is of as little consequence as the former.

The point of dispute here, was an assertion of M. Arnauld's in the same letter, to the effect, "that the grace without which we can do nothing, was wanting to St. Peter at his fall." You and I supposed that the controversy here would turn upon the great principles of grace; such as, whether grace is given to all men? Or, if it is efficacious of itself? But we were quite mistaken. You must know I have become a great theologian within this short time; and now for the proofs of it!

To ascertain the matter with certainty, I repaired to my neighbor, M. N——, doctor of Navarre, who, as you are aware, is one of the keenest opponents of the Jansenists, and my curiosity having made me almost as keen as himself, I asked him if they would not formally decide at once that "grace is given to all men," and thus set the question at rest. But he gave me a sore rebuff, and told me that that was not the point; that there were some of his party who held that grace was not given to all; that the examiners themselves had declared, in a full assembly of the Sorbonne, that that opinion was *problematical;* and that he himself held the same sentiment, which he confirmed by quoting to me what he called that celebrated passage of St. Augustine: "We know that grace is not given to all men."

I apologized for having misapprehended his sentiment, and requested him to say if they would not at least condemn that other opinion of the Jansenists which is making so much noise, "That grace is efficacious of itself, and invincibly determines our will to what is good." But in this second query I was equally unfortunate. "You know nothing about the matter," he said; "that is not a heresy—it is an orthodox opinion; all the Thomists maintain it; and I myself have defended it in my Sorbonic thesis."

I did not venture again to propose my doubts, and yet I was as far as ever from understanding where the difficulty lay; so, at last, in order to get at it, I begged him to tell me where, then, lay the heresy of M. Arnauld's proposition. "It lies here," said he, "that he does not acknowledge that the righteous have the power of obeying the commandments of God, in the manner in which we understand it."

On receiving this piece of information, I took my leave of him; and, quite proud at having discovered the knot of the question, I sought M. N——, who is gradually getting better, and was sufficiently recovered to conduct me to the house of his brother-in-law, who is a Jansenist, if ever there was one, but a very good man notwithstanding. Thinking to insure myself a better reception, I pretended to be very high on what I took to be his side, and said: "Is it possible that the Sorbonne has introduced into the Church such an error as this, 'that all the righteous have always the power of obeying the commandments of God?' "

"What say you?" replied the doctor. "Call you that an error—a sentiment so Catholic that none but Lutherans and Calvinists impugn it?"

"Indeed!" said I, surprised in my turn; "so you are not of their opinion?"

"No," he replied; "we anathematize it as heretical and impious."

Confounded by this reply, I soon discovered that I had overacted the Jansenist, as I had formerly overdone the Molinist. But not being sure if I had rightly understood him, I requested him to tell me frankly if he held "that the righteous have always a real power to observe the divine precepts?" Upon this the good man got warm (but it was with a holy zeal), and protested that he would not disguise his sentiments on any consideration—that such was, indeed, his belief, and that he and all his party would defend it to the death, as the pure doctrine of St. Thomas, and of St. Augustine their master.

This was spoken so seriously as to leave me no room for doubt; and under this impression I returned to my first doctor, and said to him, with an air of great satisfaction, that I was sure there would be peace in the Sorbonne very soon; that the Jansenists were quite at one with them in reference to the power of the righteous to obey the commandments of God; that I could pledge my word for them, and could make them seal it with their blood.

"Hold there!" said he. "One must be a theologian to see the point of this question. The difference between us is so subtle, that it is with some difficulty we can discern it ourselves—you will find it rather too much for your powers of comprehension. Content yourself, then, with knowing that it is very true the Jansenists will tell you that all the righteous have always the power of obeying the commandments; that is not the point in dispute between us; but mark you, they will not tell you that that power is *proximate*. That is the point."

This was a new and unknown word to me. Up to this moment I had managed to understand matters, but that term involved me in obscurity; and I verily believe that it has been invented for no other purpose than to mystify. I requested him to give me an explanation of it, but he made a mystery of it, and sent me back, without any further satisfaction, to demand of the Jansenists if they would admit this *proximate power*. Having charged my memory with the phrase (as to my understanding, that was out of the question), I hastened with all possible expedition, fearing that I might forget it, to my Jansenist friend, and accosted him, immediately after our first salutations, with: "Tell me, pray, if you admit *the proximate power?*" He smiled, and replied, coldly: "Tell me yourself in what sense you understand it, and I may then inform you what I think of it." As my knowledge did not extend quite so far, I was at a loss what reply to make; and yet, rather than lose the object of my visit, I said at random: "Why, I understand it in the sense of the Molinists." "To which of the Molinists do you refer me?" replied he, with the utmost coolness. I referred him to the whole of them together, as forming one body, and animated by one spirit.

"You know very little about the matter," returned he. "So far are they from being united in sentiment, that some of them are diametrically opposed to each other. But, being all united in the design to ruin M. Arnauld, they have resolved to agree on this term *proximate*, which both parties might use indiscriminately, though they understand it diversely, that thus, by a similarity of language, and an apparent conformity, they may form a large body, and get up a majority to crush him with the greater certainty."

This reply filled me with amazement; but without imbibing these impressions of the malicious designs of the Molinists, which I am unwilling to believe on his word, and with which I have no concern, I set myself simply to ascertain the various senses which they give to that mysterious word *proximate*. "I would enlighten you on the subject with all my heart," he said; "but you would discover in it such a mass of contrariety and contradiction, that you would hardly believe me. You would suspect me. To make sure of the matter, you had better learn it from some of themselves; and I shall give you some of their addresses. You have only to make a separate visit to one called M. le Moine and to Father Nicolai."

"I have no acquaintance with any of these persons," said I. "Let me see, then," he replied, "if you know any of those whom I shall name to you; they all agree in sentiment with M. le Moine."

I happened, in fact, to know some of them.

"Well, let us see if you are acquainted with any of the Dominicans whom they call the 'New Thomists,' for they are all the same with Father Nicolai."

I knew some of them also whom he named; and, resolved to profit by this counsel, and to investigate the matter, I took my leave of him, and went immediately to one of the disciples of M. le Moine. I begged him to inform me what it was to have the *proximate power* of doing a thing.

"It is easy to tell you that," he replied; "it is merely to have all that is necessary for doing it in such a manner that nothing is wanting to performance."

"And so," said I, "to have the proximate power of crossing a river, for example, is to have a boat, boatmen, oars, and all the rest, so that nothing is wanting?"

"Exactly so," said the monk.

"And to have the proximate power of *seeing*," continued I, "must be to have good eyes and the light of day; for a person with good sight in the dark would not have the proximate power of seeing, according to you, as he would want the light, without which one cannot see?"

"Precisely," said he.

"And consequently," returned I, "when you say that all the righteous have the proximate power of observing the commandments of God, you mean that they have always all the grace necessary for observing them, so that nothing is wanting to them on the part of God."

"Stay there," he replied; "they have always all that is necessary for observing the commandments, or at least for asking it of God."

"I understand you," said I; "they have all that is necessary for praying to God to assist them, without requiring any new grace from God to enable them to pray."

"You have it now," he rejoined.

"But is it not necessary that they have an efficacious grace, in order to pray to God?"

"No," said he; "not according to M. le Moine."

To lose no time, I went to the Jacobins, and requested an interview with some whom I knew to be New Thomists, and I begged them to tell me what "proximate power" was. "Is it not," said I, "that power to which nothing is wanting in order to act?"

"No," said they.

"Indeed! fathers," said I; "if anything is wanting to that power, do you call it proximate? Would you say, for instance, that a man in the night time, and without any light, had the proximate power of seeing?"

"Yes, indeed, he would have it, in our opinion, if he is not blind."

"I grant that," said I; "but M. le Moine understands it in a different manner."

"Very true," they replied; "but so it is that we understand it."

"I have no objections to that," I said; "for I never quarrel about a name, provided I am apprised of the sense in which it is understood. But I perceive from this, that when you speak of the righteous having always the proximate power of praying to God, you understand that they require another supply for praying, without which they will never pray."

"Most excellent!" exclaimed the good fathers, embracing me; "exactly the thing; for they must have, besides, an efficacious grace bestowed upon all, and which determines their wills to pray; and it is heresy to deny the necessity of that efficacious grace in order to pray."

"Most excellent!" cried I, in return; "but, according to you, the Jansenists are Catholics, and M. le Moine a heretic; for the Jansenists maintain that, while the righteous have power to pray, they require nevertheless an efficacious grace; and this is what you approve. M. le Moine, again, maintains that the righteous may pray without efficacious grace; and this is what you condemn."

"Ay," said they; "but M. le Moine calls that power *proximate power.*"

"How now! fathers," I exclaimed; "this is merely playing with words, to say that you are agreed as to the common terms which you employ, while you differ with them as to the sense of these terms."

The fathers made no reply; and at this juncture, who should come in but my old friend, the disciple of M. le Moine! I regarded this at the time as an extraordinary piece of good fortune; but I have discovered since then that such meetings are not rare—that, in fact, they are constantly mixing in each other's society.

"I know a man," said I, addressing myself to M. le Moine's disciple, "who holds that all the righteous have always the power of praying to God, but that, notwithstanding this, they will never pray without an efficacious grace which determines them, and which God does not always give to all the righteous. Is he a heretic?"

"Stay," said the doctor; "you might take me by surprise. Let us go cautiously to work. *Distinguo.* If he call that power *proximate power,* he will be a Thomist, and therefore a Catholic; if not, he will be a Jansenist, and therefore a heretic."

"He calls it neither proximate nor non-proximate," said I.

"Then he is a heretic," quoth he; "I refer you to these good fathers if he is not."

I did not appeal to them as judges, for they had already nodded assent; but I said to them: "He refuses to admit that word *proximate,* because he can meet with nobody who will explain it to him."

Upon this one of the fathers was on the point of offering his definition of the term, when he was interrupted by M. le Moine's disciple, who said to him: "Do you mean, then, to renew our broils? Have we not agreed not to explain that word *proximate,* but to use it on both sides without saying what it signifies?" To this the Jacobin gave his assent.

I was thus let into the whole secret of their plot; and rising to take my leave of them, I remarked: "Indeed, fathers, I am much afraid this is nothing better than pure chicanery; and whatever may be the result of your convocations, I venture to predict that, though the censure should pass, peace will not be established. For though it should be decided that the syllables of that word *proximate* should be pronounced, who does not see that, the meaning not being explained, each of you will be disposed to claim the victory? The Jacobins will contend that the word is to be understood in their sense; M. le Moine will insist that it must be taken in his; and thus there will be more wrangling about the explanation of the word than about its introduction. For, after all, there would be no great danger in adopting it without any sense, seeing it is through the sense only that it can do any harm. But it would be unworthy of the Sorbonne and of theology to employ equivocal and captious terms without giving any explanation of them. In short, fathers, tell me, I entreat you, for the last time, what is necessary to be believed in order to be a good Catholic?"

"You must say," they all vociferated simultaneously, "that all the righteous have the *proximate power*, abstracting from it all sense—from the sense of the Thomists and the sense of other divines."

"That is to say," I replied, in taking leave of them, "that I must pronounce that word to avoid being the heretic of a name. For, pray, is this a Scripture word?" "No," said they. "Is it a word of the Fathers, the Councils, or the Popes?" "No." "Is the word, then, used by St. Thomas?" "No." "What necessity, therefore, is there for using it since it has neither the authority of others nor any sense of itself?" "You are an opinionative fellow," said they; "but you shall say it, or you shall be a heretic, and M. Arnauld into the bargain; for we are the majority, and should it be necessary, we can bring a sufficient number of Cordeliers into the field to carry the day."

On hearing this solid argument, I took my leave of them, to write you the foregoing account of my interview, from which you will perceive that the following points remain undisputed and uncondemned by either party. *First*, That grace is not given to all men. *Second*, That all the righteous have always the power of obeying the divine commandments. *Third*, That they require, nevertheless, in order to obey them, and even to pray, an efficacious grace, which invincibly determines their will. *Fourth*, That this efficacious grace is not always granted to all the righteous, and that it depends on the pure mercy of God. So that, after all, the truth is safe, and nothing runs any risk but that word without the sense, *proximate*.

Happy the people who are ignorant of its existence!—happy those who lived before it was born!—for I see no help for it, unless the gentlemen of the Acadamy, by an act of absolute authority, banish that barbarous term, which causes so many divisions, from beyond the precincts of the Sorbonne. Unless this be done, the censure appears certain; but I can easily see that it will do no other harm than diminish the credit of the Sorbonne, and deprive it of that authority which is so necessary to it on other occasions.

Meanwhile, I leave you at perfect liberty to hold by the word *proximate* or not, just as you please; for I love you too much to persecute you under that pretext. If this account is not displeasing to you, I shall continue to apprise you of all that happens.—I am, &c.

Of sufficient grace

Paris, January 29, 1656

Sir,—Just as I had sealed up my last letter, I received a visit from our old friend M. N——. Nothing could have happened more luckily for my curiosity; for he is thoroughly informed in the questions of the day, and is completely in the secret of the Jesuits, at whose houses, including those of their leading men, he is a constant visitor. After having talked over the business which brought him to my house, I asked him to state, in a few words, what were the points in dispute between the two parties.

He immediately complied, and informed me that the principal points were two—the *first* about the *proximate power*, and the *second* about *sufficient grace*. I have enlightened you on the first of these points in my former letter, and shall now speak of the second.

In one word then, I found that their difference about sufficient grace may be defined thus: The Jesuits maintain that there is a grace given generally to all men, subject in such a way to free-will that the will renders it efficacious or inefficacious at its pleasure, without any additional aid from God, and without wanting anything on his part in order to act effectively; and hence they term this grace *sufficient*, because it suffices of itself for action. The Jansenists, on the other hand, will not allow that any grace is actually sufficient which is not also efficacious; that is, that all those kinds of grace which do not determine the will to act effectively are insuffi-

336

cient for action; for they hold that a man can never act without *efficacious grace*.

Such are the points in debate between the Jesuits and the Jansenists; and my next object was to ascertain the doctrine of the New Thomists. "It is rather an odd one," he said: "they agree with the Jesuits in admitting a *sufficient grace* given to all men; but they maintain, at the same time, that no man can act with this grace alone, but that, in order to do this, he must receive from God an efficacious grace which really determines his will to the action, and which God does not grant to all men." "So that, according to this doctrine," said I, "this grace is *sufficient* without being sufficient." "Exactly so," he replied; "for if it suffices, there is no need of anything more for acting; and if it does not suffice, why—it is not sufficient."

"But," asked I, "where, then, is the difference between them and the Jansenists?" "They differ in this," he replied, "that the Dominicans have this good qualification, that they do not refuse to say that all men have the *sufficient grace*." "I understand you," returned I; "but they say it without thinking it; for they add that, in order to act, we must have an *efficacious grace which is not given to all;* consequently, if they agree with the Jesuits in the use of a term which has no sense, they differ from them, and coincide with the Jansenists in the substance of the thing." "That is very true," said he. "How, then," said I, "are the Jesuits united with them? and why do they not combat them as well as the Jansenists, since they will always find powerful antagonists in these men, who, by maintaining the necessity of the efficacious grace which determines the will, will prevent them from establishing that grace which they hold to be of itself sufficient?"

"The Dominicans are too powerful," he replied, "and the Jesuits are too politic, to come to an open rupture with them. The Society is content with having prevailed on them so far as to admit the name of *sufficient grace*, though they understand it in another sense; by which manœuvre they gain this advantage, that they will make their opinion appear untenable, as soon as they judge it proper to do so. And this will be no difficult matter; for, let it be once granted that all men have the sufficient graces, nothing can be more natural than to conclude, that the efficacious grace is not necessary to action— the sufficiency of the general grace precluding the necessity of all others. By saying *sufficient* we express all that is necessary for action; and it will serve little purpose for the Dominicans to exclaim that they attach another sense to the expression; the people, accustomed to the common acceptation of that term, would not even listen to their explanation. Thus the Society gains a sufficient advantage from the expression which has been adopted by the Dominicans, without pressing them any further; and were you but acquainted with what passed under Popes Clement VIII. and Paul V., and knew how the Society was thwarted by the Dominicans in the establishment of the sufficient grace, you would not be surprised to find that it avoids embroiling itself in quarrels with them, and allows them to hold their own opinion, provided that of the Society is left untouched; and more especially, when the Dominicans countenance its doctrine, by agreeing to employ, on all public occasions, the term *sufficient grace*.

"The Society," he continued, "is quite satisfied with their complaisance. It does not insist on their denying the necessity of efficacious grace; this would be urging them too far. People should not tyrannize over their friends; and the Jesuits have gained quite enough. The world is content with words; few think of searching into the nature of things; and thus the name of *sufficient grace* being adopted on both sides, though in different senses, there is nobody, except the most subtle theologians, who ever dreams of doubting that the thing signified by that word is held by the Jacobins as well as by the Jesuits; and the result will show that these last are not the greatest dupes."

I acknowledged that they were a shrewd class of people, these Jesuits; and, availing myself of his advice, I went straight to the Jacobins, at whose gate I found one of my good friends, a staunch Jansenist (for you must know I have got friends among all parties), who was calling for another monk, different from him whom I was in search of. I prevailed on him, however, after much entreaty, to accompany me, and asked for one of my New Thomists. He was delighted to see me again. "How now! my dear father," I began, "it seems it is not enough that all men have a *proximate power*, with which they can never act with effect; they must have besides this a *sufficient grace*, with which they can act as little. Is not that the doctrine of your school?" "It is," said the worthy monk; "and I was upholding it this very morning in the Sorbonne. I spoke on the point during my whole half-hour; and but for the *sand-glass*, I bade fair to have reversed that wicked proverb, now so current in Paris: 'He votes without speaking, like a monk in the Sorbonne.' " "What do you mean by your half-hour and your sand-glass?" I asked; "do they cut your speeches by a certain measure?" "Yes," said he, "they have done so for some days past." "And do they oblige you to speak for half an hour?" "No; we may speak as little as we please." "But not as much as you please," said I. "O what a capital regulation for the boobies! what a blessed excuse for those who have nothing worth the saying! But, to return to the point, father; this grace given to all men is *sufficient*, is it not?" "Yes," said he. "And yet it has no effect without *efficacious grace?*" "None whatever," he replied. "And all men have the sufficient," continued I, "and all have not the efficacious?" "Exactly," said he. "That is," returned I, "all have enough of grace, and all have not enough of it—that is, this grace suffices, though it does not suffice—that is, it is sufficient in name, and insufficient in effect! In good sooth, father, this is particularly subtle doctrine! Have you forgotten, since you retired to the cloister, the meaning attached, in the world you have quitted, to the word *sufficient?*—don't you remember that it includes all that is necessary for acting? But no, you cannot have lost all recollection of it; for, to avail myself of an illustration which will come home more vividly to your feelings, let us suppose that you were supplied with no more than two ounces of bread and a glass of water daily, would you be quite pleased with your prior were he to tell you that this would be sufficient to support you, under the pretext that, along with something else, which, however, he would not give you, you would have all that would be necessary to support you? How, then, can you allow yourselves to say that all men have sufficient grace for acting, while you admit that there is another grace absolutely necessary to acting which all men have not? Is it because this is an unimportant article of belief, and you leave all men at liberty to believe that efficacious grace is necessary or not, as they choose? Is it a matter of indifference to say, that with sufficient grace a man may really act?" "How!" cried the good man; "indifference!—it is heresy—formal heresy. The necessity of *efficacious grace* for acting effectively, is a point of *faith*—it is heresy to deny it."

"Where are we now?" I exclaimed; "and which side am I to take here? If I deny the sufficient grace, I am a Jansenist. If I admit it, as the Jesuits do, in the way of denying that efficacious grace is necessary, I shall be a heretic, say you. And if I admit it, as you do, in the way of maintaining the necessity of efficacious grace, I sin against common sense, and am a blockhead, say the Jesuits. What must I do, thus reduced to the inevitable necessity of being a blockhead, a heretic, or a Jansenist? And what a sad pass are matters come to, if there are none but the Jansenists who avoid coming into collision either with the faith or with reason, and who save themselves at once from absurdity and from error!"

My Jansenist friend took this speech as a good omen, and already looked upon me as a convert. He said nothing to me, however; but, addressing the monk: "Pray, father," inquired he, "what is the point on which you agree with the Jesuits?" "We agree in this," he replied, "that the Jesuits and we acknowledge the sufficient grace given to all." "But," said the Jansenist, "there are two things in this expression *sufficient grace*—there is the sound, which is only so much breath; and there is the thing which it signifies, which is real and effectual. And, therefore, as you are agreed with the Jesuits in regard to the word *sufficient*, and opposed to them as to the sense, it is apparent that you are opposed to them in regard to the substance of that term, and that you only agree with them as to the sound. Is this what you call acting sincerely and cordially?"

"But," said the good man, "what cause have you to complain, since we deceive nobody by this mode of speaking? In our schools we openly teach that we understand it in a manner different from the Jesuits."

"What I complain of," returned my friend, "is, that you do not proclaim it everywhere, that by sufficient grace you understand the grace which is *not* sufficient. You are bound in conscience, by thus altering the sense of the ordinary terms of theology, to tell that, when you admit a sufficient grace in all men, you understand that they have not sufficient grace in effect. All classes of persons in the world understand the word sufficient in one and the same sense; the New Thomists alone understand it in another sense. All the women, who form one-half of the world, all courtiers, all military men, all magistrates, all lawyers, merchants, artisans, the whole populace—in short, all sorts of men, except the Dominicans, understand the word *sufficient* to express all that is necessary. Scarcely any one is aware of this singular exception. It is reported over the whole earth, simply that the Dominicans hold that all men have the *sufficient graces*. What other conclusion can be drawn from this, than that they hold that all men have all the graces necessary for action; especially when they are seen joined in interest and intrigue with the Jesuits, who understand the thing in that sense? Is not the uniformity of your expressions, viewed in connection with this union of party, a manifest indication and confirmation of the uniformity of your sentiments?

"The multitude of the faithful inquire of theologians: What is the real condition of human nature since its corruption? St. Augustine and his disciples reply, that it has no sufficient grace until God is pleased to bestow it. Next come the Jesuits, and they say that all have the effectually sufficient graces. The Dominicans are consulted on this contrariety of opinion; and what course do they pursue? They unite with the Jesuits; by this coalition they make up a majority; they secede from those who deny these sufficient graces; they declare that all men possess them. Who, on hearing this, would imagine anything else than that they gave their sanction to the opinion of the Jesuits? And then they add that, nevertheless, these said sufficient graces are perfectly useless without the efficacious, which are not given to all!

"Shall I present you with a picture of the Church amidst these conflicting sentiments? I consider her very like a man who, leaving his native country on a journey, is encountered by robbers, who inflict many wounds on him, and leave him half dead. He sends for three physicians resident in the neighboring towns. The first, on probing his wounds, pronounces them mortal, and assures him that none but God can restore to him his lost powers. The second, coming after the other, chooses to flatter the man—tells him that he has still sufficient strength to reach his home; and, abusing the first physician who opposed his advice, determines upon his ruin. In this dilemma, the poor patient, observing the third medical gentleman at a distance, stretches out his hands to him as the person who should determine the controversy. This practitioner, on examining his wounds, and ascertaining the opinions of the first two doctors, embraces that of the second, and uniting with him, the two combine against the first, and being the stronger party in number drive him from the field in disgrace. From this proceeding, the patient naturally concludes that the last comer is of the same opinion with the second; and, on putting the question to him, he assures him most positively that his strength is sufficient for prosecuting his journey. The wounded man, however, sensible of his own weakness, begs him to explain to him how he considered him sufficient for the journey. 'Because,' replies his adviser, 'you are still in possession of your legs, and legs are the organs which naturally suffice for walking.' 'But,' says the patient, 'have I all the strength necessary to make us of my legs? for, in my present weak condition, it humbly appears to me that they are wholly useless.' 'Certainly you have not,' replies the doctor; 'you will never walk *effectively*, unless God vouchsafes some extraordinary assistance to sustain and conduct you.' 'What!' exclaims the poor man, 'do you not mean to say that I have sufficient strength in me, so as to want for nothing to walk effectively?' 'Very far from it,' returns the physician. 'You must, then,' says the patient, 'be of a different opinion from your companion there about my real condition.' 'I must admit that I am,' replies the other.

"What do you suppose the patient said to this? Why, he complained of the strange conduct and ambiguous terms of this third physician. He censured him for taking part with the second, to whom he was opposed in sentiment, and with whom he had only the semblance of agreement, and for having driven away the first doctor, with whom he in reality agreed; and, after making a trial of his strength, and finding by experience his actual weakness, he sent them both about their business, recalled his first adviser, put himself under his care, and having, by his advice, implored from God the strength of which he confessed his need, obtained the mercy he sought, and, through divine help, reached his house in peace."

The worthy monk was so confounded with this parable that he could not find words to reply. To cheer him up a little, I said to him, in a mild tone: "But after all, my dear father, what made you think of giving the name of *sufficient* to a grace which you say it is a point of faith to believe is, in fact, insufficient?" "It is very easy for you to talk about it," said he. "You are an independent and private man; I am a monk, and in a community—cannot you estimate the difference between the two cases? We depend on superiors; they depend on others. They have promised our votes—what would you have to become of me?" We understood the hint; and this brought to our recollection the case of his brother monk, who, for a similar piece of indiscretion, has been exiled to Abbeville.

"But," I resumed, "how comes it about that your community is bound to admit this grace?" "That is another question," he replied. "All that I can tell you is, in one word, that our order has defended, to the utmost of its ability, the doctrine of St. Thomas on efficacious grace. With what ardor did it oppose, from the very commencement, the doctrine of Molina? How did it labor to establish the necessity of the efficacious grace of Jesus Christ? Don't you know what happened under Clement VIII. and Paul V., and how the former having been prevented by death, and the latter hindered by some Italian affairs from publishing his bull, our arms still sleep in the Vatican? But the Jesuits, availing themselves, since the introduction of the heresy of Luther and Calvin, of the scanty light which the people possess for discriminating between the error of these men and the truth of the doctrine of St. Thomas, disseminated their principles with such rapidity and success, that they became, ere long, masters of the popular belief; while we, on our part, found ourselves in the predicament of being denounced as Calvinists, and treated as the Jansenists are at present, unless we qualified the efficacious grace with, at least, the apparent avowal of a *sufficient*. In this extremity, what better course could we have taken for saving the truth, without losing our own credit, than by admitting the name of sufficient grace, while we denied that it was such in effect? Such is the real history of the case."

This was spoken in such a melancholy tone, that I really began to pity the man; not so, however, my companion. "Flatter not yourselves," said he to the monk, "with having saved the truth; had she not found other defenders, in your feeble hands she must have perished. By admitting into the Church the name of her enemy, you have admitted the enemy himself. Names are inseparable from things. If the term sufficient grace be once established, it will be vain for you to protest that you understand by it a grace which is *not* sufficient. Your protest will be held inadmissible. Your explanation would be scouted as odious in the world, where men speak more ingenuously about matters of infinitely less moment. The Jesuits will gain a triumph—it will be their grace, which is sufficient in fact, and not yours, which is only so in name, that will pass as established; and the converse of your creed will become an article of faith."

"We will all suffer martyrdom first," cried the father, "rather than consent to the establishment of *sufficient grace in the sense of the Jesuits*. St. Thomas, whom we have sworn to follow even to the death, is diametrically opposed to such doctrine."

To this my friend, who took up the matter more seriously than I did, replied: "Come now, father, your fraternity has received an honor which it sadly abuses. It abandons that grace which was confided to its care, and which has never been abandoned since the creation of the world. That victorious grace, which was waited for by the patriarchs, predicted by the prophets, introduced by Jesus Christ, preached by St. Paul, explained by St. Augustine, the greatest of the fathers, embraced by his followers, confirmed by St. Bernard, the last of the fathers, supported by St. Thomas, the angel of the schools, transmitted by him to your order, maintained by so many of your fathers, and so nobly defended by your monks under popes Clement and Paul—that efficacious grace, which had been committed as a sacred deposit into your hands, that it might find, in a sacred and everlasting order, a succession of preachers, who might proclaim it to the end of time—is discarded and deserted for interests the most contemptible. It is high time for other hands to arm in its quarrel. It is time for God to raise up intrepid disciples of the Doctor of grace, who, strangers to the entanglements of the world, will serve God for God's sake. Grace may not, indeed, number the Dominicans among her champions, but champions she shall never want; for, by her own almighty energy, she creates them for herself. She demands hearts pure and disengaged; nay, she herself purifies and disengages them from worldly interests, incompatible with the truths of the Gospel. Reflect seriously on this, father; and take care that God does not remove this candlestick from its place, leaving you in darkness, and without the crown, as a punishment for the coldness which you manifest to a cause so important to his Church."

He might have gone on in this strain much longer, for he was kindling as he advanced, but I interrupted him by rising to take my leave, and said: "Indeed, my dear father, had I any influence in France, I should have it proclaimed, by sound of trumpet: 'BE IT KNOWN TO ALL MEN, *that when the Jacobins* SAY *that sufficient grace is given to all, they* MEAN *that all have not the grace which actually suffices!*' After which, you might say it as often as you please, but not otherwise." And thus ended our visit.

You will perceive, therefore, that we have here a *politic sufficiency* somewhat similar to *proximate power*. Meanwhile I may tell you, that it appears to me that both the proximate power and this same sufficient grace may be safely doubted by anybody, provided he is not a Jacobin.

I have just come to learn, when closing my letter, that the censure has passed. But as I do not yet know in what terms it is worded, and as it will not be published till the 15th of February, I shall delay writing you about it till the next post.— I am, &c.

REPLY OF THE "PROVINCIAL" TO THE FIRST TWO LETTERS
OF HIS FRIEND

February 2, 1656

SIR,—Your two letters have not been confined to me. Everybody has seen them, everybody understands them, and everybody believes them. They are not only in high repute among theologians—they have proved agreeable to men of the world, and intelligible even to the ladies.

In a communication which I lately received from one of the gentlemen of the Academy—one of the most illustrious names in a society of men who are all illustrious—who had seen only your first letter, he writes me as follows: "I only wish that the Sorbonne, which owes so much to the memory of the late cardinal, would acknowledge the jurisdiction of his French Academy. The author of the letter would be satisfied; for, in the capacity of an academician, I would authoritatively condemn, I would banish, I would proscribe—I had almost said exterminate—to the extent of my power, this *proximate power*, which makes so much noise about nothing, and without knowing what it would have. The misfortune is, that our academic 'power' is a very limited and *remote* power. I am sorry for it; and still more sorry that my small power cannot discharge me from my obligations to you," &c.

My next extract is from the pen of a lady, whom I shall not indicate in any way whatever. She writes thus to a female friend who had transmitted to her the first of your letters: "You can have no idea how much I am obliged to you for the letter you sent me—it is so very ingenious, and so nicely written. It narrates, and yet it is not a narrative; it clears up

347

the most intricate and involved of all possible matters; its raillery is exquisite; it enlightens those who know little about the subject, and imparts double delight to those who understand it. It is an admirable apology; and, if they would so take it, a delicate and innocent censure. In short, that letter displays so much art, so much spirit, and so much judgment, that I burn with curiosity to know who wrote it," &c.

You too, perhaps, would like to know who the lady is that writes in this style; but you must be content to esteem without knowing her; when you come to know her, your esteem will be greatly enhanced.

Take my word for it, then, and continue your letters; and let the censure come when it may, we are quite prepared for receiving it. These words, "proximate power," and "sufficient grace," with which we are threatened, will frighten us no longer. We have learned from the Jesuits, the Jacobins, and M. le Moine, in how many different ways they may be turned, and how little solidity there is in these new-fangled terms, to give ourselves any trouble about them.—Meanwhile, I remain, &c.

LETTER III

Injustice, absurdity, and nullity of the censure on M. Arnauld

Paris, February 9, 1658

SIR,—I have just received your letter; and, at the same time, there was brought me a copy of the censure in manuscript. I find that I am as well treated in the former, as M. Arnauld is ill treated in the latter. I am afraid there is some extravagance in both cases, and that neither of us is sufficiently well known by our judges. Sure I am, that were we better known, M. Arnauld would merit the approval of the Sorbonne, and I the censure of the Academy. Thus our interests are quite at variance with each other. It is his interest to make himself known, to vindicate his innocence; whereas it is mine to remain in the dark, for fear of forfeiting my reputation. Prevented, therefore, from showing my face, I must devolve on you the task of making my acknowledgments to my illustrious admirers, while I undertake that of furnishing you with the news of the censure.

I assure you, sir, it has filled me with astonishment. I expected to find it condemning the most shocking heresy in the world, but your wonder will equal mine, when informed that these alarming preparations, when on the point of producing the grand effect anticipated, have all ended in smoke.

To understand the whole affair in a pleasant way, only recollect, I beseech you, the strange impressions which, for a long time past, we have been taught to form of the Jansenists. Recall to mind the cabals, the factions, the errors, the schisms, the outrages, with which they have been so long charged; the manner in which they have been denounced and vilified from the pulpit and the press; and the degree to which this torrent of abuse, so remarkable for its violence and duration, has swollen of late years, when they have been openly and publicly accused of being not only heretics and schismatics, but apostates and infidels—with "denying the mystery of transubstantiation, and renouncing Jesus Christ and the Gospel."

After having published these startling accusations, it was resolved to examine their writings, in order to pronounce judgment on them. For this purpose the second letter of M. Arnauld, which was reported to be full of the greatest errors, is selected. The examiners appointed are his most open and avowed enemies. They employ all their learning to discover something that they might lay hold upon, and at length they produce one proposition of a doctrinal character, which they exhibit for censure.

What else could any one infer from such proceedings, than that this proposition, selected under such remarkable circumstances, would contain the essence of the blackest heresies imaginable. And yet the proposition so entirely agrees with what is clearly and formally expressed in the passages from the fathers quoted by M. Arnauld, that I have not met with a single individual who could comprehend the difference between them. Still, however, it might be imagined that there was a very great difference; for the passages from the fathers being unquestionably Catholic, the proposition of M. Arnauld, if heretical, must be widely opposed to them.

Such was the difficulty which the Sorbonne was expected to clear up. All Christendom waited, with wide-opened eyes, to discover, in the censure of these learned doctors, the point of difference which had proved imperceptible to ordinary mortals. Meanwhile M. Arnauld gave in his defences, placing his own proposition and the passages of the fathers from which he had drawn it in parallel columns, so as to make the agreement between them apparent to the most obtuse understandings.

He shows, for example, that St. Augustine says in one

passage, that "Jesus Christ points out to us, in the person of St. Peter, a righteous man warning us by his fall to avoid presumption." He cites another passage from the same father, in which he says, "that God, in order to show us that without grace we can do nothing, left St. Peter without grace." He produces a third, from St. Chrysostom, who says, "that the fall of St. Peter happened, not through any coldness towards Jesus Christ, but because grace failed him; and that he fell, not so much through his own negligence as through the withdrawment of God, as a lesson to the whole Church, that without God we can do nothing." He then gives his own accused proposition, which is as follows: "The fathers point out to us, in the person of St. Peter, a righteous man to whom that grace without which we can do nothing, was wanting."

In vain did people attempt to discover how it could possibly be, that M. Arnauld's expression differed from those of the fathers as much as truth from error, and faith from heresy. For where was the difference to be found? Could it be in these words, "that the fathers point out to us, in the person of St. Peter, a righteous man?" St. Augustine has said the same thing in so many words. Is it because he says "that grace had failed him?" The same St. Augustine, who had said that "St. Peter was a righteous man," says "that he had not had grace on that occasion." Is it, then, for his having said, "that without grace we can do nothing?" Why, is not this just what St. Augustine says in the same place, and what St. Chrysostom had said before him, with this difference only, that he expresses it in much stronger language, as when he says "that his fall did not happen through his own coldness or negligence, but through the failure of grace, and the withdrawment of God?"

Such considerations as these kept everybody in a state of breathless suspense, to learn in what this diversity could consist, when at length, after a great many meetings, this famous and long-looked-for censure made its appearance. But, alas! it has sadly baulked our expectation. Whether it be that the Molinist doctors would not condescend so far as to enlighten us on the point, or for some other mysterious reason, the fact is, they have done nothing more than pronounce these words: "This proposition is rash, impious, blasphemous, accursed, and heretical!"

Would you believe it, sir, that most people, finding themselves deceived in their expectations, have got into bad humor, and begin to fall foul upon the censors themselves? They are drawing strange inferences from their conduct in favor of M. Arnauld's innocence. "What!" they are saying, "is this all that could be achieved, during all this time, by so many doctors joining in a furious attack on one individual? Can they find nothing in all his works worthy of reprehension, but three lines, and these extracted, word for word, from the greatest doctors of the Greek and Latin Churches? Is there any author whatever whose writings, were it intended to ruin him, would not furnish a more specious pretext for the purpose? And what higher proof could be furnished of the orthodoxy of this illustrious accused?

"How comes it to pass," they add, "that so many denunciations are launched in this censure, into which they have crowded such terms as 'poison, pestilence, horror, rashness, impiety, blasphemy, abomination, execration, anathema, heresy'—the most dreadful epithets that could be used against Arius, or Antichrist himself; and all to combat an imperceptible heresy, and that, moreover, without telling us what it is? If it be against the words of the fathers that they inveigh in this style, where is the faith and tradition? If against M. Arnauld's proposition, let them point out the difference between the two; for we can see nothing but the most perfect harmony between them. As soon as we have discovered the evil of the proposition, we shall hold it in abhorrence; but so long as we do not see it, or rather see nothing in the statement but the sentiments of the holy fathers, conceived and expressed in their own terms, how can we possibly regard it with any other feelings than those of holy veneration?"

Such is the specimen of the way in which they are giving vent to their feelings. But these are by far too deep-thinking people. You and I, who make no pretensions to such extraordinary penetration, may keep ourselves quite easy about the whole affair. What! would we be wiser than our masters? No: let us take example from them, and not undertake what they have not ventured upon. We would be sure to get boggled in such an attempt. Why it would be the easiest thing imaginable, to render this censure itself heretical. Truth, we know, is so delicate, that if we make the slightest deviation from it, we fall into error; but this alleged error is so extremely finespun, that, if we diverge from it in the slightest degree, we fall back upon the truth. There is positively nothing between this obnoxious proposition and the truth but an imperceptible point. The distance between them is so impalpable, that I was in terror lest, from pure inability to perceive it, I might, in my over-anxiety to agree with the doctors of the Sorbonne, place myself in opposition to the doctors of the Church. Under this apprehension, I judged it expedient to consult one of those who, through policy, was neutral on the first question, that from him I might learn the real state of the matter. I have accordingly had an interview with one of the most intelligent of that party, whom I requested to point out to me the difference between the two things, at the same time frankly owning to him that I could see none.

He appeared to be amused at my simplicity, and replied, with a smile: "How simple it is in you to believe that there is any difference! Why, where could it be? Do you imagine that, if they could have found out any discrepancy between M. Arnauld and the fathers, they would not have boldly pointed it out, and been delighted with the opportunity of exposing it before the public, in whose eyes they are so anxious to depreciate that gentleman?"

I could easily perceive, from these few words, that those who had been neutral on the first question, would not all prove so on the second; but anxious to hear his reasons, I asked: "Why, then, have they attacked this unfortunate proposition?"

"Is it possible," he replied, "you can be ignorant of these

two things, which I thought had been known to the veriest tyro in these matters?—that, on the one hand, M. Arnauld has uniformly avoided advancing a single tenet which is not powerfully supported by the tradition of the Church; and that, on the other hand, his enemies have determined, cost what it may, to cut that ground from under him; and, accordingly, that as the writings of the former afforded no handle to the designs of the latter, they have been obliged, in order to satiate their revenge, to seize on some proposition, it mattered not what, and to condemn it without telling why or wherefore. Do not you know how the Jansenists keep them in check, and annoy them so desperately, that they cannot drop the slightest word against the principles of the fathers without being incontinently overwhelmed with whole volumes, under the pressure of which they are forced to succumb? So that, after a great many proofs of their weakness, they have judged it more to the purpose, and much less troublesome, to censure than to reply—it being a much easier matter with them to find monks than reasons."

"Why then," said I, "if this be the case, their censure is not worth a straw; for who will pay any regard to it, when they see it to be without foundation, and refuted, as it no doubt will be, by the answers given to it?"

"If you knew the temper of people," replied my friend the doctor, "you would talk in another sort of way. Their censure, censurable as it is, will produce nearly all its designed effect for a time; and although, by the force of demonstration, it is certain that, in course of time, its invalidity will be made apparent, it is equally true that, at first, it will tell as effectually on the minds of most people as if it had been the most righteous sentence in the world. Let it only be cried about the streets: 'Here you have the censure of M. Arnauld!—here you have the condemnation of the Jansenists!' and the Jesuits will find their account in it. How few will ever read it! How few of them who do read, will understand it! How few will observe that it answers no objections! How few will take the matter to heart, or attempt to sift it to the bottom!—Mark then, how much advantage this gives to the enemies of the Jansenists. They are sure to make a triumph of it, though a vain one, as usual, for some months at least—and that is a great matter for them—they will look out afterwards for some new means of subsistence. They live from hand to mouth, sir. It is in this way they have contrived to maintain themselves down to the present day. Sometimes it is by a catechism in which a child is made to condemn their opponents; then it is by a procession, in which sufficient grace leads the efficacious in triumph; again it is by a comedy, in which Jansenius is represented as carried off by devils; at another time it is by an almanac; and now it is by this censure."

"In good sooth," said I, "I was on the point of finding fault with the conduct of the Molinists; but after what you have told me, I must say I admire their prudence and their policy. I see perfectly well that they could not have followed a safer or more judicious course."

"You are right," returned he; "their safest policy has always been to keep silent; and this led a certain learned divine to remark, 'that the cleverest among them are those who intrigue much, speak little, and write nothing.'

"It is on this principle that, from the commencement of the meetings, they prudently ordained that, if M. Arnauld came into the Sorbonne, it must be simply to explain what he believed, and not to enter the lists of controversy with any one. The examiners having ventured to depart a little from this prudent arrangement, suffered for their temerity. They found themselves rather too vigorously refuted by his second apology.

"On the same principle, they had recourse to that rare and very novel device of the half-hour and the sand-glass. By this means they rid themselves of the importunity of those troublesome doctors, who might undertake to refute all their arguments, to produce books which might convict them of forgery, to insist on a reply, and reduce them to the predicament of having none to give.

"It is not that they were so blind as not to see that this

encroachment on liberty, which has induced so many doctors to withdraw from the meetings, would do no good to their censure; and that the protest of nullity, taken on this ground by M. Arnauld before it was concluded, would be a bad preamble for securing it a favorable reception. They know very well that unprejudiced persons place fully as much weight on the judgment of seventy doctors, who had nothing to gain by defending M. Arnauld, as on that of a hundred others who had nothing to lose by condemning him. But, upon the whole, they considered that it would be of vast importance to have a censure, although it should be the act of a party only in the Sorbonne, and not of the whole body; although it should be carried with little or no freedom of debate, and obtained by a great many small manœuvres not exactly according to order; although it should give no explanation of the matter in dispute; although it should not point out in what this heresy consists, and should say as little as possible about it, for fear of committing a mistake. This very silence is a mystery in the eyes of the simple; and the censure will reap this singular advantage from it, that they may defy the most critical and subtle theologians to find in it a single weak argument.

"Keep yourself easy, then, and do not be afraid of being set down as a heretic, though you should make use of the condemned proposition. It is bad, I assure you, only as occurring in the second letter of M. Arnauld. If you will not believe this statement on my word, I refer you to M. le Moine, the most zealous of the examiners, who, in the course of conversation with a doctor of my acquaintance this very morning, on being asked by him where lay the point of difference in dispute, and if one would no longer be allowed to say what the fathers had said before him, made the following exquisite reply: 'This proposition would be orthodox in the mouth of any other—it is only as coming from M. Arnauld that the Sorbonne has condemned it!' You must now be prepared to admire the machinery of Molinism, which can produce such prodigious overturnings in the Church—that what is Catholic in the fathers becomes heretical in M. Arnauld—that what is heretical in the Semi-Pelagians becomes orthodox in the writings of the Jesuits; the ancient doctrine of St. Augustine becomes an intolerable innovation, and new inventions, daily fabricated before our eyes, pass for the ancient faith of the Church." So saying, he took his leave of me.

This information has satisfied my purpose. I gather from it that this same heresy is one of an entirely new species. It is not the sentiments of M. Arnauld that are heretical; it is only his person. This is a personal heresy. He is not a heretic for anything he has said or written, but simply because he is M. Arnauld. This is all they have to say against him. Do what he may, unless he cease to be, he will never be a good Catholic. The grace of St. Augustine will never be the true grace, so long as he continues to defend it. It would become so at once, were he to take it into his head to impugn it. That would be a sure stroke, and almost the only plan for establishing the truth and demolishing Molinism; such is the fatality attending all the opinions which he embraces.

Let us leave them, then, to settle their own differences. These are the disputes of theologians, not of theology. We, who are no doctors, have nothing to do with their quarrels. Tell our friends the news of the censure, and love me while I am, &c.

LETTER IV

On actual grace and sins of ignorance

Paris, February 25, 1656

Sir,—Nothing can come up to the Jesuits. I have seen Jacobins, doctors, and all sorts of people in my day, but such an interview as I have just had was wanting to complete my knowledge of mankind. Other men are merely copies of them. As things are always found best at the fountainhead, I paid a visit to one of the ablest among them, in company with my trusty Jansenist—the same who accompanied me to the Dominicans. Being particularly anxious to learn something of a dispute which they have with the Jansenists about what they call *actual grace,* I said to the worthy father that I would be much obliged to him if he would instruct me on this point —that I did not even know what the term meant, and would thank him to explain it. "With all my heart," the Jesuit replied; "for I dearly love inquisitive people. Actual grace, according to our definition, 'is an inspiration of God, whereby He makes us to know His will, and excites within us a desire to perform it.' "

"And where," said I, "lies your difference with the Jansenists on this subject?"

"The difference lies here," he replied; "we hold that God bestows actual grace *on all men in every case of temptation;* for we maintain, that unless a person have, whenever tempted, actual grace to keep him from sinning, his sin, whatever it may be, can never be imputed to him. The Jansenists, on the other hand, affirm that sins, though committed without actual

358

grace, are, nevertheless, imputed; but they are a pack of fools." I got a glimpse of his meaning; but, to obtain from him a fuller explanation, I observed: "My dear father, it is that phrase *actual grace* that puzzles me; I am quite a stranger to it, and if you would have the goodness to tell me the same thing over again, without employing that term, you would infinitely oblige me."

"Very good," returned the father; "that is to say, you want me to substitute the definition in place of the thing defined; that makes no alteration of the sense; I have no objections. We maintain it, then, as an undeniable principle, *that an action cannot be imputed as a sin, unless God bestow on us, before committing it, the knowledge of the evil that is in the action, and an inspiration inciting us to avoid it.* Do you understand me now?"

Astonished at such a declaration, according to which, no sins of surprise, nor any of those committed in entire forgetfulness of God, could be imputed, I turned round to my friend the Jansenist, and easily discovered from his looks that he was of a different way of thinking. But as he did not utter a word, I said to the monk, "I would fain wish, my dear father, to think that what you have now said is true, and that you have good proofs for it."

"Proofs, say you!" he instantly exclaimed: "I shall furnish you with these very soon, and the very best sort too; let me alone for that."

So saying, he went in search of his books, and I took this opportunity of asking my friend if there was any other person who talked in this manner? "Is this so strange to you?" he replied. "You may depend upon it that neither the fathers, nor the popes, nor councils, nor Scripture, nor any book of devotion, employ such language; but if you wish casuists and modern schoolmen, he will bring you a goodly number of them on his side." "O! but I care not a fig about these authors, if they are contrary to tradition," I said. "You are right," he replied.

As he spoke, the good father entered the room, laden with

books; and presenting to me the first that came to hand. "Read that," he said; "this is 'The Summary of Sins,' by Father Bauny—the fifth edition too, you see, which shows that it is a good book."

"It is a pity, however," whispered the Jansenist in my ear, "that this same book has been condemned at Rome, and by the bishops of France."

"Look at page 906," said the father. I did so, and read as follows: "In order to sin and become culpable in the sight of God, it is necessary to know that the thing we wish to do is not good, or at least to doubt that it is—to fear or to judge that God takes no pleasure in the action which we contemplate, but forbids it; and in spite of this, to commit the deed, leap the fence, and transgress."

"This is a good commencement," I remarked. "And yet," said he, "mark how far envy will carry some people. It was on that very passage that M. Hallier, before he became one of our friends, bantered Father Bauny, by applying to him these words: *Ecce qui tollit peccata mundi*—'Behold the man that taketh away the sins of the world!'"

"Certainly," said I, "according to Father Bauny, we may be said to behold a redemption of an entirely new description."

"Would you have a more authentic witness on the point?" added he. "Here is the book of Father Annat. It is the last that he wrote against M. Arnauld. Turn up to page 34, where there is a dog's ear, and read the lines which I have marked with pencil—they ought to be written in letters of gold." I then read these words: "He that has no thought of God, nor of his sins, nor any apprehension (that is, as he explained it, any knowledge) of his obligation to exercise the acts of love to God or contrition, has no actual grace for exercising those acts; but it is equally true that he is guilty of no sin in omitting them, and that, if he is damned, it will not be as a punishment for that omission." And a few lines below, he adds: "The same thing may be said of a culpable commission."

"You see," said the monk, "how he speaks of sins of *omis-*

sion and of *commission.* Nothing escapes him. What say you
to that?"

"Say!" I exclaimed. "I am delighted! What a charming
train of consequences do I discover flowing from this doctrine!
I can see the whole results already; and such mysteries present themselves before me! Why, I see more people, beyond
all comparison, justified by this ignorance and forgetfulness
of God, than by grace and the sacraments! But, my dear
father, are you not inspiring me with a delusive joy? Are you
sure there is nothing here like that *sufficiency which suffices
not?* I am terribly afraid of the *Distinguo;*—I was taken in
with that once already! Are you quite in earnest?"

"How now!" cried the monk, beginning to get angry, "here
is no matter for jesting. I assure you there is no such thing as
equivocation here."

"I am not making a jest of it," said I; "but that is what I
really dread, from pure anxiety to find it true."

"Well then," he said, "to assure yourself still more of it,
here are the writings of M. le Moine, who taught the doctrine
in a full meeting of the Sorbonne. He learned it from us, to be
sure; but he has the merit of having cleared it up most admirably. O how circumstantially he goes to work! He shows
that, in order to make out an action to be *a sin*, all these things
must have passed through the mind. Read, and weigh every
word."—I then read what I now give you in a translation
from the original Latin: "1. On the one hand, God sheds
abroad on the soul some measure of love, which gives it a bias
toward the thing commanded; and on the other, a rebellious
concupiscence solicits it in the opposite direction. 2. God inspires the soul with a knowledge of its own weakness. 3. God
reveals the knowledge of the physician who can heal it. 4. God
inspires it with a desire to be healed. 5. God inspires a desire
to pray and solicit his assistance."

"And unless all these things occur and pass through the
soul," added the monk, "the action is not properly a sin, and
cannot be imputed, as M. le Moine shows in the same place

and in what follows. Would you wish to have other authorities for this? Here they are."

"All modern ones, however," whispered my Jansenist friend.

"So I perceive," said I to him aside; and then, turning to the monk: "O my dear sir," cried I, "what a blessing this will be to some persons of my acquaintance! I must positively introduce them to you. You have never, perhaps, met with people who had fewer sins to account for all your life. For, in the first place, they never think of God at all; their vices have got the better of their reason; they have never known either their weakness or the physician who can cure it; they have never thought of 'desiring the health of their soul,' and still less of 'praying to God to bestow it'; so that, according to M. le Moine, they are still in the state of baptismal innocence. They have 'never had a thought of loving God or of being contrite for their sins'; so that, according to Father Annat, they have never committed sin through the want of charity and penitence. Their life is spent in a perpetual round of all sorts of pleasures, in the course of which they have not been interrupted by the slightest remorse. These excesses had led me to imagine that their perdition was inevitable; but you, father, inform me that these same excesses secure their salvation. Blessings on you, my good father, for this way of justifying people! Others prescribe painful austerities for healing the soul; but you show that souls which may be thought desperately distempered are in quite good health. What an excellent device for being happy both in this world and in the next! I had always supposed that the less a man thought of God, the more he sinned; but, from what I see now, if one could only succeed in bringing himself not to think upon God at all, everything would be pure with him in all time coming. Away with your half-and-half sinners, who retain some sneaking affection for virtue! They will be damned every one of them, these semi-sinners. But commend me to your arrant sinners—hardened, unalloyed, out-and-out, thorough-bred sinners. Hell is no place for them; they have cheated the devil, purely by virtue of their devotion to his service!"

The good father, who saw very well the connection between these consequences and his principle, dexterously evaded them; and maintaining his temper, either from good nature or policy, he merely replied: "To let you understand how we avoid these inconveniences, you must know that, while we affirm that these reprobates to whom you refer would be without sin if they had no thoughts of conversion and no desires to devote themselves to God, we maintain that they all actually *have* such thoughts and desires, and that God never permitted a man to sin without giving him previously a view of the evil which he contemplated, and a desire, either to avoid the offence, or at all events to implore his aid to enable him to avoid it; and none but Jansenists will assert the contrary."

"Strange! father," returned I; "is this, then, the heresy of the Jansenists, to deny that every time a man commits a sin, he is troubled with a remorse of conscience, in spite of which, he 'leaps the fence and transgresses,' as Father Bauny has it? It is rather too good a joke to be made a heretic for that. I can easily believe that a man may be damned for not having good thoughts; but it never would have entered my head to imagine that any man could be subjected to that doom for not believing that all mankind must have good thoughts! But, father, I hold myself bound in conscience to disabuse you, and to inform you that there are thousands of people who have no such desires—who sin without regret—who sin with delight —who make a boast of sinning. And who ought to know better about these things than yourself? You cannot have failed to have confessed some of those to whom I allude; for it is among persons of high rank that they are most generally to be met with. But mark, father, the dangerous consequences of your maxim. Do you not perceive what effect it may have on those libertines who like nothing better than to find out matter of doubt in religion? What a handle do you give them, when you assure them, as an article of faith, that on every occasion when they commit a sin, they feel an inward presentiment of the evil, and a desire to avoid it? Is it not obvious that, feeling convinced by their own experience of the falsity of your doctrine on this point, which you say is a matter of faith, they will extend the inference drawn from this to all the other points? They will argue that, since you are not trustworthy in one article, you are to be suspected in them all; and thus you shut them up to conclude, either that religion is false, or that you must know very little about it."

Here my friend the Jansenist, following up my remarks, said to him: "You would do well, father, if you wish to preserve your doctrine, not to explain so precisely as you have done to us, what you mean by *actual grace*. For, how could you, without forfeiting all credit in the estimation of men, openly declare that *nobody sins without having previously the knowledge of his weakness, and of a physician, or the desire of a cure, and of asking it of God?* Will it be believed, on your word, that those who are immersed in avarice, impurity, blasphemy, duelling, revenge, robbery and sacrilege, have really a desire to embrace chastity, humility, and the other Christian virtues? Can it be conceived that those philosophers who boasted so loudly of the powers of nature, knew its infirmity and its physician? Will you maintain that those who held it as a settled maxim that 'it is not God that bestows virtue, and that no one ever asked it from him,' would think of asking it for themselves? Who can believe that the Epicureans, who denied a divine providence, ever felt any inclination to pray to God?—men who said that 'it would be an insult to invoke the Deity in our necessities, as if he were capable of wasting a thought on beings like us?' In a word, how can it be imagined that idolaters and atheists, every time they are tempted to the commission of sin, in other words, infinitely often during their lives, have a desire to pray to the true God, of whom they are ignorant, that he would bestow on them virtues of which they have no conception?"

"Yes," said the worthy monk, in a resolute tone, "we will affirm it: and sooner than allow that any one sins without having the consciousness that he is doing evil, and the desire of the opposite virtue, we will maintain that the whole world, reprobates and infidels included, have these inspirations and desires in every case of temptation. You cannot show me, from the Scripture at least, that this is not the truth."

On this remark I struck in, by exclaiming: "What! father, must we have recourse to the Scripture to demonstrate a thing so clear as this? This is not a point of faith, nor even of reason. It is a matter of fact: we see it—we know it—we feel it."

But the Jansenist, keeping the monk to his own terms, addressed him as follows: "If you are willing, father, to stand or fall by Scripture, I am ready to meet you there; only you must promise to yield to its authority; and since it is written that 'God has not revealed his judgments to the Heathen, but left them to wander in their own ways,' you must not say that God has enlightened those whom the Sacred Writings assure us 'he has left in darkness and in the shadow of death.' Is it not enough to show the erroneousness of your principle, to find that St. Paul calls himself 'the chief of sinners,' for a sin which he committed 'ignorantly, and with zeal?' Is it not enough, to and from the Gospel, that those who crucified Jesus Christ had need of the pardon which he asked for them, although they knew not the malice of their action, and would never have committed it, according to St. Paul, if they had known it? Is it not enough that Jesus Christ apprises us that there will be persecutors of the Church, who, while making every effort to ruin her, will 'think that they are doing God service'; teaching us that this sin, which in the judgment of the apostle, is the greatest of all sins, may be committed by persons who, so far from knowing that they were sinning, would think that they sinned by not committing it? In fine, is it not enough that Jesus Christ himself has taught us that there are two kinds of sinners, the one of whom sin with 'knowledge of their Master's will,' and the other without knowledge; and that both of them will be 'chastised,' although, indeed, in a different manner?"

Sorely pressed by so many testimonies from Scripture, to which he had appealed, the worthy monk began to give way;

and, leaving the wicked to sin without inspiration, he said: "You will not deny that *good men*, at least, never sin unless God give them"—"You are flinching," said I, interrupting him; "you are flinching now, my good father; you abandon the general principle, and finding that it will not hold good in regard to the wicked, you would compound the matter, by making it apply at least to the righteous. But in this point of view the application of it is, I conceive, so circumscribed, that it will hardly apply to anybody, and it is scarcely worth while to dispute the point."

My friend, however, who was so ready on the whole question, that I am inclined to think he had studied it all that very morning, replied: "This, father, is the last entrenchment to which those of your party who are willing to reason at all are sure to retreat; but you are far from being safe even here. The example of the saints is not a whit more in your favor. Who doubts that they often fall into sins of surprise, without being conscious of them? Do we not learn from the saints themselves how often concupiscence lays hidden snares for them; and how generally it happens, as St. Augustine complains of himself in his Confessions, that, with all their discretion, they 'give to pleasure what they mean only to give to necessity?'

"How usual is it to see the more zealous friends of truth betrayed by the heat of controversy into sallies of bitter passion for their personal interests, while their consciences, at the time, bear them no other testimony than that they are acting in this manner purely for the interests of truth, and they do not discover their mistake till long afterwards!

"What, again, shall we say of those who, as we learn from examples in ecclesiastical history, eagerly involve themselves in affairs which are really bad, because they believe them to be really good; and yet this does not hinder the fathers from condemning such persons as having sinned on these occasions?

"And were this not the case, how could the saints have their secret faults? How could it be true that God alone knows the magnitude and the number of our offences; that no one knows whether he is worthy of hatred or love; and that the best of saints, though unconscious of any culpability, ought always, as St. Paul says of himself, to remain in 'fear and trembling?'

"You perceive, then, father, that this knowledge of the evil, and love of the opposite virtue, which you imagine to be essential to constitute sin, are equally disproved by the examples of the righteous and of the wicked. In the case of the wicked, their passion for vice sufficiently testifies that they have no desire for virtue; and in regard to the righteous, the love which they bear to virtue plainly shows that they are not always conscious of those sins which, as the Scripture teaches, they are daily committing.

"So true is it, indeed, that the righteous often sin through ignorance, that the greatest saints rarely sin otherwise. For how can it be supposed that souls so pure, who avoid with so much care and zeal the least things that can be displeasing to God as soon as they discover them, and who yet sin many times every day, could possibly have, every time before they fell into sin, 'the knowledge of their infirmity on that occasion, and of their physician, and the desire of their souls' health, and of praying to God for assistance,' and that, in spite of these inspirations, these devoted souls 'nevertheless transgress,' and commit the sin?

"You must conclude then, father, that neither sinners nor yet saints have always that knowledge, or those desires and inspirations every time they offend; that is, to use your own terms, they have not always actual grace. Say no longer, with your modern authors, that it is impossible for those to sin who do not know righteousness; but rather join with St. Augustine and the ancient fathers in saying that it is impossible *not* to sin, when we do not know righteousness: *Necesse est ut peccet, a quo ignoratur justitia.*"

The good father, though thus driven from both of his positions, did not lose courage, but after ruminating a little, "Ha!" he exclaimed, "I shall convince you immediately." And again taking up Father Bauny, he pointed to the same place he had before quoted, exclaiming, "Look now—see the ground on which he establishes his opinion! I was sure he would not be deficient in good proofs. Read what he quotes from Aristotle, and you will see that after so express an authority, you must either burn the books of this prince of philosophers or adopt our opinion. Hear, then, the principles which support Father Bauny: Aristotle states first, *'that an action cannot be imputed as blameworthy, if it be involuntary.'* "

"I grant that," said my friend.

"This is the first time you have agreed together," said I. "Take my advice, father, and proceed no further."

"That would be doing nothing," he replied; "we must know what are the conditions necessary to constitute an action voluntary."

"I am much afraid," returned I, "that you will get at loggerheads on that point."

"No fear of that," said he; "this is sure ground—Aristotle is on my side. Hear, now, what Father Bauny says: 'In order that an action be voluntary, it must proceed from a man who perceives, knows, and comprehends what is good and what is evil in it. *Voluntarium est*—that is a voluntary action, as we commonly say with the philosopher' (that is Aristotle, you know, said the monk, squeezing my hand); *'quod fit a principio cognoscente singula in quibus est actio*—which is done by a person knowing the particulars of the action; so that when the will is led inconsiderately, and without mature reflection, to embrace or reject, to do or omit to do anything, before the understanding has been able to see whether it would be right or wrong, such an action is neither good nor evil; because previous to this mental inquisition, view, and reflection on the good or bad qualities of the matter in question, the act by which it is done is not voluntary.' Are you satisfied now?" said the father.

"It appears," returned I, "that Aristotle agrees with Father Bauny; but that does not prevent me from feeling surprised at this statement. What, sir! is it not enough to make an action voluntary that the man knows what he is doing, and does it just because he chooses to do it? Must we suppose, besides this, that he 'perceives, knows, and comprehends what is good and evil in the action?' Why, on this supposition there would be hardly such a thing in nature as voluntary actions, for no one scarcely thinks about all this. How many oaths in gambling—how many excesses in debauchery—how many riotous extravagances in the carnival, must, on this principle, be excluded from the list of voluntary actions, and consequently neither good nor bad, because not accompanied by those 'mental reflections on the good and evil qualities' of the action? But is it possible, father, that Aristotle held such a sentiment? I have always understood that he was a sensible man."

"I shall soon convince you of that," said the Jansenist, and requesting a sight of Aristotle's Ethics, he opened it at the beginning of the third book, from which Father Bauny had taken the passage quoted, and said to the monk: "I excuse you, my dear sir, for having believed, on the word of Father Bauny, that Aristotle held such a sentiment; but you would have changed your mind had you read him for yourself. It is true that he teaches, that 'in order to make an action voluntary, we must know the particulars of that action'—*singula in quibus est actio*. But what else does he mean by that, than the *particular circumstances* of the action? The examples which he adduces clearly show this to be his meaning, for they are exclusively confined to cases in which the persons were ignorant of some of the circumstances; such as that of 'a person who, wishing to exhibit a machine, discharges a dart which wounds a bystander; and that of Merope, who killed her own son instead of her enemy,' and such like.

"Thus you see what is the kind of ignorance that renders actions involuntary; namely, that of the particular circumstances, which is termed by divines, as you must know, *ignorance of the fact*. But with respect to *ignorance of the right*—ignorance of the good or evil in an action—which is the only point in question, let us see if Aristotle agrees with Father Bauny. Here are the words of the philosopher: 'All wicked men are ignorant of what they ought to do, and what they ought to avoid; and it is this very ignorance which makes them wicked and vicious. Accordingly, a man cannot be said to act involuntarily merely because he is ignorant of what it is proper for him to do in order to fulfil his duty. This ignorance in the choice of good and evil does not make the action involuntary; it only makes it vicious. The same thing may be affirmed of the man who is ignorant generally of the rules of his duty; such ignorance is worthy of blame, not of excuse. And consequently, the ignorance which renders actions involuntary and excusable is simply that which relates to the fact and its particular circumstances. In this case the person is excused and forgiven, being considered as having acted contrary to his inclination.'

"After this, father, will you maintain that Aristotle is of your opinion? And who can help being astonished to find that a Pagan philosopher had more enlightened views than your doctors, in a matter so deeply affecting morals, and the direction of conscience, too, as the knowledge of those conditions which render actions voluntary or involuntary, and which, accordingly, charge or discharge them as sinful? Look for no more support, then, father, from the prince of philosophers, and no longer oppose yourselves to the prince of theologians, who has thus decided the point in the first book of his Retractations, chapter xv.: 'Those who sin through ignorance, though they sin without meaning to sin, commit the deed only because they *will* commit it. And, therefore, even this sin of ignorance cannot be committed except by the will of him who commits it, though by a will which incites him to the action merely, and not to the sin; and yet the action itself is nevertheless sinful, for it is enough to constitute it such that he has done what he was bound not to do.' "

The Jesuit seemed to be confounded more with the passage from Aristotle, I thought, than that from St. Augustine; but while he was thinking on what he could reply, a messenger came to inform him that Madame la Maréchale of ——, and Madame the Marchioness of ——, requested his attendance. So taking a hasty leave of us, he said: "I shall speak about it to our fathers. They will find an answer to it, I warrant you; we have got some long heads among us."

We understood him perfectly well; and on our being left alone, I expressed to my friend my astonishment at the subversion which this doctrine threatened to the whole system of morals. To this he replied that he was quite astonished at my astonishment. "Are you not yet aware," he said, "that they have gone to far greater excess in morals than in any other matter?" He gave me some strange illustrations of this, promising me more at some future time. The information which I may receive on this point, will, I hope, furnish the topic of my next communication.—I am, &c.

LETTER V

Design of the Jesuits in establishing a new system of morals—two sorts of casuists among them, a great many lax, and some severe ones—reason of this difference—explanation of the doctrine of probability—a multitude of modern and unknown authors substituted in the place of the holy fathers

Paris, March 20, 1656

Sir,—According to my promise, I now send you the first outlines of the morals taught by those good fathers the Jesuits —"those men distinguished for learning and sagacity, who are all under the guidance of divine wisdom—a surer guide than all philosophy." You imagine, perhaps, that I am in jest, but I am perfectly serious; or rather, they are so when they speak thus of themselves in their book entitled "The Image of the First Century." I am only copying their own words, and may now give you the rest of the eulogy: "They are a society of men, or rather let us call them angels, predicted by Isaiah in these words, 'Go, ye swift and ready angels.'" The prediction is as clear as day, is it not? "They have the spirit of eagles; they are a flock of phœnixes (a late author having demonstrated that there are a great many of these birds); they have changed the face of Christendom!" Of course, we must believe all this, since they have said it; and in one sense you will find the account amply verified by the sequel of this communication, in which I propose to treat of their maxims.

Determined to obtain the best possible information, I did not trust to the representations of our friend the Jansenist, but sought an interview with some of themselves. I found, however, that he told me nothing but the bare truth, and I am persuaded he is an honest man. Of this you may judge from the following account of these conferences.

In the conversation I had with the Jansenist, he told me so many strange things about these fathers, that I could with difficulty believe them, till he pointed them out to me in their writings; after which he left me nothing more to say in their defence, than that these might be the sentiments of some individuals only, which it was not fair to impute to the whole fraternity. And, indeed, I assured him that I knew some of them who were as severe as those whom he quoted to me were lax. This led him to explain to me the spirit of the Society, which is not known to every one; and you will perhaps have no objections to learning something about it.

"You imagine," he began, "that it would tell considerably in their favor to show that some of their fathers are as friendly to Evangelical maxims as others are opposed to them; and you would conclude from that circumstance, that these loose opinions do not belong to the whole Society. That I grant you; for had such been the case, they would not have suffered persons among them holding sentiments so diametrically opposed to licentiousness. But as it is equally true that there are among them those who hold these licentious doctrines, you are bound also to conclude that the Spirit of the Society is not that of Christian severity; for had such been the case, they would not have suffered persons among them holding sentiments so diametrically opposed to that severity."

"And what, then," I asked, "can be the design of the whole as a body? Perhaps they have no fixed principle, and every one is left to speak out at random whatever he thinks."

"That cannot be," returned my friend; "such an immense body could not subsist in such a haphazard sort of way, or without a soul to govern and regulate its movements; besides, it is one of their express regulations, that none shall print a page without the approval of their superiors."

"But," said I, "how can these same superiors give their consent to maxims so contradictory?"

"That is what you have yet to learn," he replied. "Know, then, that their object is not the corruption of manners—that is not their design. But as little is it their sole aim to reform them—that would be bad policy. Their idea is briefly this: They have such a good opinion of themselves as to believe that it is useful, and in some sort essentially necessary to the good of religion, that their influence should extend everywhere, and that they should govern all consciences. And the Evangelical or severe maxims being best fitted for managing some sorts of people, they avail themselves of these when they find them favorable to their purpose. But as these maxims do not suit the views of the great bulk of the people, they waive them in the case of such persons, in order to keep on good terms with all the world. Accordingly, having to deal with persons of all classes and of all different nations, they find it necessary to have casuists assorted to match this diversity.

"On this principle, you will easily see that if they had none but the looser sort of casuists, they would defeat their main design, which is to embrace all; for those that are truly pious are fond of a stricter discipline. But as there are not many of that stamp, they do not require many severe directors to guide them. They have a few for the select few; while whole multitudes of lax casuists are provided for the multitudes that prefer laxity.

"It is in virtue of this 'obliging and accommodating, conduct,' as Father Petau calls it, that they may be said to stretch out a helping hand to all mankind. Should any person present himself before them, for example, fully resolved to make restitution of some ill-gotten gains, do not suppose that they would dissuade him from it. By no means; on the contrary, they would applaud and confirm him in such a holy resolution. But suppose another should come who wishes to be absolved without restitution, and it will be a particularly hard case indeed, if they cannot furnish him with means of evading the duty, of one kind or another, the lawfulness of which they will be ready to guarantee.

"By this policy they keep all their friends, and defend

themselves against all their foes; for, when charged with extreme laxity, they have nothing more to do than produce their austere directors, with some books which they have written on the severity of the Christian code of morals; and simple people, or those who never look below the surface of things, are quite satisfied with these proofs of the falsity of the accusation.

"Thus are they prepared for all sorts of persons, and so ready are they to suit the supply to the demand, that when they happen to be in any part of the world where the doctrine of a crucified God is accounted foolishness, they suppress the offence of the cross, and preach only a glorious and not a suffering Jesus Christ. This plan they followed in the Indies and in China, where they permitted Christians to practise idolatry itself, with the aid of the following ingenious contrivance:— they made their converts conceal under their clothes an image of Jesus Christ, to which they taught them to transfer mentally those adorations which they rendered ostensibly to the idol of Cachinchoam and Keum-fucum. This charge is brought against them by Gravina, a Dominican, and is fully established by the Spanish memorial presented to Philip IV., king of Spain, by the Cordeliers of the Philippine Islands, quoted by Thomas Hurtado, in his 'Martyrdom of the Faith,' page 427. To such a length did this practice go, that the Congregation *De Propaganda* were obliged expressly to forbid the Jesuits, on pain of excommunication, to permit the worship of idols on any pretext whatever, or to conceal the mystery of the cross from their catechumens; strictly enjoining them to admit none to baptism who were not thus instructed, and ordering them to expose the image of the crucifix in their churches:—all of which is amply detailed in the decree of that Congregation, dated the 9th of July, 1646, and signed by Cardinal Capponi.

"Such is the manner in which they have spread themselves over the whole earth, aided by *the doctrine of probable opinions*, which is at once the source and the basis of all this licentiousness. You must get some of themselves to explain this doctrine to you. They make no secret of it, any more than of what you have already learned; with this difference only, that they conceal their carnal and worldly policy under the garb of divine and Christian prudence; as if the faith, and tradition, its ally, were not always one and the same at all times and in all places; as if it were the part of the rule to bend in conformity to the subject which it was meant to regulate; and as if souls, to be purified from their pollutions, had only to corrupt the law of the Lord, in place of 'the law of the Lord, which is clean and pure, converting the soul which lieth in sin,' and bringing it into conformity with its salutary lessons!

"Go and see some of these worthy fathers, I beseech you, and I am confident that you will soon discover, in the laxity of their moral system, the explanation of their doctrine about grace. You will then see the Christian virtues exhibited in such a strange aspect, so completely stripped of the charity which is the life and soul of them—you will see so many crimes palliated and irregularities tolerated, that you will no longer be surprised at their maintaining that 'all men have always enough of grace' to lead a pious life, in the sense in which they understand piety. Their morality being entirely Pagan, nature is quite competent to its observance. When we maintain the necessity of efficacious grace, we assign it another sort of virtue for its object. Its office is not to cure one vice by means of another; it is not merely to induce men to practise the external duties of religion: it aims at a virtue higher than that propounded by Pharisees, or the greatest sages of Heathenism. The law and reason are 'sufficient graces' for these purposes. But to disenthral the soul from the love of the world—to tear it from what it holds most dear—to make it die to itself—to lift it up and bind it wholly, only, and forever, to God—can be the work of none but an all-powerful hand. And it would be as absurd to affirm that we have the full power of achieving such objects, as it would be to allege that those virtues, devoid of the love of God, which these fathers confound with the virtues of Christianity, are beyond our power."

Such was the strain of my friend's discourse, which was delivered with much feeling; for he takes these sad disorders very much to heart. For my own part, I began to entertain a high admiration for these fathers, simply on account of the ingenuity of their policy; and following his advice, I waited on a good casuist of the Society, one of my old acquaintances, with whom I now resolved purposely to renew my former intimacy. Having my instructions how to manage them, I had no great difficulty in getting him afloat. Retaining his old attachment, he received me immediately with a profusion of kindness; and after talking over some indifferent matters, I took occasion from the present season, to learn something from him about fasting, and thus slip insensibly into the main subject. I told him, therefore, that I had difficulty in supporting the fast. He exhorted me to do violence to my inclinations; but as I continued to murmur, he took pity on me, and began to search out some ground for a dispensation. In fact he suggested a number of excuses for me, none of which happened to suit my case, till at length he bethought himself of asking me, whether I did not find it difficult to sleep without taking supper. "Yes, my good father," said I; "and for that reason I am obliged often to take a refreshment at mid-day, and supper at night."

"I am extremely happy," he replied, "to have found out a way of relieving you without sin: go in peace—you are under no obligation to fast. However, I would not have you depend on my word: step this way to the library."

On going thither with him he took up a book, exclaiming, with great rapture, "Here is the authority for you: and, by my conscience, such an authority! It is ESCOBAR!"

"Who is Escobar?" I inquired.

"What! not know Escobar!" cried the monk; "the member of our Society who compiled this Moral Theology from twenty-four of our fathers, and on this founds an analogy, in his preface, between his book and 'that in the Apocalypse which was sealed with seven seals,' and states that 'Jesus presents it thus sealed to the four living creatures, Suarez, Vasquez, Molina, and Valencia, in presence of the four-and-twenty Jesuits who represent the four-and-twenty elders."

He read me, in fact, the whole of that allegory, which he pronounced to be admirably appropriate, and which conveyed to my mind a sublime idea of the excellence of the work. At length, having sought out the passage on fasting, "Oh, here it is!" he said; "treatise 1, example 13, no. 67: 'If a man cannot sleep without taking supper, is he bound to fast? Answer: *By no means!*' Will that not satisfy you?"

"Not exactly," replied I; "for I might sustain the fast by taking my refreshment in the morning, and supping at night."

"Listen, then, to what follows; they have provided for all that: 'And what is to be said, if the person might make a shift with a refreshment in the morning and supping at night?'"

"That's my case exactly."

"'Answer: Still he is not obliged to fast; because no person is obliged to change the order of his meals.'"

"A most excellent reason!" I exclaimed.

"But tell me, pray," continued the monk, "do you take much wine?"

"No, my dear father," I answered; "I cannot endure it."

"I merely put the question," returned he, "to apprise you that you might, without breaking the fast, take a glass or so in the morning, or whenever you felt inclined for a drop; and that is always something in the way of supporting nature. Here is the decision at the same place, no. 57: 'May one, without breaking the fast, drink wine at any hour he pleases, and even in a large quantity? Yes, he may: and a dram of hippocrass too.' I had no recollection of the hippocrass," said the monk; "I must take a note of that in my memorandum-book."

"He must be a nice man, this Escobar," observed I.

"Oh! everybody likes him," rejoined the father; "he has such delightful questions! Only observe this one in the same place, no. 38: 'If a man doubt whether he is twenty-one years old, is he obliged to fast? No. But suppose I were to be twenty-one to-night an hour after midnight, and to-morrow were the fast, would I be obliged to fast to-morrow? No; for you were at liberty to eat as much as you pleased for an hour after midnight, not being till then fully twenty-one; and therefore having a right to break the fast day, you are not obliged to keep it.'"

"Well, that is vastly entertaining!" cried I.

"Oh," rejoined the father, "it is impossible to tear one's self away from the book: I spend whole days and nights in reading it; in fact, I do nothing else."

The worthy monk, perceiving that I was interested, was quite delighted, and went on with his quotations. "Now," said he, "for a taste of Filiutius, one of the four-and-twenty Jesuits: 'Is a man who has exhausted himself any way—by profligacy, for example—obliged to fast? By no means. But if he has exhausted himself expressly to procure a dispensation from fasting, will he be held obliged? He will not, even though he should have had that design.' There now! would you have believed that?"

"Indeed, good father, I do not believe it yet," said I. "What! is it no sin for a man not to fast when he has it in his power? And is it allowable to court occasions of committing sin, or rather, are we not bound to shun them? That would be easy enough, surely."

"Not always so," he replied; "that is just as it may happen."

"Happen, how?" cried I.

"Oh!" rejoined the monk, "so you think that if a person experience some inconvenience in avoiding the occasions of sin, he is still bound to do so? Not so thinks Father Bauny. 'Absolution,' says he, 'is not to be refused to such as continue in the proximate occasions of sin, if they are so situated that they cannot give them up without becoming the common talk of the world, or subjecting themselves to personal inconvenience.'"

"I am glad to hear it, father," I remarked; "and now that we are not obliged to avoid the occasions of sin, nothing more remains but to say that we may deliberately court them."

"Even that is occasionally permitted," added he; "the celebrated casuist Basil Ponce has said so, and Father Bauny quotes his sentiment with approbation, in his Treatise on Penance, as follows: 'We may seek an occasion of sin directly and designedly—*primo et per se*—when our own or our neighbor's spiritual or temporal advantage induces us to do so.'"

"Truly," said I, "it appears to be all a dream to me, when I hear grave divines talking in this manner! Come now, my dear father, tell me conscientiously, do *you* hold such a sentiment as that?"

"No, indeed," said he, "I do not."

"You are speaking, then, against your conscience," continued I.

"Not at all," he replied; "I was speaking on that point not according to my own conscience, but according to that of Ponce and Father Bauny, and them you may follow with the utmost safety, for I assure you that they are able men."

"What, father! because they have put down these three lines in their books, will it therefore become allowable to court the occasions of sin? I always thought that we were bound to take the Scripture and the tradition of the Church as our only rule, and not your casuists."

"Goodness!" cried the monk, "I declare you put me in mind of these Jansenists. Think you that Father Bauny and Basil Ponce are not able to render their opinion *probable?*"

"Probable won't do for me," said I; "I must have certainty."

"I can easily see," replied the good father, "that you know nothing about our doctrine of *probable opinions*. If you did, you would speak in another strain. Ah! my dear sir, I must really give you some instructions on this point; without knowing this, positively you can understand nothing at all. It is the foundation—the very A, B, C, of our whole moral philosophy."

Glad to see him come to the point to which I had been

drawing him on, I expressed my satisfaction, and requested him to explain what was meant by a probable opinion?

"That," he replied, "our authors will answer better than I can do. The generality of them, and, among others, our four-and-twenty elders, describe it thus: 'An opinion is called probable, when it is founded upon reasons of some consideration. Hence it may sometimes happen that a single *very grave doctor* may render an opinion probable.' The reason is added: 'For a man particularly given to study would not adhere to an opinion unless he was drawn to it by a good and sufficient reason.'"

"So it would appear," I observed, with a smile, "that a single doctor may turn consciences round about and upside down as he pleases, and yet always land them in a safe position."

"You must not laugh at it, sir," returned the monk; "nor need you attempt to combat the doctrine. The Jansenists tried this; but they might have saved themselves the trouble —it is too firmly established. Hear Sanchez, one of the most famous of our fathers: 'You may doubt, perhaps, whether the authority of a single good and learned doctor renders an opinion probable. I answer, that it does; and this is confirmed by Angelus, Sylvester, Navarre, Emanuel Sa, &c. It is proved thus: A probable opinion is one that has a considerable foundation. Now the authority of a learned and pious man is entitled to very great consideration; because (mark the reason), if the testimony of such a man has great influence in convincing us that such and such an event occurred, say at Rome, for example, why should it not have the same weight in the case of a question in morals?'"

"An odd comparison this," interrupted I, "between the concerns of the world and those of conscience!"

"Have a little patience," rejoined the monk; "Sanchez answers that in the very next sentence: 'Nor can I assent to the qualification made here by some writers, namely, that the authority of such a doctor, though sufficient in matters of human right, is not so in those of divine right. It is of vast weight in both cases.' "

"Well, father," said I, frankly, "I really cannot admire that rule. Who can assure me, considering the freedom your doctors claim to examine everything by reason, that what appears safe to one may seem so to all the rest? The diversity of judgments is so great"—

"You don't understand it," said he, interrupting me; "no doubt they are often of different sentiments, but what signifies that?—each renders his own opinion probable and safe. We all know well enough that they are far from being of the same mind; what is more, there is hardly an instance in which they ever agree. There are very few questions, indeed, in which you do not find the one saying yes, and the other saying no. Still, in all these cases, each of the contrary opinions is probable. And hence Diana says on a certain subject: 'Ponce and Sanchez hold opposite views of it; but, as they are both learned men, each renders his own opinion probable.' "

"But, father," I remarked, "a person must be sadly embarrassed in choosing between them!"—"Not at all," he rejoined; "he has only to follow the opinion which suits him best."—"What! if the other is more probable?" "It does not signify."—"And if the other is the safer?" "It does not signify," repeated the monk; "this is made quite plain by Emanuel Sa, of our Society, in his Aphorisms: 'A person may do what he considers allowable according to a probable opinion, though the contrary may be the safer one. The opinion of a single grave doctor is all that is requisite.' "

"And if an opinion be at once the less probable and the less safe, is it allowable to follow it," I asked, "even in the way of rejecting one which we believe to be more probable and safe?"

"Once more, I say yes," replied the monk. "Hear what Filiutius, that great Jesuit of Rome, says: 'It is allowable to follow the less probable opinion, even though it be the less

safe one. That is the common judgment of modern authors.'
Is not that quite clear?"

"Well, reverend father," said I, "you have given *us* elbow-room, at all events! Thanks to your probable opinions, we have got liberty of conscience with a witness! And are you casuists allowed the same latitude in giving your responses?"

"Oh, yes," said he, "we answer just as we please; or rather, I should say, just as it may please those who ask our advice. Here are our rules, taken from Fathers Layman, Vasquez, Sanchez, and the four-and-twenty worthies, in the words of Layman: 'A doctor, on being consulted, may give an advice, not only probable according to his own opinion, but contrary to his opinion, provided this judgment happens to be more favorable or more agreeable to the person that consults him— *si forte hæc favorabilior seu exoptatior sit.* Nay, I go further, and say, that there would be nothing unreasonable in his giving those who consult him a judgment held to be probable by some learned person, even though he should be satisfied in his own mind that it is absolutely false.' "

"Well, seriously, father," I said, "your doctrine is a most uncommonly comfortable one! Only think of being allowed to answer yes or no, just as you please! It is impossible to prize such a privilege too highly. I see now the advantage of the contrary opinions of your doctors. One of them always serves your turn, and the other never gives you any annoyance. If you do not find your account on the one side, you fall back on the other, and always land in perfect safety."

"That is quite true," he replied; "and accordingly, we may always say with Diana, on his finding that Father Bauny was on his side, while Father Lugo was against him: *Sæpe premente deo, fert deus alter opem.*"

"I understand you," resumed I; "but a practical difficulty has just occurred to me, which is this, that supposing a person to have consulted one of your doctors, and obtained from him a pretty liberal opinion, there is some danger of his getting into a scrape by meeting a confessor who takes a different view of the matter, and refuses him absolution unless he recant the sentiment of the casuist. Have you not provided for such a case as that, father?"

"Can you doubt it?" he replied. "We have bound them, sir, to absolve their penitents who act according to probable opinions, under the pain of mortal sin, to secure their compliance. 'When the penitent,' says Father Bauny, 'follows a probable opinion, the confessor is bound to absolve him, though his opinion should differ from that of his penitent.'"

"But he does not say it would be a mortal sin not to absolve him," said I.

"How hasty you are!" rejoined the monk; "listen to what follows; he has expressly decided that, 'to refuse absolution to a penitent who acts according to a probable opinion, is a sin which is in its nature mortal.' And to settle that point, he cites the most illustrious of our fathers—Suarez, Vasquez, and Sanchez."

"My dear sir," said I, "that is a most prudent regulation. I see nothing to fear now. No confessor can dare to be refractory after this. Indeed, I was not aware that you had the power of issuing your orders on pain of damnation. I thought that your skill had been confined to the taking away of sins; I had no idea that it extended to the introduction of new ones. But from what I now see, you are omnipotent."

"That is not a correct way of speaking," rejoined the father. "We do not introduce sins; we only pay attention to them. I have had occasion to remark, two or three times during our conversation, that you are no great scholastic."

"Be that as it may, father, you have at least answered my difficulty. But I have another to suggest. How do you manage when the Fathers of the Church happen to differ from any of your casuists?"

"You really know very little of the subject," he replied. "The Fathers were good enough for the morality of their own times; but they lived too far back for that of the present age, which is no longer regulated by them, but by the modern casuists. On this Father Cellot, following the famous Reginald, remarks: 'In questions of morals, the modern casuists are to be preferred to the ancient fathers, though those lived nearer to the times of the apostles.' And following out this maxim, Diana thus decides: 'Are beneficiaries bound to restore their revenue when guilty of mal-appropriation of it? The ancients would say yes, but the moderns say no; let us, therefore, adhere to the latter opinion, which relieves from the obligation of restitution.' "

"Delightful words these, and most comfortable they must be to a great many people!" I observed.

"We leave the fathers," resumed the monk, "to those who deal with positive divinity. As for us, who are the directors of conscience, we read very little of them, and quote only the modern casuists. There is Diana, for instance, a most voluminous writer; he has prefixed to his works a list of his authorities, which amount to two hundred and ninety-six, and the most ancient of them is only about eighty years old."

"It would appear, then," I remarked, "that all these have come into the world since the date of your Society?"

"Thereabouts," he replied.

"That is to say, dear father, on your advent, St. Augustine, St. Chrysostom, St. Ambrose, St. Jerome, and all the rest, in so far as morals are concerned, disappeared from the stage. Would you be so kind as let me know the names, at least, of those modern authors who have succeeded them?"

"A most able and renowned class of men they are," replied the monk. "Their names are, Villalobos, Conink, Llamas, Achokier, Dealkozer, Dellacruz, Veracruz, Ugolin, Tambourin, Fernandez, Martinez, Suarez, Henriquez, Vasquez, Lopez, Gomez, Sanchez, De Vechis, De Grassis, De Grassalis, De Pitigianis, De Graphæis, Squilanti, Bizozeri, Barcola, De Bobadilla, Simanacha, Perez de Lara, Aldretta, Lorca, De Scarcia, Quaranta, Scophra, Pedrezza, Cabrezza, Bisbe, Dias, De Clavasio, Villagut, Adam à Manden, Iribarne, Binsfeld, Volfangi à Vorberg, Vosthery, Strevesdorf."

"O my dear father!" cried I, quite alarmed, "were all these people Christians?"

"How! Christians!" returned the casuist; "did I not tell

you that these are the only writers by whom we now govern Christendom?"

Deeply affected as I was by this announcement, I concealed my emotion from the monk, and only asked him if all these authors were Jesuits?

"No," said he; "but that is of little consequence; they have said a number of good things for all that. It is true the greater part of these same good things are extracted or copied from our authors, but we do not stand on ceremony with them on that score, more especially as they are in the constant habit of quoting our authors with applause. When Diana, for example, who does not belong to our Society, speaks of Vasquez, he calls him 'that phœnix of genius'; and he declares more than once, 'that Vasquez alone is to him worth all the rest of men put together'—*instar omnium.* Accordingly, our fathers often make use of this good Diana; and if you understand our doctrine of probability, you will see that this is no small help in its way. In fact, we are anxious that others besides the Jesuits would render their opinions probable, to prevent people from ascribing them all to us; for you will observe, that when any author, whoever he may be, advances a probable opinion, we are entitled, by the doctrine of probability, to adopt it if we please; and yet, if the author does not belong to our fraternity, we are not responsible for its soundness."

"I understand all that," said I. "It is easy to see that all are welcome that come your way, except the ancient fathers; you are masters of the field, and have only to walk the course. But I foresee three or four serious difficulties and powerful barriers which will oppose your career."

"And what are these?" cried the monk, looking quite alarmed.

"They are the Holy Scriptures," I replied, "the popes, and the councils, whom you cannot gainsay, and who are all in the way of the Gospel."

"Is that all?" he exclaimed; "I declare you put me in a fright. Do you imagine that we would overlook such an obvious scruple as that, or that we have not provided against it?

A good idea, forsooth, to suppose that we would contradict Scripture, popes, and councils! I must convince you of your mistake; for I should be sorry you should go away with an impression that we are deficient in our respect to these authorities. You have doubtless taken up this notion from some of the opinions of our fathers, which are apparently at variance with their decisions, though in reality they are not. But to illustrate the harmony between them would require more leisure than we have at present; and as I would not like you to retain a bad impression of us, if you agree to meet with me to-morrow, I shall clear it all up then."

Thus ended our interview, and thus shall end my present communication, which has been long enough, besides, for one letter. I am sure you will be satisfied with it, in the prospect of what is forthcoming.—I am, &c.

Various artifices of the Jesuits to elude the authority of the Gospel, of councils, and of the popes—some consequences which result from their doctrine of probability—their relaxation in favor of beneficiaries, priests, monks, and domestics—story of John D'Alba

Paris, April 10, 1656

Sir,—I mentioned, at the close of my last letter, that my good friend the Jesuit had promised to show me how the casuists reconcile the contrarieties between their opinions and the decisions of the popes, the councils, and the Scripture. This promise he fulfilled at our last interview, of which I shall now give you an account.

"One of the methods," resumed the monk, "in which we reconcile these apparent contradictions, is by the interpretation of some phrase. Thus, Pope Gregory XIV. decided that assassins are not worthy to enjoy the benefit of sanctuary in churches, and ought to be dragged out of them; and yet our four-and-twenty elders affirm that 'the penalty of this bull is not incurred by all those that kill in treachery.' This may appear to you a contradiction; but we get over this by interpreting the word *assassin* as follows: 'Are assassins unworthy of sanctuary in churches? Yes, by the bull of Gregory XIV. they are. But by the word *assassins* we understand those that have received money to murder one; and accordingly, such as kill without taking any reward for the deed, but merely *to oblige their friends*, do not come under the category of assassins.' "

"Take another instance: It is said in the Gospel, 'Give alms of your superfluity.' Several casuists, however, have contrived to discharge the wealthiest from the obligation of alms-giving. This may appear another paradox, but the matter is easily put to rights by giving such an interpretation to the word *superfluity* that it will seldom or never happen that any one is troubled with such an article. This feat has been accomplished by the learned Vasquez, in his Treatise on Alms, c. 4: 'What men of the world lay up to improve their circumstances, or those of their relatives, cannot be termed superfluity; and accordingly, such a thing as superfluity is seldom to be found among men of the world, not even excepting kings.' Diana, too, who generally founds on our fathers, having quoted these words of Vasquez, justly concludes, 'that as to the question whether the rich are bound to give alms of their superfluity, even though the affirmative were true, it will seldom or never happen to be obligatory in practice.' "

"I see very well how that follows from the doctrine of Vasquez," said I. "But how would you answer this objection, that, in working out one's salvation, it would be as safe, according to Vasquez, to give no alms, provided one can muster as much ambition as to have no superfluity; as it is safe, according to the Gospel, to have no ambition at all, in order to have some superfluity for the purpose of alms-giving?"

"Why," returned he, "the answer would be, that both of these ways are safe according to the Gospel; the one according to the Gospel in its more literal and obvious sense, and the other according to the same Gospel as interpreted by Vasquez. There you see the utility of interpretations. When the terms are so clear, however," he continued, "as not to admit of an interpretation, we have recourse to the observation of favorable circumstances. A single example will illustrate this. The popes have denounced excommunication on monks who lay aside their canonicals; our casuists, notwithstanding, put it as a question, 'On what occasions may a monk lay aside his religious habits without incurring excommunication?' They mention a number of cases in which they may,

and among others the following: 'If he has laid it aside for
an infamous purpose, such as to pick pockets or to go *incognito*
into haunts of profligacy, meaning shortly after to resume it.'
It is evident the bulls have no reference to cases of that description."

I could hardly believe that, and begged the father to show
me the passage in the original. He did so, and under the chapter headed "Practice according to the School of the Society of
Jesus"—*Praxis ex Societatis Jesu Schola*—I read these very
words: *Si habitum dimittat ut furetur occulte, vel fornicetur.*
He showed me the same thing in Diana, in these terms: *Ut
eat incognitus ad lupanar.* "And why, father," I asked, "are
they discharged from excommunication on such occasions?"

"Don't you understand it?" he replied. "Only think what
a scandal it would be, were a monk surprised in such a predicament with his canonicals on! And have you never heard," he
continued, "how they answer the first bull *contra sollicitantes*
and how our four-and-twenty, in another chapter of the
Practice according to the School of our Society, explain the
bull of Pius V. *contra clericos,* &c.?"

"I know nothing about all that," said I.

"Then it is a sign you have not read much of Escobar,"
returned the monk.

"I got him only yesterday, father," said I; "and I had no
small difficulty, too, in procuring a copy. I don't know how it
is, but everybody of late has been in search of him."

"The passage to which I referred," returned the monk,
"may be found in treatise 1, example 8, no. 102. Consult it at
your leisure when you go home."

I did so that very night; but it is so shockingly bad, that I
dare not transcribe it.

The good father then went on to say: "You now understand
what use we make of favorable circumstances. Sometimes,
however, obstinate cases will occur, which will not admit of
this mode of adjustment; so much so, indeed, that you would
almost suppose they involved flat contradictions. For example,
three popes have decided that monks who are bound by a

particular vow to a Lenten life, cannot be absolved from it even though they should become bishops. And yet Diana avers that notwithstanding this decision they *are* absolved."

"And how does he reconcile that?" said I.

"By the most subtle of all the modern methods, and by the nicest possible application of probability," replied the monk. "You may recollect you were told the other day, that the affirmative and negative of most opinions have each, according to our doctors, some probability—enough, at least, to be followed with a safe conscience. Not that the *pro* and *con* are both true in the same sense—that is impossible—but only they are both probable, and therefore safe, as a matter of course. On this principle our worthy friend Diana remarks: 'To the decision of these three popes, which is contrary to my opinion, I answer, that they spoke in this way by adhering to the affirmative side—which, in fact, even in my judgment, is probable; but it does not follow from this that the negative may not have its probability too.' And in the same treatise, speaking of another subject on which he again differs from a pope, he says: 'The pope, I grant, has said it as the head of the Church; but his decision does not extend beyond the sphere of the probability of his own opinion.' Now you perceive this is not doing any harm to the opinions of the popes; such a thing would never be tolerated at Rome, where Diana is in high repute. For he does not say that what the popes have decided is not probable; but leaving their opinion within the sphere of probability, he merely says that the contrary is also probable."

"That is very respectful," said I.

"Yes," added the monk, "and rather more ingenious than the reply made by Father Bauny, when his books were censured at Rome; for when pushed very hard on this point by M. Hallier, he made bold to write: 'What has the censure of Rome to do with that of France?' You now see how, either by the interpretation of terms, by the observation of favorable circumstances, or by the aid of the double probability of *pro* and *con*, we always contrive to reconcile those seeming contradictions which occasioned you so much surprise, without ever touching on the decisions of Scripture, councils, or popes."

"Reverend father," said I, "how happy the world is in having such men as you for its masters! And what blessings are these probabilities! I never knew the reason why you took such pains to establish that a single doctor, *if a grave one*, might render an opinion probable, and that the contrary might be so too, and that one may choose any side one pleases, even though he does not believe it to be the right side, and all with such a safe conscience, that the confessor who should refuse him absolution on the faith of the casuists would be in a state of damnation. But I see now that a single casuist may make new rules of morality at his discretion, and dispose, according to his fancy, of everything pertaining to the regulation of manners."

"What you have now said," rejoined the father, "would require to be modified a little. Pay attention now, while I explain our method, and you will observe the progress of a new opinion, from its birth to its maturity. First, the grave doctor who invented it exhibits it to the world, casting it abroad like seed, that it may take root. In this state it is very feeble; it requires time gradually to ripen. This accounts for Diana, who has introduced a great many of these opinions, saying: 'I advance this opinion; but as it is new, I give it time to come to maturity—*relinquo tempori maturandum*.' Thus in a few years it becomes insensibly consolidated; and after a considerable time it is sanctioned by the tacit approbation of the Church, according to the grand maxim of Father Bauny, 'that if an opinion has been advanced by some casuist, and has not been impugned by the Church, it is a sign that she approves of it.' And, in fact, on this principle he authenticates one of his own principles in his sixth treatise, p. 312."

"Indeed, father!" cried I, "why, on this principle the Church would approve of all the abuses which she tolerates, and all the errors in all the books which she does not censure!"

"Dispute the point with Father Bauny," he replied. "I am

merely quoting his words, and you begin to quarrel with *me*. There is no disputing with facts, sir. Well, as I was saying, when time has thus matured an opinion, it thenceforth becomes completely probable and safe. Hence the learned Caramuel, in dedicating his Fundamental Theology to Diana, declares that this great Diana has rendered many opinions probable which were not so before—*quæ antea non erant;* and that, therefore, in following them, persons do not sin now, though they would have sinned formerly—*jam non peccant, licet ante peccaverint.*"

"Truly, father," I observed, "it must be worth one's while living in the neighborhood of your doctors. Why, of two individuals who do the same actions, he that knows nothing about their doctrine sins, while he that knows it does no sin. It seems, then, that their doctrine possesses at once an edifying and a justifying virtue! The law of God, according to St. Paul, made transgressors; but this law of yours makes nearly all of us innocent. I beseech you, my dear sir, let me know all about it. I will not leave you till you have told me all the maxims which your casuists have established."

"Alas!" the monk exclaimed, "our main object, no doubt, should have been to establish no other maxims than those of the Gospel in all their strictness: and it is easy to see, from the Rules for the regulation of our manners, that if we tolerate some degree of relaxation in others, it is rather out of complaisance than through design. The truth is, sir, we are forced to it. Men have arrived at such a pitch of corruption nowadays, that unable to make them come to us, we must e'en go to them, otherwise they would cast us off altogether; and what is worse, they would become perfect castaways. It is to retain such characters as these that our casuists have taken under consideration the vices to which people of various conditions are most addicted, with the view of laying down maxims which, while they cannot be said to violate the truth, are so gentle that he must be a very impracticable subject indeed who is not pleased with them. The grand project of our Society, for the good of religion, is never to repulse any one, let him be what he may, and so avoid driving people to despair.

"They have got maxims, therefore, for all sorts of persons; for beneficiaries, for priests, for monks; for gentlemen, for servants; for rich men, for commercial men; for people in embarrassed or indigent circumstances; for devout women, and women that are not devout; for married people, and irregular people. In short, nothing has escaped their foresight."

"In other words," said I, "they have got maxims for the clergy, the nobility, and the commons. Well, I am quite impatient to hear them."

"Let us commence," resumed the father, "with the beneficiaries. You are aware of the traffic with benefices that is now carried on, and that were the matter referred to St. Thomas and the ancients who have written on it, there might chance to be some simoniacs in the Church. This rendered it highly necessary for our fathers to exercise their prudence in finding out a palliative. With what success they have done so will appear from the following words of Valencia, who is one of Escobar's 'four living creatures.' At the end of a long discourse, in which he suggests various expedients, he propounds the following at page 2039, vol. iii., which, to my mind, is the best: 'If a person gives a temporal in exchange for a spiritual good'—that is, if he gives money for a benefice—'and gives the money as the price of the benefice, it is manifest simony. But if he gives it merely as the motive which inclines the will of the patron to confer on him the living, it is not simony, even though the person who confers it considers and expects the money as the principal object.' Tanner, who is also a member of our Society, affirms the same thing, vol. iii., p. 1519, although he 'grants that St. Thomas is opposed to it; for he expressly teaches that it is always simony to give a spiritual for a temporal good, if the temporal is the end in view.' By this means we prevent an immense number of simoniacal transactions; for who would be so desperately wicked as to refuse, when giving money for a benefice, to take the simple precaution of so directing his intentions as to give it as *a motive* to induce the beneficiary to part with it, instead of giving it as *the price* of the benefice? No man, surely, can be so far left to himself as that would come to."

"I agree with you there," I replied; "all men, I should think, have *sufficient grace* to make a bargain of that sort."

"There can be no doubt of it," returned the monk. "Such, then, is the way in which we soften matters in regard to the beneficiaries. And now for the priests—we have maxims pretty favorable to them also. Take the following, for example, from our four-and-twenty elders: 'Can a priest, who has received money to say a mass, take an additional sum upon the same mass? Yes, says Filiutius, he may, by applying that part of the sacrifice which belongs to himself as a priest to the person who paid him last; provided he does not take a sum equivalent to a whole mass, but only a part, such as the third of a mass.' "

"Surely, father," said I, "this must be one of those cases in which the *pro* and the *con* have both their share of probability. What you have now stated cannot fail, of course, to be probable, having the authority of such men as Filiutius and Escobar; and yet, leaving that within the sphere of probability, it strikes me that the contrary opinion might be made out to be probable too, and might be supported by such reasons as the following: That, while the Church allows priests who are in poor circumstances to take money for their masses, seeing it is but right that those who serve at the altar should live by the altar, she never intended that they should barter the sacrifice for money, and still less, that they should deprive themselves of those benefits which they ought themselves, in the first place, to draw from it; to which I might add, that, according to St. Paul, the priests are to offer sacrifice first for themselves, and then for the people; and that accordingly, while permitted to participate with others in the benefit of the sacrifice, they are not at liberty to forego their share, by transferring it to another for a third of a mass, or, in other words, for the matter of fourpence or fivepence. Verily, father, little as I pretend to be a *grave* man, I might contrive to make this opinion probable."

"It would cost you no great pains to do that," replied the

monk; "it is visibly probable already. The difficulty lies in discovering probability in the converse of opinions manifestly good; and this is a feat which none but great men can achieve. Father Bauny shines in this department. It is really delightful to see that learned casuist examining with characteristic ingenuity and subtlety, the negative and affirmative of the same question, and proving both of them to be right! Thus in the matter of priests, he says in one place: 'No law can be made to oblige the curates to say mass every day; for such a law would unquestionably (*haud dubie*) expose them to the danger of saying it sometimes in mortal sin.' And yet in another part of the same treatise, he says, 'that priests who have received money for saying mass every day ought to say it every day, and that they cannot excuse themselves on the ground that they are not always in a fit state for the service; because it is in their power at all times to do penance, and if they neglect this they have themselves to blame for it, and not the person who made them say mass.' And to relieve their minds from all scruples on the subject, he thus resolves the question: 'May a priest say mass on the same day in which he has committed a mortal sin of the worst kind, in the way of confessing himself beforehand?' Villalobos says no, because of his impurity; but Sancius says, He may without any sin; and I hold his opinion to be safe, and one which may be followed in practice—*et tuta et sequenda in praxi*."

"Follow this opinion in practice!" cried I. "Will any priest who has fallen into such irregularities, have the assurance on the same day to approach the altar, on the mere word of Father Bauny? Is he not bound to submit to the ancient laws of the Church, which debarred from the sacrifice forever, or at least for a long time, priests who had committed sins of that description—instead of following the modern opinions of casuists, who would admit him to it on the very day that witnessed his fall?"

"You have a very short memory," returned the monk. "Did I not inform you a little ago that, according to our fathers

Cellot and Reginald, 'in matters of morality we are to follow, not the ancient fathers, but the modern casuists?' "

"I remember it perfectly," said I; "but we have something more here: we have the laws of the Church."

"True," he replied; "but this shows you do not know another capital maxim of our fathers, 'that the laws of the Church lose their authority when they have gone into desuetude—*cum jam desuetudine abierunt*—as Filiutius says. We know the present exigencies of the Church much better than the ancients could do. Were we to be so strict in excluding priests from the altar, you can understand there would not be such a great number of masses. Now a multitude of masses brings such a revenue of glory to God and of good to souls, that I may venture to say, with Father Cellot, that there would not be too many priests, 'though not only all men and women, were that possible, but even inanimate bodies, and even brute beasts—*bruta animalia*—were transformed into priests to celebrate mass.' "

I was so astounded at the extravagance of this imagination, that I could not utter a word, and allowed him to go on with his discourse. "Enough, however, about priests; I am afraid of getting tedious: let us come to the *monks*. The grand difficulty with them is the obedience they owe to their superiors; now observe the palliative which our fathers apply in this case. Castro Palao of our Society has said: 'Beyond all dispute, a monk who has a probable opinion of his own, is not bound to obey his superior, though the opinion of the latter is the more probable. For the monk is at liberty to adopt the opinion which is more agreeable to himself—*quæ sibi gratior fuerit*—as Sanchez says. And though the order of his superior be just, that does not oblige you to obey him, for it is not just at all points or in every respect—*non undequaque juste præcepit*—but only probably so; and consequently, you are only probably bound to obey him, and probably not bound—*probabiliter obligatus, et probabiliter deobligatus.*' "

"Certainly, father," said I, "it is impossible too highly to estimate this precious fruit of the double probability."

"It is of great use indeed," he replied; "but we must be brief. Let me only give you the following specimen of our famous Molina in favor of monks who are expelled from their convents for irregularities. Escobar quotes him thus: 'Molina asserts that a monk expelled from his monastery is not obliged to reform in order to get back again, and that he is no longer bound by his vow of obedience.' "

"Well, father," cried I, "this is all very comfortable for the clergy. Your casuists, I perceive, have been very indulgent to them, and no wonder—they were legislating, so to speak, for themselves. I am afraid people of other conditions are not so liberally treated. Every one for himself in this world."

"There you do us wrong," returned the monk; "they could not have been kinder to themselves than we have been to them. We treat all, from the highest to the lowest, with an even-handed charity, sir. And to prove this, you tempt me to tell you our maxims for servants. In reference to this class, we have taken into consideration the difficulty they must experience, when they are men of conscience, in serving profligate masters. For if they refuse to perform all the errands in which they are employed, they lose their places; and if they yield obedience, they have their scruples. To relieve them from these, our four-and-twenty fathers have specified the services which they may render with a safe conscience; such as 'carrying letters and presents, opening doors and windows, helping their master to reach the window, holding the ladder which he is mounting. All this,' say they, 'is allowable and indifferent; it is true that, as to holding the ladder, they must be threatened, more than usually, with being punished for refusing; for it is doing an injury to the master of a house to enter it by the window.' You perceive the judiciousness of that observation, of course?"

"I expected nothing less," said I, "from a book edited by four-and-twenty Jesuits."

"But," added the monk, "Father Bauny has gone beyond this; he has taught valets how to perform these sorts of offices for their masters quite innocently, by making them direct their intention, not to the sins to which they are accessary, but to the gain which is to accrue from them. In his Summary of Sins, p. 710, first edition, he thus states the matter: 'Let confessors observe,' says he, 'that they cannot absolve valets who perform base errands, if they consent to the sins of their masters; but the reverse holds true, if they have done the thing merely from a regard to their temporal emolument.' And that, I should conceive, is no difficult matter to do; for why should they insist on consenting to sins of which they taste nothing but the trouble? The same Father Bauny has established a prime maxim in favor of those who are not content with their wages: 'May servants who are dissatisfied with their wages, use means to raise them by laying their hands on as much of the property of their masters as they may consider necessary to make the said wages equivalent to their trouble? They may, in certain circumstances; as when they are so poor that, in looking for a situation, they have been obliged to accept the offer made to them, and when other servants of the same class are gaining more than they, elsewhere.' "

"Ha, father!" cried I, "that is John d'Alba's passage, I declare."

"What John d'Alba?" inquired the father: "what do you mean?"

"Strange, father!" returned I: "do you not remember what happened in this city in the year 1647? Where in the world were you living at that time?"

"I was teaching cases of conscience in one of our colleges far from Paris," he replied.

"I see you don't know the story, father: I must tell it you. I heard it related the other day by a man of honor, whom I met in company. He told us that this John d'Alba, who was in the service of your fathers in the College of Clermont, in the Rue St. Jacques, being dissatisfied with his wages, had purloined something to make himself amends; and that your fathers, on discovering the theft, had thrown him into prison on the charge of larceny. The case was reported to the court, if I recollect right, on the 16th of April, 1647; for he was very minute in his statements, and indeed they would hardly have been credible otherwise. The poor fellow, on being questioned, confessed to having taken some pewter plates, but maintained that for all that he had not *stolen* them; pleading in his defence this very doctrine of Father Bauny, which he produced before the judges, along with a pamphlet by one of your fathers, under whom he had studied cases of conscience, and who had taught him the same thing. Whereupon M. de Montrouge, one of the most respected members of the court, said, in giving his opinion, 'that he did not see how, on the ground of the writings of these fathers—writings containing a doctrine so illegal, pernicious, and contrary to all laws, natural, divine, and human, and calculated to ruin all families, and sanction all sorts of household robbery—they could discharge the accused. But his opinion was, that this too faithful disciple should be whipped before the college gate, by the hand of the common hangman; and that, at the same time, this functionary should burn the writings of these fathers which treated of larceny, with certification that they were prohibited from teaching such doctrine in future, upon pain of death.'

"The result of this judgment, which was heartily approved of, was waited for with much curiosity, when some incident occurred which made them delay procedure. But in the meantime the prisoner disappeared, nobody knew how, and nothing more was heard about the affair; so that John d'Alba got off, pewter plates and all. Such was the account he gave us, to which he added, that the judgment of M. de Montrouge was entered on the records of the court, where any one may consult it. We were highly amused at the story."

"What are you trifling about now?" cried the monk. "What does all that signify? I was explaining the maxims of our casuists, and was just going to speak of those relating to gentlemen, when you interrupt me with impertinent stories."

"It was only something put in by the way, father," I observed; "and besides, I was anxious to apprise you of an important circumstance, which I find you have overlooked in establishing your doctrine of probability."

"Ay, indeed!" exclaimed the monk, "what defect can this be, that has escaped the notice of so many ingenious men?"

"You have certainly," continued I, "contrived to place your disciples in perfect safety so far as God and the conscience are concerned; for they are quite safe in that quarter, according to you, by following in the wake of a grave doctor. You have also secured them on the part of the confessors, by obliging priests, on the pain of mortal sin, to absolve all who follow a probable opinion. But you have neglected to secure them on the part of the judges; so that, in following your probabilities, they are in danger of coming into contact with the whip and the gallows. This is a sad oversight."

"You are right," said the monk; "I am glad you mentioned it. But the reason is, we have no such power over magistrates as over the confessors, who are obliged to refer to us in cases of conscience, in which we are the sovereign judges."

"So I understand," returned I; "but if, on the one hand, you are the judges of the confessors, are you not, on the other hand, the confessors of the judges? Your power is very extensive. Oblige them, on pain of being debarred from the sacraments, to acquit all criminals who act on a probable opinion; otherwise it may happen, to the great contempt and scandal of probability, that those whom you render innocent in theory may be whipped or hanged in practice. Without something of this kind, how can you expect to get disciples?"

"The matter deserves consideration," said he; "it will never do to neglect it. I shall suggest it to our father Provincial. You might, however, have reserved this advice to some other time, without interrupting the account I was about to give you of the maxims which we have established in favor of gentlemen; and I shall not give you any more information, except on condition that you do not tell me any more stories."

This is all you shall have from me at present; for it would require more than the limits of one letter to acquaint you with all that I learned in a single conversation.—Meanwhile I am, &c.

LETTER VII

Method of directing the intention adopted by the casuists—permission to kill in defence of honor and property, extended even to priests and monks—curious question raised by Caramuel, as to whether Jesuits may be allowed to kill Jansenists

Paris, April 25, 1656

SIR,—Having succeeded in pacifying the good father, who had been rather disconcerted by the story of John d'Alba, he resumed the conversation, on my assuring him that I would avoid all such interruptions in future, and spoke of the maxims of his casuists with regard to gentlemen, nearly in the following terms:—

"You know," he said, "that the ruling passion of persons in that rank of life is 'the point of honor,' which is perpetually driving them into acts of violence apparently quite at variance with Christian piety; so that, in fact, they would be almost all of them excluded from our confessionals, had not our fathers relaxed a little from the strictness of religion, to accommodate themselves to the weakness of humanity. Anxious to keep on good terms both with the Gospel, by doing their duty to God, and with the men of the world, by showing charity to their neighbor, they needed all the wisdom they possessed to devise expedients for so nicely adjusting matters as to permit these gentlemen to adopt the methods usually resorted to for vindicating their honor, without wounding their consciences, and thus reconcile two things apparently so opposite to each other as piety and the point of honor. But, sir, in proportion to the utility of the design, was the difficulty of the execution. You cannot fail, I should think, to realize the magnitude and arduousness of such an enterprise?"

"It astonishes me, certainly," said I, rather coldly.

"It astonishes you, forsooth!" cried the monk. "I can well believe that; many besides you might be astonished at it. Why, don't you know that, on the one hand, the Gospel commands us 'not to render evil for evil, but to leave vengeance to God'; and that, on the other hand, the laws of the world forbid our enduring an affront without demanding satisfaction from the offender, and that often at the expense of his life? You have never, I am sure, met with anything, to all appearance, more diametrically opposed than these two codes of morals; and yet, when told that our fathers have reconciled them, you have nothing more to say than simply that this astonishes you!"

"I did not sufficiently explain myself, father. I should certainly have considered the thing perfectly impracticable, if I had not known, from what I have seen of your fathers, that they are capable of doing with ease what is impossible to other men. This led me to anticipate that they must have discovered some method for meeting the difficulty—a method which I admire even before knowing it, and which I pray you to explain to me."

"Since that is your view of the matter," replied the monk, "I cannot refuse you. Know, then, that this marvellous principle is our grand method of *directing the intention*—the importance of which, in our moral system, is such, that I might almost venture to compare it with the doctrine of probability. You have had some glimpses of it in passing, from certain maxims which I mentioned to you. For example, when I was showing you how servants might execute certain troublesome jobs with a safe conscience, did you not remark that it was simply by diverting their intention from the evil to which they were accessary, to the profit which they might reap from the transaction? Now that is what we call *directing the intention*. You saw, too, that were it not for a similar divergence of the mind, those who give money for benefices might be downright simoniacs. But I will now show you this grand method in all its glory, as it applies to the subject of homicide —a crime which it justifies in a thousand instances; in order that, from this startling result, you may form an idea of all that it is calculated to effect."

"I foresee already," said I, "that, according to this mode, everything will be permitted; it will stick at nothing."

"You always fly from the one extreme to the other," replied the monk: "prithee avoid that habit. For just to show you that we are far from permitting everything, let me tell you that we never suffer such a thing as a formal intention to sin, with the sole design of sinning; and if any person whatever should persist in having no other end but evil in the evil that he does, we break with him at once: such conduct is diabolical. This holds true, without exception of age, sex, or rank. But when the person is not of such a wretched disposition as this, we try to put in practice our method of *directing the intention*, which simply consists in his proposing to himself, as the end of his actions, some allowable object. Not that we do not endeavour, as far as we can, to dissuade men from doing things forbidden; but when we cannot prevent the action, we at least purify the motive, and thus correct the viciousness of the means by the goodness of the end. Such is the way in which our fathers have contrived to permit those acts of violence to which men usually resort in vindication of their honor. They have no more to do than to turn off their intention from the desire of vengeance, which is criminal, and direct it to a desire to defend their honor, which, according to us, is quite warrantable. And in this way our doctors discharge all their duty towards God and towards man. By permitting the action, they gratify the world; and by purifying the intention, they give satisfaction to the Gospel. This is a secret, sir, which was entirely unknown to the ancients; the world is indebted for the discovery entirely to our doctors. You understand it now, I hope?"

"Perfectly well," was my reply. "To men you grant the outward material effect of the action; and to God you give the inward and spiritual movement of the intention; and by this equitable partition, you form an alliance between the laws of God and the laws of men. But, my dear sir, to be frank with you, I can hardly trust your premisses, and I suspect that your authors will tell another tale."

"You do me injustice," rejoined the monk; "I advance nothing but what I am ready to prove, and that by such a rich array of passages, that altogether their number, their authority, and their reasonings, will fill you with admiration. To show you, for example, the alliance which our fathers have formed between the maxims of the Gospel and those of the world, by thus regulating the intention, let me refer you to Reginald: 'Private persons are forbidden to avenge themselves; for St. Paul says to the Romans (ch. 12th), "Recompense to no man evil for evil"; and Ecclesiasticus says (ch. 28th), "He that taketh vengeance shall draw on himself the vengeance of God, and his sins will not be forgotten." Besides all that is said in the Gospel about forgiving offences, as in the 6th and 18th chapters of St. Matthew.' "

"Well, father, if after that he says anything contrary to the Scripture, it will not be from lack of scriptural knowledge, at any rate. Pray, how does he conclude?"

"You shall hear," he said. "From all this it appears that a military man may demand satisfaction on the spot from the person who has injured him—not, indeed, with the intention of rendering evil for evil, but with that of preserving his honor—'*non ut malum pro malo reddat, sed ut conservet honorem.*' See you how carefully they guard against the intention of rendering evil for evil, because the Scripture condemns it? This is what they will tolerate on no account. Thus Lessius observes, that 'if a man has received a blow on the face, he must on no account have an intention to avenge himself; but he may lawfully have an intention to avert infamy, and may, with that view, repel the insult immediately, even at the point of the sword—*etiam cum gladio!*' So far are we from permitting any one to cherish the design of taking vengeance on his enemies, that our fathers will not allow any even to *wish their death*—by a movement of hatred. 'If your enemy is disposed to injure you,' says Escobar, 'you have no right to wish his death, by a movement of hatred; though you may, with a view to save yourself from harm.' So legitimate, indeed, is this wish, with such an intention, that our great Hurtado de Mendoza says, that 'we may *pray God* to visit with speedy death those who are bent on persecuting us, if there is no other way of escaping from it.' "

"May it please your reverence," said I, "the Church has forgotten to insert a petition to that effect among her prayers."

"They have not put in everything into the prayers that one may lawfully ask of God," answered the monk. "Besides, in the present case the thing was impossible, for this same opinion is of more recent standing than the Breviary. You are not a good chronologist, friend. But, not to wander from the point, let me request your attention to the following passage, cited by Diana from Gaspar Hurtado, one of Escobar's four-and-twenty fathers: 'An incumbent may, without any mortal sin, desire the decease of a life-renter on his benefice, and a son that of his father, and rejoice when it happens; provided always it is for the sake of the profit that is to accrue from the event, and not from personal aversion.' "

"Good!" cried I. "That is certainly a very happy hit; and I can easily see that the doctrine admits of a wide application. But yet there are certain cases, the solution of which, though of great importance for gentlemen, might present still greater difficulties."

"Propose them, if you please, that we may see," said the monk.

"Show me, with all your directing of the intention," returned I, "that it is allowable to fight a duel."

"Our great Hurtado de Mendoza," said the father, "will satisfy you on that point in a twinkling. 'If a gentleman,' says he, in a passage cited by Diana, 'who is challenged to fight a duel, is well known to have no religion, and if the vices to which he is openly and unscrupulously addicted are such as would lead people to conclude, in the event of his refusing to fight, that he is actuated, not by the fear of God, but by cowardice, and induce them to say of him that he was a *hen*, and not a man—*gallina, et non vir;* in that case he may, to save his honor, appear at the appointed spot—not, indeed, with the express intention of fighting a duel, but merely with that of defending himself, should the person who challenged him come there unjustly to attack him. His action in this case, viewed by itself, will be perfectly indifferent; for what moral evil is there in one stepping into a field, taking a stroll in expectation of meeting a person, and defending one's self in the event of being attacked? And thus the gentleman is guilty of no sin whatever; for in fact it cannot be called accepting a challenge at all, his intention being directed to other circumstances, and the acceptance of a challenge consisting in an express intention to fight, which we are supposing the gentleman never had.' "

"You have not kept your word with me, sir," said I. "This is not, properly speaking, to permit duelling; on the contrary, the casuist is so persuaded that this practice is forbidden, that, in licensing the action in question, he carefully avoids calling it a duel."

"Ah!" cried the monk, "you begin to get knowing on my hand, I am glad to see. I might reply, that the author I have quoted grants all that duellists are disposed to ask. But since you must have a categorical answer, I shall allow our Father Layman to give it for me. He permits duelling in so many words, provided that, in accepting the challenge, the person directs his intention solely to the preservation of his honor or his property: 'If a soldier or a courtier is in such a predicament that he must lose either his honor or his fortune unless he accepts a challenge, I see nothing to hinder him from doing so in self-defence.' The same thing is said by Peter Hurtado, as quoted by our famous Escobar; his words are: 'One may fight a duel even to defend one's property, should that be necessary; because every man has a right to defend his property, though at the expense of his enemy's life!' "

I was struck, on hearing these passages, with the reflection that while the piety of the king appears in his exerting all his power to prohibit and abolish the practice of duelling in the State, the piety of the Jesuits is shown in their employing all their ingenuity to tolerate and sanction it in the Church. But the good father was in such an excellent key for talking, that it would have been cruel to have interrupted him; so he went on with his discourse.

"In short," said he, "Sanchez (mark, now, what great names I am quoting to you!) Sanchez, sir, goes a step further; for he shows how, simply by managing the intention rightly, a person may not only receive a challenge, but give one. And our Escobar follows him."

"Prove that, father," said I, "and I shall give up the point: but I will not believe that he has written it, unless I see it in print."

"Read it yourself, then," he replied: and, to be sure, I read the following extract from the Moral Theology of Sanchez: "It is perfectly reasonable to hold that a man may fight a duel to save his life, his honor, or any considerable portion of his property, when it is apparent that there is a design to deprive him of these unjustly, by law-suits and chicanery, and when there is no other way of preserving them. Navarre justly observes, that in such cases, it is lawful either to accept or to send a challenge—*licet acceptare et offerre duellum*. The same author adds, that there is nothing to prevent one from despatching one's adversary in a private way. Indeed, in the circumstances referred to, it is advisable to avoid employing the method of the duel, if it is possible to settle the affair by privately killing our enemy; for, by this means, we escape at once from exposing our life in the combat, and from participating in the sin which our opponent would have committed by fighting the duel!"

"A most pious assassination!" said I. "Still, however, pious though it be, it is assassination, if a man is permitted to kill his enemy in a treacherous manner."

"Did I say that he might kill him treacherously?" cried the monk. "God forbid! I said he might kill him *privately,* and you conclude that he may kill him *treacherously*, as if that were the same thing! Attend, sir, to Escobar's definition before allowing yourself to speak again on this subject: 'We call it killing in treachery, when the person who is slain had no reason to suspect such a fate. He, therefore, that slays his *enemy* cannot be said to kill him in treachery, even although the blow should be given insidiously and behind his back— *licet per insidias aut a tergo percutiat.*' And again: 'He that kills his enemy, with whom he was reconciled under a promise of never again attempting his life, cannot be *absolutely* said to kill in treachery, unless there was between them all the stricter friendship—*arctior amicitia.*' You see now you do not even understand what the terms signify, and yet you pretend to talk like a doctor."

"I grant you this is something quite new to me," I replied; "and I should gather from that definition that few, if any, were ever killed in treachery; for people seldom take it into their heads to assassinate any but their enemies. Be this as it may, however, it seems that, according to Sanchez, a man may freely slay (I do not say *treacherously*, but only insidiously, and behind his back) a calumniator, for example, who prosecutes us at law?"

"Certainly he may," returned the monk, "always, however, in the way of giving a right direction to the intention: you constantly forget the main point. Molina supports the same doctrine; and what is more, our learned brother Reginald maintains that we may despatch the false witnesses whom he summons against us. And, to crown the whole, according to our great and famous fathers Tanner and Emanuel Sa, it is lawful to kill both the false witnesses and *the judge himself*, if he has had any collusion with them. Here are Tanner's very words: 'Sotus and Lessius think that it is not lawful to kill the false witnesses and the magistrate who conspire together to put an innocent person to death; but Emanuel Sa and other authors with good reason impugn that sentiment, at least so far as the conscience is concerned.' And he goes on to show that it is quite lawful to kill both the witnesses and the judge."

"Well, father," said I, "I think I now understand pretty well your principle regarding the direction of the intention; but I should like to know something of its consequences, and all the cases in which this method of yours arms a man with the power of life and death. Let us go over them again, for fear of mistake, for equivocation here might be attended with dangerous results. Killing is a matter which requires to be well-timed, and to be backed with a good probable opinion. You have assured me, then, that by giving a proper turn to the intention, it is lawful, according to your fathers, for the preservation of one's honor, or even property, to accept a challenge to a duel, to give one sometimes, to kill in a private way a false accuser, and his witnesses along with him, and even the judge who has been bribed to favor them; and you have also told me that he who has got a blow, may, without avenging himself, retaliate with the sword. But you have not told me, father, to what length he may go."

"He can hardly mistake there," replied the father, "for he may go all the length of killing his man. This is satisfactorily proved by the learned Henriquez, and others of our fathers quoted by Escobar, as follows: 'It is perfectly right to kill a person who has given us a box on the ear, although he should run away, provided it is not done through hatred or revenge, and there is no danger of giving occasion thereby to murders of a gross kind and hurtful to society. And the reason is, that it is as lawful to pursue the thief that has stolen our honor, as him that has run away with our property. For, although your honor cannot be said to be in the hands of your enemy in the same sense as your goods and chattels are in the hands of the thief, still it may be recovered in the same way—by showing proofs of greatness and authority, and thus acquiring the esteem of men. And, in point of fact, is it not certain that the man who has received a buffet on the ear is held to be under disgrace, until he has wiped off the insult with the blood of his enemy?'"

I was so shocked on hearing this, that it was with great

difficulty I could contain myself; but, in my anxiety to hear the rest, I allowed him to proceed.

"Nay," he continued, "it is allowable to prevent a buffet, by killing him that meant to give it, if there be no other way to escape the insult. This opinion is quite common with our fathers. For example, Azor, one of the four-and-twenty elders, proposing the question, 'Is it lawful for a man of honor to kill another who threatens to give him a slap on the face, or strike him with a stick?' replies, 'Some say he may not; alleging that the life of our neighbour is more precious than our honor, and that it would be an act of cruelty to kill a man merely to avoid a blow. Others, however, think that it is allowable; and I certainly consider it probable, when there is no other way of warding off the insult; for, otherwise, the honor of the innocent would be constantly exposed to the malice of the insolent.' The same opinion is given by our great Filiutius; by Father Hereau, in his Treatise on Homicide; by Hurtado de Mendoza, in his Disputations; by Becan, in his Summary; by our Fathers Flahaut and Lecourt, in those writings which the University, in their third petition, quoted at length, in order to bring them into disgrace (though in this they failed); and by Escobar. In short, this opinion is so general, that Lessius lays it down as a point which no casuist has contested; he quotes a great many that uphold, and none that deny it; and particularly Peter Navarre, who, speaking of affronts in general (and there is none more provoking than a box on the ear), declares that 'by the universal consent of the casuists, it is lawful to kill the calumniator, if there be no other way of averting the affront—*ex sententia omnium, licet contumeliosum occidere, si aliter ea injuria arceri nequit.*' Do you wish any more authorities?" asked the monk.

I declared I was much obliged to him; I had heard rather more than enough of them already. But just to see how far this damnable doctrine would go, I said, "But father, may not one be allowed to kill for something still less? Might not a person so direct his intention as lawfully to kill another for telling a lie, for example?"

"He may," returned the monk; "and according to Father Baldelle, quoted by Escobar, 'you may lawfully take the life of another for saying, You have told a lie; if there is no other way of shutting his mouth.' The same thing may be done in the case of slanders. Our Fathers Lessius and Hereau agree in the following sentiments: 'If you attempt to ruin my character by telling stories against me in the presence of men of honor, and I have no other way of preventing this than by putting you to death, may I be permitted to do so? According to the modern authors, I may, and that even though I have been really guilty of the crime which you divulge, provided it is a secret one, which you could not establish by legal evidence. And I prove it thus: If you mean to rob me of my honor by giving me a box on the ear, I may prevent it by force of arms; and the same mode of defence is lawful when you would do me the same injury with the tongue. Besides, we may lawfully obviate affronts, and therefore slanders. In fine, honor is dearer than life; and as it is lawful to kill in defence of life, it must be so to kill in defence of honor.' There, you see, are arguments in due form; this is demonstration, sir— not mere discussion. And, to conclude, this great man Lessius shows, in the same place, that it is lawful to kill even for a simple gesture, or a sign of contempt. 'A man's honor,' he remarks, 'may be attacked or filched away in various ways—in all of which vindication appears very reasonable; as, for instance, when one offers to strike us with a stick, or give us a slap on the face, or affront us either by words or signs—*sive per signa.*' "

"Well, father," said I, "it must be owned that you have made every possible provision to secure the safety of reputation; but it strikes me that human life is greatly in danger, if any one may be conscientiously put to death simply for a defamatory speech or a saucy gesture."

"That is true," he replied; "but as our fathers are very circumspect, they have thought it proper to forbid putting this doctrine into practice on such trifling occasions. They say, at least, 'that it ought *hardly* to be reduced to practice—

practice vix probari potest.' And they have a good reason for that, as you shall see."

"Oh, I know what it will be," interrupted I; "because the law of God forbids us to kill, of course."

"They do not exactly take that ground," said the father; "as a matter of conscience, and viewing the thing abstractly, they hold it allowable."

"And why, then, do they forbid it?"

"I shall tell you that, sir. It is because, were we to kill all the defamers among us, we should very shortly depopulate the country. 'Although,' says Reginald, 'the opinion that we may kill a man for calumny is not without its probability in theory, the contrary one ought to be followed in practice; for, in our mode of defending ourselves, we should always avoid doing injury to the commonwealth; and it is evident that by killing people in this way there would be too many murders.' 'We should be on our guard,' says Lessius, 'lest the practice of this maxim prove hurtful to the State; for in this case it ought not to be permitted—*tunc enim non est permittendus.*' "

"What, father! is it forbidden only as a point of policy, and not of religion? Few people, I am afraid, will pay any regard to such a prohibition, particularly when in a passion. Very probably they might think they were doing no harm to the State, by ridding it of an unworthy member."

"And accordingly," replied the monk, "our Filiutius has fortified that argument with another, which is of no slender importance, namely, 'that for killing people after this manner, one might be punished in a court of justice.' "

"There now, father; I told you before, that you will never be able to do anything worth the while, unless you get the magistrates to go along with you."

"The magistrates," said the father, "as they do not penetrate into the conscience, judge merely of the outside of the action, while we look principally to the intention; and hence it occasionally happens that our maxims are a little different from theirs."

"Be that as it may, father; from yours, at least, one thing

may be fairly inferred—that, by taking care not to injure the commonwealth, we may kill defamers with a safe conscience, provided we can do it with a sound skin. But, sir, after having seen so well to the protection of honor, have you done nothing for property? I am aware it is of inferior importance, but that does not signify; I should think one might direct one's intention to kill for its preservation also."

"Yes," replied the monk; "and I gave you a hint to that effect already, which may have suggested the idea to you. All our casuists agree in that opinion; and they even extend the permission to those cases 'where no further violence is apprehended from those that steal our property; as, for example, where the thief runs away.' Azor, one of our Society, proves that point."

"But, sir, how much must the article be worth, to justify our proceeding to that extremity?"

"According to Reginald and Tanner, 'the article must be of great value in the estimation of a judicious man.' And so think Layman and Filiutius."

"But, father, that is saying nothing to the purpose; where am I to find 'a judicious man' (a rare person to meet with at any time), in order to make this estimation? Why do they not settle upon an exact sum at once?"

"Ay, indeed!" retorted the monk; "and was it so easy, think you, to adjust the comparative value between the life of a man, and a Christian man, too, and money? It is here I would have you feel the need of our casuists. Show me any of your ancient fathers who will tell for how much money we may be allowed to kill a man. What will they say, but '*Non occides*—Thou shalt not kill?'"

"And who, then, has ventured to fix that sum?" I inquired.

"Our great and incomparable Molina," he replied—"the glory of our Society—who has, in his inimitable wisdom, estimated the life of a man 'at six or seven ducats; for which sum he assures us it is warrantable to kill a thief, even though he should run off'; and he adds, 'that he would not venture to condemn that man as guilty of any sin who should kill another for taking away an article worth a crown, or even less—*unius aurei, vel minoris adhuc valoris*'; which has led Escobar to lay it down as a general rule, 'that a man may be killed quite regularly, according to Molina, for the value of a crown-piece.'"

"O father," cried I; "where can Molina have got all this wisdom to enable him to determine a matter of such importance, without any aid from Scripture, the councils, or the fathers? It is quite evident that he has obtained an illumination peculiar to himself, and is far beyond St. Augustine in the matter of homicide, as well as of grace. Well, now, I suppose I may consider myself master of this chapter of morals; and I see perfectly that, with the exception of ecclesiastics, nobody need refrain from killing those who injure them in their property or reputation."

"What say you?" exclaimed the monk. "Do you then suppose that it would be reasonable that those who ought of all men to be most respected, should alone be exposed to the insolence of the wicked? Our fathers have provided against that disorder; for Tanner declares that 'Churchmen, and even monks, are permitted to kill, for the purpose of defending not only their lives, but their property, and that of their community.' Molina, Escobar, Becan, Reginald, Layman, Lessius, and others, hold the same language. Nay, according to our celebrated Father Lamy, priests and monks may lawfully prevent those who would injure them by calumnies from carrying their ill designs into effect, by putting them to death. Care, however, must always be taken to direct the intention properly. His words are: 'An ecclesiastic or a monk may warrantably kill a defamer who threatens to publish the scandalous crimes of his community, or his own crimes, when there is no other way of stopping him; if, for instance, he is prepared to circulate his defamations unless promptly despatched. For, in these circumstances, as the monk would be allowed to kill one who threatened to take his life, he is also warranted to kill him who would deprive him of his reputation or his property, in the same way as the men of the world.'"

"I was not aware of that," said I; "in fact, I have been accustomed simply enough to believe the very reverse, without reflecting on the matter, in consequence of having heard that the Church had such an abhorrence of bloodshed as not even to permit ecclesiastical judges to attend in criminal cases."

"Never mind that," he replied; "our Father Lamy has completely proved the doctrine I have laid down, although, with a humility which sits uncommonly well on so great a man, he submits it to the judgment of his *judicious readers. Caramuel, too, our famous champion, quoting it in his Fundamental Theology, p. 543, thinks it so certain, that he declares the contrary opinion to be destitute of probability, and draws some admirable conclusions from it, such as the following, which he calls 'the conclusion of conclusions—*conclusionum conclusio:*' 'That a priest not only may kill a slanderer, but there are certain circumstances in which it may be his *duty* to do so—*etiam aliquando debet occidere.*' He examines a great many new questions on this principle, such as the following, for instance: '*May the Jesuits kill the Jansenists?*' "

"A curious point of divinity that, father!" cried I. "I hold the Jansenists to be as good as dead men, according to Father Lamy's doctrine."

"There now, you are in the wrong," said the monk: "Caramuel infers the very reverse from the same principles."

"And how so, father?"

"Because," he replied, "it is not in the power of the Jansenists to injure our reputation. 'The Jansenists,' says he, 'call the Jesuits Pelagians; may they not be killed for that? No; inasmuch as the Jansenists can no more obscure the glory of the Society than an owl can eclipse that of the sun; on the contrary, they have, though against their intention, enhanced it—*occidi non possunt, quia nocere non potuerunt.*' "

"Ha, father! do the lives of the Jansenists, then, depend on the contingency of their injuring your reputation? If so, I reckon them far from being in a safe position; for supposing it should be thought in the slightest degree *probable* that they might do you some mischief, why, they are *killable* at once!

You have only to draw up a syllogism in due form, and, with a direction of the intention, you may despatch your man at once with a safe conscience. Thrice happy must those hot spirits be who cannot bear with injuries, to be instructed in this doctrine! But woe to the poor people who have offended them! Indeed, father, it would be better to have to do with persons who have no religion at all, than with those who have been taught on this system. For, after all, the intention of the wounder conveys no comfort to the wounded. The poor man sees nothing of that secret direction of which you speak; he is only sensible of the direction of the blow that is dealt him. And I am by no means sure but a person would feel much less sorry to see himself brutally killed by an infuriated villain, than to find himself conscientiously stilettoed by a devotee. To be plain with you, father, I am somewhat staggered at all this; and these questions of Father Lamy and Caramuel do not please me at all."

"How so?" cried the monk. "Are you a Jansenist?"

"I have another reason for it," I replied. "You must know I am in the habit of writing from time to time, to a friend of mine in the country, all that I can learn of the maxims of your doctors. Now, although I do no more than simply report and faithfully quote their own words, yet I am apprehensive lest my letter should fall into the hands of some stray genius, who may take into his head that I have done you injury, and may draw some mischievous conclusion from your premisses."

"Away!" cried the monk; "no fear of danger from that quarter, I'll give you my word for it. Know that what our fathers have themselves printed, with the approbation of our superiors, it cannot be wrong to read nor dangerous to publish."

I write you, therefore, on the faith of this worthy father's word of honor. But, in the meantime, I must stop for want of paper—not of passages; for I have got as many more in reserve, and good ones too, as would require volumes to contain them.—I am, &c.

*Corrupt maxims of the casuists relating to judges—usurers—the
contract mohatra—bankrupts—restitution—divers ridiculous no-
tions of these same casuists*

Paris, May 28, 1656

SIR,—You did not suppose that anybody would have the
curiosity to know who we were; but it seems there are people
who are trying to make it out, though they are not very happy
in their conjectures. Some take me for a doctor of the Sorbonne; others ascribe my letters to four or five persons, who,
like me, are neither priests nor Churchmen. All these false
surmises convince me that I have succeeded pretty well in
my object, which was to conceal myself from all but yourself and the worthy monk, who still continues to bear with
my visits, while I still contrive, though with considerable
difficulty, to bear with his conversations. I am obliged, however, to restrain myself; for were he to discover how much I
am shocked at his communications, he would discontinue
them, and thus put it out of my power to fulfil the promise I
gave you, of making you acquainted with their morality. You
ought to think a great deal of the violence which I thus do
to my own feelings. It is no easy matter, I can assure you,
to stand still and see the whole system of Christian ethics
undermined by such a set of monstrous principles, without
daring to put in a word of flat contradiction against them.
But after having borne so much for your satisfaction, I am
resolved I shall burst out for my own satisfaction in the end,
when his stock of information has been exhausted. Meanwhile, I shall repress my feelings as much as I possibly can
for I find that the more I hold my tongue, he is the more

communicative. The last time I saw him, he told me so many things, that I shall have some difficulty in repeating them all. On the point of restitution you will find they have some most convenient principles. For, however the good monk palliates his maxims, those which I am about to lay before you really go to sanction corrupt judges, usurers, bankrupts, thieves, prostitutes and sorcerers—all of whom are most liberally absolved from the obligation of restoring their ill-gotten gains. It was thus the monk resumed the conversation:—

"At the commencement of our interviews, I engaged to explain to you the maxims of our authors for all ranks and classes; and you have already seen those that relate to beneficiaries, to priests, to monks, to domestics, and to gentlemen. Let us now take a cursory glance at the remaining, and begin with the judges.

"Now I am going to tell you one of the most important and advantageous maxims which our fathers have laid down in their favor. Its author is the learned Castro Palao, one of our four-and-twenty elders. His words are: 'May a judge, in a question of right and wrong, pronounce according to a probable opinion, in preference to the more probable opinion? He may, even though it should be contrary to his own judgment—*imo contra propriam opinionem.*' "

"Well, father," cried I, "that is a very fair commencement! The judges, surely, are greatly obliged to you; and I am surprised that they should be so hostile, as we have sometimes observed, to your probabilities, seeing these are so favorable to them. For it would appear from this, that you give them the same power over men's fortunes, as you have given to yourselves over their consciences."

"You perceive we are far from being actuated by self-interest," returned he; "we have had no other end in view than the repose of their consciences; and to the same useful purpose has our great Molina devoted his attention, in regard to the presents which may be made them. To remove any scruples which they might entertain in accepting of these on certain occasions, he has been at the pains to draw out a list of all those cases in which bribes may be taken with a good conscience, provided, at least, there be no special law forbidding them. He says: 'Judges may receive presents from parties when they are given them either for friendship's sake, or in gratitude for some former act of justice, or to induce them to give justice in future, or to oblige them to pay particular attention to their case, or to engage them to despatch it promptly.' The learned Escobar delivers himself to the same effect: 'If there be a number of persons, none of whom have more right than another to have their causes disposed of, will the judge who accepts of something from one of them on condition—*ex pacto*—of taking up his cause first, be guilty of sin? Certainly not, according to Layman; for, in common equity, he does no injury to the rest, by granting to one, in consideration of his present, what he was at liberty to grant to any of them he pleased; and besides, being under an equal obligation to them all in respect of their right, he becomes more obliged to the individual who furnished the donation, who thereby acquired for himself a preference above the rest —a preference which seems capable of a pecuniary valuation —*quæ obligatio videtur pretio æstimabilis.*' "

"May it please your reverence," said I, "after such a permission, I am surprised that the first magistrates of the kingdom should know no better. For the first president has actually carried an order in Parliament to prevent certain clerks of court from taking money for that very sort of preference—a sign that he is far from thinking it allowable in judges; and everybody has applauded this as a reform of great benefit to all parties."

The worthy monk was surprised at this piece of intelligence, and replied: "Are you sure of that? I heard nothing about it. Our opinion, recollect, is only probable; the contrary is probable also."

"To tell you the truth, father," said I, "people think that the first president has acted more than probably well, and that he has thus put a stop to a course of public corruption which has been too long winked at."

"I am not far from being of the same mind," returned he; "but let us waive that point, and say no more about the judges."

"You are quite right, sir," said I; "indeed, they are not half thankful enough for all you have done for them."

"That is not my reason," said the father: "but there is so much to be said on all the different classes, that we must study brevity on each of them. Let us now say a word or two about men of business. You are aware that our great difficulty with these gentlemen is to keep them from usury—an object to accomplish which our fathers have been at particular pains; for they hold this vice in such abhorrence, that Escobar declares 'it is heresy to say that usury is no sin;' and Father Bauny has filled several pages of his Summary of Sins with the pains and penalties due to usurers. He declares them 'infamous during their life, and unworthy of sepulture after their death.' "

"O dear!" cried I, "I had no idea he was so severe."

"He can be severe enough when there is occasion for it," said the monk; "but then this learned casuist, having observed that some are allured into usury merely from the love of gain, remarks in the same place, that 'he would confer no small obligation on society, who, while he guarded it against the evil effects of usury, and of the sin which gives birth to it, would suggest a method by which one's money might secure as large, if not a larger profit, in some honest and lawful employment, than he could derive from usurious dealings.' "

"Undoubtedly, father, there would be no more usurers after that."

"Accordingly," continued he, "our casuist has suggested 'a general method for all sorts of persons—gentlemen, presidents, councillors,' &c.; and a very simple process it is, consisting only in the use of certain words which must be pronounced by the person in the act of lending his money; after which he may take his interest for it without fear of being a usurer, which he certainly would be on any other plan."

"And pray what may those mysterious words be, father?"

"I will give you them exactly in his own words," said the father; "for he has written his Summary in French, you know, 'that it may be understood by everybody,' as he says in the preface: 'The person from whom the loan is asked, must answer, then, in this manner: I have got no money to *lend;* I have got a little, however, to lay out for an honest and lawful profit. If you are anxious to have the sum you mention in order to make something of it by your industry, dividing the profit and loss between us, I may perhaps be able to accommodate you. But now I think of it, as it may be a matter of difficulty to agree about the profit, if you will secure me a certain portion of it, and give me so much for my principal, so that it incur no risk, we may come to terms much sooner, and you shall touch the cash immediately.' Is not that an easy plan for gaining money without sin? And has not Father Bauny good reason for concluding with these words: 'Such, in my opinion, is an excellent plan by which a great many people, who now provoke the just indignation of God by their usuries, extortions, and illicit bargains, might save themselves, in the way of making good, honest, and legitimate profits?' "

"O sir!" I exclaimed, "what potent words these must be! Doubtless they must possess some latent virtue to chase away the demon of usury which I know nothing of, for, in my poor judgment, I always thought that that vice consisted in recovering more money than what was lent."

"You know little about it indeed," he replied. "Usury, according to our fathers, consists in little more than the intention of taking the interest as usurious. Escobar, accordingly, shows you how you may avoid usury by a simple shift of the intention. 'It would be downright usury,' says he 'to take interest from the borrower, if we should exact it as due in point of justice; but if only exacted as due in point of gratitude, it is not usury. Again, it is not lawful to have directly the intention of profiting by the money lent; but to claim it through the medium of the benevolence of the borrower— *media benevolentia*—is not usury.' These are subtle methods;

but, to my mind, the best of them all (for we have a great choice of them) is that of the Mohatra bargain."

"The Mohatra, father!"

"You are not acquainted with it, I see," returned he. "The name is the only strange thing about it. Escobar will explain it to you: 'The Mohatra bargain is effected by the needy person purchasing some goods at a high price and on credit, in order to sell them over again, at the same time and to the same merchant, for ready money and at a cheap rate.' This is what we call the Mohatra—a sort of bargain, you perceive, by which a person receives a certain sum of ready money, by becoming bound to pay more."

"But, sir, I really think nobody but Escobar has employed such a term as that; is it to be found in any other book?"

"How little you do know of what is going on, to be sure!" cried the father. "Why, the last work on theological morality, printed at Paris this very year, speaks of the Mohatra, and learnedly, too. It is called *Epilogus Summarum*, and is an abridgment of all the summaries of divinity—extracted from Suarez, Sanchez, Lessius, Fagundez, Hurtado, and other celebrated casuists, as the title bears. There you will find it said, on p. 54, that 'the Mohatra bargain takes place when a man who has occasion for twenty pistoles purchases from a merchant goods to the amount of thirty pistoles, payable within a year, and sells them back to him on the spot for twenty pistoles ready money.' This shows you that the Mohatra is not such an unheard-of term as you supposed."

"But, father, is that sort of bargain lawful?"

"Escobar," replied he, 'tells us in the same place, that there are laws which prohibit it under very severe penalties."

"It is useless, then, I suppose?"

"Not at all; Escobar, in the same passage, suggests expedients for making it lawful: 'It is so, even though the principal intention both of the buyer and seller is to make money by the transaction, provided the seller, in disposing of the goods, does not exceed their highest price, and in repurchasing them does not go below their lowest price, and that no previous

bargain has been made, expressly or otherwise.' Lessius, however, maintains, that 'even though the merchant has sold his
goods, with the intention of re-purchasing them at the lowest
price, he is not bound to make restitution of the profit thus
acquired, unless, perhaps, as an act of charity, in the case of
the person from whom it has been exacted being in poor circumstances, and not even then, if he cannot do it without inconvenience—*si commode non potest.*' This is the utmost
length to which they could go."

"Indeed, sir," said I, "any further indulgence would, I
should think, be rather too much."

"Oh, our fathers know very well when it is time for them
to stop!" cried the monk. "So much, then, for the utility of
the Mohatra. I might have mentioned several other methods,
but these may suffice; and I have now to say a little in regard
to those who are in embarrassed circumstances. Our casuists
have sought to relieve them, according to their condition of
life. For, if they have not enough of property for a decent
maintenance, and at the same time for paying their debts,
they permit them to secure a portion by making a bankruptcy
with their creditors. This has been decided by Lessius, and
confirmed by Escobar, as follows: 'May a person who turns
bankrupt, with a good conscience keep back as much of his
personal estate as may be necessary to maintain his family
in a respectable way—*ne indecore vivat?* I hold, with Lessius,
that he may, even though he may have acquired his wealth
unjustly and by notorious crimes—*ex injustitia et notorio
delicto;* only, in this case, he is not at liberty to retain so large
an amount as he otherwise might.' "

"Indeed, father! what a strange sort of charity is this, to
allow property to remain in the hands of the man who has
acquired it by rapine, to support him in his extravagance
rather than go into the hands of his creditors, to whom it legitimately belongs!"

"It is impossible to please everybody," replied the father;
"and we have made it our particular study to relieve these
unfortunate people. This partiality to the poor has induced

our great Vasquez, cited by Castro Palao, to say, that 'if one saw a thief going to rob a poor man, it would be lawful to divert him from his purpose by pointing out to him some rich individual, whom he might rob in place of the other.' If you have not access to Vasquez or Castro Palao, you will find the same thing in your copy of Escobar; for, as you are aware, his work is little more than a compilation from twenty-four of the most celebrated of our fathers. You will find it in his treatise, entitled 'The Practice of our Society, in the matter of Charity towards our Neighbors.' "

"A very singular kind of charity this," I observed, "to save one man from suffering loss, by inflicting it upon another! But I suppose that, to complete the charity, the charitable adviser would be bound in conscience to restore to the rich man the sum which he had made him lose?"

"Not at all, sir," returned the monk; "for he did not rob the man—he only advised the other to do it. But only attend to this notable decision of Father Bauny, on a case which will still more astonish you, and in which you would suppose there was a much stronger obligation to make restitution. Here are his identical words: 'A person asks a soldier to beat his neighbor, or to set fire to the barn of a man that has injured him. The question is, whether, in the essence of the soldier, the person who employed him to commit these outrages is bound to make reparation out of his own pocket for the damage that has followed? My opinion is, that he is not. For none can be held bound to restitution, where there has been no violation of justice; and is justice violated by asking another to do us a favor? As to the nature of the request which he made, he is at liberty either to acknowledge or deny it; to whatever side he may incline, it is a matter of mere choice; nothing obliges him to it, unless it may be the goodness, gentleness, and easiness of his disposition. If the soldier, therefore, makes no reparation for the mischief he has done, it ought not to be exacted from him at whose request he injured the innocent.' "

This sentence had very nearly broken up the whole conversation, for I was on the point of bursting into a laugh at the idea of the *goodness and gentleness* of a burner of barns, and at these strange sophisms which would exempt from the duty of restitution the principal and real incendiary, whom the civil magistrate would not exempt from the halter. But had I not restrained myself, the worthy monk, who was perfectly serious, would have been displeased; he proceeded, therefore, without any alteration of countenance, in his observations.

"From such a mass of evidence, you ought to be satisfied now of the futility of your objections; but we are losing sight of our subject. To revert, then, to the succor which our fathers apply to persons in straitened circumstances, Lessius, among others, maintains that 'it is lawful to steal, not only in a case of extreme necessity, but even where the necessity is *grave,* though not extreme.'"

"This is somewhat startling, father," said I. "There are very few people in this world who do not consider their cases of necessity to be *grave* ones, and to whom, accordingly, you would not give the right of stealing with a good conscience. And though you should restrict the permission to those only who are really and truly in that condition, you open the door to an infinite number of petty larcenies which the magistrates would punish in spite of your 'grave necessity,' and which you ought to repress on a higher principle—you who are bound by your office to be the conservators, not of justice only, but of charity between man and man, a grace which this permission would destroy. For after all, now, is it not a violation of the law of charity, and of our duty to our neighbor, to deprive a man of his property in order to turn it to our own advantage? Such, at least, is the way I have been taught to think hitherto."

"That will not always hold true," replied the monk; "for our great Molina has taught us that 'the rule of charity does not bind us to deprive ourselves of a profit, in order thereby to save our neighbor from a corresponding loss.' He advances this in corroboration of what he had undertaken to prove—

'that one is not bound in conscience to restore the goods which another had put into his hands in order to cheat his creditors.' Lessius holds the same opinion, on the same ground. Allow me to say, sir, that you have too little compassion for people in distress. Our fathers have had more charity than that comes to: they render ample justice to the poor, as well as the rich; and, I may add, to sinners as well as saints. For, though far from having any predilection for criminals, they do not scruple to teach that the property gained by crime may be lawfully retained. 'No person,' says Lessius, speaking generally, 'is bound, either by the law of nature or by positive laws (that is, *by any law*), to make restitution of what has been gained by committing a criminal action, such as adultery, even though that action is contrary to justice.' For, as Escobar comments on this writer, 'though the property which a woman acquires by adultery is certainly gained in an illicit way, yet once acquired, the possession of it is lawful—*quamvis mulier illicite acquisat, licite tamen retinet acquisita.*' It is on this principle that the most celebrated of our writers have formally decided that the bribe received by a judge from one of the parties who has a bad case, in order to procure an unjust decision in his favor, the money got by a soldier for killing a man, or the emoluments gained by infamous crimes, may be legitimately retained. Escobar, who has collected this from a number of our authors, lays down this general rule on the point, that 'the means acquired by infamous courses, such as murder, unjust decisions, profligacy, &c., are legitimately possessed, and none are obliged to restore them.' And further, 'they may dispose of what they have received for homicide, profligacy, &c., as they please; for the possession is just, and they have acquired a propriety in the fruits of their iniquity.' "

"My dear father," cried I, "this is a mode of acquisition which I never heard of before; and I question much if the law will hold it good, or if it will consider assassination, injustice, and adultery, as giving valid titles to property."

"I do not know what your law-books may say on the point," returned the monk; "but I know well that our books, which are the genuine rules for conscience, bear me out in what I say. It is true they make one exception, in which restitution is positively enjoined; that is, in the case of any receiving money from those who have no right to dispose of their property, such as *minors and monks*. 'Unless,' says the great Molina, 'a woman has received money from one who cannot dispose of it, such as a monk or a minor—*nisi mulier accepisset ab eo qui alienare non potest, ut a religioso et filio familias*. In this case she must give back the money.' And so says Escobar."

"May it please your reverence," said I, "the monks, I see, are more highly favored in this way than other people."

"By no means," he replied; "have they not done as much generally for all minors, in which class monks may be viewed as continuing all their lives? It is barely an act of justice to make them an exception; but with regard to all other people, there is no obligation whatever to refund to them the money received from them for a criminal action. For, as has been amply shown by Lessius, 'a wicked action may have its price fixed in money, by calculating the advantage received by the person who orders it to be done, and the trouble taken by him who carries it into execution; on which account the latter is not bound to restore the money he got for the deed, whatever that may have been—homicide, injustice, or a foul act' (for such are the illustrations which he uniformly employs in this question); 'unless he obtained the money from those having no right to dispose of their property. You may object, perhaps, that he who has obtained money for a piece of wickedness is sinning, and therefore ought neither to receive nor retain it. But I reply, that after the thing is done, there can be no sin either in giving or in receiving payment for it.' The great Filiutius enters still more minutely into details, remarking, 'that a man is *bound in conscience*, to vary his payments for actions of this sort, according to the different conditions of the individuals who commit them, and some may bring a higher price than others.' This he confirms by very solid arguments."

He then pointed out to me, in his authors, some things of this nature so indelicate that I should be ashamed to repeat them; and indeed the monk himself, who is a good man, would have been horrified at them himself, were it not for the profound respect which he entertains for his fathers, and which makes him receive with veneration everything that proceeds from them. Meanwhile, I held my tongue, not so much with the view of allowing him to enlarge on this matter, as from pure astonishment at finding the books of men in holy orders stuffed with sentiments at once so horrible, so iniquitous, and so silly. He went on, therefore, without interruption in his discourse, concluding as follows:—

"From these premises, our illustrious Molina decides the following question (and after this, I think you will have got enough): 'If one has received money to perpetrate a wicked action, is he obliged to restore it? We must distinguish here,' says this great man; 'if he has not done the deed, he must give back the cash; if he has, he is under no such obligation!' Such are some of our principles touching restitution. You have got a great deal of instruction to-day; and I should like, now, to see what proficiency you have made. Come, then, answer me this question: 'Is a judge, who has received a sum of money from one of the parties before him, in order to pronounce a judgment in his favor, obliged to make restitution?' "

"You were just telling me a little ago, father, that he was not."

"I told you no such thing," replied the father; "did I express myself so generally? I told you he was not bound to make restitution, provided he succeeded in gaining the cause for the party who had the wrong side of the question. But if a man has justice on his side, would you have him to purchase the success of his cause, which is his legitimate right? You are very unconscionable. Justice, look you, is a debt which the judge owes, and therefore he cannot sell it; but he cannot be said to owe injustice, and therefore he may lawfully receive money for it. All our leading authors, accordingly, agree in teaching 'that though a judge is bound to restore the money he had received for doing an act of justice, unless it was given him out of mere generosity, he is not obliged to restore what he has received from a man in whose favor he has pronounced an unjust decision.'"

This preposterous decision fairly dumbfounded me, and while I was musing on its pernicious tendencies, the monk had prepared another question for me. "Answer me again," said he, "with a little more circumspection. Tell me now, 'if a man who deals in divination is obliged to make restitution of the money he has acquired in the exercise of his art?'"

"Just as you please, your reverence," said I.

"Eh! what!—just as I please! Indeed, but you are a pretty scholar! It would seem, according to your way of talking, that the truth depended on our will and pleasure. I see that, in the present case, you would never find it out yourself: so I must send you to Sanchez for a solution of the problem—no less a man than Sanchez. In the first place, he makes a distinction between 'the case of the diviner who has recourse to astrology and other natural means, and that of another who employs the diabolical art. In the one case, he says, the diviner is bound to make restitution; in the other he is not.' Now, guess which of them is the party bound?"

"It is not difficult to find out that," said I.

"I see what you mean to say," he replied. "You think that he ought to make restitution in the case of his having employed the agency of demons. But you know nothing about it; it is just the reverse. 'If,' says Sanchez, 'the sorcerer has not taken care and pains to discover, by means of the devil, what he could not have known otherwise, he must make restitution —*si nullam operam apposuit ut arte diaboli id sciret;* but if he has been at that trouble, he is not obliged.'"

"And why so, father?"

"Don't you see?" returned he. "It is because men may truly divine by the aid of the devil, whereas astrology is a mere sham."

"But, sir, should the devil happen not to tell the truth (and he is not much more to be trusted than astrology), the magician must, I should think, for the same reason, be obliged to make restitution?"

"Not always," replied the monk: "*Distinguo,* as Sanchez says, here. If the magician be ignorant of the diabolic art—*si sit artis diabolicæ ignarus*—he is bound to restore: but if he is an expert sorcerer, and has done all in his power to arrive at the truth, the obligation ceases; for the industry of such a magician may be estimated at a certain sum of money.'"

"There is some sense in that," I said; "for this is an excellent plan to induce sorcerers to aim at proficiency in their art, in the hope of making an honest livelihood, as you would say, by faithfully serving the public."

"You are making a jest of it, I suspect," said the father: "that is very wrong. If you were to talk in that way in places where you were not known, some people might take it amiss, and charge you with turning sacred subjects into ridicule."

"That, father, is a charge from which I could very easily vindicate myself; for certain I am that whoever will be at the trouble to examine the true meaning of my words will find my object to be precisely the reverse; and perhaps, sir, before our conversations are ended, I may find an opportunity of making this very amply apparent."

"Ho, ho," cried the monk, "there is no laughing in your head now."

"I confess," said I, "that the suspicion that I intended to laugh at things sacred, would be as painful for me to incur, as it would be unjust in any to entertain it."

"I did not say it in earnest," returned the father; "but let us speak more seriously."

"I am quite disposed to do so, if you prefer it; that depends upon you, father. But I must say, that I have been astonished to see your friends carrying their attentions to all sorts and conditions of men so far as even to regulate the legitimate gains of sorcerers."

"One cannot write for too many people," said the monk, "nor be too minute in particularising cases, nor repeat the same things too often in different books. You may be convinced of this by the following anecdote, which is related by one of the gravest of our fathers, as you may well suppose, seeing he is our present Provincial—the reverend Father Cellot: 'We know a person,' says he, 'who was carrying a large sum of money in his pocket to restore it, in obedience to the orders of his confessor, and who, stepping into a bookseller's shop by the way, inquired if there was anything new?— *numquid novi?*—when the bookseller showed him a book on moral theology, recently published; and turning over the leaves carelessly, and without reflection, he lighted upon a passage describing his own case, and saw that he was under no obligation to make restitution: upon which, relieved from the burden of his scruples, he returned home with a purse no less heavy, and a heart much lighter, than when he left it:— *abjecta scrupuli sarcina, retento auri pondere, levior domum repetiit.*'

"Say, after hearing that, if it is useful or not to know our maxims? Will you laugh at them now? or rather, are you not prepared to join with Father Cellot in the pious reflection which he makes on the blessedness of that incident? 'Accidents of that kind,' he remarks, 'are, with God, the effect of his providence; with the guardian angel, the effect of his good guidance; with the individuals to whom they happen, the effect of their predestination. From all eternity, God decided that the golden chain of their salvation should depend on such and such an author, and not upon a hundred others who say the same thing, because they never happen to meet with them. Had that man not written, this man would not have been saved. All, therefore, who find fault with the multitude of our authors, we would beseech, in the bowels of Jesus Christ, to beware of envying others those books which the eternal election of God and the blood of Jesus Christ have purchased for them!' Such are the eloquent terms in which this learned man proves so successfully the proposition which he had advanced, namely, 'How useful it must be to have a great many writers on moral theology—*quam utile sit de theologia morali multos scribere!*' "

"Father," said I, "I shall defer giving you my opinion of that passage to another opportunity; in the meantime, I shall only say that as your maxims are so useful, and as it is so important to publish them, you ought to continue to give me further instruction in them. For I can assure you that the person to whom I send them shows my letters to a great many people. Not that we intend to avail ourselves of them in our own case; but indeed we think it will be useful for the world to be informed about them."

"Very well," rejoined the monk, "you see I do not conceal them; and, in continuation, I am ready to furnish you, at our next interview, with an account of the comforts and indulgences which our fathers allow, with the view of rendering salvation easy, and devotion agreeable; so that in addition to what you have hitherto learned as to particular conditions of men, you may learn what applies in general to all classes, and thus you will have gone through a complete course of instruction."—So saying, the monk took his leave of me.—I am, &c.

P. S.—I have always forgot to tell you that there are different editions of Escobar. Should you think of purchasing him, I would advise you to choose the Lyons edition, having on the title page the device of a lamb lying on a book sealed with seven seals; or the Brussels edition of 1651. Both of these are better and larger than the previous editions published at Lyons in the years 1644 and 1646.

False worship of the Virgin introduced by the Jesuits—devotion made easy—their maxims on ambition, envy, gluttony, equivocation, and mental reservations—female dress—gaming—hearing Mass

Paris, July 3, 1656

SIR,—I shall use as little ceremony with you as the worthy monk did with me, when I saw him last. The moment he perceived me, he came forward with his eyes fixed on a book which he held in his hand, and accosted me thus: " 'Would you not be infinitely obliged to any one who should open to you the gates of paradise? Would you not give millions of gold to have a key by which you might gain admittance whenever you thought proper? You need not be at such expense; here is one—here are a hundred for much less money.' "

At first I was at a loss to know whether the good father was reading, or talking to me, but he soon put the matter beyond doubt by adding:

"These, sir, are the opening words of a fine book, written by Father Barry of our Society; for I never give you anything of my own."

"What book is it?" asked I.

"Here is its title," he replied: " *'Paradise opened to Philagio, in a Hundred Devotions to the Mother of God, easily practised.'* "

"Indeed, father! and is each of these easy devotions a sufficient passport to heaven?"

"It is," returned he. "Listen to what follows: 'The devotions to the Mother of God, which you will find in this book, are so many celestial keys, which will open wide to you the gates of paradise, provided you practise them'; and accordingly, he says at the conclusion, 'that he is satisfied if you practise only one of them.' "

"Pray, then, father, do teach me one of the easiest of them."

"They are all easy," he replied, "for example—'Saluting the Holy Virgin when you happen to meet her image—saying the little chaplet of the pleasures of the Virgin—fervently pronouncing the name of Mary—commissioning the angels to bow to her for us—wishing to build her as many churches as all the monarchs on earth have done—bidding her good morrow every morning, and good night in the evening—saying the *Ave Maria* every day, in honor of the heart of Mary'— which last devotion, he says, possesses the additional virtue of securing us the heart of the Virgin."

"But, father," said I, "only provided we give her our own in return, I presume?"

"That," he replied, "is not absolutely necessary, when a person is too much attached to the world. Hear Father Barry: 'Heart for heart would, no doubt, be highly proper; but yours is rather too much attached to the world, too much bound up in the creature, so that I dare not advise you to offer, at present, that *poor little slave* which you call your heart.' And so he contents himself with the *Ave Maria* which he had prescribed."

"Why, this is extremely easy work," said I, "and I should really think that nobody will be damned after that."

"Alas!" said the monk, "I see you have no idea of the hardness of some people's hearts. There are some, sir, who would never engage to repeat, every day, even these simple words, *Good day, Good evening,* just because such a practice would require some exertion of memory. And, accordingly, it became necessary for Father Barry to furnish them with expedients still easier, such as wearing a chaplet night and day on the arm, in the form of a bracelet, or carrying about one's person a rosary, or an image of the Virgin. 'And, tell me now,' as Father Barry says, 'if I have not provided you with easy devotions to obtain the good graces of Mary?'"

"Extremely easy indeed, father," I observed.

"Yes," he said, "it is as much as could possibly be done, and I think should be quite satisfactory. For he must be a wretched creature indeed, who would not spare a single moment in all his lifetime to put a chaplet on his arm, or a rosary in his pocket, and thus secure his salvation; and that, too, with so much certainty that none who have tried the experiment have ever found it to fail, in whatever way they may have lived; though, let me add, we exhort people not to omit holy living. Let me refer you to the example of this, given at p. 34; it is that of a female who, while she practised daily the devotion of saluting the images of the Virgin, spent all her days in mortal sin, and yet was saved after all, by the merit of that single devotion."

"And how so?" cried I.

"Our Saviour," he replied, "raised her up again, for the very purpose of showing it. So certain it is, that none can perish who practise any one of these devotions."

"My dear sir," I observed, "I am fully aware that the devotions to the Virgin are a powerful means of salvation, and that the least of them, if flowing from the exercise of faith and charity, as in the case of the saints who have practised them, are of great merit; but to make persons believe that, by practising these without reforming their wicked lives, they will be converted by them at the hour of death, or that God will raise them up again, does appear calculated rather to keep sinners going on in their evil courses, by deluding them with false peace and foolhardy confidence, than to draw them off from sin by that genuine conversion which grace alone can effect."

"What does it matter," replied the monk, "by what road we enter paradise, provided we do enter it? as our famous Father Binet, formerly our Provincial, remarks on a similar subject, in his excellent book, On the Mark of Predestination.

'Be it by hook or by crook,' as he says, 'what need we care, if we reach at last the celestial city.' "

"Granted," said I; "but the great question is, if we will get there at all."

"The Virgin will be answerable for that," returned he; "so says Father Barry in the concluding lines of his book: 'If, at the hour of death, the enemy should happen to put in some claim upon you, and occasion disturbance in the little commonwealth of your thoughts, you have only to say that Mary will answer for you, and that he must make his application to her.' "

"But, father, it might be possible to puzzle you, were one disposed to push the question a little further. Who, for example, has assured us that the Virgin will be answerable in this case?"

"Father Barry will be answerable for her," he replied. " 'As for the profit and happiness to be derived from these devotions,' he says, 'I will be answerable for that; I will stand bail for the good Mother.' "

"But, father, who is to be answerable for Father Barry?"

"How!" cried the monk; "for Father Barry? is he not a member of our Society; and do you need to be told that our Society is answerable for all the books of its members? It is highly necessary and important for you to know about this. There is an order in our Society, by which all booksellers are prohibited from printing any work of our fathers without the approbation of our divines and the permission of our superiors. This regulation was passed by Henry III., 10th May 1583, and confirmed by Henry IV., 20th December 1603, and by Louis XIII., 14th February 1612; so that the whole of our body stands responsible for the publications of each of the brethren. This is a feature quite peculiar to our community. And, in consequence of this, not a single work emanates from us which does not breathe the spirit of the Society. That, sir, is a piece of information quite *apropos*."

"My good father," said I, "you oblige me very much, and I only regret that I did not know this sooner, as it will induce me to pay considerably more attention to your authors."

"I would have told you sooner," he replied, "had an opportunity offered; I hope, however, you will profit by the information in future, and, in the meantime, let us prosecute our subject. The methods of securing salvation which I have mentioned are, in my opinion, very easy, very sure, and sufficiently numerous; but it was the anxious wish of our doctors that people should not stop short at this first step, where they only do what is absolutely necessary for salvation, and nothing more. Aspiring, as they do without ceasing, after the greater glory of God, they sought to elevate men to a higher pitch of piety; and as men of the world are generally deterred from devotion by the strange ideas they have been led to form of it by some people, we have deemed it of the highest importance to remove this obstacle which meets us at the threshold. In this department Father Le Moine has acquired much fame, by his work entitled Devotion Made Easy, composed for this very purpose. The picture which he draws of devotion in this work is perfectly charming. None ever understood the subject before him. Only hear what he says in the beginning of his work: 'Virtue has never as yet been seen aright; no portrait of her, hitherto produced, has borne the least verisimilitude. It is by no means surprising that so few have attempted to scale her rocky eminence. She has been held up as a cross-tempered dame, whose only delight is in solitude; she has been associated with toil and sorrow; and, in short, represented as the foe of sports and diversions, which are, in fact, the flowers of joy and the seasoning of life.' "

"But, father, I am sure, I have heard at least, that there have been great saints who led extremely austere lives."

"No doubt of that," he replied; "but still, to use the language of the doctor, 'there have always been a number of genteel saints, and well-bred devotees'; and this difference in their manners, mark you, arises entirely from a difference of humors. 'I am far from denying,' says my author, 'that there are devout persons to be met with, pale and melancholy in their temperament, fond of silence and retirement, with phlegm instead of blood in their veins, and with faces of clay; but there are many others of a happier complexion, and who possess that sweet and warm humor, that genial and rectified blood, which is the true stuff that joy is made of.'

"You see," resumed the monk, "that the love of silence and retirement is not common to all devout people; and that, as I was saying, this is the effect rather of their complexion than their piety. Those austere manners to which you refer, are, in fact, properly the character of a savage and barbarian, and, accordingly, you will find them ranked by Father Le Moine among the ridiculous and brutal manners of a moping idiot. The following is the description he has drawn of one of these in the seventh book of his Moral Pictures: 'He has no eyes for the beauties of art or nature. Were he to indulge in anything that gave him pleasure, he would consider himself oppressed with a grievous load. On festival days, he retires to hold fellowship with the dead. He delights in a grotto rather than a palace, and prefers the stump of a tree to a throne. As to injuries and affronts, he is as insensible to them as if he had the eyes and ears of a statue. Honor and glory are idols with whom he has no acquaintance, and to whom he has no incense to offer. To him a beautiful woman is no better than a spectre; and those imperial and commanding looks—those charming tyrants who hold so many slaves in willing and chainless servitude—have no more influence over his optics than the sun over those of owls,' &c."

"Reverend sir," said I, "had you not told me that Father Le Moine was the author of that description, I declare I would have guessed it to be the production of some profane fellow, who had drawn it expressly with the view of turning the saints into ridicule. For if that is not the picture of a man entirely denied to those feelings which the Gospel obliges us to renounce, I confess that I know nothing of the matter."

"You may now perceive, then, the extent of your ignorance," he replied; "for these are the features of a feeble, uncultivated mind, 'destitute of those virtuous and natural affections which it ought to possess,' as Father Le Moine says at the close of that description. Such is his way of teaching 'Christian virtue and philosophy,' as he announces in his advertisement; and, in truth, it cannot be denied that this method of treating devotion is much more agreeable to the taste of the world than the old way in which they went to work before our times."

"There can be no comparison between them," was my reply, "and I now begin to hope that you will be as good as your word."

"You will see that better by-and-by," returned the monk. "Hitherto I have only spoken of piety in general, but, just to show you more in detail how our fathers have disencumbered it of its toils and troubles, would it not be most consoling to the ambitious to learn that they may maintain genuine devotion along with an inordinate love of greatness?"

"What, father! even though they should run to the utmost excess of ambition?"

"Yes," he replied; "for this would be only a venial sin, unless they sought after greatness in order to offend God and injure the State more effectually. Now venial sins do not preclude a man from being devout, as the greatest saints are not exempt from them. 'Ambition,' says Escobar, 'which consists in an inordinate appetite for place and power, is of itself a venial sin; but when such dignities are coveted for the purpose of hurting the commonwealth, or having more opportunity to offend God, these adventitious circumstances render it mortal.'"

"Very savory doctrine, indeed, father."

"And is it not still more savory," continued the monk, "for misers to be told, by the same authority, 'that the rich are not guilty of mortal sin by refusing to give alms out of their superfluity to the poor in the hour of their greatest need?—*scio in gravi pauperum necessitate divites non dando superflua, non peccare mortaliter.*'"

"Why truly," said I, "if that be the case, I give up all pretension to skill in the science of sins."

"To make you still more sensible of this," returned he,

"you have been accustomed to think, I suppose, that a good opinion of one's self, and a complacency in one's own works, is a most dangerous sin? Now, will you not be surprised if I can show you that such a good opinion, even though there should be no foundation for it, is so far from being a sin, that it is, on the contrary, *the gift of God?*"

"Is it possible, father?"

"That it is," said the monk; "and our good Father Garasse shows it in his French work, entitled Summary of the Capital Truths of Religion: 'It is a result of commutative justice that all honest labor should find its recompense either in praise or in self-satisfaction. When men of good talents publish some excellent work, they are justly remunerated by public applause. But when a man of weak parts has wrought hard at some worthless production, and fails to obtain the praise of the public, in order that his labor may not go without its reward, God imparts to him a personal satisfaction, which it would be worse than barbarious injustice to envy him. It is thus that God, who is infinitely just, has given even to frogs a certain complacency in their own croaking.'"

"Very fine decisions in favor of vanity, ambition, and avarice!" cried I; "and envy, father, will it be more difficult to find an excuse for it?"

"That is a delicate point," he replied. "We require to make use here of Father Bauny's distinction, which he lays down in his Summary of Sins: 'Envy of the spiritual good of our neighbor is mortal, but envy of his temporal good is only venial.'"

"And why so, father?"

"You shall hear," said he. " 'For the good that consists in temporal things is so slender, and so insignificant in relation to heaven, that it is of no consideration in the eyes of God and his saints.'"

"But, father, if temporal good is so *slender,* and of so little consideration, how do you come to permit men's lives to be taken away in order to preserve it?"

"You mistake the matter entirely," returned the monk;

"you were told that temporal good was of no consideration in the eyes of God, but not in the eyes of men."

"That idea never occurred to me," I replied; "and now, it is to be hoped that, in virtue of these same distinctions, the world will get rid of mortal sins altogether."

"Do not flatter yourself with that," said the father; "there are still such things as mortal sins—there is sloth, for example."

"Nay, then, father dear!" I exclaimed, "after that, farewell to all 'the joys of life!'"

"Stay," said the monk, "when you have heard Escobar's definition of that vice, you will perhaps change your tone: 'Sloth,' he observes, 'lies in grieving that spiritual things are spiritual, as if one should lament that the sacraments are the sources of grace; which would be a mortal sin.'"

"O my dear sir!" cried I, "I don't think that anybody ever took it into his head to be slothful in that way."

"And accordingly," he replied, "Escobar afterwards remarks: 'I must confess that it is very rarely that a person falls into the sin of sloth.' You see now how important it is to *define* things properly?"

"Yes, father, and this brings to my mind your other definitions about assassinations, ambuscades, and superfluities. But why have you not extended your method to all cases, and given definitions of all vices in your way, so that people may no longer sin in gratifying themselves?"

"It is not always essential," he replied, "to accomplish that purpose by changing the definitions of things. I may illustrate this by referring to the subject of good cheer, which is accounted one of the greatest pleasures of life, and which Escobar thus sanctions in his 'Practice according to our Society': 'Is it allowable for a person to eat and drink to repletion, unnecessarily, and solely for pleasure? Certainly he may, according to Sanchez, provided he does not thereby injure his health; because the natural appetite may be permitted to enjoy its proper functions.'"

"Well, father, that is certainly the most complete passage,

and the most finished maxim in the whole of your moral system! What comfortable inferences may be drawn from it! Why, and is gluttony, then, not even a venial sin?"

"Not in the shape I have just referred to," he replied; "but, according to the same author, it would be a venial sin 'were a person to gorge himself, unnecessarily, with eating and drinking, to such a degree as to produce vomiting.' So much for that point. I would now say a little about the facilities we have invented for avoiding sin in worldly conversations and intrigues. One of the most embarrassing of these cases is how to avoid telling lies, particularly when one is anxious to induce a belief in what is false. In such cases, our doctrine of equivocations has been found of admirable service, according to which, as Sanchez has it, 'it is permitted to use ambiguous terms, leading people to understand them in another sense from that in which we understand them ourselves.'"

"I know that already, father," said I.

"We have published it so often," continued he, "that at length, it seems, everybody knows of it. But do you know what is to be done when no equivocal words can be got?"

"No, father."

"I thought as much," said the Jesuit; "this is something new, sir: I mean the doctrine of mental reservations. 'A man may swear,' as Sanchez says in the same place, 'that he never did such a thing (though he actually did it), meaning within himself that he did not do so on a certain day, or before he was born, or understanding any other such circumstance, while the words which he employs have no such sense as would discover his meaning. And this is very convenient in many cases, and quite innocent, when necessary or conducive to one's health, honor, or advantage.'"

"Indeed, father! is that not a lie, and perjury to boot?"

"No," said the father: "Sanchez and Filiutius prove that it is not; for, says the latter, 'it is the intention that determines the quality of the action.' And he suggests a still surer method for avoiding falsehood, which is this: After saying aloud, *I swear that I have not done that*, to add, in a low voice, *to-day;* or after saying aloud, *I swear,* to interpose in a whisper, *that I say,* and then continue aloud, *that I have done that.* This, you perceive, is telling the truth."

"I grant it," said I; "it might possibly, however, be found to be telling the truth in a low key, and falsehood in a loud one; besides, I should be afraid that many people might not have sufficient presence of mind to avail themselves of these methods."

"Our doctors," replied the Jesuit, "have taught, in the same passage, for the benefit of such as might not be expert in the use of these reservations, that no more is required of them, to avoid lying, than simply to say that *they have not done* what they have done, provided 'they have, in general, the intention of giving to their language the sense which an *able man* would give to it.' Be candid, now, and confess if you have not often felt yourself embarrassed, in consequence of not knowing this?"

"Sometimes," said I.

"And will you not also acknowledge," continued he, "that it would often prove very convenient to be absolved in conscience from keeping certain engagements one may have made?"

"The most convenient thing in the world!" I replied.

"Listen, then, to the general rule laid down by Escobar: 'Promises are not binding, when the person in making them had no intention to bind himself. Now, it seldom happens that any have such an intention, unless when they confirm their promises by an oath or contract; so that when one simply says, *I will do it,* he means that he will do it if he does not change his mind; for he does not wish, by saying that, to deprive himself of his liberty.' He gives other rules in the same strain, which you may consult for yourself, and tells us, in conclusion, 'that all this is taken from Molina and our other authors, and is therefore settled beyond all doubt.'"

"My dear father," I observed, "I had no idea that the direction of the intention possessed the power of rendering promises null and void."

"You must perceive," returned he, "what facility this affords for prosecuting the business of life. But what has given us the most trouble has been to regulate the commerce between the sexes; our fathers being more chary in the matter of chastity. Not but that they have discussed questions of a very curious and very indulgent character, particularly in reference to married and betrothed persons."

At this stage of the conversation I was made acquainted with the most extraordinary questions you can well imagine. He gave me enough of them to fill many letters; but as you show my communications to all sorts of persons, and as I do not choose to be the vehicle of such reading to those who would make it the subject of diversion, I must decline even giving the quotations.

The only thing to which I can venture to allude, out of all the books which he showed me, and these in French, too, is a passage which you will find in Father Bauny's Summary, p. 165, relating to certain little familiarities, which, provided the intention is well directed, he explains *"as passing for gallant"*; and you will be surprised to find, on p. 148, a principle of morals, as to the power which daughters have to dispose of their persons without the leave of their relatives, couched in these terms: "When that is done with the consent of the daughter, although the father may have reason to complain, it does not follow that she, or the person to whom she has sacrificed her honor, has done him any wrong, or violated the rules of justice in regard to him; for the daughter has possession of her honor, as well as of her body, and can do what she pleases with them, bating death or mutilation of her members." Judge, from that specimen, of the rest. It brings to my recollection a passage from a Heathen poet, a much better casuist, it would appear, than these reverend doctors; for he says, "that the person of a daughter does not belong wholly to herself, but partly to her father and partly to her mother, without whom she cannot dispose of it, even in marriage." And I am much mistaken if there is a single judge in the land who would not lay down as law the very reverse of this maxim of Father Bauny.

This is all I dare tell you of this part of our conversation, which lasted so long that I was obliged to beseech the monk to change the subject. He did so, and proceeded to entertain me with their regulations about female attire.

"We shall not speak," he said, "of those who are actuated by impure intentions; but as to others, Escobar remarks, that 'if the woman adorn herself without any evil intention, but merely to gratify a natural inclination to vanity—*ob naturalem fastus inclinationem*—this is only a venial sin, or rather no sin at all.' And Father Bauny maintains, that 'even though the woman knows the bad effect which her care in adorning her person may have upon the virtue of those who may behold her, all decked out in rich and precious attire, she would not sin in so dressing.' And among others, he cites our Father Sanchez as being of the same mind."

"But, father, what do your authors say to those passages of Scripture which so strongly denounce everything of that sort?"

"Lessius has well met that objection," said the monk, "by observing, 'that these passages of Scripture have the force of precepts only in regard to the women of that period, who were expected to exhibit, by their modest demeanor, an example of edification to the Pagans.' "

"And where did he find that, father?"

"It does not matter where he found it," replied he; "it is enough to know that the sentiments of these great men are always probable of themselves. It deserves to be noticed, however, that Father Le Moine has qualified this general permission; for he will on no account allow it to be extended to *the old ladies*. 'Youth,' he observes, 'is naturally entitled to adorn itself, nor can the use of ornament be condemned at an age which is the flower and verdure of life. But there it should be allowed to remain: it would be strangely out of season seek for roses on the snow. The stars alone have a right to be always dancing, for they have the gift of perpetual youth. The wisest course in this matter, therefore, for old women, would be to consult good sense and a good mirror, to yield to decency and necessity, and to retire at the first approach of the shades of night.' "

"A most judicious advice," I observed.

"But," continued the monk, "just to show you how careful our fathers are about everything you can think of, I may mention that, after granting the ladies permission to gamble, and foreseeing that, in many cases, this license would be of little avail unless they had something to gamble with, they have established another maxim in their favor, which will be found in Escobar's chapter on larceny, no. 13: 'A wife,' says he, 'may gamble, and for this purpose may pilfer money from her husband.' "

"Well, father, that is capital!"

"There are many other good things besides that," said the father; "but we must waive them, and say a little about those more important maxims, which facilitate the practice of holy things—the manner of attending mass, for example. On this subject our great divines, Gaspard Hurtado, and Coninck, have taught 'that it is quite sufficient to be present at mass in body, though we may be absent in spirit, provided we maintain an outwardly respectful deportment.' Vasquez goes a step further, maintaining 'that one fulfils the precept of hearing mass, even though one should go with no such intention at all.' All this is repeatedly laid down by Escobar, who, in one passage, illustrates the point by the example of those who are dragged to mass by force, and who put on a fixed resolution not to listen to it."

"Truly, sir," said I, "had any other person told me that, I would not have believed it."

"In good sooth," he replied, "it requires all the support which the authority of these great names can lend it; and so does the following maxim by the same Escobar, 'that even a wicked intention, such as that of ogling the women, joined to that of hearing mass rightly, does not hinder a man from fulfilling the service.' But another very convenient device, suggested by our learned brother Turrian, is, that 'one may hear the half of a mass from one priest, and the other half from another; and that it makes no difference though he should hear first the conclusion of the one, and then the commencement of the other.' I might also mention that it has been decided by several of our doctors, to be lawful 'to hear the two halves of a mass at the same time, from the lips of two diferent priests, one of whom is commencing the mass, while the other is at the elevation; it being quite possible to attend to both parties at once, and two halves of a mass making a whole —*duæ medietates unam missam constituunt.*' 'From all which,' says Escobar, 'I conclude, that you may hear mass in a very short period of time; if, for example, you should happen to hear four masses going on at the same time, so arranged that when the first is at the commencement, the second is at the gospel, the third at the consecration, and the last at the communion.' "

"Certainly, father, according to that plan, one may hear mass any day at Notre Dame in a twinkling."

"Well," replied he, "that just shows how admirably we have succeeded in facilitating the hearing of mass. But I am anxious now to show you how we have softened the use of the sacraments, and particularly that of penance. It is here that the benignity of our fathers shines in its truest splendor; and you will be really astonished to find that devotion, a thing which the world is so much afraid of, should have been treated by our doctors with such consummate skill, that, to use the words of Father Le Moine, in his Devotion Made Easy, demolishing the bugbear which the devil had placed at its threshold, they have rendered it easier than vice, and more agreeable than pleasure; so that, in fact, simply to live is incomparably more irksome than to live well. Is that not a marvellous change, now?"

"Indeed, father, I cannot help telling you a bit of my mind: I am sadly afraid that you have overshot the mark, and that this indulgence of yours will shock more people than it will attract. The mass, for example, is a thing so grand and so holy, that, in the eyes of a great many, it would be enough to blast the credit of your doctors forever, to show them how you have spoken of it."

"With a certain class," replied the monk, "I allow that may be the case; but do you not know that we accommodate ourselves to all sorts of persons? You seem to have lost all recollection of what I have repeatedly told you on this point. The first time you are at leisure, therefore, I propose that we make this the theme of our conversation, deferring till then the lenitives we have introduced into the confessional. I promise to make you understand it so well that you will never forget it."

With these words we parted, so that our next conversation, I presume, will turn on the policy of the Society.—I am, &c.

P. S.—Since writing the above, I have seen "Paradise Opened by a Hundred Devotions Easily Practised," by Father Barry; and also the "Mark of Predestination," by Father Binet; both of them pieces well worth the seeing.

Palliatives applied by the Jesuits to the sacrament of penance, in their maxims regarding confession, satisfaction, absolution, proximate occasions of sin, contrition and the love of God

Paris, August 2, 1656

SIR,—I have not come yet to the policy of the Society, but shall first introduce you to one of its leading principles. I refer to the palliatives which they have applied to confession, and which are unquestionably the best of all the schemes they have fallen upon to "attract all and repel none." It is absolutely necessary to know something of this before going any further; and, accordingly, the monk judged it expedient to give me some instructions on the point, nearly as follows:—

"From what I have already stated," he observed, "you may judge of the success with which our doctors have labored to discover, in their wisdom, that a great many things, formerly regarded as forbidden, are innocent and allowable; but as there are some sins for which one can find no excuse, and for which there is no remedy but confession, it became necessary to alleviate, by the methods I am now going to mention, the difficulties attending that practice. Thus, having shown you, in our previous conversations, how we relieve people from troublesome scruples of conscience, by showing them that what they believed to be sinful was indeed quite innocent, I proceed now to illustrate our convenient plan for expiating what is really sinful, which is effected by making confession as easy a process as it was formerly a painful one."

"And how do you manage that, father?"

"Why," said he, "it is by those admirable subtleties which are peculiar to our Company, and have been styled by our fathers in Flanders, in 'The Image of the First Century,' 'the pious finesse, the holy artifice of devotion—*piam et religiosam calliditatem, et pietatis solertiam.*' By the aid of these inventions, as they remark in the same place, 'crimes may be expiated nowadays *alacrius*—with more zeal and alacrity than they were committed in former days, and a great many people may be washed from their stains almost as cleverly as they contracted them—*plurimi vix citius maculas contrahunt quam eluunt.*' "

"Pray, then, father, do teach me some of these most salutary lessons of *finesse.*"

"We have a good number of them," answered the monk; "for there are a great many irksome things about confession, and for each of these we have devised a palliative. The chief difficulties connected with this ordinance are the shame of confessing certain sins, the trouble of specifying the circumstances of others, the penance exacted for them, the resolution against relapsing into them, the avoidance of the proximate occasions of sins, and the regret for having committed them. I hope to convince you to-day, that it is now possible to get over all this with hardly any trouble at all; such is the care we have taken to allay the bitterness and nauseousness of this very necessary medicine. For, to begin with the difficulty of confessing certain sins, you are aware it is of importance often to keep in the good graces of one's confessor; now, must it not be extremely convenient to be permitted, as you are by our doctors, particularly Escobar and Suarez, 'to have two confessors, one for the mortal sins and another for the venial, in order to maintain a fair character with your ordinary confessor—*uti bonam famam apud ordinarium tueatur*—provided you do not take occasion from thence to indulge in mortal sin?' This is followed by another ingenious contrivance for confessing a sin, even to the ordinary confessor, without his perceiving that it was committed since the last confession, which is, 'to make a general confession, and huddle this last sin in a lump among the rest which we confess.' And I am sure you will own that the following decision of Father Bauny goes far to alleviate the shame which one must feel in confessing his relapses, namely, 'that, except in certain cases, which rarely occur, the confessor is not entitled to ask his penitent if the sin of which he accuses himself is an habitual one, nor is the latter obliged to answer such a question; because the confessor has no right to subject his penitent to the shame of disclosing his frequent relapses.' "

"Indeed, father! I might as well say that a physician has no right to ask his patient if it is long since he had the fever. Do not sins assume quite a different aspect according to circumstances? and should it not be the object of a genuine penitent to discover the whole state of his conscience to his confessor, with the same sincerity and open-heartedness as if he were speaking to Jesus Christ himself, whose place the priest occupies? If so, how far is he from realizing such a disposition, who, by concealing the frequency of his relapses, conceals the aggravations of his offence!"

I saw that this puzzled the worthy monk, for he attempted to elude rather than resolve the difficulty, by turning my attention to another of their rules, which only goes to establish a fresh abuse, instead of justifying in the least the decision of Father Bauny; a decision which, in my opinion, is one of the most pernicious of their maxims, and calculated to encourage profligate men to continue in their evil habits.

"I grant you," replied the father, "that habit aggravates the malignity of a sin, but it does not alter its nature; and that is the reason why we do not insist on people confessing it, according to the rule laid down by our fathers, and quoted by Escobar, 'that one is only obliged to confess the circumstances that alter the species of the sin, and not those that aggravate it.' Proceeding on this rule, Father Granados says, 'that if one has eaten flesh in Lent, all he needs to do is to confess that he has broken the fast, without specifying whether it was by eating flesh, or by taking two fish meals.' And, according to Reginald, 'a sorcerer who has employed the diabolical art is not obliged to reveal that circumstance; it is enough to say that he has dealt in magic, without expressing

whether it was by palmistry or by a paction with the devil.'
Fagundez, again, has decided that 'rape is not a circumstance
which one is bound to reveal, if the woman give her consent.'
All this is quoted by Escobar, with many other very curious
decisions as to these circumstances, which you may consult at
your leisure."

"These 'artifices of devotion' are vastly convenient in their
way," I observed.

"And yet," said the father, "notwithstanding all that, they
would go for nothing, sir, unless we had proceeded to mollify
penance, which, more than anything else, deters people from
confession. Now, however, the most squeamish have nothing
to dread from it, after what we have advanced in our theses
of the College of Clermont, where we hold that if the confessor
imposes a suitable penance, and the penitent be unwilling to
submit himself to it, the latter may go home, 'waiving both
the penance and the absolution.' Or, as Escobar says, in giving
the Practice of our Society, 'if the penitent declare his willing-
ness to have his penance remitted to the next world, and to
suffer in purgatory all the pains due to him, the confessor
may, for the honor of the sacrament, impose a very light
penance on him, particularly if he has reason to believe that
this penitent would object to a heavier one.' "

"I really think," said I, "that, if that is the case, we ought
no longer to call confession the sacrament of penance."

"You are wrong," he replied; "for we always administer
something in the way of penance, for the form's sake."

"But, father, do you suppose that a man is worthy of receiving absolution, when he will submit to nothing painful to
expiate his offences? And, in these circumstances, ought you
not to retain rather than remit their sins? Are you not aware
of the extent of your ministry, and that you have the power
of binding and loosing? Do you imagine that you are at liberty
to give absolution indifferently to all who ask it, and without
ascertaining beforehand if Jesus Christ looses in heaven those
whom you loose on earth?"

"What!" cried the father, "do you suppose that we do not

know that 'the confessor (as one remarks) ought to sit in judgment on the disposition of his penitent, both because he is bound not to dispense the sacraments to the unworthy, Jesus Christ having enjoined him to be a faithful steward, and not give that which is holy unto dogs; and because he is a judge, and it is the duty of a judge to give righteous judgment, by loosing the worthy and binding the unworthy, and he ought not to absolve those whom Jesus Christ condemns.' "

"Whose words are these, father?"

"They are the words of our father Filiutius," he replied.

"You astonish me," said I; "I took them to be a quotation from one of the fathers of the Church. At all events, sir, that passage ought to make an impression on the confessors, and render them very circumspect in the dispensation of this sacrament, to ascertain whether the regret of their penitents is sufficient, and whether their promises of future amendment are worthy of credit."

"That is not such a difficult matter," replied the father; "Filiutius had more sense than to leave confessors in that dilemma, and accordingly he suggests an easy way of getting out of it, in the words immediately following: 'The confessor may easily set his mind at rest as to the disposition of his penitent; for, if he fail to give sufficient evidence of sorrow, the confessor has only to ask him if he does not detest the sin in his heart, and if he answers that he does, he is bound to believe it. The same thing may be said of resolutions as to the future, unless the case involves an obligation to restitution, or to avoid some proximate occasion of sin.' "

"As to that passage, father, I can easily believe that it is Filiutius' own."

"You are mistaken though," said the father, "for he has extracted it, word for word, from Suarez."

"But, father, that last passage from Filiutius overturns what he had laid down in the former. For confessors can no longer be said to sit as judges on the disposition of their penitents, if they are bound to take it simply upon their word, in the absence of all satisfying signs of contrition. Are the professions made on such occasions so infallible, that no other sign is needed? I question much if experience has taught your fathers, that all who make fair promises are remarkable for keeping them; I am mistaken if they have not often found the reverse."

"No matter," replied the monk; "confessors are bound to believe them for all that; for Father Bauny, who has probed this question to the bottom, has concluded 'that at whatever time those who have fallen into frequent relapses, without giving evidence of amendment, present themselves before a confessor, expressing their regret for the past, and a good purpose for the future, he is bound to believe them on their simple averment, although there may be reason to presume that such resolution only came from the teeth outwards. Nay,' says he, 'though they should indulge subsequently to greater excess than ever in the same delinquencies, still, in my opinion, they may receive absolution.' There now! that, I am sure, should silence you."

"But, father," said I, "you impose a great hardship, I think, on the confessors, by thus obliging them to believe the very reverse of what they see."

"You don't understand it," returned he; "all that is meant is, that they are obliged to act and absolve *as if* they believed that their penitents would be true to their engagements, though, in point of fact, they believe no such thing. This is explained, immediately afterwards, by Suarez and Filiutius. After having said that 'the priest is bound to believe the penitent on his word,' they add, 'It is not necessary that the confessor should be convinced that the good resolution of his penitent will be carried into effect, nor even that he should judge it probable; it is enough that he thinks the person has at the time the design in general, though he may very shortly after relapse. Such is the doctrine of all our authors—*ita docent omnes autores*.' Will you presume to doubt what has been taught by our authors?"

"But, sir, what then becomes of what Father Petau himself is obliged to own, in the preface to his Public Penance, 'that the holy fathers, doctors, and councils of the Church agree in holding it as a settled point, that the penance preparatory to the eucharist must be genuine, constant, resolute, and not languid and sluggish, or subject to after-thoughts and relapses?' "

"Don't you observe," replied the monk, "that Father Petau is speaking of the *ancient Church?* But all that is now *so little in season*, to use a common saying of our doctors, that, according to Father Bauny, the reverse is the only true view of the matter. 'There are some,' says he, 'who maintain that absolution ought to be refused to those who fall frequently into the same sin, more especially if, after being often absolved, they evince no signs of amendment; and others hold the opposite view. But the only true opinion is, that they ought not to be refused absolution; and though they should be nothing the better of all the advice given them, though they should have broken all their promises to lead new lives, and been at no trouble to purify themselves, still it is of no consequence; whatever may be said to the contrary, the true opinion which ought to be followed is, that even in all these cases, they ought to be absolved.' And again: 'Absolution ought neither to be denied nor delayed in the case of those who live in habitual sins against the law of God, of nature, and of the Church, although there should be no apparent prospect of future amendment—*etsi emendationis futuræ nulla spes appareat.*' "

"But, father, this certainty of always getting absolution may induce sinners—"

"I know what you mean," interrupted the Jesuit; "but listen to Father Bauny, q. 15: 'Absolution may be given even to him who candidly avows that the hope of being absolved induced him to sin with more freedom than he would otherwise have done.' And Father Caussin, defending this proposition, says, 'that were this not true, confession would be interdicted to the greater part of mankind; and the only resource left poor sinners would be a branch and a rope.' "

"O father, how these maxims of yours will draw people to your confessionals!"

"Yes," he replied, "you would hardly believe what numbers are in the habit of frequenting them; 'we are absolutely oppressed and overwhelmed, so to speak, under the crowd of our penitents—*penitentium numero obruimur'*—as is said in 'The Image of the First Century.' "

"I could suggest a very simple method," said I, "to escape from this inconvenient pressure. You have only to oblige sinners to avoid the proximate occasions of sin; that single expedient would afford you relief at once."

"We have no wish for such a relief," rejoined the monk; "quite the reverse; for, as is observed in the same book, 'the great end of our Society is to labor to establish the virtues, to wage war on the vices, and to save a great number of souls.' Now, as there are very few souls inclined to quit the proximate occasions of sin, we have been obliged to define what a proximate occasion is. 'That cannot be called a proximate occasion,' says Escobar, 'where one sins but rarely, or on a sudden transport—say three or four times a year'; or, as Father Bauny has it, 'once or twice in a month.' Again, asks this author, 'what is to be done in the case of masters and servants, or cousins, who, living under the same roof, are by this occasion tempted to sin?' "

"They ought to be separated," said I.

"That is what he says, too, 'if their relapses be very frequent: but if the parties offend rarely, and cannot be separated without trouble and loss, they may, according to Suarez and other authors, be absolved, provided they promise to sin no more, and are truly sorry for what is past.' "

This required no explanation, for he had already informed me with what sort of evidence of contrition the confessor was bound to rest satisfied.

"And Father Bauny," continued the monk, "permits those who are involved in the proximate occasions of sin, 'to remain as they are, when they cannot avoid them without becoming the common talk of the world, or subjecting themselves to inconvenience.' 'A priest,' he remarks in another work, 'may and ought to absolve a woman who is guilty of living with a paramour, if she cannot put him away honorably, or has some reason for keeping him—*si non potest honeste ejicere, aut habeat aliquam causam retinendi*—provided she promises to act more virtuously for the future.' "

"Well, father," cried I, "you have certainly succeeded in relaxing the obligation of avoiding the occasions of sin to a very comfortable extent, by dispensing with the duty as soon as it becomes inconvenient; but I should think your fathers will at least allow it be binding when there is no difficulty in the way of its performance?"

"Yes," said the father, "though even then the rule is not without exceptions. For Father Bauny says, in the same place, 'that any one may frequent profligate houses, with the view of converting their unfortunate inmates, though the probability should be that he fall into sin, having often experienced before that he has yielded to their fascinations. Some doctors do not approve of this opinion, and hold that no man may voluntarily put his salvation in peril to succor his neighbor; yet I decidedly embrace the opinion which they controvert.' "

"A novel sort of preachers these, father! But where does Father Bauny find any ground for investing them with such a mission?"

"It is upon one of his own principles," he replied, "which he announces in the same place after Basil Ponce. I mentioned it to you before, and I presume you have not forgotten it. It is, 'that one may seek an occasion of sin, directly and expressly—*primo et per se*—to promote the temporal or spiritual good of himself or his neighbor.' "

On hearing these passages, I felt so horrified that I was on the point of breaking out; but, being resolved to hear him to an end, I restrained myself, and merely inquired: "How, father, does this doctrine comport with that of the Gospel, which binds us to 'pluck out the right eye,' and 'cut off the right hand,' when they 'offend,' or prove prejudicial to salvation? And how can you suppose that the man who wilfully indulges in the occasions of sins, sincerely hates sin? It it not evident, on the contrary, that he has never been properly touched with a sense of it, and that he has not yet experienced that genuine conversion of heart, which makes a man love God as much as he formerly loved the creature?"

"Indeed!" cried he, "do you call that genuine contrition? It seems you do not know that, as Father Pintereau says, 'all our fathers teach, with one accord, that it is an error, and almost a heresy, to hold that *contrition* is necessary; or that *attrition* alone, induced by the *sole* motive, the fear of the pains of hell, which excludes a disposition to offend, is not sufficient with the sacrament?'"

"What, father! do you mean to say that it is almost an article of faith, that attrition, induced merely by fear of punishment, is sufficient with the sacrament? That idea, I think, is peculiar to your fathers; for those other doctors who hold that attrition is sufficient along with the sacrament, always take care to show that it must be accompanied with some love to God at least. It appears to me, moreover, that even your own authors did not always consider this doctrine of yours so certain. Your Father Suarez, for instance, speaks of it thus: 'Although it is a probable opinion that attrition is sufficient with the sacrament, yet it is not certain, and it may be false—*non est certa, et potest esse falsa.* And if it is false, attrition is not sufficient to save a man; and he that dies knowingly in this state, wilfully exposes himself to the grave peril of eternal damnation. For this opinion is neither very ancient nor very common—*nec valde antiqua, nec multum communis.*' Sanchez was not more prepared to hold it as infallible, when he said in his Summary, that 'the sick man and his confessor, who content themselves at the hour of death with attrition and the sacrament, are both chargeable with mortal sin, on account of the great risk of damnation to which the penitent would be exposed, if the opinion that attrition is sufficient with the sacrament should not turn out to be true.'

Comitolus, too, says that 'we should not be too sure that attrition suffices with the sacrament.'"

Here the worthy father interrupted me. "What!" he cried, "you read our authors then, it seems? That is all very well; but it would be still better were you never to read them without the precaution of·having one of *us* beside you. Do you not see, now, that, from having read them alone, you have concluded, in your simplicity, that these passages bear hard on those who have more lately supported our doctrine of attrition? Whereas it might be shown that nothing could set them off to greater advantage. Only think what a triumph it is for our fathers of the present day to have succeeded in disseminating their opinion in such short time, and to such an extent that, with the exception of theologians, nobody almost would ever suppose but that our modern views on this subject had been the uniform belief of the faithful in all ages! So that, in fact, when you have shown, from our fathers themselves, that, a few years ago, 'this opinion was not certain,' you have only succeeded in giving our modern authors the whole merit of its establishment!

"Accordingly," he continued, "our cordial friend Diana, to gratify us, no doubt, has recounted the various steps by which the opinion reached its present position. 'In former days, the ancient schoolmen maintained that contrition was necessary as soon as one had committed a mortal sin; since then, however, it has been thought that it is not binding except on festival days; afterwards, only when some great calamity threatened the people; others, again, that it ought not to be long delayed at the approach of death. But our fathers, Hurtado and Vasquez, have ably refuted all these opinions, and established that one is not bound to contrition unless he cannot be absolved in any other way, or at the point of death!' But, to continue the wonderful progress of this doctrine, I might add, what our fathers, Fagundez, Granados, and Escobar, have decided, 'that contrition is not necessary even at death; because,' say they, 'if attrition with the sacrament did not suffice at death, it would follow that attrition would not be sufficient with the sacrament. And the learned Hurtado, cited by Diana and Escobar, goes still further; for he asks, 'Is that sorrow for sin which flows solely from apprehension of its temporal consequences, such as having lost health or money, sufficient? We must distinguish. If the evil is not regarded as sent by the hand of God, such a sorrow does not suffice; but if the evil is viewed as sent by God, as, in fact, all evil, says Diana, except sin, comes from him, that kind of sorrow is sufficient.' Our Father Lamy holds the same doctrine."

"You surprise me, father; for I see nothing in all that attrition of which you speak but what is natural; and in this way a sinner may render himself worthy of absolution without supernatural grace at all. Now everybody knows that this is a heresy condemned by the Council."

"I should have thought with you," he replied; "and yet it seems this must not be the case, for the fathers of our College of Clermont have maintained (in their Theses of the 23rd May and 6th June 1644) 'that attrition may be holy and sufficient for the sacrament, although it may not be supernatural'; and (in that of August 1643) 'that attrition, though merely natural, is sufficient for the sacrament, provided it is honest.' I do not see what more could be said on the subject, unless we choose to subjoin an inference, which may be easily drawn from these principles, namely, that contrition, so far from being necessary to the sacrament, is rather prejudicial to it, inasmuch as, by washing away sins of itself, it would leave nothing for the sacrament to do at all. That is, indeed, exactly what the celebrated Jesuit Father Valencia remarks. (Tom. iv., disp. 7, q. 8, p. 4.) 'Contrition,' says he, 'is by no means necessary in order to obtain the principal benefit of the sacrament; on the contrary, it is rather an obstacle in the way of it—*imo obstat potius quominus effectus sequatur.*' Nobody could well desire more to be said in commendation of attrition."

"I believe that, father," said I; "but you must allow me to tell you my opinion, and to show you to what a dreadful length this doctrine leads. When you say that 'attrition, induced by the mere dread of punishment,' is sufficient, with the sacrament, to justify sinners, does it not follow that a person may always expiate his sins in this way, and thus be saved without ever having loved God all his lifetime? Would your fathers venture to hold that?"

"I perceive," replied the monk, "from the strain of your remarks, that you need some information on the doctrine of our fathers regarding the love of God. This is the last feature of their morality, and the most important of all. You must have learned something of it from the passages about contrition which I have quoted to you. But here are others still more definite on the point of love to God—Don't interrupt me, now; for it is of importance to notice the connection. Attend to Escobar, who reports the different opinions of our authors, in his 'Practice of the Love of God according to our Society.' The question is: 'When is one obliged to have an actual affection for God?' Suarez says, it is enough if one loves him before being *articulo mortis*—at the point of death —without determining the exact time. Vasquez, that it is sufficient even at the very point of death. Others, when one has received baptism. Others, again, when one is bound to exercise contrition. And others, on festival days. But our father, Castro Palao, combats all these opinions, and with good reason—*merito*. Hurtado de Mendoza insists that we are obliged to love God once a year; and that we ought to regard it as a great favor that we are not bound to do it oftener. But our Father Coninck thinks that we are bound to it only once in three or four years; Henriquez, once in five years; and Filiutius says that it is *probable* that we are not strictly bound to it even once in five years. How often, then, do you ask? Why, he refers it to the judgment of the judicious."

I took no notice of all this badinage, in which the ingenuity of man seems to be sporting, in the height of insolence, with the love of God.

"But," pursued the monk, "our Father Antony Sirmond surpasses all on this point, in his admirable book, 'The Defence of Virtue,' where, as he tells the reader, 'he speaks French in France,' as follows: 'St. Thomas says that we are obliged to love God as soon as we come to the use of reason: that is rather too soon! Scotus says, every Sunday, pray, for what reason? Others say, when we are sorely tempted: yes, if there be no other way of escaping the temptation. Scotus says, when we have received a benefit from God: good, in the way of thanking him for it. Others say, at death: rather late! As little do I think it binding at the reception of any sacrament: attrition in such cases is quite enough, along with confession, if convenient. Suarez says that it is binding at some time or another; but at what time?—he leaves you to judge of that for yourself—he does not know; and what that doctor did not know I know not who should know.' In short, he concludes that we are not strictly bound to more than to keep the other commandments, without any affection for God, and without giving Him our hearts, provided that we do not hate Him. To prove this is the sole object of his second treatise. You will find it in every page; more especially where he says: 'God, in commanding us to love Him, is satisfied with our obeying Him in his other commandments. If God had said, whatever obedience thou yieldest me, if thy heart is not given to me, I will destroy thee!—would such a motive, think you, be well fitted to promote the end which God must, and only can, have in view? Hence it is said that we shall love God by doing his will, *as if* we loved him with affection, as if the motive in this case was real charity. If that is really our motive, so much the better; if not, still we are strictly fulfilling the commandment of love, by having its works, so that (such is the goodness of God!) we are commanded, not so much to love him, as not to hate him.'

"Such is the way in which our doctors have discharged men from the 'painful' obligation of actually loving God. And this doctrine is so advantageous, that our Fathers Annat, Pintereau, Le Moine, and Antony Sirmond himself, have strenuously defended it when it has been attacked. You have only to consult their answers to the 'Moral Theology.' That of

Father Pintereau, in particular, will enable you to form some idea of the value of this dispensation, from the price which he tells us that it cost, which is no less than the blood of Jesus Christ. This crowns the whole. It appears, that this dispensation from the 'painful' obligation to love God, is the privilege of the Evangelical law, in opposition to the Judaical. 'It was reasonable,' he says, 'that, under the law of grace in the New Testament, God should relieve us from that trouble-some and arduous obligation which existed under the law of bondage, to exercise an act of perfect contrition, in order to be justified; and that the place of this should be supplied by the sacraments, instituted in aid of an easier disposition. Otherwise, indeed, Christians, who are the children, would have no greater facility in gaining the good graces of their Father than the Jews, who were the slaves, had in obtaining the mercy of their Lord and Master.' "

"O father!" cried I; "no patience can stand this any longer. It is impossible to listen without horror to the sentiments I have just heard."

"They are not my sentiments," said the monk.

"I grant it, sir," said I; "but you feel no aversion to them; and, so far from detesting the authors of these maxims, you hold them in esteem. Are you not afraid that your consent may involve you in a participation of their guilt? and are you not aware that St. Paul judges worthy of death, not only the authors of evil things, but also 'those who have pleasure in them that do them?' Was it not enough to have permitted men to indulge in so many forbidden things under the covert of your palliations? Was it necessary to go still further, and hold out a bribe to them to commit even those crimes which you found it impossible to excuse, by offering them an easy and certain absolution; and for this purpose nullifying the power of the priests, and obliging them, more as slaves than as judges, to absolve the most inveterate sinners—without any amendment of life—without any sign of contrition except promises a hundred times broken—without penance 'unless they choose to accept of it'—and without abandoning the occasions of their vices, 'if they should thereby be put to any inconvenience?'

"But your doctors have gone even beyond this; and the license which they have assumed to tamper with the most holy rules of Christian conduct amounts to a total subversion of the law of God. They violate 'the great commandment on which hang all the law and the prophets'; they strike at the very heart of piety; they rob it of the spirit that giveth life; they hold that to love God is not necessary to salvation; and go so far as to maintain that 'this dispensation from loving God is the privilege which Jesus Christ has introduced into the world!' This, sir, is the very climax of impiety. The price of the blood of Jesus Christ paid to obtain us a dispensation from loving him! Before the incarnation, it seems men were obliged to love God; but since 'God has so loved the world as to give his only begotten Son,' the world, redeemed by him, is released from loving him! Strange divinity of our days—to dare to take off the 'anathema' which St. Paul denounces on those 'that love not the Lord Jesus!' To cancel the sentence of St. John: 'He that loveth not, abideth in death!' and that of Jesus Christ himself: 'He that loveth me not keepeth not my precepts!' and thus to render those worthy of enjoying God through eternity who never loved God all their life! Behold the Mystery of Iniquity fulfilled! Open your eyes at length, my dear father, and if the other aberrations of your casuists have made no impression on you, let these last, by their very extravagance, compel you to abandon them. This is what I desire from the bottom of my heart, for your own sake and for the sake of your doctors; and my prayer to God is, that he would vouchsafe to convince them how false the light must be that has guided them to such precipices; and that he would fill their hearts with that love of himself from which they have dared to give man a dispensation!"

After some remarks of this nature, I took my leave of the monk, and I see no great likelihood of my repeating my visits to him. This, however, need not occasion you any regret; for, should it be necessary to continue these communications on their maxims, I have studied their books sufficiently to tell you as much of their morality, and more, perhaps, of their policy, than he could have done himself.—I am, &c.

TO THE REVEREND FATHERS,
THE JESUITS

*Ridicule a fair weapon when employed against absurd opinions—
rules to be observed in the use of this weapon—the profane buffoonery of Fathers Le Moine and Garasse*

August 18, 1656

REVEREND FATHERS,—I have seen the letters which you
are circulating in opposition to those which I wrote to one of
my friends on your morality; and I perceive that one of the
principal points of your defence is, that I have not spoken of
your maxims with sufficient seriousness. This charge you repeat in all your productions, and carry it so far as to allege,
that I have been "guilty of turning sacred things into ridicule."

Such a charge, fathers, is no less surprising than it is unfounded. Where do you find that I have turned sacred things
into ridicule? You specify "the Mohatra contract, and the
story of John d'Alba." But are these what you call "sacred
things?" Does it really appear to you that the Mohatra is
something so venerable that it would be blasphemy not to
speak of it with respect? And the lessons of Father Bauny
on larceny, which led John d'Alba to practise it at your expense, are they so sacred as to entitle you to stigmatize all
who laugh at them as profane people?

What, fathers! must the vagaries of your doctors pass for
the verities of the Christian faith, and no man be allowed to
ridicule Escobar, or the fantastical and unchristian dogmas

of your authors, without being stigmatized as jesting at religion? Is it possible you can have ventured to reiterate so often an idea so utterly unreasonable? Have you no fears that, in blaming me for laughing at your absurdities, you may only afford me fresh subject of merriment; that you may make the charge recoil on yourselves, by showing that I have really selected nothing from your writings as the matter of raillery, but what was truly ridiculous; and that thus, in making a jest of your morality, I have been as far from jeering at holy things, as the doctrine of your casuists is far from being the holy doctrine of the Gospel?

Indeed, reverend sirs, there is a vast difference between laughing at religion, and laughing at those who profane it by their extravagant opinions. It were impiety to be wanting in respect for the verities which the Spirit of God has revealed; but it were no less impiety of another sort, to be wanting in contempt for the falsities which the spirit of man opposes to them.

For, fathers (since you will force me into this argument), I beseech you to consider that, just in proportion as Christian truths are worthy of love and respect, the contrary errors must deserve hatred and contempt; there being two things in the truths of our religion—a divine beauty that renders them lovely, and a sacred majesty that renders them venerable; and two things also about errors—an impiety, that makes them horrible, and an impertinence that renders them ridiculous. For these reasons, while the saints have ever cherished towards the truth the twofold sentiment of love and fear—the whole of their wisdom being comprised between fear, which is its beginning, and love, which is its end—they have, at the same time, entertained towards error the twofold feeling of hatred and contempt, and their zeal has been at once employed to repel, by force of reasoning, the malice of the wicked, and to chastise, by the aid of ridicule, their extravagance and folly.

Do not then expect, fathers, to make people believe that it is unworthy of a Christian to treat error with derision. Nothing is easier than to convince all who were not aware of it before, that this practice is perfectly just—that it is common with the fathers of the Church, and that it is sanctioned by Scripture, by the example of the best of saints, and even by that of God himself.

Do we not find that God at once hates and despises sinners; so that even at the hour of death, when their condition is most sad and deplorable, Divine Wisdom adds mockery to the vengeance which consigns them to eternal punishment? *"In interitu vestro ridebo et subsannabo*—I will laugh at your calamity." The saints, too, influenced by the same feeling, will join in the derision; for, according to David, when they witness the punishment of the wicked, "they shall fear, and yet laugh at it—*videbunt justi et timebunt, et super eum ridebunt.*" And Job says: *"Innocens subsannabit eos*—The innocent shall laugh at them."

It is worthy of remark here, that the very first words which God addressed to man after his fall, contain, in the opinion of the fathers, "bitter irony" and mockery. After Adam had disobeyed his Maker, in the hope, suggested by the devil, of being like God, it appears from Scripture that God, as a punishment, subjected him to death; and after having reduced him to this miserable condition, which was due to his sin, he taunted him in that state with the following terms of derision: "Behold, the man has become as one of us!—*Ecce Adam quasi unus ex nobis!*"—which, according to St. Jerome and the interpreters, is "a grievous and cutting piece of irony," with which God "stung him to the quick." "Adam," says Rupert, "deserved to be taunted in this manner, and he would be naturally made to feel his folly more acutely by this ironical expression than by a more serious one." St. Victor, after making the same remark, adds, "that this irony was due to his sottish credulity, and that this species of raillery is an act of justice, merited by him against whom it was directed."

Thus you see, fathers, that ridicule is, in some cases, a very appropriate means of reclaiming men from their errors, and that it is accordingly an act of justice, because, as Jeremiah says, "the actions of those that err are worthy of derision, because of their vanity—*vana sunt et risu digna*." And so far from its being impious to laugh at them, St. Augustine holds it to be the effect of divine wisdom: "The wise laugh at the foolish, because they are wise, not after their own wisdom, but after that divine wisdom which shall laugh at the death of the wicked."

The prophets, accordingly, filled with the Spirit of God, have availed themselves of ridicule, as we find from the examples of Daniel and Elias. In short, examples of it are not wanting in the discourses of Jesus Christ himself. St. Augustine remarks that, when he would humble Nicodemus, who deemed himself so expert in his knowledge of the law, "perceiving him to be puffed up with pride, from his rank as doctor of the Jews, he first beats down his presumption by the magnitude of his demands, and having reduced him so low that he was unable to answer, What! says he, you a master in Israel, and not know these things!—as if he had said, Proud ruler, confess that thou knowest nothing." St. Chrysostom and St. Cyril likewise observe upon this, that "he deserved to be ridiculed in this manner."

You may learn from this, fathers, that should it so happen, in our day, that persons who enact the part of "masters" among Christians, as Nicodemus and the Pharisees did among the Jews, show themselves so ignorant of the first principles of religion as to maintain, for example, that "a man may be saved who never loved God all his life," we only follow the example of Jesus Christ, when we laugh at such a combination of ignorance and conceit.

I am sure, fathers, these sacred examples are sufficient to convince you, that to deride the errors and extravagances of man is not inconsistent with the practice of the saints; otherwise we must blame that of the greatest doctors of the Church, who have been guilty of it—such as St. Jerome, in his letters and writings against Jovinian, Vigilantius, and the Pelagians; Tertullian, in his Apology against the follies of idolaters; St. Augustine against the monks of Africa, whom he styles "the hairy men"; St. Irenæus the Gnostics; St. Bernard and the other fathers of the Church, who, having been the imitators of the apostles, ought to be imitated by the faithful in all time coming; for, say what we will, they are the true models for Christians, even of the present day.

In following such examples, I conceived that I could not go far wrong; and, as I think I have sufficiently established this position, I shall only add, in the admirable words of Tertullian, which give the true explanation of the whole of my proceeding in this matter: "What I have now done is only a little sport before the real combat. I have rather indicated the wounds that might be given you, than inflicted any. If the reader has met with passages which have excited his risibility, he must ascribe this to the subjects themselves. There are many things which deserve to be held up in this way to ridicule and mockery, lest, by a serious refutation, we should attach a weight to them which they do not deserve. Nothing is more due to vanity than laughter; and it is the Truth properly that has a right to laugh, because she is cheerful, and to make sport of her enemies, because she is sure of the victory. Care must be taken, indeed, that the raillery is not too low, and unworthy of the truth; but, keeping this in view, when ridicule may be employed with effect, it is a duty to avail ourselves of it." Do you not think fathers, that this passage is singularly applicable to our subject? The letters which I have hitherto written are "merely a little sport before a real combat." As yet I have been only playing with the foils, and "rather indicating the wounds that might be given you than inflicting any." I have merely exposed your passages to the light, without making scarcely a reflection on them. "If the reader has met with any that have excited his risibility, he must ascribe this to the subjects themselves." And, indeed, what is more fitted to raise a laugh, than to see a matter so grave as that of Christian morality decked out with fancies so grotesque as those in which you have exhibited it? One is apt to form such high anticipations of these maxims, from being told that "Jesus Christ himself has revealed them to the fathers of the Society," that when one discovers among them such absurdities as "that a priest receiving money to say a mass, may take additional sums from other persons by giving up to them his own share in the sacrifice"; "that a monk is not to be excommunicated for putting off his habit, provided it is to dance, swindle, or go incognito into infamous houses"; and "that the duty of hearing mass may be fulfilled by listening to four quarters of a mass at once from different priests"—when, I say, one listens to such decisions as these, the surprise is such that it is impossible to refrain from laughing; for nothing is more calculated to produce that emotion than a startling contrast between the thing looked for and the thing looked at. And why should the greater part of these maxims be treated in any other way? As Tertullian says, "To treat them seriously would be to sanction them."

What! is it necessary to bring up all the forces of Scripture and tradition, in order to prove that running a sword through a man's body, covertly and behind his back, is to murder him in treachery? or, that to give one money as a motive to resign a benefice, is to purchase the benefice? Yes, there are things which it is duty to despise, and which "deserve only to be laughed at." In short, the remark of that ancient author, "that nothing is more due to vanity than derision," with what follows, applies to the case before us so justly and so convincingly, as to put it beyond all question that we may laugh at errors without violating propriety.

And let me add, fathers, that this may be done without any breach of charity either, though this is another of the charges you bring against me in your publications. For, according to St. Augustine, "charity may sometimes oblige us to ridicule the errors of men, that they may be induced to laugh at them in their turn, and renounce them—*Hæc tu misericorditer irride, ut eis ridenda ac fugienda commendes.*" And the same charity may also, at other times, bind us to repel them with indignation, according to that other saying of St. Gregory of Nazianzen: "The spirit of meekness and charity hath its emotions and its heats." Indeed, as St. Augustine observes, "who would venture to say that truth ought to stand disarmed against falsehood, or that the enemies of the faith shall be at liberty to frighten the faithful with hard words, and jeer at them with lively sallies of wit; while the Catholics ought never to write except with a coldness of style enough to set the reader asleep?"

Is it not obvious that, by following such a course, a wide door would be opened for the introduction of the most extravagant and pernicious dogmas into the Church; while none would be allowed to treat them with contempt, through fear of being charged with violating propriety, or to confute them with indignation, from the dread of being taxed with want of charity?

Indeed, fathers! shall you be allowed to maintain, "that it is lawful to kill a man to avoid a box on the ear or an affront," and must nobody be permitted publicly to expose a public error of such consequence? Shall you be at liberty to say, "that a judge may in conscience retain a fee received for an act of injustice," and shall no one be at liberty to contradict you? Shall you print, with the privilege and approbation of your doctors, "that a man may be saved without ever having loved God"; and will you shut the mouth of those who defend the true faith, by telling them that they would violate brotherly love by attacking you, and Christian modesty by laughing at your maxims? I doubt, fathers, if there be any persons whom you could make believe this; if however, there be any such, who are really persuaded that, by denouncing your morality, I have been deficient in the charity which I owe to you, I would have them examine, with great jealousy, whence this feeling takes its rise within them. They may imagine that it proceeds from a holy zeal, which will not allow them to see their neighbor impeached without being scandalized at it; but I would entreat them to consider, that it is not impossible that it may flow from another source, and that it is even extremely likely that it may spring from that secret, and often self-concealed dissatisfaction, which the unhappy corruption within us seldom fails to stir up against those who oppose the relaxation of morals. And to furnish them with a rule which may enable them to ascertain the real principle from which it proceeds, I will ask them, if while they lament the way in which the religious have been treated, they lament still more the manner in which these religious have treated the truth. If they are incensed, not only against the letters, but still more against the maxims quoted in them. I shall grant it to be barely possible that their resentment proceeds from some zeal, though not of the most enlightened kind; and, in this case, the passages I have just cited from the fathers will serve to enlighten them. But if they are merely angry at the reprehension, and not at the things reprehended, truly, fathers, I shall never scruple to tell them that they are grossly mistaken, and that their zeal is miserably blind.

Strange zeal, indeed! which gets angry at those that censure public faults, and not at those that commit them! Novel charity this, which groans at seeing error confuted, but feels no grief at seeing morality subverted by that error. If these persons were in danger of being assassinated, pray, would they be offended at one advertising them of the stratagem that had been laid for them; and instead of turning out of their way to avoid it, would they trifle away their time in whining about the little charity manifested in discovering to them the criminal design of the assassins? Do they get waspish when one tells them not to eat such an article of food, because it is poisoned? or not to enter such a city, because it has the plague?

Whence comes it, then, that the same persons who set down a man as wanting in charity, for exposing maxims hurtful to religion, would, on the contrary, think him equally deficient in that grace were he not to disclose matters hurtful to health and life, unless it be from this, that their fondness for life induces them to take in good part every hint that contributes to its preservation, while their indifference to truth leads them, not only to take no share in its defence, but even to view with pain the efforts made for the extirpation of falsehood?

Let them seriously ponder, as in the sight of God, how shameful, and how prejudicial to the Church, is the morality which your casuists are in the habit of propagating; the scandalous and unmeasured license which they are introducing into public manners; the obstinate and violent hardihood with which you support them. And if they do not think it full time to rise against such disorders, their blindness is as much to be pitied as yours, fathers; and you and they have equal reason to dread that saying of St. Augustine, founded on the words of Jesus Christ, in the Gospel: "Woe to the blind leaders! woe to the blind followers!—*Væ cæcis ducentibus! væ cæcis sequentibus!*"

But to leave you no room in future, either to create such impressions on the minds of others, or to harbor them in your own, I shall tell you, fathers (and I am ashamed I should have to teach you what I should have rather learnt from you), the marks which the fathers of the Church have given for judging when our animadversions flow from a principle of piety and charity, and when from a spirit of malice and impiety.

The first of these rules is, that the spirit of piety always prompts us to speak with sincerity and truthfulness; whereas malice and envy make use of falsehood and calumny. *"Splendentia et vehementia, sed rebus veris*—Splendid and vehement in words, but true in things," as St. Augustine says. The dealer in falsehood is an agent of the devil. No direction of the intention can sanctify slander; and though the conversion of the whole earth should depend on it, no man may warrantably calumniate the innocent: because none may do the least evil, in order to accomplish the greatest good; and, as the Scripture says, "the truth of God stands in no need of our lie." St. Hilary observes, that "it is the bounden duty of the advocates of truth, to advance nothing in its support but true things." Now, fathers, I can declare before God, that there is nothing that I detest more than the slightest possible deviation from the truth, and that I have ever taken the greatest care, not only not to falsify (which would be horrible), but not to alter or wrest, in the slightest possible degree, the sense of a single passage. So closely have I adhered to this rule, that if I may presume to apply them to the present case, I may safely say, in the words of the same St. Hilary: "If we advance things that are false, let our statements be branded with infamy; but if we can show that they are public and notorious, it is no breach of apostolic modesty or liberty to expose them."

It is not enough, however, to tell nothing but the truth; we must not always tell everything that is true; we should publish only those things which it is useful to disclose, and not those which can only hurt, without doing any good. And, therefore, as the first rule is to speak with truth, the second is to speak with discretion. "The wicked," says St. Augustine, "in persecuting the good, blindly follow the dictates of their passion; but the good, in their prosecution of the wicked, are guided by a wise discretion, even as the surgeon warily considers where he is cutting, while the murderer cares not where he strikes." You must be sensible, fathers, that in selecting from the maxims of your authors, I have refrained from quoting those which would have galled you most, though I might have done it, and that without sinning against discretion, as others who were both learned and Catholic writers, have done before me. All who have read your authors know how far I have spared you in this respect. Besides, I have taken no notice whatever of what might be brought against individual characters among you; and I would have been extremely sorry to have said a word about secret and personal failings, whatever evidence I might have of them, being persuaded that this is the distinguishing property of malice, and a practice which ought never to be resorted to, unless where it is urgently demanded for the good of the Church. It is obvious, therefore, that in what I have been compelled to advance against your moral maxims, I have been by no means wanting in due consideration: and that you have more reason to congratulate yourself on my moderation than to complain of my indiscretion.

The third rule, fathers, is: That when there is need to employ a little raillery, the spirit of piety will take care to employ it against error only, and not against things holy; whereas the spirit of buffoonery, impiety, and heresy, mocks at all that is most sacred. I have already vindicated myself on that score; and indeed there is no great danger of falling into that vice so long as I confine my remarks to the opinions which I have quoted from your authors.

In short, fathers, to abridge these rules, I shall only mention another, which is the essence and the end of all the rest: That the spirit of charity prompts us to cherish in the heart a desire for the salvation of those against whom we dispute, and to address our prayers to God while we direct our accusations to men. "We ought ever," says St. Augustine, "to preserve charity in the heart, even while we are obliged to pursue a line of external conduct which to man has the appearance of harshness; we ought to smite them with a sharpness, severe but kindly, remembering that their advantage is more to be studied than their gratification." I am sure, fathers, that there is nothing in my letters, from which it can be inferred that I have not cherished such a desire towards you; and as you can find nothing to the contrary in them, charity obliges you to believe that I have been really actuated by it. It appears, then, that you cannot prove that I have offended against this rule, or against any of the other rules which charity inculcates; and you have no right to say, therefore, that I have violated it.

But, fathers, if you should now like to have the pleasure of seeing, within a short compass, a course of conduct directly at variance with each of these rules, and bearing the genuine stamp of the spirit of buffoonery, envy, and hatred, I shall give you a few examples of it; and that they may be of the sort best known and most familiar to you, I shall extract them from your own writings.

To begin, then, with the unworthy manner in which your

authors speak of holy things, whether in their sportive and gallant effusions, or in their more serious pieces, do you think that the parcel of ridiculous stories, which your father Binet has introduced into his "Consolation to the Sick," are exactly suitable to his professed object, which is that of imparting Christian consolation to those whom God has chastened with affliction? Will you pretend to say, that the profane, foppish style in which your Father Le Moine has talked of piety in his "Devotion made Easy," is more fitted to inspire respect than contempt for the picture that he draws of Christian virtues? What else does his whole book of "Moral Pictures" breathe, both in its prose and poetry, but a spirit full of vanity, and the follies of this world? Take, for example, that ode in his seventh book, entitled, "Eulogy on Bashfulness, showing that all beautiful things are red, or inclined to redden." Call you that a production worthy of a priest? The ode is intended to comfort a lady, called Delphina, who was sadly addicted to blushing. Each stanza is devoted to show that certain red things are the best of things, such as roses, pomegranates, the mouth, the tongue; and it is in the midst of this badinage, so disgraceful in a clergyman, that he has the effrontery to introduce those blessed spirits that minister before God, and of whom no Christian should speak without reverence:—

> "The cherubim—those glorious choirs—
>   Composed of head and plumes,
> Whom God with his own Spirit inspires,
>   And with his eyes illumes.
> These splendid faces, as they fly,
> Are ever red and burning high,
> With fire angelic or divine;
> And while their mutual flames combine,
> The waving of their wings supplies
> A fan to cool their ecstasies!
> But redness shines with better grace,
> Delphina, on thy beauteous face,
> Where modesty sits revelling—
> Arrayed in purple, like a king," &c.

What think you of this, fathers? Does this preference of the blushes of Delphina to the ardor of those spirits, which is neither more nor less than the ardor of divine love, and this simile of the fan applied to their mysterious wings, strike you as being very Christian-like in the lips which consecrate the adorable body of Jesus Christ? I am quite aware that he speaks only in the character of a gallant, and to raise a smile; but this is precisely what is called laughing at things holy. And is it not certain, that, were he to get full justice, he could not save himself from incurring a censure? although, to shield himself from this, he pleads an excuse which is hardly less censurable than the offence, "that the Sorbonne has no jurisdiction over Parnassus, and that the errors of that land are subject neither to censure nor the Inquisition";—as if one could act the blasphemer and profane fellow only in prose! There is another passage, however, in the preface, where even this excuse fails him, when he says, "that the water of the river, on whose banks he composes his verses, is so apt to make poets, that, though it were converted into *holy water,* it would not chase away the demon of poesy." To match this, I may add the following flight of your Father Garasse, in his "Summary of the Capital Truths in Religion," where, speaking of the sacred mystery of the incarnation, he mixes up blasphemy and heresy in this fashion: "The human personality was grafted, as it were, or *set on horseback,* upon the personality of the Word!" And omitting many others, I might mention another passage from the same author, who, speaking on the subject of the name of Jesus, ordinarily written thus, I. H. S. observes that "some have taken away the cross from the top of it, leaving the characters barely thus, I. H. S.—which," says he, "is a stripped Jesus!"

Such is the indecency with which you treat the truths of religion, in the face of the inviolable law which binds us always to speak of them with reverence. But you have sinned no less flagrantly against the rule which obliges us to speak of them with truth and discretion. What is more common in your writings than calumny? Can those of Father Brisacier be called sincere? Does he speak with truth when he says, that "the nuns of Port-Royal do not pray to the saints, and have no images in their church?" Are not these most outrageous falsehoods, when the contrary appears before the eyes of all Paris? And can he be said to speak with discretion, when he stabs the fair reputation of these virgins, who lead a life so pure and austere, representing them as "impenitent, unsacramentalists, uncommunicants, foolish virgins, visionaries, Calagans, desperate creatures, and anything you please," loading them with many other slanders, which have justly incurred the censure of the late Archbishop of Paris? Or when he calumniates priests of the most irreproachable morals, by asserting "that they practise novelties in confession, to entrap handsome innocent females, and that he would be horrified to tell the abominable crimes which they commit." Is it not a piece of intolerable assurance, to advance slanders so black and base, not merely without proof, but without the slightest shadow, or the most distant semblance of truth? I shall not enlarge on this topic, but defer it to a future occasion, for I have something more to say to you about it; but what I have now produced is enough to show that you have sinned at once against truth and discretion.

But it may be said, perhaps, that you have not offended against the last rule at least, which binds you to desire the salvation of those whom you denounce, and that none can charge you with this, except by unlocking the secrets of your breasts, which are only known to God. It is strange, fathers, but true, nevertheless, that we can convict you even of this offence; that while your hatred to your opponents has carried you so far as to wish their eternal perdition, your infatuation has driven you to discover the abominable wish, that so far from cherishing in secret desires for their salvation, you have offered up prayers in public for their damnation; and that, after having given utterance to that hideous vow in the city of Caen, to the scandal of the whole Church, you have since then ventured, in Paris, to vindicate, in your printed books, the diabolical transaction. After such gross offences against piety, first ridiculing and speaking lightly of things the most sacred; next falsely and scandalously calumniating priests and virgins; and lastly, forming desires and prayers for their damnation, it would be difficult to add anything worse. I cannot conceive, fathers, how you can fail to be ashamed of yourselves, or how you could have thought for an instant of charging me with a want of charity, who have acted all along with so much truth and moderation, without reflecting on your own horrid violations of charity, manifested in those deplorable exhibitions, which make the charge recoil against yourselves.

In fine, fathers, to conclude with another charge which you bring against me, I see you complain that among the vast number of your maxims which I quote, there are some which have been objected to already, and that I "say over again, what others have said before me." To this I reply, that it is just because you have not profited by what has been said before, that I say it over again. Tell me now what fruit has appeared from all the castigations you have received in all the books written by learned doctors, and even the whole University? What more have your fathers Annat, Caussin, Pintereau, and Le Moine done, in the replies they have put forth, except loading with reproaches those who had given them salutary admonitions? Have you suppressed the books in which these nefarious maxims are taught? Have you restrained the authors of these maxims? Have you become more circumspect in regard to them? On the contrary, is it not the fact, that since that time Escobar has been repeatedly reprinted in France and in the Low Countries, and that your fathers Cellot, Bagot, Bauny, Lamy, Le Moine, and others, persist in publishing daily the same maxims over again, or new ones as licentious as ever? Let us hear no more complaints, then, fathers, either because I have charged you with maxims which you have not disavowed, or because I have objected to some new ones against you, or because I have laughed equally at them all. You have only to sit down and look at them, to see at once your own confusion and my defence. Who can look without laughing at the decision of Bauny, respecting the person who employs another to set fire to his neighbor's barn; that of Cellot on restitution; the rule of Sanchez in favor of sorcerers; the plan of Hurtado for avoiding the sin of duelling by taking a walk through a field, and waiting for a man; the compliments of Bauny for escaping usury; the way of avoiding simony by a detour of the intention, and keeping clear of falsehood by speaking high and low; and such other opinions of your most grave and reverend doctors? Is there anything more necessary, fathers, for my vindication? And as Tertullian says, "can anything be more justly due to the vanity and weakness of these opinions than laughter?" But, fathers, the corruption of manners to which your maxims lead, deserves another sort of consideration; and it becomes us to ask, with the same ancient writer, "Whether ought we to laugh at their folly, or deplore their blindness?—*Rideam vanitatem, an exprobrem cæcitatem?*" My humble opinion is, that one may either laugh at them or weep over them, as one is in the humor. *Hæc tolerabilius vel ridentur, vel flentur,* as St. Augustine says. The Scripture tells us that "there is a time to laugh, and a time to weep;" and my hope is, fathers, that I may not find verified, in your case, these words in the Proverbs: "If a wise man contendeth with a foolish man, whether he rage or laugh, there is no rest."

P. S.—On finishing this letter, there was put in my hands one of your publications, in which you accuse me of falsification, in the case of six of your maxims quoted by me, and also with being in correspondence with heretics. You will shortly receive, I trust, a suitable reply; after which, fathers, I rather think you will not feel very anxious to continue this species of warfare.

TO THE REVEREND FATHERS, THE JESUITS

Refutation of their chicaneries regarding alms-giving and simony

September 9, 1656

REVEREND FATHERS,—I was prepared to write you on the subject of the abuse with which you have for some time past been assailing me in your publications, in which you salute me with such epithets as "reprobate," "buffoon," "blockhead," "merry-Andrew," "impostor," "slanderer," "cheat," "heretic," "Calvinist in disguise," "disciple of Du Moulin," "possessed with a legion of devils," and everything else you can think of. As I should be sorry to have all this believed of me, I was anxious to show the public why you treated me in this manner; and I had resolved to complain of your calumnies and falsifications, when I met with your Answers, in which you bring these same charges against myself. This will compel me to alter my plan; though it will not prevent me from prosecuting it in some sort, for I hope, while defending myself, to convict you of impostures more genuine than the imaginary ones which you have ascribed to me. Indeed, fathers, the suspicion of foul play is much more sure to rest on you than on me. It is not very likely, standing as I do, alone, without power or any human defence, against such a large body, and having no support but truth and integrity, that I would expose myself to lose everything, by laying myself open to be convicted of imposture. It is too easy to discover falsifications in matters of fact such as the present.

483

In such a case there would have been no want of persons to accuse me, nor would justice have been denied them. With you, fathers, the case is very different; you may say as much as you please against me, while I may look in vain for any to complain to. With such a wide difference between our positions, though there had been no other consideration to restrain me, it became me to study no little caution. By treating me, however, as a common slanderer, you compel me to assume the defensive, and you must be aware that this cannot be done without entering into a fresh exposition, and even into a fuller disclosure of the points of your morality. In provoking this discussion, I fear you are not acting as good politicians. The war must be waged within your own camp, and at your own expense; and although you imagine that, by embroiling the questions with scholastic terms, the answers will be so tedious, thorny, and obscure, that people will lose all relish for the controversy, this may not, perhaps, turn out to be exactly the case; I shall use my best endeavors to tax your patience as little as possible with that sort of writing. Your maxims have something diverting about them, which keeps up the good humor of people to the last. At all events, remember that it is you that oblige me to enter upon this *eclaircissement*, and let us see which of us comes off best in self-defence.

The first of your Impostures, as you call them, is on the opinion of Vasquez upon alms-giving. To avoid all ambiguity, then, allow me to give a simple explanation of the matter in dispute. It is well known, fathers, that according to the mind of the Church, there are two precepts touching alms— 1st, "To give out of our superfluity in the case of the ordinary necessities of the poor;" and 2dly, "To give even out of our necessaries, according to our circumstances, in cases of extreme necessity." Thus says Cajetan, after St. Thomas; so that, to get at the mind of Vasquez on this subject, we must consider the rules he lays down, both in regard to necessaries and superfluities:

With regard to superfluity, which is the most common

source of relief to the poor, it is entirely set aside by that single maxim which I have quoted in my Letters: "That what the men of the world keep with the view of improving their own condition and that of their relatives, is not properly superfluity; so that, such a thing as superfluity is rarely to be met with among men of the world, not even excepting kings." It is very easy to see, fathers, that according to this definition, none can have superfluity, provided they have ambition; and thus, so far as the greater part of the world is concerned, alms-giving is annihilated. But even though a man should happen to have superfluity, he would be under no obligation, according to Vasquez, to give it away in the case of ordinary necessity; for he protests against those who would thus bind the rich. Here are his own words: "Corduba," says he, "teaches, that when we have a superfluity we are bound to give out of it in cases of ordinary necessity; but *this does not please me—sed hoc non placet—*for we have demonstrated the contrary against Cajetan and Navarre." So, fathers, the obligation to this kind of alms is wholly set aside, according to the good pleasure of Vasquez.

With regard to necessaries, out of which we are bound to give in cases of extreme and urgent necessity, it must be obvious, from the conditions by which he has limited the obligation, that the richest man in all Paris may not come within its reach once in a lifetime. I shall only refer to two of these. The first is, That *"we must know* that the poor man cannot be relieved from any other quarter—*hæc intelligo et cætera omnia, quando* SCIO *nullum alium opem laturum."* What say you to this, fathers? Is it likely to happen frequently in Paris, where there are so many charitable people, that I *must know* that there is not another soul but myself, to relieve the poor wretch who begs an alms from me? And yet, according to Vasquez, if I have not ascertained that fact, I may send him away with nothing. The second condition is, That the poor man be reduced to such straits "that he is menaced with some fatal accident, or the ruin of his character"—none of them very common occurrences. But what marks still more the rarity of the cases in which one is bound to give charity, is his remark, in another passage, that the poor man must be so ill off, "that he may conscientiously rob the rich man!" This must surely be a very extraordinary case, unless he will insist that a man may be ordinarily allowed to commit robbery. And so, after having cancelled the obligation to give alms out of our superfluities, he obliges the rich to relieve the poor only in those cases when he would allow the poor to rifle the rich! Such is the doctrine of Vasquez, to whom you refer your readers for their edification!

I now come to your pretended Impostures. You begin by enlarging on the obligation to alms-giving which Vasquez imposes on ecclesiastics. But on this point I have said nothing; and I am prepared to take it up whenever you choose. This, then, has nothing to do with the present question. As for laymen, who are the only persons with whom we have now to do, you are apparently anxious to have it understood that, in the passage which I quoted, Vasquez is giving not his own judgment, but that of Cajetan. But as nothing could be more false than this, and as you have not said it in so many terms, I am willing to believe, for the sake of your character, that you did not intend to say it.

You next loudly complain that, after quoting that maxim of Vasquez, "Such a thing as superfluity is rarely if ever to be met with among men of the world, not excepting kings," *I have inferred* from it, "that the rich are rarely, if ever, bound to give alms out of their superfluity." But what do you mean to say, fathers? If it be true that the rich have almost never superfluity, is it not obvious that they will almost never be bound to give alms out of their superfluity? I might have put it into the form of a syllogism for you, if Diana, who has such an esteem for Vasquez that he calls him "the phœnix of genius," had not drawn the same conclusion from the same premises; for, after quoting the maxim of Vasquez, he concludes, "that, with regard to the question, whether the rich are obliged to give alms out of their superfluity, though the affirmation were true, it would seldom, or almost never, happen to be obligatory in practice." I have followed this language word for word. What, then, are we to make of this, fathers? When Diana quotes with approbation the sentiments of Vasquez—when he finds them probable, and "very convenient for rich people," as he says in the same place, he is no slanderer, no falsifier, and we hear no complaints of misrepresenting his author; whereas, when I cite the same sentiments of Vasquez, though without holding him up as a phœnix, I am a slanderer, a fabricator, a corrupter of his maxims. Truly, fathers, you have some reason to be apprehensive, lest your very different treatment of those who agree in their representation, and differ only in their estimate of your doctrine, discover the real secret of your hearts, and provoke the conclusion, that the main object you have in view is to maintain the credit and glory of your Company. It appears that, provided your accommodating theology is treated as judicious complaisance, you never disavow those that publish it, but laud them as contributing to your design; but let it be held forth as pernicious laxity, and the same interest of your Society prompts you to disclaim the maxims which would injure you in public estimation. And thus you recognize or renounce them, not according to the truth, which never changes, but according to the shifting exigencies of the times, acting on that motto of one of the ancients, *"Omnia pro tempore, nihil pro veritate*—Anything for the times, nothing for the truth." Beware of this, fathers; and that you may never have it in your power again to say that I drew from the principle of Vasquez a conclusion which he had disavowed, I beg to inform you that he has drawn it himself: "According to the opinion of Cajetan, and according to MY OWN—*et secundum nostram*—(he says, chap. i., no. 27), one is hardly obliged to give alms at all, when one is only obliged to give them out of one's superfluity." Confess then, fathers, on the testimony of Vasquez himself, that I have exactly copied his sentiment; and think how you could have the conscience to say, that "the reader, on consulting the original, would see to his astonishment, that he there teaches the very reverse!"

In fine, you insist, above all, that if Vasquez does not bind the rich to give alms out of their superfluity, he obliges them to atone for this by giving out of the necessaries of life. But you have forgotten to mention the list of conditions which he declares to be essential to constitute that obligation, which I have quoted, and which restrict it in such a way as almost entirely to annihilate it. In place of giving this honest statement of his doctrine, you tell us, in general terms, that he obliges the rich to give even what is necessary to their condition. This is proving too much, fathers; the rule of the Gospel does not go so far; and it would be an error, into which Vasquez is very far, indeed, from having fallen. To cover his laxity, you attribute to him an excess of severity which would be reprehensible; and thus you lose all credit as faithful reporters of his sentiments. But the truth is, Vasquez is quite free from any such suspicion; for he has maintained, as I have shown, that the rich are not bound, either in justice or in charity, to give of their superfluities, and still less of their necessaries, to relieve the ordinary wants of the poor; and that they are not obliged to give of the necessaries, except in cases so rare that they almost never happen.

Having disposed of your objections against me on this head, it only remains to show the falsehood of your assertion, that Vasquez is more severe than Cajetan. This will be very easily done. That cardinal teaches "that we are bound in justice to give alms out of our superfluity, even in the ordinary wants of the poor; because, according to the holy fathers, the rich are merely the dispensers of their superfluity, which they are to give to whom they please, among those who have need of it." And accordingly, unlike Diana, who says of the maxims of Vasquez, that they will be "very convenient and agreeable to the rich and their confessors," the cardinal, who has no such consolation to afford them, declares that he has nothing to say to the rich but these words of Jesus Christ: "It is easier for a camel to go through the eye of a needle,

than for a rich man to enter into heaven;" and to their confessors: "If the blind lead the blind, both shall fall into the
ditch." So indispensable did he deem this obligation! This,
too, is what the fathers and all the saints have laid down as
a certain truth. "There are two cases," says St. Thomas, "in
which we are bound to give alms as a matter of justice—*ex
debito legali:* one, when the poor are in danger; the other,
when we possess superfluous property." And again: "The
three-tenths which the Jews were bound to eat with the poor,
have been augmented under the new law; for Jesus Christ
wills that we give to the poor, not the tenth only, but the
whole of our superfluity." And yet it does not seem good to
Vasquez that we should be obliged to give even a fragment of
our superfluity; such is his complaisance to the rich, such his
hardness to the poor, such his opposition to those feelings of
charity which teach us to relish the truth contained in the
following words of St. Gregory, harsh as it may sound to the
rich of this world: "When we give the poor what is necessary
to them, we are not so much bestowing on them what is our
property, as rendering to them what is their own; and it may
be said to be an act of justice, rather than a work of mercy."

It is thus that the saints recommend the rich to share with
the poor the good things of this earth, if they would expect
to possess with them the good things of heaven. While you
make it your business to foster in the breasts of men that
ambition which leaves no superfluity to dispose of, and that
avarice which refuses to part with it, the saints have labored
to induce the rich to give up their superfluity, and to convince
them that they would have abundance of it, provided they
measured it, not by the standard of covetousness, which
knows no bounds to its cravings, but by that of piety, which
is ingenious in retrenchments, so as to have wherewith to
diffuse itself in the exercise of charity. "We will have a great
deal of superfluity," says St. Augustine, "if we keep only
what is necessary: but if we seek after vanities, we will never
have enough. Seek, brethren, what is sufficient for the work
of God"—that is, for nature—"and not for what is sufficient

for your covetousness," which is the work of the devil: "and remember that the superfluities of the rich are the necessaries of the poor."

I would fondly trust, fathers, that what I have now said to you may serve, not only for my vindication—that were a small matter—but also to make you feel and detest what is corrupt in the maxims of your casuists, and thus unite us sincerely under the sacred rules of the Gospel, according to which we must all be judged.

As to the second point, which regards simony, before proceeding to answer the charges you have advanced against me, I shall begin by illustrating your doctrine on this subject. Finding yourselves placed in an awkward dilemma, between the canons of the Church, which impose dreadful penalties upon simoniacs, on the one hand, and the avarice of many who pursue this infamous traffic on the other, you have recourse to your ordinary method, which is to yield to men what they desire, and give the Almighty only words and shows. For what else does the simoniac want, but money, in return for his benefice? And yet this is what you exempt from the charge of simony. And as the name of simony must still remain standing, and a subject to which it may be ascribed, you have substituted, in the place of this, an imaginary idea, which never yet crossed the brain of a simoniac, and would not serve him much though it did—the idea, namely, that simony lies in estimating the money considered in itself as highly as the spiritual gift or office considered in itself. Who would ever take it into his head to compare things so utterly disproportionate and heterogeneous? And yet, provided this metaphysical comparison be not drawn, any one may, according to your authors, give away a benefice, and receive money in return for it, without being guilty of simony.

Such is the way in which you sport with religion, in order to gratify the worst passions of men; and yet only see with what gravity your Father Valentia delivers his rhapsodies in the passage cited in my letters. He says: "One may give a spiritual for a temporal good in two ways—first, in the way of prizing the temporal more than the spiritual, and that would be simony; secondly, in the way of taking the temporal as the motive and end inducing one to give away the spiritual, but without prizing the temporal more than the spiritual, and then it is not simony. And the reason is, that simony consists in receiving something temporal, as the just price of what is spiritual. If, therefore, the temporal is sought —*si petatur temporale*—not as the *price,* but only as the *motive* determining us to part with the spiritual, it is by no means simony, even although the possession of the temporal may be principally intended and expected—*minime erit simonia, etiamsi temporale principaliter intendatur et expectetur.*" Your redoubtable Sanchez has been favored with a similar revelation; Escobar quotes him thus: "If one give a spiritual for a temporal good, not as the *price,* but as a *motive* to induce the collator to give it, or as an *acknowledgment* if the benefice has been actually received, is that simony? Sanchez assures us that it is not." In your Caen Theses of 1644, you say: "It is a probable opinion, taught by many Catholics, that it is not simony to exchange a temporal for a spiritual good, when the former is not given as a price." And as to Tanner, here is his doctrine, exactly the same with that of Valentia; and I quote it again to show you how far wrong it is in you to complain of me for saying that it does not agree with that of St. Thomas, for he avows it himself in the very passage which I quoted in my letter: "There is properly and truly no simony," says he, "unless when a temporal good is taken as the price of a spiritual; but when taken merely as the motive for giving the spiritual, or as an acknowledgment for having received it, this is not simony, at least in point of conscience." And again: "The same thing may be said although the temporal should be regarded as the principal end, and even preferred to the spiritual; although St. Thomas and others appear to hold the reverse, inasmuch as they maintain it to be downright simony to exchange a spiritual for a temporal good, when the temporal is the end of the transaction."

Such, then, being your doctrine on simony, as taught by

your best authors, who follow each other very closely in this point, it only remains now to reply to your charges of misrepresentation. You have taken no notice of Valentia's opinion, so that his doctrine stands as it was before. But you fix on that of Tanner, maintaining that he has merely decided it to be no simony by divine right; and you would have it to be believed that, in quoting the passage, I have suppressed these words, *divine right*. This, fathers, is a most unconscionable trick; for these words, *divine right*, never existed in that passage. You add that Tanner declares it to be simony according to *positive right*. But you are mistaken; he does not say that generally, but only of particular cases, or, as he expresses it, *in casibus a jure expressis,* by which he makes an exception to the general rule he had laid down in that passage, "that it is not simony in point of conscience," which must imply that it is not so in point of positive right, unless you would have Tanner made so impious as to maintain that simony, in point of positive right, is not simony in point of conscience. But it is easy to see your drift in mustering up such terms as "divine right, positive right, natural right, internal and external tribunal, expressed cases, outward presumption," and others equally little known; you mean to escape under this obscurity of language, and make us lose sight of your aberrations. But, fathers, you shall not escape by these vain artifices; for I shall put some questions to you so simple, that they will not admit of coming under your *distinguo*.

I ask you, then, without speaking of "positive rights," of "outward presumptions," or "external tribunals"—I ask if, according to your authors, a beneficiary would be simoniacal, were he to give a benefice worth four thousand livres of yearly rent, and to receive ten thousand francs ready money, not as the price of the benefice, but merely as a motive inducing him to give it? Answer me plainly, fathers: What must we make of such a case as this according to your authors? Will not Tanner tell us decidedly that "this is not simony in point of conscience, seeing that the temporal good is not the price of the benefice, but only the motive inducing to dispose of it?"

Will not Valentia, will not your own Theses of Caen, will not Sanchez and Escobar agree in the same decision, and give the same reason for it? Is anything more necessary to exculpate that beneficiary from simony? And, whatever might be your private opinion of the case, durst you deal with that man as a simonist in your confessionals, when he would be entitled to stop your mouth by telling you that he acted according to the advice of so many grave doctors? Confess candidly, then, that, according to your views, that man would be no simonist; and, having done so, defend the doctrine as you best can.

Such, fathers, is the true mode of treating questions, in order to unravel, instead of perplexing them, either by scholastic terms, or, as you have done in your last charge against me here, by altering the state of the question. Tanner, you say, has, at any rate, declared that such an exchange is a great sin; and you blame me for having maliciously suppressed this circumstance, which, you maintain, *"completely justifies him."* But you are wrong again, and that in more ways than one. For, first, though what you say had been true, it would be nothing to the point, the question in the passage to which I referred being, not if it was *sin,* but if it was *simony.* Now, these are two very different questions. Sin, according to your maxims, obliges only to confession—simony obliges to restitution; and there are people to whom these may appear two very different things. You have found expedients for making confession a very easy affair; but you have not fallen upon ways and means to make restitution an agreeable one. Allow me to add, that the case which Tanner charges with sin, is not simply that in which a spiritual good is exchanged for a temporal, the latter being the principal end in view, but that in which the party "prizes the temporal above the spiritual," which is the imaginary case already spoken of. And it must be allowed he could not go far wrong in charging such a case as that with sin, since that man must be either very wicked or very stupid who, when permitted to exchange the one thing for the other, would not avoid the sin of the transaction by such a simple process as that of abstaining from comparing the two things together. Besides, Valentia, in the place quoted, when treating the question, if it be sinful to give a spiritual good for a temporal, the latter being the main consideration, and after producing the reasons given for the affirmative, adds, *"Sed hoc non videtur mihi satis certum*—But this does not appear to my mind sufficiently certain."

Since that time, however, your father, Erade Bille, professor of cases of conscience at Caen, has decided that there is no sin at all in the case supposed; for probable opinions, you know, are always in the way of advancing to maturity. This opinion he maintains in his writings of 1644, against which M. Dupré, doctor and professor at Caen, delivered that excellent oration, since printed and well known. For though this Erade Bille confesses that Valentia's doctrine, adopted by Father Milhard, and condemned by the Sorbonne, "is contrary to the common opinion, suspected of simony, and punishable at law when discovered in practice," he does not scruple to say that it is a probable opinion, and consequently sure in point of conscience, and that there is neither simony nor sin in it. "It is a probable opinion," he says, "taught by many Catholic doctors, that there is neither any simony *nor any sin* in giving money, or any other temporal thing, for a benefice, either in the way of acknowledgment, or as a motive, without which it would not be given, provided it is not given as a price equal to the benefice." This is all that could possibly be desired. In fact, according to these maxims of yours, simony would be so exceedingly rare, that we might exempt from this sin even Simon Magus himself, who desired to purchase the Holy Spirit, and is the emblem of those simonists that buy spiritual things; and Gehazi, who took money for a miracle, and may be regarded as the prototype of the simonists that sell them. There can be no doubt that when Simon, as we read in the Acts, "offered the apostles money, saying, Give me also this power;" he said nothing about buying or selling, or fixing the price; he did no more than offer the money as a motive to induce them to give him that spiritual gift; which being, according to you, no simony at all, he might, had he but been instructed in your maxims, have escaped the anathema of St. Peter. The same unhappy ignorance was a great loss to Gehazi, when he was struck with leprosy by Elisha; for, as he accepted the money from the prince who had been miraculously cured, simply as an acknowledgment, and not as a price equivalent to the divine virtue which had effected the miracle, he might have insisted on the prophet healing him again on pain of mortal sin; seeing, on this supposition, he would have acted according to the advice of your grave doctors, who, in such cases, oblige confessors to absolve their penitents, and to wash them from that spiritual leprosy of which the bodily disease is the type.

Seriously, fathers, it would be extremely easy to hold you up to ridicule in this matter, and I am at a loss to know why you expose yourselves to such treatment. To produce this effect, I have nothing more to do than simply to quote Escobar, in his "Practice of Simony according to the Society of Jesus;" "Is it simony when two Churchmen become mutually pledged thus: Give me your vote for my election as Provincial, and I shall give you mine for your election as prior? By no means." Or take another: "It is not simony to get possession of a benefice by promising a sum of money, when one has no intention of actually paying the money; for this is merely making a show of simony, and is as far from being real simony as counterfeit gold is from the genuine." By this quirk of conscience, he has contrived means, in the way of adding swindling to simony, for obtaining benefices without simony and without money.

But I have no time to dwell longer on the subject, for I must say a word or two in reply to your third accusation, which refers to the subject of bankrupts. Nothing can be more gross than the manner in which you have managed this charge. You rail at me as a libeller in reference to a sentiment of Lessius, which I did not quote myself, but took from a passage in Escobar; and therefore, though it were true that Lessius does not hold the opinion ascribed to him by Escobar, what can be more unfair than to charge me with the misrepresentation? When I quote Lessius or others of your authors myself, I am quite prepared to answer for it; but as Escobar has collected the opinions of twenty-four of your writers, I beg to ask, if I am bound to guarantee anything beyond the correctness of my citations from his book? Or if I must, in addition, answer for the fidelity of all his quotations of which I may avail myself? This would be hardly reasonable; and yet this is precisely the case in the question before us. I produced in my letter the following passage from Escobar, and you do not object to the fidelity of my translation: "May the bankrupt, with a good conscience, retain as much of his property as is necessary to afford him an honorable maintenance—*nè indecore vivat?* I answer, with Lessius, that he may—*cum Lessio assero posse.*" You tell me that Lessius does not hold that opinion. But just consider for a moment the predicament in which you involve yourselves. If it turns out that he does hold that opinion, you will be set down as impostors for having asserted the contrary; and if it is proved that he does not hold it, Escobar will be the impostor; so it must now of necessity follow, that one or other of the Society will be convicted of imposture. Only think what a scandal! You cannot, it would appear, foresee the consequences of things. You seem to imagine that you have nothing more to do than to cast aspersions upon people, without considering on whom they may recoil. Why did you not acquaint Escobar with your objection before venturing to publish it? He might have given you satisfaction. It is not so very troublesome to get word from Valladolid, where he is living in perfect health, and completing his grand work on Moral Theology, in six volumes, on the first of which I mean to say a few words by-and-by. They have sent him the first ten letters; you might as easily have sent him your objection, and I am sure he would have soon returned you an answer, for he has doubtless seen in Lessius the passage from which he took the *ne indecore vivat.* Read him yourselves, fathers, and you will find it word for word, as I have done. Here it is: "The same thing is apparent from the authorities cited, particularly in regard to that property which he acquires after his failure, out of which even the delinquent debtor may retain as much as is necessary for his honorable maintenance, according to his station of life—*ut non indecore vivat*. Do you ask if this rule applies to goods which he possessed at the time of his failure? Such seems to be the judgment of the doctors."

I shall not stop here to show how Lessius, to sanction his maxim, perverts the law that allows bankrupts nothing more than a mere livelihood, and that makes no provision for "honorable maintenance." It is enough to have vindicated Escobar from such an accusation—it is more, indeed, than what I was in duty bound to do. But you, fathers, have not done your duty. It still remains for you to answer the passage of Escobar, whose decisions, by the way, have this advantage, that being entirely independent of the context, and condensed in little articles, they are not liable to your distinctions. I quoted the whole of the passage, in which "bankrupts are permitted to keep their goods, though unjustly acquired, to provide an honorable maintenance for their families"—commenting on which in my letters, I exclaim: "Indeed, father! by what strange kind of charity would you have the ill-gotten property of a bankrupt appropriated to his own use, instead of that of his lawful creditors?" This is the question which must be answered; but it is one that involves you in a sad dilemma, and from which you in vain seek to escape by altering the state of the question, and quoting other passages from Lessius, which have no connection with the subject. I ask you, then, May this maxim of Escobar be followed by bankrupts with a safe conscience, or no? And take care what you say. If you answer, no, what becomes of your doctor, and your doctrine of probability? If you say, yes—I delate you to the Parliament.

In this predicament I must now leave you, fathers; for my limits will not permit me to overtake your next accusation, which respects homicide. This will serve for my next letter, and the rest will follow.

In the meanwhile, I shall make no remarks on the advertisements which you have tagged to the end of each of your charges, filled as they are with scandalous falsehoods. I mean to answer all these in a separate letter, in which I hope to show the weight due to your calumnies. I am sorry, fathers, that you should have recourse to such desperate resources. The abusive terms which you heap on me will not clear up our disputes, nor will your manifold threats hinder me from defending myself. You think you have power and impunity on your side; and I think I have truth and innocence on mine. It is a strange and tedious war, when violence attempts to vanquish truth. All the efforts of violence cannot weaken truth, and only serve to give it fresh vigor. All the lights of truth cannot arrest violence, and only serve to exasperate it. When force meets force, the weaker must succumb to the stronger; when argument is opposed to argument, the solid and the convincing triumphs over the empty and the false; but violence and verity can make no impression on each other. Let none suppose, however, that the two are, therefore, equal to each other; for there is this vast difference between them, that violence has only a certain course to run, limited by the appointment of Heaven, which overrules its effects to the glory of the truth which it assails; whereas verity endures forever, and eventually triumphs over its enemies, being eternal and almighty as God himself.

TO THE REVEREND FATHERS OF THE SOCIETY OF JESUS

The doctrine of Lessius on homicide the same with that of Valentia—how easy it is to pass from speculation to practice —why the Jesuits have recourse to this distinction, and how little it serves for their vindication

September 30, 1656

REVEREND FATHERS,—I have just seen your last production, in which you have continued your list of Impostures up to the twentieth, and intimate that you mean to conclude with this the first part of your accusations against me, and to proceed to the second, in which you are to adopt a new mode of defence, by showing that there are other casuists besides those of your Society who are as lax as yourselves. I now see the precise number of charges to which I have to reply; and as the fourth, to which we have now come, relates to homicide, it may be proper, in answering it, to include the 11th, 13th, 14th, 15th, 16th, 17th, and 18th, which refer to the same subject.

In the present letter, therefore, my object shall be to vindicate the correctness of my quotations from the charges of falsity which you bring against me. But as you have ventured, in your pamphlets, to assert that "the sentiments of your authors on murder are agreeable to the decisions of popes and ecclesiastical laws," you will compel me, in my next letter, to confute a statement at once so unfounded and so injurious to the Church. It is of some importance to show that she is innocent of your corruptions, in order that heretics may be prevented from taking advantage of your aberrations, to draw conclusions tending to her dishonor. And thus, viewing on the one hand your pernicious maxims, and on the other the canons of the Church which have uniformly condemned them, people will see, at one glance, what they should shun and what they should follow.

Your fourth charge turns on a maxim relating to murder, which you say I have falsely ascribed to Lessius. It is as follows: "That if a man has received a buffet, he may immediately pursue his enemy, and even return the blow with the sword, not to avenge himself, but to retrieve his honor." This, you say, is the opinion of the casuist Victoria. But this is nothing to the point. There is no inconsistency in saying that it is at once the opinion of Victoria and of Lessius; for Lessius himself says that it is also held by Navarre and Henriquez, who teach identically the same doctrine. The only question, then, is, if Lessius holds this view as well as his brother casuists. You maintain "that Lessius quotes this opinion solely for the purpose of refuting it, and that I therefore attribute to him a sentiment which he produces only to overthrow—the basest and most disgraceful act of which a writer can be guilty." Now I maintain, fathers, that he quotes the opinion solely for the purpose of supporting it. Here is a question of fact, which it will be very easy to settle. Let us see, then, how you prove your allegation, and you will see afterwards how I prove mine.

To show that Lessius' is not of that opinion, you tell us that he condemns the practice of it; and in proof of this, you quote one passage of his (l. 2, c. 9, n. 92), in which he says, in so many words, "I condemn the practice of it." I grant that, on looking for these words, at number 92, to which you refer, they will be found there. But what will people say, fathers, when they discover, at the same time, that he is treating in that place of a question totally different from that of which we are speaking, and that the opinion of which he there says that he condemns the practice, has no connection with that now in dispute, but is quite distinct? And yet to be convinced that this is the fact, we have only to open the book to which you refer, and there we find the whole subject in its connection as follows: At number 79 he treats the question, "If it is lawful to kill for a buffet?" and at number 80 he finishes this matter without a single word of condemnation. Having disposed of this question, he opens a new one at art. 81, namely, "If it is lawful to kill for slanders?" and it is when speaking of *this* question that he employs the words you have quoted—"I condemn the practice of it."

Is it not shameful, fathers, that you should venture to produce these words to make it be believed that Lessius condemns the opinion that it is lawful to kill for a buffet? and that, on the ground of this single proof, you should chuckle over it, as you have done, by saying: "Many persons of honor in Paris have already discovered this notorious falsehood by consulting Lessius, and have thus ascertained the degree of credit due to that slanderer?" Indeed! and is it thus that you abuse the confidence which those persons of honor repose in you? To show them that Lessius does not hold a certain opinion, you open the book to them at a place where he is condemning another opinion; and these persons not having begun to mistrust your good faith, and never thinking of examining whether the author speaks in that place of the subject in dispute, you impose on their credulity. I make no doubt, fathers, that to shelter yourselves from the guilt of such a scandalous lie, you had recourse to your doctrine of equivocations; and that, having read the passage *in a loud voice,* you would say, *in a lower key,* that the author was speaking there of something else. But I am not so sure whether this saving clause, which is quite enough to satisfy your consciences, will be a very satisfactory answer to the just complaint of those "honorable persons," when they shall discover that you have hoodwinked them in this style.

Take care, then, fathers, to prevent them by all means from seeing my letters; for this is the only method now left to you to preserve your credit for a short time longer. This is not the way in which I deal with your writings: I send them to all my friends: I wish everybody to see them. And I verily believe that both of us are in the right for our own interests; for after having published with such parade this fourth Imposture, were it once discovered that you have made it up by foisting in one passage for another, you would be instantly denounced. It will be easily seen, that if you could have found what you wanted in the passage where Lessius treated of this matter, you would not have searched for it elsewhere, and that you had recourse to such a trick only because you could find nothing in that passage favorable to your purpose.

You would have us believe that we may find in Lessius what you assert, "that he does *not* allow that this opinion (that a man may be lawfully killed for a buffet) is probable in theory;" whereas Lessius distinctly declares, at number 80: "This opinion, that a man may kill for a buffet, *is* probable in theory." Is not this, word for word, the reverse of your assertion? And can we sufficiently admire the hardihood with which you have advanced, in set phrase, the very reverse of a matter of fact! To your conclusion, from a fabricated passage, that Lessius was *not* of that opinion, we have only to place Lessius himself, who, in the genuine passage, declares that he *is* of that opinion.

Again, you would have Lessius to say "that he condemns the practice of it;" and, as I have just observed, there is not in the original a single word of condemnation; all that he says is: "It appears that it ought not to be EASILY permitted in practice—*In praxi non videtur* FACILE *permittenda.*" Is that, fathers, the language of a man who *condemns* a maxim? Would you say that adultery and incest ought not to be *easily permitted* in practice? Must we not, on the contrary, conclude, that as Lessius says no more than that the practice ought not to be easily permitted, his opinion is, that it may be permitted sometimes, though rarely? And, as if he had been anxious to apprise everybody when it might be permitted, and to relieve those who have received affronts from being troubled with unreasonable scruples, from not knowing on what occasions they might lawfully kill in practice, he has been at pains to inform them what they ought to avoid in order to practise the doctrine with a safe conscience. Mark his words: "It seems," says he, "that it ought not to be easily permitted, *because* of the danger that persons may act in this matter out of hatred or revenge, or with excess, or that this may occasion too many murders." From this it appears that murder is freely permitted by Lessius, if one avoids the inconveniences referred to—in other words, if one can act without hatred or revenge, and in circumstances that may not open the door to a great many murders. To illustrate the matter, I may give you an example of recent occurrence—the case of the buffet of Compiègne. You will grant that the person who received the blow on that occasion has shown by the way in which he has acted, that he was sufficiently master of the passions of hatred and revenge. It only remained for him, therefore, to see that he did not give occasion to too many murders; and you need hardly be told, fathers, it is such a rare spectacle to find Jesuits bestowing buffets on the officers of the royal household, that he had no great reason to fear that a murder committed on this occasion would be likely to draw many others in its train. You cannot, accordingly, deny that the Jesuit who figured on that occasion was *killable* with a safe conscience, and that the offended party might have converted him into a practical illustration of the doctrine of Lessius. And very likely, fathers, this might have been the result had he been educated in your school, and learnt from Escobar that the man who has received a buffet is held to be disgraced until he has taken the life of him who insulted him. But there is ground to believe, that the very different instructions which he received from a curate, who is no great favorite of yours, have contributed not a little in this case to save the life of a Jesuit.

Tell us no more, then, of inconveniences which may, in many instances, be so easily got over, and in the absence of which, according to Lessius, murder is permissible even in practice. This is frankly avowed by your authors, as quoted by Escobar, in his "Practice of Homicide, according to your Society." "Is it allowable," asks this casuist, "to kill him who has given me a buffet? Lessius says it is permissible in speculation, though not to be followed in practice—*non consulendum in praxi*—on account of the risk of hatred, or of murders prejudicial to the State. Others, however, have judged that, BY AVOIDING THESE INCONVENIENCES, THIS IS PERMISSIBLE AND SAFE IN PRACTICE—*in praxi probabilem et tutam judicarunt Henriquez,*" &c. See how your opinions mount up, by little and little, to the climax of probabilism! The present one you have at last elevated to this position, by permitting murder without any distinction between speculation and practice, in the following terms: "It is lawful, when one has received a buffet, to return the blow immediately with the sword, not to avenge one's self, but to preserve one's honor." Such is the decision of your fathers of Caen in 1644, embodied in their publications produced by the university before parliament, when they presented their third remonstrance against your doctrine of homicide, as shown in the book then emitted by them, on page 339.

Mark, then, fathers, that your own authors have themselves demolished this absurd distinction between speculative and practical murder—a distinction which the university treated with ridicule, and the invention of which is a secret of your policy, which it may now be worth while to explain. The knowledge of it, besides being necessary to the right understanding of your 15th, 16th, 17th, and 18th charges, is well calculated, in general, to open up, by little and little, the principles of that mysterious policy.

In attempting, as you have done, to decide cases of conscience in the most agreeable and accommodating manner, while you met with some questions in which religion alone was concerned—such as those of contrition, penance, love to God, and others only affecting the inner court of conscience—you encountered another class of cases in which civil society was interested as well as religion—such as those relating to usury, bankruptcy, homicide, and the like. And it is truly distressing to all that love the Church, to observe that, in a vast number of instances, in which you had only Religion to contend with, you have violated her laws without reservation, without distinction, and without compunction; because you knew that it is not here that God visibly administers his justice. But in those cases in which the State is interested as well as Religion, your apprehension of man's justice has induced you to divide your decisions into two shares. To the first of these you give the name of *speculation;* under which category crimes, considered in themselves, without regard to society, but merely to the law of God, you have permitted, without the least scruple, and in the way of trampling on the divine law which condemns them. The second you rank under the denomination of *practice;* and here, considering the injury which may be done to society, and the presence of magistrates who look after the public peace, you take care, in order to keep yourselves on the safe side of the law, not to approve always in practice the murders and other crimes which you have sanctioned in speculation. Thus, for example, on the question, "If it be lawful to kill for slanders?" your authors, Filiutius, Reginald, and others, reply: "This is permitted in speculation—*ex probabile opinione licet;* but is not to be approved in *practice*, on account of the great number of murders which might ensue, and which might injure the State, if all slanderers were to be killed, *and also because one might be punished in a court of justice for having killed another for that matter.*" Such is the style in which your opinions begin to develop themselves, under the shelter of this distinction, in virtue of which, without doing any sensible injury to society, you only ruin religion. In acting thus, you consider yourselves quite safe. You suppose that, on the one hand, the influence you have in the Church will effectually shield from punishment your assaults on truth; and that, on the other, the precautions you have taken against too easily reducing your permissions to practice will save you on the part of the civil powers, who, not being judges in cases of conscience, are properly concerned only with the outward practice. Thus an opinion which would be condemned under the name of practice, comes out quite safe under the name of speculation. But

this basis once established, it is not difficult to erect on it the
rest of your maxims. There is an infinite distance between
God's prohibition of murder, and your speculative permission
of the crime; but between that permission and the practice
the distance is very small indeed. It only remains to show,
that what is allowable in speculation is also so in practice;
and there can be no want of reasons for this. You have contrived to find them in far more difficult cases. Would you like
to see, fathers, how this may be managed? I refer you to the
reasoning of Escobar, who has distinctly decided the point in
the first of the six volumes of his grand Moral Theology, of
which I have already spoken—a work in which he shows quite
another spirit from that which appears in his former compilation from your four-and-twenty elders. At that time he
thought that there might be opinions probable in speculation,
which might not be safe in practice; but he has now come to
form an opposite judgment, and has, in this, his latest work,
confirmed it. Such is the wonderful growth attained by the
doctrine of probability in general, as well as by every probable
opinion in particular, in the course of time. Attend, then, to
what he says: "I cannot see how it can be that an action which
seems allowable in speculation should not be so likewise in
practice; because what may be done in practice depends on
what is found to be lawful in speculation, and the things differ
from each other only as cause and effect. Speculation is that
which determines to action. WHENCE IT FOLLOWS THAT OPIN-
IONS PROBABLE IN SPECULATION MAY BE FOLLOWED WITH A
SAFE CONSCIENCE IN PRACTICE, and that even with more safety
than those which have not been so well examined as matters
of speculation."

Verily, fathers, your friend Escobar reasons uncommonly
well sometimes; and, in point of fact, there is such a close
connection between speculation and practice, that when the
former has once taken root, you have no difficulty in permitting the latter, without any disguise. A good illustration of
this we have in the permission "to kill for a buffet," which,
from being a point of simple speculation, was boldly raised

by Lessius into a practice "which ought not easily to be allowed;" from that promoted by Escobar to the character of "an easy practice;" and from thence elevated by your fathers of Caen, as we have seen, without any distinction between theory and practice, into a full permission. Thus you bring your opinions to their full growth very gradually. Were they presented all at once in their finished extravagance, they would beget horror; but this slow imperceptible progress gradually habituates men to the sight of them, and hides their offensiveness. And in this way the permission to murder, in itself so odious both to Church and State, creeps first into the Church, and then from the Church into the State.

A similar success has attended the opinion of "killing for slander," which has now reached the climax of a permission without any distinction. I should not have stopped to quote my authorities on this point from your writings, had it not been necessary in order to put down the effrontery with which you have asserted, twice over, in your fifteenth Imposture, "that there never was a Jesuit who permitted killing for slander." Before making this statement, fathers, you should have taken care to prevent it from coming under my notice, seeing that it is so easy for me to answer it. For not to mention that your fathers Reginald, Filiutius, and others, have permitted it in speculation, as I have already shown, and that the principle laid down by Escobar leads us safely on to the practice, I have to tell you that you have authors who have permitted it in so many words, and among others Father Hereau in his public lectures, on the conclusion of which the king put him under arrest in your house, for having taught, among other errors, that when a person who has slandered us in the presence of men of honor, continues to do so after being warned to desist, it is allowable to kill him, not publicly, indeed, for fear of scandal, but IN A PRIVATE WAY—*sed clam.*

I have had occasion already to mention Father Lamy, and you do not need to be informed that his doctrine on this subject was censured in 1649 by the University of Louvain. And yet two months have not elapsed since your Father Des Bois maintained this very censured doctrine of Father Lamy, and taught that "it was allowable for a monk to defend the honor which he acquired by his virtue, EVEN BY KILLING the person who assails his reputation—*etiam cum morte invasoris;*" which has raised such a scandal in that town, that the whole of the curés united to impose silence on him, and to oblige him, by a canonical process, to retract his doctrine. The case is now pending in the Episcopal court.

What say you now, fathers? Why attempt, after that, to maintain that "no Jesuit ever held that it was lawful to kill for slander?" Is anything more necessary to convince you of this than the very opinions of your fathers which you quote, since they do not condemn murder in speculation, but only in practice, and that, too, "on account of the injury that might thereby accrue to the State?" And here I would just beg to ask, whether the whole matter in dispute between us is not simply and solely to ascertain if you have or have not subverted the law of God which condemns murder? The point in question is, not whether you have injured the commonwealth, but whether you have injured religion. What purpose, then, can it serve, in a dispute of this kind, to show that you have spared the State, when you make it apparent, at the same time, that you have destroyed the faith? Is this not evident from your saying that the meaning of Reginald, on the question of killing for slanders, is, "that a private individual has a right to employ that mode of defence, viewing it simply *in itself?*" I desire nothing beyond this concession to confute you. "A private individual," you say, "has a right to employ that mode of defence" (that is, killing for slanders), "viewing the thing in itself;" and, consequently, fathers, the law of God, which forbids us to kill, is nullified by that decision.

It serves no purpose to add, as you have done, "that such a mode is unlawful and criminal, even according to the law of God, on account of the murders and disorders which would follow in society, because the law of God obliges us to have regard to the good of society." This is to evade the question: for there are two laws to be observed—one forbidding us to kill, and another forbidding us to harm society. Reginald has not perhaps, broken the law which forbids us to do harm to society; but he has most certainly violated that which forbids us to kill. Now this is the only point with which we have to do. I might have shown, besides, that your other writers, who have permitted these murders in practice, have subverted the one law as well as the other. But, to proceed, we have seen that you *sometimes* forbid doing harm to the State; and you allege that your design in that is to fulfil the law of God, which obliges us to consult the interests of society. That may be true, though it is far from being certain, as you might do the same thing purely from fear of the civil magistrate. With your permission, then, we shall scrutinize the real secret of this movement.

Is it not certain, fathers, that if you had really any regard to God, and if the observance of his law had been the prime and principal object in your thoughts, this respect would have invariably predominated in all your leading decisions and would have engaged you at all times on the side of religion? But if it turns out, on the contrary, that you violate, in innumerable instances, the most sacred commands that God has laid upon men, and that, as in the instances before us, you annihilate the law of God, which forbids these actions as criminal in themselves, and that you only scruple to approve of them in practice, from bodily fear of the civil magistrate, do you not afford us ground to conclude that you have no respect to God in your apprehensions, and that if you yield an apparent obedience to his law, in so far as regards the obligation to do no harm to the State, this is not done out of any regard to the law itself, but to compass your own ends, as has ever been the way with politicians of no religion?

What, fathers! will you tell us that, looking simply to the law of God, which says, "Thou shalt not kill," we have a right to kill for slanders? And after having thus trampled on the eternal law of God, do you imagine that you atone for the scandal you have caused, and can persuade us of your reverence for him, by adding that you prohibit the practice for

State reasons, and from dread of the civil arm? Is not this, on the contrary, to raise a fresh scandal?—I mean not by the respect which you testify for the magistrate; that is not my charge against you, and it is ridiculous in you to banter, as you have done, on this matter. I blame you, not for fearing the magistrate, but for fearing none but the magistrate. And I blame you for this, because it is making God less the enemy of vice than man. Had you said that to kill for slander was allowable according to men, but not according to God, that might have been something more endurable; but when you maintain, that what is too criminal to be tolerated among men, may yet be innocent and right in the eyes of that Being who is righteousness itself, what is this but to declare before the whole world, by a subversion of principle as shocking in itself as it is alien to the spirit of the saints, that while you can be braggarts before God, you are cowards before men?

Had you really been anxious to condemn these homicides, you would have allowed the commandment of God which forbids them to remain intact; and had you dared at once to permit them, you would have permitted them openly, in spite of the laws of God and men. But your object being to permit them imperceptibly, and to cheat the magistrate, who watches over the public safety, you have gone craftily to work. You separate your maxims into two portions. On the one side, you hold out "that it is lawful in speculation to kill a man for slander;"—and nobody thinks of hindering you from taking a speculative view of matters. On the other side, you come out with this detached axiom, "that what is permitted in speculation is also permissible in practice;"—and what concern does society seem to have in this general and metaphysical-looking proposition? And thus these two principles, so little suspected, being embraced in their separate form, the vigilance of the magistrate is eluded; while it is only necessary to combine the two together, to draw from them the conclusion which you aim at—namely, that it is lawful in practice to put a man to death for a simple slander.

It is, indeed, fathers, one of the most subtle tricks of your policy, to scatter through your publications the maxims which you club together in your decisions. It is partly in this way that you establish your doctrine of probabilities, which I have frequently had occasion to explain. That general principle once established, you advance propositions harmless enough when viewed apart, but which, when taken in connection with that pernicious dogma, become positively horrible. An example of this, which demands an answer, may be found in the 11th page of your "Impostures," where you allege that "several famous theologians have decided that it is lawful to kill a man for a box on the ear." Now, it is certain, that if that had been said by a person who did not hold probabilism, there would be nothing to find fault with in it; it would in this case amount to no more than a harmless statement, and nothing could be elicited from it. But you, fathers, and all who hold that dangerous tenet, "that whatever has been approved by celebrated authors is probable and safe in conscience," when *you* add to this "that several celebrated authors are of opinion that it is lawful to kill a man for a box on the ear," what is this but to put a dagger into the hand of all Christians, for the purpose of plunging it into the heart of the first person that insults them, and to assure them that, having the judgment of so many grave authors on their side, they may do so with a perfectly safe conscience?

What monstrous species of language is this, which, in announcing that certain authors hold a detestable opinion, is at the same time giving a decision in favor of that opinion—which solemnly teaches whatever it simply tells! We have learnt, fathers, to understand this peculiar dialect of the Jesuitical school; and it is astonishing that you have the hardihood to speak it out so freely, for it betrays your sentiments somewhat too broadly. It convicts you of permitting murder for a buffet, as often as you repeat that many celebrated authors have maintained that opinion.

This charge, fathers, you will never be able to repel; nor will you be much helped out by those passages from Vasquez and Suarez that you adduce against me, in which they con-

demn the murders which their associates have approved.
These testimonies, disjoined from the rest of your doctrine,
may hoodwink those who know little about it; but we, who
know better, put your principles and maxims together. You
say, then, that Vasquez condemns murders; but what say you
on the other side of the question, my reverend fathers? Why,
"that the probability of one sentiment does not hinder the
probability of the opposite sentiment; and that it is warrantable to follow the less probable and less safe opinion,
giving up the more probable and more safe one." What follows
from all this taken in connection, but that we have perfect
freedom of conscience to adopt any one of these conflicting
judgments which pleases us best? And what becomes of all
the effect which you fondly anticipate from your quotations?
It evaporates in smoke, for we have no more to do than to
conjoin for your condemnation the maxims which you have
disjoined for your exculpation. Why, then, produce those passages of your authors which I have not quoted, to qualify
those which I have quoted, as if the one could excuse the
other? What right does that give you to call me an "impostor?"
Have I said that all your fathers are implicated in the same
corruptions? Have I not, on the contrary, been at pains to
show that your interest lay in having them of all different
minds, in order to suit all your purposes? Do you wish to kill
your man?—here is Lessius for you. Are you inclined to spare
him?—here is Vasquez. Nobody need go away in ill humor—
nobody without the authority of a grave doctor. Lessius will
talk to you like a Heathen on homicide, and like a Christian,
it may be, on charity. Vasquez, again, will descant like a
Heathen on charity, and like a Christian on homicide. But by
means of probabilism, which is held both by Vasquez and
Lessius, and which renders all your opinions common property, they will lend their opinions to one another, and each
will be held bound to absolve those who have acted according
to opinions which each of them has condemned. It is this very
variety, then, that confounds you. Uniformity, even in evil,
would be better than this. Nothing is more contrary to the

orders of St. Ignatius and the first generals of your Society, than this confused medley of all sorts of opinions, good and bad. I may, perhaps, enter on this topic at some future period; and it will astonish many to see how far you have degenerated from the original spirit of your institution, and that your own generals have foreseen that the corruption of your doctrine on morals might prove fatal, not only to your Society, but to the Church universal.

Meanwhile, I repeat that you can derive no advantage from the doctrine of Vasquez. It would be strange, indeed, if, out of all the Jesuits that have written on morals, one or two could not be found who may have hit upon a truth which has been confessed by all Christians. There is no glory in maintaining the truth, according to the Gospel, that it is unlawful to kill a man for smiting us on the face; but it is foul shame to deny it. So far, indeed, from justifying you, nothing tells more fatally against you than the fact that, having doctors among you who have told you the truth, you abide not in the truth, but love the darkness rather than the light. You have been taught by Vasquez that it is a Heathen, and not a Christian, opinion to hold that we may knock down a man for a blow on the cheek; and that it is subversive both of the Gospel and of the decalogue to say that we may kill for such a matter. The most profligate of men will acknowledge as much. And yet you have allowed Lessius, Escobar, and others, to decide, in the face of these well-known truths, and in spite of all the laws of God against manslaughter, that it is quite allowable to kill a man for a buffet!

What purpose, then, can it serve to set this passage of Vasquez over against the sentiment of Lessius, unless you mean to show that, in the opinion of Vasquez, Lessius is a "Heathen" and a "profligate?" and that, fathers, is more than I durst have said myself. What else can be deduced from it than that Lessius "subverts both the Gospel and the decalogue;" that, at the last day, Vasquez will condemn Lessius on this point, as Lessius will condemn Vasquez on another; and that all your fathers will rise up in judgment one against another, mutually condemning each other for their sad outrages on the law of Jesus Christ?

To this conclusion, then, reverend fathers, must we come at length, that as your probabilism renders the good opinions of some of your authors useless to the Church, and useful only to your policy, they merely serve to betray, by their contrariety, the duplicity of your hearts. This you have completely unfolded, by telling us, on the one hand, that Vasquez and Suarez are against homicide, and on the other hand, that many celebrated authors are for homicide; thus presenting two roads to our choice, and destroying the simplicity of the Spirit of God, who denounces his anathema on the deceitful and the double-hearted: *"Væ duplici corde, et ingredienti duabus viis!*—Woe be to the double hearts, and the sinner that goeth two ways!"

TO THE REVEREND FATHERS, THE JESUITS

*In which the maxims of the Jesuits on murder are refuted from
the Fathers—Some of their calumnies answered by the way—And
their doctrine compared with the forms observed in criminal trials*

October 23, 1656

REVEREND FATHERS,—If I had merely to reply to the three
remaining charges on the subject of homicide, there would
be no need for a long discourse, and you will see them refuted
presently in a few words; but as I think it of much more importance to inspire the public with a horror at your opinions
on this subject, than to justify the fidelity of my quotations,
I shall be obliged to devote the greater part of this letter to the
refutation of your maxims, to show you how far you have departed from the sentiments of the Church, and even of nature
itself. The permissions of murder, which you have granted
in such a variety of cases, render it very apparent, that you
have so far forgotten the law of God, and quenched the light
of nature, as to require to be remanded to the simplest principles of religion and of common sense.

What can be a plainer dictate of nature than that "no private individual has a right to take away the life of another?"
"So well are we taught this of ourselves," says St. Chrysostom,
"that God, in giving the commandment not to kill, did not
add as a reason that homicide was an evil; because," says that
father, "the law supposes that nature has taught us that truth
already." Accordingly, this commandment has been binding

on men in all ages. The Gospel has confirmed the requirement of the law; and the decalogue only renewed the command which man had received from God before the law, in the person of Noah, from whom all men are descended. On that renovation of the world, God said to the patriarch: "At the hand of man, and at the hand of every man's brother, will I require the life of man. Whoso sheddeth man's blood, by man shall his blood be shed; for man is made in the image of God." (Gen. ix. 5, 6.) This general prohibition deprives man of all power over the life of man. And so exclusively has the Almighty reserved this prerogative in his own hand, that, in accordance with Christianity, which is at utter variance with the false maxims of Paganism, man has no power even over his own life. But, as it has seemed good to his providence to take human society under his protection, and to punish the evildoers that give it disturbance, he has himself established laws for depriving criminals of life; and thus those executions which, without his sanction, would be punishable outrages, become, by virtue of his authority, which is the rule of justice, praiseworthy penalties. St. Augustine takes an admirable view of this subject. "God," he says, "has himself qualified this general prohibition against manslaughter, both by the laws which he has instituted for the capital punishment of malefactors, and by the special orders which he has sometimes issued to put to death certain individuals. And when death is inflicted in such cases, it is not man that kills, but God, of whom man may be considered as only the instrument, in the same way as a sword in the hand of him that wields it. But, these instances excepted, whosoever kills incurs the guilt of murder."

It appears, then, fathers, that the right of taking away the life of man is the sole prerogative of God, and that having ordained laws for executing death on criminals, he has deputed kings or commonwealths as the depositaries of that power—a truth which St. Paul teaches us, when, speaking of the right which sovereigns possess over the lives of their subjects, he deduces it from Heaven in these words: "He beareth not the sword in vain; for he is the minister of God to execute wrath upon him that doeth evil." (Rom. xiii. 4.) But as it is God who has put this power into their hands, so he requires them to exercise it in the same manner as he does himself; in other words, with perfect justice; according to what St. Paul observes in the same passage: "Rulers are not a terror to good works, but to the evil. Wilt thou, then, not be afraid of the power? Do that which is good: for he is the minister of God to thee for good." And this restriction, so far from lowering their prerogative, exalts it, on the contrary, more than ever; for it is thus assimilated to that of God, who has no power to do evil, but is all-powerful to do good; and it is thus distinguished from that of devils, who are impotent in that which is good, and powerful only for evil. There is this difference only to be observed betwixt the King of Heaven and earthly sovereigns, that God, being justice and wisdom itself, may inflict death instantaneously on whomsoever and in whatsoever manner he pleases; for, besides his being the sovereign Lord of human life, it is certain that he never takes it away either without cause or without judgment, because he is as incapable of injustice as he is of error. Earthly potentates, however, are not at liberty to act in this manner; for, though the ministers of God, still they are but men, and not gods. They may be misguided by evil counsels, irritated by false suspicions, transported by passion, and hence they find themselves obliged to have recourse, in their turn also, to human agency, and appoint magistrates in their dominions, to whom they delegate their power, that the authority which God has bestowed on them may be employed solely for the purpose for which they received it.

I hope you understand, then, fathers, that to avoid the crime of murder, we must act at once by the authority of God, and according to the justice of God; and that when these two conditions are not united, sin is contracted; whether it be by taking away life with his authority, but without his justice; or by taking it away with justice, but without his authority. From this indispensable connection it follows, according to St. Augustine, "that he who, without proper au-

thority, kills a criminal, becomes a criminal himself, chiefly
for this reason, that he usurps an authority which God has not
given him"; and on the other hand, magistrates, though they
possess this authority, are nevertheless chargeable with murder, if, contrary to the laws which they are bound to follow,
they inflict death on an innocent man.

Such are the principles of public safety and tranquillity
which have been admitted at all times and in all places, and on
the basis of which all legislators, sacred and profane, from the
beginning of the world, have founded their laws. Even
Heathens have never ventured to make an exception to this
rule, unless in cases where there was no other way of escaping the loss of chastity or life, when they conceived, as Cicero
tells us, "that the law itself seemed to put its weapons into
the hands of those who were placed in such an emergency."

But with this single exception, which has nothing to do with
my present purpose, that such a law was ever enacted, au-
thorizing or tolerating, as you have done, the practice of
putting a man to death, to atone for an insult, or to avoid the
loss of honor or property, where life is not in danger at the
same time; that, fathers, is what I deny was ever done, even
by infidels. They have, on the contrary, most expressly forbidden the practice. The law of the Twelve Tables of Rome
bore, "that it is unlawful to kill a robber in the daytime, when
he does not defend himself with arms"; which, indeed, had
been prohibited long before in the 22d chapter of Exodus.
And the law *Furem,* in the *Lex Cornelia,* which is borrowed
from Ulpian, forbids the killing of robbers even by night, if
they do not put us in danger of our lives.

Tell us now, fathers, what authority you have to permit
what all laws, human as well as divine, have forbidden; and
who gave Lessius a right to use the following language? "The
book of Exodus forbids the killing of thieves by day, when
they do not employ arms in their defence; and in a court of
justice, punishment is inflicted on those who kill under these
circumstances. *In conscience,* however, no blame can be attached to this practice, when a person is not sure of being able

otherwise to recover his stolen goods, or entertains a doubt on the subject, as Sotus expresses it; for he is not obliged to run the risk of losing any part of his property merely to save the life of a robber. The same privilege extends even to clergymen." Such extraordinary assurance! The law of Moses punishes those who kill a thief when he does not threaten our lives, and the law of the Gospel, according to you, will absolve them! What, fathers! has Jesus Christ come to destroy the law, and not to fulfil it? "The civil judge," says Lessius, "would inflict punishment on those who should kill under such circumstances; but no blame can be attached to the deed in conscience." Must we conclude, then, that the morality of Jesus Christ is more sanguinary, and less the enemy of murder, than that of Pagans, from whom our judges have borrowed their civil laws which condemn that crime? Do Christians make more account of the good things of this earth, and less account of human life, than infidels and idolaters? On what principle do you proceed, fathers? Assuredly not upon any law that ever was enacted either by God or man—on nothing, indeed, but this extraordinary reasoning: "The laws," say you, "permit us to defend ourselves against robbers, and to repel force by force; self-defence, therefore, being permitted, it follows that murder, without which self-defence is often impracticable, may be considered as permitted also."

It is false, fathers, that because self-defence is allowed, murder may be allowed also. This barbarous method of self-vindication lies at the root of all your errors, and has been justly stigmatized by the Faculty of Louvain, in their censure of the doctrine of your friend Father Lamy, as "*a murderous defence—defensio occisiva.*" I maintain that the laws recognize such a wide difference between murder and self-defence, that in those very cases in which the latter is sanctioned, they have made a provision against murder, when the person is in no danger of his life. Read the words, fathers, as they run in the same passage of Cujas: "It is lawful to repulse the person who comes to invade our property; but *we are not permitted to kill him.*" And again: "If any should threaten to strike us, and not to deprive us of life, it is quite allowable to repulse him; but *it is against all law to put him to death.*"

Who, then, has given you a right to say, as Molina, Reginald, Filiutius, Escobar, Lessius, and others among you, have said, "that it is lawful to kill the man who offers to strike us a blow?" or, "that it is lawful to take the life of one who means to insult us, by the common consent of all the casuists," as Lessius says. By what authority do you, who are mere private individuals, confer upon other private individuals, not excepting clergymen, this right of killing and slaying? And how dare you usurp the power of life and death, which belongs essentially to none but God, and which is the most glorious mark of sovereign authority? These are the points that demand explanation; and yet you conceive that you have furnished a triumphant reply to the whole, by simply remarking, in your thirteenth Imposture, "that the value for which Molina permits us to kill a thief, who flies without having done us any violence, is not so small as I have said, and that it must be a much larger sum than six ducats!" How extremely silly! Pray, fathers, where would you have the price to be fixed? At fifteen or sixteen ducats? Do not suppose that this will produce any abatement in my accusations. At all events, you cannot make it exceed the value of a horse; for Lessius is clearly of opinion, "that we may lawfully kill the thief that runs off with our horse." But I must tell you, moreover, that I was perfectly correct when I said that Molina estimates the value of the thief's life at six ducats; and, if you will not take it upon my word, we shall refer it to an umpire, to whom you cannot object. The person whom I fix upon for this office is your own Father Reginald, who, in his explanation of the same passage of Molina (l. 28, n. 68), declares that "Molina there DETERMINES the sum for which it is not allowable to kill at three, or four, or five ducats." And thus, fathers, I shall have Reginald in addition to Molina, to bear me out.

It will be equally easy for me to refute your fourteenth Imposture, touching Molina's permission to "kill a thief who offers to rob us of a crown." This palpable fact is attested by

Escobar, who tells us "that Molina has regularly determined the sum for which it is lawful to take away life, at one crown." And all you have to lay to my charge in the fourteenth Imposture is, that I have suppressed the last words of this passage, namely, "that in this matter every one ought to study the moderation of a just self-defence." Why do you not complain that Escobar has also omitted to mention these words? But how little tact you have about you! You imagine that nobody understands what you mean by self-defence. Don't we know that it is to employ "*a murderous defence?*" You would persuade us that Molina meant to say, that if a person, in defending his crown, finds himself in danger of his life, he is then at liberty to kill his assailant, in self-preservation. If that were true, fathers, why should Molina say in the same place, that "in this matter he was of a contrary judgment from Carrer and Bald," who give permission to kill in self-preservation? I repeat, therefore, that his plain meaning is, that provided the person can save his crown without killing the thief, he ought not to kill him; but that, if he cannot secure his object without shedding blood, even though he should run no risk of his own life, as in the case of the robber being unarmed, he is permitted to take up arms and kill the man, in order to save his crown; and in so doing, according to him, the person does not transgress "the moderation of a just defence." To show you that I am in the right, just allow him to explain himself: "One does not exceed the moderation of a just defence," says he, "when he takes up arms against a thief who has none, or employs weapons which give him the advantage over his assailant. I know there are some who are of a contrary judgment; but I do not approve of their opinion, even in the external tribunal."

Thus, fathers, it is unquestionable that your authors have given permission to kill in defence of property and honor, though life should be perfectly free from danger. And it is upon the same principle that they authorize duelling, as I have shown by a great variety of passages from their writings, to which you have made no reply. You have animadverted in your writings only on a single passage taken from Father Layman, who sanctions the above practice, "when otherwise a person would be in danger of sacrificing his fortune or his honor"; and here you accuse me with having suppressed what he adds, "that such a case happens very rarely." You astonish me, fathers: these are really curious impostures you charge me withal. You talk as if the question were, whether that is a rare case? when the real question is, if, in such a case, duelling is lawful? These are two very different questions. Layman, in the quality of a casuist, ought to judge whether duelling is lawful in the case supposed; and he declares that it is. We can judge without his assistance, whether the case be a rare one; and we can tell him that it is a very ordinary one. Or, if you prefer the testimony of your good friend Diana, he will tell you that "the case is exceedingly common." But be it rare or not, and let it be granted that Layman follows in this the example of Navarre, a circumstance on which you lay so much stress, is it not shameful that he should consent to such an opinion as that, to preserve a false honor, it is lawful in conscience to accept of a challenge, in the face of the edicts of all Christian states, and of all the canons of the Church, while, in support of these diabolical maxims, you can produce neither laws, nor canons, nor authorities from Scripture, or from the fathers, nor the example of a single saint, nor, in short, anything but the following impious syllogism: "Honor is more than life; it is allowable to kill in defence of life; therefore it is allowable to kill in defence of honor!" What, fathers! because the depravity of men disposes them to prefer that factitious honor before the life which God hath given them to be devoted to his service, must they be permitted to murder one another for its preservation? To love that honor more than life, is in itself a heinous evil; and yet this vicious passion, which, when proposed as the end of our conduct, is enough to tarnish the holiest of actions, is considered by you capable of sanctifying the most criminal of them!

What a subversion of all principle is here, fathers! And who does not see to what atrocious excesses it may lead? It is obvious, indeed, that it will ultimately lead to the commission of murder for the most trifling things imaginable, when one's honor is considered to be staked for their preservation—murder, I venture to say, even *for an apple!* You might complain of me, fathers, for drawing sanguinary inferences from your doctrine with a malicious intent, were I not fortunately supported by the authority of the grave Lessius, who makes the following observation, in number 68: "It is not allowable to take life for an article of small value, such as for a crown or *for an apple—aut pro pomo*—unless it would be deemed dishonorable to lose it. In this case, one may recover the article, and even, if necessary, *kill the aggressor*, for this is not so much defending one's property as retrieving one's honor." This is plain speaking, fathers; and, just to crown your doctrine with a maxim which includes all the rest, allow me to quote the following from Father Hereau, who has taken it from Lessius: "The right of self-defence extends to whatever is necessary to protect ourselves from all injury."

What strange consequences does this inhuman principle involve! and how imperative is the obligation laid upon all, and especially upon those in public stations, to set their face against it! Not the general good alone, but their own personal interest should engage them to see well to it; for the casuists of your school whom I have cited in my letters, extend their permissions to kill far enough to reach even them. Factious men, who dread the punishment of their outrages, which never appear to them in a criminal light, easily persuade themselves that they are the victims of violent oppression, and will be led to believe at the same time, "that the right of self-defence extends to whatever is necessary to protect themselves from all injury." And thus, relieved from contending against the checks of conscience, which stifle the greater number of crimes at their birth, their only anxiety will be to surmount external obstacles.

I shall say no more on this subject, fathers; nor shall I dwell on the other murders, still more odious and important to governments, which you sanction, and of which Lessius, in common with many others of your authors, treats in the most unreserved manner. It was to be wished that these horrible maxims had never found their way out of hell; and that the devil, who is their original author, had never discovered men sufficiently devoted to his will to publish them among Christians.

From all that I have hitherto said, it is easy to judge what a contrariety there is betwixt the licentiousness of your opinions and the severity of civil laws, not even excepting those of Heathens. How much more apparent must the contrast be with ecclesiastical laws, which must be incomparably more holy than any other, since it is the Church alone that knows and possesses the true holiness! Accordingly, this chaste spouse of the Son of God, who, in imitation of her heavenly husband, can shed her own blood for others, but never the blood of others for herself, entertains a horror at the crime of murder altogether singular, and proportioned to the peculiar illumination which God has vouchsafed to bestow upon her. She views man, not simply as man, but as the image of the God whom she adores. She feels for every one of the race a holy respect, which imparts to him, in her eyes, a venerable character, as redeemed by an infinite price, to be made the temple of the living God. And therefore she considers the death of a man, slain without the authority of his Maker, not as murder only, but as sacrilege, by which she is deprived of one of her members; for whether he be a believer or an unbeliever, she uniformly looks upon him, if not as one, at least as capable of becoming one, of her own children.

Such, fathers, are the holy reasons which, ever since the time that God became man for the redemption of men, have rendered their condition an object of such consequence to the Church, that she uniformly punishes the crime of homicide, not only as destructive to them, but as one of the grossest outrages that can possibly be perpetrated against God. In proof of this I shall quote some examples, not from the idea that all the severities to which I refer ought to be kept up (for I am aware that the Church may alter the arrangement of such exterior discipline), but to demonstrate her immutable spirit upon this subject. The penances which she ordains for murder may differ according to the diversity of the times, but no change of time can ever effect an alteration of the horror with which she regards the crime itself.

For a long time the Church refused to be reconciled, till the very hour of death, to those who had been guilty of wilful murder, as those are to whom you give your sanction. The celebrated Council of Ancyra adjudged them to penance during their whole lifetime; and, subsequently, the Church deemed it an act of sufficient indulgence to reduce that term to a great many years. But, still more effectually to deter Christians from wilful murder, she has visited with most severe punishment even those acts which have been committed through inadvertence, as may be seen in St. Basil, in St. Gregory of Nyssen, and in the decretals of Popes Zachary and Alexander II. The canons quoted by Isaac, bishop of Langres (tr. 2. 13), "ordain seven years of penance for having killed another in self-defence." And we find St. Hildebert, bishop of Mans, replying to Yves de Chartres, "that he was right in interdicting for life a priest who had, in self-defence, killed a robber with a stone."

After this, you cannot have the assurance to persist in saying that your decisions are agreeable to the spirit or the canons of the Church. I defy you to show one of them that permits us to kill solely in defence of our property (for I speak not of cases in which one may be called upon to defend his life— *se suaqae liberando*); your own authors, and, among the rest, Father Lamy, confess that no such canon can be found. "There is no authority," he says, "human or divine, which gives an express permission to kill a robber who makes no resistance." And yet this is what you permit most expressly. I defy you to show one of them that permits us to kill in vindication of honor, for a buffet, for an affront, or for a slander. I defy you to show one of them that permits the killing of witnesses, judges, or magistrates, whatever injustice we may apprehend from them. The spirit of the church is diametrically opposite to these seditious maxims, opening the door to insurrections to which the mob is naturally prone enough already. She has invariably taught her children that they ought not to render evil for evil; that they ought to give place unto wrath; to make no resistance to violence; to give unto every one his due—honor, tribute, submission; to obey magistrates and superiors, even though they should be unjust, because we ought always to respect in them the power of that God who has placed them over us. She forbids them, still more strongly than is done by the civil law, to take justice into their own hands; and it is in her spirit that Christian kings decline doing so in cases of high treason, and remit the criminals charged with this grave offence into the hands of the judges, that they may be punished according to the laws and the forms of justice, which in this matter exhibit a contrast to your mode of management, so striking and complete that it may well make you blush for shame.

As my discourse has taken this turn, I beg you to follow the comparison which I shall now draw between the style in which you would dispose of your enemies, and that in which the judges of the land dispose of criminals. Everybody knows, fathers, that no private individual has a right to demand the death of another individual; and that though a man should have ruined us, maimed our body, burnt our house, murdered our father, and was prepared, moreover, to assassinate ourselves, or ruin our character, our private demand for the death of that person would not be listened to in a court of justice. Public officers have been appointed for that purpose, who make the demand in the name of the king, or rather, I would say, in the name of God. Now, do you conceive, fathers, that Christian legislators have established this regulation out of mere show and grimace? Is it not evident that their object was to harmonize the laws of the state with those of the Church, and thus prevent the external practice of justice from clashing with the sentiments which all Christians are bound to cherish in their hearts? It is easy to see how this, which forms the commencement of a civil process, must stagger you; its subsequent procedure absolutely overwhelms you.

Suppose, then, fathers, that these official persons have demanded the death of the man who has committed all the above-mentioned crimes, what is to be done next? Will they instantly plunge a dagger in his breast? No, fathers; the life of man is too important to be thus disposed of; they go to work with more decency; the laws have committed it, not to all sorts of persons, but exclusively to the judges, whose probity and competency have been duly tried. And is one judge sufficient to condemn a man to death? No; it requires seven at the very least; and of these seven there must not be one who has been injured by the criminal, lest his judgment should be warped or corrupted by passion. You are aware also, fathers, that the more effectually to secure the purity of their minds, they devote the hours of the morning to these functions. Such is the care taken to prepare them for the solemn action of devoting a fellow-creature to death; in performing which they occupy the place of God, whose ministers they are, appointed to condemn such only as have incurred his condemnation.

For the same reason, to act as faithful administrators of the divine power of taking away human life, they are bound to form their judgment solely according to the depositions of the witnesses, and according to all the other forms prescribed to them; after which they can pronounce conscientiously only according to law, and can judge worthy of death those only whom the law condemns to that penalty. And then, fathers, if the command of God obliges them to deliver over to punishment the bodies of the unhappy culprits, the same divine statute binds them to look after the interests of their guilty souls, and binds them the more to this just because they are guilty; so that they are not delivered up to execution till after they have been afforded the means of providing for their consciences. All this is quite fair and innocent; and yet, such is the abhorrence of the Church to blood, that she judges those to be incapable of ministering at her altars who have borne any share in passing or executing a sentence of death, accompanied though it be with these religious circumstances; from which we may easily conceive what idea the Church entertains of murder.

Such, then, being the manner in which human life is disposed of by the legal forms of justice, let us now see how you dispose of it. According to your modern system of legislation, there is but one judge, and that judge is no other than the offended party. He is at once the judge, the party, and the executioner. He himself demands from himself the death of his enemy; he condemns him, he executes him on the spot; and, without the least respect either for the soul or the body of his brother, he murders and damns him for whom Jesus Christ died; and all this for the sake of avoiding a blow on the cheek, or a slander, or an offensive word, or some other offence of a similar nature, for which, if a magistrate, in the exercise of legitimate authority, were condemning any to die, he would himself be impeached; for, in such cases, the laws are very far indeed from condemning any to death. In one word, to crown the whole of this extravagance, the person who kills his neighbor in this style, without authority, and in the face of all law, contracts no sin and commits no disorder, though he should be religious, and even a priest! Where are we, fathers? Are these really religious, and priests, who talk in this manner? Are they Christians? are they Turks? are they men? or are they demons? And are these "the mysteries revealed by the Lamb to his Society?" or are they not rather abominations suggested by the Dragon to those who take part with him?

To come to the point, with you, fathers, whom do you wish to be taken for?—for the children of the Gospel, or for the enemies of the Gospel? You must be ranged either on the one side or on the other; for there is no medium here. "He that is not with Jesus Christ is against him." Into these two classes all mankind are divided. There are, according to St. Augustine, two peoples and two worlds, scattered abroad over the earth. There is the world of the children of God, who form one body, of which Jesus Christ is the king and the head; and there is the world at enmity with God, of which the devil is the king and the head. Hence Jesus Christ is called the King and God of the world, because he has everywhere his subjects and worshippers; and hence the devil is also termed in Scripture the prince of this world, and the god of this world, because he has everywhere his agents and his slaves. Jesus Christ has imposed upon the Church, which is his empire, such laws as he, in his eternal wisdom, was pleased to ordain; and the devil has imposed on the world, which is his kingdom, such laws as he chose to establish. Jesus Christ has associated honor with suffering; the devil with not suffering. Jesus Christ has told those who are smitten on the one cheek to turn the other also; and the devil has told those who are threatened with a buffet to kill the man that would do them such an injury. Jesus Christ pronounces those happy who share in his reproach; and the devil declares those to be unhappy who lie under ignominy. Jesus Christ says, Woe unto you when men shall speak well of you! and the devil says, Woe unto those of whom the world does not speak with esteem!

Judge, then, fathers, to which of these kingdoms you belong. You have heard the language of the city of peace, the mystical Jerusalem; and you have heard the language of the city of confusion, which Scripture terms "the spiritual Sodom." Which of these two languages do you understand? which of them do you speak? Those who are on the side of Jesus Christ have, as St. Paul teaches us, the same mind which was also in him; and those who are the children of the devil—*ex patre diabolo*—who has been a murderer from the beginning, according to the saying of Jesus Christ, follow the maxims of the devil. Let us hear, therefore, the language of your school. I put this question to your doctors: When a person has given me a blow on the cheek, ought I rather to submit to the injury than kill the offender? or may I not kill the man in order to escape the affront? Kill him by all means—it is quite lawful! exclaim, in one breath, Lessius, Molina, Escobar, Reginald, Filiutius, Baldelle, and other Jesuits. Is that the language of Jesus Christ? One question more: Would I lose my honor by tolerating a box on the ear, without killing the person that gave it? "Can there be a doubt," cries Escobar, "that so long as a man suffers another to live who has given him a buffet, that man remains without honor?" Yes, fathers, without that honor which the devil transfuses, from his own proud spirit into that of his proud children. This is the honor which has ever been the idol of worldly-minded men. For the preservation of this false glory, of which the god of this world is the appropriate dispenser, they sacrifice their lives by yielding to the madness of duelling; their honor, by exposing themselves to ignominious punishments; and their salvation, by involving themselves in the peril of damnation—a peril which, according to the canons of the Church, deprives them even of Christian burial. We have reason to thank God, however, for having enlightened the mind of our monarch with ideas much purer than those of your theology. His edicts bearing so severely on this subject, have not made duelling a crime— they only punish the crime which is inseparable from duelling. He has checked, by the dread of his rigid justice, those who were not restrained by the fear of the justice of God; and his piety has taught him that the honor of Christians consists in their observance of the mandates of Heaven and the rules of Christianity, and not in the pursuit of that phantom which, airy and unsubstantial as it is, you hold to be a legitimate apology for murder. Your murderous decisions being thus universally detested, it is highly advisable that you should now change your sentiments, if not from religious principle, at least from motives of policy. Prevent, fathers, by a spontaneous condemnation of these inhuman dogmas, the melancholy consequences which may result from them, and for which you will be responsible. And to impress your minds with a deeper horror at homicide, remember that the first crime of fallen man was a murder, committed on the person of the first holy man; that the greatest crime was a murder, perpetrated on the person of the King of saints; and that of all crimes, murder is the only one which involves in a common destruction the Church and the state, nature and religion.

I have just seen the answer of your apologist to my Thirteenth Letter; but if he has nothing better to produce in the shape of a reply to that letter, which obviates the greater part of his objections, he will not deserve a rejoinder. I am sorry to see him perpetually digressing from his subject, to indulge in rancorous abuse both of the living and the dead. But, in order to gain some credit to the stories with which you have furnished him, you should not have made him publicly disavow a fact so notorious as that of the buffet of Compiègne. Certain it is, fathers, from the deposition of the injured party, that he received upon his cheek a blow from the hand of a Jesuit; and all that your friends have been able to do for you has been to raise a doubt whether he received the blow with the back or the palm of the hand, and to discuss the question whether a stroke on the cheek with the back of the hand can be properly denominated a buffet. I know not to what tribunal it belongs to decide this point; but shall content myself, in the meantime, with believing that it was, to say the very least, *a probable buffet*. This gets me off with a safe conscience.

TO THE REVEREND FATHERS, THE JESUITS

Showing that the Jesuits first exclude calumny from their catalogue of crimes, and then employ it in denouncing their opponents

November 25, 1656

REVEREND FATHERS,—As your scurrilities are daily increasing, and as you are employing them in the merciless abuse of all pious persons opposed to your errors, I feel myself obliged, for their sake and that of the Church, to bring out that grand secret of your policy, which I promised to disclose some time ago, in order that all may know, through means of your own maxims, what degree of credit is due to your calumnious accusations.

I am aware that those who are not very well acquainted with you, are at a great loss what to think on this subject, as they find themselves under the painful necessity, either of believing the incredible crimes with which you charge your opponents, or (what is equally incredible) of setting you down as slanderers. "Indeed!" they exclaim, "were these things not true, would clergymen publish them to the world—would they debauch their consciences and damn themselves by venting such libels?" Such is their way of reasoning, and thus it is that the palpable proof of your falsifications coming into collision with their opinion of your honesty, their minds hang in a state of suspense between the evidence of truth which they cannot gainsay, and the demands of charity which they would not violate. It follows, that since their high esteem for you is the only thing that prevents them from discrediting your calumnies, if we can succeed in convincing them that you have quite a different idea of calumny from that which they suppose you to have, and that you actually believe that in blackening and defaming your adversaries you are working out your own salvation, there can be little question that the weight of truth will determine them immediately to pay no regard to your accusations. This, fathers, will be the subject of the present letter.

My design is not simply to show that your writings are full of calumnies; I mean to go a step beyond this. It is quite possible for a person to say a number of false things believing them to be true; but the character of a liar implies the intention to tell lies. Now I undertake to prove, fathers, that it is your deliberate intention to tell lies, and that it is both knowingly and purposely that you load your opponents with crimes of which you know them to be innocent, because you believe that you may do so without falling from a state of grace. Though you doubtless know this point of your morality as well as I do, this need not prevent me from telling you about it; which I shall do, were it for no other purpose than to convince all men of its existence, by showing them that I can maintain it to your face, while you cannot have the assurance to disavow it, without confirming, by that very disavowment, the charge which I bring against you.

The doctrine to which I allude is so common in your schools, that you have maintained it not only in your books, but, such is your assurance, even in your public theses; as, for example, in those delivered at Louvain in the year 1645, where it occurs in the following terms: "What is it but a venial sin to culminate and forge false accusations to ruin the credit of those who speak evil of us?" So settled is this point among you, that if any one dare to oppose it, you treat him as a blockhead and a hare-brained idiot. Such was the way in which you treated Father Quiroga, the German Capuchin, when he was so unfortunate as to impugn the doctrine. The poor man was instantly attacked by Dicastille, one of your fraternity; and the following is a specimen of the manner in which he manages the dispute: "A certain rueful-visaged, bare-footed, cowled friar—*cucullatus gymnopoda*—whom I do not choose to name, had the boldness to denounce this opinion, among some women and ignorant people, and to allege that it was scandalous and pernicious against all good manners, hostile to the peace of states and societies, and, in short, contrary to the judgment not only of all Catholic doctors, but of all true Catholics. But in opposition to him I maintained, as I do still, that calumny, when employed against a calumniator, though it should be a falsehood, is not a mortal sin, either against justice or charity: and to prove the point, I referred him to the whole body of our fathers, and to whole universities, exclusively composed of them, whom I had consulted on the subject; and among others the reverend Father John Gans, confessor to the emperor; the reverend Father Daniel Bastele, confessor to the archduke Leopold; Father Henri, who was preceptor to these two princes; all the public and ordinary professors of the university of Vienna" (wholly composed of Jesuits); "all the professors of the university of Gratz" (all Jesuits); "all the professors of the university of Prague" (where Jesuits are the masters);—"from all of whom I have in my possession approbations of my opinions, written and signed with their own hands; besides having on my side the reverend Father Panalossa, a Jesuit, preacher to the emperor and the king of Spain; Father Pilliceroli, a Jesuit, and many others, who had all judged this opinion to be probable, before our dispute began." You perceive, fathers, that there are few of your opinions which you have been at more pains to establish than the present, as indeed there were few of them of which you stood more in need. For this reason, doubtless, you have authenticated it so well, that the casuists appeal to it as an indubitable principle. "There can be no doubt," says Caramuel, "that it is a probable opinion that we contract no mortal sin by calumniating another, in order to preserve our own reputation. For it is maintained by more than twenty grave doctors, by Gaspard Hurtado, and Dicastille, Jesuits,

&c.; so that, were this doctrine not probable, it would be difficult to find any one such in the whole compass of theology."

Wretched indeed must that theology be, and rotten to the very core, which, unless it has been decided to be safe in conscience to defame our neighbor's character to preserve our own, can hardly boast of a safe decision on any other point! How natural is it, fathers, that those who hold this principle should occasionally put it in practice! The corrupt propensity of mankind leans so strongly in that direction of itself, that the obstacle of conscience once being removed, it would be folly to suppose that it will not burst forth with all its native impetuosity. If you desire an example of this, Caramuel will furnish you with one that occurs in the same passage: "This maxim of Father Dicastille," he says, "having been communicated by a German countess to the daughters of the empress, the belief thus impressed on their minds that calumny was only a venial sin, gave rise in the course of a few days to such an immense number of false and scandalous tales, that the whole court was thrown into a flame and filled with alarm. It is easy, indeed, to conceive what a fine use these ladies would make of the new light they had acquired. Matters proceeded to such a length, that it was found necessary to call in the assistance of a worthy Capuchin friar, a man of exemplary life, called Father Quiroga" (the very man whom Dicastille rails at so bitterly), "who assured them that the maxim was most pernicious, especially among women, and was at the greatest pains to prevail upon the empress to abolish the practice of it entirely." We have no reason, therefore, to be surprised at the bad effects of this doctrine; on the contrary, the wonder would be, if it had failed to produce them. Self-love is always ready enough to whisper in our ear, when we are attacked, that we suffer wrongfully; and more particularly in your case, fathers, whom vanity has blinded so egregiously as to make you believe that to wound the honor of your Society, is to wound that of the Church. There would have been good ground to look on it as something miraculous, if you had *not* reduced this maxim to practice. Those who do not know you are ready to say, How could these good fathers slander their enemies, when they cannot do so but at the expense of their own salvation? But if they knew you better, the question would be, How could these good fathers forego the advantage of decrying their enemies, when they have it in their power to do so without hazarding their salvation? Let none, therefore, henceforth be surprised to find the Jesuits calumniators; they can exercise this vocation with a safe conscience; there is no obstacle in heaven or on earth to prevent them. In virtue of the credit they have acquired in the world, they can practise defamation without dreading the justice of mortals; and, on the strength of their self-assumed authority in matters of conscience, they have invented maxims for enabling them to do it without any fear of the justice of God.

This, fathers, is the fertile source of your base slanders. On this principle was Father Brisacier led to scatter his calumnies about him, with such zeal as to draw down on his head the censure of the late Archbishop of Paris. Actuated by the same motives, Father D'Anjou launched his invectives from the pulpit of the Church of St. Benedict in Paris on the 8th of March, 1655, against those honorable gentlemen who were intrusted with the charitable funds raised for the poor of Picardy and Champagne, to which they themselves had largely contributed; and, uttering a base falsehood, calculated (if your slanders had been considered worthy of any credit) to dry up the stream of that charity, he had the assurance to say, "that he knew, from good authority, that certain persons had diverted that money from its proper use, to employ it against the Church and the State"; a calumny which obliged the curate of the parish, who is a doctor of the Sorbonne, to mount the pulpit the very next day, in order to give it the lie direct. To the same source must be traced the conduct of your Father Crasset, who preached calumny at such a furious rate in Orleans that the archbishop of that place was under the necessity of interdicting him as a public slanderer. In this mandate, dated the 9th of September last, his lordship declares, "That whereas he had been informed that Brother Jean Crasset, priest of the Society of Jesus, had delivered from the pulpit a discourse filled with falsehoods and calumnies against the ecclesiastics of this city, falsely and maliciously charging them with maintaining impious and heretical propositions, such as, That the commandments of God are impracticable; that internal grace is irresistible; that Jesus Christ did not die for all men; and others of a similar kind, condemned by Innocent X.: he therefore hereby interdicts the aforesaid Crasset from preaching in his diocese, and forbids all his people to hear him, on pain of mortal disobedience." The above, fathers, is your ordinary accusation, and generally among the first that you bring against all whom it is your interest to denounce. And although you should find it as impossible to substantiate the charge against any of them, as Father Crasset did in the case of the clergy of Orleans, your peace of conscience will not be in the least disturbed on that account; for you believe that this mode of calumniating your adversaries is permitted you with such certainty, that you have no scruple to avow it in the most public manner, and in the face of a whole city.

A remarkable proof of this may be seen in the dispute you had with M. Puys, curate of St. Nisier at Lyons; and the story exhibits so complete an illustration of your spirit, that I shall take the liberty of relating some of its leading circumstances. You know, fathers, that, in the year 1649, M. Puys translated into French an excellent book, written by another Capuchin friar, "On the duty which Christians owe to their own parishes, against those that would lead them away from them," without using a single invective, or pointing to any monk or any order of monks in particular. Your fathers, however, were pleased to put the cap on their own heads; and without any respect to an aged pastor, a judge in the Primacy of France, and a man who was held in the highest esteem by the whole city, Father Alby wrote a furious tract against him, which you sold in your own church upon Assumption Day; in which book, among other various charges, he accused him of having "made himself scandalous by his gallantries," described him as suspected of having no religion, as a heretic, excommunicated, and, in short, worthy of the stake. To this M. Puys made a reply; and Father Alby, in a second publication, supported his former allegations. Now, fathers, is it not a clear point, either that you were calumniators, or that you believed all that you alleged against that worthy priest to be true; and that, on this latter assumption, it became you to see him purified from all these abominations before judging him worthy of your friendship? Let us see, then, what happened at the accommodation of the dispute, which took place in the presence of a great number of the principal inhabitants of the town on the 25th of September, 1650. Before all these witnesses M. Puys made a declaration, which was neither more nor less than this: "That what he had written was not directed against the fathers of the Society of Jesus; that he had spoken in general of those who alienated the faithful from their parishes, without meaning by that to attack the Society; and that so far from having such an intention, the Society was the object of his esteem and affection." By virtue of these words alone, without either retraction or absolution, M. Puys recovered, all at once, from his apostasy, his scandals, and his excommunication; and Father Alby immediately thereafter addressed him in the following express terms: "Sir, it was in consequence of my believing that you meant to attack the Society to which I have the honor to belong, that I was induced to take up the pen in its defence; and I considered that the mode of reply which I adopted was *such as I was permitted to employ*. But, on a better understanding of your intention, I am now free to declare, that *there is nothing in your work* to prevent me from regarding you as a man of genius, enlightened in judgment, profound and *orthodox* in doctrine, and *irreproachable* in manners; in one word, as a pastor worthy of your Church. It is with much pleasure that I make this declaration, and I beg these gentlemen to remember what I have now said."

They do remember it, fathers; and, allow me to add, they were more scandalized by the reconciliation than by the quarrel. For who can fail to admire this speech of Father Alby? He does not say that he retracts, in consequence of having learnt that a change had taken place in the faith and manners of M. Puys, but solely because, *having understood that he had no intention of attacking your Society,* there was nothing further to prevent him from regarding the author as a good Catholic. He did not then believe him to be actually a heretic! And yet, after having, contrary to his conviction, accused him of this crime, he will not acknowledge he was in the wrong, but has the hardihood to say, that he considered the method he adopted to be "such as he was *permitted* to employ!"

What can you possibly mean, fathers, by so publicly avowing the fact, that you measure the faith and the virtue of men only by the sentiments they entertain towards your Society? Had you no apprehension of making yourselves pass, by your own acknowledgment, as a band of swindlers and slanderers? What, fathers! must the same individual without undergoing any personal transformation, but simply according as you judge him to have honored or assailed your community, be "pious" or "impious," "irreproachable" or "excommunicated," "a pastor worthy of the Church," or "worthy of the stake"; in short, "a Catholic" or "a heretic"? To attack your Society and to be a heretic, are, therefore, in your language, convertible terms! An odd sort of heresy this, fathers! And so it would appear, that when we see many good Catholics branded, in your writings, by the name of heretics, it means nothing more than that *you think they attack you!* It is well, fathers, that we understand this strange dialect, according to which there can be no doubt that I must be a great heretic. It is in *this* sense, then, that you so often favor me with this appellation! Your sole reason for cutting me off from the Church is, because you conceive that my letters have done you harm; and, accordingly, all that I have to do, in order to become a good Catholic, is either to approve of your extravagant morality, or to convince you that my sole aim in exposing it has been your advantage. The former I could not do without renouncing every sentiment of piety that I ever possessed; and

the latter you will be slow to acknowledge till you are well
cured of your errors. Thus am I involved in heresy, after a very
singular fashion; for, the purity of my faith being of no avail
for my exculpation, I have no means of escaping from the
charge, except either by turning traitor to my own conscience,
or by reforming yours. Till one or other of these events happen, I must remain a reprobate and a slanderer; and, let me be
ever so faithful in my citations from your writings, you will
go about crying everywhere, "What an instrument of the devil
must that man be, to impute to us things of which there is not
the least mark or vestige to be found in our books!" And, by
doing so, you will only be acting in conformity with your
fixed maxim and your ordinary practice: to such latitude does
your privilege of telling lies extend! Allow me to give you an
example of this, which I select on purpose; it will give me an
opportunity of replying, at the same time, to your ninth Imposture: for, in truth, they only deserve to be refuted in
passing.

About ten or twelve years ago, you were accused of holding
that maxim of Father Bauny, "that it is permissible to seek
directly (*primo et per se*) a proximate occasion of sin, for the
spiritual or temporal good of ourselves or our neighbor" (tr.
4, q. 14); as an example of which, he observes, "It is allowable to visit infamous places, for the purpose of converting
abandoned females, even although the practice should be very
likely to lead into sin, as in the case of one who has found from
experience that he has frequently yielded to their temptations." What answer did your Father Caussin give to this
charge in the year 1644? "Just let any one look at the passage
in Father Bauny," said he, "let him peruse the page, the
margins, the preface, the appendix, in short, the whole book
from beginning to end, and he will not discover the slightest
vestige of such a sentence, which could only enter into the
mind of a man totally devoid of conscience, and could hardly
have been forged by any other but an instrument of Satan."
Father Pintereau talks in the same style: "That man must be
lost to all conscience who would teach so detestable a doctrine;

but he must be worse than a devil who attributes it to Father Bauny. Reader, there is not a single trace or vestige of it in the whole of his book." Who would not believe that persons talking in this tone have good reason to complain, and that Father Bauny has, in very deed, been misrepresented? Have you ever asserted anything against me in stronger terms? And, after such a solemn asseveration, that "there was not a single trace or vestige of it in the whole book," who would imagine that the passage is to be found, word for word, in the place referred to?

Truly, fathers, if this be the means of securing your reputation, so long as you remain unanswered, it is also, unfortunately, the means of destroying it forever, so soon as an answer makes its appearance. For so certain is it that you told a lie at the period before mentioned, that you make no scruple of acknowledging, in your apologies of the present day, that the maxim in question is to be found in the very place which had been quoted; and what is most extraordinary, the same maxim which, twelve years ago, was "detestable," has now become so innocent, that in your ninth Imposture (p. 10) you accuse me of "ignorance and malice, in quarrelling with Father Bauny for an opinion which has not been rejected in the School." What an advantage it is, fathers, to have to do with people that deal in contradictions! I need not the aid of any but yourselves to confute you; for I have only two things to show—first, That the maxim in dispute is a worthless one; and, secondly, That it belongs to Father Bauny; and I can prove both by your own confession. In 1644, you confessed that it was "detestable"; and, in 1656, you avow that it is Father Bauny's. This double acknowledgment completely justifies me, fathers; but it does more, it discovers the spirit of your policy. For, tell me, pray, what is the end you propose to yourselves in your writings? Is it to speak with honesty? No, fathers; that cannot be, since your defences destroy each other. Is it to follow the truth of the faith? As little can this be your end; since, according to your own showing, you authorize a "detestable" maxim. But, be it observed, that while you said the maxim was "detestable," you denied, at the same time, that it was the property of Father Bauny, and so he was innocent; and when you now acknowledge it to be his, you maintain, at the same time, that it is a good maxim, and so he is innocent still. The innocence of this monk, therefore, being the only thing common to your two answers, it is obvious that this was the sole end which you aimed at in putting them forth; and that, when you say of one and the same maxim, that it is in a certain book, and that it is not; that it is a good maxim, and that it is a bad one; your sole object is to white-wash some one or other of your fraternity; judging in the matter, not according to the truth, which never changes, but according to your own interest, which is varying every hour. Can I say more than this? You perceive that it amounts to a demonstration; but it is far from being a singular instance, and, to omit a multitude of examples of the same thing, I be-lieve you will be contented with my quoting only one more.

You have been charged, at different times, with another proposition of the same Father Bauny, namely, "That absolu-tion ought to be neither denied nor deferred in the case of those who live in the habits of sin against the law of God, of nature, and of the Church, although there should be no ap-parent prospect of future amendment—*etsi emendationis fu-turæ spes nulla appareat*." Now, with regard to this maxim, I beg you to tell me, fathers, which of the apologies that have been made for it is most to your liking; whether that of Father Pintereau, or that of Father Brisacier, both of your Society, who have defended Father Bauny, in your *two different* modes —the one by condemning the proposition, but disavowing it to be Father Bauny's; the other by allowing it to be Father Bauny's, but vindicating the proposition? Listen, then, to their respective deliverances. Here comes that of Father Pin-tereau (p. 8): "I know not what can be called a transgression of all the bounds of modesty, a step beyond all ordinary impu-dence, if the imputation to Father Bauny of so damnable a doctrine is not worthy of that designation. Judge, reader, of the baseness of that calumny; see what sort of creatures the

Jesuits have to deal with; and say, if the author of so foul a slander does not deserve to be regarded from henceforth as the interpreter of the father of lies." Now for Father Brisacier: "It is true, Father Bauny says what you allege." (That gives the lie direct to Father Pintereau, plain enough.) "But," adds he, in defence of Father Bauny, "if you who find so much fault with this sentiment, wait, when a penitent lies at your feet, till his guardian angel find security for his rights in the inheritance of heaven; if you wait till God the Father, swear by himself that David told a lie, when he said by the Holy Ghost, that 'all men are liars,' fallible and perfidious; if you wait till the penitent be no longer a liar, no longer frail and changeable, no longer a sinner, like other men; if you wait, I say, till then, you will never apply the blood of Jesus Christ to a single soul."

What do you really think now, fathers, of these impious and extravagant expressions? According to them, if we would wait "till there be some hope of amendment" in sinners before granting their absolution, we must wait "till God the Father swear by himself," that they will never fall into sin any more! What, fathers! is no distinction to be made between *hope* and *certainty?* How injurious is it to the grace of Jesus Christ, to maintain that it is so impossible for Christians ever to escape from crimes against the laws of God, nature, and the Church, that such a thing cannot be looked for, without supposing "that the Holy Ghost has told a lie"; and if absolution is not granted to those who give no hope of amendment, the blood of Jesus Christ will be useless, forsooth, and "would never be applied to a single soul!" To what a sad pass have you come, fathers, by this extravagant desire of upholding the glory of your authors, when you can find only two ways of justifying them—by imposture or by impiety; and when the most innocent mode by which you can extricate yourselves, is by the barefaced denial of facts as patent as the light of day!

This may perhaps account for your having recourse so frequently to that very convenient practice. But this does not complete the sum of your accomplishments in the art of self-

defence. To render your opponents odious, you have had recourse to the forging of documents, such as that *Letter of a
Minister to M. Arnauld,* which you circulated through all
Paris, to induce the belief that the work on Frequent Communion, which had been approved by so many bishops and
doctors, but which, to say the truth, was rather against you,
had been concocted through secret intelligence with the ministers of Charenton. At other times, you attribute to your
adversaries writings full of impiety, such as the *Circular Letter
of the Jansenists,* the absurd style of which renders the fraud
too gross to be swallowed, and palpably betrays the malice
of your Father Meynier, who has the impudence to make use
of it for supporting his foulest slanders. Sometimes, again, you
will quote books which were never in existence, such as *The
Constitution of the Holy Sacrament,* from which you extract
passages, fabricated at pleasure, and calculated to make the
hair on the heads of certain good simple people, who have no
idea of the effrontery with which you can invent and propagate
falsehoods, actually to bristle with horror. There is not, indeed, a single species of calumny which you have not put into
requisition; nor is it possible that the maxim which excuses the
vice could have been lodged in better hands.

But those sorts of slander to which we have adverted are
rather too easily discredited; and, accordingly, you have
others of a more subtle character, in which you abstain from
specifying particulars, in order to preclude your opponents
from getting any hold, or finding any means of reply; as, for
example, when Father Brisacier says that "his enemies are
guilty of abominable crimes, *which he does not choose to mention.*" Would you not think it were impossible to prove a
charge so vague as this to be a calumny? An able man, however, has found out the secret of it; and it is a Capuchin again,
fathers. You are unlucky in Capuchins, as times now go; and I
foresee that you may be equally so some other time in Benedictines. The name of this Capuchin is Father Valerien, of
the house of the Counts of Magnis. You shall hear, by this
brief narrative, how he answered your calumnies. He had

happily succeeded in converting Prince Ernest, the Landgrave of Hesse-Rheinsfelt. Your fathers, however, seized, as it would appear, with some chagrin at seeing a sovereign prince converted without their having had any hand in it, immediately wrote a book against the friar (for good men are everywhere the objects of your persecution), in which, by falsifying one of his passages, they ascribed to him an heretical doctrine. They also circulated a letter against him, in which they said: "Ah, we have such things to disclose" (without mentioning what) "as will gall you to the quick! If you don't take care, we shall be forced to inform the pope and the cardinals about it." This manœuvre was pretty well executed; and I doubt not, fathers, but you may speak in the same style of me; but take warning from the manner in which the friar answered in his book, which was printed last year at Prague (p. 112, &c.): "What shall I do," he says, "to counteract these vague and indefinite insinuations? How shall I refute charges which have never been specified? Here, however, is my plan. I declare, loudly and publicly, to those who have threatened me, that they are notorious slanderers, and most impudent liars, if they do not discover these crimes before the whole world. Come forth, then, mine accusers! and publish your lies upon the house tops, in place of telling them in the ear, and keeping yourselves out of harm's way by telling them in the ear. Some may think this a scandalous way of managing the dispute. It was scandalous, I grant, to impute to me such a crime as heresy, and to fix upon me the suspicion of many others besides; but, by asserting my innocence, I am merely applying the proper remedy to the scandal already in existence."

Truly, fathers, never were your reverences more roughly handled, and never was a poor man more completely vindicated. Since you have made no reply to such a peremptory challenge, it must be concluded that you are unable to discover the slightest shadow of criminality against him. You have had very awkward scrapes to get through occasionally; but experience has made you nothing the wiser. For, some time after this happened, you attacked the same individual in a similar strain, upon another subject; and he defended himself after the same spirited manner, as follows: "This class of men, who have become an intolerable nuisance to the whole of Christendom, aspire, under the pretext of good works, to dignities and domination, by perverting to their own ends almost all laws, human and divine, natural and revealed. They gain over to their side, by their doctrine, by the force of fear, or of persuasion, the great ones of the earth, whose authority they abuse for the purpose of accomplishing their detestable intrigues. Meanwhile their enterprises, criminal as they are, are neither punished nor suppressed; on the contrary, they are rewarded; and the villains go about them with as little fear or remorse as if they were doing God service. Everybody is aware of the fact I have now stated; everybody speaks of it with execration; but few are found capable of opposing a despotism so powerful. This, however, is what I have done. I have already curbed their insolence; and, by the same means, I shall curb it again. I declare, then, that *they are most impudent liars*—MENTIRIS IMPUDENTISSIME. If the charges they have brought against me be true, let them prove it; otherwise they stand convicted of falsehood, aggravated by the grossest effrontery. Their procedure in this case will show who has the right upon his side. I desire all men to take a particular observation of it; and beg to remark, in the meantime, that this precious cabal, who will not suffer the most trifling charge which they can possibly repel to lie upon them, made a show of enduring, with great patience, those from which they cannot vindicate themselves, and conceal, under a counterfeit virtue, their real impotency. My object, therefore, in provoking their modesty, by this sharp retort, is to let the plainest people understand that if my enemies hold their peace, their forbearance must be ascribed, not to the meekness of their natures, but to the power of a guilty conscience." He concludes with the following sentence: "These gentry, whose history is well known throughout the whole world, are so glaringly iniquitous in their measures, and have become so insolent in their impunity, that if I did not detest their conduct, and pub-

licly express my detestation too, not merely for my own
vindication, but to guard the simple against its seducing influence, I must have renounced my allegiance to Jesus Christ
and his Church."

Reverend fathers, there is no room for tergiversation. You
must pass for convicted slanderers, and take comfort in your
old maxim, that calumny is no crime. This honest friar has
discovered the secret of shutting your mouths; and it must
be employed on all occasions when you accuse people without proof. We have only to reply to each slander as it appears,
in the words of the Capuchin, *Mentiris impudentissime*—
"You are most impudent liars." For instance, what better
answer does Father Brisacier deserve when he says of his
opponents that they are "the gates of hell; the devil's bishops;
persons devoid of faith, hope, and charity; the builders of
Antichrist's exchequer"; adding, "I say this of him, not by
way of insult, but from deep conviction of its truth?" Who
would be at the pains to demonstrate that he is not "a gate
of hell," and that he has no concern with "the building up of
Antichrist's exchequer"?

In like manner, what reply is due to all the vague speeches
of this sort which are to be found in your books and advertisements on my letters; such as the following, for example:
"That restitutions have been converted to private uses, and
thereby creditors have been reduced to beggary; that bags
of money have been offered to learned monks, who declined
the bribe; that benefices are conferred for the purpose of disseminating heresies against the faith; that pensioners are
kept in the houses of the most eminent churchmen, and in
the courts of sovereigns; that I also am a pensioner of Port-
Royal; and that, before writing my letters, I had composed
romances"—I, who never read one in my life, and who do
not know so much as the names of those which your apologist has published? What can be said in reply to all this,
fathers, if you do not mention the names of all these persons
you refer to, their words, the time, and the place, except—
Mentiris impudentissime? You should either be silent alto-

gether, or relate and prove all the circumstances, as I did when I told you the anecdotes of Father Alby and John d'Alba. Otherwise, you will hurt none but yourselves. Your numerous fables might, perhaps, have done you some service, before your principles were known; but now that the whole has been brought to light, when you begin to whisper as usual, "A man of honor, who desired us to conceal his name, has told us some horrible stories of these same people"—you will be cut short at once, and reminded of the Capuchin's *Mentiris impudentissime*. Too long by far have you been permitted to deceive the world, and to abuse the confidence which men were ready to place in your calumnious accusations. It is high time to redeem the reputation of the multitudes whom you have defamed. For what innocence can be so generally known, as not to suffer some injury from the daring aspersions of a body of men scattered over the face of the earth, and who, under religious habits, conceal minds so utterly irreligious, that they perpetrate crimes like calumny, not in opposition to, but in strict accordance with, their moral maxims? I cannot, therefore, be blamed for destroying the credit which might have been awarded you, seeing it must be allowed to be a much greater act of justice to restore to the victims of your obloquy the character which they did not deserve to lose, than to leave you in the possession of a reputation for sincerity which you do not deserve to enjoy. And as the one could not be done without the other, how important was it to show you up to the world as you really are! In this letter I have commenced the exhibition; but it will require some time to complete it. Published it shall be, fathers, and all your policy will be inadequate to save you from the disgrace; for the efforts which you may make to avert the blow, will only serve to convince the most obtuse observers that you were terrified out of your wits, and that, your consciences anticipating the charges I had to bring against you, you have put every oar in the water to prevent the discovery.

TO THE REVEREND FATHERS, THE JESUITS

Shameful calumnies of the Jesuits against pious clergymen and innocent nuns

December 4, 1656.

REVEREND FATHERS,—I now come to consider the rest of your calumnies, and shall begin with those contained in your advertisements, which remain to be noticed. As all your other writings, however, are equally well stocked with slander, they will furnish me with abundant materials for entertaining you on this topic as long as I may judge expedient. In the first place, then, with regard to the fable which you have propagated in all your writings against the bishop of Ypres, I beg leave to say, in one word, that you have maliciously wrested the meaning of some ambiguous expressions in one of his letters, which being capable of a good sense, ought, according to the spirit of the Gospel, to have been taken in good part, and could only be taken otherwise according to the spirit of your Society. For example, when he says to a friend, "Give yourself no concern about your nephew; I will furnish him with what he requires from the money that lies in my hands," what reason have you to interpret this to mean, that he would take that money without restoring it, and not that he merely advanced it with the purpose of replacing it? And how extremely imprudent was it for you to furnish a refutation of your own lie, by printing the other letters of the Bishop of Ypres, which clearly show that, in point of fact, it was merely *advanced* money, which he was bound to refund. This appears, to your confusion, from the following terms in the letter, to which you give the date of July 30, 1619: "Be not uneasy about the money advanced, he shall want for nothing so long as he is here"; and likewise from another, dated January 6, 1620, where he says: "You are in too great haste; when the account shall become due, I have no fear but that the little credit which I have in this place will bring me as much money as I require."

If you are convicted slanderers on this subject, you are no less so in regard to the ridiculous story about the charity-box of St. Merri. What advantage, pray, can you hope to derive from the accusation which one of your worthy friends has trumped up against that ecclesiastic? Are we to conclude that a man is guilty, because he is accused? No, fathers. Men of piety, like him, may expect to be perpetually accused, so long as the world contains calumniators like you. We must judge of him, therefore, not from the accusation, but from the sentence; and the sentence pronounced on the case (February 23, 1656) justifies him completely. Moreover, the person who had the temerity to involve himself in that iniquitous process, was disavowed by his colleagues, and himself compelled to retract his charge. And as to what you allege, in the same place, about "that famous director, who pocketed at once nine hundred thousand livres," I need only refer you to Messieurs the curés of St. Roch and St. Paul, who will bear witness, before the whole city of Paris, to his perfect disinterestedness in the affair, and to your inexcusable malice in that piece of imposition.

Enough, however, for such paltry falsities. These are but the first raw attempts of your novices, and not the masterstrokes of your "grand professed." To these do I now come, fathers; I come to a calumny which is certainly one of the basest that ever issued from the spirit of your Society. I refer to the insufferable audacity with which you have imputed to holy nuns, and to their directors, the charge of "disbelieving the mystery of transubstantiation, and the real presence of

Jesus Christ in the eucharist." Here, fathers, is a slander worthy of yourselves. Here is a crime which God alone is capable of punishing, as you alone were capable of committing it. To endure it with patience, would require an humility as great as that of these calumniated ladies; to give it credit would demand a degree of wickedness equal to that of their wretched defamers. I propose not, therefore, to vindicate them; they are beyond suspicion. Had they stood in need of defence, they might have commanded abler advocates than me. My object in what I say here is to show, not their innocence, but your malignity. I merely intend to make you ashamed of yourselves, and to let the whole world understand that, after this, there is nothing of which you are not capable.

You will not fail, I am certain, notwithstanding all this, to say that I belong to Port-Royal; for this is the first thing you say to every one who combats your errors: as if it were only at Port-Royal that persons could be found possessed of sufficient zeal to defend, against your attacks, the purity of Christian morality. I know, fathers, the work of the pious recluses who have retired to that monastery, and how much the Church is indebted to their truly solid and edifying labors. I know the excellence of their piety and their learning. For, though I have never had the honor to belong to their establishment, as you, without knowing who or what I am, would fain have it believed, nevertheless, I do know some of them, and honor the virtue of them all. But God has not confined within the precincts of that society all whom he means to raise up in opposition to your corruptions. I hope, with his assistance, fathers, to make you feel this; and if he vouchsafe to sustain me in the design he has led me to form, of employing in his service all the resources I have received from him, I shall speak to you in such a strain as will, perhaps, give you reason to regret that you have *not* had to do with a man of Port-Royal. And to convince you of this, fathers, I must tell you that, while those whom you have abused with this notorious slander content themselves with lifting up their groans to Heaven to obtain your forgiveness for the outrage, I feel myself obliged, not being in the least affected by your slander, to make you blush in the face of the whole Church, and so bring you to that wholesome shame of which the Scripture speaks, and which is almost the only remedy for a hardness of heart like yours: *"Imple facies eorum ignominia, et quærent nomen tuum, Domine*—Fill their faces with shame, that they may seek thy name, O Lord."

A stop must be put to this insolence, which does not spare the most sacred retreats. For who can be safe after a calumny of this nature? For shame, fathers! to publish in Paris such a scandalous book, with the name of your Father Meynier on its front, and under this infamous title, "Port-Royal and Geneva in concert against the most holy Sacrament of the Altar," in which you accuse of this apostasy, not only Monsieur the abbé of St. Cyran, and M. Arnauld, but also Mother Agnes, his sister, and all the nuns of that monastery, alleging that "their faith, in regard to the eucharist, is as suspicious as that of M. Arnauld," whom you maintain to be "a downright Calvinist." I here ask the whole world if there be any class of persons within the pale of the Church, on whom you could have advanced such an abominable charge with less semblance of truth. For tell me, fathers, if these nuns and their directors, had been "in concert with Geneva against the most holy sacrament of the altar" (the very thought of which is shocking), how they should have come to select as the principal object of their piety that very sacrament which they held in abomination? How should they have assumed the habit of the holy sacrament? taken the name of the Daughters of the Holy Sacrament? called their church the Church of the Holy Sacrament? How should they have requested and obtained from Rome the confirmation of that institution, and the right of saying every Thursday the office of the holy sacrament, in which the faith of the Church is so perfectly expressed, if they had conspired with Geneva to banish that faith from the Church? Why would they have bound themselves, by a particular devotion, also sanctioned by the pope, to have some of their sisterhood, night and day without intermission, in presence of the sacred host, to compensate, by their perpetual adorations towards that perpetual sacrifice, for the impiety of the heresy that aims at its annihilation? Tell me, fathers, if you can, why, of all the mysteries of our religion, they should have passed by those in which they believed, to fix upon that in which they believed not? and how they should have devoted themselves, so fully and entirely, to that mystery of our faith, if they took it, as the heretics do, for the mystery of iniquity? And what answer do you give to these clear evidences, embodied not in words only, but in actions; and not in some particular actions, but in the whole tenor of a life expressly dedicated to the adoration of Jesus Christ, dwelling on our altars? What answer, again, do you give to the books which you ascribe to Port-Royal, all of which are full of the most precise terms employed by the fathers and the councils to mark the essence of that mystery? It is at once ridiculous and disgusting to hear you replying to these, as you have done throughout your libel. M. Arnauld, say you, talks very well about transubstantiation; but he understands, perhaps, only "a significative transubstantiation." True, he professes to believe in "the real presence"; who can tell, however, but he means nothing more than "a true and real figure"? How now, fathers! whom, pray, will you not make pass for a Calvinist whenever you please, if you are to be allowed the liberty of perverting the most canonical and sacred expressions by the wicked subtleties of your modern equivocations? Who ever thought of using any other terms than those in question, especially in simple discourses of devotion, where no controversies are handled? And yet the love and the reverence in which they hold this sacred mystery, have induced them to give it such a prominence in all their writings, that I defy you, fathers, with all your cunning, to detect in them either the least appearance of ambiguity, or the slightest correspondence with the sentiments of Geneva.

Everybody knows, fathers, that the essence of the Genevan heresy consists, as it does according to your own showing, in their believing that Jesus Christ is not contained (*enfermé*), in this sacrament; that it is impossible he can be in many places at once; that he is, properly speaking, only in heaven, and that it is as there alone that he ought to be adored, and not on the altar; that the substance of the bread remains; that the body of Jesus Christ does not enter into the mouth or the stomach; that he can only be eaten by faith, and accordingly wicked men do not eat him at all; and that the mass is not a sacrifice, but an abomination. Let us now hear, then, in what way "Port-Royal is in concert with Geneva." In the writings of the former we read, to your confusion, the following statement: That "the flesh and blood of Jesus Christ are contained under the species of bread and wine"; that "the Holy of Holies is present in the sanctuary, and that there he ought to be adored"; that "Jesus Christ dwells in the sinners who communicate, by the real and veritable presence of his body in their stomach, although not by the presence of his Spirit in their hearts"; that "the dead ashes of the bodies of the saints derive their principal dignity from that seed of life which they retain from the touch of the immortal and vivifying flesh of Jesus Christ"; that "it is not owing to any natural power, but to the almighty power of God, to whom nothing is impossible, that the body of Jesus Christ is comprehended under the host, and under the smallest portion of every host"; that "the divine virtue is present to produce the effect which the words of consecration signify"; that "Jesus Christ, while he is lowered (*rabaissé*), and hidden upon the altar, is, at the same time, elevated in his glory; that he subsists, of himself and by his own ordinary power, in divers places at the same time—in the midst of the Church triumphant, and in the midst of the Church militant and travelling"; that "the sacramental species remain suspended, and subsist extraordinarily, without being upheld by any subject; and that the body of Jesus Christ is also suspended under the species, and that it does not depend upon these, as substances depend upon accidents"; that "the substance of the bread is changed, the immutable accidents remaining the same"; that "Jesus Christ reposes in the eucharist with the same glory that he has in heaven"; that "his glorious humanity resides in the tabernacles of the Church, under the species of bread, which forms its visible covering; and that, knowing the grossness of our natures, he conducts us to the adoration of his divinity, which is present in all places, by the adoring of his humanity, which is present in a particular place"; that "we receive the body of Jesus Christ upon the tongue, which is sanctified by its divine touch"; "that it enters into the mouth of the priest"; that "although Jesus Christ has made himself accessible in the holy sacrament, by an act of his love and graciousness, he preserves, nevertheless, in that ordinance, his inaccessibility, as an inseparable condition of his divine nature; because, although the body alone and the blood alone are there, by virtue of the words *vi verborum,* as the schoolmen say, his whole divinity may, notwithstanding, be there also, as well as his whole humanity, by a necessary conjunction." In fine, that "the eucharist is at the same time sacrament and sacrifice"; and that "although this sacrifice is a commemoration of that of the cross, yet there is this difference between them, that the sacrifice of the mass is offered for the Church only, and for the faithful in her communion; whereas that of the cross has been offered for all the world, as the Scripture testifies."

I have quoted enough, fathers, to make it evident that there was never, perhaps, a more imprudent thing attempted than what you have done. But I will go a step farther, and make you pronounce this sentence against yourselves. For what do you require from a man, in order to remove all suspicion of his being in concert and correspondence with Geneva? "If M. Arnauld," says your Father Meynier, p. 93, "had said that in this adorable mystery, there is no substance of the bread under the species, but only the flesh and the blood of Jesus Christ, I should have confessed that he had declared himself absolutely against Geneva." Confess it, then, ye revilers! and make him a public apology. How often have you seen this declaration made in the passages I have just cited? Besides this, however, the Familiar Theology of M. de St.

Cyran having been approved by M. Arnauld, it contains the
sentiments of both. Read, then, the whole of lesson 15th, and
particularly article 2d, and you will there find the words you
desiderate, even more formally stated than you have done
yourselves. "Is there any bread in the host, or any wine in the
chalice? No: for all the substance of the bread and the wine
is taken away, to give place to that of the body and blood of
Jesus Christ, the which substance alone remains therein, covered by the qualities and species of bread and wine."

How now, fathers! will you still say that Port-Royal teaches
"nothing that Geneva does not receive," and that M. Arnauld
has said nothing in his second letter "which might not have
been said by a minister of Charenton?" See if you can persuade Mestrezat to speak as M. Arnauld does in that letter,
on page 237? Make him say, that it is an infamous calumny
to accuse him of denying transubstantiation; that he takes for
the fundamental principle of his writings the truth of the real
presence of the Son of God, in opposition to the heresy of the
Calvinists; and that he accounts himself happy for living in
a place where the Holy of Holies is continually adored in the
sanctuary"—a sentiment which is still more opposed to the
belief of the Calvinists than the real presence itself; for as
Cardinal Richelieu observes in his Controversies (p. 536):
"The new ministers of France having agreed with the Lutherans, who believe the real presence of Jesus Christ in the
eucharist; they have declared that they remain in a state of
separation from the Church on the point of this mystery, only
on account of the adoration which Catholics render to the
eucharist." Get all the passages which I have extracted from
the books of Port-Royal subscribed at Geneva, and not the
isolated passages merely, but the entire treatises regarding
this mystery, such as the Book of Frequent Communion, the
Explication of the Ceremonies of the Mass, the Exercise during Mass, the Reasons of the Suspension of the Holy Sacrament, the Translation of the Hymns in the Hours of Port-
Royal, &c.; in one word, prevail upon them to establish at
Charenton that holy institution of adoring, without intermis-

sion, Jesus Christ contained in the eucharist, as is done at Port-Royal, and it will be the most signal service which you could render to the Church; for in this case it will turn out, not that Port-Royal is in concert with Geneva, but that Geneva is in concert with Port-Royal, and with the whole Church.

Certainly, fathers, you could not have been more unfortunate than in selecting Port-Royal as the object of attack for not believing in the eucharist; but I will show what led you to fix upon it. You know I have picked up some small acquaintance with your policy; in this instance you have acted upon its maxims to admiration. If Monsieur the abbé of St. Cyran, and M. Arnauld, had only spoken of what ought to be believed with great respect to this mystery, and said nothing about what ought to be done in the way of preparation for its reception, they might have been the best Catholics alive; and no equivocations would have been discovered in their use of the terms "real presence" and "transubstantiation." But since all who combat your licentious principles must needs be heretics, and heretics too, in the very point in which they condemn your laxity, how could M. Arnauld escape falling under this charge on the subject of the eucharist, after having published a book expressly against your profanations of that sacrament? What! must he be allowed to say, with impunity, that "the body of Jesus Christ ought not to be given to those who habitually lapse into the same crimes, and who have no prospect of amendment; and that such persons ought to be excluded, for some time, from the altar, to purify themselves by sincere penitence, that they may approach it afterwards with benefit"? Suffer no one to talk in this strain, fathers, or you will find that fewer people will come to your confessionals. Father Brisacier says, that "were you to adopt this course, you would never apply the blood of Jesus Christ to a single individual." It would be infinitely more for your interest were every one to adopt the views of your Society, as set forth by your Father Mascarenhas, in a book approved by your doctors, and even by your reverend Father-General, namely, "That persons of every description, and even priests, may receive the body of

Jesus Christ on the very day they have polluted themselves with odious crimes; that so far from such communions implying irreverence, persons who partake of them in this manner act a commendable part; that confessors ought not to keep them back from the ordinance, but, on the contrary, ought to advise those who have recently committed such crimes to communicate immediately; because, although the Church has forbidden it, this prohibition is annulled by the universal practice in all places of the earth."

See what it is, fathers, to have Jesuits in all places of the earth! Behold the universal practice which you have introduced, and which you are anxious everywhere to maintain! It matters nothing that the tables of Jesus Christ are filled with abominations, provided that your churches are crowded with people. Be sure, therefore, cost what it may, to set down all that dare to say a word against your practice, as heretics on the holy sacrament. But how can you do this, after the irrefragable testimonies which they have given of their faith? Are you not afraid of my coming out with the four grand proofs of their heresy which you have adduced? You ought, at least, to be so, fathers, and I ought not to spare your blushing. Let us, then, proceed to examine proof the first.

"M. de St. Cyran," says Father Meynier, "consoling one of his friends upon the death of his mother (tom. i., let. 14), says that the most acceptable sacrifice that can be offered up to God on such occasions, is that of patience; therefore he is a Calvinist." This is marvellously shrewd reasoning, fathers; and I doubt if anybody will be able to discover the precise point of it. Let us learn it, then, from his own mouth. "Because," says this mighty controversialist, "it is obvious that he does not believe in the sacrifice of the mass; for this is, of all other sacrifices, the most acceptable unto God." Who will venture to say now that the Jesuits do not know how to reason? Why, they know the art to such perfection, that they will extract heresy out of anything you choose to mention, not even excepting the Holy Scripture itself! For example, might it not be heretical to say, with the wise man in Ecclesiasticus,

"There is nothing worse than to love money"; as if adultery, murder, or idolatry, were not far greater crimes? Where is the man who is not in the habit of using similar expressions every day? May we not say, for instance, that the most acceptable of all sacrifices in the eyes of God is that of a contrite and humbled heart; just because, in discourses of this nature, we simply mean to compare certain internal virtues with one another, and not with the sacrifice of the mass, which is of a totally different order, and infinitely more exalted? Is this not enough to make you ridiculous, fathers? And is it necessary, to complete your discomfiture, that I should quote the passages of that letter in which M. de St. Cyran speaks of the sacrifice of the mass, as "the most excellent" of all others, in the following terms? "Let there be presented to God, daily and in all places, the sacrifice of the body of his Son, who could not find *a more excellent way* than that by which he might honor his Father." And afterwards: "Jesus Christ has enjoined us to take, when we are dying, his sacrificed body, to render more acceptable to God the sacrifice of our own, and to join himself with us at the hour of dissolution; to the end that he may strengthen us for the struggle, sanctifying, by his presence, the last sacrifice which we make to God of our life and our body?" Pretend to take no notice of all this, fathers, and persist in maintaining, as you do in page 39, that he refused to take the communion on his death-bed, and that he did not believe in the sacrifice of the mass. Nothing can be too gross for calumniators by profession.

Your second proof furnishes an excellent illustration of this. To make a Calvinist of M. de St. Cyran, to whom you ascribe the book of *Petrus Aurelius,* you take advantage of a passage (page 80) in which Aurelius explains in what manner the Church acts towards priests, and even bishops, whom she wishes to degrade or depose. "The Church," he says, "being incapable of depriving them of the power of the order, the character of which is indelible, she does all that she can do;— she banishes from her memory the character which she cannot banish from the souls of the individuals who have been once invested with it; she regards them in the same light as if they were not bishops or priests; so that, according to the ordinary language of the Church, it may be said they are no longer such, although they always remain such, in as far as the character is concerned—*ob indelebilitatem characteris.*" You perceive, fathers, that this author, who has been approved by three general assemblies of the clergy of France, plainly declares that the character of the priesthood is indelible; and yet you make him say, on the contrary, in the very same passage, that "the character of the priesthood is *not* indelible." This is what I would call a notorious slander; in other words, according to your nomenclature, a small venial sin. And the reason is, this book has done you some harm, by refuting the heresies of your brethren in England touching the Episcopal authority. But the folly of the charge is equally remarkable; for, after having taken it for granted, without any foundation, that M. de St. Cyran holds the priestly character to be not indelible, you conclude from this that he does not believe in the real presence of Jesus Christ in the eucharist.

Do not expect me to answer this, fathers. If you have got no common sense, I am not able to furnish you with it. All who possess any share of it will enjoy a hearty laugh at your expense. Nor will they treat with greater respect your third proof, which rests upon the following words, taken from the Book of Frequent Communion: "In the eucharist God vouchsafes us *the same food* that he bestows on the saints in heaven, with this difference only, that here he withholds from us its sensible sight and taste, reserving both of these for the heavenly world." These words express the sense of the Church so distinctly, that I am constantly forgetting what reason you have for picking a quarrel with them, in order to turn them to a bad use; for I can see nothing more in them than what the Council of Trent teaches (sess. xiii., c. 8), namely, that there is no difference between Jesus Christ in the eucharist and Jesus Christ in heaven, except that here he is veiled, and there he is not. M. Arnauld does not say that there is no difference in the manner of receiving Jesus Christ, but only that there is no difference in Jesus Christ who is received. And yet you would, in the face of all reason, interpret his language in this passage to mean, that Jesus Christ is no more eaten with the mouth in this world than he is in heaven; upon which you ground the charge of heresy against him.

You really make me sorry for you, fathers. Must we explain this further to you? Why do you confound that divine nourishment with the manner of receiving it? There is but one point of difference, as I have just observed, betwixt that nourishment upon earth and in heaven, which is, that here it is hidden under veils which deprive us of its sensible sight and taste; but there are various points of dissimilarity in the manner of receiving it here and there, the principal of which is, as M. Arnauld expresses it (p. 3, ch. 16), "that here it enters into the mouth and the breast both of the good and of the wicked," which is not the case in heaven.

And if you require to be told the reason of this diversity, I may inform you, fathers, that the cause of God's ordaining these different modes of receiving the same food, is the difference that exists betwixt the state of Christians in this life and that of the blessed in heaven. The state of the Christian, as Cardinal Perron observes after the fathers, holds a middle place between the state of the blessed and the state of the Jews. The spirits in bliss possess Jesus Christ really, without veil or figure. The Jews possessed Jesus Christ only in figures and veils, such as the manna and the paschal lamb. And Christians possess Jesus Christ in the eucharist really and truly, although still concealed under veils. "God," says St. Eucher, "has made three tabernacles—the synagogue, which had the shadows only, without the truth; the Church, which has the truth and shadows together; and heaven, where there is no shadow, but the truth alone." It would be a departure from our present state, which is the state of faith, opposed by St. Paul alike to the law and to open vision, did we possess the figures only, without Jesus Christ; for it is the property of the law to have the mere figure, and not the substance of things. And it would be equally a departure from our present state if we possessed him visibly; because faith, according to the same apostle, deals not with things that are seen. And thus the eucharist, from its including Jesus Christ truly, though under a veil, is in perfect accordance with our state of faith. It follows, that this state would be destroyed, if, as the heretics maintain, Jesus Christ were not really under the species of bread and wine; and it would be equally destroyed if we received him openly, as they do in heaven: since, on these suppositions, our state would be confounded, either with the state of Judaism or with that of glory.

Such, fathers, is the mysterious and divine reason of this most divine mystery. This it is that fills us with abhorrence at the Calvinists, who would reduce us to the condition of the Jews; and this it is that makes us aspire to the glory of the beatified, where we shall be introduced to the full and eternal enjoyment of Jesus Christ. From hence you must see that there are several points of difference between the manner in which he communicates himself to Christians and to the blessed; and that, amongst others, he is in this world received by the mouth, and not so in heaven; but that they all depend solely on the distinction between our state of faith and their state of immediate vision. And this is precisely, fathers, what M. Arnauld has expressed, with great plainness, in the following terms: "There can be no other difference between the purity of those who receive Jesus Christ in the eucharist and that of the blessed, than what exists between faith and the open vision of God, upon which alone depends the different manner in which he is eaten upon earth and in heaven." You were bound in duty, fathers, to have revered in these words the sacred truths they express, instead of wresting them for the purpose of detecting an heretical meaning which they never contained, nor could possibly contain, namely, that Jesus Christ is eaten by faith only, and not by the mouth; the malicious perversion of your Fathers Annat and Meynier, which forms the capital count of their indictment.

Conscious, however, of the wretched deficiency of your proofs, you have had recourse to a new artifice, which is nothing less than to falsify the Council of Trent, in order to convict M. Arnauld of nonconformity with it; so vast is your store of methods for making people heretics. This feat has been achieved by Father Meynier, in fifty different places of his book, and about eight or ten times in the space of a single page (the 54th), wherein he insists that to speak like a true Catholic, it is not enough to say, "I believe that Jesus Christ is really present in the eucharist," but we must say, "I believe, *with the council,* that he is present by a true *local presence,* or locally." And in proof of this, he cites the council, session xiii., canon 3d, canon 4th, and canon 6th. Who would not suppose, upon seeing the term *local presence* quoted from three canons of a universal council, that the phrase was actually to be found in them? This might have served your turn very well, before the appearance of my fifteenth letter; but as matters now stand, fathers, the trick has become too stale for us. We go our way and consult the council, and discover only that you are falsifiers. Such terms as *local presence, locally,* and *locality,* never existed in the passages to which you refer; and let me tell you further, they are not to be found in any other canon of that council, nor in any other previous council, nor in any father of the Church. Allow me, then, to ask you, fathers, if you mean to cast the suspicion of Calvinism upon all that have not made use of that peculiar phrase? If this be the case, the Council of Trent must be suspected of heresy, and all the holy fathers without exception. Have you no other way of making M. Arnauld heretical, without abusing so many other people who never did you any harm, and among the rest, St. Thomas, who is one of the greatest champions of the eucharist, and who, so far from employing that term, has expressly rejected it— *"Nullo modo corpus Christi est in hoc sacramento localiter?* —By no means is the body of Christ in this sacrament *locally?"* Who are you, then, fathers, to pretend, on your authority, to impose new terms, and ordain them to be used by all for rightly expressing their faith; as if the profession of the faith, drawn up by the popes according to the plan of the council, in which this term has no place, were defective, and left an ambiguity in the creed of the faithful which you had the sole merit of discovering? Such a piece of arrogance, to prescribe these terms, even to learned doctors! such a piece of forgery, to attribute them to general councils! and such ignorance, not to know the objections which the most enlightened saints have made to their reception! "Be ashamed of the error of your ignorance," as the Scripture says of ignorant impostors like you—*De mendacio ineruditionis tuæ confundere.*

Give up all further attempts, then, to act the masters; you have neither character nor capacity for the part. If, however, you would bring forward your propositions with a little more modesty, they might obtain a hearing. For although this phrase, *local presence,* has been rejected, as you have seen, by St. Thomas, on the ground that the body of Jesus Christ is not in the eucharist, in the ordinary extension of bodies in their places, the expression has, nevertheless, been adopted by some modern controversial writers, who understand it simply to mean that the body of Jesus Christ is truly under the species, which being in a particular place, the body of Jesus Christ is there also. And in this sense M. Arnauld will make no scruple to admit the term, as M. de St. Cyran and he have repeatedly declared that Jesus Christ in the eucharist is truly in a particular place, and miraculously in many places at the same time. Thus all your subtleties fall to the ground; and you have failed to give the slightest semblance of plausibility to an accusation, which ought not to have been allowed to show its face, without being supported by the most unanswerable proofs.

But what avails it, fathers, to oppose their innocence to your calumnies? You impute these errors to them, not in the belief that they maintain heresy, but from the idea that they have done you injury. That is enough, according to your theology, to warrant you to calumniate them without criminality; and you can, without either penance or confession, say mass, at the very time that you charge priests, who say it every day, with holding it to be pure idolatry; which, were it true, would amount to sacrilege no less revolting than that of your own Father Jarrige, whom you yourselves ordered to be hanged in effigy, for having said mass "at the time he was in agreement with Geneva."

What surprises me, therefore, is not the little scrupulosity with which you load them with crimes of the foulest and falsest description, but the little prudence you display, by fixing on them charges so destitute of plausibility. You dispose of sins, it is true, at your pleasure; but do you mean to dispose of men's beliefs too? Verily, fathers, if the suspicion of Calvinism must needs fall either on them or on you, you would stand, I fear, on very ticklish ground. Their language is as Catholic as yours; but their conduct confirms their faith, and your conduct belies it. For if you believe, as well as they do, that the bread is really changed into the body of Jesus Christ, why do you not require, as they do, from those whom you advise to approach the altar, that the heart of stone and ice should be sincerely changed into a heart of flesh and of love? If you believe that Jesus Christ is in that sacrament in a state of death, teaching those that approach it to die to the world, to sin, and to themselves, why do you suffer those to profane it in whose breasts evil passions continue to reign in all their life and vigor? And how do you come to judge those worthy to eat the bread of heaven, who are not worthy to eat that of earth?

Precious votaries, truly, whose zeal is expended in persecuting those who honor this sacred mystery by so many holy communions, and in flattering those who dishonor it by so many sacrilegious desecrations! How comely is it in these champions of a sacrifice so pure and so venerable, to collect around the table of Jesus Christ a crowd of hardened profligates, reeking from their debaucheries; and to plant in the midst of them a priest, whom his own confessor has hurried from his obscenities to the altar; there, in the place of Jesus Christ, to offer up that most holy victim to the God of holiness, and convey it, with his polluted hands, into mouths as thoroughly polluted as his own! How well does it become those who pursue this course "in all parts of the world," in con-

formity with maxims sanctioned by their own general to impute to the author of Frequent Communion, and to the Sisters
of the Holy Sacrament, the crime of not believing in that
sacrament!

Even this, however, does not satisfy them. Nothing less
will satiate their rage than to accuse their opponents of having renounced Jesus Christ and their baptism. This is no air-
built fable, like those of your invention; it is a fact, and
denotes a delirious frenzy, which marks the fatal consummation of your calumnies. Such a notorious falsehood as this
would not have been in hands worthy to support it, had it
remained in those of your good friend Filleau, through whom
you ushered it into the world: your Society has openly adopted
it; and your Father Meynier maintained it the other day to
be "*a certain truth*," that Port-Royal has, for the space of
thirty-five years, been forming a secret plot, of which M. de
St. Cyran and M. d'Ypres have been the ringleaders, "to ruin
the mystery of the incarnation—to make the Gospel pass for
an apocryphal fable—to exterminate the Christian religion,
and to erect Deism upon the ruins of Christianity." Is this
enough, fathers? Will you be satisfied if all this be believed of
the objects of your hate? Would your animosity be glutted
at length, if you could but succeed in making them odious,
not only to all within the Church, by the charge of "*consenting
with Geneva,*" of which you accuse them, but even to all who
believe in Jesus Christ, though beyond the pale of the Church,
by the imputation of *Deism?*

But whom do you expect to convince, upon your simple
asseveration, without the slightest shadow of proof, and in
the face of every imaginable contradiction, that priests who
preach nothing but the grace of Jesus Christ, the purity of the
Gospel, and the obligations of baptism, have renounced at
once their baptism, the Gospel, and Jesus Christ? Who will
believe it, fathers? Wretched as you are, do you believe it
yourselves? What a sad predicament is yours, when you must
either prove that they do not believe in Jesus Christ, or must
pass for the most abandoned calumniators. Prove it, then,

fathers. Name that *"worthy clergyman,"* who, you say, attended that assembly at Bourg-Fontaine in 1621, and discovered to Brother Filleau the design there concerted of overturning the Christian religion. Name those six persons whom you allege to have formed that conspiracy. Name the *individual who is designated by the letters A. A.,* who you say *"was not Antony Arnauld"* (because he convinced you that he was at that time only nine years of age), *"but another person, who you say is still in life, but too good a friend of M. Arnauld not to be known to him."* You know him, then, fathers; and consequently, if you are not destitute of religion yourselves, you are bound to delate that impious wretch to the king and parliament, that he may be punished according to his deserts. You must speak out, fathers; you must name the person, or submit to the disgrace of being henceforth regarded in no other light than as common liars, unworthy of being ever credited again. Good Father Valerien has taught us that this is the way in which such characters should be "put to the rack," and brought to their senses. Your silence upon the present challenge will furnish a full and satisfactory confirmation of this diabolical calumny. Your blindest admirers will be constrained to admit, that it will be "the result, not of your goodness, but your impotency"; and to wonder how you could be so wicked as to extend your hatred even to the nuns of Port-Royal, and to say, as you do in page 14, that *The Secret Chaplet of the Holy Sacrament,* composed by one of their number, was the first fruit of that conspiracy against Jesus Christ; or, as in page 95, that "they have imbibed all the detestable principles of that work"; which is, according to your account, "a lesson in Deism." Your falsehoods regarding that book have already been triumphantly refuted, in the defence of the censure of the late Archbishop of Paris against Father Brisacier. That publication you are incapable of answering; and yet you do not scruple to abuse it in a more shameful manner than ever, for the purpose of charging women, whose piety is universally known, with the vilest blasphemy.

Cruel, cowardly persecutors! Must, then, the most retired

cloisters afford no retreat from your calumnies? While these consecrated virgins are employed, night and day, according to their institution, in adoring Jesus Christ in the holy sacrament, you cease not, night nor day, to publish abroad that they do not believe that he is either in the eucharist or even at the right hand of his Father; and you are publicly excommunicating them from the Church, at the very time when they are in secret praying for the whole Church, and for you! You blacken with your slanders those who have neither ears to hear nor mouths to answer you! But Jesus Christ, in whom they are now hidden, not to appear till one day together with him, hears you, and answers for them. At the moment I am now writing, that holy and terrible voice is heard which confounds nature and consoles the Church. And I fear, fathers, that those who now harden their hearts, and refuse with obstinacy to hear him, while he speaks in the character of God, will one day be compelled to hear him with terror, when he speaks to them in the character of a Judge. What account, indeed, fathers, will you be able to render to him of the many calumnies you have uttered, seeing that he will examine them, in that day, not according to the fantasies of Fathers Dicastille, Gans, and Pennalossa, who justify them, but according to the eternal laws of truth, and the sacred ordinances of his own Church, which, so far from attempting to vindicate that crime, abhors it to such a degree that she visits it with the same penalty as wilful murder? By the first and second councils of Arles she has decided that the communion shall be denied to slanderers as well as murderers, till the approach of death. The Council of Lateran has judged those unworthy of admission into the ecclesiastical state who have been convicted of the crime, even though they may have reformed. The popes have even threatened to deprive of the communion at death those who have calumniated bishops, priests, or deacons. And the authors of a defamatory libel, who fail to prove what they have advanced, are condemned by Pope Adrian *to be whipped;* —yes, reverend fathers, *flagellentur* is the word. So strong has been the repugnance of the Church at all times to the errors of your Society—a Society so thoroughly depraved as to invent excuses for the grossest of crimes, such as calumny, chiefly that it may enjoy the greater freedom in perpetrating them itself. There can be no doubt, fathers, that you would be capable of producing abundance of mischief in this way, had God not permitted you to furnish with your own hands the means of preventing the evil, and of rendering your slanders perfectly innocuous; for, to deprive you of all credibility, it was quite enough to publish the strange maxim, that it is no crime to calumniate. Calumny is nothing, if not associated with a high reputation for honesty. The defamer can make no impression, unless he has the character of one that abhors defamation, as a crime of which he is incapable. And thus, fathers, you are betrayed by your own principle. You establish the doctrine to secure yourselves a safe conscience, that you might slander without risk of damnation, and be ranked with those "pious and holy calumniators" of whom St. Athanasius speaks. To save yourselves from hell, you have embraced a maxim which promises you this security on the faith of your doctors; but this same maxim, while it guarantees you, according to their idea, against the evils you dread in the future world, deprives you of all the advantage you may have expected to reap from it in the present; so that, in attempting to escape the guilt, you have lost the benefit of calumny. Such is the self-contrariety of evil, and so completely does it confound and destroy itself by its own intrinsic malignity.

You might have slandered, therefore, much more advantageously for yourselves, had you professed to hold, with St. Paul, that evil speakers are not worthy to see God; for in this case, though you would indeed have been condemning yourselves, your slanders would at least have stood a better chance of being believed. But by maintaining, as you have done, that calumny against your enemies is no crime, your slanders will be discredited, and you yourselves damned into the bargain; for two things are certain, fathers—first, That it will never be in the power of your grave doctors to annihilate the justice of God; and secondly, That you could not give more certain evidence that you are not of the Truth than by your resorting to falsehood. If the Truth were on your side, she would fight for you—she would conquer for you; and whatever enemies you might have to encounter, "the Truth would set you free" from them, according to her promise. But you have had recourse to falsehood, for no other design than to support the errors with which you flatter the sinful children of this world, and to bolster up the calumnies with which you persecute every man of piety who sets his face against these delusions. The truth being diametrically opposed to your ends, it behooved you, to use the language of the prophet, "to put your confidence in lies." You have said, "The scourges which afflict mankind shall not come nigh unto us; for we have made lies our refuge, and under falsehood have we hid ourselves." But what says the prophet in reply to such? "Forasmuch," says he, "as ye have put your trust in calumny and tumult,—*sperastis in calumnia et in tumultu*—this iniquity and your ruin shall be like that of a high wall whose breaking cometh suddenly at an instant. And he shall break it as the breaking of the potter's vessel that is shivered in pieces"—with such violence that "there shall not be found in the bursting of it a shred to take fire from the hearth, or to take water withal out of the pit." "Because," as another prophet says, "ye have made the heart of the righteous sad, whom I have not made sad; and ye have flattered and strengthened the malice of the wicked; I will therefore deliver my people out of your hands, and ye shall know that I am their Lord and yours."

Yes, fathers, it is to be hoped that if you do not repent, God will deliver out of your hands those whom you have so long deluded, either by flattering them in their evil courses with your licentious maxims, or by poisoning their minds with your slanders. He will convince the former that the false rules of your casuists will not screen them from his indignation; and he will impress on the minds of the latter the just dread of losing their souls by listening and yielding credit to your slanders, as you lose yours by hatching these slanders and disseminating them through the world. Let no man be deceived; God is not mocked; none may violate with impunity the commandment which he has given us in the Gospel, not to condemn our neighbor without being well assured of his guilt. And consequently, what profession soever of piety those may make who lend a willing ear to your lying devices, and under what pretence soever of devotion they may entertain them, they have reason to apprehend exclusion from the kingdom of God, solely for having imputed crimes of such a dark complexion as heresy and schism to Catholic priests and holy nuns, upon no better evidence than such vile fabrications as yours. "The devil," says M. de Geneve, "is on the tongue of him that slanders, and in the ear of him that listens to the slanderer." "And evil speaking," says St. Bernard, "is a poison that extinguishes charity in both of the parties; so that a single calumny may prove mortal to an infinite numbers of souls, killing not only those who publish it, but all those besides by whom it is not repudiated."

Reverend fathers, my letters were not wont either to be so prolix, or to follow so closely on one another. Want of time must plead my excuse for both of these faults. The present letter is a very long one, simply because I had no leisure to make it shorter. You know the reason of this haste better than I do. You have been unlucky in your answers. You have done well, therefore, to change your plan; but I am afraid that you will get no credit for it, and that people will say it was done for fear of the Benedictines.

I have just come to learn that the person who was generally reported to be the author of your Apologies, disclaims them, and is annoyed at their having been ascribed to him. He has good reason, and I was wrong to have suspected him of any such thing; for, in spite of the assurances which I received, I ought to have considered that he was a man of too much good sense to believe your accusations, and of too much honor to publish them if he did not believe them. There are few people in the world capable of your extravagances; they are peculiar to yourselves, and mark your character too plainly to admit of any excuse for having failed to recognize your hand in their concoction. I was led away by the common report; but this apology, which would be too good for you, is not sufficient for me, who profess to advance nothing without certain proof. In no other instance have I been guilty of departing from this rule. I am sorry for what I said. I retract it; and I only wish that you may profit by my example.

TO THE REVEREND
FATHER ANNAT, JESUIT

*The author of the letters vindicated from the charge of heresy—
an heretical phantom—popes and general councils not infallible
in questions of fact*

January 23, 1657

REVEREND FATHER,—Your former behavior had induced
me to believe that you were anxious for a truce in our hostili-
ties and I was quite disposed to agree that it should be so.
Of late, however, you have poured forth such a volley of
pamphlets, in such rapid succession, as to make it apparent
that peace rests on a very precarious footing when it depends
on the silence of Jesuits. I know not if this rupture will prove
very advantageous to you; but, for my part, I am far from
regretting the opportunity which it affords me of rebutting
that stale charge of heresy with which your writings abound.

It is full time, indeed, that I should, once for all, put a
stop to the liberty you have taken to treat me as a heretic—
a piece of gratuitous impertinence which seems to increase by
indulgence, and which is exhibited in your last book in a style
of such intolerable assurance, that were I not to answer the
charge as it deserves, I might lay myself open to the suspicion
of being actually guilty. So long as the insult was confined to
your associates I despised it, as I did a thousand others with
which they interlarded their productions. To these my fifteenth letter was a sufficient reply. But you now repeat the

charge with a different air: you make it the main point of your vindication. It is, in fact, almost the only thing in the shape of argument that you employ. You say that, "as a complete answer to my fifteen letters, it is enough to say fifteen times that I am a heretic; and having been pronounced such, I deserve no credit." In short, you make no question of my apostasy, but assume it as a settled point, on which you may build with all confidence. You are serious then, father, it would seem, in deeming me a heretic. I shall be equally serious in replying to the charge.

You are well aware, sir, that heresy is a charge of so grave a character, that it is an act of high presumption to advance, without being prepared to substantiate it. I now demand your proofs. When was I seen at Charenton? When did I fail in my presence at mass, or in my Christian duty to my parish church? What act of union with heretics, or of schism with the Church, can you lay to my charge? What council have I contradicted? What papal constitution have I violated? You *must* answer, father, else—— You know what I mean. And what *do* you answer? I beseech all to observe it: First of all, you assume "that the author of the letters is a Port-Royalist"; then you tell us "that Port-Royal is declared to be heretical"; and, therefore, you conclude, "the author of the letters must be a heretic." It is not on me, then, father, that the weight of this indictment falls, but on Port-Royal; and I am only involved in the crime because you suppose me to belong to that establishment; so that it will be no difficult matter for me to exculpate myself from the charge. I have no more to say than that I am not a member of that community; and to refer you to my letters, in which I have declared that "I am a private individual"; and again in so many words, that "I am not of Port-Royal," as I said in my sixteenth letter, which preceded your publication.

You must fall on some other way, then, to prove me heretic, otherwise the whole world will be convinced that it is beyond your power to make good your accusation. Prove from my writings that I do not receive the constitution. My letters are not very voluminous—there are but sixteen of them—and I defy you or anybody else to detect in them the slightest foundation for such a charge. I shall, however, with your permission, produce something out of them to prove the reverse. When, for example, I say in the fourteenth that, "by killing our brethren in mortal sin, according to your maxims, we are damning those for whom Jesus Christ died," do I not plainly acknowledge that Jesus Christ died for those who may be damned, and, consequently, declare it to be false "that he died only for the predestinated," which is the error condemned in the fifth proposition? Certain it is, father, that I have not said a word in behalf of these impious propositions, which I detest with all my heart. And even though Port-Royal should hold them, I protest against your drawing any conclusion from this against me, as, thank God, I have no sort of connection with any community except the Catholic, Apostolic and Roman Church, in the bosom of which I desire to live and die, in communion with the pope, the head of the Church, and beyond the pale of which I am persuaded there is no salvation.

How are you to get at a person who talks in this way, father? On what quarter will you assail me, since neither my words nor my writings afford the slightest handle to your accusations, and the obscurity in which my person is enveloped forms my protection against your threatenings? You feel yourselves smitten by an invisible hand—a hand, however, which makes your delinquencies visible to all the earth; and in vain do you endeavor to attack me in the person of those with whom you suppose me to be associated. I fear you not, either on my own account or on that of any other, being bound by no tie either to a community or to any individual whatsoever. All the influence which your Society possesses can be of no avail in my case. From this world I have nothing to hope, nothing to dread, nothing to desire. Through the goodness of God, I have no need of any man's money or any man's patronage. Thus, my father, I elude all your attempts to lay hold of me. You may touch Port-Royal if you choose, but you shall not touch me. You may turn people out of the Sorbonne, but that will not turn me out of my domicile. You may contrive plots against priests and doctors, but not against me, for I am neither the one nor the other. And thus, father, you never perhaps had to do, in the whole course of your experience, with a person so completely beyond your reach, and therefore so admirably qualified for dealing with your errors—one perfectly free—one without engagement, entanglement, relationship, or business of any kind—one, too, who is pretty well versed in your maxims, and determined, as God shall give him light, to discuss them, without permitting any earthly consideration to arrest or slacken his endeavors.

Since, then, you can do nothing against me, what good purpose can it serve to publish so many calumnies, as you and your brethren are doing, against a class of persons who are in no way implicated in our disputes? You shall not escape under these subterfuges: you shall be made to feel the force of the truth in spite of them. How does the case stand? I tell you that you are ruining Christian morality by divorcing it from the love of God, and dispensing with its obligation; and you talk about "the death of Father Mester"—a person whom I never saw in my life. I tell you that your authors permit a man to kill another for the sake of an apple, when it would be dishonorable to lose it; and you reply by informing me that somebody "has broken into the poor-box at St. Merri!" Again, what can you possibly mean by mixing me up perpetually with the book "On the Holy Virginity," written by some father of the Oratory, whom I never saw, any more than his book?" It is rather extraordinary, father, that you should thus regard all that are opposed to you as if they were one person. Your hatred would grasp them all at once, and would hold them as a body of reprobates, every one of whom is responsible for all the rest.

There is a vast difference between Jesuits and all their opponents. There can be no doubt that you compose one body, united under one head; and your regulations, as I have shown, prohibit you from printing anything without the approbation of your superiors, who are responsible for all the errors of individual writers, and who "cannot excuse themselves by saying that they did not observe the errors in any publication, for they ought to have observed them." So say your ordinances, and so say the letters of your generals, Aquaviva, Vitelleschi, &c. We have good reason, therefore, for charging upon you the errors of your associates, when we find they are sanctioned by your superiors and the divines of your Society. With me, however, father, the case stands otherwise. I have not subscribed to the book of the Holy Virginity. All the almsboxes in Paris may be broken into, and yet I am not the less a good Catholic for all that. In short, I beg to inform you, in the plainest terms, that nobody is responsible for my letters but myself, and that I am responsible for nothing but my letters.

Here, father, I might fairly enough have brought our dispute to an issue, without saying a word about those other persons whom you stigmatize as heretics, in order to comprehend me under the condemnation. But as I have been the occasion of their ill treatment, I consider myself bound in some sort to improve the occasion, and I shall take advantage of it in three particulars. One advantage, not inconsiderable in its way, is that it will enable me to vindicate the innocence of so many calumniated individuals. Another, not inappropriate to my subject, will be to disclose, at the same time, the artifices of your policy in this accusation. But the advantage which I prize most of all is, that it affords me an opportunity of apprising the world of the falsehood of that scandalous report which you have been so busily disseminating, namely, "that the Church is divided by a new heresy." And as you are deceiving multitudes into the belief that the points on which you are raising such a storm are essential to the faith, I consider it of the last importance to quash these unfounded impressions, and distinctly to explain here what these points are, so as to show that, in point of fact, there are no heretics in the Church.

I presume, then, that were the question to be asked, Wherein consists the heresy of those called Jansenists? the immediate reply would be, "These people hold that the commandments of God are impracticable to men—that grace is irresistible—that we have not free will to do either good or evil—that Jesus Christ did not die for all men, but only for the elect; in short, they maintain the five propositions condemned by the pope." Do you not give it out to all that this is the ground on which you persecute your opponents? Have you not said as much in your books, in your conversations, in your catechisms? A specimen of this you gave at the late Christmas festival at St. Louis. One of your little shepherdesses was questioned thus:—

"For whom did Jesus Christ come into the world, my dear?"

"For all men, father."

"Indeed, my child; so you are not one of those new heretics who say that he came only for the elect?"

Thus children are led to believe you, and many others besides children; for you entertain people with the same stuff in your sermons, as Father Crasset did at Orleans, before he was laid under an interdict. And I frankly own that, at one time, I believed you myself. You had given me precisely the same idea of these good people; so that when you pressed them on these propositions, I narrowly watched their answer, determined never to see them more, if they did not renounce them as palpable impieties.

This, however, they have done in the most unequivocal way. M. de Sainte-Beuve, king's professor in the Sorbonne, censured these propositions in his published writings long before the pope; and other Augustinian doctors, in various publications, and, among others, in a work "On Victorious Grace," reject the same articles as both heretical and strange doctrines. In the preface to that work they say that these propositions are "heretical and Lutheran, forged and fabricated at pleasure, and are neither to be found in Jansenius, nor in his defenders." They complain of being charged with such sentiments, and address you in the words of St. Prosper, the first disciple of St. Augustine their master, to whom the semi-Pelagians of France had ascribed similar opinions, with the view of bringing him into disgrace: "There are persons who denounce us, so blinded by passion that they have adopted means for doing so which ruin their own reputation. They have, for this purpose, fabricated propositions of the most impious and blasphemous character, which they industriously circulate, to make people believe that we maintain them in the wicked sense which they are pleased to attach to them. But our reply will show at once our innocence, and the malignity of these persons who have ascribed to us a set of impious tenets, of which they are themselves the sole inventors."

Truly, father, when I found that they had spoken in this way before the appearance of the papal constitution—when I saw that they afterwards received that decree with all possible respect, that they offered to subscribe it, and that M. Arnauld had declared all this in his second letter, in stronger terms than I can report him, I should have considered it a sin to doubt their soundness in the faith. And, in fact, those who were formerly disposed to refuse absolution to M. Arnauld's friends, have since declared, that after his explicit disclaimer of the errors imputed to him, there was no reason left for cutting off either him or them from the communion of the Church. Your associates, however, have acted very differently; and it was this that made me begin to suspect that you were actuated by prejudice.

You threatened first to compel them to sign that constitution, so long as you thought they would resist it; but no sooner did you see them quite ready of their own accord to submit to it, than we heard no more about this. Still, however, though one might suppose this ought to have satisfied you, you persisted in calling them heretics, "because," said you, "their heart belies their hand; they are Catholics outwardly, but inwardly they are heretics."

This, father, struck me as very strange reasoning; for where is the person of whom as much may not be said at any time? And what endless trouble and confusion would ensue, were it allowed to go on! "If," says Pope St. Gregory, "we refuse to believe a confession of faith made in conformity to the sentiments of the Church, we cast a doubt over the faith of all Catholics whatsoever." I am afraid, father, to use the words of the same pontiff, when speaking of a similar dispute this time, "that your object is to make these persons heretics in spite of themselves; because to refuse to credit those who testify by their confession that they are in the true faith, is not to purge heresy, but to create it—*hoc non est hæresim purgare, sed facere*. But what confirmed me in my persuasion that there was indeed no heretic in the Church, was finding that our so-called heretics had vindicated themselves so successfully, that you were unable to accuse them of a single error in the faith, and that you were reduced to the necessity of assailing them on questions of *fact* only, touching Jansenius, which could not possibly be construed into heresy. You insist, it now appears, on their being compelled to acknowledge "that these propositions are contained in Jansenius, word for word, every one of them, in so many terms," or, as you express it, *Singulares, individuæ, totidem verbis apud Jansenium contentæ*.

Thenceforth your dispute became, in my eyes, perfectly indifferent. So long as I believed that you were debating the truth or falsehood of the propositions, I was all attention, for that quarrel touched the faith; but when I discovered that the bone of contention was whether they were to be found, word for word, in Jansenius or not, as religion ceased to be interested in the controversy, I ceased to be interested in it also. Not but that there was some presumption that you were speaking the truth; because to say that such and such expressions are to be found, word for word, in an author, is a matter in which there can be no mistake. I do not wonder, therefore, that so many people, both in France and at Rome, should have been led to believe, on the authority of a phrase so little liable to suspicion, that Jansenius has actually taught these obnoxious tenets. And for the same reason, I was not a little surprised to learn that this same point of fact, which you had propounded as so certain and so important, was false; and that after being challenged to quote the pages of Jansenius, in which you had found these propositions "word for word," you have not been able to point them out to this day.

I am the more particular in giving this statement, because, in my opinion, it discovers, in a very striking light, the spirit of your Society in the whole of this affair; and because some people will be astonished to find that, notwithstanding all the facts above mentioned, you have not ceased to publish that they are heretics still. But you have only altered the heresy to suit the time; for no sooner had they freed themselves from one charge than your fathers, determined that they should never want an accusation, substituted another in its place. Thus, in 1653, their heresy lay in the *quality* of the propositions; then came the *word for word* heresy; after that, we had the *heart* heresy. And now we hear nothing of any of these, and they must be heretics, forsooth, unless they sign a declaration to the effect, *"that the sense of the doctrine of Jansenius is contained in the sense of the five propositions."*

Such is your present dispute. It is not enough for you that they condemn the five propositions, and everything in Jansenius that bears any resemblance to them, or is contrary to St. Augustine; for all that they have done already. The point at issue is not, for example, if Jesus Christ died for the elect only —they condemn that as much as you do; but, is Jansenius of that opinion, or not? And here I declare, more strongly than ever, that your quarrel affects me as little as it affects the Church. For although I am no doctor, any more than you, father, I can easily see, nevertheless, that it has no connection with the faith. The only question is, to ascertain what is the sense of Jansenius. Did they believe that his doctrine corresponded to the proper and literal sense of these propositions, they would condemn it; and they refuse to do so, because they are convinced it is quite the reverse; so that although they should misunderstand it, still they would not be heretics, seeing they understand it only in a Catholic sense.

To illustrate this by an example, I may refer to the conflicting sentiments of St. Basil and St. Athanasius, regarding the writings of St. Denis of Alexandria, which St. Basil, conceiving that he found in them the sense of Arius against the equality of the Father and the Son, condemned as heretical, but which St. Athanasius, on the other hand, judging them to contain the genuine sense of the Church, maintained to be perfectly orthodox. Think you, then, father, that St. Basil, who held these writings to be Arian, had a right to brand St. Athanasius as a heretic, because he defended them? And what ground would he have had for so doing, seeing that it was not Arianism that his brother defended, but the true faith which he considered these writings to contain? Had these two saints agreed about the true sense of these writings, and had both recognized this heresy in them, unquestionably St. Athanasius could not have approved of them without being guilty of heresy; but as they were at variance respecting the sense of the passage, St. Athanasius was orthodox in vindicating them, even though he may have understood them wrong; because in that case it would have been merely an error in a matter of fact, and because what he defended was really the Catholic faith, which he supposed to be contained in these writings.

I apply this to you, father. Suppose you were agreed upon the sense of Jansenius, and your adversaries were ready to admit with you that he held, for example, *that grace cannot be resisted;* those who refused to condemn him would be heretical. But as your dispute turns upon the meaning of that author, and they believe that, according to his doctrine, *grace may be resisted*, whatever heresy you may be pleased to attribute to him, you have no ground to brand them as heretics, seeing they condemn the sense which you put on Jansenius, and you dare not condemn the sense which they put on him. If, therefore, you mean to convict them, show that the sense which they ascribe to Jansenius is heretical; for then they will be heretical themselves. But how could you accomplish this, since it is certain, according to your own showing, that the meaning which they give to his language has never been condemned?

To elucidate the point still further, I shall assume as a principle what you yourselves acknowledge—*that the doctrine of efficacious grace has never been condemned, and that the pope has not touched it by his constitution.* And, in fact, when he proposed to pass judgment on the five propositions, the question of efficacious grace was protected against all censure. This is perfectly evident from the judgments of the consulters, to whom the pope committed them for examination. These judgments I have in my possession, in common with many other persons in Paris, and, among the rest, the bishop of Montpelier, who brought them from Rome. It appears from this document, that they were divided in their sentiments; that the chief persons among them, such as the Master of the Sacred Palace, the commissary of the Holy Office, the General of the Augustinians, and others, conceiving that these propositions might be understood in the sense of *efficacious grace,* were of opinion that they ought not to be censured; whereas the rest, while they agreed that the propositions would not have merited condemnation, had they borne that sense, judged that they ought to be censured, because, as they contended, this was very far from being their proper and natural sense. The pope, accordingly, condemned them; and all parties have acquiesced in his judgment.

It is certain, then, father, that efficacious grace has not been condemned. Indeed, it is so powerfully supported by St. Augustine, by St. Thomas, and all his school, by a great many popes and councils, and by all tradition, that to tax it with heresy would be an act of impiety. Now, all those whom you condemn as heretics declare that they find nothing in Jansenius, but this doctrine of efficacious grace. And this was the only point which they maintained at Rome. You have acknowledged this yourself, when you declare that, "when pleading before the pope, they did not say a single word about the propositions, but occupied the whole time in talking about efficacious grace." So that whether they be right or wrong in this supposition, it is undeniable, at least, that what they suppose to be the sense is not heretical sense; and that, consequently, they are no heretics; for, to state the matter in two words, either Jansenius has merely taught the doctrine of efficacious grace, and in this case he has no errors; or he has taught some other thing, and in this case he has no defenders. The whole question turns on ascertaining whether Jansenius has actually maintained something different from efficacious grace; and should it be found that he has, you will have the honor of having better understood him, but they will not have the misfortune of having erred from the faith.

It is matter of thankfulness to God, then, father, that there is in reality no heresy in the Church. The question relates entirely to a point of fact, of which no heresy can be made; for the Church, with divine authority, decides the points of *faith,* and cuts off from her body all who refuse to receive them. But she does not act in the same manner in regard to matters of *fact.* And the reason is, that our salvation is attached to the faith which has been revealed to us, and which is preserved in the Church by tradition, but that it has no dependence on facts which have not been revealed by God. Thus we are bound to believe that the commandments of God are not impracticable; but we are under no obligation to know what Jansenius has said upon that subject. In the determination of points of faith God guides the Church by the aid of His unerring Spirit; whereas in matters of fact, He leaves her to the direction of reason and the senses, which are the natural judges of such matters. None but God was able to instruct the Church in the faith; but to learn whether this or that proposition is contained in Jansenius, all we require to do is to read his book. And from hence it follows, that while it is heresy to resist the decisions of the faith, because this amounts to an opposing of our own spirit to the Spirit of God, it is no heresy, though it may be an act of presumption, to disbelieve certain particular facts, because this is no more than opposing reason—it may be enlightened reason—to an authority which is great indeed, but in this matter not infallible.

What I have now advanced is admitted by all theologians, as appears from the following axiom of Cardinal Bellarmine, a member of your Society: "General and lawful councils are incapable of error in defining the dogmas of faith; but they may err in questions of fact." In another place he says: "The pope, as pope, and even as the head of a universal council, may err in particular controversies of fact, which depend principally on the information and testimony of men." Cardinal Baronius speaks in the same manner: "Implicit submission is due to the decisions of councils in points of faith; but, in so far as persons and their writings are concerned, the censures which have been pronounced against them have not been so rigorously observed, because there is none who may not chance to be deceived in such matters." I may add that, to prove this point, the Archbishop of Toulouse has deduced the following rule from the letters of two great popes—St. Leon and Pelagius II.: "That the proper object of councils is the faith; and whatsoever is determined by them, independently of the faith, may be reviewed and examined anew: whereas nothing ought to be re-examined that has been decided in a matter of faith; because, as Tertullian observes, the rule of faith alone is immovable and irrevocable."

Hence it has been seen that, while general and lawful councils have never contradicted one another in points of faith, because, as M. de Toulouse has said, "it is not allowable to examine *de novo* decisions in matters of faith"; several instances have occurred in which these same councils have disagreed in points of fact, where the discussion turned upon the sense of an author; because, as the same prelate observes, quoting the popes as his authorities, "everything determined in councils, not referring to the faith, may be reviewed and examined *de novo*." An example of this contrariety was furnished by the fourth and fifth councils, which differed in their interpretation of the same authors. The same thing happened in the case of two popes, about a proposition maintained by certain monks of Scythia. Pope Hormisdas, understanding it in a bad sense, had condemned it; but Pope John II., his successor, upon re-examining the doctrine, understood it in a good sense, approved it, and pronounced it to be orthodox. Would you say that for this reason one of these popes was a heretic? And must you not consequently acknowledge that, provided a person condemn the heretical sense which a pope may have ascribed to a book, he is no heretic because he declines condemning that book, while he understands it in a sense which it is certain the pope has not condemned? If this cannot be admitted, one of these popes must have fallen into error.

I have been anxious to familiarize you with these discrepancies among Catholics regarding questions of fact, which involve the understanding of the sense of a writer, showing you father against father, pope against pope, and council against council, to lead you from these to other examples of opposition, similar in their nature, but somewhat more disproportioned in respect of the parties concerned. For, in the instances I am now to adduce, you will see councils and popes ranged on one side, and Jesuits on the other; and yet you have never charged your brethren, for this opposition, even with presumption, much less with heresy.

You are well aware, father, that the writings of Origen were condemned by a great many popes and councils, and particularly by the fifth general council, as chargeable with certain heresies, and, among others, that of *the reconciliation of the devils at the day of judgment*. Do you suppose that, after this, it became absolutely imperative, as a test of Catholicism, to confess that Origen actually maintained these errors, and that it is not enough to condemn them, without attributing them to him? If this were true, what would become of your worthy Father Halloix, who has asserted the purity of Origen's faith, as well as many other Catholics, who have attempted the same thing, such as Pico Mirandola, and Genebrard, doctor of the Sorbonne? Is it not, moreover, a certain fact, that the same fifth general council condemned the writings of Theodoret against St. Cyril, describing them as impious, "contrary to the true faith, and tainted with the Nestorian heresy?" And yet this has not prevented Father Sirmond, a Jesuit, from defending him, or from saying, in his life of that father, that "his writings are entirely free from the heresy of Nestorius."

It is evident, therefore, that as the Church, in condemning a book, assumes that the error which she condemns is contained in that book, it is a point of faith to hold that error as condemned; but it is not a point of faith to hold that the book, in fact, contains the error which the Church supposes it does. Enough has been said, I think, to prove this; I shall, therefore, conclude my examples by referring to that of Pope Honorius, the history of which is so well known. At the commencement of the seventh century, the Church being troubled by the heresy of the Monothelites, that pope, with the view of terminating the controversy, passed a decree which seemed favorable to these heretics, at which many took offence. The affair, nevertheless, passed over without making much disturbance during his pontificate; but fifty years after, the Church being assembled in the sixth general council, in which Pope Agathon presided by his legates, this decree was impeached, and, after being read and examined, was condemned as containing the heresy of the Monothelites, and under that character burnt, in open court, along with the other writings of these heretics. Such was the respect paid to this decision, and such the unanimity with which it was received throughout the whole Church, that it was afterwards ratified by two other general councils, and likewise by two popes, Leon II. and Adrian II., the latter of whom lived two hundred years after it had passed; and this universal and harmonious agreement remained undisturbed for seven or eight centuries. Of late years, however, some authors, and among the rest Cardinal Bellarmine, without seeming to dread the imputation of heresy, have stoutly maintained, against all this array of popes and councils, that the writings of Honorius are free from the error which had been ascribed to them; "because," says the cardinal, "general councils being liable to err in questions of fact, we have the best grounds for asserting that the sixth council was mistaken with regard to the fact now under consideration; and that, misconceiving the sense of the Letters of Honorius, it has placed this pope most unjustly in the ranks of heretics." Observe, then, I pray you, father, that a man is not heretical for saying that Pope Honorius was not a heretic; even though a great many popes and councils, after examining his writings, should have declared that he was so.

I now come to the question before us, and shall allow you to state your case as favorably as you can. What will you then say, father, in order to stamp your opponents as heretics? That "Pope Innocent X. has declared that the error of the five propositions is to be found in Jansenius?" I grant you that; what inference do you draw from it? That "it is heretical to deny that the error of the five propositions is to be found in Jansenius"? How so, father? Have we not here a question of fact exactly similar to the preceding examples? The pope has declared that the error of the five propositions is contained in Jansenius, in the same way as his predecessors decided that the errors of the Nestorians and the Monothelites polluted the pages of Theodoret and Honorius. In the latter case, your writers hesitate not to say, that while they condemn the heresies, they do not allow that these authors actually maintained them; and, in like manner, your opponents now say, that they condemn the five propositions, but cannot admit that Jansenius has taught them. Truly, the two cases are as like as they could well be; and if there be any disparity between them, it is easy to see how far it must go in favor of the present question, by a comparison of many particular circumstances, which, as they are self-evident, I do not specify. How comes it to pass, then, that when placed in precisely the same predicament, your friends are Catholics and your opponents heretics? On what strange principle of exception do you deprive the latter of a liberty which you freely award to all the rest of the faithful? What answer will you make to this, father? Will you say, "The pope has confirmed his constitution by a brief." To this I would reply, that two general councils and two popes confirmed the condemnation of the letters of Honorius. But what argument do you found upon the language of that brief, in which all that the pope says is, that "he has condemned the doctrine of Jansenius in these five propositions"? What does that add to the constitution, or what more can you infer from it? Nothing, certainly, except that as the sixth council condemned the doctrine of Honorius, in the belief that it was the same with that of the Monothelites, so the pope has said that he has condemned the doctrine of Jansenius in these five propositions, because he was led to suppose it was the same with that of the five propositions. And how could he do otherwise than suppose it? Your Society published nothing else; and you yourself, father, who have asserted that the said propositions were in that author "word for word," happened to be in Rome (for I know all your motions) at the time when the censure was passed. Was he to distrust the sincerity or the competence of so many grave ministers of religion? And how could he help being convinced of the fact, after the assurance which you had given him that the propositions were in that author "word for word"? It is evident, therefore, that in the event of its being found that Jansenius has not supported these doctrines, it would be wrong to say, as your writers have done in the cases before mentioned, that the pope has deceived himself in this point of fact, which it is painful and offensive to publish at any time; the proper phrase is, that you have deceived the pope, which, as you are now pretty well known, will create no scandal.

Determined, however, to have a heresy made out, let it cost what it may, you have attempted, by the following manœuvre, to shift the question from the point of fact, and make it bear upon a point of faith. "The pope," say you, "declares that he has condemned the doctrine of Jansenius in these five propositions; therefore it is essential to the faith to hold that the doctrine of Jansenius touching these five propositions is heretical, *let it be what it may*." Here is a strange point of faith, that a doctrine is heretical *be what it may*. What! if Jansenius should happen to maintain that *"we are capable of resisting internal grace,"* and that *"it is false to say that Jesus*

Christ died for the elect only," would this doctrine be condemned just because it is his doctrine? Will the proposition, that *"man has a freedom of will to do good or evil,"* be true when found in the pope's constitution, and false when discovered in Jansenius? By what fatality must he be reduced to such a predicament, that truth, when admitted into his book, becomes heresy? You must confess, then, that he is only heretical on the supposition that he is friendly to the errors condemned, seeing that the constitution of the pope is the rule which we must apply to Jansenius, to judge if his character answer the description there given of him; and, accordingly, the question, *Is his doctrine heretical?* must be resolved by another question of fact, *Does it correspond to the natural sense of these propositions?* as it must necessarily be heretical if it does correspond to that sense, and must necessarily be orthodox if it be of an opposite character. For, in one word, since, according to the pope and the bishops, "the propositions are condemned *in their proper and natural sense,"* they cannot possibly be condemned in the sense of Jansenius, except on the understanding that the sense of Jansenius is the same with the proper and natural sense of these propositions; and this I maintain to be purely a question of fact.

The question, then, still rests upon the point of fact, and cannot possibly be tortured into one affecting the faith. But though incapable of twisting it into a matter of heresy, you have it in your power to make it a pretext for persecution, and might, perhaps, succeed in this, were there not good reason to hope that nobody will be found so blindly devoted to your interests as to countenance such a disgraceful proceeding, or inclined to compel people, as you wish to do, to sign a declaration *that they condemn these propositions in the sense of Jansenius,* without explaining what the sense of Jansenius is. Few people are disposed to sign a blank confession of faith. Now this would really be to sign one of that description, leaving you to fill up the blank afterwards with whatsoever you pleased, as you would be at liberty to interpret according to your own taste the unexplained sense of Jansenius. Let it be explained, then, beforehand, otherwise we shall have, I fear, another version of your *proximate power,* without any sense at all—*abstrahendo ab omni sensu.* This mode of proceeding, you must be aware, does not take with the world. Men in general detest all ambiguity, especially in the matter of religion, where it is highly reasonable that one should know at least what one is asked to condemn. And how is it possible for doctors, who are persuaded that Jansenius can bear no other sense than that of efficacious grace, to consent to declare that they condemn his doctrine without explaining it, since, with their present convictions, which no means are used to alter, this would be neither more nor less than to condemn efficacious grace, which cannot be condemned without sin? Would it not, therefore, be a piece of monstrous tyranny to place them in such an unhappy dilemma, that they must either bring guilt upon their souls in the sight of God, by signing that condemnation against their consciences, or be denounced as heretics for refusing to sign it?

But there is a mystery under all this. You Jesuits cannot move a step without a stratagem. It remains for me to explain why you do not explain the sense of Jansenius. The sole purpose of my writing is to discover your designs, and, by discovering, to frustrate them. I must, therefore, inform those who are not already aware of the fact, that your great concern in this dispute being to uphold the *sufficient grace* of your Molina, you could not effect this without destroying the *efficacious grace* which stands directly opposed to it. Perceiving, however, that the latter was now sanctioned at Rome, and by all the learned in the Church, and unable to combat the doctrine on its own merits, you resolved to attack it in a clandestine way, under the name of the doctrine of Jansenius. You were resolved, accordingly, to get Jansenius condemned without explanation; and, to gain your purpose, gave out that his doctrine was not that of efficacious grace, so that every one might think he was at liberty to condemn the one without denying the other. Hence your efforts, in the present day, to impress this idea upon the minds of such as have no acquaintance with that author; an object which you yourself, father, have attempted, by means of the following ingenious syllogism: "The pope has condemned the doctrine of Jansenius; but the pope has not condemned efficacious grace: therefore, the doctrine of efficacious grace must be different from that of Jansenius." If this mode of reasoning were conclusive, it might be demonstrated in the same way that Honorius and all his defenders are heretics of the same kind. "The sixth council has condemned the doctrine of Honorius; but the council has not condemned the doctrine of the Church: therefore the doctrine of Honorius is different from that of the Church; and therefore, all who defend him are heretics." It is obvious that no conclusion can be drawn from this; for the pope has done no more than condemn the doctrine of the five propositions, which was represented to him as the doctrine of Jansenius.

But it matters not; you have no intention to make use of this logic for any length of time. Poor as it is, it will last sufficiently long to serve your present turn. All that you wish to effect by it, in the meantime, is to induce those who are unwilling to condemn efficacious grace to condemn Jansenius with less scruple. When this object has been accomplished, your argument will soon be forgotten, and their signatures remaining as an eternal testimony in condemnation of Jansenius, will furnish you with an occasion to make a direct attack upon efficacious grace, by another mode of reasoning much more solid than the former, which shall be forthcoming in proper time. "The doctrine of Jansenius," you will argue, "has been condemned by the universal subscriptions of the Church. Now this doctrine is manifestly that of efficacious grace" (and it will be easy for you to prove that); "therefore the doctrine of efficacious grace is condemned even by the confession of his defenders."

Behold your reason for proposing to sign the condemnation of a doctrine without giving an explanation of it! Behold the advantage you expect to gain from subscriptions thus procured! Should your opponents, however, refuse to subscribe, you have another trap laid for them. Having dexterously combined the question of faith with that of fact, and not allowing them to separate between them, nor to sign the one without the other, the consequence will be, that, because they could not subscribe the two together, you will publish it in all directions that they have refused the two together. And thus though, in point of fact, they simply decline acknowledging that Jansenius has maintained the propositions which they condemn, which cannot be called heresy, you will boldly assert that they have refused to condemn the propositions themselves, and that it is this that constitutes their heresy.

Such is the fruit which you expect to reap from their refusal, and which will be no less useful to you than what you might have gained from their consent. So that, in the event of these signatures being exacted, they will fall into your snares, whether they sign or not, and in both cases you will gain your point; such is your dexterity in uniformly putting matters into a train for your own advantage, whatever bias they may happen to take in their course!

How well I know you, father! and how grieved am I to see that God has abandoned you so far as to allow you such happy success in such an unhappy course! Your good fortune deserves commiseration, and can excite envy only in the breasts of those who know not what truly good fortune is. It is an act of charity to thwart the success you aim at in the whole of this proceeding, seeing that you can only reach it by the aid of falsehood, and by procuring credit to one of two lies —either that the Church has condemned efficacious grace, or that those who defend that doctrine maintain the five condemned errors.

The world must, therefore, be apprised of two facts: First, That, by your own confession, efficacious grace has not been condemned; and secondly, That nobody supports these errors. So that it may be known that those who may refuse to sign what you are so anxious to exact from them, refuse merely in consideration of the question of *fact;* and that, being quite ready to subscribe that of *faith,* they cannot be deemed heretical on that account; because, to repeat it once more, though it be matter of faith to believe these propositions to be heretical, it will never be matter of faith to hold that they are to be found in the pages of Jansenius. They are innocent of all error; that is enough. It may be that they interpret Jansenius too favorably; but it may be also that you do not interpret him favorably enough. I do not enter upon this question. All that I know is, that, according to your maxims, you believe that you may, without sin, publish him to be a heretic contrary to your own knowledge; whereas, according to their maxims, they cannot, without sin, declare him to be a Catholic, unless they are persuaded that he is one. They are, therefore, more honest than you, father; they have examined Jansenius more faithfully than you; they are no less intelligent than you; they are, therefore, no less credible witnesses than you. But come what may of this point of fact, they are certainly Catholics; for, in order to be so, it is not necessary to declare that another man is not a Catholic; it is enough, in all conscience, if a person, without charging error upon anybody else, succeed in discharging himself.

Reverend Father,—If you have found any difficulty in deciphering this letter, which is certainly not printed in the best possible type, blame nobody but yourself. Privileges are not so easily granted to me as they are to you. You can procure them even for the purpose of combating miracles; I cannot have them even to defend myself. The printing-houses are perpetually haunted. In such circumstances, you yourself would not advise me to write you any more letters, for it is really a sad annoyance to be obliged to have recourse to an Osnabruck impression.

TO THE REVEREND FATHER ANNAT, JESUIT

Showing still more plainly, on the authority of Father Annat him-self, that there is really no heresy in the Church, and that in questions of fact we must be guided by our senses, and not by authority even of the popes

March 24, 1657

REVEREND FATHER,—Long have you labored to discover some error in the creed or conduct of your opponents; but I rather think you will have to confess, in the end, that it is a more difficult task than you imagined to make heretics of people who are not only no heretics, but who hate nothing in the world so much as heresy. In my last letter I succeeded in showing that you accuse them of one heresy after another, without being able to stand by one of the charges for any length of time; so that all that remained for you was to fix on their refusal to condemn "the sense of Jansenius," which you insist on their doing without explanation. You must have been sadly in want of heresies to brand them with, when you were reduced to this. For who ever heard of a heresy which nobody could explain? The answer was ready, therefore, that if Jansenius has no errors, it is wrong to condemn him; and if he has, you were bound to point them out, that we might know at least what we were condemning. This, how-ever, you have never yet been pleased to do; but you have attempted to fortify your position by decrees, which made nothing in your favor, as they gave no sort of explanation of the sense of Jansenius, said to have been condemned in the five propositions. This was not the way to terminate the dispute. Had you mutually agreed as to the genuine sense of Jansenius, and had the only difference between you been as to whether that sense was heretical or not, in that case the decisions which might pronounce it to be heretical, would have touched the real question in dispute. But the great dispute being about the sense of Jansenius, the one party saying that they could see nothing in it inconsistent with the sense of St. Augustine and St. Thomas, and the other party asserting that they saw in it an heretical sense which they would not express. It is clear that a constitution which does not say a word about this difference of opinion, and which only condemns in general and without explanation the sense of Jansenius, leaves the point in dispute quite undecided.

You have accordingly been repeatedly told, that as your discussion turns on a matter of fact, you would never be able to bring it to a conclusion without declaring what you understand by the sense of Jansenius. But, as you continued obstinate in your refusal to make this explanation, I endeavored, as a last resource, to extort it from you, by hinting, in my last letter, that there was some mystery under the efforts you were making to procure the condemnation of this sense without explaining it, and that your design was to make this indefinite censure recoil some day or other, upon the doctrine of efficacious grace, by showing, as you could easily do, that this was exactly the doctrine of Jansenius. This has reduced you to the necessity of making a reply; for, had you pertinaciously refused, after such an insinuation, to explain your views of that sense, it would have been apparent, to persons of the smallest penetration, that you condemned it in the sense of efficacious grace—a conclusion which, considering the veneration in which the Church holds holy doctrine, would have overwhelmed you with disgrace.

You have, therefore, been forced to speak out your mind; and we find it expressed in your reply to that part of my letter in which I remarked, that "if Jansenius was capable of any other sense than that of efficacious grace, he had no defenders; but if his writings bore no other sense, he had no errors to defend." You found it impossible to deny this position, father; but you have attempted to parry it by the following distinction: "It is not sufficient," say you, "for the vindication of Jansenius, to allege that he merely holds the doctrine of efficacious grace, for that may be held in two ways—the one heretical, according to Calvin, which consists in maintaining that the will, when under the influence of grace, has not the power of resisting it; the other orthodox, according to the Thomists and the Sorbonists, which is founded on the principles established by the councils, and which is, that efficacious grace of itself governs the will in such a way that it still has the power of resisting it."

All this we grant, father; but you conclude by adding: "Jansenius would be orthodox, if he defended efficacious grace in the sense of the Thomists; but he is heretical, because he opposes the Thomists, and joins issue with Calvin, who denies the power of resisting grace." I do not here enter upon the question of fact, whether Jansenius really agrees with Calvin. It is enough for my purpose that you assert that he does, and that you now inform me that by the sense of Jansenius you have all along understood nothing more than the sense of Calvin. Was this all you meant, then, father? Was it only the error of Calvin that you were so anxious to get condemned, under the name of "the sense of Jansenius?" Why did you not tell us this sooner? You might have saved yourself a world of trouble; for we were all ready, without the aid of bulls or briefs, to join with you in condemning that error. What urgent necessity there was for such an explanation! What a host of difficulties has it removed! We were quite at a loss, my dear father, to know what error the popes and bishops meant to condemn, under the name of "the sense of Jansenius." The whole Church was in the utmost perplexity about it, and not a soul would relieve us by an explanation. This, however, has now been done by you, father

—you, whom the whole of your party regard as the chief and prime mover of all their councils, and who are acquainted with the whole secret of this proceeding. You, then, have told us that the sense of Jansenius is neither more nor less than the sense of Calvin, which has been condemned by the council. Why, this explains everything. We know now that the error which they intended to condemn, under these terms —*the sense of Jansenius*—is neither more nor less than the sense of Calvin; and that, consequently, we, by joining with them in the condemnation of Calvin's doctrine, have yielded all due obedience to these decrees. We are no longer surprised at the zeal which the popes and some bishops manifested against "the sense of Jansenius." How, indeed, could they be otherwise than zealous against it, believing, as they did, the declarations of those who publicly affirmed that it was identically the same with that of Calvin?

I must maintain, then, father, that you have no further reason to quarrel with your adversaries; for they detest that doctrine as heartily as you do. I am only astonished to see that you are ignorant of this fact, and that you have such an imperfect acquaintance with their sentiments on this point, which they have so repeatedly expressed in their published works. I flatter myself that, were you more intimate with these writings, you would deeply regret your not having made yourself acquainted sooner, in the spirit of peace, with a doctrine which is in every respect so holy and so Christian, but which passion, in the absence of knowledge, now prompts you to oppose. You would find, father, that they not only hold that an effective resistance may be made to those feebler graces which go under the name of *exciting* or *inefficacious*, from their not terminating in the good with which they inspire us; but that they are, moreover, as firm in maintaining, in opposition to Calvin, the power which the will has to resist even efficacious and victorious grace, as they are in contending against Molina for the power of this grace over the will, and fully as jealous for the one of these truths as they are for the other. They know too well that man, of his own nature,

has always the power of sinning and of resisting grace; and
that, since he became corrupt, he unhappily carries in his
breast a fount of concupiscence which infinitely augments
that power; but that, notwithstanding this, when it pleases
God to visit him with his mercy, he makes the soul do what
he wills, and in the manner he wills it to be done, while, at
the same time, the infallibility of the divine operation does
not in any way destroy the natural liberty of man, in consequence of the secret and wonderful ways by which God
operates this change. This has been most admirably explained
by St. Augustine, in such a way as to dissipate all those
imaginary inconsistencies which the opponents of efficacious
grace suppose to exist between the sovereign power of grace
over the free-will and the power which the free-will has to
resist grace. For, according to this great saint, whom the
popes and the Church have held to be a standard authority on
this subject, God transforms the heart of man, by shedding
abroad in it a heavenly sweetness, which, surmounting the
delights of the flesh, and inducing him to feel, on the one
hand, his own mortality and nothingness, and to discover, on
the other hand, the majesty and eternity of God, makes him
conceive a distaste for the pleasures of sin, which interpose
between him and incorruptible happiness. Finding his chiefest
joy in the God who charms him, his soul is drawn towards
him infallibly, but of its own accord, by a motion perfectly
free, spontaneous, love-impelled; so that it would be its
torment and punishment to be separated from him. Not but
that the person has always the power of forsaking his God,
and that he may not actually forsake him, provided he choose
to do it. But how *could* he choose such a course, seeing that
the will always inclines to that which is most agreeable to it,
and that in the case we now suppose, nothing can be more
agreeable than the possession of that *one good,* which com-
prises in itself all other good things? *"Quod enim* (says St.
Augustine) *amplius nos delectat, secundum operemur necesse
est*—Our actions are necessarily determined by that which
affords us the greatest pleasure."

Such is the manner in which God regulates the free will of man without encroaching on its freedom, and in which the free will, which always may, but never will, resist his grace, turns to God with a movement as voluntary as it is irresistible, whensoever he is pleased to draw it to himself by the sweet constraint of his efficacious inspirations.

These, father, are the divine principles of St. Augustine and St. Thomas, according to which it is equally true that *we have the power of resisting grace,* contrary to Calvin's opinion, and that, nevertheless, to employ the language of Pope Clement VIII., in his paper addressed to the Congregation *de Auxiliis,* "God forms within us the motion of our will, and effectually disposes of our hearts, by virtue of that empire which his supreme majesty has over the volitions of men, as well as over the other creatures under heaven, according to St. Augustine."

On the same principle, it follows that we act of ourselves, and thus, in opposition to another error of Calvin, that we have merits which are truly and properly *ours;* and yet, as God is the first principle of our actions, and as, in the language of St. Paul, he "worketh in us that which is pleasing in his sight"; "our merits are the gifts of God," as the Council of Trent says.

By means of this distinction we demolish the profane sentiment of Luther, condemned by that Council, namely, that "we co-operate in no way whatever towards our salvation, any more than inanimate things"; and, by the same mode of reasoning, we overthrow the equally profane sentiment of the school of Molina, who will not allow that it is by the strength of divine grace that we are enabled to co-operate with it in the work of our salvation, and who thereby comes into hostile collision with that principle of faith established by St. Paul, "That it is God who worketh in us both to will and to do."

In fine, in this way we reconcile all those passages of Scripture which seem quite inconsistent with each other such as the following: "Turn ye unto God"—"Turn thou us, and we shall be turned"—"Cast away iniquity from you"—"It is God who taketh away iniquity from his people"—"Bring forth works meet for repentance"—"Lord, thou hast wrought all our works in us"—"Make ye a new heart and a new spirit"—"A new spirit will I give you, and a new heart will I create within you," &c.

The only way of reconciling these apparent contrarieties, which ascribe our good actions at one time to God, and at another time to ourselves, is to keep in view the distinction, as stated by St. Augustine, that "our actions are ours in respect of the free will which produces them; but that they are also of God, in respect of his grace which enables our free will to produce them"; and that, as the same writer elsewhere remarks, "God enables us to do what is pleasing in his sight, by making us will to do even what we might have been unwilling to do."

It thus appears, father, that your opponents are perfectly at one with the modern Thomists, for the Thomists hold, with them, both the power of resisting grace, and the infallibility of the effect of grace; of which latter doctrine they profess themselves the most strenuous advocates, if we may judge from a common maxim of their theology, which Alvarez, one of the leading men among them, repeats so often in his book, and expresses in the following terms (disp. 72, n. 4): "When efficacious grace moves the free will, it infallibly consents; because the effect of grace is such, that, although the will has the power of withholding its consent, it nevertheless consents in effect." He corroborates this by a quotation from his master, St. Thomas: "The will of God cannot fail to be accomplished; and, accordingly, when it is his pleasure that a man should consent to the influence of grace, he consents infallibly, and even necessarily, not by an absolute necessity, but by a necessity of infallibility." In effecting this, divine grace does not trench upon "the power which man has to resist it, if he wishes to do so"; it merely prevents him from wishing to resist it. This has been acknowledged by your Father Petau, in the following passage (tom. i.

p. 602): "The grace of Jesus Christ insures infallible perseverance in piety, though not by necessity; for a person may refuse to yield his consent to grace, if he be so inclined, as the council states; but that same grace provides that he shall never be so inclined."

This, father, is the uniform doctrine of St. Augustine, of St. Prosper, of the fathers who followed them, of the councils, of St. Thomas, and of all the Thomists in general. It is likewise, whatever you may think of it, the doctrine of your opponents. And let me add, it is the doctrine which you yourself have lately sealed with your approbation. I shall quote your own words: "The doctrine of efficacious grace, which admits that we have a power of resisting it, is orthodox, founded on the councils, and supported by the Thomists and Sorbonists." Now, tell us the plain truth, father; if you had known that your opponents really held this doctrine, the interests of your Society might perhaps have made you scruple before pronouncing this public approval of it; but, acting on the supposition that they were hostile to the doctrine, the same powerful motive has induced you to authorize sentiments which you know in your heart to be contrary to those of your Society; and by this blunder, in your anxiety to ruin their principles, you have yourself completely confirmed them. So that, by a kind of prodigy, we now behold the advocates of efficacious grace vindicated by the advocates of Molina—an admirable instance of the wisdom of God in making all things concur to advance the glory of the truth.

Let the whole world observe, then, that by your own admission, the truth of this efficacious grace, which is so essential to all the acts of piety, which is so dear to the Church, and which is the purchase of her Saviour's blood, is so indisputably Catholic, that there is not a single Catholic, not even among the Jesuits, who would not acknowledge its orthodoxy. And let it be noticed, at the same time, that, according to your own confession, not the slightest suspicion of error can fall on those whom you have so often stigmatized with it. For so long as you charged them with clandestine heresies, without choosing to specify them by name, it was as difficult for them to defend themselves, as it was easy for you to bring such accusations. But now, when you have come to declare that the error which constrains you to oppose them, is the heresy of Calvin which you supposed them to hold, it must be apparent to every one that they are innocent of all error; for so decidedly hostile are they to this, the only error you charge upon them, that they protest, by their discourses, by their books, by every mode, in short, in which they can testify their sentiments, that they condemn that heresy with their whole heart, and in the same manner as it has been condemned by the Thomists, whom you acknowledge, without scruple, to be Catholics, and who have never been suspected to be anything else.

What will you say against them now, father? Will you say that they are heretics still, because, although they do not adopt the sense of Calvin, they will not allow that the sense of Jansenius is the same with that of Calvin? Will you presume to say that this is matter of heresy? Is it not a pure question of fact, with which heresy has nothing to do? It would be heretical to say that we have not the power of resisting efficacious grace; but would it be so to doubt that Jansenius held that doctrine? Is this a revealed truth? Is it an article of faith which must be believed, on pain of damnation? Or is it not, in spite of you, a point of fact, on account of which it would be ridiculous to hold that there were heretics in the Church?

Drop this epithet, then, father, and give them some other name, more suited to the nature of your dispute. Tell them, they are ignorant and stupid—that they misunderstand Jansenius. These would be charges in keeping with your controversy; but it is quite irrelevant to call them heretics. As this, however, is the only charge from which I am anxious to defend them, I shall not give myself much trouble to show that they rightly understand Jansenius. All I shall say on the point, father, is, that it appears to me that were he to be judged according to your own rules, it would be difficult to prove him not to be a good Catholic. We shall try him by the test you have proposed. "To know," say you, "whether Jansenius is sound or not, we must inquire whether he defends efficacious grace in the manner of Calvin, who denies that man has the power of resisting it—in which case he would be heretical; or in the manner of the Thomists, who admit that it may be resisted—for then he would be Catholic." Judge, then, father, whether he holds that grace may be resisted, when he says, "That we have always a power to resist grace, according to the council; that free will may always act or not act, will or not will, consent or not consent, do good or do evil; and that man, in this life, has always these two liberties, which may be called by some contradictions." Judge, likewise, if he be not opposed to the error of Calvin, as you have described it, when he occupies a whole chapter (21st) in showing "that the Church has condemned that heretic who denies that efficacious grace acts on the free will in the manner which has been so long believed in the Church, so as to leave it in the power of free will to consent or not to consent; whereas, according to St. Augustine and the council, we have always the power of withholding our consent if we choose; and according to St. Prosper, God bestows even upon his elect the will to persevere, in such a way as not to deprive them of the power to will the contrary." And, in one word, judge if he does not agree with the Thomists, from the following declaration in chapter 4th: "That all that the Thomists have written with the view of reconciling the efficaciousness of grace with the power of resisting it, so entirely coincides with his judgment, that to ascertain his sentiments on this subject, we have only to consult their writings."

Such being the language he holds on these heads, my opinion is, that he believes in the power of resisting grace; that he differs from Calvin, and agrees with the Thomists, because he has said so; and that he is, therefore, according to your own showing, a Catholic. If you have any means of knowing the sense of an author otherwise than by his expressions; and if, without quoting any of his passages, you are disposed to maintain, in direct opposition to his own words, that he denies this power of resistance, and that he is for Calvin and against the Thomists, do not be afraid, father, that I will accuse you of heresy for that. I shall only say, that you do not seem properly to understand Jansenius; but we shall not be the less on that account children of the same Church.

How comes it, then, father, that you manage this dispute in such a passionate spirit, and that you treat as your most cruel enemies, and as the most pestilent of heretics, a class of persons whom you cannot accuse of any error, nor of anything whatever, except that they do not understand Jansenius as you do? For what else in the world do you dispute about, except the sense of that author? You would have them to condemn it. They ask what you mean them to condemn. You reply, that you mean the error of Calvin. They rejoin that they condemn that error; and with this acknowledgment (unless it is syllables you wish to condemn, and not the thing which they signify), you ought to rest satisfied. If they refuse to say that they condemn the sense of Jansenius, it is because they believe it to be that of St. Thomas, and thus this unhappy phrase has a very equivocal meaning betwixt you. In your mouth it signifies the sense of Calvin; in theirs the sense of St. Thomas. Your dissensions arise entirely from the different ideas which you attach to the same term. Were I made umpire in the quarrel, I would interdict the use of the word Jansenius, on both sides; and thus, by obliging you merely to express what you understand by it, it would be seen that you ask nothing more than the condemnation of Calvin, to which they willingly agree; and that they ask nothing more than the vindication of the sense of St. Augustine and St. Thomas, in which you again perfectly coincide.

I declare, then, father, that for my part I shall continue to regard them as good Catholics, whether they condemn Jansenius, on finding him erroneous, or refuse to condemn him, from finding that he maintains nothing more than what you yourself acknowledge to be orthodox; and that I shall say to them what St. Jerome said to John, bishop of Jerusalem, who was accused of holding the eight propositions of Origen: "Either condemn Origen, if you acknowledge that he has maintained these errors, or else deny that he has maintained them—*Aut nega hoc dixisse eum qui arguitur; aut si locutus est talia, eum damna qui dixerit.*"

See, father, how these persons acted, whose sole concern was with principles, and not with persons; whereas you who aim at persons more than principles, consider it a matter of no consequence to condemn errors, unless you procure the condemnation of the individuals to whom you choose to impute them.

How ridiculously violent your conduct is, father! and how ill calculated to insure success! I told you before, and I repeat it, violence and verity can make no impression on each other. Never were your accusations more outrageous, and never was the innocence of your opponents more discernible: never has efficacious grace been attacked with greater subtilty, and never has it been more triumphantly established. You have made the most desperate efforts to convince people that your disputes involved points of faith; and never was it more apparent that the whole controversy turned upon a mere point of fact. In fine, you have moved heaven and earth to make it appear that this point of fact is founded on truth; and never were people more disposed to call it in question. And the obvious reason of this is, that you do not take the natural course to make them believe a point of fact, which is to convince their senses, and point out to them in a book the words which you allege are to be found in it. The means you have adopted are so far removed from this straightforward course, that the most obtuse minds are unavoidably struck by observing it. Why did you not take the plan which I followed in bringing to light the wicked maxims of your authors—which was to cite faithfully the passages of their writings from which they were extracted? This was the mode followed by the curés of Paris, and it never fails to produce conviction. But, when you were charged by them with holding, for example, the proposition of Father Lamy, that a "monk may kill a person who threatens to publish calumnies against himself or his order, when he cannot otherwise prevent the publication,"—what would you have thought, and what would the public have said, if they had not quoted the place where that sentiment is literally to be found? or if, after having been repeatedly demanded to quote their authority, they still obstinately refused to do it? or if, instead of acceding to this, they had gone off to Rome, and procured a bull, ordaining all men to acknowledge the truth of their statement? Would it not be undoubtedly concluded that they had surprised the pope, and that they would never have had recourse to this extraordinary method, but for want of the natural means of substantiating the truth, which matters of fact furnish to all who undertake to prove them? Accordingly, they had no more to do than to tell us that Father Lamy teaches this doctrine *in tome* 5, *disp.* 36, *n.* 118, *page* 544, *of the Douay edition;* and by this means everybody who wished to see it found it out, and nobody could doubt about it any longer. This appears to be a very easy and prompt way of putting an end to controversies of fact, when one has got the right side of the question.

How comes it, then, father, that you do not follow this plan? You said, in your book, that the five propositions are in Jansenius, word for word, in the identical terms—*iisdem verbis.* You were told they were not. What had you to do after this, but either to cite the page, if you had really found the words, or to acknowledge that you were mistaken. But you have done neither the one nor the other. In place of this, on finding that all the passages from Jansenius, which you sometimes adduce for the purpose of hoodwinking the people, are not "the condemned propositions in their individual identity," as you had engaged to show us, you present us with Constitutions from Rome, which, without specifying any particular place, declare that the propositions have been extracted from his book.

I am sensible, father, of the respect which Christians owe to the Holy See, and your antagonists give sufficient evidence of their resolution ever to abide by its decisions. Do not imagine that it implied any deficiency in this due deference on their part, that they represented to the pope, with all the submission which children owe to their father, and members to their head, that it was possible he might be deceived on this point of fact—that he had not caused it to be investigated during his pontificate; and that his predecessor, Innocent X., had merely examined into the heretical character of the propositions, and not into the fact of their connection with Jansenius. This they stated to the commissary of the Holy Office, one of the principal examiners, stating, that they could not be censured, according to the sense of any author, because they had been presented for examination on their own merits; and without considering to what author they might belong: further, that upwards of sixty doctors, and a vast number of other persons of learning and piety, had read that book carefully over, without ever having encountered the proscribed propositions, and that they have found some of a quite opposite description: that those who had produced that impression on the mind of the pope, might be reasonably presumed to have abused the confidence he reposed in them, inasmuch as they had an interest in decrying that author, who has convicted Molina of upwards of fifty errors: that what renders this supposition still more probable is, that they have a certain maxim among them, one of the best authenticated in their whole system of theology, which is, "that they may, without criminality, calumniate those by whom they conceive themselves to be unjustly attacked;" and that, accordingly, their testimony being so suspicious, and the testimony of the other party so respectable, they had some ground for supplicating his holiness, with the most profound humility, that he would ordain an investigation to be made into this fact, in the presence of doctors belonging to both parties, in order that a solemn and regular decision might be formed on the point in dispute. "Let there be a convocation of able judges (says St. Basil on a similar occasion, Ep. 75); let each of them be left at perfect freedom; let them examine my writings; let them judge if they contain errors against the faith; let them read the objections and the replies; that so a judgment may be given in due form, and with proper knowledge of the case, and not a defamatory libel without examination."

It is quite vain for you, father, to represent those who would act in the manner I have now supposed as deficient in proper subjection to the Holy See. The popes are very far from being disposed to treat Christians with that imperiousness which some would fain exercise under their name. "The Church," says Pope St. Gregory, "which has been trained in the school of humility, does not command with authority, but persuades by reason, her children whom she believes to be in error, to obey what she has taught them." And so far from deeming it a disgrace to review a judgment into which they may have been surprised, we have the testimony of St. Bernard for saying that they glory in acknowledging the mistake. "The Apostolic See (he says, Ep. 180) can boast of this recommendation, that it never stands on the point of honor, but willingly revokes a decision that has been gained from it by surprise; indeed, it is highly just to prevent any from profiting by an act of injustice, and more especially before the Holy See."

Such, father, are the proper sentiments with which the popes ought to be inspired; for all divines are agreed that they may be surprised, and that their supreme character, so far from warranting them against mistakes, exposes them the more readily to fall into them, on account of the vast number of cares which claim their attention. This is what the same St. Gregory says to some persons who were astonished at the circumstance of another pope having suffered himself to be deluded: "Why do you wonder," says he, "that we should be deceived, we who are but men? Have you not read that David, a king who had the spirit of prophecy, was induced, by giving credit to the falsehoods of Ziba, to pronounce an unjust judgment against the son of Jonathan? Who will think it strange, then, that we, who are not prophets, should sometimes be imposed upon by deceivers? A multiplicity of affairs presses on us, and our minds, which, by being obliged to attend to so many things at once, apply themselves less closely to each in particular, are the more easily liable to be imposed upon in individual cases." Truly, father, I should suppose that the popes know better than you whether they may be deceived or not. They themselves tell us that popes, as well as the greatest princes, are more exposed to deception than individuals who are less occupied with important avocations. This must be believed on their testimony. And it is easy to imagine by what means they come to be thus overreached. St. Bernard, in the letter which he wrote to Innocent II., gives us the following description of the process: "It is no wonder, and no novelty, that the human mind may be deceived, and is deceived. You are surrounded by monks who come to you in the spirit of lying and deceit. They have filled your ears with stories against a bishop, whose life has been most exemplary, but who is the object of their hatred. These persons bite like dogs, and strive to make good appear evil. Meanwhile, most holy father, you put yourself into a rage against your own son. Why have you afforded matter of joy to his enemies? Believe not every spirit, but try the spirits whether they be of God. I trust that, when you have ascertained the truth, all this delusion, which rests on a false report, will be dissipated. I pray the spirit of truth to grant you the grace to separate light from darkness, and to favor the good by rejecting the evil." You see, then, father, that the eminent rank of the popes does not exempt them from the influence of delusion; and I may now add, that it only serves to render their mistakes more dangerous and important than those of other men. This is the light in which St. Bernard represents them to Pope Eugenius: "There is another fault, so common among the great of this world, that I never met one of them who was free from it; and that is, holy father, an excessive credulity, the source of numerous disorders. From this proceed violent persecutions against the innocent, unfounded prejudices against the absent, and tremendous storms about nothing (*pro nihilo*). This, holy father, is a universal evil, from the influence of which, if you are exempt, I shall only say, you are the only individual among all your compeers who can boast of that privilege."

I imagine, father, that the proofs I have brought are beginning to convince you that the popes are liable to be surprised. But, to complete your conversion, I shall merely remind you of some examples, which you yourself have quoted in your book, of popes and emperors whom heretics have actually deceived. You will remember, then, that you have told us that Apollinarius surprised Pope Damasius, in the same way that Celestius surprised Zozimus. You inform us, besides, that one called Athanasius deceived the Emperor Heraclius, and prevailed on him to persecute the Catholics. And lastly, that Sergius obtained from Honorius that infamous decretal which was burned at the sixth council, "by playing the busy-body," as you say, "about the person of that pope."

It appears, then, father, by your own confession, that those who act this part about the persons of kings and popes, do sometimes artfully entice them to persecute the faithful defenders of the truth, under the persuasion that they are persecuting heretics. And hence the popes, who hold nothing in greater horror than these surprisals, have, by a letter of Alexander III., enacted an ecclesiastical statute, which is inserted in the canonical law, to permit the suspension of the execution of their bulls and decretals, when there is ground to suspect that they have been imposed upon. "If," says that pope to the Archbishop of Ravenna, "we sometimes send decretals to your fraternity which are opposed to your sentiments, give yourselves no distress on that account. We shall expect you either to carry them respectfully into execution, or to send us the reason why you conceive they ought not to be executed; for we deem it right that you should not execute a decree which may have been procured from us by artifice and surprise." Such has been the course pursued by the popes, whose sole object is to settle the disputes of Christians, and not to follow the passionate counsels of those who strive to involve them in trouble and perplexity. Following the advice of St. Peter and St. Paul, who in this followed the commandment of Jesus Christ, they avoid domination. The spirit which appears in their whole conduct is that of peace and truth. In this spirit they ordinarily insert in their letters this clause, which is tacitly understood in them all—"*Si ita est—si preces- veritate nitantur*—If it be so as we have heard it —if the facts be true.*" It is quite clear, if the popes themselves give no force to their bulls, except in so far as they are founded on genuine facts, that it is not the bulls alone that prove the truth of the facts, but that, on the contrary, even according to the canonists, it is the truth of the facts which renders the bulls lawfully admissible.

In what way, then, are we to learn the truth of facts? It must be by the eyes, father, which are the legitimate judges of such matters, as reason is the proper judge of things natural and intelligible, and faith of things supernatural and revealed. For, since you will force me into this discussion, you must allow me to tell you, that, according to the sentiments of the two greatest doctors of the Church, St. Augustine and St. Thomas, these three principles of our knowledge, the senses, reason, and faith, have each their separate objects, and their own degrees of certainty. And as God has been pleased to employ the intervention of the senses to give entrance to faith (for "faith cometh by hearing"), it follows, that so far from faith destroying the certainty of the senses, to call in question the faithful report of the senses would lead to the destruction of faith. It is on this principle that St. Thomas explicitly states that God has been pleased that the sensible accidents should subsist in the eucharist, in order that the senses, which judge only of these accidents, might not be deceived.

We conclude, therefore, from this, that whatever the proposition may be that is submitted to our examination, we must first determine its nature, to ascertain to which of those three principles it ought to be referred. If it relate to a supernatural truth, we must judge of it neither by the senses nor by reason, but by Scripture and the decisions of the Church. Should it concern an unrevealed truth, and something within the reach of natural reason, reason must be its proper judge. And if it embrace a point of fact, we must yield to the testimony of the senses, to which it naturally belongs to take cognizance of such matters.

So general is this rule, that, according to St. Augustine and St. Thomas, when we meet with a passage even in the Scripture, the literal meaning of which, at first sight, appears contrary to what the senses or reason are certainly persuaded of, we must not attempt to reject their testimony in this case, and yield them up to the authority of that apparent sense of the Scripture, but we must interpret the Scripture, and seek out therein another sense agreeable to that sensible truth; because, the Word of God being infallible in the facts which it records, and the information of the senses and of reason, acting in their sphere, being certain also, it follows that there must be an agreement between these two sources of knowledge. And as Scripture may be interpreted in different ways, whereas the testimony of the senses is uniform, we must in these matters adopt as the true interpretation of Scripture that view which corresponds with the faithful report of the senses. "Two things," says St. Thomas, "must be observed, according to the doctrine of St. Augustine: first, That Scripture has always one true sense; and secondly, That as it may receive various senses, when we have discovered one which reason plainly teaches to be false, we must not persist in maintaining that this is the natural sense, but search out another with which reason will agree."

St. Thomas explains his meaning by the example of a passage in Genesis, where it is written that "God created two great lights, the sun and the moon, and also the stars," in which the Scriptures appear to say that the moon is greater than all the stars; but as it is evident, from unquestionable demonstration, that this is false, it is not our duty, says that saint, obstinately to defend the literal sense of that passage; another meaning must be sought, consistent with the truth of the fact, such as the following, "That the phrase *great light*, as applied to the moon, denotes the greatness of that luminary merely as it appears in our eyes, and not the magnitude of its body considered in itself."

An opposite mode of treatment, so far from procuring respect to the Scripture, would only expose it to the contempt of infidels; because, as St. Augustine says, "when they found that we believed, on the authority of Scripture, in things which they assuredly knew to be false, they would laugh at our credulity with regard to its more recondite truths, such as the resurrection of the dead and eternal life." "And by this means," adds St. Thomas, "we should render our religion contemptible in their eyes, and shut up its entrance into their minds."

And let me add, father, that it would in the same manner be the likeliest means to shut up the entrance of Scripture into the minds of heretics, and to render the pope's authority contemptible in their eyes, to refuse all those the name of Catholics who would not believe that certain words were in a certain book, where they are not to be found, merely because a pope by mistake has declared that they are. It is only by examining a book that we can ascertain what words it contains. Matters of fact can only be proved by the senses. If the position which you maintain be true, show it, or else ask no man to believe it—that would be to no purpose. Not all the powers on earth can, by the force of authority, persuade us of a point of fact, any more than they can alter it; for nothing can make that to be not which really is.

It was to no purpose, for example, that the monks of Ratisbon procured from Pope St. Leo IX. a solemn decree, by which he declared that the body of St. Denis, the first bishop of Paris, who is generally held to have been the Areopagite, had been transported out of France, and conveyed into the chapel of their monastery. It is not the less true, for all this, that the body of that saint always lay, and lies to this hour, in the celebrated abbey which bears his name, and within the walls of which you would find it no easy matter to obtain a cordial reception to this bull, although the pope has therein assured us that he has examined the affair "with all possible diligence (*diligentissime*), and with the advice of many bishops and prelates; so that he strictly enjoins all the French (*districte præcipientes*) to own and confess that these holy relics are no longer in their country." The French, however, who knew that fact to be untrue, by the evidence of their own eyes, and who, upon opening the shrine, found all those relics entire, as the historians of that period inform us, believed then, as they have always believed since, the reverse of what that holy pope had enjoined them to believe, well knowing that even saints and prophets are liable to be imposed upon.

It was to equally little purpose that you obtained against Galileo a decree from Rome, condemning his opinion respecting the motion of the earth. It will never be proved by such an argument as this that the earth remains stationary; and if it can be demonstrated by sure observation that it is the earth and not the sun that revolves, the efforts and arguments of all mankind put together will not hinder our planet from revolving, nor hinder themselves from revolving along with her.

Again, you must not imagine that the letters of Pope Zachary, excommunicating St. Virgilius for maintaining the existence of the antipodes, have annihilated the New World; nor must you suppose that, although he declared that opinion to be a most dangerous heresy, the king of Spain was wrong in giving more credence to Christopher Columbus, who came from the place, than to the judgment of the pope, who had never been there, or that the Church has not derived a vast benefit from the discovery, inasmuch as it has brought the knowledge of the Gospel to a great multitude of souls, who might otherwise have perished in their infidelity.

You see, then, father, what is the nature of matters of fact, and on what principles they are to be determined; from all which, to recur to our subject, it is easy to conclude, that if the five propositions are not in Jansenius, it is impossible that they can have been extracted from him; and that the only way to form a judgment on the matter, and to produce universal conviction, is to examine that book in a regular conference, as you have been desired to do long ago. Until that be done, you have no right to charge your opponents with contumacy; for they are as blameless in regard to the point of fact as they are of errors in point of faith—Catholics in doctrine, reasonable in fact, and innocent in both.

Who can help feeling astonishment, then, father, to see on the one side a vindication so complete, and on the other accusations so outrageous! Who would suppose that the only question between you relates to a single fact of no importance, which the one party wishes the other to believe without showing it to them! And who would ever imagine that such a noise should have been made in the Church for nothing (*pro nihilo*), as good St. Bernard says! But this is just one of the principal tricks of your policy, to make people believe that everything is at stake, when, in reality, there is nothing at stake; and to represent to those influential persons who listen to you, that the most pernicious errors of Calvin, and the most vital principles of the faith, are involved in your disputes, with the view of inducing them, under this conviction, to employ all their zeal and all their authority against your opponents, as if the safety of the Catholic religion depended upon it; whereas, if they came to know that the whole dispute was about this paltry point of fact, they would give themselves no concern about it, but would, on the contrary, regret extremely that, to gratify your private passions, they had made such exertions in an affair of no consequence to the Church. For, in fine, to take the worst view of the matter, even though it should be true that Jansenius maintained these propositions, what great misfortune would accrue from some persons doubting of the fact, provided they detested the propositions, as they have publicly declared that they do? Is it not enough that they are condemned by everybody, without exception, and that, too, in the sense in which you have explained that you wish them to be condemned? Would they be more severely censured by saying that Jansenius maintained them?

What purpose, then, would be served by exacting this acknowledgment, except that of disgracing a doctor and bishop, who died in the communion of the Church? I cannot see how that should be accounted so great a blessing as to deserve to be purchased at the expense of so many disturbances. What interest has the state, or the pope, or bishops, or doctors, or the Church at large, in this conclusion? It does not affect them in any way whatever, father; it can affect none but your Society, which would certainly enjoy some pleasure from the defamation of an author who has done you some little injury. Meanwhile everything is in confusion, because you have made people believe that everything is in danger. This is the secret spring giving impulse to all those mighty commotions, which would cease immediately were the real state of the controversy once known. And therefore, as the peace of the Church depended on this explanation, it was, I conceive, of the utmost importance that it should be given, that, by exposing all your disguises, it might be manifest to the whole world that your accusations were without foundation, your opponents without error, and the Church without heresy.

Such, father, is the end which it has been my desire to accomplish; an end which appears to me, in every point of view, so deeply important to religion, that I am at a loss to conceive how those to whom you furnish so much occasion for speaking can contrive to remain in silence. Granting that they are not affected with the personal wrongs which you have committed against them, those which the Church suffers ought, in my opinion, to have forced them to complain. Besides, I am not altogether sure if ecclesiastics ought to make a sacrifice of their reputation to calumny, especially in the matter of religion. They allow you, nevertheless, to say whatever you please; so that, had it not been for the opportunity which, by mere accident, you afforded me of taking their part, the scandalous impressions which you are circulating against them in all quarters would, in all probability, have gone forth without contradiction. Their patience, I confess, astonishes me; and the more so, that I cannot suspect it of proceeding either from timidity or from incapacity, being well assured that they want neither arguments for their own vindication, nor zeal for the truth. And yet I see them religiously bent on silence, to a degree which appears to me altogether unjustifiable. For my part, father, I do not believe that I can possibly follow their example. Leave the Church in peace, and I shall leave you as you are, with all my heart; but so long as you make it your sole business to keep her in confusion, doubt not but that there shall always be found within her bosom children of peace, who will consider themselves bound to employ all their endeavors to preserve her tranquillity.

LETTER XIX

Fragment of a nineteenth provincial letter, addressed to Father Annat

REVEREND SIR,—If I have caused you some dissatisfaction, in former Letters, by my endeavors to establish the innocence of those whom you were laboring to asperse, I shall afford you pleasure in the present, by making you acquainted with the sufferings which you have inflicted upon them. Be comforted, my good father, the objects of your enmity are in distress! And if the Reverend the Bishops should be induced to carry out, in their respective dioceses, the advice you have given them, to cause to be subscribed and sworn a certain matter of fact, which is, in itself, not credible, and which it cannot be obligatory upon any one to believe—you will indeed succeed in plunging your opponents to the depth of sorrow, at witnessing the Church brought into so abject a condition.

Yes, sir, I have seen them; and it was with a satisfaction inexpressible! I have seen these holy men; and this was the attitude in which they were found. They were not wrapt up in a philosophic magnanimity; they did not affect to exhibit that indiscriminate firmness which urges implicit obedience to every momentary impulsive duty; nor yet were they in a frame of weakness and timidity, which would prevent them from either discerning the truth, or following it when discerned. But I found them with minds pious, composed, and unshaken; impressed with a meek deference for ecclesiastical authority; with tenderness of spirit, zeal for truth, and a desire to ascertain and obey her dictates: filled with a salutary suspicion of themselves, distrusting their own infirmity, and regretting that it should be thus exposed to trial; yet withal, sustained by a modest hope that their Lord will deign to instruct them by his illuminations, and sustain them by his power; and believing, that that peace of their Saviour, whose sacred influences it is their endeavor to maintain, and for whose cause they are brought into suffering, will be at once their guide and their support! I have, in fine, seen them maintaining a character of Christian piety, whose power

. . . .

I found them surrounded by their friends, who had hastened to impart those counsels which they deemed the most fitting in their present exigency. I have heard those counsels; I have observed the manner in which they were received, and the answers given: and truly, my father, had you yourself been present, I think you would have acknowledged that, in their whole procedure, there was the entire absence of a spirit of insubordination and schism; and that their only desire and aim was to preserve inviolate two things—to them infinitely precious—peace and truth.

For, after due representations had been made to them of the penalties they would draw upon themselves by their refusal to sign the Constitution, and the scandal it might cause in the Church, their reply was . . . .

. . . .